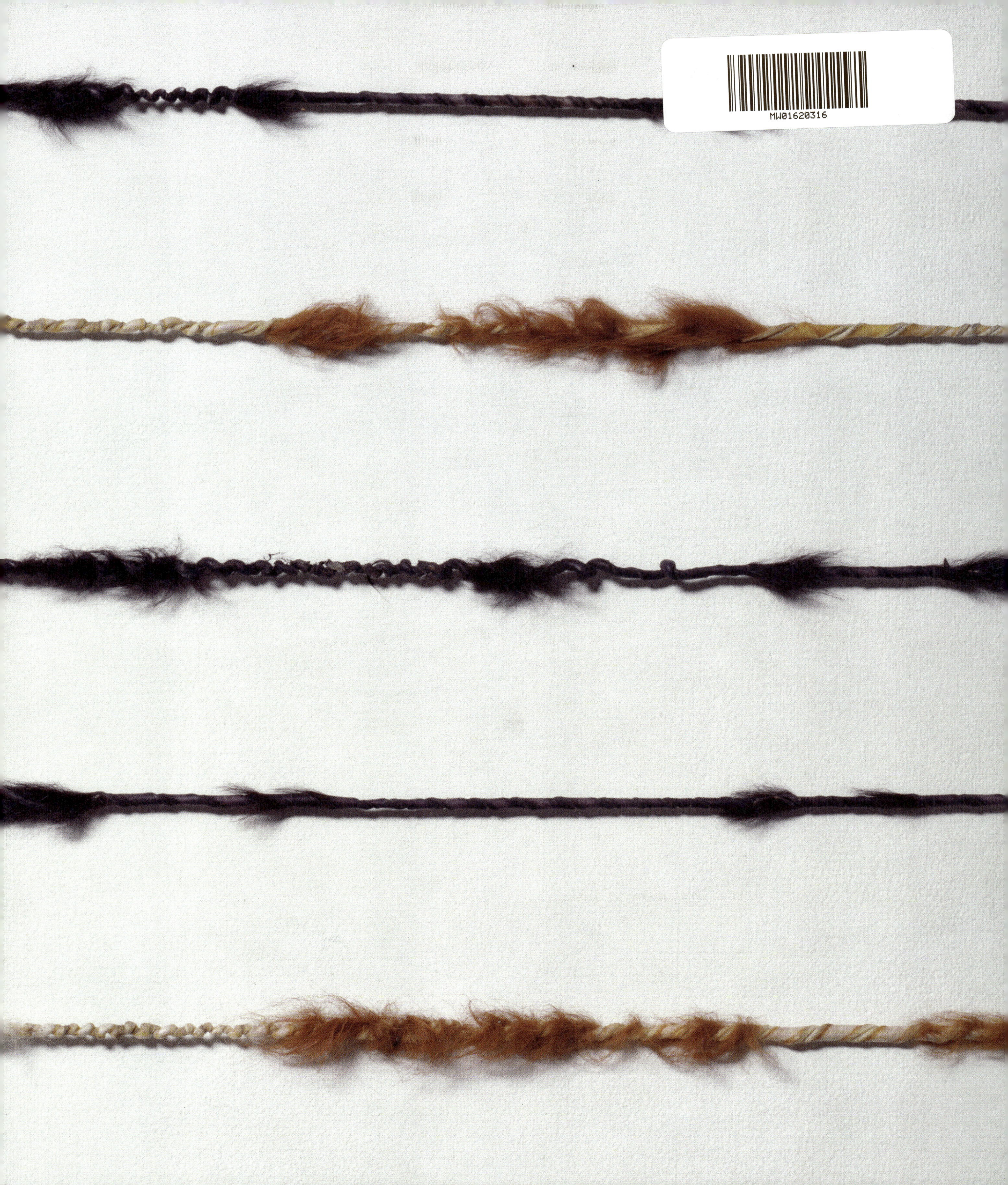

Martin Puryear
Nexus

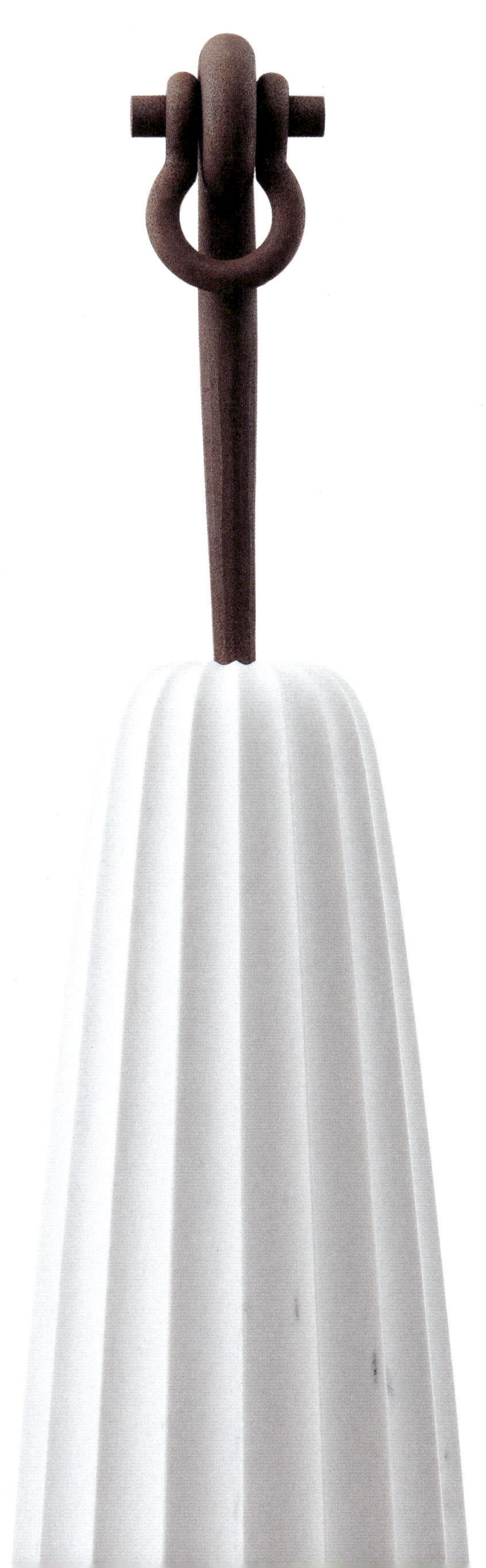

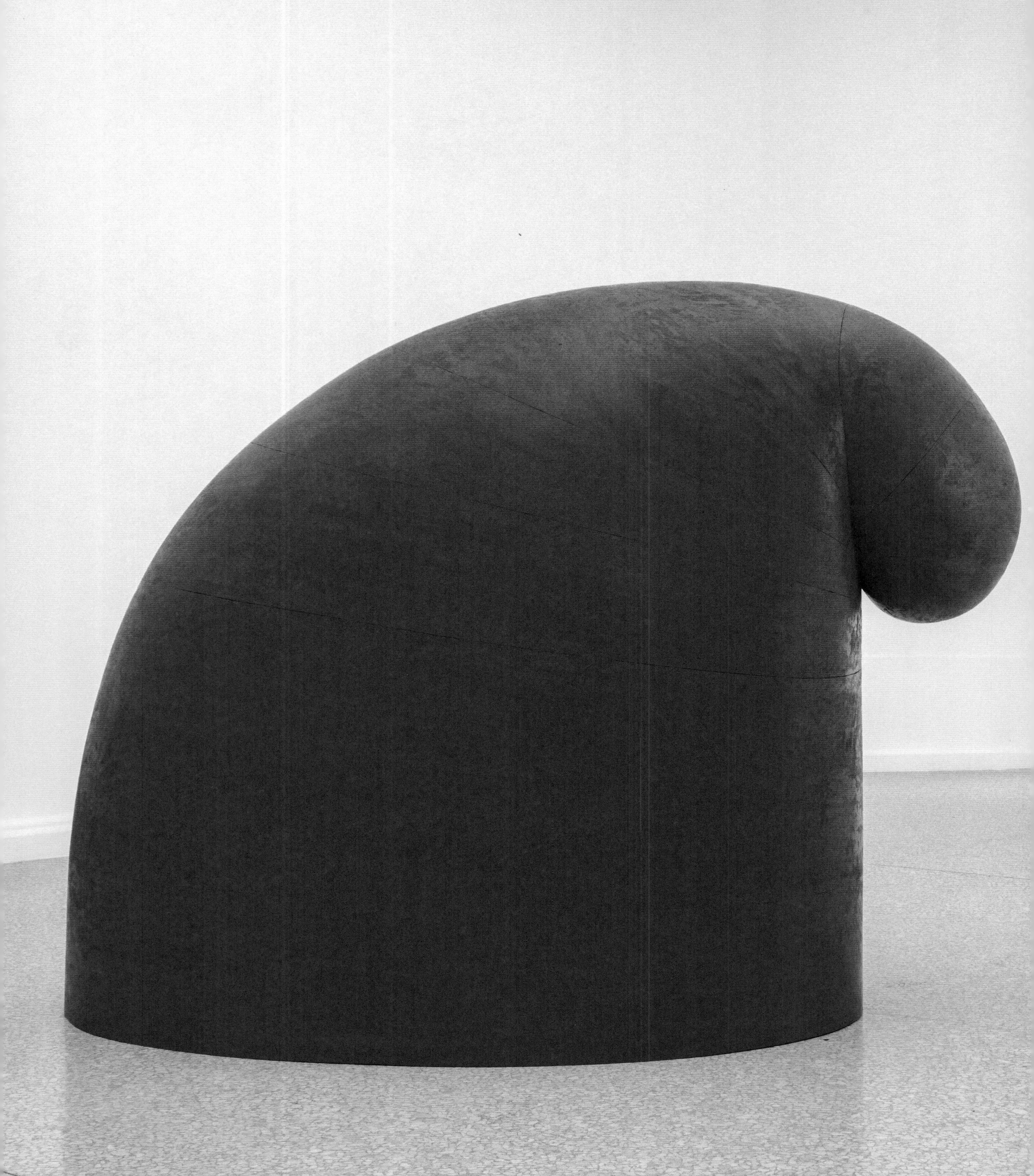

Martin Puryear
Nexus

Edited by Emily Liebert
with Reto Thüring

Contributions by
Rizvana Bradley
Joan Kee
Michelle Millar Fisher
Ugochukwu-Smooth Nzewi

and
Nairy Baghramian
Alex Da Corte
Thelma Golden
Tom Joyce
Maya Lin
Kerry James Marshall
Pam Paulson
Julia Phillips
Charles Ray
Gabriella Shypula
Billie Tsien

The Cleveland Museum of Art
Distributed by Yale University Press, New Haven and London

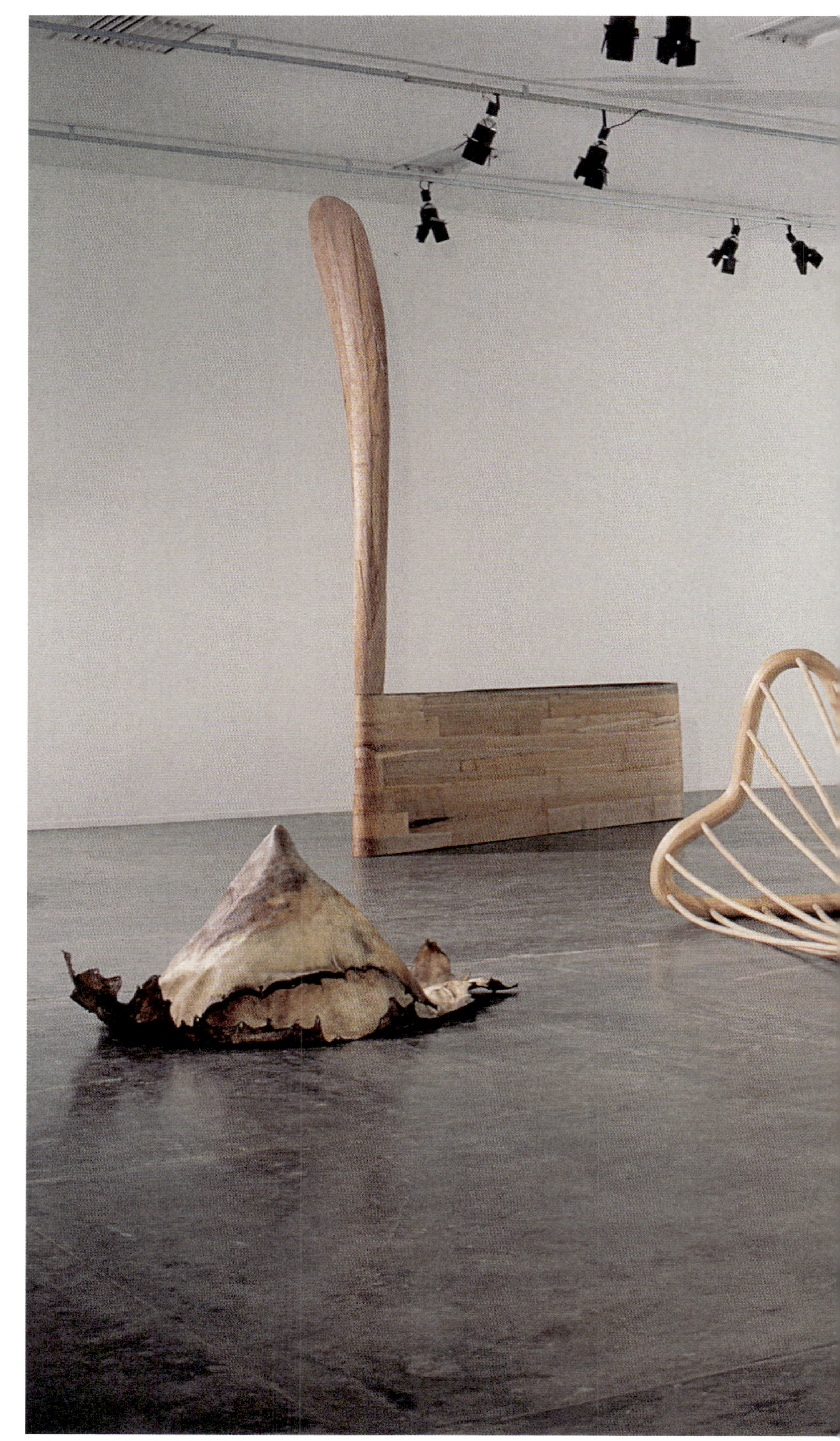

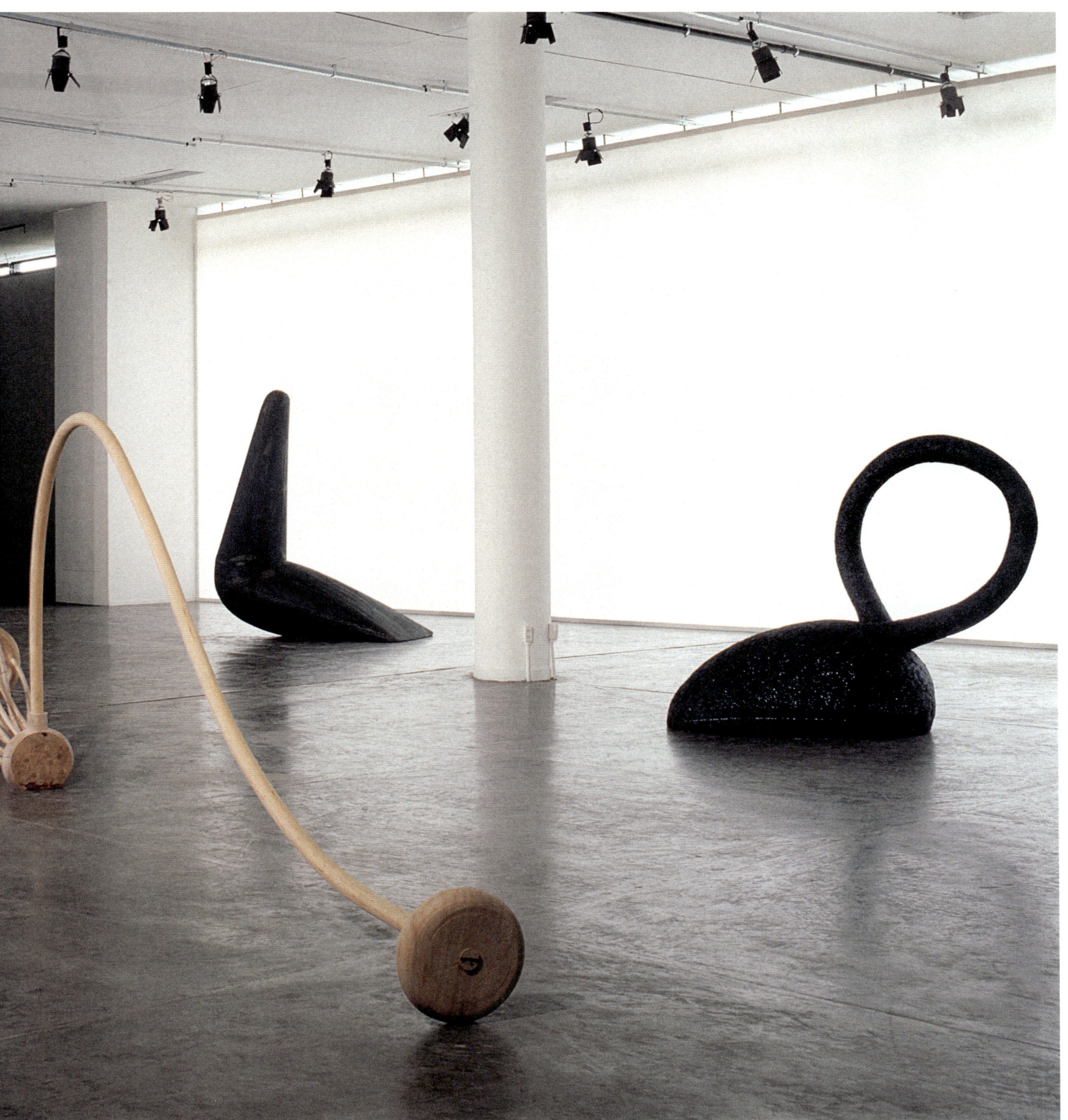

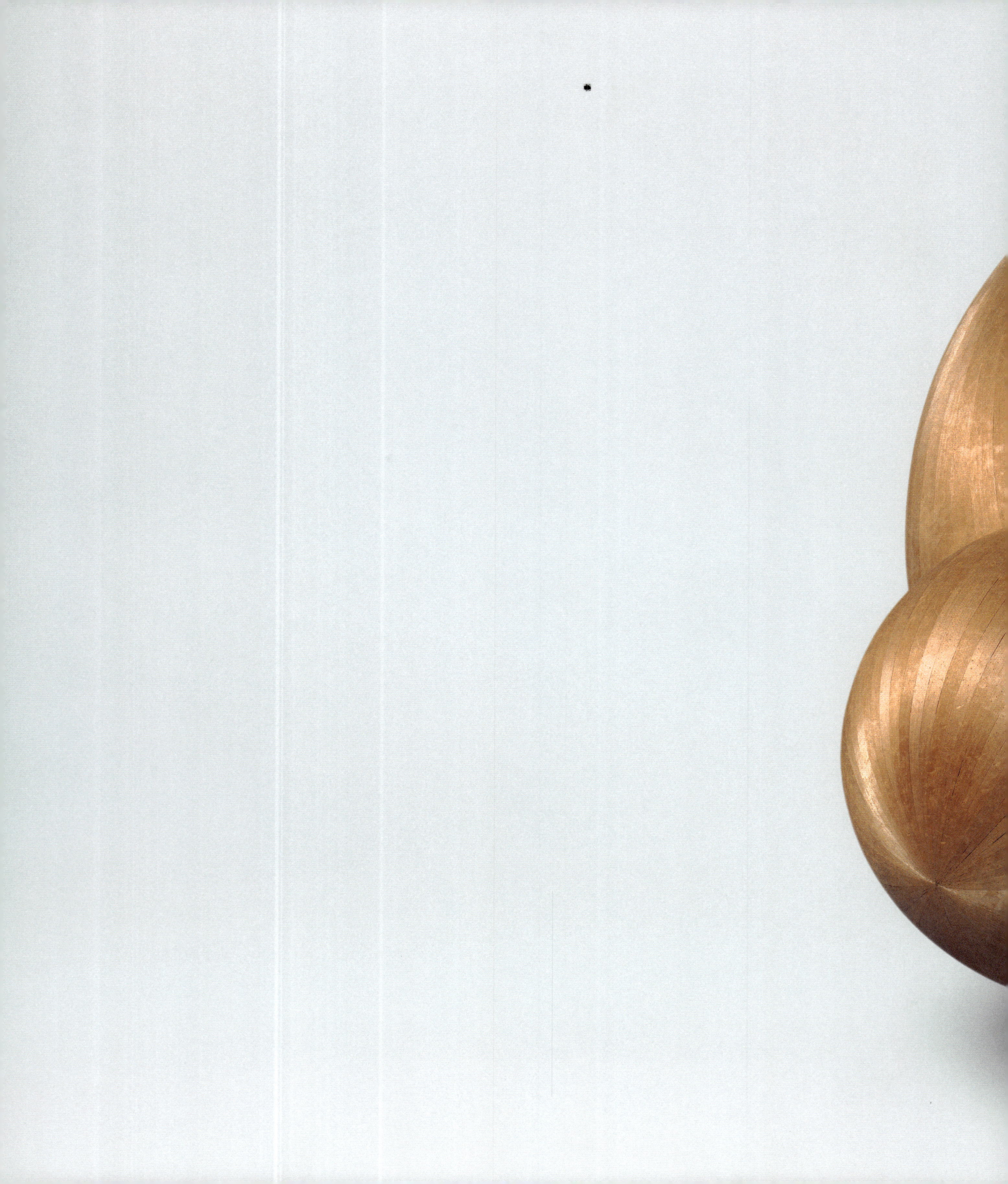

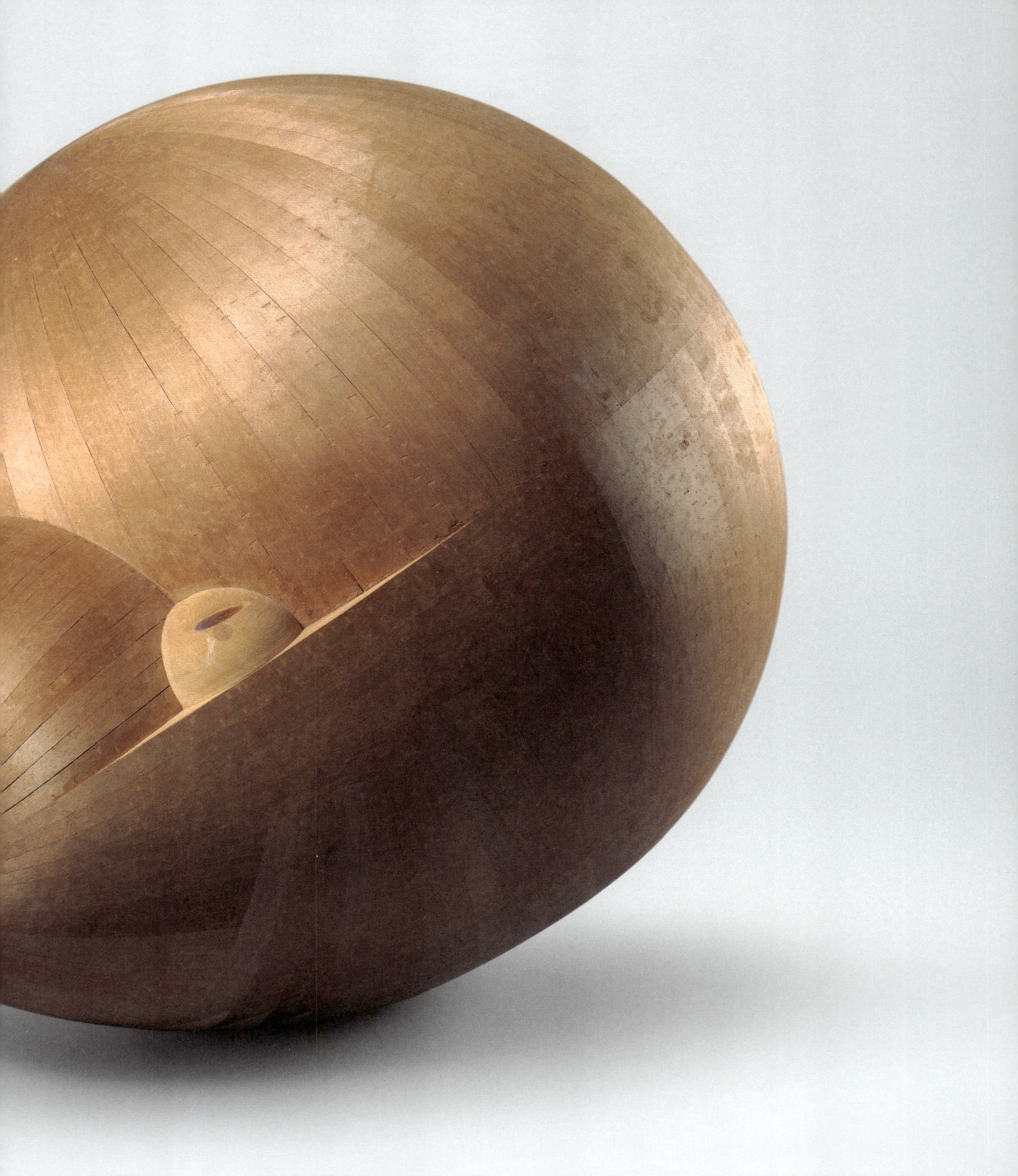

Glenstone

ABRAMS
FOUNDATION

THE CARL AND RUTH
SHAPIRO
FAMILY FOUNDATION

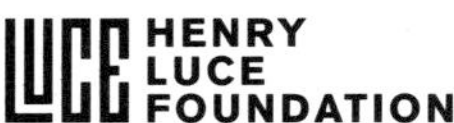

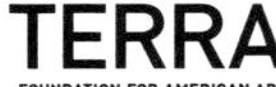

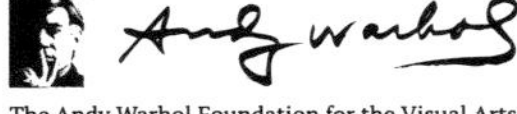

Principal support for the exhibition catalogue is provided by the Glenstone Foundation.

This publication is made possible in part by the Andrew W. Mellon Foundation

Published on the occasion of the exhibition *Martin Puryear: Nexus*, on view at the Museum of Fine Arts, Boston, from September 27, 2025, to February 1, 2026, the Cleveland Museum of Art from April 12 to August 9, 2026, and High Museum of Art, Atlanta from September 25, 2026, to January 17, 2027.

The exhibition at the Museum of Fine Arts, Boston is sponsored by the Abrams Foundation. Generous support is provided by the Carl and Ruth Shapiro Family Foundation, the Terra Foundation for American Art and the Henry and Lois Foster Fund for Contemporary Exhibitions. Additional support is provided by Davis and Carol Noble, the Callaghan Family Fund for Contemporary Exhibitions, the Amy and Jonathan Poorvu Fund for the Exhibition of Contemporary Art and Sculpture, the Robert and Jane Burke Fund for Exhibitions, and the Barbara Jane Anderson Fund.

Principal support for the exhibition at the Cleveland Museum of Art is provided by Agnes Gund, the Henry Luce Foundation, the Terra Foundation for American Art, and the Andy Warhol Foundation for the Visual Arts. Generous support is provided by the Gottlob family in loving memory of Milford Gottlob, MD. Additional support is provided by Kenneth H. Kirtz and family.

All exhibitions at the Cleveland Museum of Art are underwritten by the CMA Fund for Exhibitions. Principal annual support is provided by Michael Frank and the late Pat Snyder, the Kelvin and Eleanor Smith Foundation, the John and Jeanette Walton Exhibition Fund, and Margaret and Loyal Wilson. Major annual support is provided by the late Dick Blum and Harriet Warm and the Frankino-Dodero Family Fund for Exhibitions Endowment. Generous annual support is provided by two anonymous donors, Gini and Randy Barbato, Cynthia and Dale Brogan, Dr. Ben and Julia Brouhard, Brenda and Marshall Brown, Gail and Bill Calfee, the Leigh H. Carter family, Dr. William A. Chilcote Jr. and Dr. Barbara S. Kaplan, Joseph and Susan Corsaro, Ron and Cheryl Davis, Richard and Dian Disantis, the Jeffery Wallace Ellis Trust in memory of Lloyd H. Ellis Jr., Leigh and Andy Fabens, Florence Kahane Goodman, Janice Hammond and Edward Hemmelgarn, Robin Heiser, the late Marta and the late Donald M. Jack Jr., the estate of Walter and Jean Kalberer, Mrs. Nancy M. Lavelle, Eva and Rudolf Linnebach, the William S. Lipscomb Fund, Bill and Joyce Litzler, Lu Anne and the late Carl Morrison, Jeffrey Mostade and Eric Nilson and Varun Shetty, Sarah Nash, Courtney and Michael Novak, Tim O'Brien and Breck Platner, Dr. Nicholas and Anne Ogan, William J. and Katherine T. O'Neill, Henry Ott-Hansen, the Pickering Foundation, Christine Fae Powell, Peter and Julie Raskind, Michael and Cindy Resch, Marguerite and James Rigby, William Roj and Mary Lynn Durham, Betty T. and David M. Schneider, Elizabeth and Tim Sheeler, Saundra K. Stemen, Paula and Eugene Stevens, the Womens Council of the Cleveland Museum of Art, and Claudia Woods and David Osage.

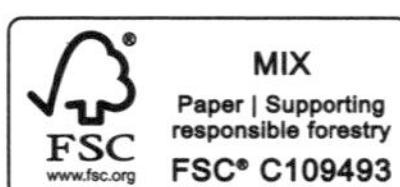

NOTES TO THE READER
All measurements are in centimeters; height precedes width precedes depth. Catalogue numbers appear in [brackets].

Library of Congress Control Number: 2025937413

Authorized Representative in the EU: Easy Access System Europe, Mustamäe tee 50, 10621 Tallinn, Estonia, gpsr.requests@easproject.com

ISBN: 978-0-300-28392-1

Designed by Tom Barnard, Director of Publications

Emily Mears, Director of Exhibitions

Rachel Beamer, Senior Publications Project Manager

Edited by Jane Friedman

Proofread by Annie Jun

Color management by Maurizio Brivio

Printed and bound by SYL The Art of Books, S.L. in Barcelona, Spain

The Cleveland Museum of Art
11150 East Boulevard
Cleveland, OH 44106-1797
www.clevelandart.org

Distributed by
Yale University Press
302 Temple Street
P.O. Box 209040
New Haven, CT 06520-9040
www.yalebooks.com/art

Cover: *Alien Huddle* (1993–95; [30])

Back cover: *On the Tundra* (1986; [26]). Photo © 2025 Museum of Fine Arts, Boston

Page 1: *A Column for Sally Hemings* (2021; detail, [62]). Photo: Matthew Marks Gallery

Page 2: *Big Phrygian*, (2010–14; [55]). Photo: Ron Amstutz

Page 4–5: Installation view of 20th Bienal Internacional de São Paulo, 1989. Pictured: *Rawhide Cone* (1980; [18]), *Lever #1* (1988–89; [28]), *Lever #2* (1989), *Lever #4* (1989), *Untitled* (1987). Photo: Sarah Wells

Pages 6–7: *Alien Huddle* (1993–95; [30])

Page 9: *On the Tundra* (1986; [26]). Photo © 2025 MFA Boston

Endpapers: *Some Lines for Jim Beckwourth*, (1978; detail, [15]). Photo: Donald Young Gallery, Chicago, IL

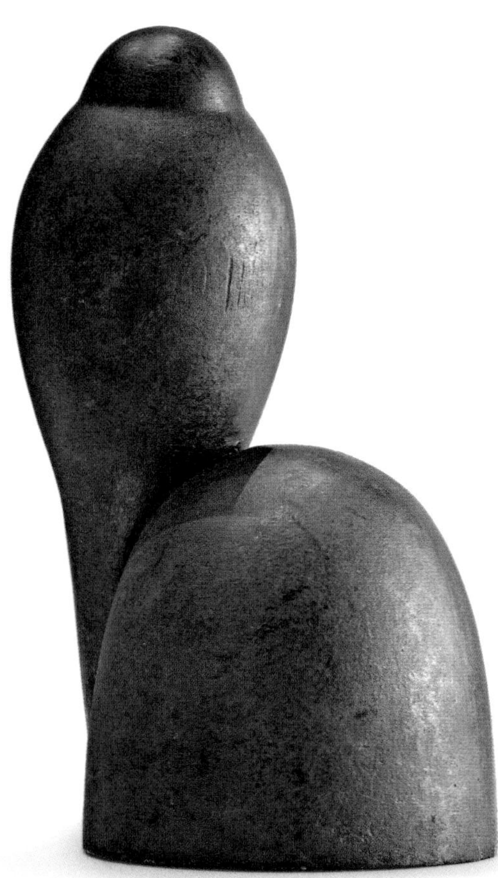

Directors' Foreword

The art of Martin Puryear (American, b. 1941) arrests us with its beauty and moves us with its invitation to see with fresh eyes the world that we inhabit. For more than five decades, Puryear has been making sculptures, as well as prints and drawings, that are informed by numerous traditions of material culture, social history, and the natural world. The result is a body of work that is global in its scope, engaging in its content, and unparalleled in its formal elegance.

Given the expansive range of aesthetic traditions and histories of making that inform Puryear's art, it is fitting that his career retrospective is being presented by two museums whose collections have roots around the world and span thousands of years of history. We hope that the works in *Martin Puryear: Nexus* offer visitors new ways to encounter our museums' holdings of, for example, Indigenous baskets, European modernist furniture, Mughal painting, and African masks. These are among the art forms that have inspired Puryear, and their traces can be found throughout this exhibition. Conversely, viewers' encounters with such works may shed light on Puryear's art. Our contemporary programs at the Cleveland Museum of Art (CMA) and the Museum of Fine Arts, Boston (MFA, Boston), afford us a special opportunity to situate the present in the context of the history from which it stems and to interpret the past through the future that it has yielded. Martin Puryear's art has a particular ability to inspire imaginative leaps across time and place.

It is through the generosity of individuals and foundations that we are able to realize *Martin Puryear: Nexus.* For this, we are deeply grateful. Principal support for the exhibition catalogue is provided by the Glenstone Foundation. The publication is also made possible with support from the Andrew W. Mellon Foundation. At the MFA, Boston, the exhibition is sponsored by the Abrams Foundation. Generous support is provided by the Carl and Ruth Shapiro Family Foundation, the Terra Foundation for American Art and the Henry and Lois Foster Fund for Contemporary Exhibitions. Additional support is provided by Davis and Carol Noble, the Callaghan Family Fund for Contemporary Exhibitions, the Amy and Jonathan Poorvu Fund for the Exhibition of Contemporary Art and Sculpture, the Robert and Jane Burke Fund for Exhibitions, and the Barbara Jane Anderson Fund. Principal support for the exhibition at the Cleveland Museum of Art is provided by Agnes Gund, the Henry Luce Foundation, the Terra Foundation for American Art, and the Andy Warhol Foundation for the Visual Arts. Additional support is provided by Kenneth H. Kirtz and family. All exhibitions at the Cleveland Museum of Art are underwritten by the CMA Fund for Exhibitions.

We thank Matthew Teitelbaum, former Ann and Graham Gund Director and CEO of the MFA, Boston, for his enthusiastic support for this project during its development. We are grateful for our collaboration with Randall Suffolk, Director of the High Museum of Art. We are thrilled that this has resulted in a tour that brings Martin Puryear's art to audiences in Atlanta.

We appreciate curators Emily Liebert, Lauren Rich Fine Curator of Contemporary Art, Chair of Art of the Americas and Modern and Contemporary Art at the CMA, and Reto Thüring, former Beal Family Chair, Department of Contemporary Art at the MFA Boston, for their stewardship of this project throughout the various stages of its evolution. Their great respect for, and dedication to, Puryear's work animates both museum presentations as well as the pages of this catalogue. We are also grateful to our staffs across departments at the CMA and the MFA, Boston, whose exceptional talents have supported and enhanced *Martin Puryear: Nexus* at every turn.

Numerous institutions and individuals parted with their artworks so that we could include them in this exhibition. We sincerely appreciate the generosity of all the lenders to *Martin Puryear: Nexus*, named elsewhere in this catalogue.

Our greatest debt of gratitude is to the artist himself. It has been a privilege to work with Martin Puryear, whose immense talent, intelligence, and exquisite sensitivity are manifested in his life's work. We are honored to share that work with our audiences, who will, no doubt, savor the work's lasting impact as we do.

William M. Griswold
Sarah S. and Alexander M. Cutler Director
The Cleveland Museum of Art

Pierre Terjanian
Ann and Graham Gund Director and CEO
Museum of Fine Arts, Boston

Phrygian (Cap in the Air) (2012; [54]). Martin Puryear (American, b. 1941). Photo © 2025 MFA Boston

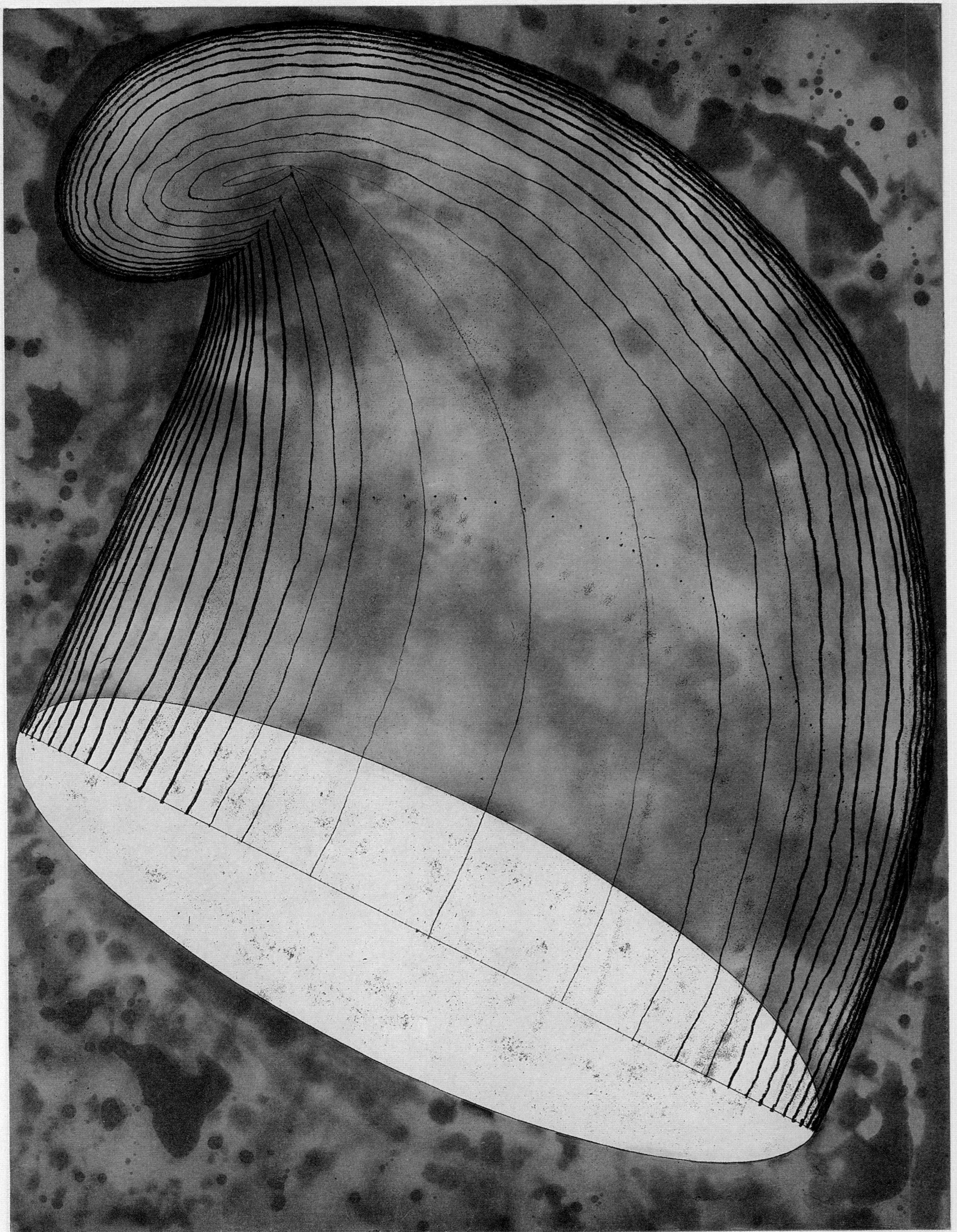

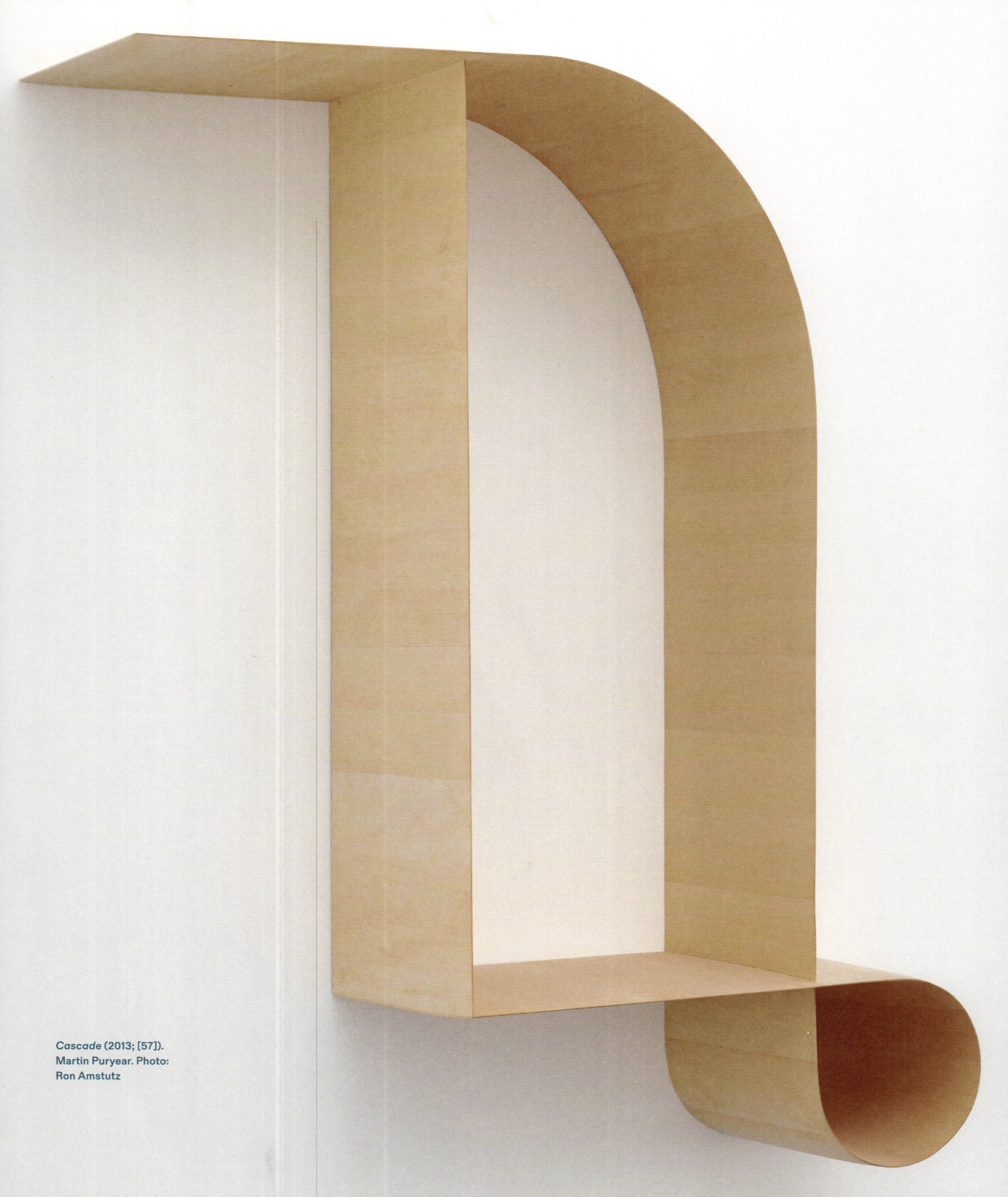

Cascade (2013; [57]). Martin Puryear. Photo: Ron Amstutz

Curators' Acknowledgments

On a snowy day in February 2022, we met Martin Puryear at his home in Upstate New York. We had come to share with him our idea for an exhibition and catalogue that would introduce his work of the last five-plus decades to new audiences. We felt the time was ripe for a career survey that would highlight the global aesthetic histories and production techniques that have informed Puryear's thinking and his art. There seemed no better setting for this than two major American art museums with comprehensive collections spanning time and place. Following this visit, and time spent together at the Cleveland Museum of Art and the Museum of Fine Arts, Boston, Puryear agreed to the collaboration. In the years since that initial visit it has been our great privilege and honor to get to know Puryear and to gain greater insight into his work.

Puryear's art is startlingly beautiful, and his care for detail is tangible from every meticulously crafted joint to the precision of each print's execution. But beyond their formal distinction, what has kept us returning again and again to his sculptures, as well as his prints and drawings, is a dynamism that is particular to his work. We believe this derives from the singular way in which Puryear integrates materials and translates processes from all corners of the world that he has observed on his travels and studied in his books. Puryear has acquired the extraordinary breadth of knowledge that informs his work through more than curiosity. His lifelong pursuit of learning is motivated by a profound respect and empathy for many ways of being in the world. In this sense, Puryear's art models humanity. What more can we ask of art in our present moment?

We thank our generous supporters, named by our directors, who enabled us to celebrate and amplify Puryear's art through their commitment to this exhibition and its catalogue. We are grateful to William M. Griswold, Director and President, CMA, and Pierre Terjanian, Director and CEO, MFA Boston, for their vision and steadfast support in recognizing the importance of sharing Puryear's work with our audiences.

This exhibition and catalogue have come to fruition because of the talent and commitment of our extraordinary colleagues at both institutions. We are especially grateful to our most immediate collaborators and thought partners on the project: at the CMA, Gabriella Shypula, Leigh and Mary Carter Director's Research Fellow, has greatly enriched *Martin Puryear: Nexus* through her creativity, resourcefulness, and attentive care; at the MFA Boston, Ian Alteveer, Beal Family Chair, and Daisy Alejandre, Curatorial Assistant, of the Department of Contemporary Art, have helped shape the project in crucial ways. Beyond this core team, at the CMA we would like to acknowledge the essential participation of Jane Alexander, Alyssa Arend, Rachel Arzuaga, Barry Austin, Tom Barnard, Rachel Beamer, Arthur Beukemann, Joe Blaser, Jacqueline Bon, David Brichford, Philip Brutz, Tony Cisneros, Jihad Dennis, Andria Derstine, Beth Edelstein, Jacob Emmett, Jim Engelmann, Erin Fletcher, Stephanie Foster, Matthew Gengler, Andrew Gutierrez, Jamie Hardis, Haley Kedziora, James Kohler, Peter Kratcoski, Chrysta LaFay, Bruce Loessin, Cameron McConnell, Emily Mears, Todd Mesek, Sara Miller, Alyssa Morasco, Marsha Morrow, Beth Owens, Sharon Robinson, Andrew Robison, Elizabeth Saluk, Sarah Scaturro, Tessa Shlonsky, Aumaine Rose Smith, Amy Sparks, Mark Spisak, Moyna Stanton, Heidi Strean, Joshua Sulser, Mary Thomas, Deirdre Vodanoff, and Jason Willis. At the MFA Boston we thank Kat Bossi, Meghan Campbell, Indigo Casais, Keith Crippen, Jessica Doonan, Kristen Hoskins, Jill Kennedy-Kernohan, Christine Mitchell, Angie Morrow, Katrina Newbury, Rachel Nicholson, Bryan Owen, Katherine ter Kuile, Emilie Tréhu, and Christina Yu Yu. We are thrilled that beyond Cleveland and Boston, audiences in Atlanta will enjoy this exhibition thanks to a rich collaboration with Randall Suffolk, Director of the High Museum and Michael Rooks, the High's Wieland Family Senior Curator of Modern and Contemporary Art.

Martin Puryear: Nexus has benefited greatly from the invaluable knowledge, expertise, and devotion of Puryear's studio manager, Jeanne Englert, and his studio assistant, Rob Horton. We would like to extend our gratitude to Jeanne Gordon, Puryear's wife, for her warm hospitality in welcoming us each time we visited, and for her support throughout the project.

We appreciate and admire the contributors to this catalogue, who bring innovative insights to Puryear's work: Nairy Baghramian, Rizvana Bradley, Alex Da Corte, Thelma Golden, Tom Joyce, Joan Kee, Maya Lin, Kerry James Marshall, Michelle Millar Fisher, Ugochukwu-Smooth Nzewi, Pam Paulson, Julia Phillips, Charles Ray, Gabriella Shypula, and Billie Tsien. Their individual perspectives will broaden and enrich Puryear's work for generations to come. We are also grateful for the keen eyes of our editor, Jane Friedman and proofreader, Annie Jun.

For their critical archival research support, we are sincerely thankful to David Conway, Senior Archivist, David C. Driskell Center for the Visual Arts and Culture of African Americans and the African Diaspora; Katherine Coward, Archival and Curatorial Assistant, Burchfield Penney Art Center; Annakarin Lindberg, Head of Archive and Library, Royal Academy of Fine Arts, Stockholm; and Katherine Markoski, Adjunct Professor in Art History, Corcoran School of the Arts and Design, George Washington University.

At the Matthew Marks Gallery, we would like to thank Matthew Marks, Founding Partner, and Stephanie Dorsey, Senior Director who have been instrumental supporters throughout all stages of this undertaking.

We offer our most unlimited appreciation to the artist, Martin Puryear. Our collaboration with him continues to be a source of energy and inspiration that we will draw upon for years to come.

Emily Liebert
Lauren Rich Fine Curator of Contemporary Art
Chair of Art of the Americas and Modern and Contemporary Art
The Cleveland Museum of Art

Reto Thüring
Head of Culture at the Foundation for Art, Culture, and History in Winterthur, Switzerland and former Beal Family Chair, Department of Contemporary Art
The Museum of Fine Arts, Boston

An Attitude Toward Sculpture

Emily Liebert and Reto Thüring

In Martin Puryear's foundational sculpture *Bower* (1980; fig. 1 [19]), strips of spruce and pine, loosely woven together, delineate a large, open volume. Its rounded shape pitches forward, resolving in a bulbous peak. The work's construction brings to mind basketry, an art form Puryear has long admired and collected.[1] *Bower* is the first in a succession of works in which a web of woven wood outlines a similar form: *Old Mole* (1985; fig. 2) followed soon after, *Brunhilde* (1998–2000; fig. 3) came next, and *Aso Oke* (2019; [60]) materialized nearly four decades later. The works' titles connect their forms with wide-ranging references—a dwelling, an animal, a character from Norse mythology, and a man's hat made of handwoven cloth indigenous to the Yoruba region of Nigeria (see fig. 56), respectively. During a recent conversation with Puryear, when we asked about his use of woven lines to define volume, he expanded this web of allusions still further, retrieving from his extensive library three volumes on the Florentine Renaissance painter and mathematician Paolo Uccello (1397–1475).[2] Thumbing his way to the reproduction of Uccello's perspectival drawing of a chalice from 1430 (fig. 4), he described the influence on his own process of the Old Master's technique of building up a dense network of lines to render forms in space.[3]

Indeed, Puryear's unique sculptural language—his "attitude toward sculpture," as he puts it—has always been informed by his deep engagement with artistic and cultural traditions from around the world.[4] Since growing up in Washington, DC, the artist has lived in disparate places that include, in chronological order: Sierra Leone (1964–66); Stockholm (1966–68); New Haven (1969–71); Nashville (1971–73); New York City (1973–78); Chicago (1978–90); and Upstate New York, which has been his home since 1992. From these various bases, Puryear has traveled extensively within North America and well beyond domestic borders. Countries and regions of particular sustained interest—as explored elsewhere in this catalogue—include France, Japan, Korea, Scandinavia, and West Africa. Beyond the sheer beauty and elegance of Puryear's art, its draw and indelible impact stem from the ways in which he combines the distinctive techniques of production and the formal histories he has encountered through his movements and migrations, research and study.

It was Puryear's range of sources that provided some of the initial inspiration for this exhibition at the Cleveland Museum of Art and the Museum of Fine Arts, Boston. As internationally renowned repositories for objects spanning vast reaches of time and geography, both institutions offer a rich and fitting context in which to consider Puryear's oeuvre. *Martin Puryear: Nexus* and its accompanying publication highlight the global histories that have shaped Puryear's practice, offering a fresh and timely perspective on his powerful body of work. While celebrating the visual allure of Puryear's art, this exhibition looks beyond form, illuminating the ways in which Puryear's artistic vocabulary has been informed by his enduring interests in myriad traditions of material culture as well as social history and the natural world. In these ways, Puryear's body of work demonstrates the expressive potential for abstraction in our time.

Martin Puryear: Nexus is an expansive presentation, introducing new audiences to the full career of one of the most inventive and influential living artists. The exhibition begins with work from the early 1960s and follows Puryear's innovations in form, material, and process since then. Visitors will encounter new works that make their first appearance in this show, alongside iconic sculptures and works that have not been exhibited publicly in decades.

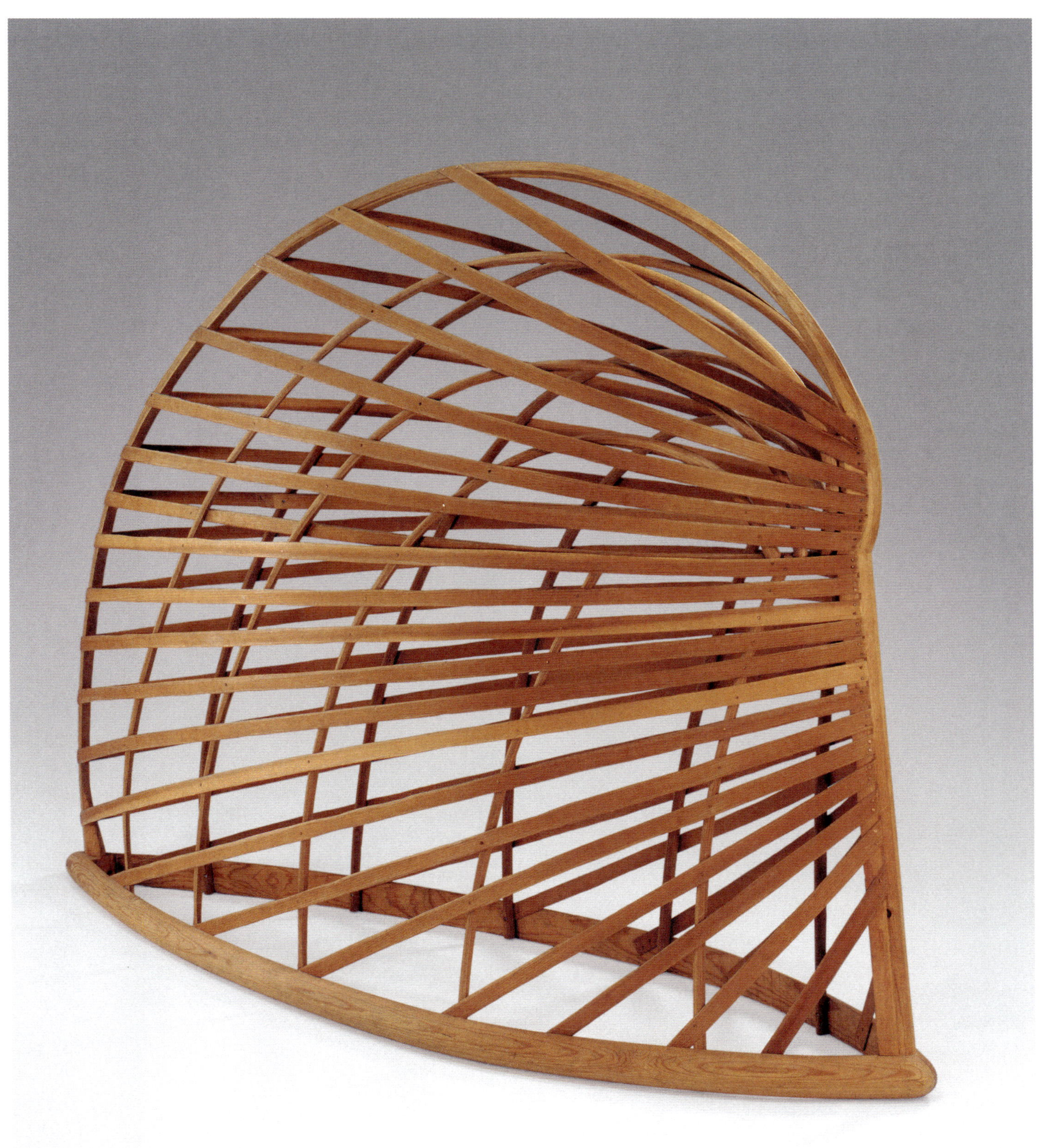

Figure 1. *Bower* (1980; [19]). Martin Puryear. Photo: Smithsonian American Art Museum, Washington, DC / Art Resource, NY

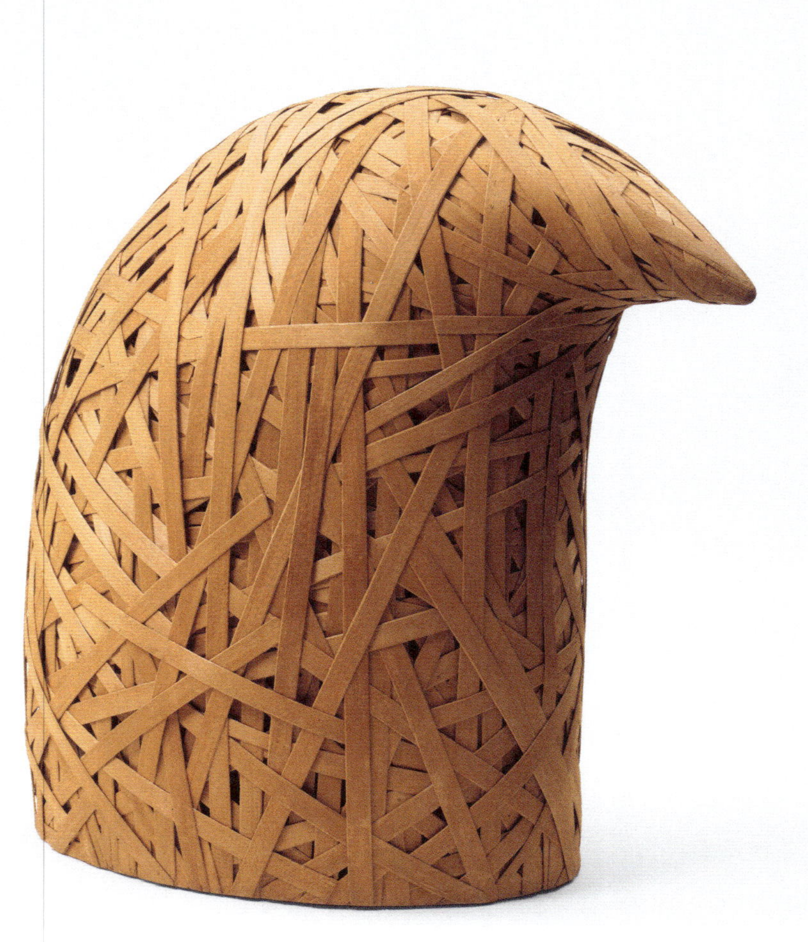

Figure 2. *Old Mole* (1985). Martin Puryear. Red cedar; 154.9 x 154.8 cm. Philadelphia Museum of Art, Purchased with gifts (by exchange) of Samuel S. White, 3rd and Vera White, and Mr. and Mrs. Charles C. G. Chaplin and with funds contributed by Marion Boulton Stroud, Mr. and Mrs. Robert Kardon, Gisela and Dennis Alter, and Mrs. H. Gates Lloyd. Photo: The Philadelphia Museum of Art / Art Resource, NY

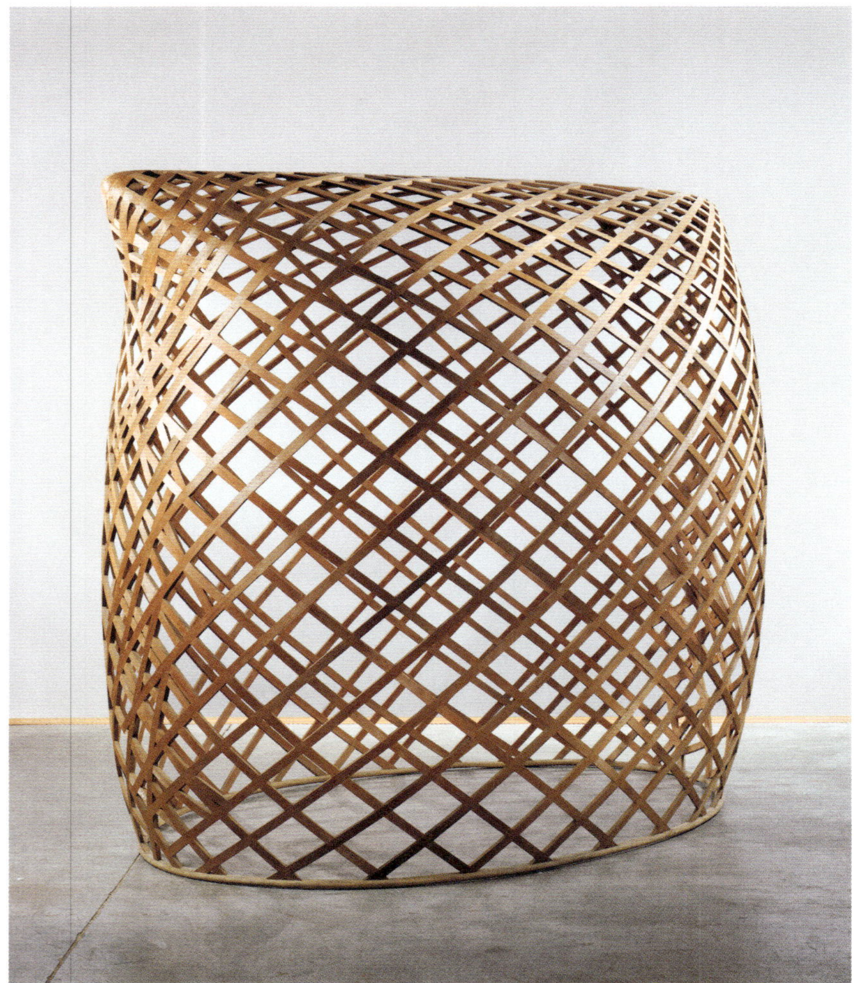

Figure 3. *Brunhilde* (1998–2000). Martin Puryear. Cedar and rattan; 243.8 x 285 x 187.9 cm. Collection of the artist. Photo: Richard Goodbody

Puryear's first solo exhibition was a presentation of his prints and small sculptures at the Gröna Paletten Galleri, Stockholm, in 1968. Ever since, he has consistently exhibited his work both in the United States and internationally. Notably, a career survey spanning thirty years of Puryear's sculpture opened in 2007 at the Museum of Modern Art, New York (see figs. 7, 38, 83, and 124), and toured the United States until 2009.[5] A traveling survey of Puryear's works on paper, organized by the Art Institute of Chicago, opened at the Morgan Library & Museum in 2015, illuminating what had up until then be a less-known facet of his practice (see fig. 116).[6] In 2023, the opening of *Lookout* (see figs. 29a–c; [70]), a permanent brick sculpture at Storm King Art Center, was the occasion for an exhibition that demonstrated the importance of site-specific outdoor sculpture in his oeuvre.[7] The show presented these mostly permanent works spread across the globe—from Washington, DC, and Chicago to Norway and Japan—through sketches, photographic documentation, and exquisitely crafted maquettes, populated with the artist's hand-carved figures for scale. Building on the contributions of these foundational exhibitions, *Martin Puryear: Nexus* frames the artist's primarily sculptural practice in relation to his prints, drawings, and documentation of the outdoor works to reveal how he has translated forms and ideas across mediums throughout his career.

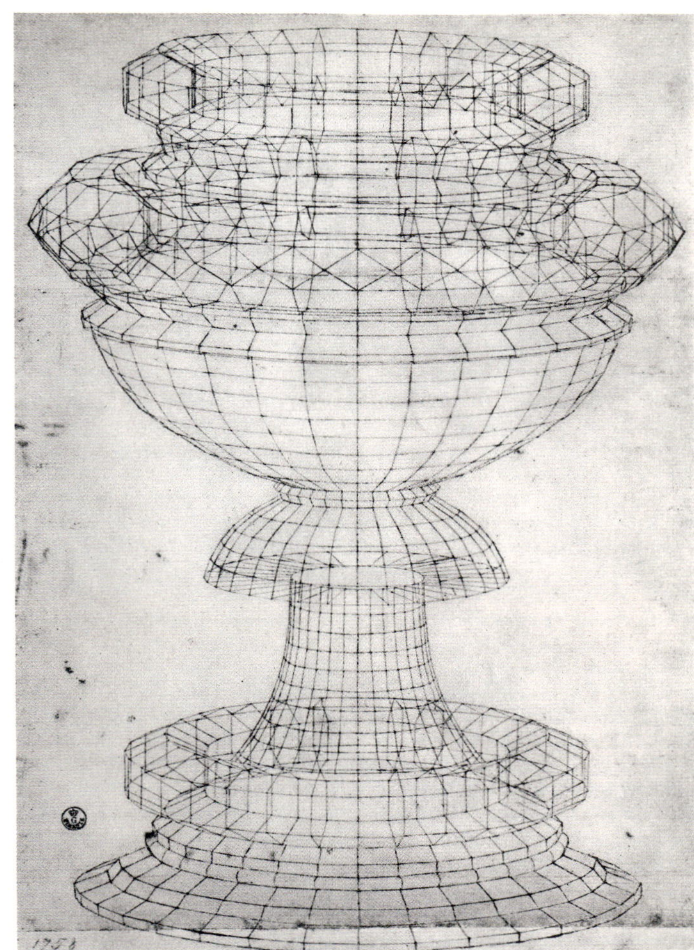

Figure 4. Paolo Uccello (Italian, 1397–1475), *Perspective Study of a Chalice*, 1430. Pen and ink on paper; 29 x 24.5 cm. Gabinetto dei Disegni, Uffizi, Florence

Puryear has long described the arc of his career as a spiral in which interests, materials, and forms endure but are regularly reimagined and transformed at different points in time.[8] Responding to that characterization, art historian Nancy Princenthal writes that for Puryear, "a survey is . . . as much an opportunity to review how his work's meaning has shifted in relationship to new contexts as to plot the development of his career."[9] In the terms offered by this reflection, this exhibition asks: How does Puryear's work make meaning at our current moment in history?

While Puryear's art never delivers explicit commentary on current events or politics, it manifests the artist's deep engagements with the social and material histories that shape our everyday environments. One of Puryear's most direct articulations of these engagements took form when he represented the United States at the 58th Venice Biennale in 2019 (see figs. 28 and 60). Against the backdrop of Donald Trump's first presidency, Puryear felt that his installation in the American Pavilion needed to reflect—albeit in characteristically subtle and nuanced ways—the crisis that he believed the country was experiencing.[10]

The critique that permeated *Martin Puryear: Liberty / Libertà* was most perceptible in the two works that were site-specific to the presentation: *Swallowed Sun (Monstrance and Volute)* (2019; see figs. 5, 6, 28, and [63–65]) and *A Column for Sally Hemings* (2019; fig. 60).[11] Visitors encountered the monumental *Swallowed Sun* in the forecourt of the American Pavilion. The work's tall and wide screen, made of laminated plywood, partially obscured the pavilion's facade and prevented entrance through its front door (see fig. 5). By hindering physical passage into this space, Puryear undermined the elegance of the pavilion's entrance and the building's lofty ambitions: to celebrate the United States' role in global culture and democracy. When visitors did make it around the partition, they encountered the work's support structure: a dark, coiled mass evoking the tail of a dragon (see fig. 6).

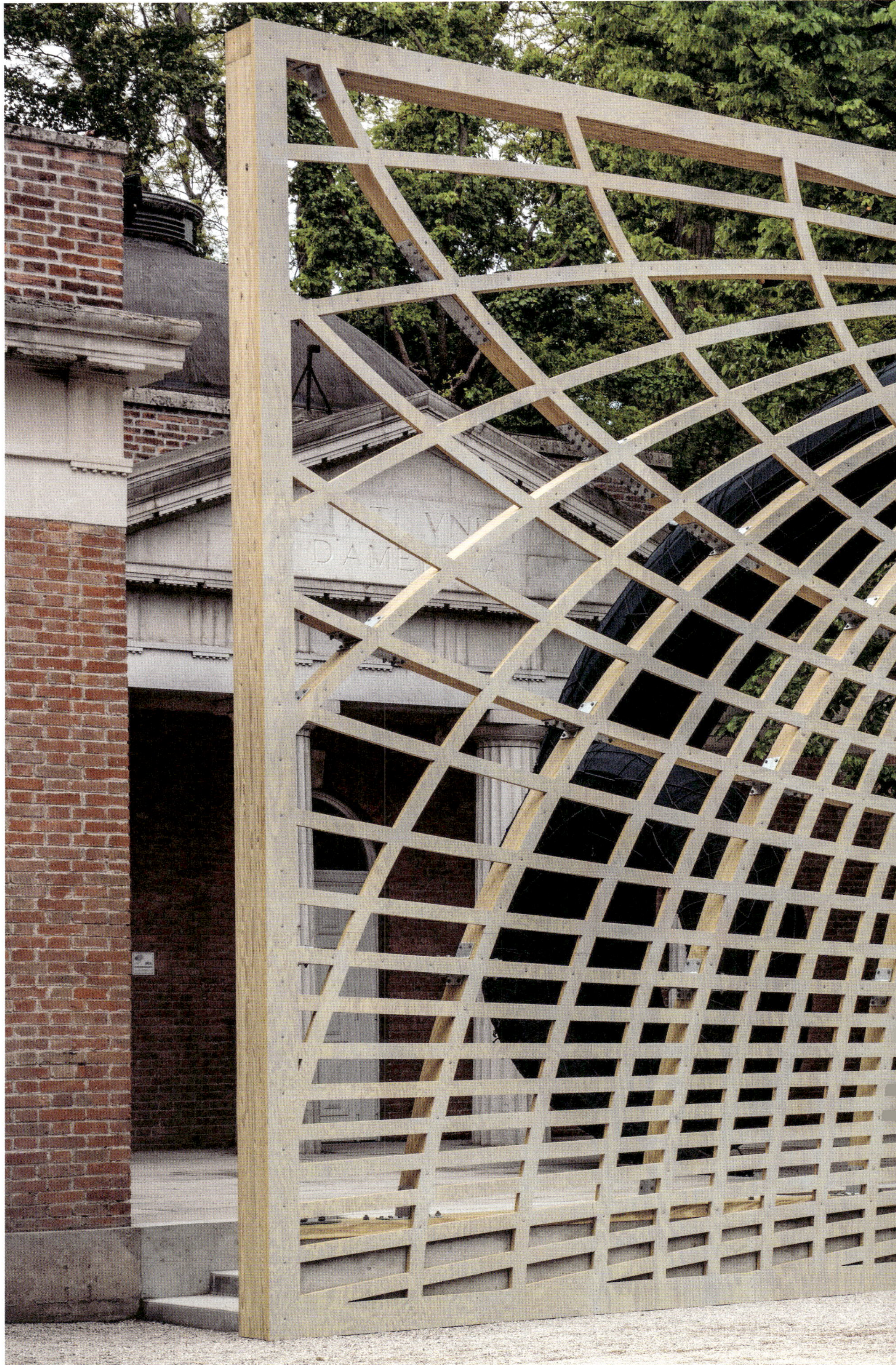

Figure 5. Installation view of *Swallowed Sun (Monstrance and Volute)* (2019), Venice Biennale, 2019. Southern yellow pine, steel, polyester, and rope; two parts, overall 691.1 x 1341.1 x 739.1 cm. Photo: Joshua White

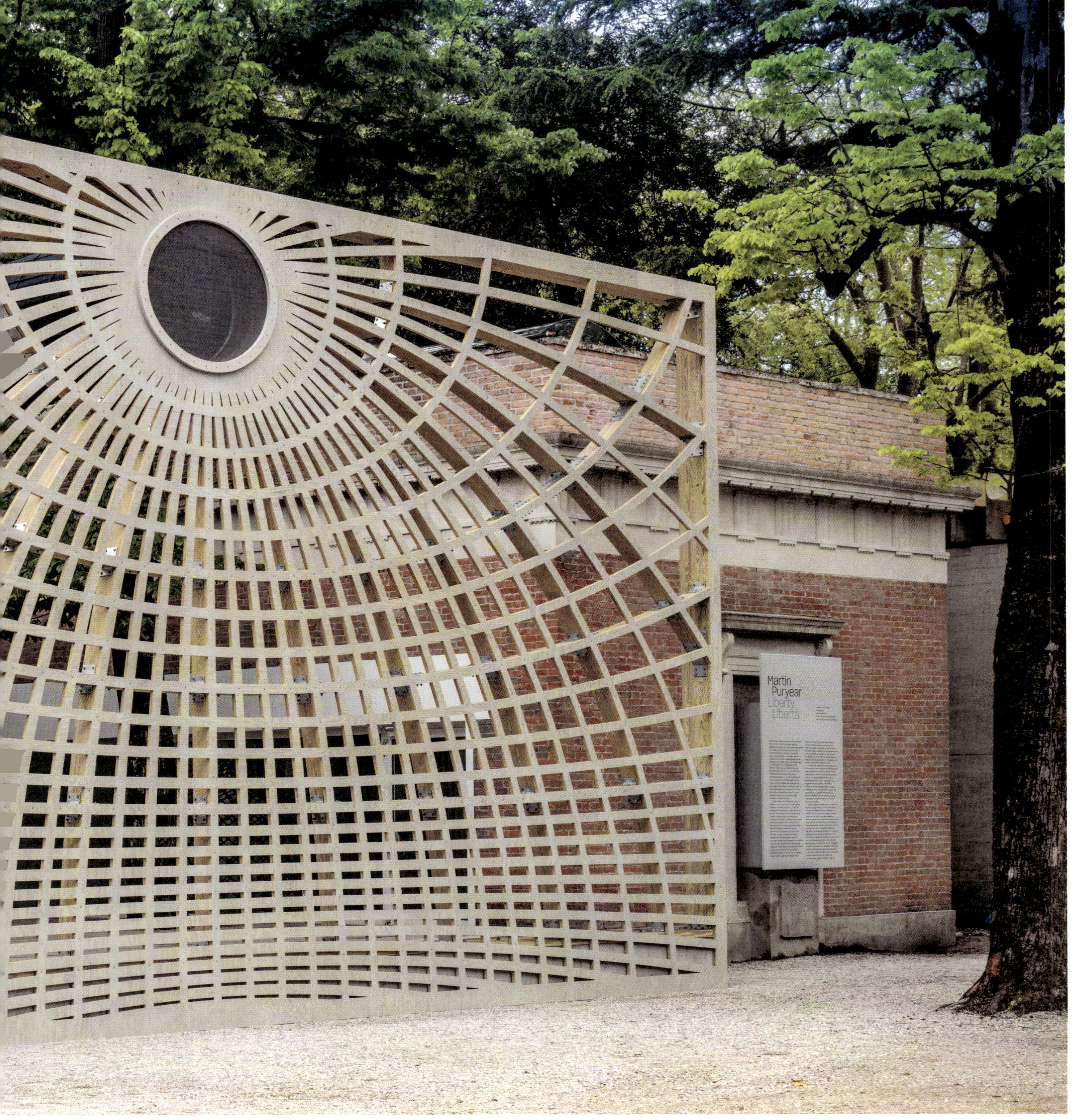
Martin
Puryear
Liberty
Libertà

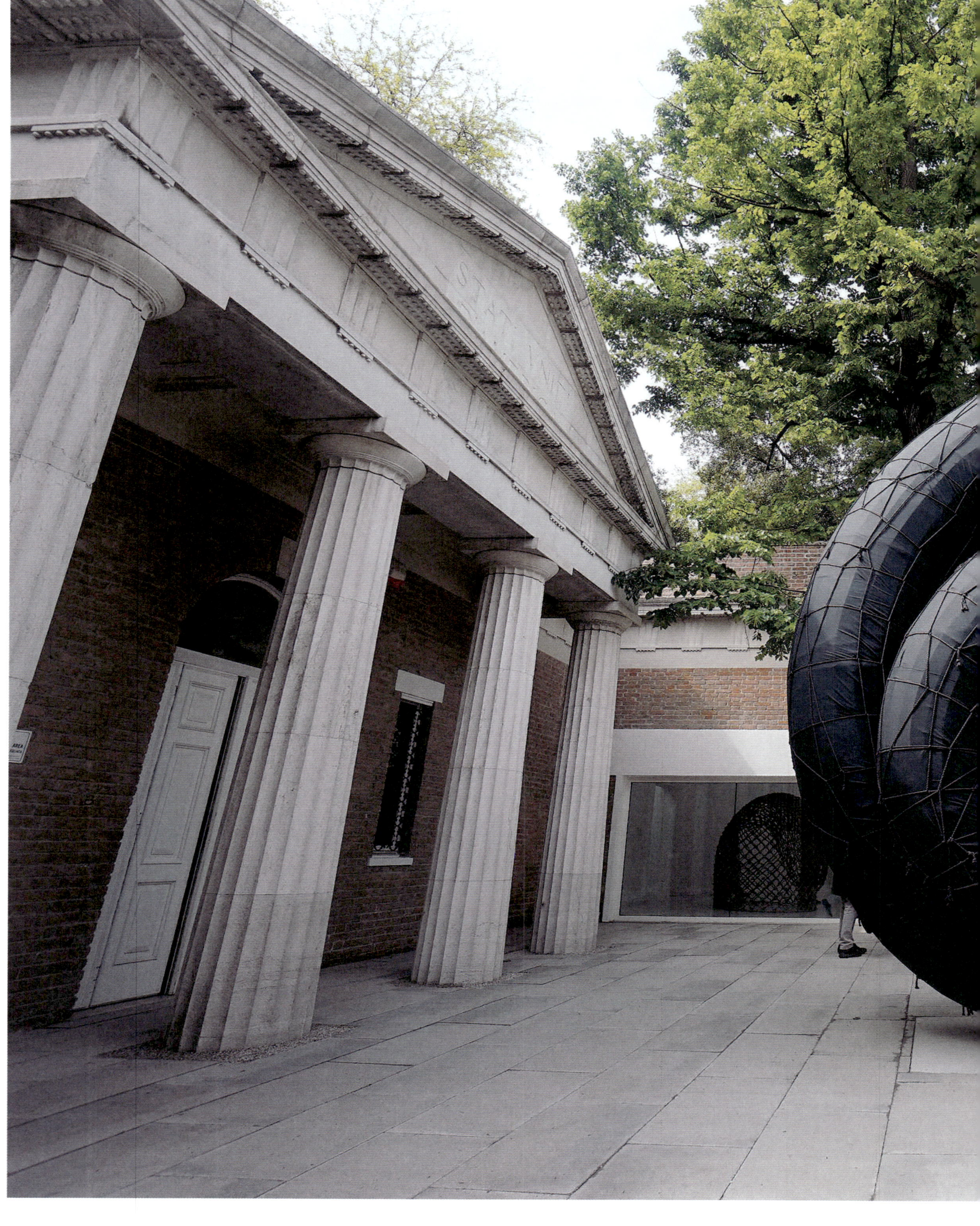

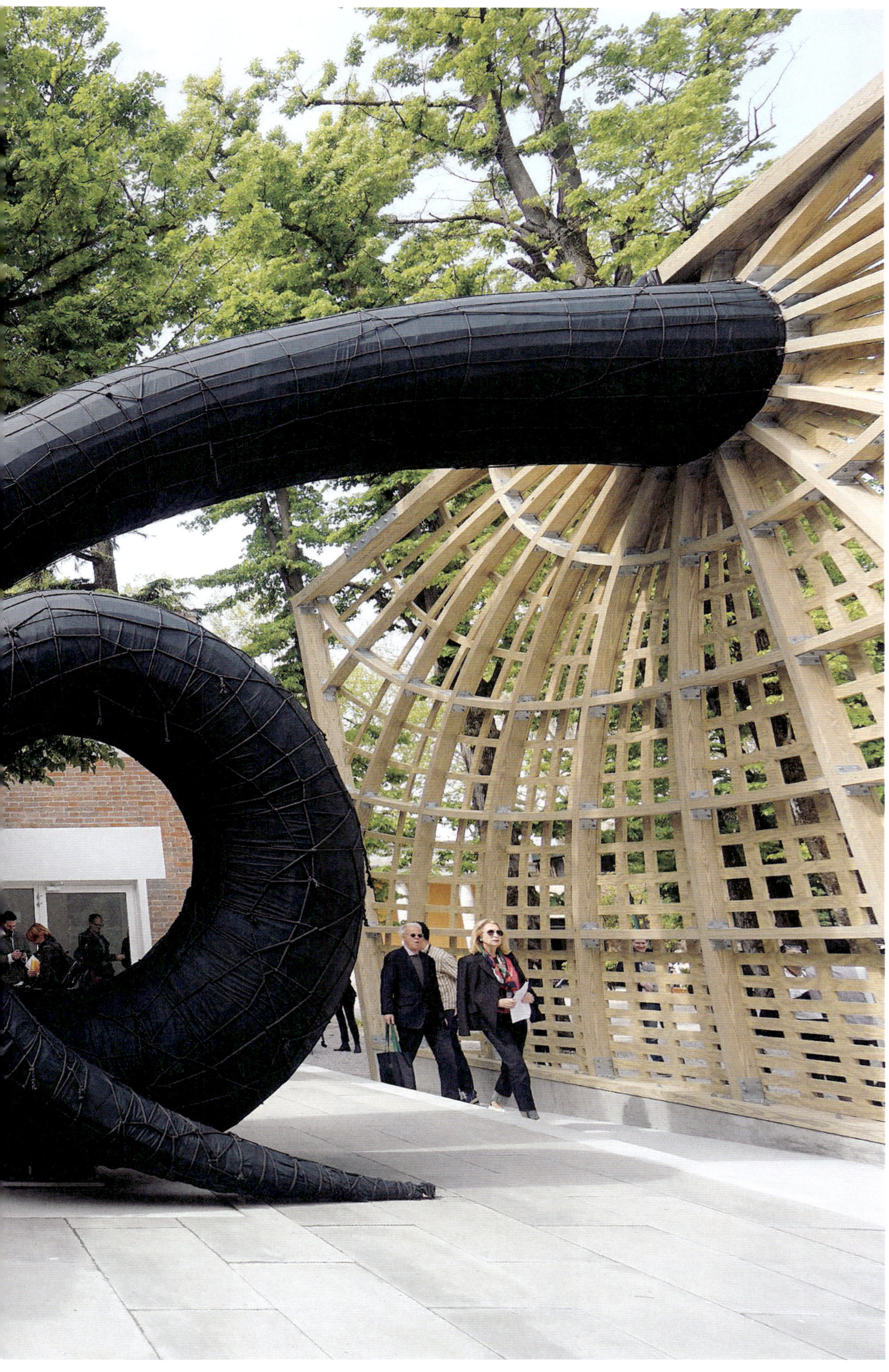

Figure 6. Installation view of *Swallowed Sun (Monstrance and Volute)* (2019), Venice Biennale, 2019. Photo: Andrea Merola / EPA-EFE / Shutterstock

Inside the pavilion, *A Column for Sally Hemings* brought the history of the woman enslaved by Thomas Jefferson and mother to at least six of his children into *Liberty / Libertà*. As discussed more extensively elsewhere in this publication, Puryear created this work in response to the American Pavilion's architecture, which was modeled on Monticello, Jefferson's home in Charlottesville, Virginia (see fig. 59).[12]

The Venice presentation afforded its curator, Brooke Kamin Rapaport, an occasion to question the dominance of formalism in the discourse surrounding Puryear's work. The "persistent classification of his work as pure abstraction," she explains, "limits full analysis and interpretation."[13] If this assertion was especially born out in the Biennale's American Pavilion, a thorough consideration of Puryear's career up until that point shows that formalism on its own has never been a sufficient interpretive model for understanding the artist's work. Now, as new and veteran audiences encounter an expansive presentation of Puryear's career through this exhibition, the time is ripe to bring a fresh set of readings to his art that illuminate the astonishing breadth of its sources, content, and underlying ideas.

Five essays by a new generation of scholars offer valuable insights on these topics. Emily Liebert traces Puryear's attunement to and extensive knowledge of nature and wildlife from childhood to the present. Liebert shows that throughout his career, the natural world has offered a way to elucidate social experience, including the constructed opposition between science and culture. Ugochukwu-Smooth Nzewi addresses the many ways that Puryear's time in Sierra Leone, where he was a Peace Corps volunteer from 1964 to 1966, shaped his practice as an artist. Nzewi's text interprets the formal, aesthetic, and ethical characteristics of Puryear's art in relation to analogous qualities in African art and artisanal histories. Michelle Millar Fisher considers Puryear's art in relation to a history of contemporary craft. In Fisher's analysis, that history does not comprise a series of material or technical innovations but rather a philosophy and ethos that she locates at the core of Puryear's practice. Fisher begins her essay in Sweden, where Puryear, then a student at the Royal Academy of Fine Arts, Stockholm, had his first of multiple formative encounters with the celebrated woodworker, furniture maker, and educator James Krenov (1920–2009). Joan Kee explores Puryear's engagement with Asian histories of making and inhabiting space. Through that perspective Kee reveals the nuanced role of influence and allusion in Puryear's practice, arguing that "kinship" is a more useful interpretive lens than "inherited ties" for locating the relevant affinities. Rizvana Bradley traces the ways in which Puryear's art carries history into the present, focusing on its capacity for multiple, even irreconcilable interpretations. This, Bradley contends, manifests a broader resistance to linear treatments of history that have not sufficiently attended to Black lives, art, and culture.

Through entries on individual works of their choosing, ten thinkers and makers from a range of disciplines, many of them longtime interlocutors of the artist, bring additional viewpoints into this book. Nairy Baghramian, Alex Da Corte, Thelma Golden, Tom Joyce, Maya Lin, Kerry James Marshall, Pam Paulson, Julia Phillips, Charles Ray, and Billie Tsien offer incisive and often personal accounts of Puryear's art spanning time and material. Gabriella Shypula's chronology of exhibitions, commissions, and special projects charts in words and pictures the public life of Puryear's art from 1962 up to the present moment.

Thanks to Martin Puryear's generous exchanges with the authors in this catalogue, the publication is suffused with his erudition and focus, curiosity and empathy, grace and wit—elements of a humanity that this singular artist's work conveys with beauty and power.

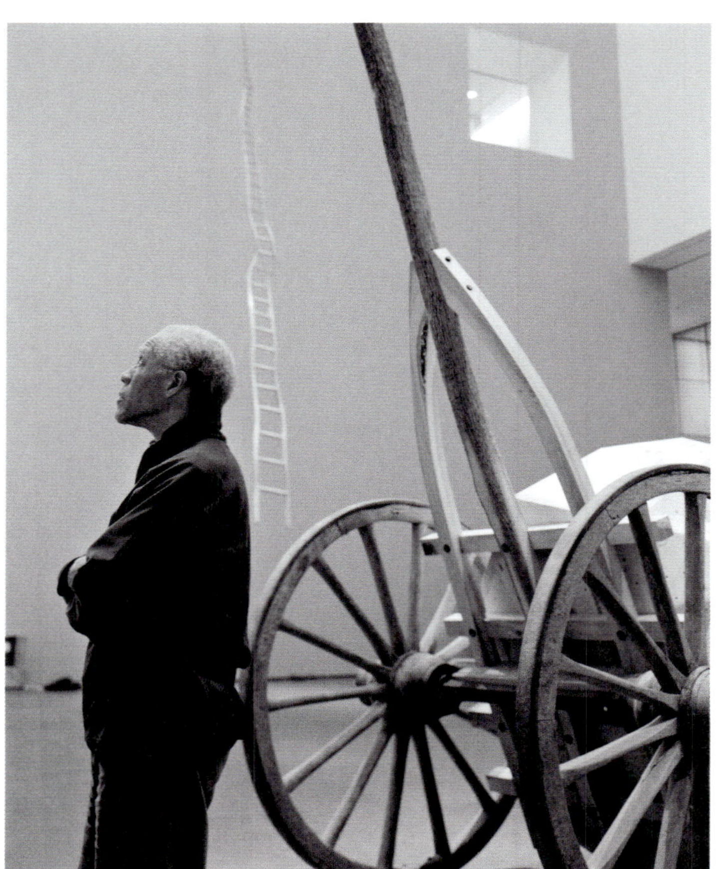

Figure 7. Martin Puryear with *Ladder for Booker T. Washington* (1996) and *Ad Astra* (2007) in *Martin Puryear*, The Museum of Modern Art, New York, 2007. Photo: Yola Monakhov Stockton

1. For an insightful account of the ways in which Puryear's work reflects his interest in basketry, see Lynne Cooke, "Modernist Histories: Braided, Interlaced, and Aligned," in *Woven Histories: Textiles and Modern Abstraction*, ed. Lynne Cooke, exh. cat. (Washington, DC: National Gallery of Art; Chicago and London: University of Chicago Press, 2023), 19.

2. John Pope-Hennessy, *Paolo Uccello: Complete Edition* (London and New York: Phaidon, 1950); Franco and Stefano Borsi, *Paolo Uccello* (Paris: Hazan, 1992); and Paolo D'Ancona, *Paolo Uccello* (London: Oldbourne Press, 1960).

3. Martin Puryear, conversation with the authors, June 14, 2024.

4. Martin Puryear, conversation with the authors, March 23, 2023.

5. Organized by John Elderfield, *Martin Puryear* was on view at the Museum of Modern Art from November 4, 2007, to January 14, 2008; it traveled to the Modern Art Museum of Fort Worth (February 24–May 18, 2008); the National Gallery of Art, Washington, DC (June 22–September 28, 2008); and the San Francisco Museum of Modern Art (November 8, 2008–January 25, 2009).

6. Organized by Mark Pascale, *Martin Puryear: Multiple Dimensions* was on view at the Art Institute of Chicago from February 5 to May 1, 2016. The show opened at the Morgan Library & Museum (October 9, 2015–January 10, 2016), and concluded its tour at the Smithsonian American Art Museum (May 26–September 4, 2016).

7. Organized by Nora Lawrence, *Martin Puryear: Process and Scale* was on view at Storm King Art Center from September 23 to December 17, 2023.

8. Puryear, conversation with the authors, June 14, 2024. See also Puryear quoted in Peter W. Boswell, "Martin Puryear," in Martin Friedman et al., *Sculpture Inside Outside*, exh. cat. (Minneapolis: Walker Art Center; New York: Rizzoli, 1988), 189; and cited in John Elderfield, "Martin Puryear: Ideas of Otherness," in *Martin Puryear*, ed. John Elderfield, exh. cat. (New York: Museum of Modern Art, 2007), 13.

9. Nancy Princenthal, "Puryear's Tall Tales," *Art in America* 96, no. 2 (February 2008): 118.

10. Puryear, conversation with the authors, June 14, 2024.

11. The artist made two editions of *A Column for Sally Hemings*, one in 2019 and the other in 2021. The 2019 edition, exhibited at the Venice Biennale that same year, was created in white-painted poplar and cast iron, see fig. 60; the 2021 edition, featured in *Martin Puryear: Nexus* [62], was created in marble and cast iron.

12. See Emily Liebert's essay in this volume, p. 126; Ugochukwu-Smooth Nzewi's essay in volume, p. 142.

13. Brooke Kamin Rapaport, "Martin Puryear: Liberty / Libertà," in Brooke Kamin Rapaport et al., *Martin Puryear: Liberty / Libertà*, exh. cat. (New York: Madison Square Park Conservancy and Gregory R. Miller; Berlin: Hatje Cantz, 2019), 32.

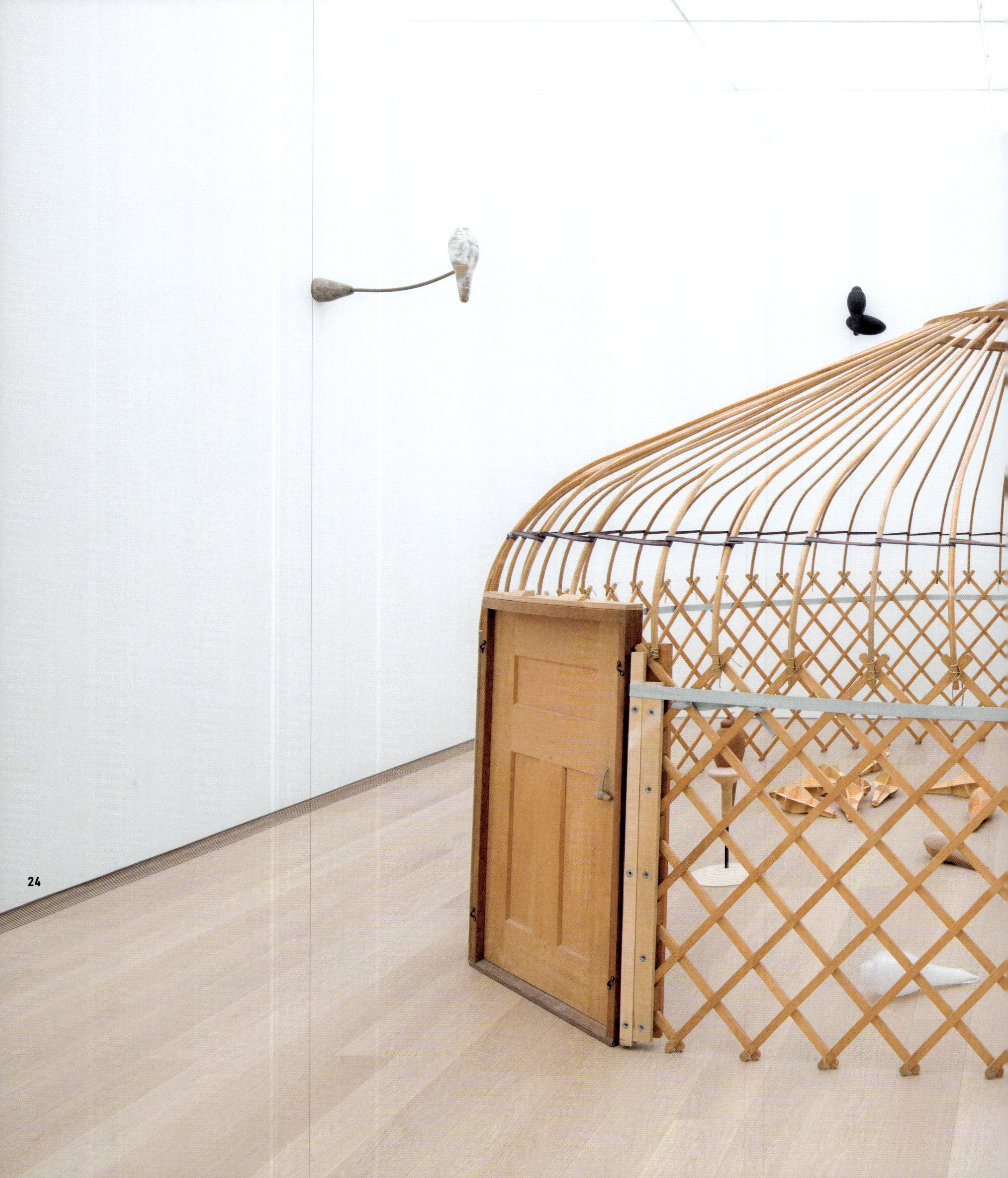

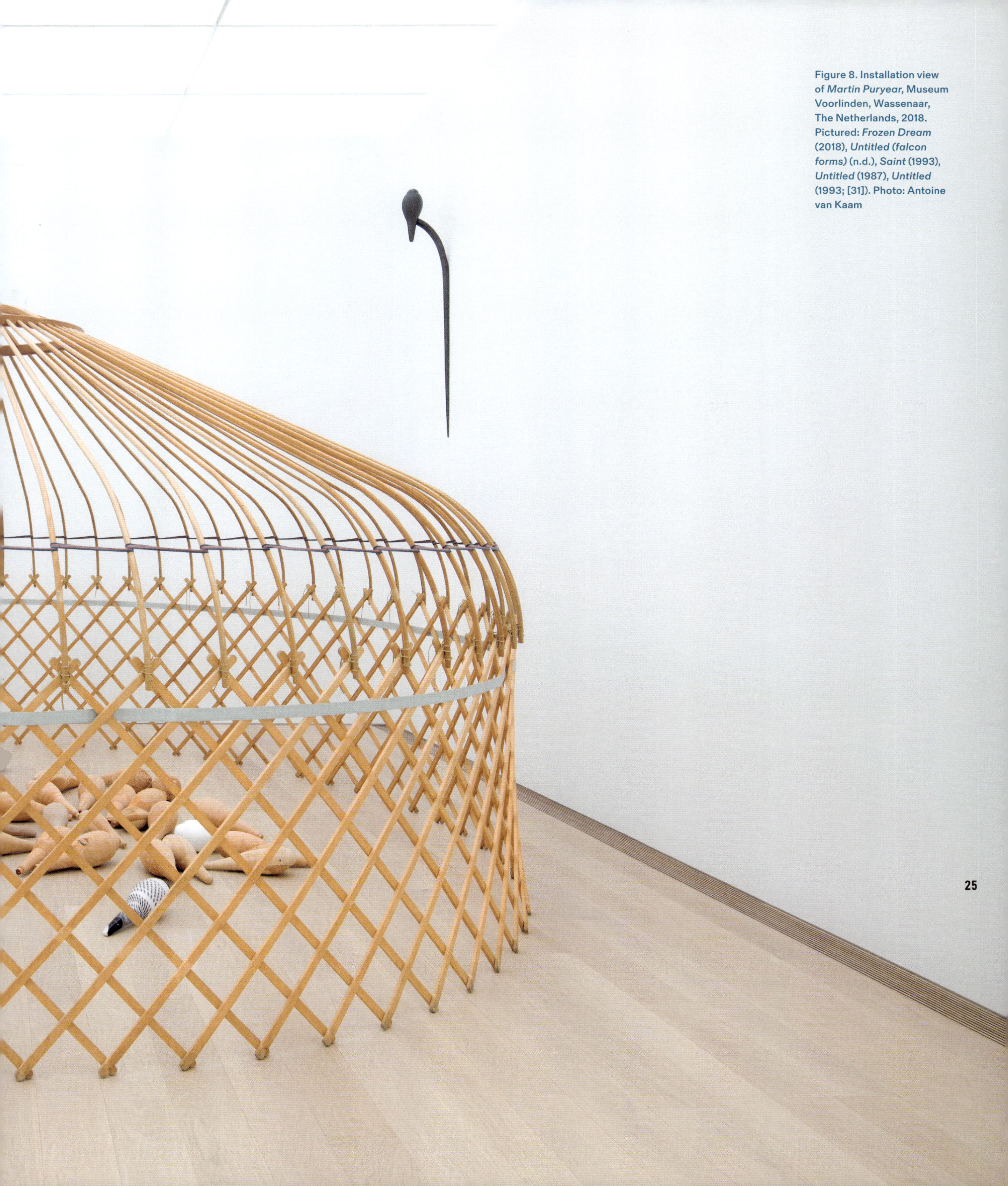

Figure 8. Installation view of *Martin Puryear*, Museum Voorlinden, Wassenaar, The Netherlands, 2018. Pictured: *Frozen Dream* (2018), *Untitled (falcon forms)* (n.d.), *Saint* (1993), *Untitled* (1987), *Untitled* (1993; [31]). Photo: Antoine van Kaam

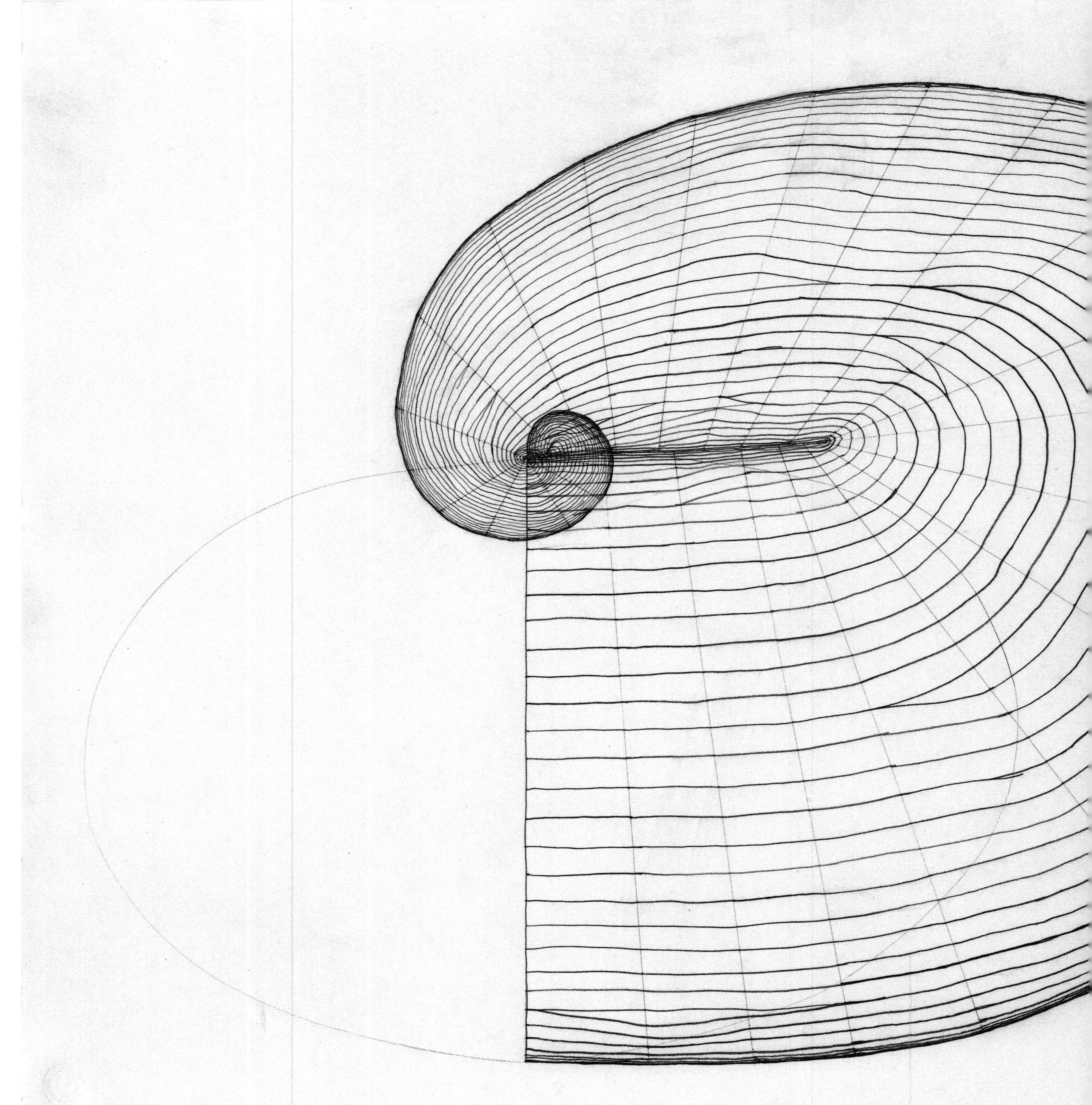

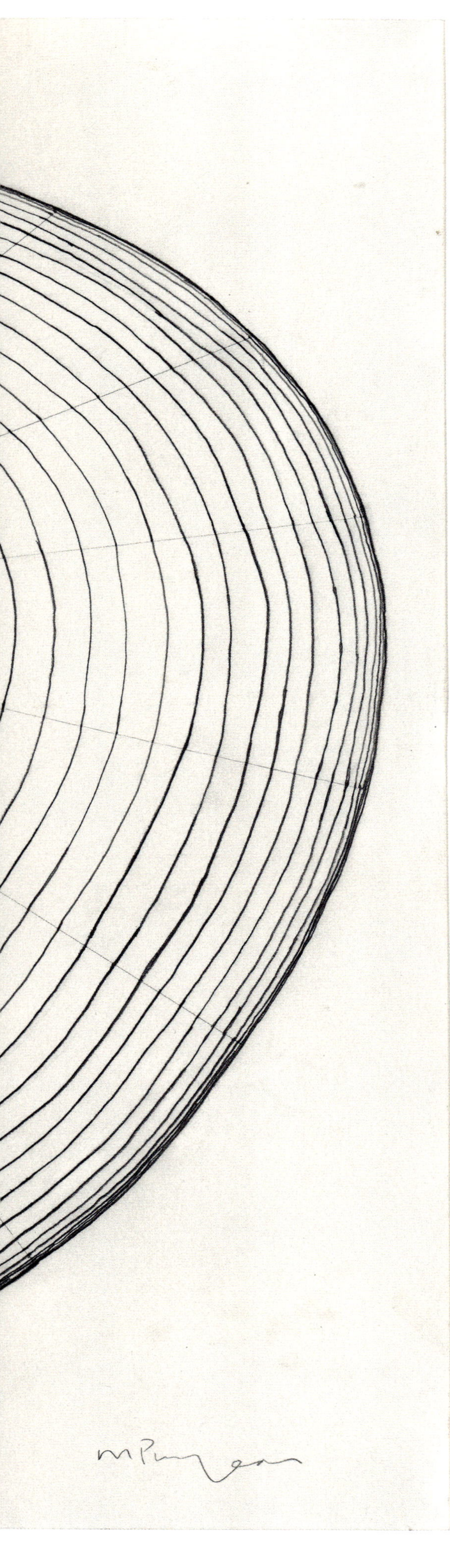

Figure 9. *Untitled* (c. 2003; [47]). Martin Puryear. Collection of the artist. Photo: The Art Institute of Chicago

Plates and Responses

Responses

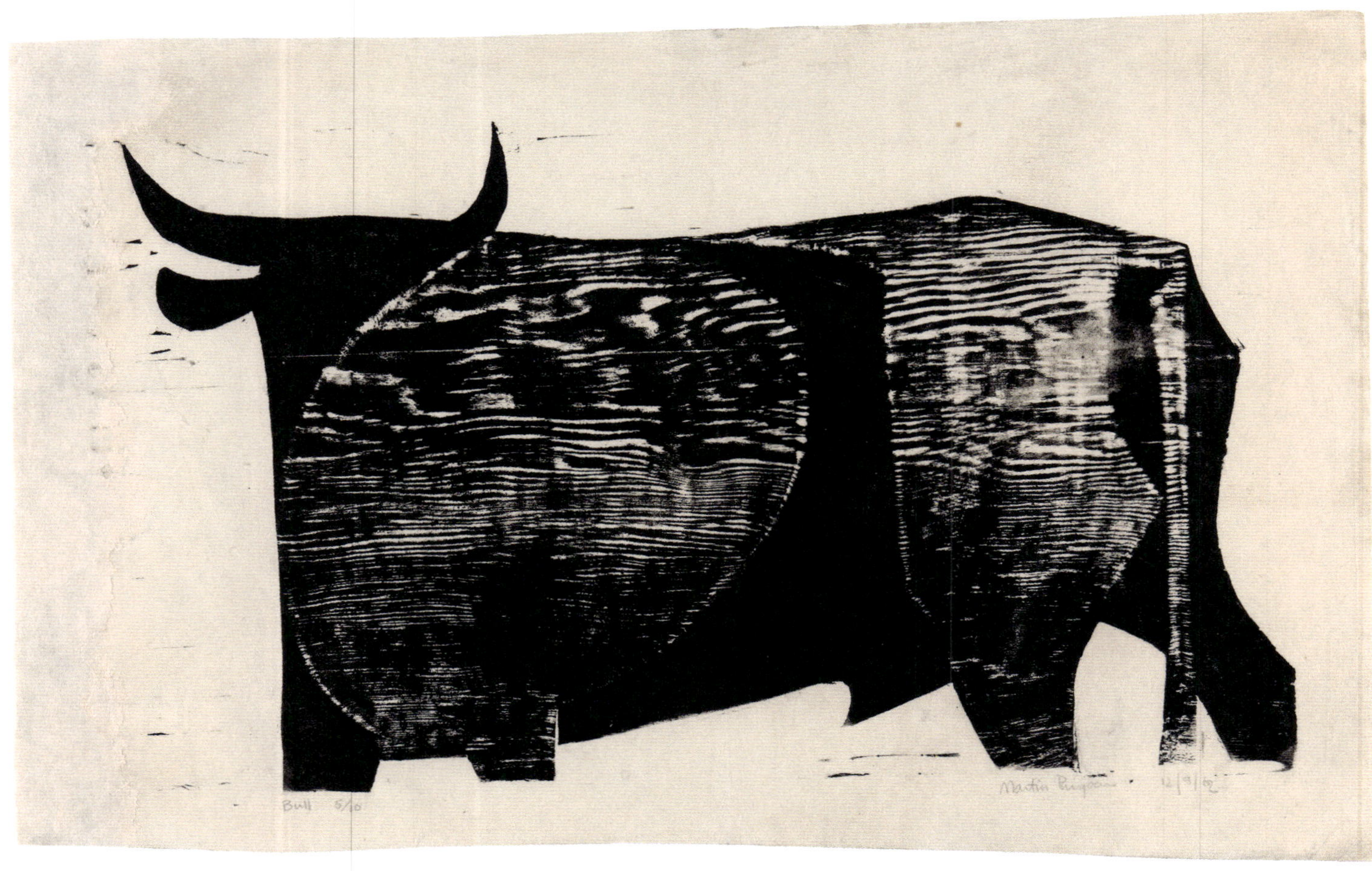

1

Bull, 1962

Woodcut on Japanese paper; block: 27.5 x 49 cm; sheet: 35 x 54.4 cm

Collection of the artist

Photo: The Art Institute of Chicago

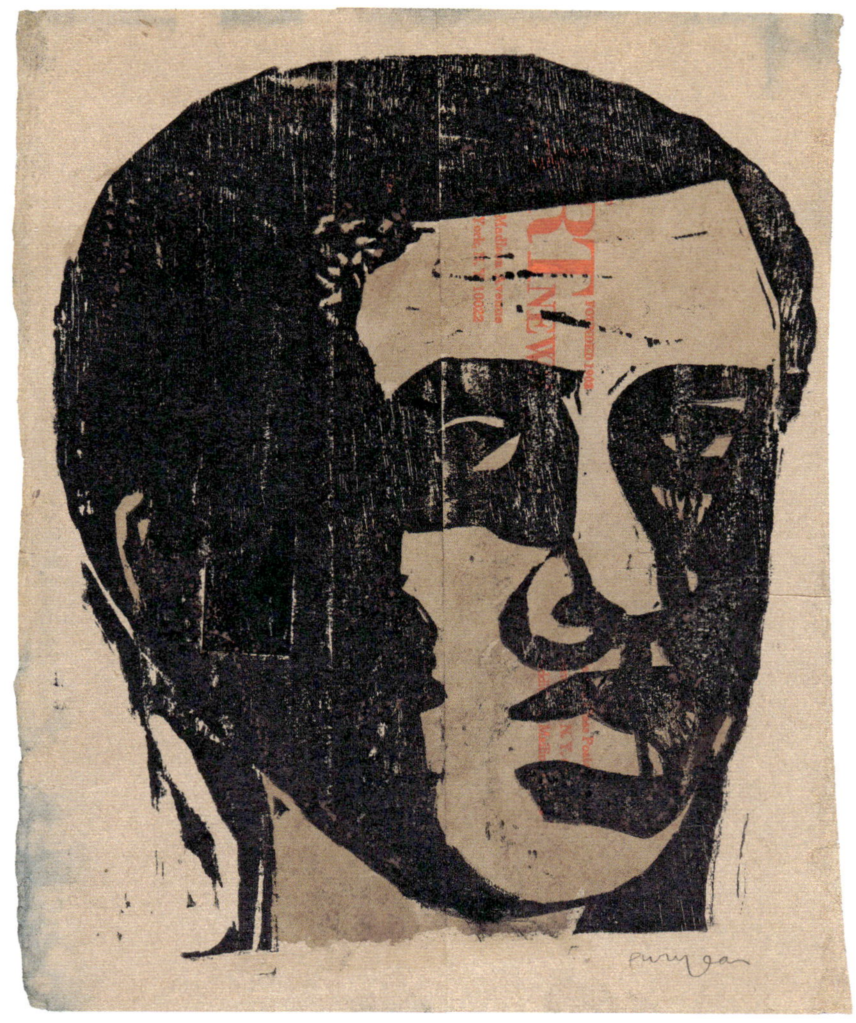

2

Head, 1965

Woodcut (*ARTnews* wrapper); block: 27 x 22 cm; sheet: 29.9 x 24 cm

Collection of the artist

Photo: The Art Institute of Chicago

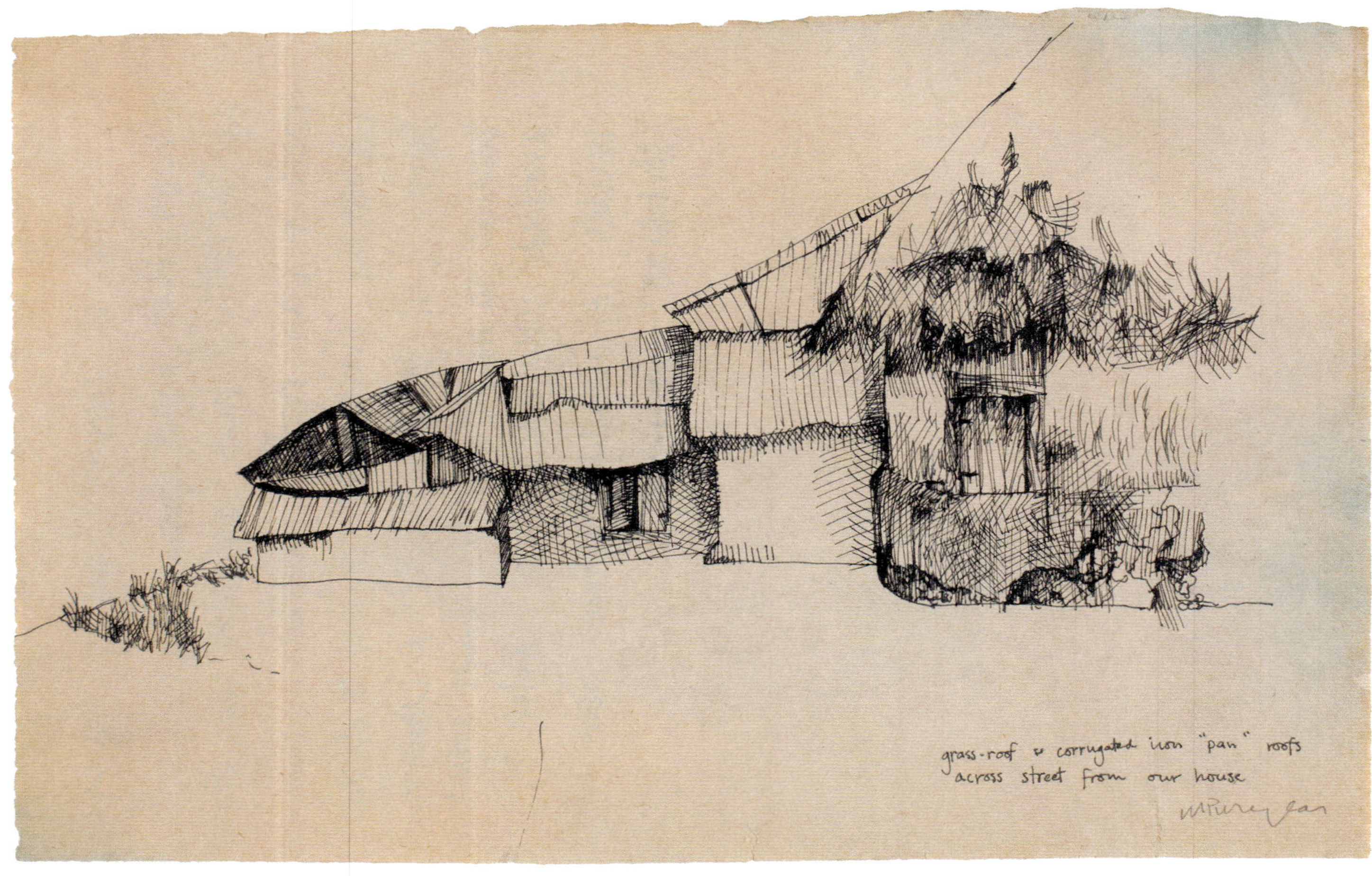

3

Untitled, 1964/1966

Pen and black ink on tan wove paper; 21.9 x 34 cm

Collection of the artist

Photo: The Art Institute of Chicago

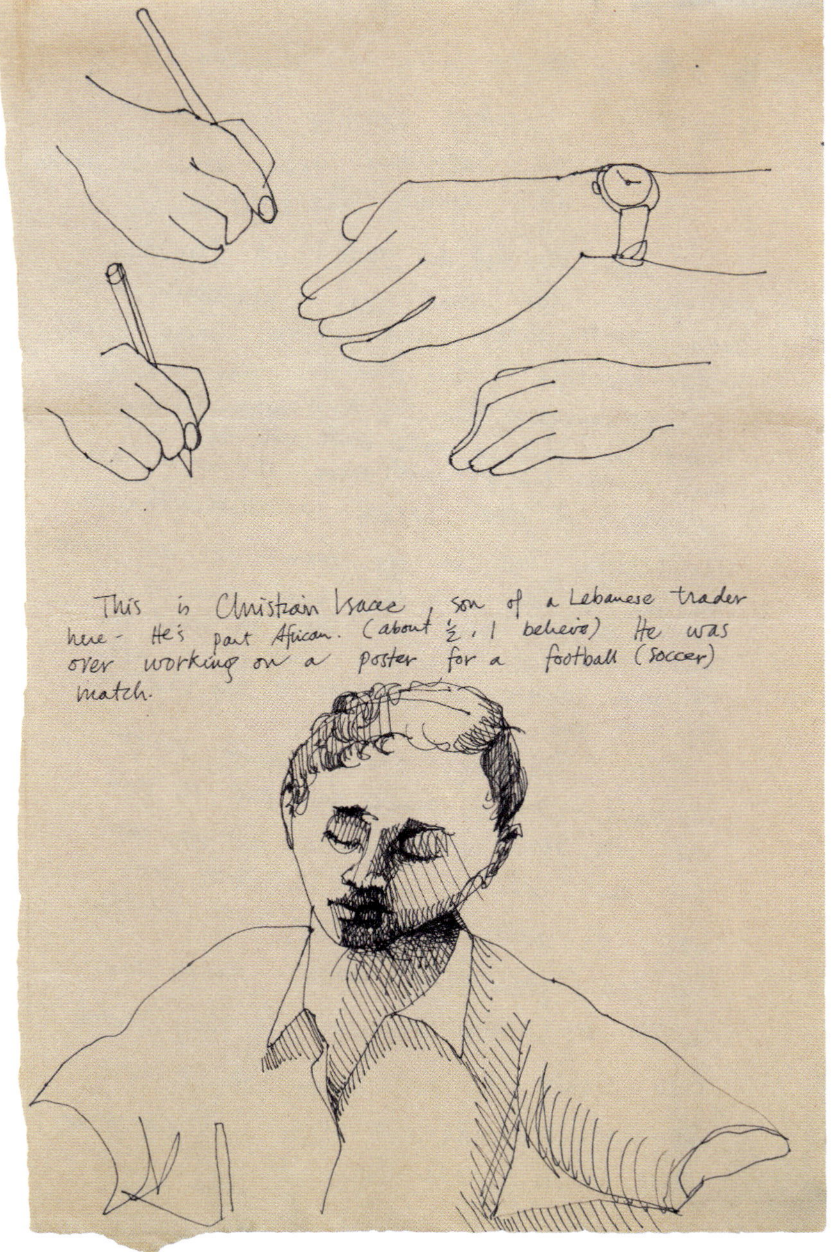

4

Untitled, 1965

Pen and black ink on paper; 34.3 x 21.6 cm.

Collection of the artist

Photo: Matthew Marks Gallery

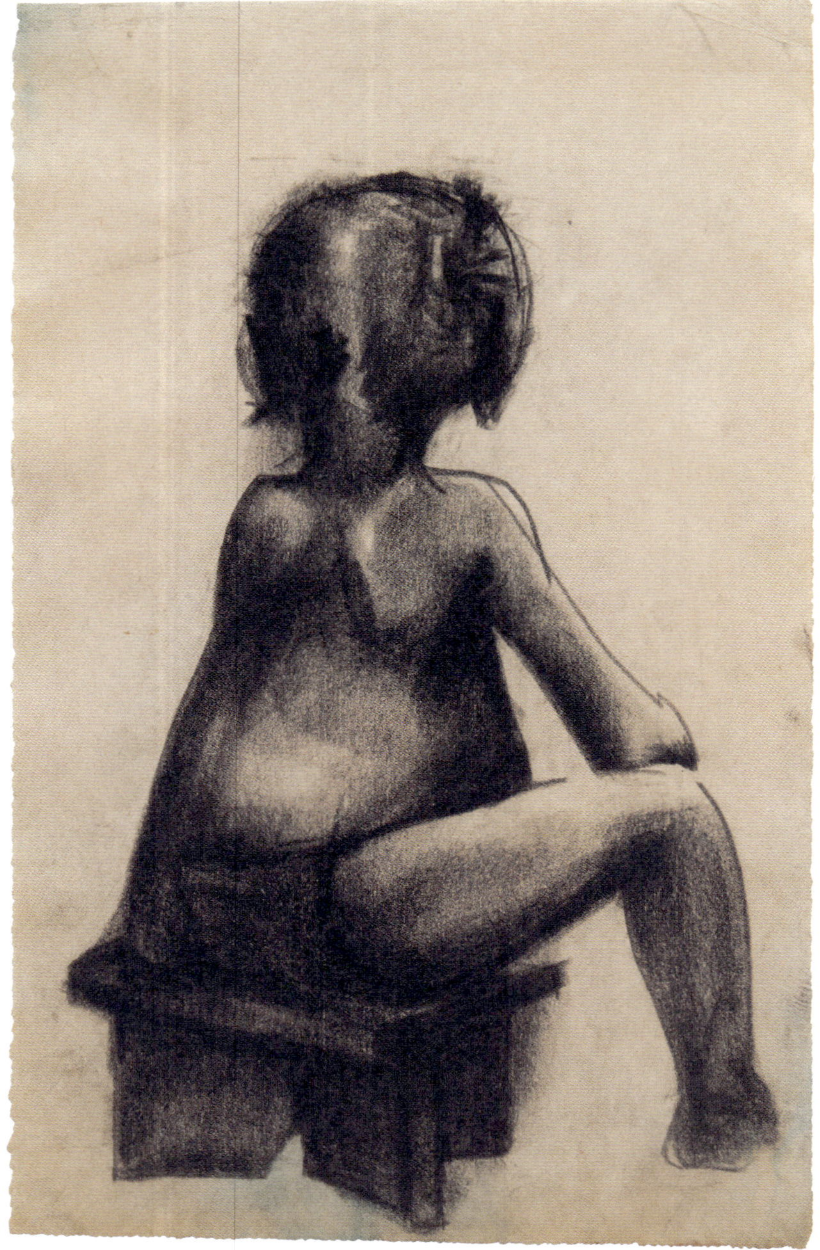

5

Untitled, 1964/1966

Charcoal on paper;
35.1 x 21.9 cm

Collection of the artist

Photo: Matthew Marks
Gallery

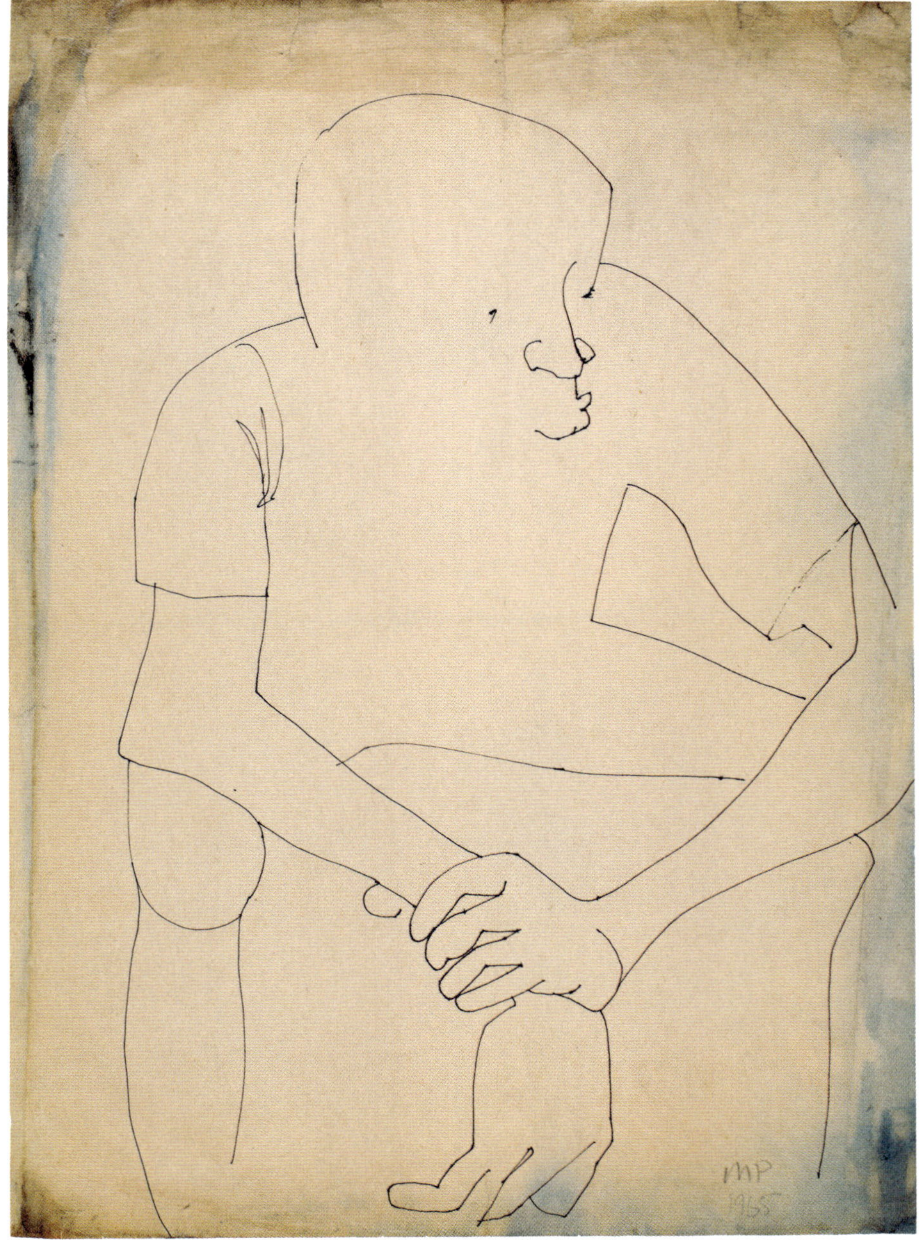

6

Untitled (Joseph Momoh), 1965

Pen and ink paper; 41.9 x 29.6 cm

Collection of the artist

Photo: The Art Institute of Chicago

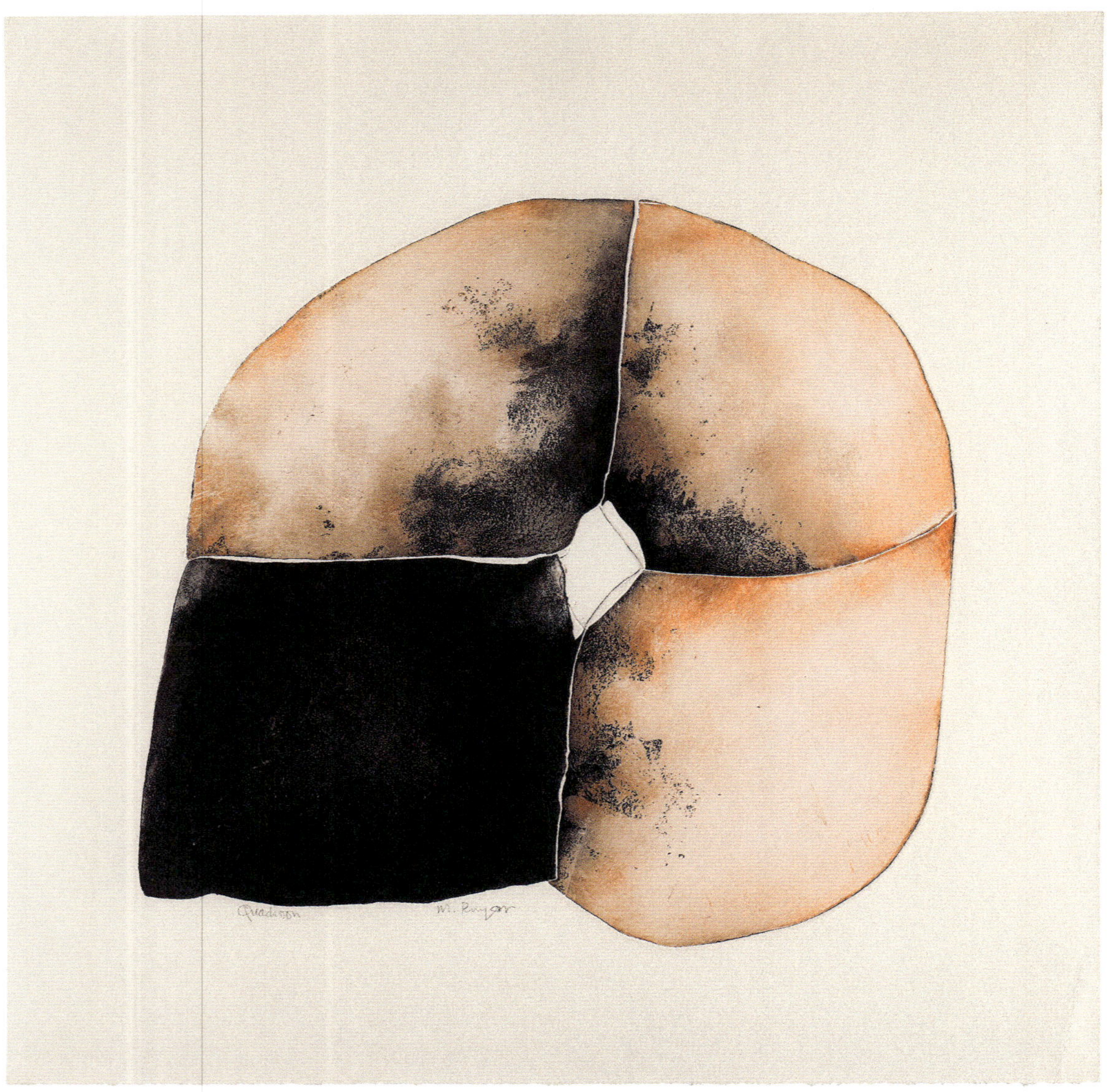

7

Quadroon, 1966–67

Soft ground etching and aquatint; image / plate: 39 x 40.1 cm; sheet: 55.4 x 56.2 cm

Collection of the artist

Photo: The Art Institute of Chicago

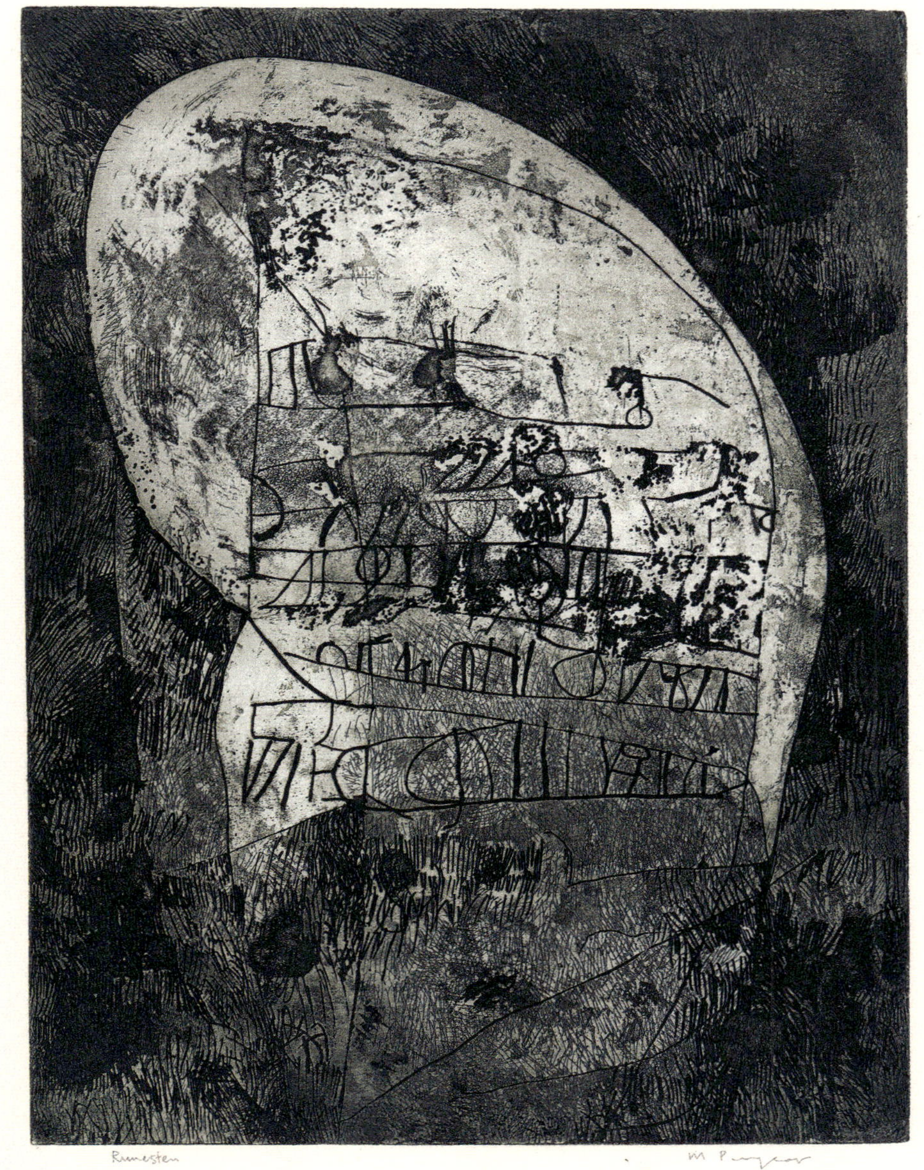

8

Rune Stone, 1966

Soft ground etching, aquatint, and open bite; image / plate: 49.3 x 37 cm; sheet: 59.2 x 46 cm

Collection of the artist

Photo: The Art Institute of Chicago

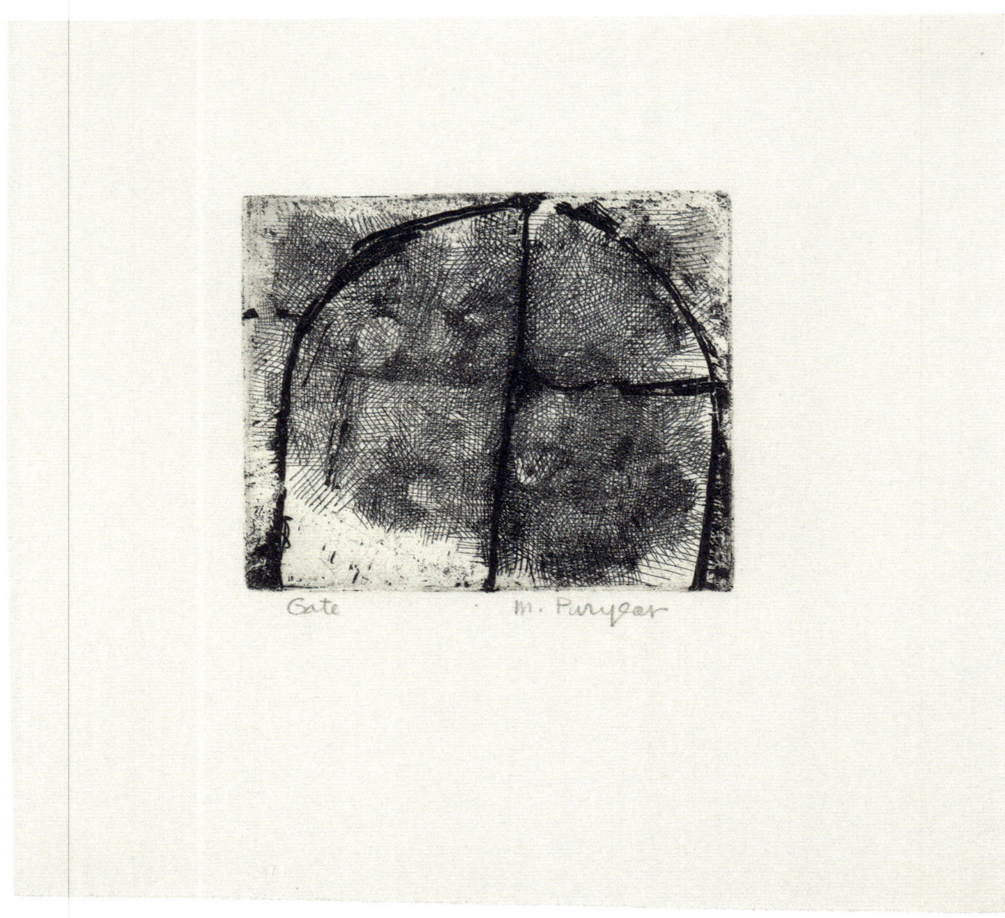

9

Gate, 1966

Soft ground etching; image / plate: 10.5 x 12.6 cm; sheet: 23.5 x 38.4 cm

Collection of the artist

Photo: The Art Institute of Chicago

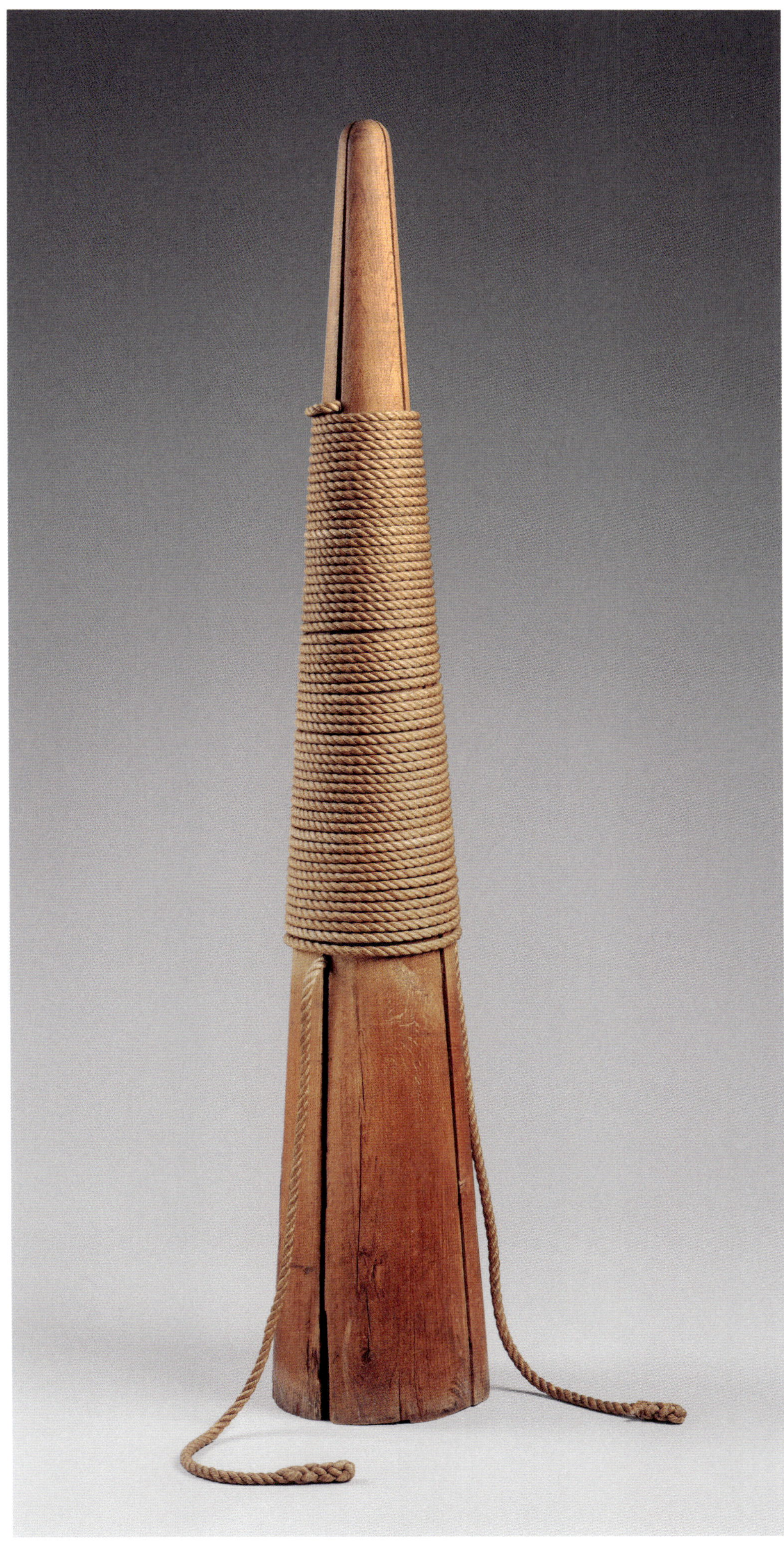

10

Bound Cone, 1972–73

Red oak and hemp rope; 176.2 x 27.9 x 27.9 cm

Toledo Museum of Art, Ohio, Gift of David K. and Georgia E. Welles, 2025.14

Photo: Richard Goodbody

11

Bask, 1976

Stained pine; 30.5 x 372.7 x 55.9 cm

Solomon R. Guggenheim Museum, New York, Exxon Corporation Purchase Award, 1978, 78.2430

Photo: The Solomon R. Guggenheim Foundation / Art Resource, NY

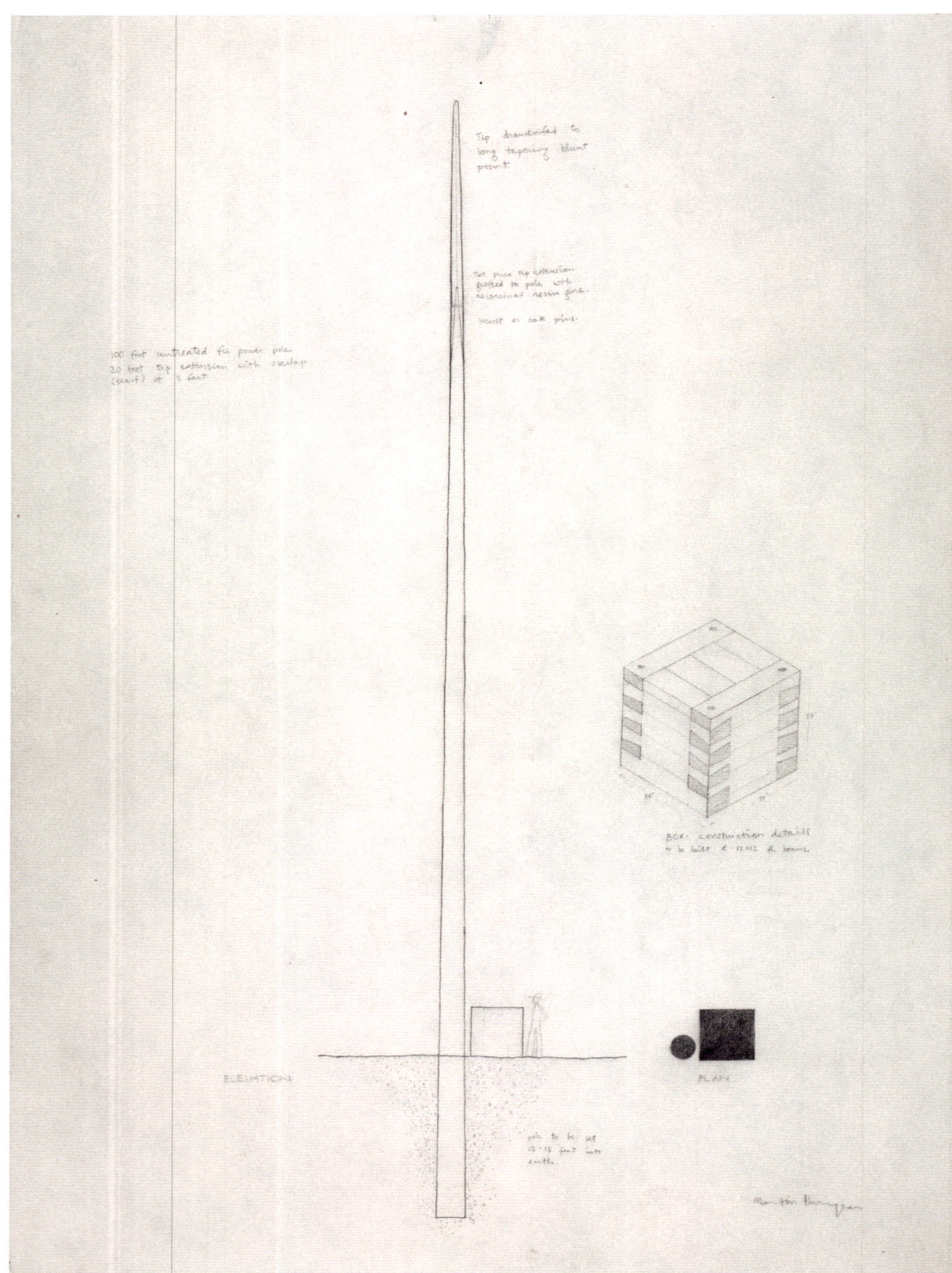

12

Drawing for *Box and Pole*, 1977

Graphite on paper; 73.7 x 53.3 cm

Collection of the artist

Photo: Buffalo AKG Art Museum

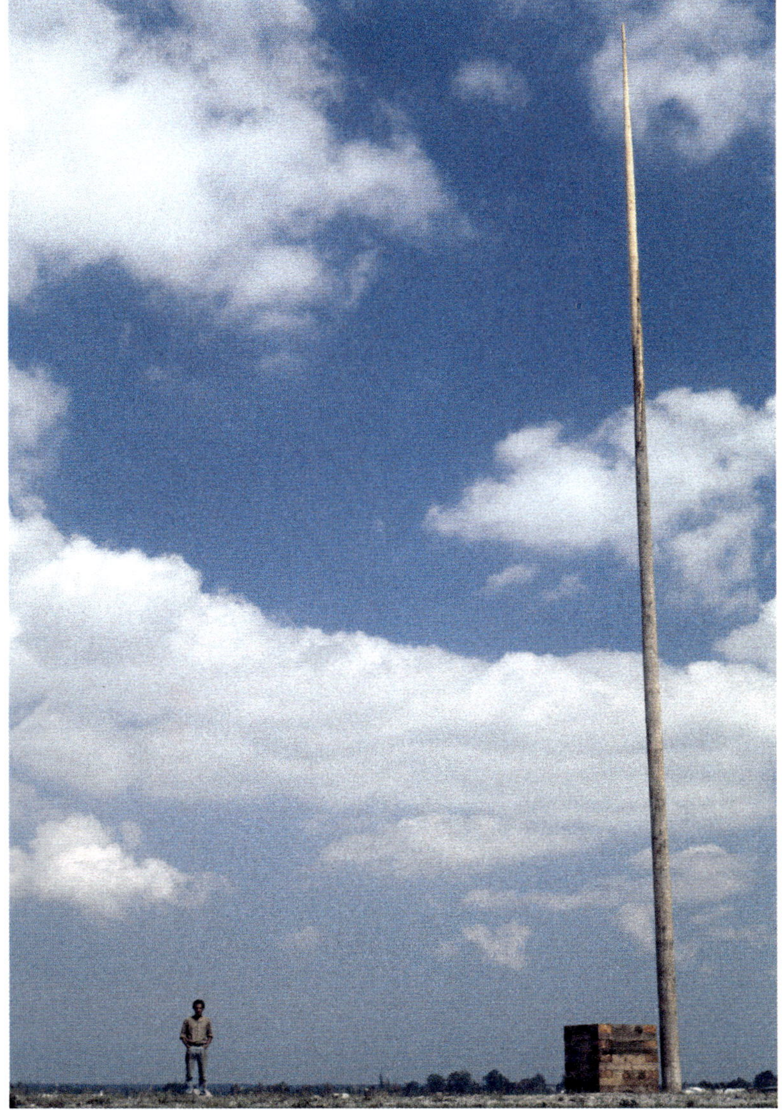

Figure 10. Martin Puryear standing next to *Box and Pole* (1977), temporary installation at Artpark, Lewistown, New York, 1977. Canadian hemlock and southern yellow pine; box: 137.2 x 137.2 x 137.2 cm; pole: 30.5 m (height). Photo: Burchfield Penney Art Center

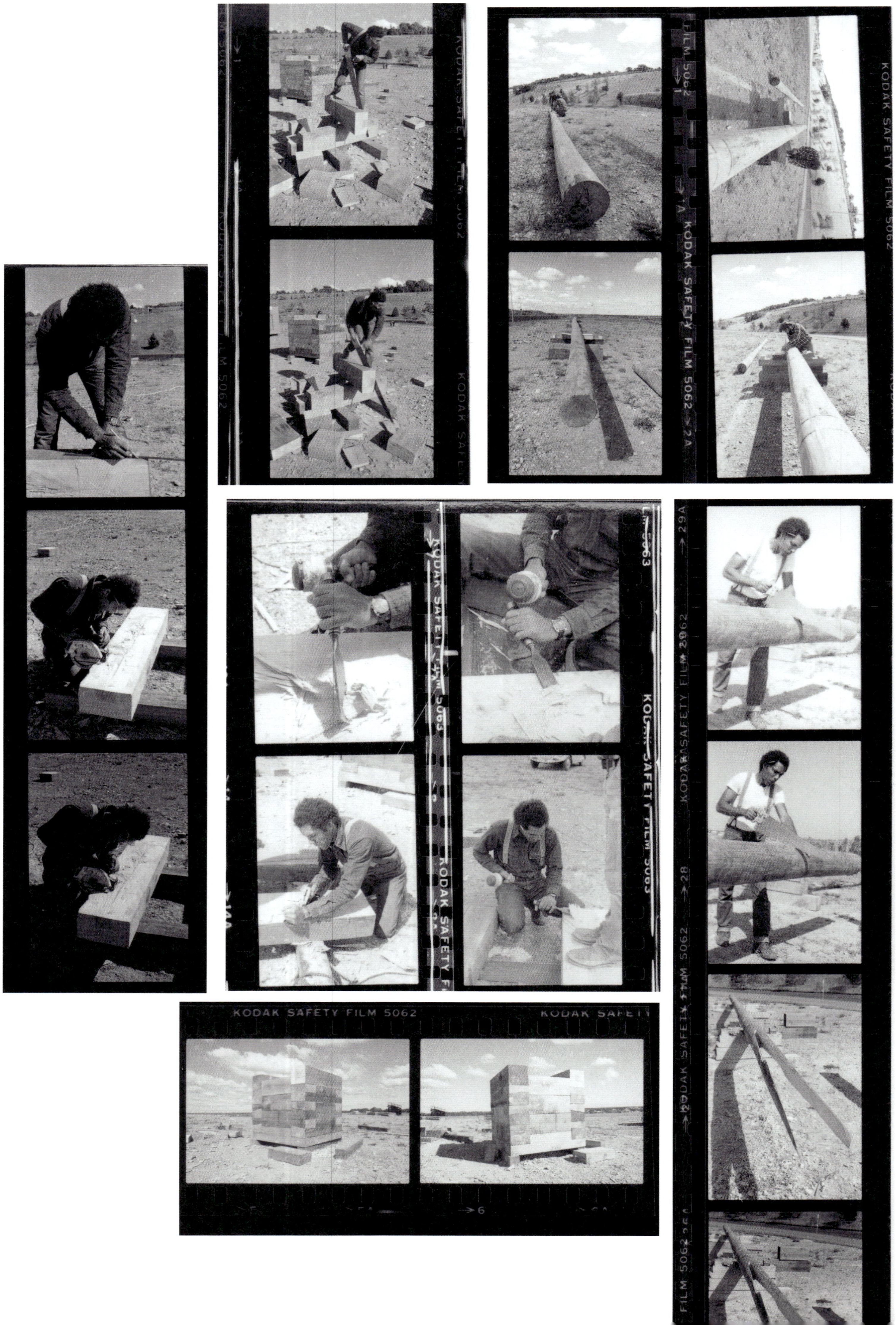

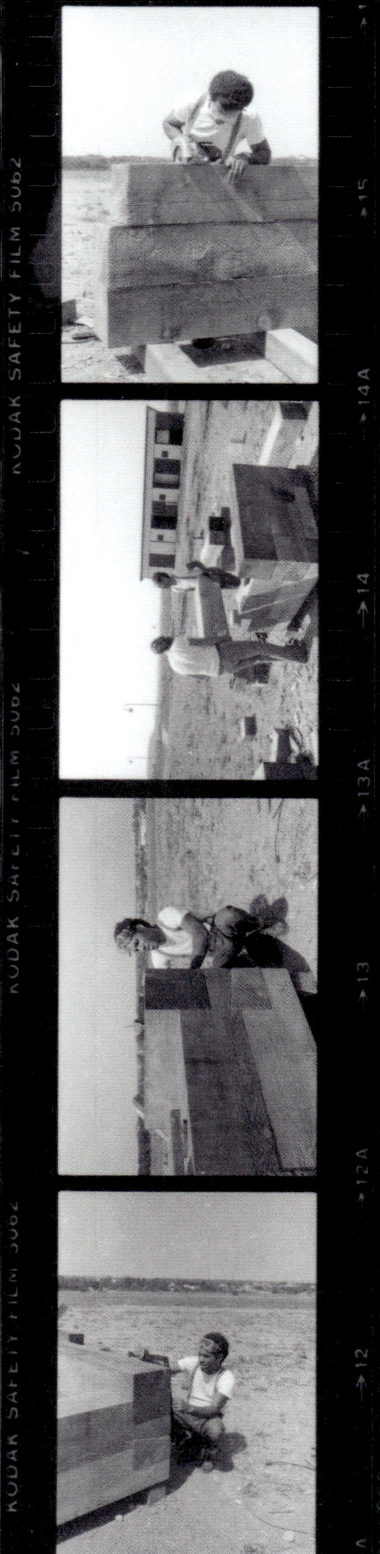

Figure 11. Martin Puryear constructing *Box and Pole* (1977), temporary installation at Artpark, Lewiston, New York, 1977. Photos: Burchfield Penney Art Center

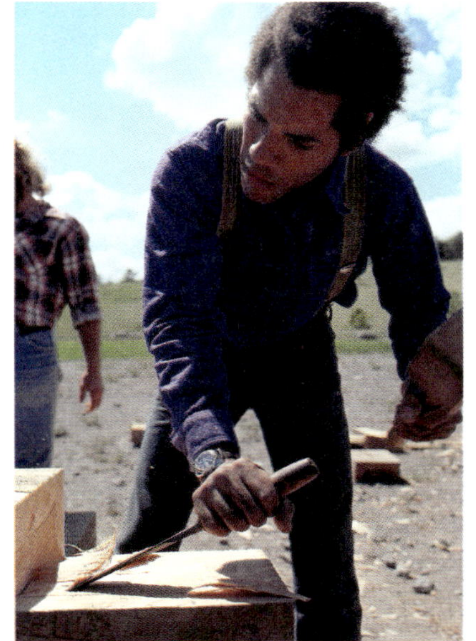

Figure 12. Martin Puryear constructing *Box and Pole* (1977), temporary installation at Artpark, Lewiston, New York, 1977. Photo: Burchfield Penney Art Center

The effect of memory

Charles Ray

As a young artist, perhaps more importantly as a young man, Martin Puryear, ten years my senior, made a work of art that affected me, my life, and my career in a positive manner. This relatively unknown work *Box and Pole* is a large-scale outdoor sculpture the artist made for Artpark in Lewiston, New York, in 1977. I never saw this work in person, and when I asked Puryear about it, he said something to the effect that we were all young once, and he was a young man when he made it. I agree, but I also believe an eighteen-year-old could make a major work of art that a twenty-year-old could not. As we pass through doors made from years, Rembrandt's self-portraits are an example. The rowdy pride embedded in the portrait he painted when he was a young man makes it a great work of art. Yet it is eons from the portrait that he made in later years of an artist as an old man, where light itself is rendered as emanating from the artist himself. *The artist as a light source* could not have been comprehended by an artist even ten years younger.

What initially drew me to Martin Puryear's *Box and Pole* sculpture was a photograph and his artist's statement, which I first discovered in 1980. Puryear talked about the challenge of working in an outdoor space with the acreage of a small farm, so open a space to be filled only by him. It didn't matter how huge it was physically. What I could superimpose myself on was the challenge and opportunity not to *build in*, but to *sculpt with*. Work has sources, and our sources have sources. As the ancient philosopher said, it's turtles all the way down. Influence is both a beautiful and a surprising aspect of a work of art. To simply copy is to ignore the gift of inspiration.

I learned much from Puryear's writing on a work that I never saw, and through the photographic image I could at least approach it in my mind. There is a clear Minimalist image: a tapered pole a hundred feet tall and a box, forty by forty inches, in close proximity. Both were Minimal forms, but without the shock and surprise of early Minimalism—a Donald Judd box or a Robert Morris fiberglass sculpture in a white cube gallery or museum. The box and pole were just as much found familiar fine art objects already embedded in contemporary Post-Minimalist culture. I bring this into focus because the art—the innovation—was not located in visual gestalt but in a cultural quality of craft. These forms had an American characteristic found in woodworking: trestle building, cabin construction, covered bridges of New England, even Amish barn raising. There is a quality in Puryear's works that indicates that they were honed and built by one man—not in a fetish for woodworking, but by the necessity of means and making. This equation translates over to one's necessity of viewing. We use our minds as well as our American cultural understanding to fall in line not with what is made in a Puryear sculpture, but with what is built.

What struck me most of all was his description of the work in a huge space that he could not fill horizontally. He turned to verticality, dividing the horizon itself into two. The viewer approaches and looks up into the sky, rather than across the grassy landscape next to the tapered pole. The box is a dovetailed cube built of twelve-by-twelve-inch lumber. One sees its craft and man-made-ness. The pole is also joined at a splice, quieter but just as powerful as the dovetails of the box. Puryear's statement that he brought two separate events into close proximity reinforced for me as a young artist that sculpture could be an event rather than an image. Sculpture as a verb rather than a noun.

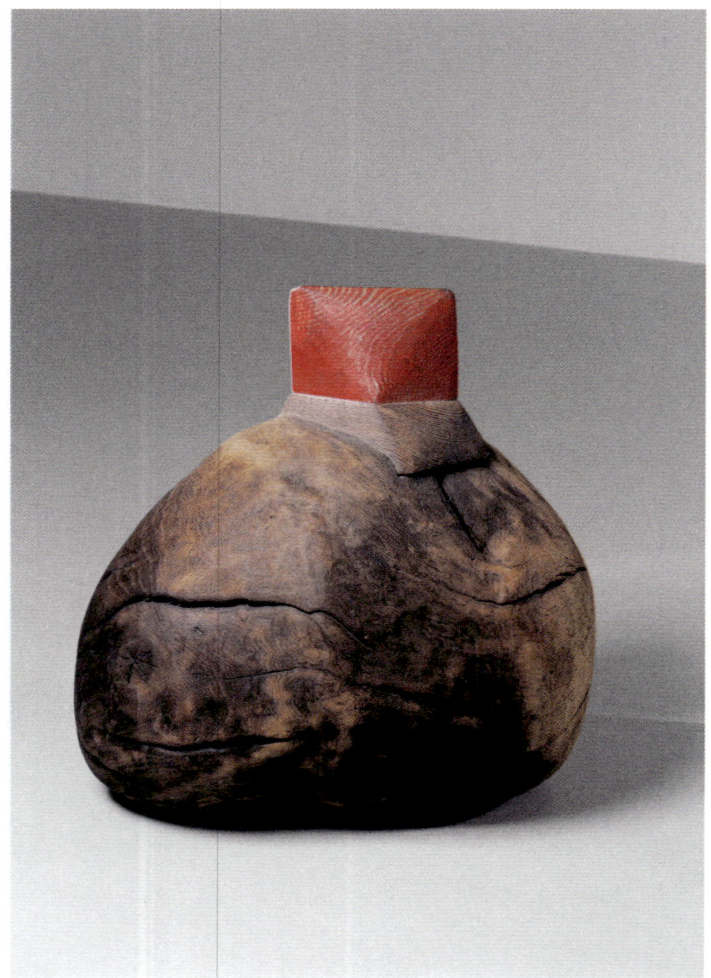

13

Believer, 1977–82

Tulip poplar and pine;
59.1 x 59.4 x 44.1 cm

Collection of the artist

Photo: Donald Young
Gallery, Chicago

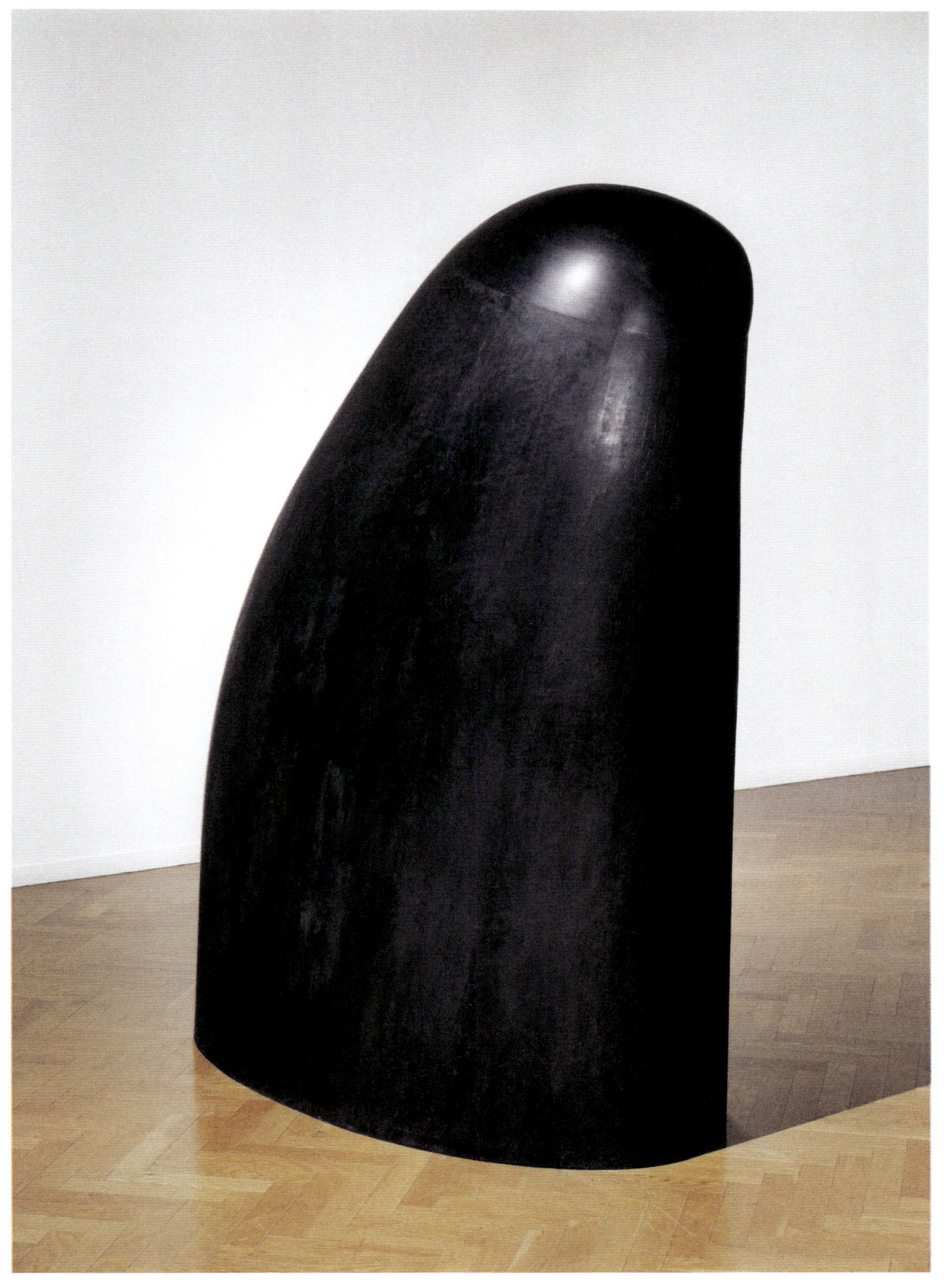

14

Self, 1978

Stained and painted red cedar and mahogany; 175.3 x 121.9 x 63.5 cm

Joslyn Art Museum, Omaha, Nebraska, Museum purchase in memory of Elinor Ashton, 1980.63.

Photo: Donald Young Gallery, Chicago, IL

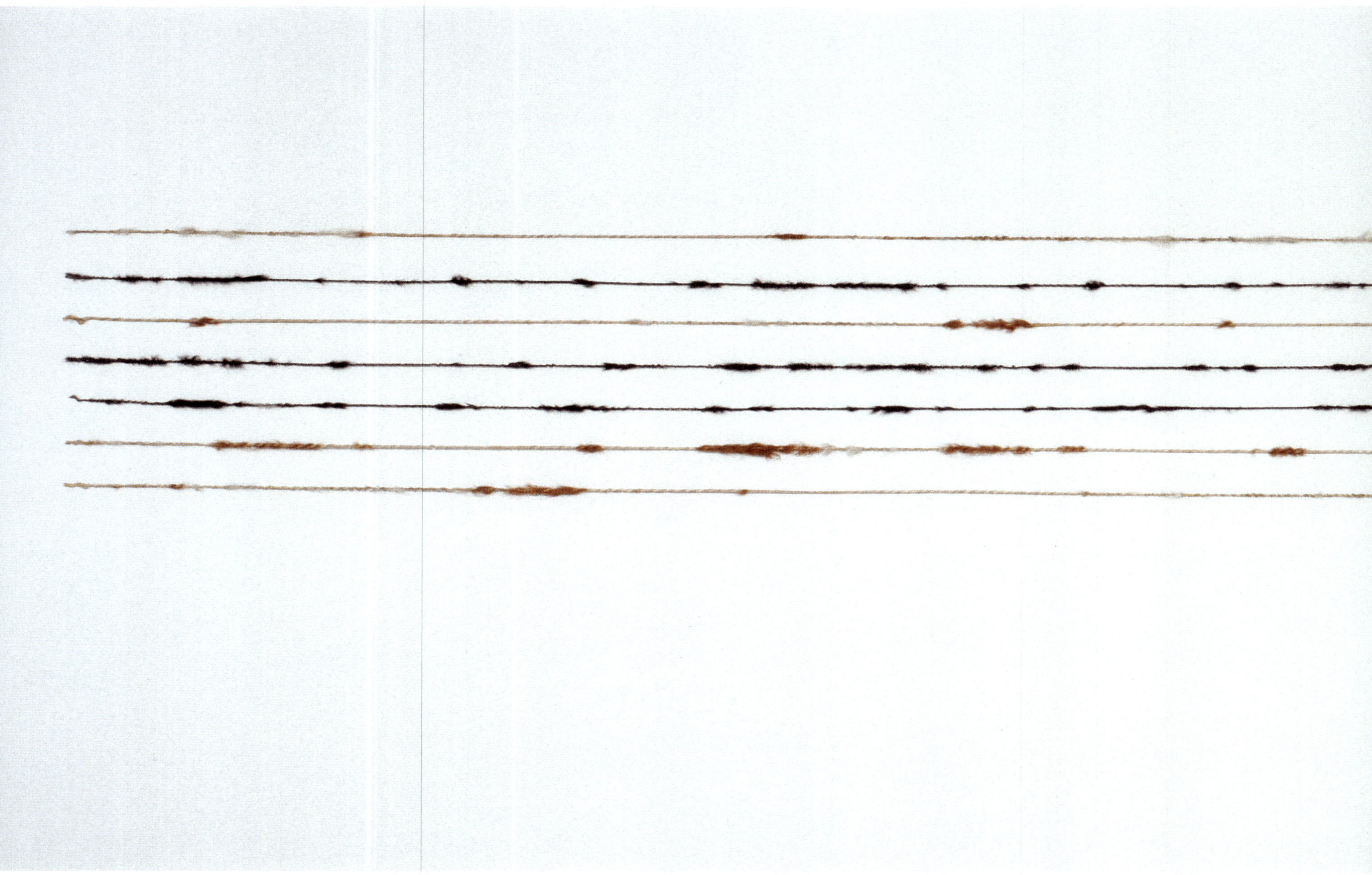

15

Some Lines for Jim Beckwourth, 1978

Twisted rawhide; 690.9 cm (length); height variable

Collection of the artist

Photo: Donald Young Gallery, Chicago

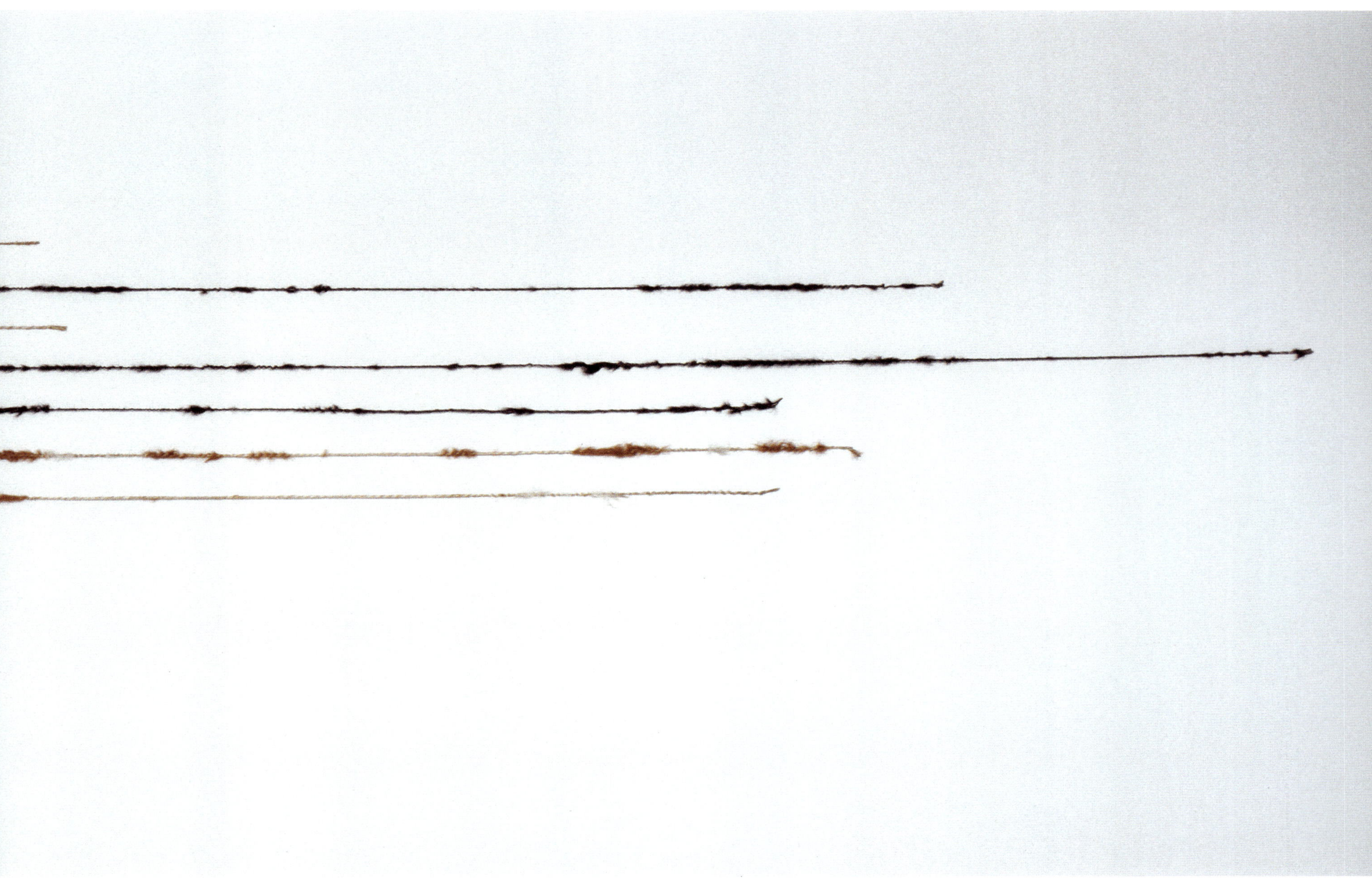

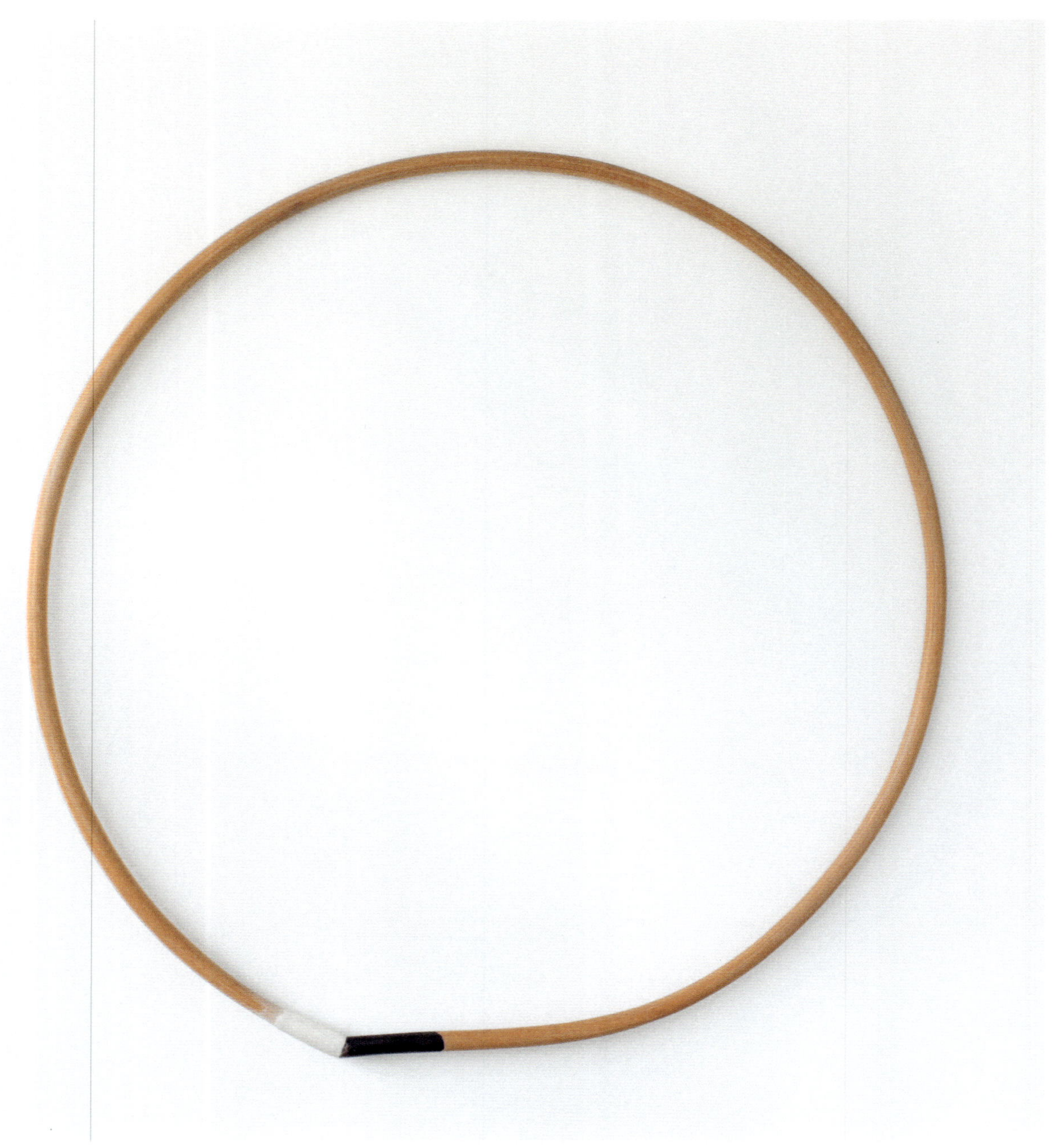

16

Nexus, 1979

Alaskan yellow cedar, pigment, and gesso; 114.3 x 114.3 x 3.8 cm

Collection of halley k harrisburg and Michael Rosenfeld, New York

Photo: Michael Rosenfeld Gallery LLC, New York, NY

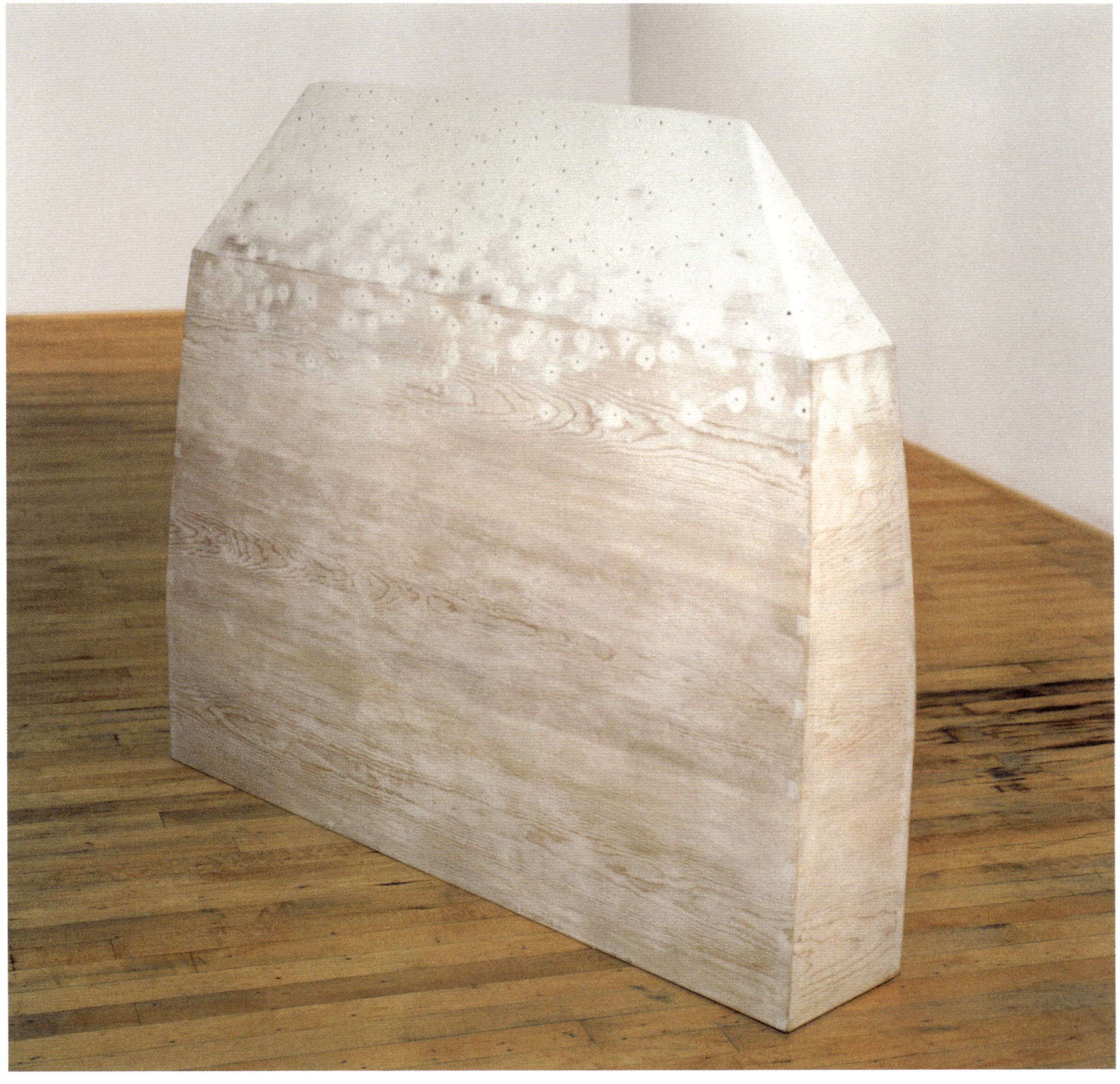

17

Reliquary, 1980

Gessoed pine; 106.7 x 120.7 x 22.9 cm

Andrew L. and Gayle Shaw Camden Collection

Photo: Donald Young Gallery, Chicago, IL

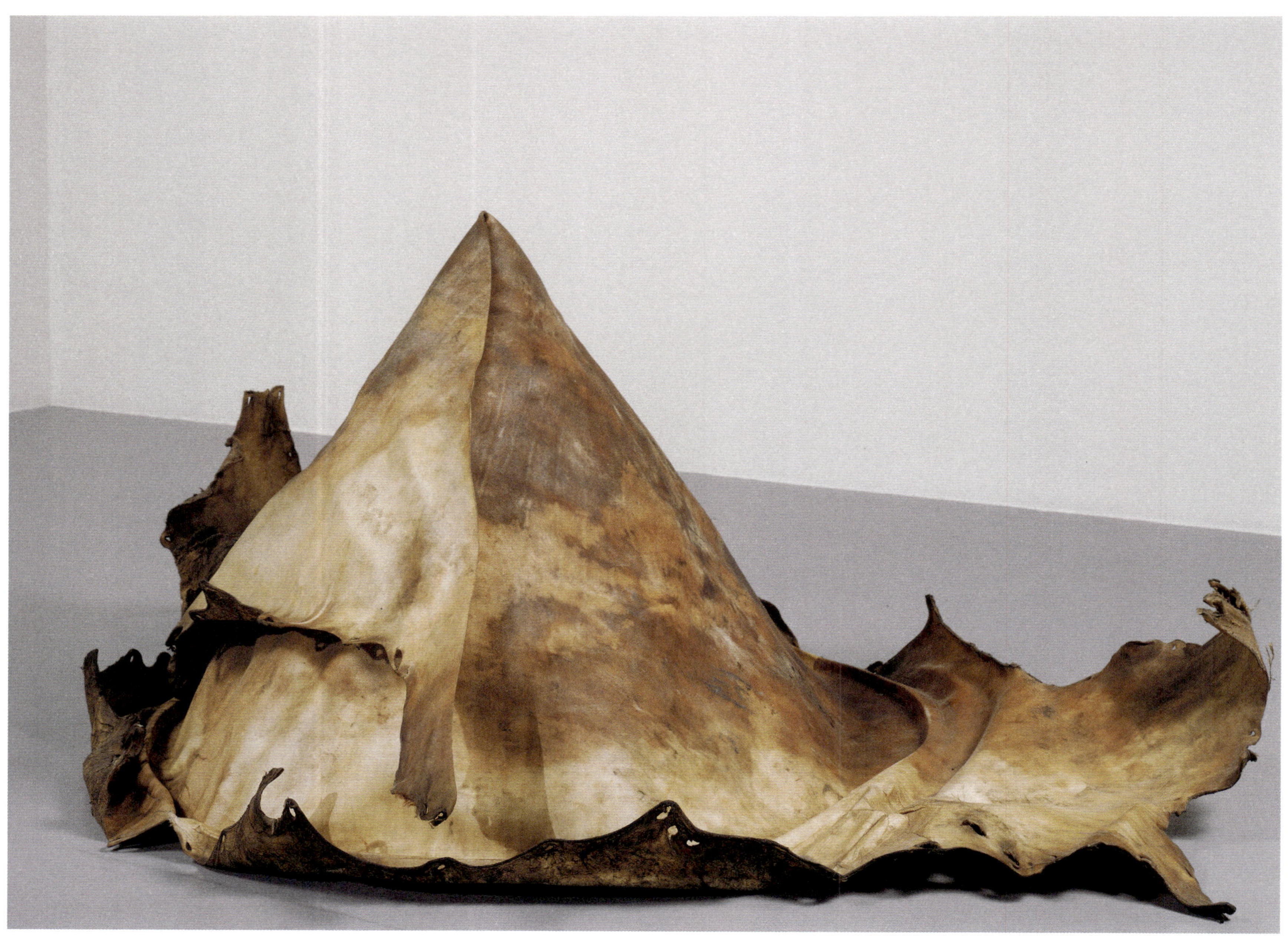

18

Rawhide Cone, 1980

Molded rawhide; 74.9 x 152.4 x 116.8 cm

Collection of the artist

Photo: Michael Tropea

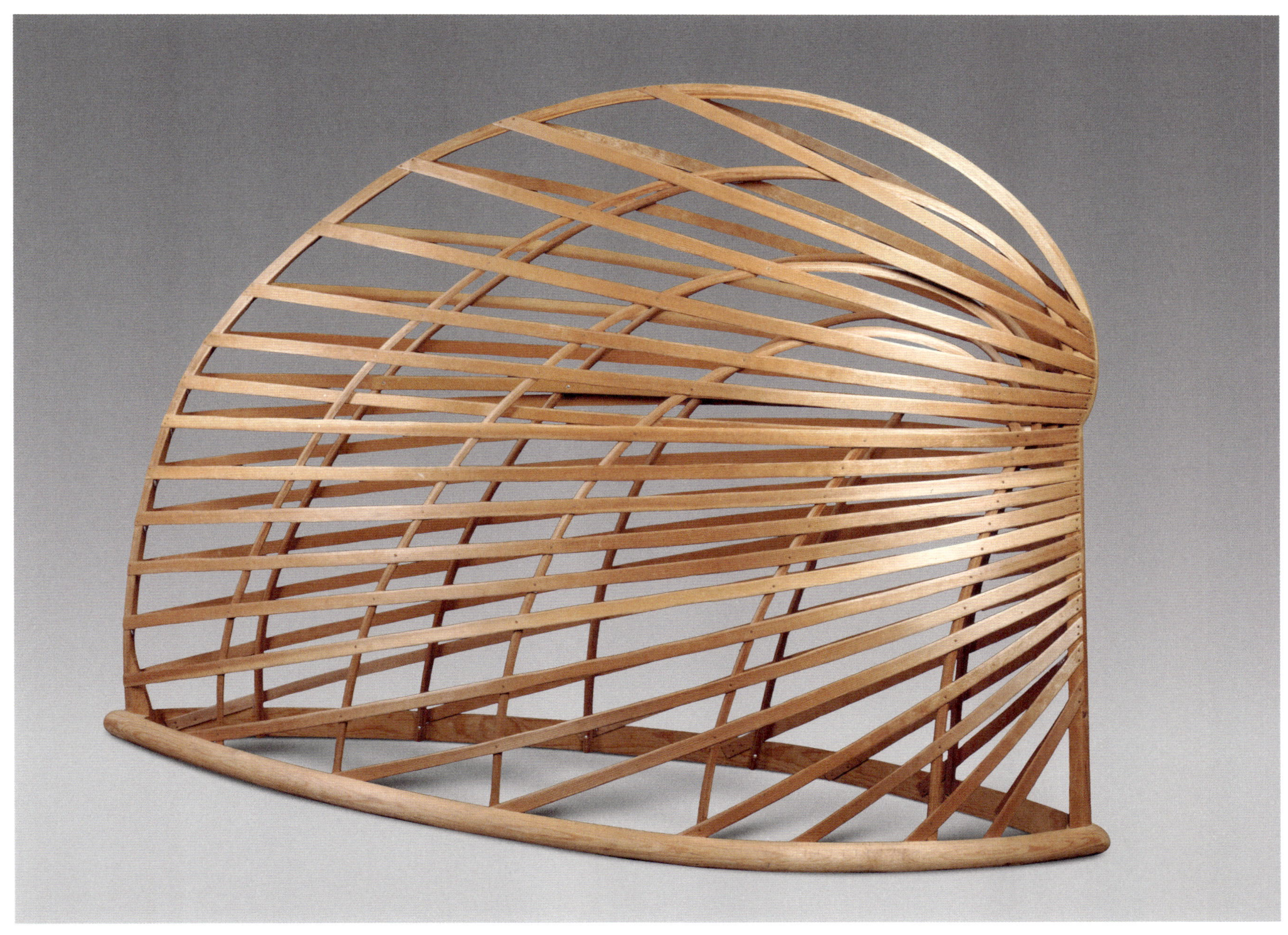

19

Bower, 1980

Sitka spruce, pine, and copper tacks; 163.3 x 240.2 x 66 cm

Smithsonian American Art Museum, Museum purchase made possible through the Luisita L. and Franz H. Denghausen Endowment, Alexander Calder, Frank Wilbert Stokes, and the Ford Motor Company, 2002.18

Photo: Smithsonian American Art Museum, Washington, DC / Art Resource, NY

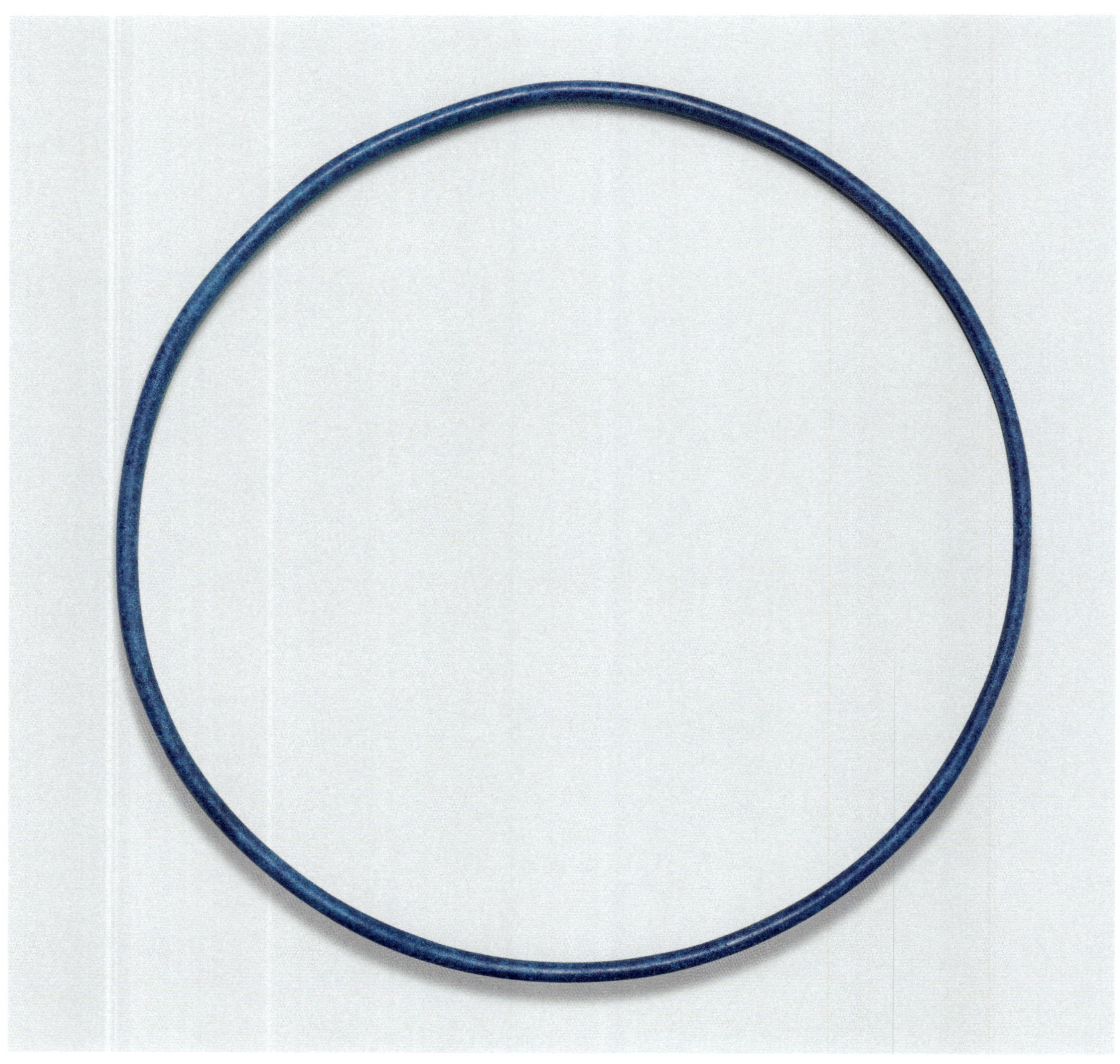

20

Azul-Azul, 1981

Painted basswood;
162.5 x 162.5 x 4.4 cm

Collection of Pamela and
Arthur Sanders

Photo: McKee Gallery, NY

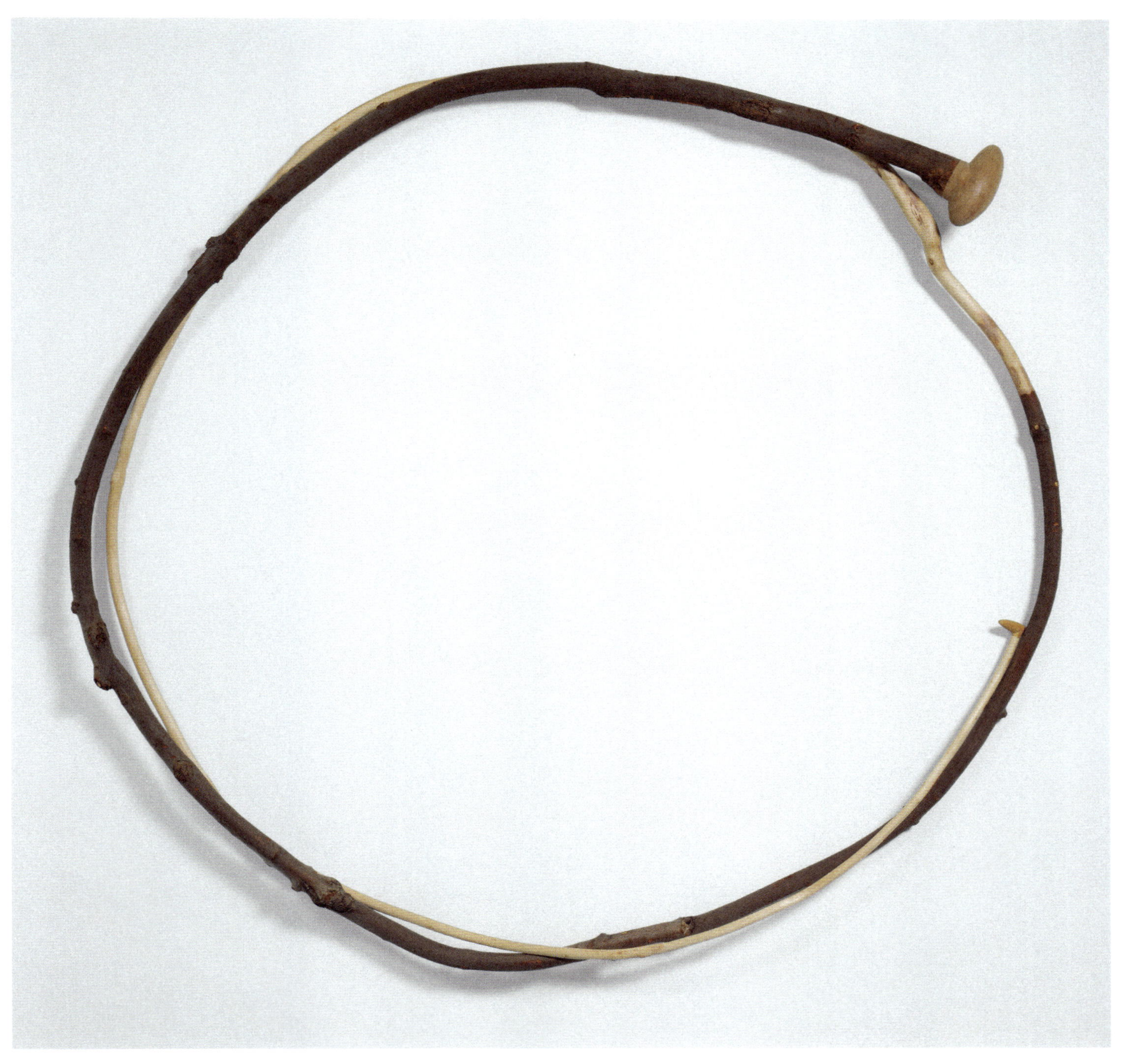

21

Untitled, 1982

Maple sapling, pear wood, and yellow cedar; 149.9 x 167.6 x 12.7 cm

Yale University Art Gallery, Gift of the Neisser Family, Judith Neisser, David Neisser, Kate Neisser, and Stephen Burns, in memory of Edward Neisser, B.A. 1952, 2019.123.2

Photo: Yale University Art Gallery

22

Sanctuary, 1982

Pine, maple, and cherry; 320 x 61 x 45.7 cm

The Art Institute of Chicago, Mr. and Mrs. Frank G. Logan Purchase Prize Fund, 1982.1473

Photo: Thomas Cinoman, The Art Institute of Chicago

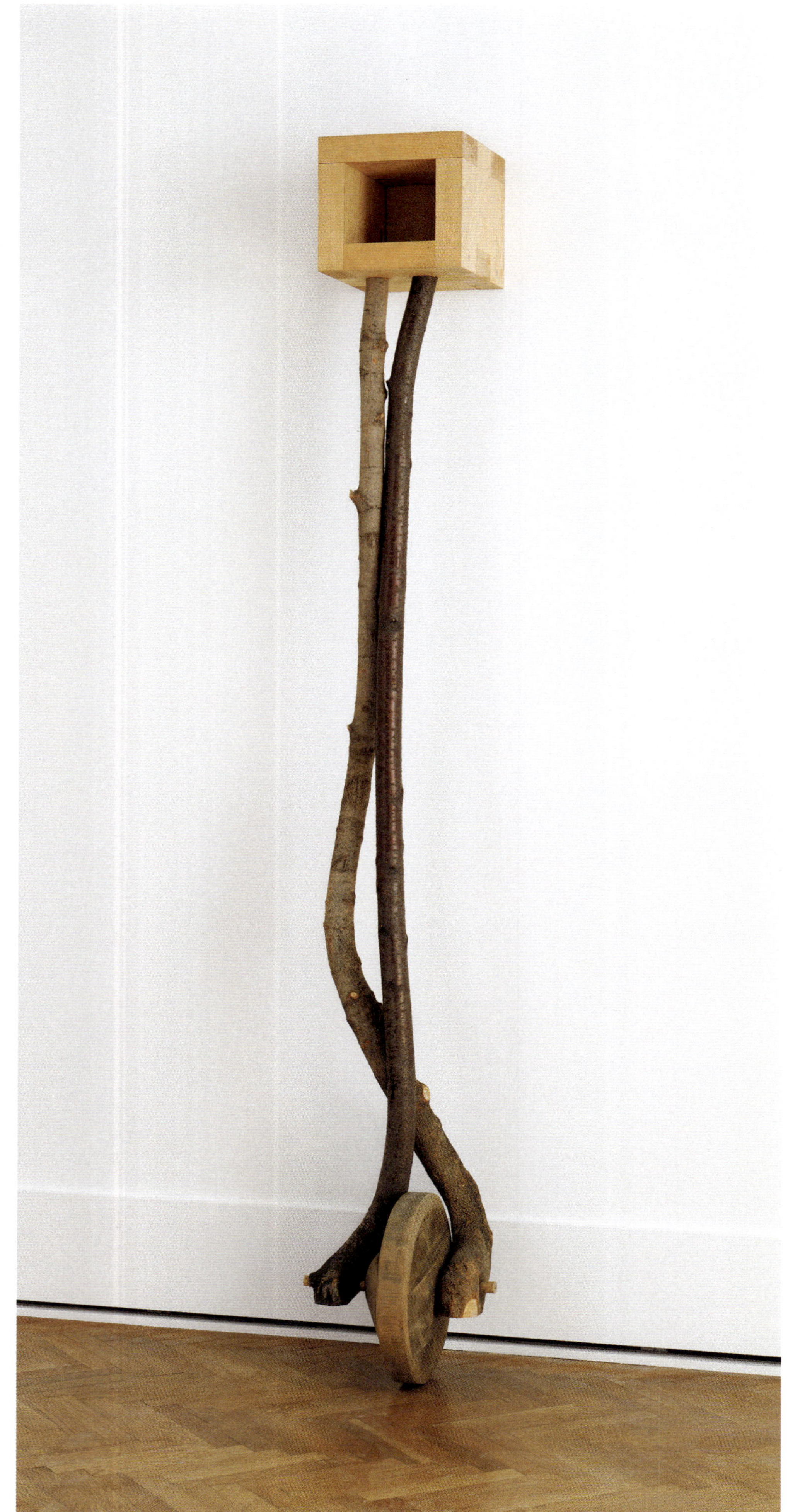

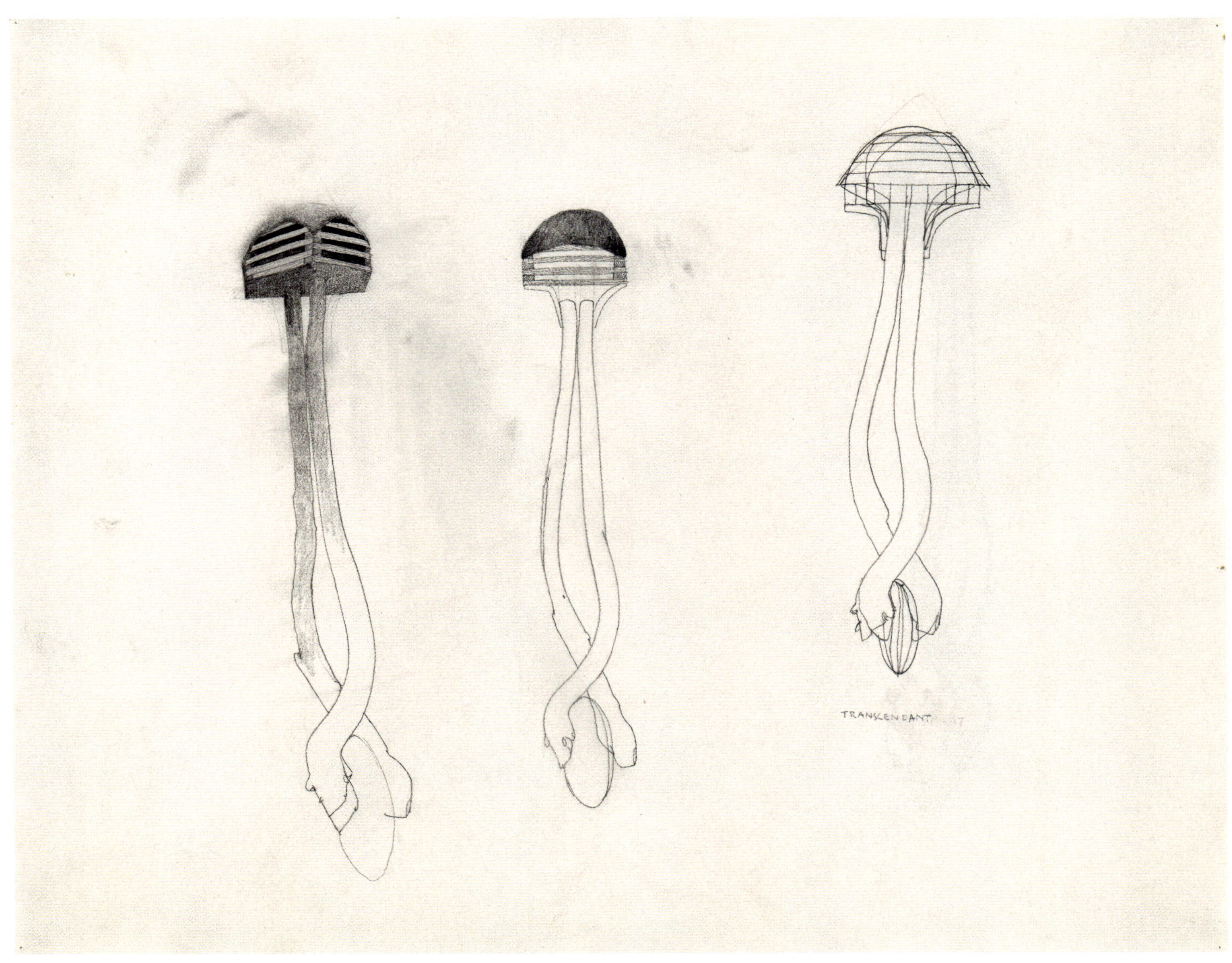

23

Untitled, drawing for *Sanctuary*, c. 1982

Graphite on paper; 58.7 x 73.8 cm

The Art Institute of Chicago, Gift of Martin Puryear, 1996.641

Photo: The Art Institute of Chicago / Art Resource, NY

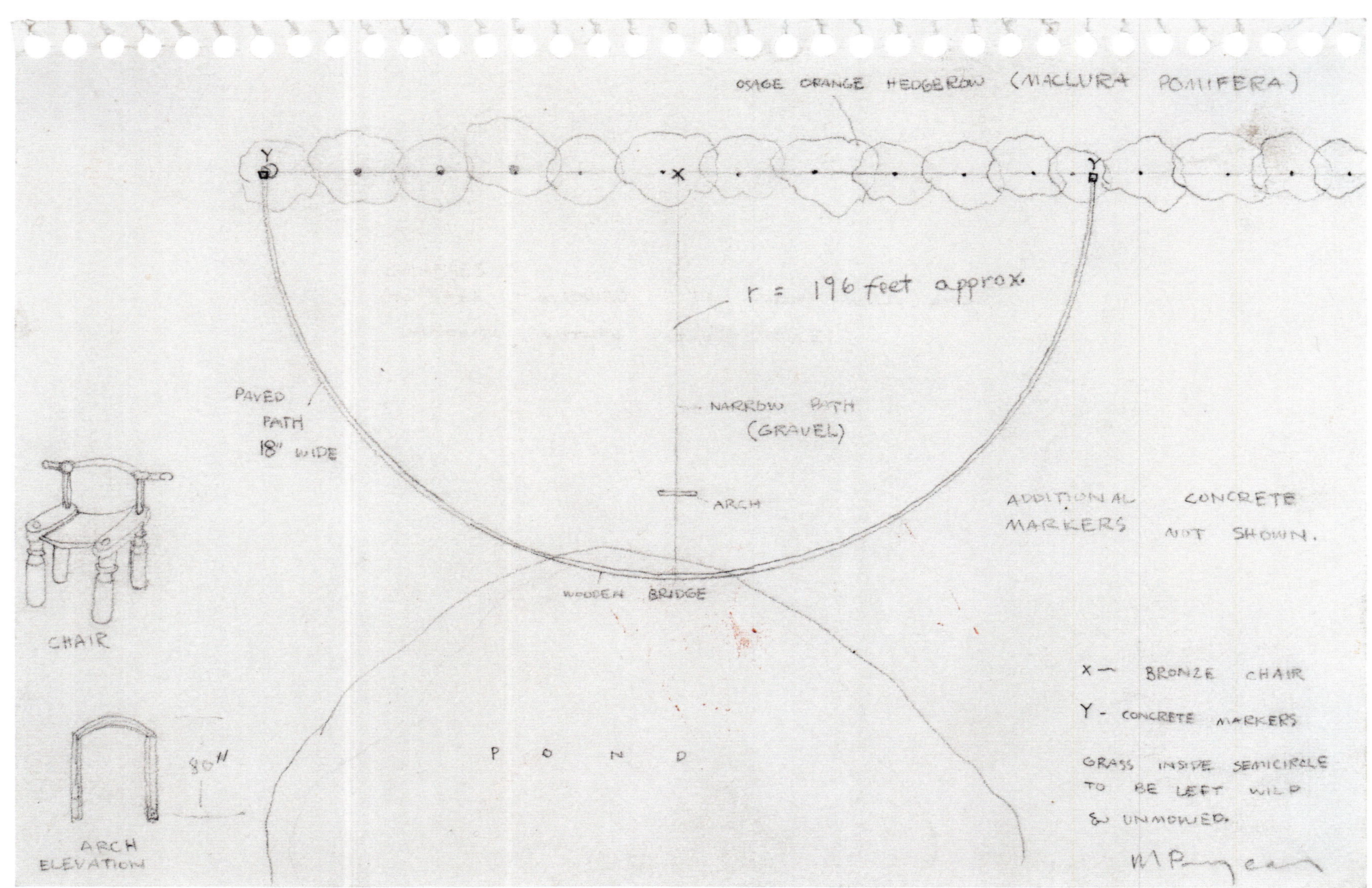

24

Drawing for *Bodark Arc*, 1982

Graphite on paper; 15.2 x 22.9 cm

Collection of the artist

Photo: Jeffrey Jenkins

Figure 13. Installation view of *Bodark Arc* (1982) at the Nathan Manilow Sculpture Park, Governors State University, University Park, Illinois. Martin Puryear. Earth, wood, Osage orange trees, asphalt, stones, and cast bronze; 119.5 m (diameter). Photos: Courtesy of the Nathan Manilow Sculpture Park

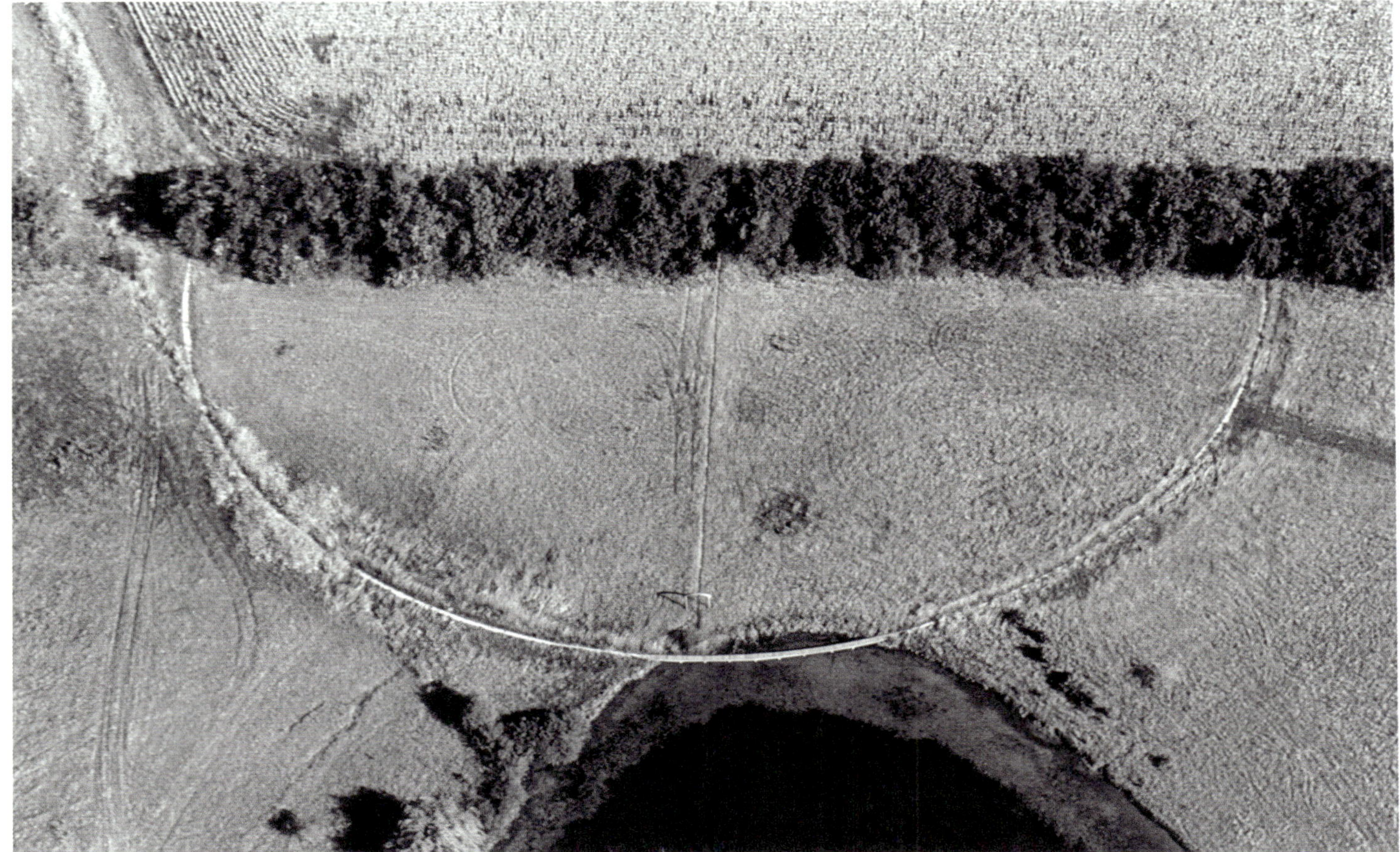

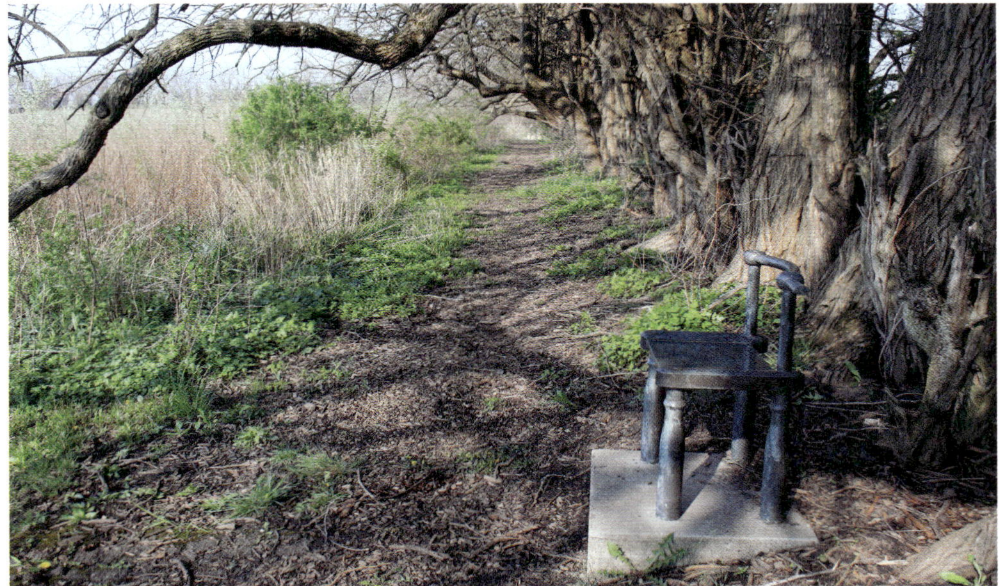

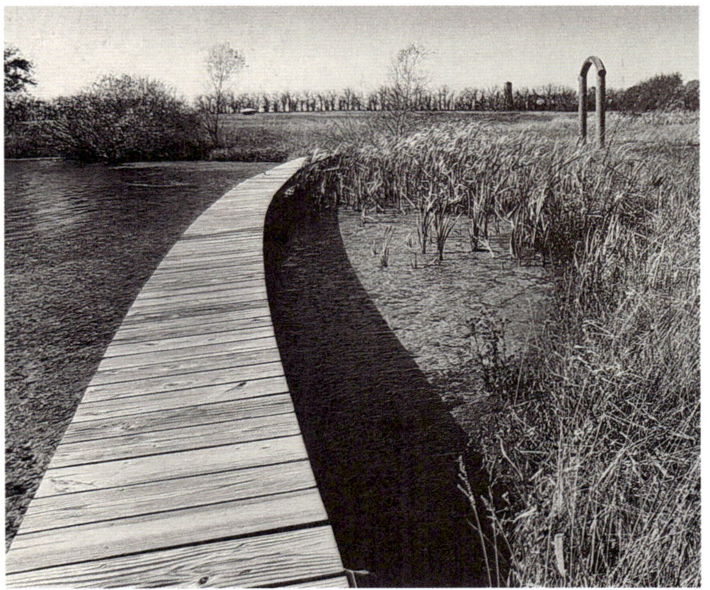

Figure 14. Detail view of the chair in *Bodark Arc* (1982) at the Nathan Manilow Sculpture Park, Governors State University, University Park, Illinois

Figure 15. Detail view of the bridge and arch in *Bodark Arc* (1982) at the Nathan Manilow Sculpture Park, Governors State University, University Park, Illinois

25

Night and Day, 1984

Painted pine and wire; 212.1 x 301 x 12.7 cm

Nasher Sculpture Center, Dallas, Raymond and Patsy Nasher Collection, NC.1985.A.04

Photo: David Heald

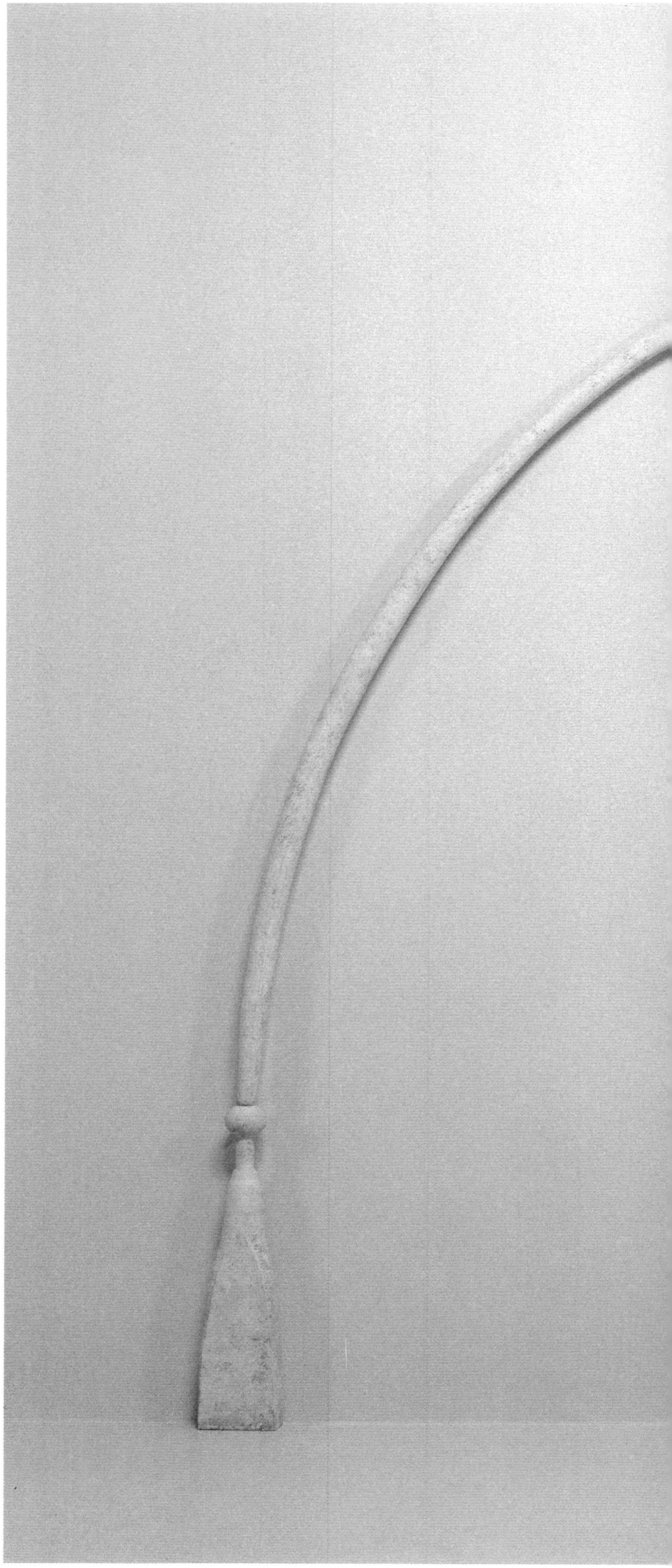

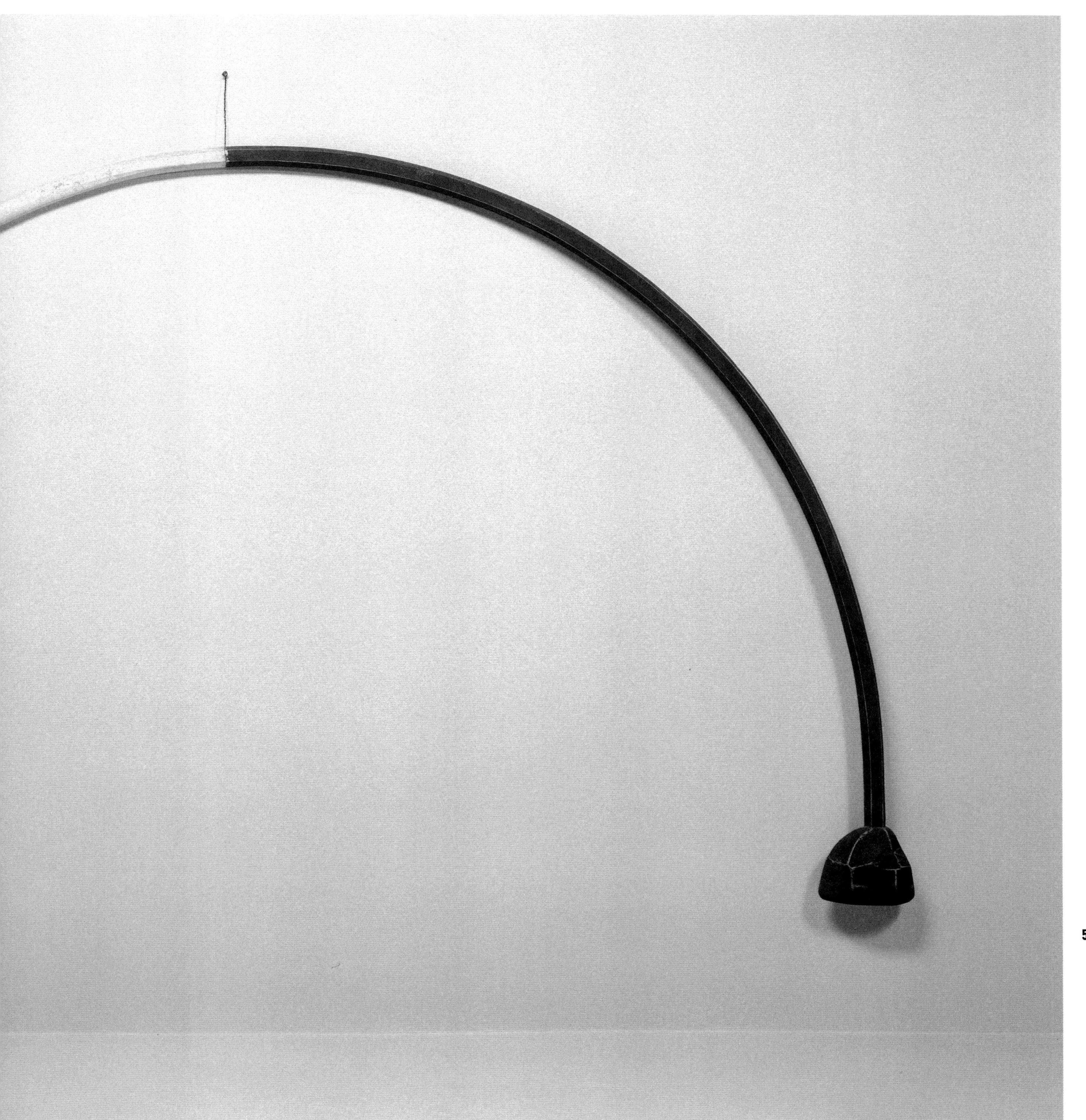

On the Tundra

Billie Tsien

She has her back turned to you.
She chooses to look away.
She is waiting.
It is a she.

Because I want her to be a she, and because falconers prefer to use female falcons since they are larger and better hunters than the males.

Martin has talked about being a falconer, and in his studio he has the tiny hood he made from the kind of leather that is used to quiet the falcon. Indeed, so much of his work feels as if it is trying to make the world more quiet.

When I look at art in museums or galleries, I always decide which piece I would steal. I would choose this piece, *On the Tundra* (1986). At 19 ½ inches tall it might be possible to carry the work but, being made of cast iron, its weight would be immense. The work is rooted to the ground. The rock on which she perches reaches down to the center of the earth. It cannot be moved. Yet she, when she wants to, is capable of flight at a burning speed. The tension between the two is delicate and unbearable.

As architects, we are always trying to make work that feels connective to its site and rooted in the topography of the place. We do not have the opportunity to imagine an apparatus that can take flight as part of what we do. So, we try for the rock on which she perches—but we will never have the bird.

I hope she never turns her head. Seeing her in this photograph gives me the benefit of observing her only from this one vantage point.

There is a power in her refusal to acknowledge the presence of others.

She holds this power within her, and it is what draws me to her.

I wait.

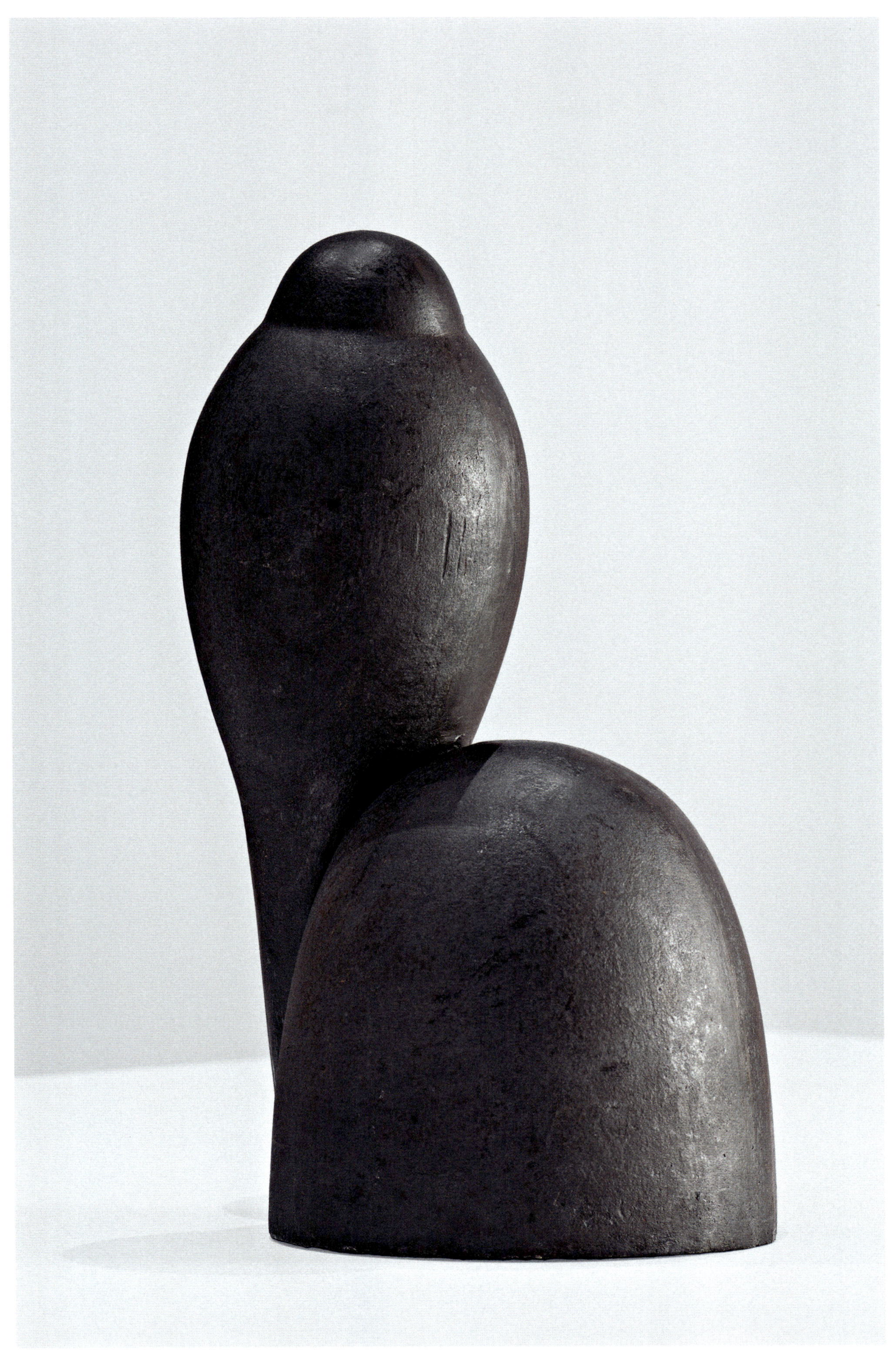

26

On the Tundra, 1986

Cast iron; 49.5 x 24.1 x 29.2 cm

Museum of Fine Arts, Boston, Curator's Grant Program of the Peter Norton Family Foundation, 1991.620

Photo © 2025 MFA Boston

More Than Is Necessary, Less Than Required

Kerry James Marshall

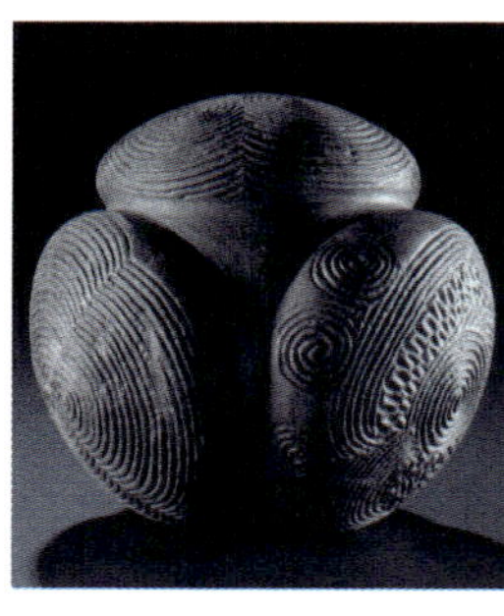

Figure 16. Towie carved stone ball, Neolithic, 3200–2500 BCE. Stone; four projecting discs and incised ornaments; 7.6 cm (diameter). National Museums, Scotland, X.AS 10. Photo © National Museums, Scotland

In preparation for these remarks about Martin Puryear's sculpture *Noblesse O.* (1987), I was looking through the book *30,000 Years of Art*.[1] What became increasingly clear page after page, from the earliest representation to the last, was just how deliberate and consistent human beings have been at exercising their creative capacities.

The special category "art" arose from the tendency among many people to embellish utilitarian objects with more features than were necessary for the performance of those objects' function. Except that it pleases us, there is no reason for a water pot to be decorated with an intricate pattern or a spoon handle to be carved in the shape of an animal or a naked woman.

Even abstraction, the practice of reduction and stylization claimed for modern art, has origins much more ancient than we tend to suppose. See, for instance, the Towie carved stone ball, made 3200–2500 BCE, housed in the National Museums in Scotland (fig. 16). The rhythm of forms and constellations of shapes alone have elicited admiration and awe for millennia.

Even the denial of function and the emphasis on process, essential to the autonomy of art objects under modernist analysis, is likely not exclusively a twentieth-century phenomenon. So, from Constantin Brâncuși (1876–1957) to Henry Moore (1898–1986), to Carl Andre (1935–2024), to Richard Serra (1938–2024), what I see is the continuity of a tradition. That tradition re-creates the wonders of nature and the handiworks of humankind as comprehensible and inspirational diversions to be marveled at and thought about. The late philosopher and art critic Arthur C. Danto summed up the practice in the title of one of his books: *The Transfiguration of the Commonplace: A Philosophy of Art*.[2]

So it is with Martin Puryear's sculpture. His referential source images are never completely obscured; neither are the materials and methods of their making concealed. His synthesis of subject, medium, and style consistently results in objects that are simultaneously curious and familiar. I have often compared this effect to the performance program of magicians, such as Penn and Teller, who will do a trick, show how the trick was done, then repeat the trick without losing the amazement. This is the kind of magic that Martin makes with ordinary materials like wood, wire, and stone.

In almost every instance these materials are assembled and finished with a sensitivity respecting their inherent character. The only exception I know of is the work *Noblesse O.* Made of cedar, this tall, conical form, over eight feet in height, sits on the floor like an inverted funnel. A large rim at the base and a small rim at the top suggest the possibility that it might be open to a hollow interior. Otherwise, it has a pretty solid presence. The whole thing is evenly covered with aluminum paint that obliterates and contradicts its organic substrate. It looks metallic. A close examination, though, shows the telltale signs of hand-hewn woodworking. Indeed, the shiny surface seems to exaggerate the surface irregularities. Chips, cracks, scratches, nicks, and gaps stand out more because their edges catch and reflect highlights in ways that wood generally does not. The misdirection set up by *Noblesse O.* seems out of character for Martin's work, which generally allows materials to appear as themselves.

More than a few of his sculptures are derived from literary and historical sources and references to the body. With that in mind, the inverted funnel became, for me, the hat of the Tin Woodman from the children's novel *The Wizard of Oz* (1900). This DIY persona, cobbled together from a variety of found parts, could be an alter ego for Martin himself, a woodchopper, who, like the Wizard, supplies the feeling heart to an arrangement of otherwise inert materials.

1. Phaidon Editors, *30,000 Years of Art: The Story of Human Creativity across Time and Space* (London: Phaidon, 2007).

2. Arthur C. Danto, *The Transfiguration of the Commonplace: A Philosophy of Art* (Cambridge, MA: Harvard University Press, 1981).

27

Noblesse O., 1987

Red cedar and aluminum paint; 249.9 x 147.3 x 116.8 cm

Dallas Museum of Art, General Acquisitions Fund and a gift of The 500, Inc., 1987.350

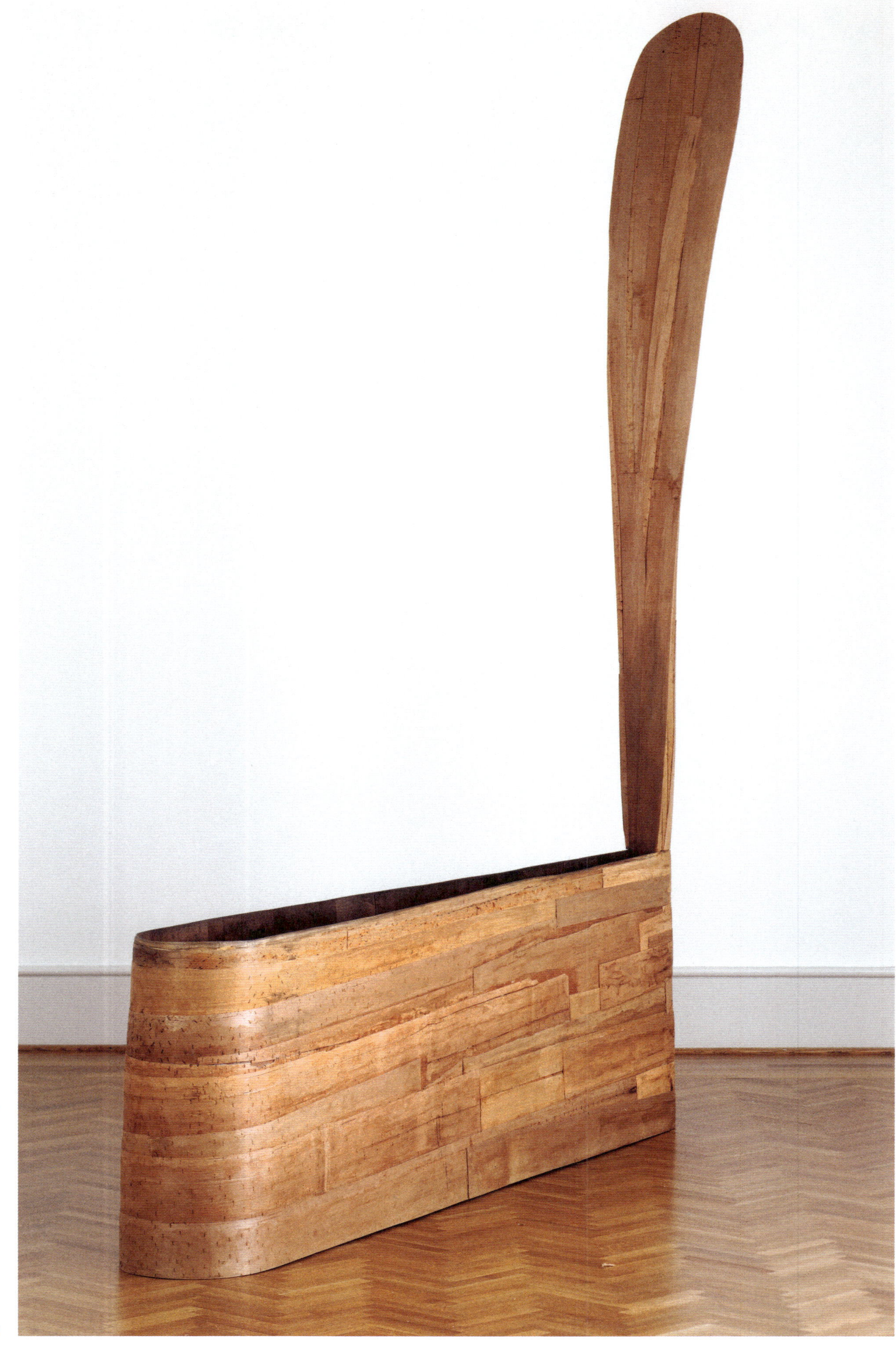

28

Lever #1, 1988–89

Red cedar, cypress, poplar, and ash;
429.3 x 340.4 x 45.1 cm

The Art Institute of Chicago, A. James Speyer Memorial, UNR Industries in honor of James W. Alsdorf, and Barbara Neff Smith and Solomon Byron Smith funds, 1989.385a–b

Photo: The Art Institute of Chicago / Art Resource, NY

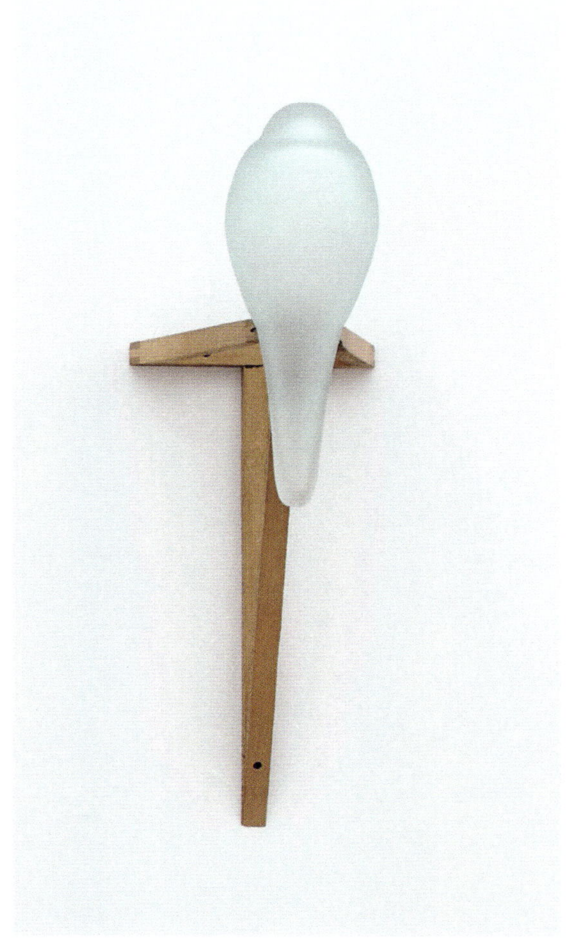

29

Untitled, 1992

Glass and wood;
81.3 x 27.9 x 35.6 cm

Collection of Margaret V. B. Wurtele

Photo: Antoine van Kaam / Voorlinden Museum & Gardens

Alien Huddle

Tom Joyce

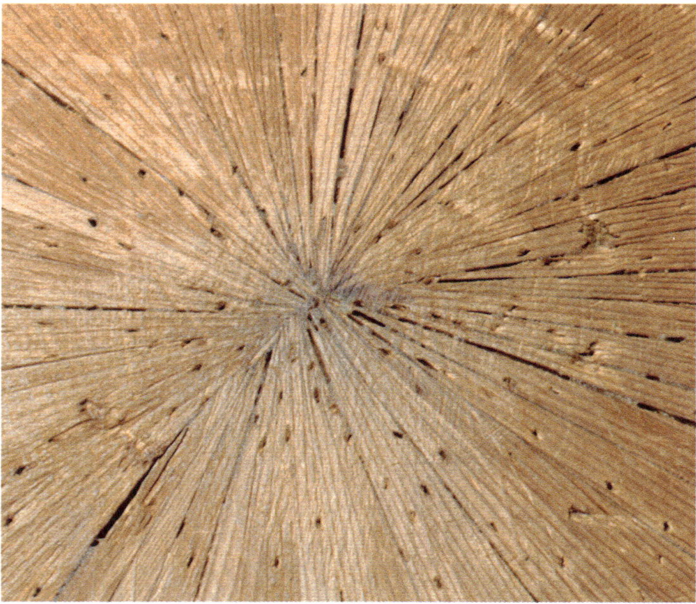

Figure 17. Detail of *Alien Huddle* (1993–95; [30])

Every time I visit the Cleveland Museum of Art, I circumnavigate *Alien Huddle* (1993–95) in an earthbound orbit tethered to the center of its buoyant, teetering mass. The sculpture is bisected by two distinct radii that define the parameters of each conjoined orb. As I walk, equidistance, around the sphere's major axis, I imagine the arc Martin's compass draws with Euclidean precision when laying out the patterns he will transfer onto thin red cedar planks. The proportionally balanced geometry he applies to construct this seemingly simple yet complex form asks a lot of himself and the material he employs. Carefully selected for straight grain, free of knots, each gore-shaped stave he fashions radiates across longitudinal meridians exactly as a cartographer divides a globe into as many equal segments. Cut, contoured, and curved over a hemispherical substructure invisible beneath this skin, 174 pieces are meticulously joined with a sly nod toward wooden-hull assembling of the past. The orderly regiment of long strips of spherical triangles are methodically laid down "eye sweet," as a shipwright would approvingly acknowledge. Waterproof the joints, and, no doubt, this vessel would be seaworthy!

With consummate hand skills evident at every glance, Martin is undeniably a maker's maker. Viewers cannot help but appreciate the shimmering surface of *Alien Huddle* reflecting thousands of razor-sharp plane-induced facets that refine its spherical exterior, achieved after he glued and removed staples that temporarily secured the cladding to its armature. Profoundly respected among peers for his seasoned approach, Martin's work never rests on hard-won laurels of studio practice; rather, it generously supports his vision as a resolute artist with a packed slate of multivalent messages amplified by the conceptual integrity emanating from its core.

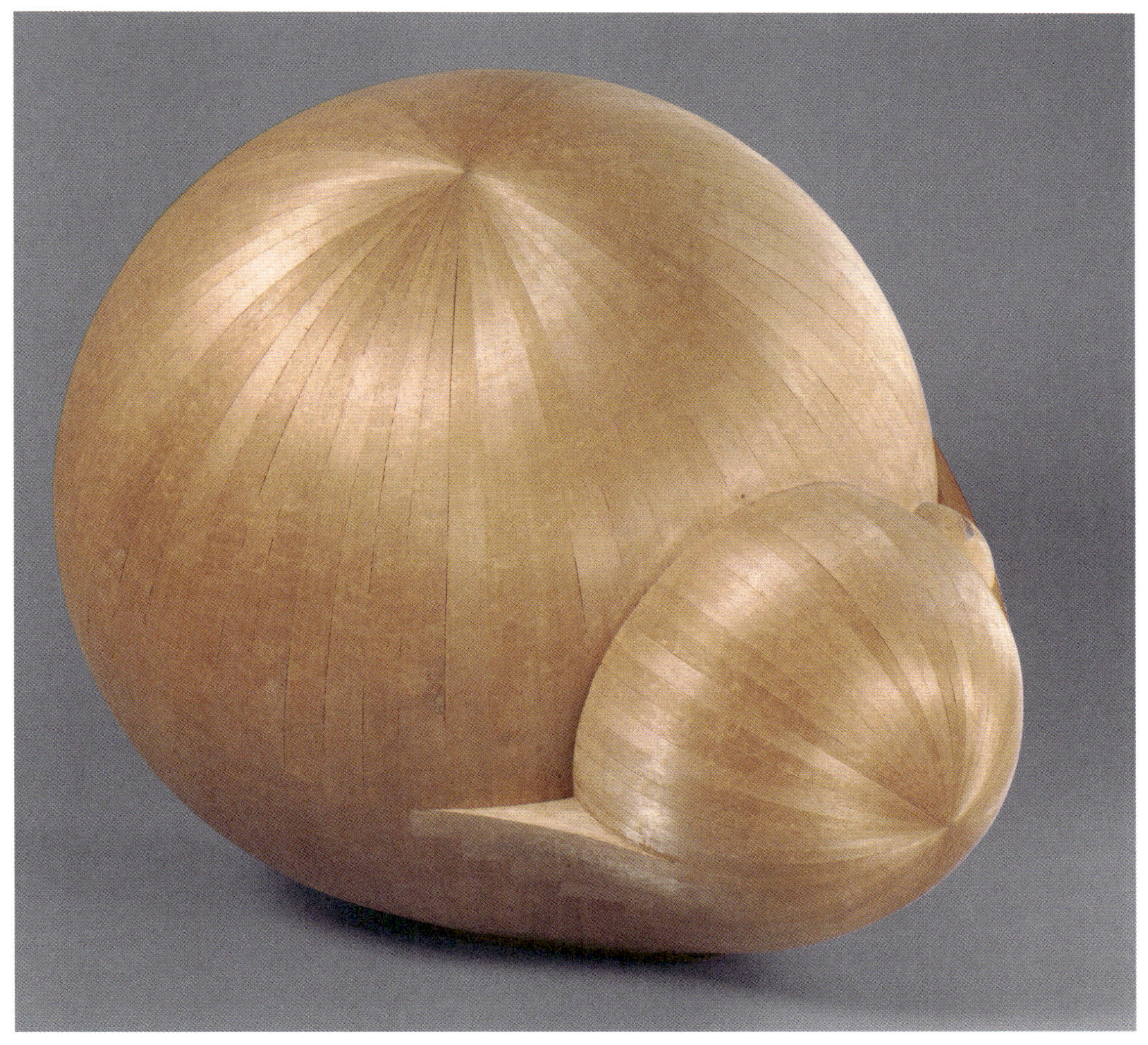

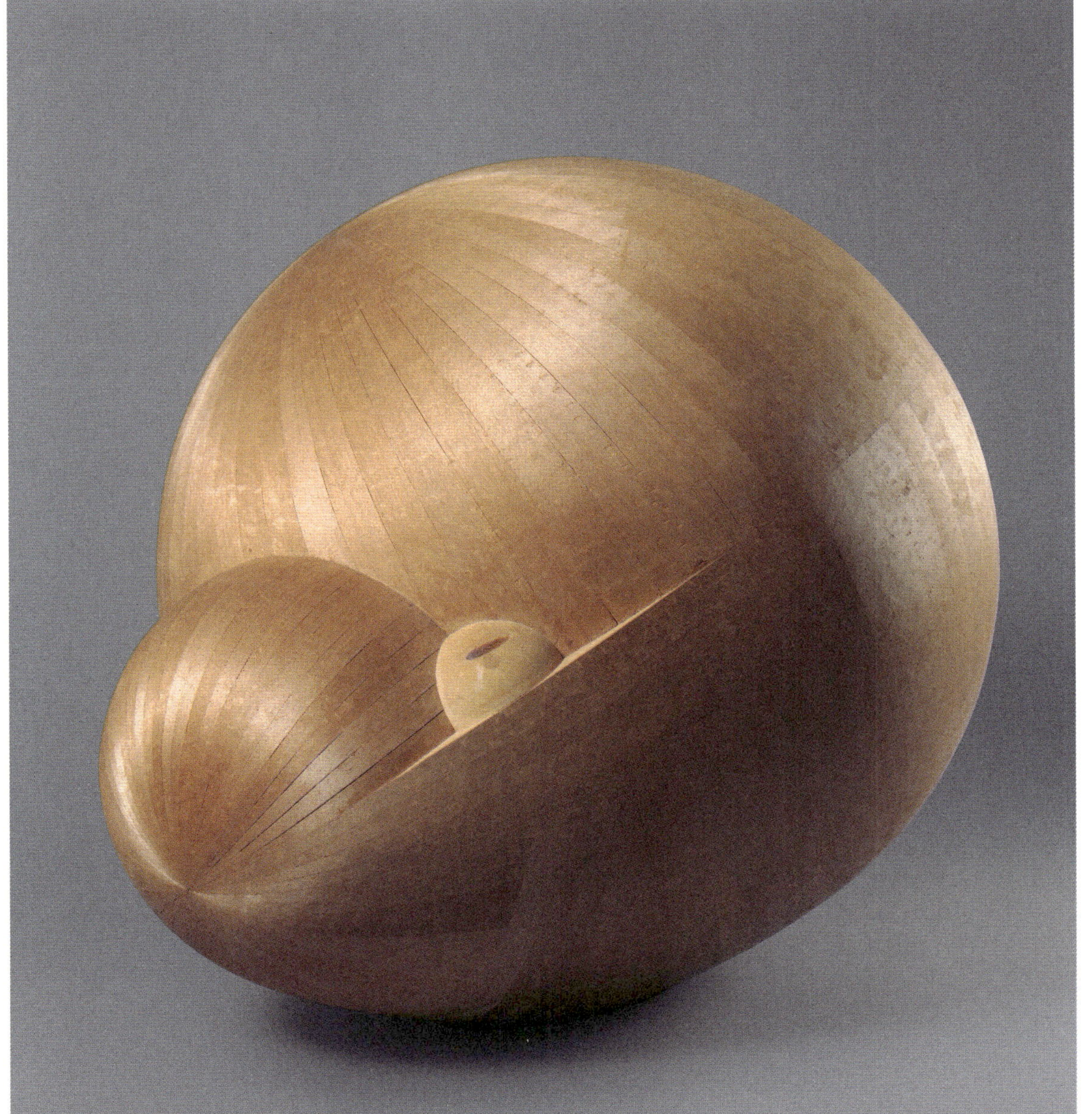

30

Alien Huddle, 1993–95

Red cedar and pine, overall: 134.6 x 162.6 x 134.6 cm

The Cleveland Museum of Art, Gift of Agnes Gund and Daniel Shapiro, 2002.65

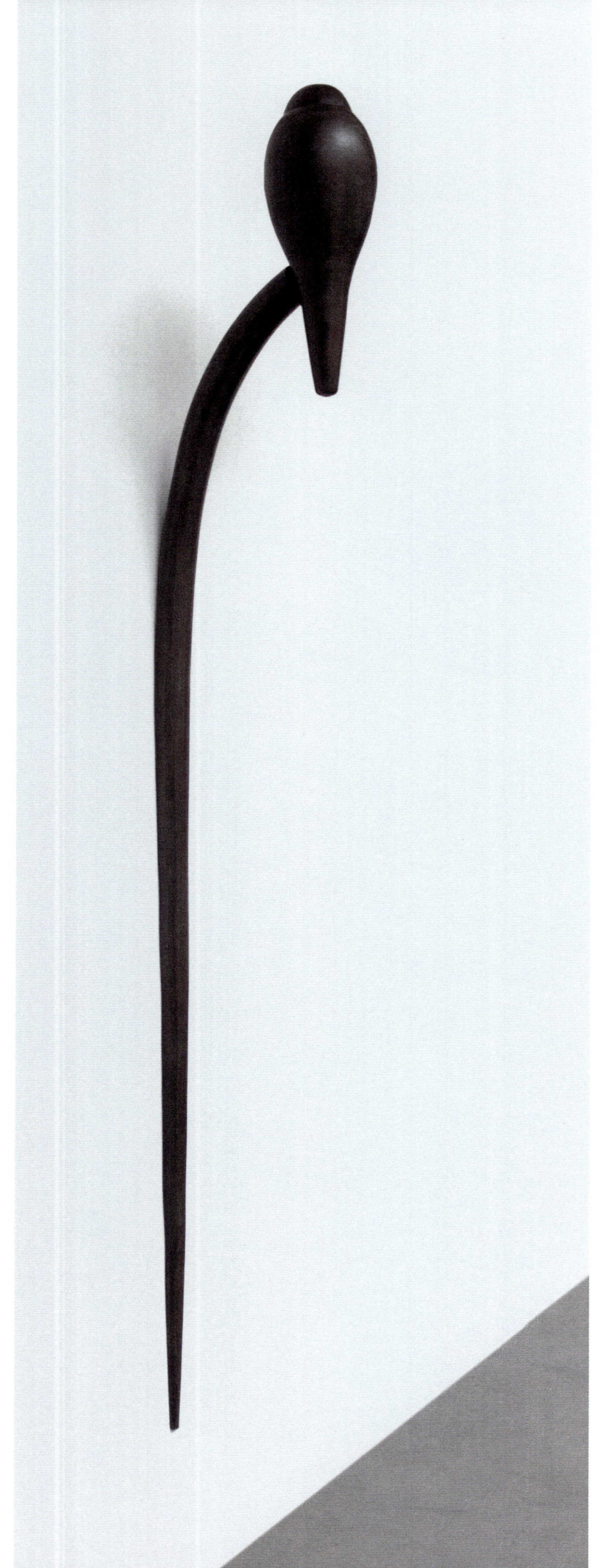

31

Untitled, 1993

Bronze; 196.8 x 14 x 34.9 cm

Collection of the artist

Photo: Jeanne Englert

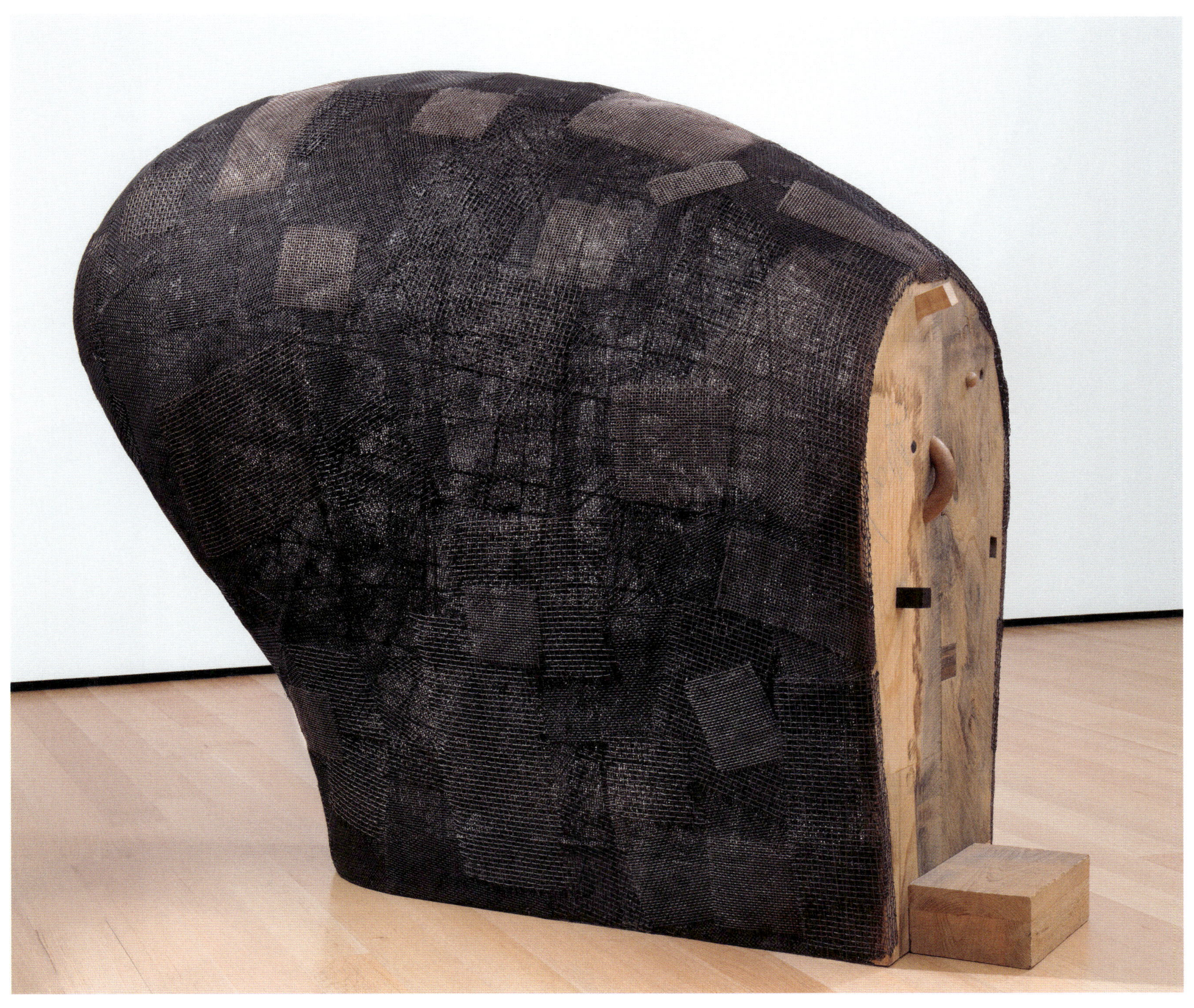

32

Confessional, 1996–2000

Wire mesh, staples, nails, steel rods, tar, and various woods; 196.2 x 247 x 114.3 cm

Museum of Fine Arts, Boston, Museum purchase with funds donated by the Ives Family Fund, Towles Contemporary Art Fund, Catherine and Paul Buttenwieser Fund, The Heritage Fund for a Diverse Collection, Joyce Linde, Carol Wall, and partial gift of Mickey Cartin, 2012.1019

Photo © 2025 Museum of Fine Arts, Boston

33

Drawing for *Tokyo International Forum*, 1995

Graphite on tracing paper; 38.4 x 237.5 cm

Collection of the artist

Photo: Jeffrey Jenkins

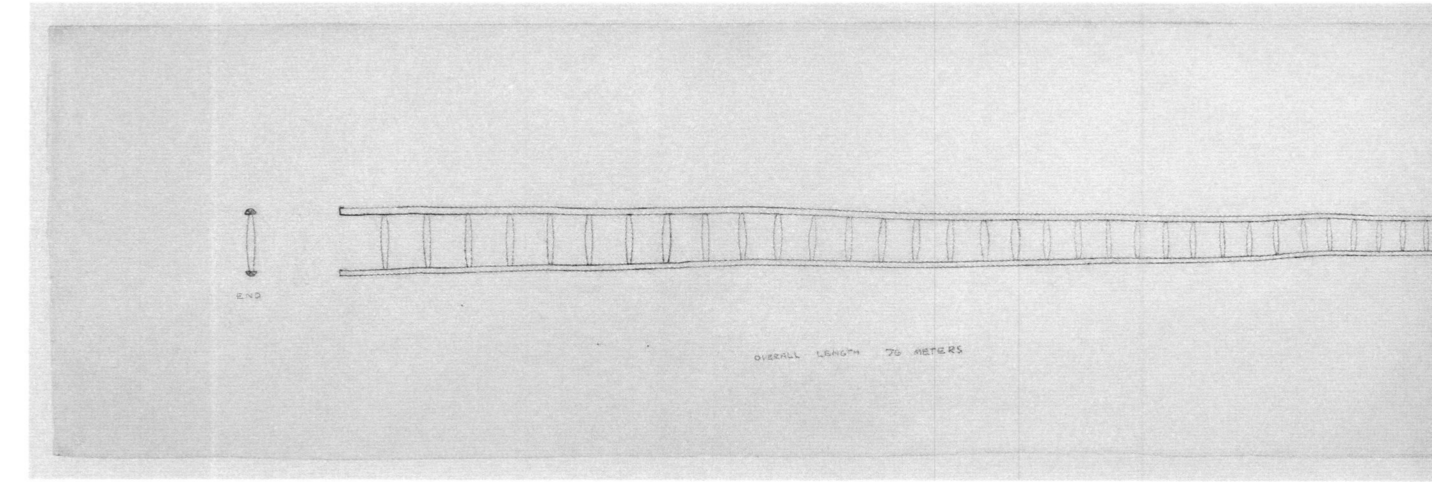

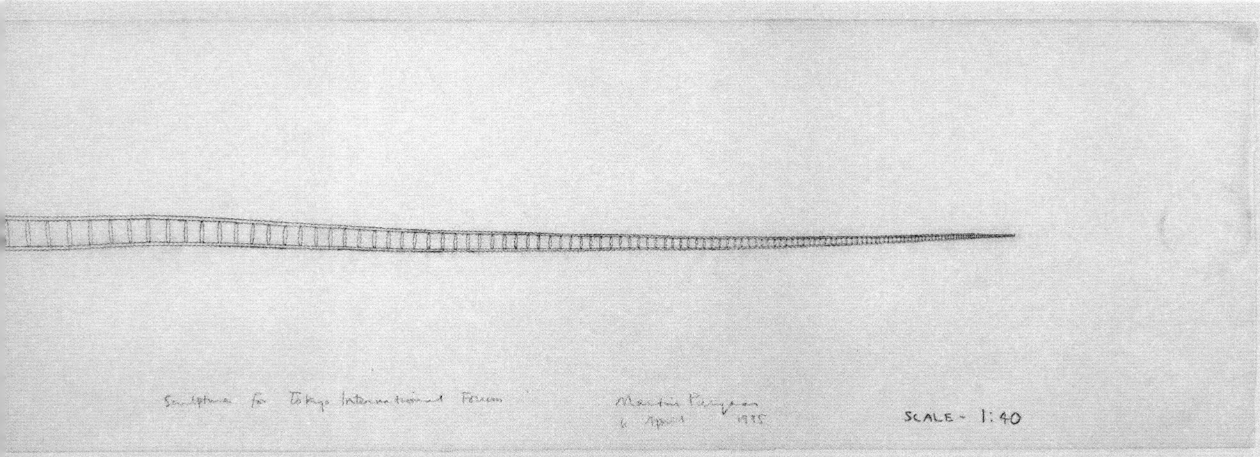
SCALE - 1:40

Ladder for Booker T. Washington

Alex Da Corte

On the last day of the world
I planted an ash tree,
and in time that tree would become a ladder.

In 1996 Martin Puryear made a ladder. The ladder was deceptively simple, appearing to have a life of its own. Extending nearly thirty-six feet in height, Puryear followed the meandering path of the young sapling as it reached toward the sky, splitting the trunk evenly, in two. Two wandering roads in time will inevitably converge. For every rung moving upward from the ground, there is a loss of lateral width between the rails. What begins as two paths eighteen inches apart becomes a point. Only then is its optical magic made apparent, its title a poem, a mist that gives it lift. Puryear says this work was not made to be about transcendence but rather about his desire to create "a kind of artificial perspective through sculpture."[1] Ladders do take you places, but Puryear doesn't offer us an exit from the world, just a reminder that many seasons are contained within today. Saplings, once green and pliant, become soldiers, now unyielding, and tomorrows become yesterdays.

Puryear's technique of forced perspective is twofold. First, there is his adjustment of the scale of the rungs in relation to the viewer. This tricks the viewer into perceiving a ladder that stretches further into the distance than it really does, confounding the connection between the top and the bottom or the beginning and the end. Is the ground plane I am on the roof or the basement? Second, if we look to the title of the ladder, we will recall Booker T. Washington's (1856–1915) gradualist ideology regarding equality and the ways in which he negotiated the dismantling of systemic racism through incremental and subtle actions. This is in contrast to the teachings of W. E. B. Du Bois (1868–1963), which espouse a more active and forceful perspective in pursuit of equal rights.

In 1985, on the heels of the wildly successful *Purple Rain* (1984), Prince embarked on the making of an album in search of equilibrium. In a world plagued by famine, earthquakes, police brutality, and the AIDS epidemic, Prince considered what it was to be an active participant, with eyes open to raw reality, and still find peace. He wanted the album to challenge listeners to "look inside [themselves] to find perfection."[2] The album cover for *Around the World in a Day* features a motley assortment of individuals: some crying, some making music, a clown juggling, a doctor. They are all gathered around a body of water. In the center, splitting the pool, is a ladder, the rails two slight diagonals opening up from the sky, only bending when they breach the water's edge. I can't help but think of Puryear's amorphous ladder as I listen to a song from this album, "America," with its forward and backward sludgy beat behind Prince's wails for Freedom, Love, Joy, Peace . . .

Maybe like Puryear's young ash tree, tomorrow comes from within.

1. Martin Puryear in Michael Auping, "A Form of Carving" (interview), in *30 Years: Interviews and Outtakes* (Fort Worth: Modern Art Museum of Fort Worth, 2007), 249.

2. Neal Karlen, "Prince Talks," *Rolling Stone*, no. 456 (September 12, 1985): 30.

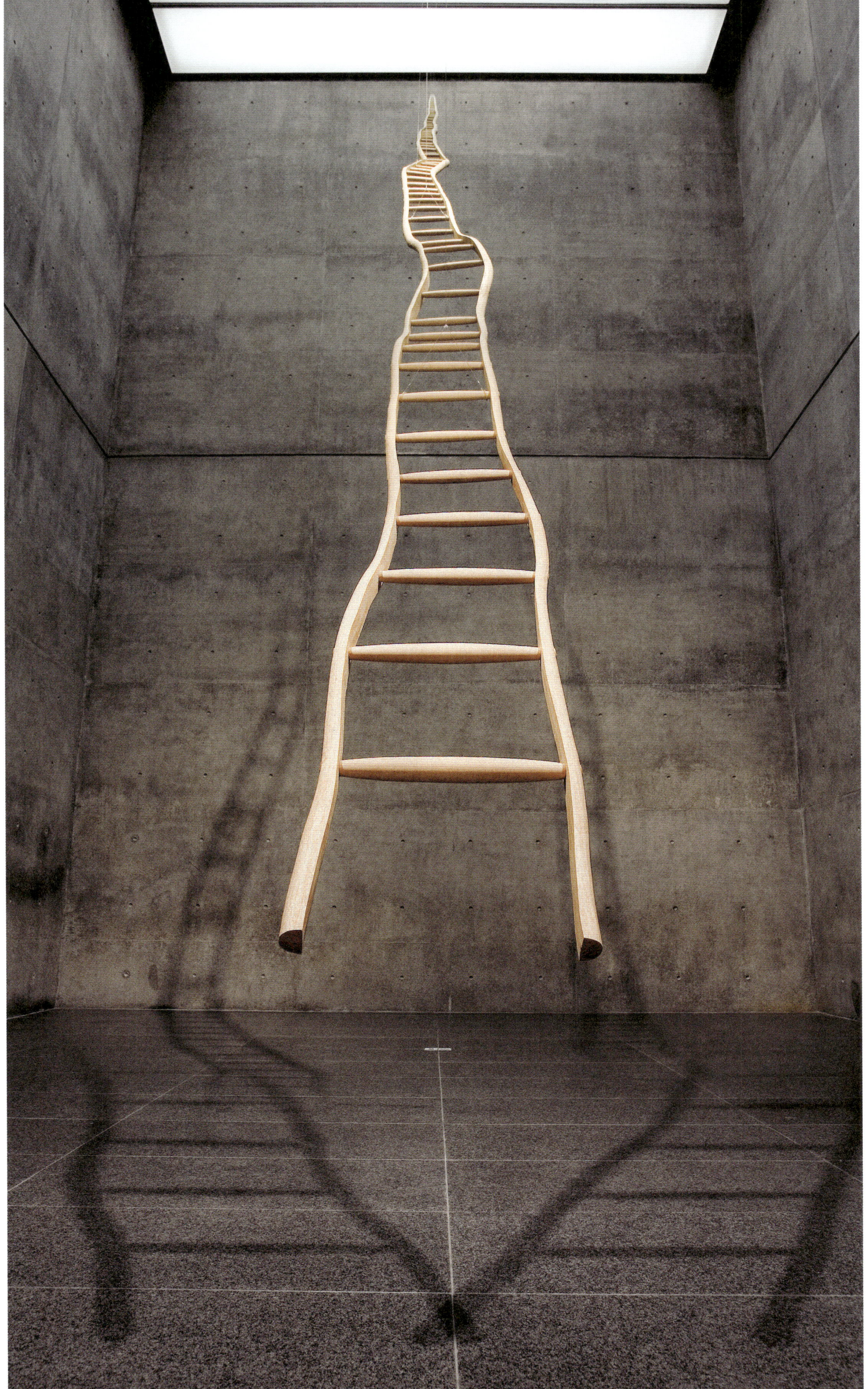

Figure 18. Installation view of *Ladder for Booker T. Washington* (1996), Modern Art Museum of Fort Worth. Ash and maple; 1097.3 x 57.8 (narrowing to 3.2 at top) x 7.6 cm. Photo: Modern Art Museum of Fort Worth, Texas

Meditation in a Beech Wood

Maya Lin

In 2003 I was invited to Wanås Konst in Knislinge, Sweden, to create a new work for the sculpture park.[1] On my first day there, as I was walking through the landscape to identify a site, I wandered into an open beech glade and encountered a Buddha-like sculpture that was perfectly framed within the woods. The form had a slight curve, giving the piece an anthropogenic quality, and the sculpture was made of freshly crafted thatch, a building material historically used for rooftops in the area.

The experience was transformative.

After all these years, the beauty and simplicity and power of *Meditation in a Beech Wood* still lingers (fig. 19). It was perfectly situated in an opening in the grove that let in the sunlight. It was fall when I encountered the piece, and the coppery red of the leaves made the grove and the sculpture glow.

The form—slightly bent, truncated at the top—felt very much like a human presence but abstracted, quiet, subtle. The sculpture reached and was framed by the surrounding majestic and very large beech trees. It set up a dialogue in scale and proportion with the forest itself. I could recognize that it was Martin's work. I have always admired and appreciated his indoor wood sculptures, and this outdoor sculpture captured the warmth and intimate quality of the works I knew.

The thatch had a soft, subtle presence, so the form felt very much a natural part of the grove. Even though it was created to be a permanent outdoor work, the sculpture has needed periodic rethatching so the ephemeral and fragile quality of the piece remains. It ages and changes with time and is then reborn again. It reminds me of the Ise Shrine in Japan, which is rebuilt every twenty years.

I have since traveled back to Wanås to see the work as it transformed with the seasons and through time. This transmutable character gives it a quality that reinforces its organic and living aspect.

It is one of the most powerful and moving works of art I have ever encountered.

Figure 19. Installation view of *Meditation in a Beech Wood* (1996) at Wanås Foundation, Knislinge, Sweden. Martin Puryear. Water reed thatched over timber frame (wood, concrete, and steel); 444.8 x 500.4 x 340.4 cm. Photo: Anders Norrsell

1. *Eleven Minute Line*, 2004, 66.1 x 294.1 x 3.7 m, Wanås Foundation, Knislinge, Sweden.

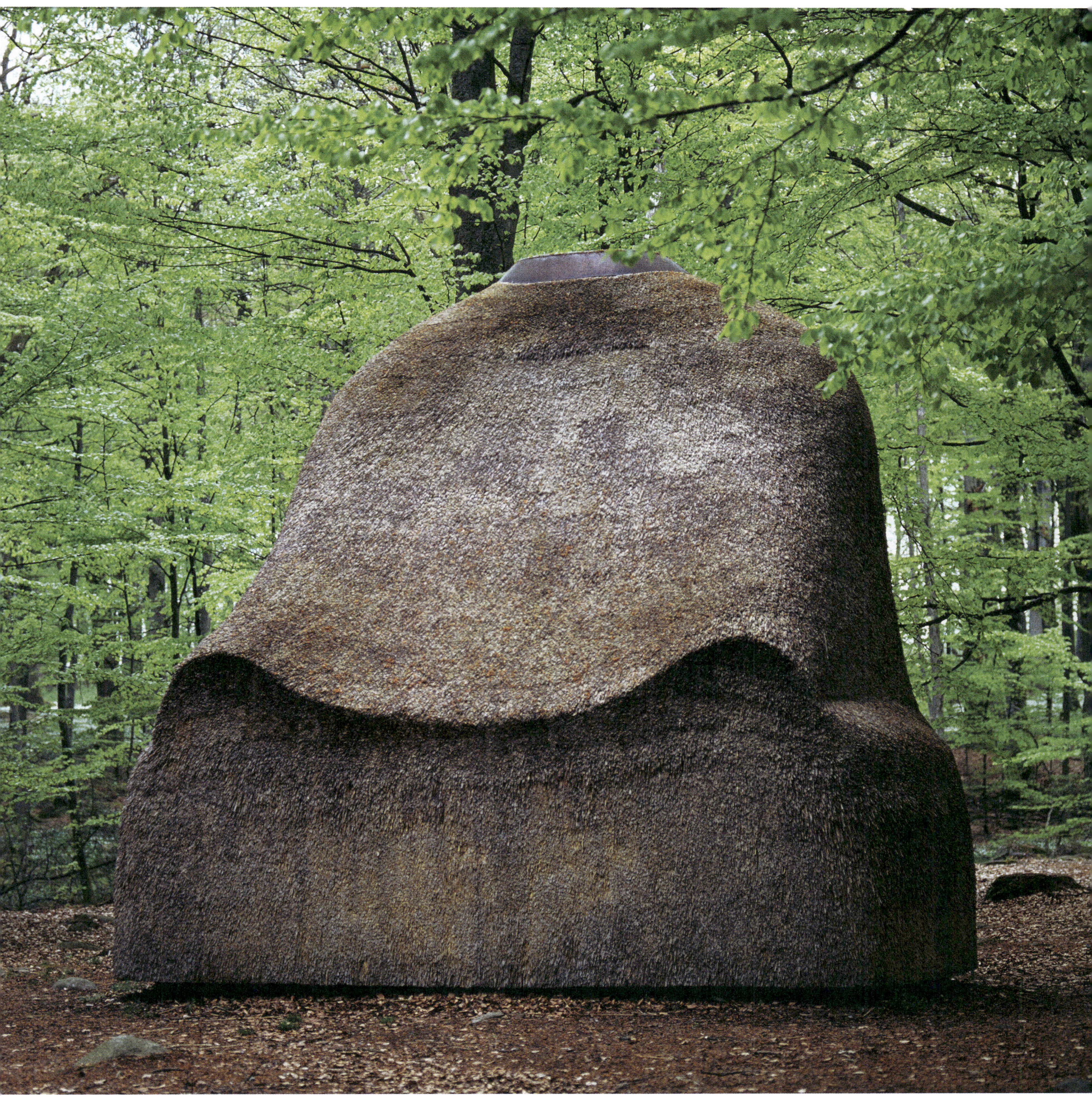

Untitled (1997)

Nairy Baghramian

If there is a syntax that Martin Puryear's works share, it lies in their incommensurability and diversity. While formal or material echoes may occasionally surface, evoking a sense of déjà vu—much like recognizing a musical motif one believes to have heard in a different context—unambiguity, in the sense of effortless recognition, is hardly intended. Each sculpture operates as a discrete entity in which much resonates but nothing is articulated as explicitly as to elicit a narrative on which we all could immediately agree. The forms conjure memories of both the quotidian and the historical, and one is never certain whether Puryear adds to the austere vocabulary of minimal art or whether he is engaging in a process of reduction from the figurative or the everyday without eschewing formalism. In any case, what we may recognize remains deliberately elusive, and the works defy any need to become signifiers of a predetermined content. Puryear draws from a wide-ranging formal repertoire, crafting a distinct yet universal visual language in which references remain allusions; this allows them to evade the burden of definitive meaning, embracing the potential for multiple interpretations.

Such a methodical and composed use of sculpture as an aesthetic vessel of information—where there exists a foreground as well as concealed layers of meaning in which strata of color, form, material, and language can be both added and subtracted—recalls the iconographic practice of Robert Indiana (1928–2018). Indiana's works are deeply embedded in our collective cultural consciousness, and through their pop-cultural directness they seem to offer the possibility of accessing them with immediacy. Yet once one learns, for example, that the top layer of his work *LOVE*—its coloration—was derived from the chromatic vocabulary of his former partner Ellsworth Kelly (1923–2015), hinting at a lover's dedication, coded depths are revealed that suggest a complexity far beyond the initial, surface interpretation.

Puryear's *Self* (1978; [14]), provokes a similar sentiment. Upon encountering its familiar yet opaque presence, it feels like meeting an old acquaintance. Upon closer examination of the materials, however, and upon contemplating the weight and volumes, and trying to discern what lies behind or beneath, one uncovers a profound stratification that imbues Martin Puryear's works with compelling expressiveness. Engaging deeply with sculptures such as *Self*, *Bower* (1980; [19]), *Big Phrygian* (2010–14; [55]), and *Phrygian Spirit* (2012–14) and considering their chronological evolution reveals that, on the one hand, Puryear is exploring the concept of seriality by revisiting a particular form over the course of many years; on the other hand, each of these closely related forms is imbued with its own significance.

The resonance of recurring forms and materials, with their deceptive fullness and spectral contours, culminates in *Untitled* (1997). It is infused with the layers of meaning accrued by its predecessors and successors, and it draws the viewer into a deeper realm of ambiguous abstraction, a realm whose untitled status stands in for the vast multitude of the "nameless."

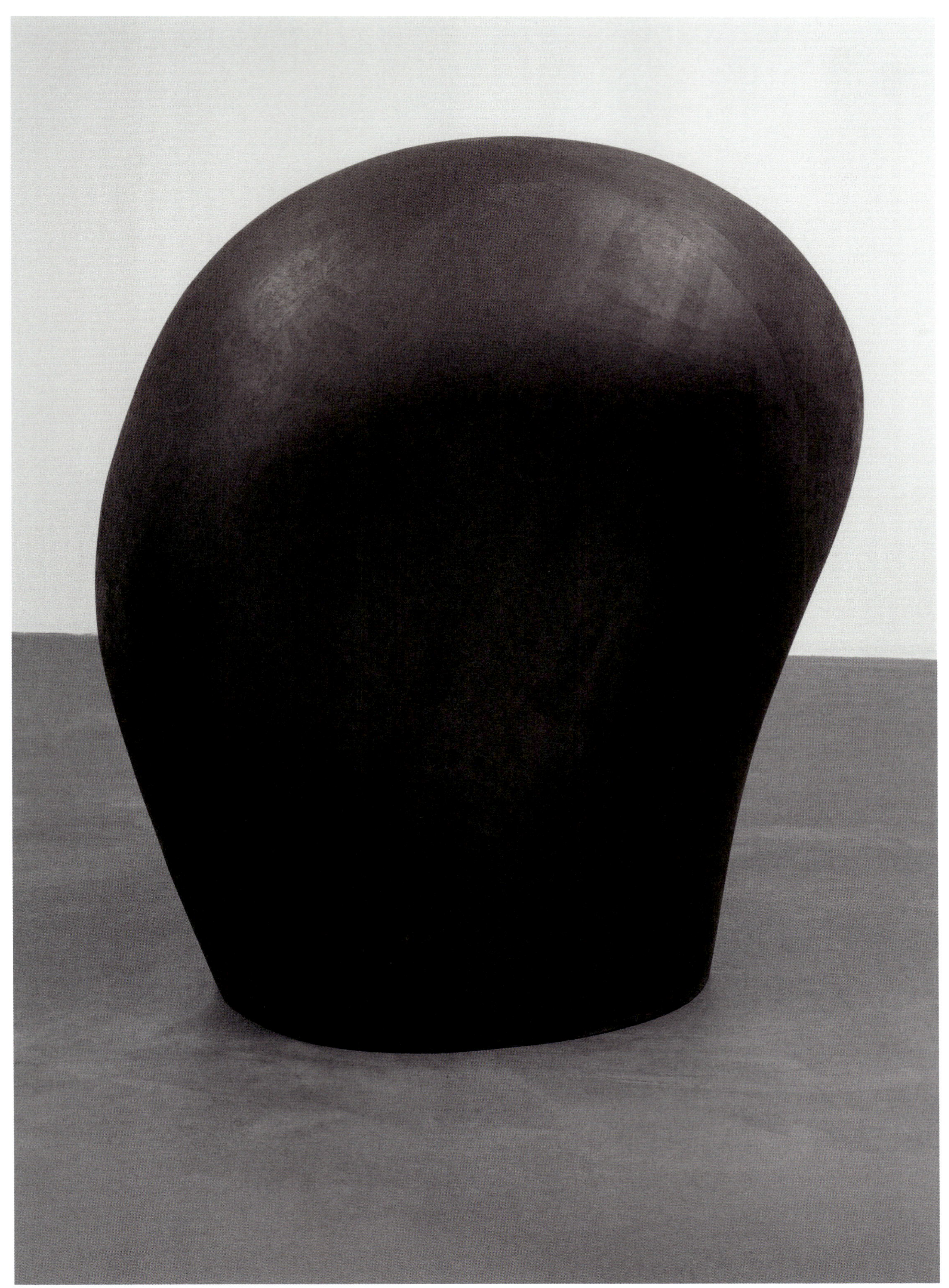

34

Untitled, 1997

Painted red cedar and pine; 172.7 x 144.8 x 129.5 cm

The Museum of Modern Art, New York, Gift of Agnes Gund in honor of Tom Cahill, 1997, 651.1997

Photo: John Wronn

Digital Image © The Museum of Modern Art/ Licensed by SCALA / Art Resource, NY

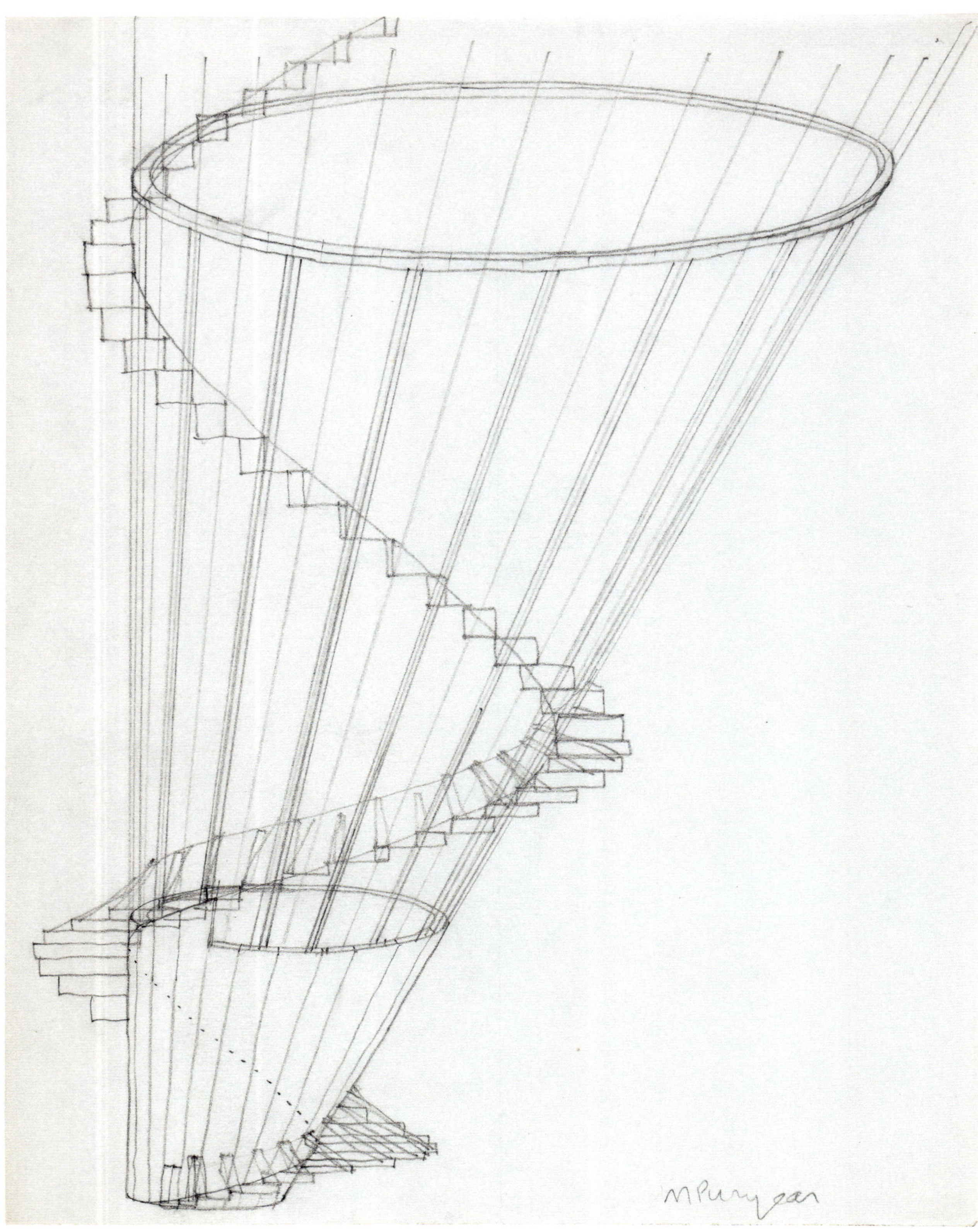

35

Drawing for *This Mortal Coil*, 1998

Graphite on paper; 35.6 x 27.9 cm

Collection of the artist

Photo: Jeffrey Jenkins

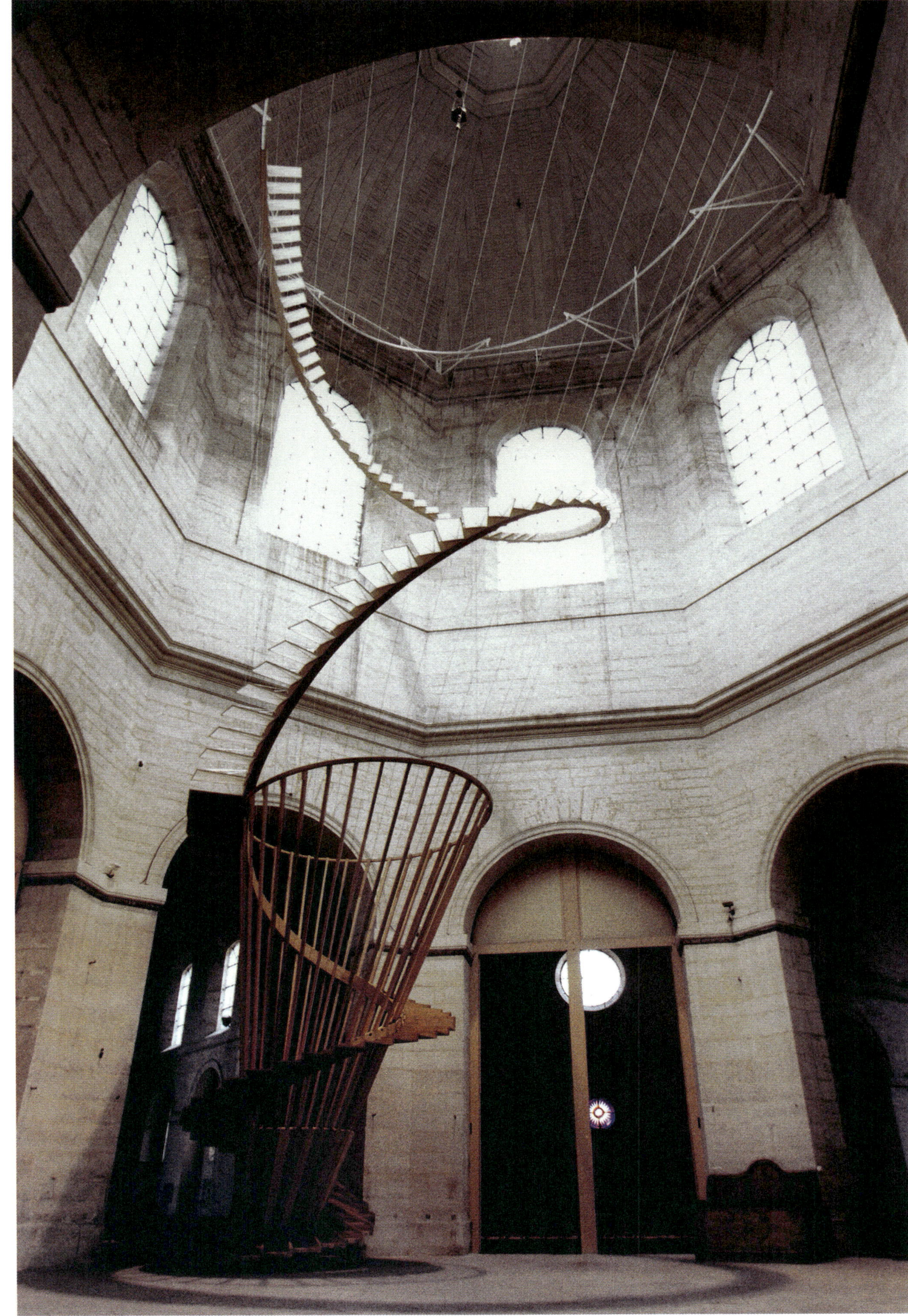

Figure 20. Installation view of *This Mortal Coil* (1999) at Chapelle Saint-Louis de la Salpêtrière, Paris. Martin Puryear. Red cedar, stainless-steel cable, aluminum, and muslin; 26 x 12 x 16 m. Courtesy of the Festival d'Automne à Paris

Photo: Pascal Victor

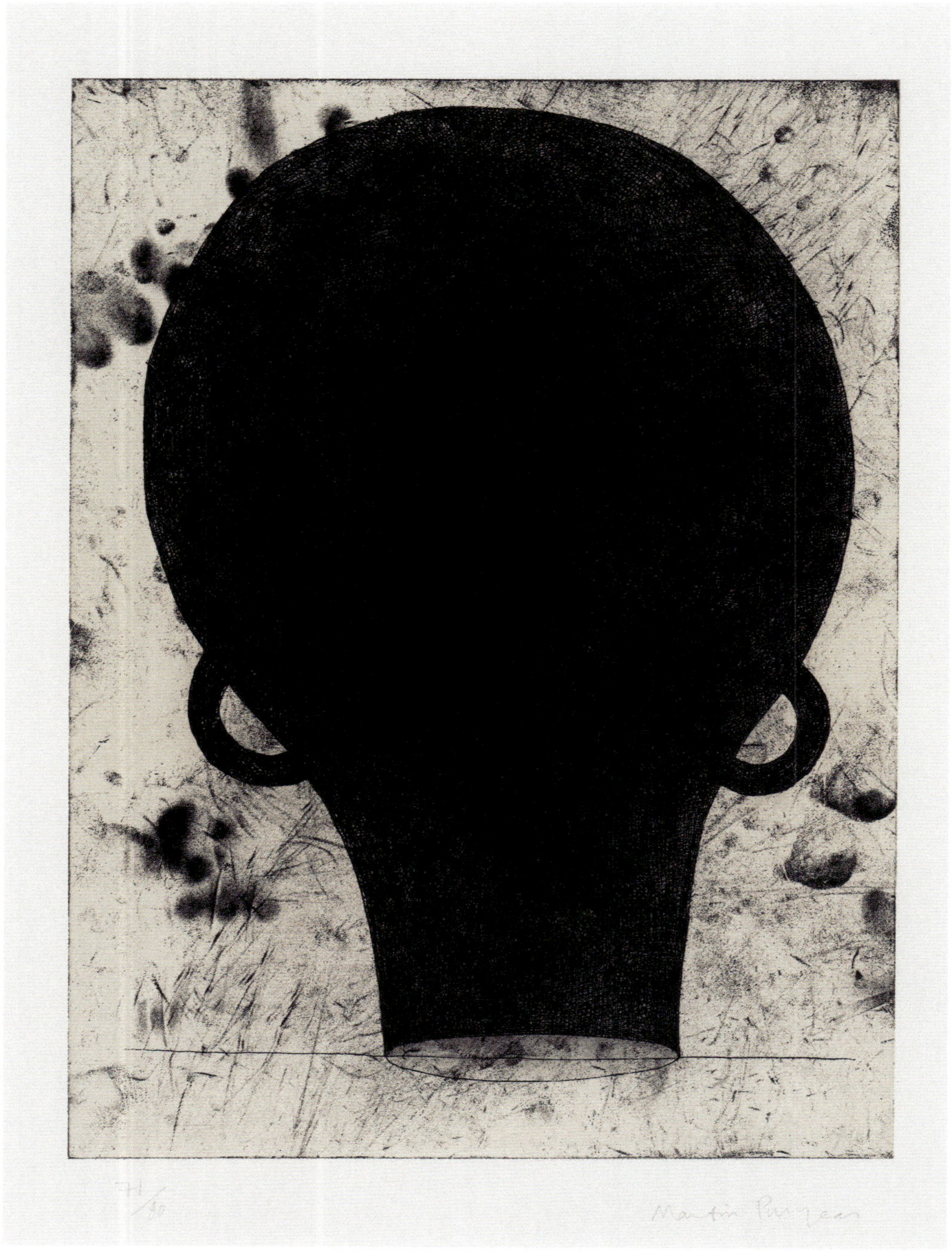

36

Untitled (LA MoCA Portfolio), 1999

Hard and soft ground etching and aquatint with chine collé; platemark: 61 x 45.4 cm; sheet: 76.3 x 55.3 cm

Museum of Fine Arts, Boston, Museum purchase with funds donated by the Board of Trustees in honor of Stokley Towles, Chair of the Board of Trustees, 2007–2010, and Sylvia Quarles Simmons, Chair of the Board of Overseers, 2008–2010, 2010.625

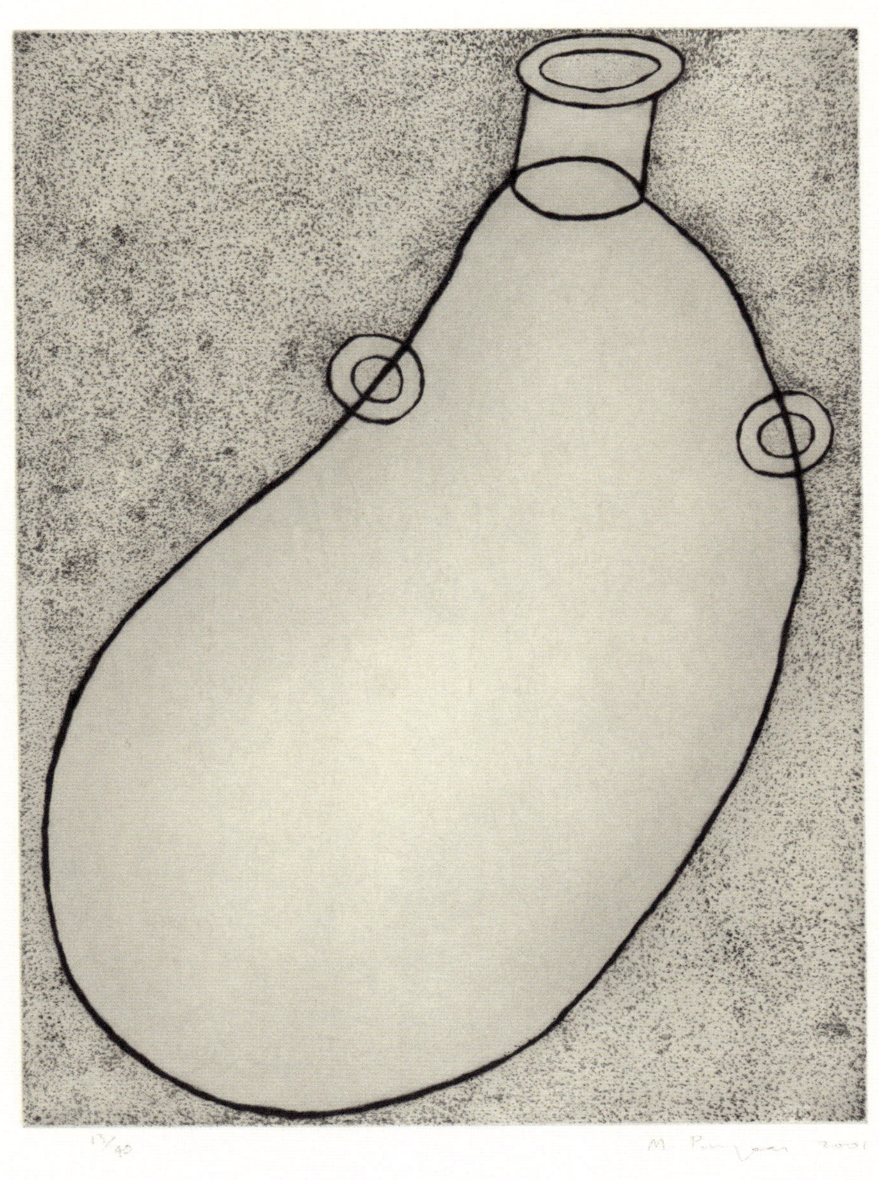

37

Jug, 2001

Printer and publisher: Paulson Bott Press, Berkeley, CA

Hard and soft ground etching, with drypoint and chine collé; image / plate: 60.3 x 45 cm; sheet: 87.8 x 70.1 cm

The Art Institute of Chicago, Mr. and Mrs. Robert O. Delaney Fund, 2007.91

Photo: The Art Institute of Chicago / Art Resource, NY

Martin Puryear's *Cane*

Thelma Golden

Martin Puryear's work has long concerned itself with rooting out the symbols, experiences, and materials of African and African American history. So in the late 1990s, when Arion Press approached Puryear to produce an artist's book to accompany a special edition of Jean Toomer's (1894–1967) novel *Cane* (1923), his response was informed by the same historical close looking that has inspired his practice for years. Puryear accepted. A canonical piece of literature from the Harlem Renaissance, *Cane* deftly captures the lives of African Americans—from the South and the North—during the Great Migration. Structurally, *Cane* was genre-busting and experimental. Composed of poetry, prose, and playscript, all written in Toomer's unique lyrical voice, the book defied literary categorizations of the early 1920s and represents so acutely the myriad groundbreaking literature, art, music, and philosophical thinking that emerged throughout the movement.

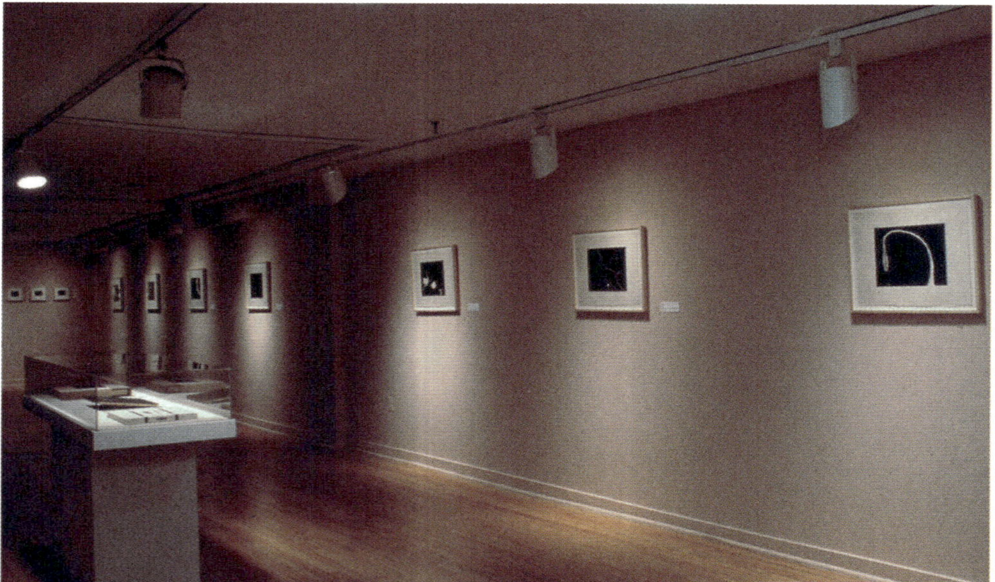

Figure 21. Installation view of *Martin Puryear: The Cane Project*, Studio Museum in Harlem, New York, 2000. Photo: Courtesy of the Studio Museum in Harlem Archives

Much like Toomer's book, Puryear's seven woodblock prints based on *Cane* evade easy classification. They are inspired by seven vignettes in *Cane* and take as their titles the names of the text's key female characters— Avey, Becky, Bona, Carma, Esther, Fern, and Karintha—most of whom are Black women from the South. But Puryear's prints are not portraits. Like his revered sculptures in wood, these images employ abstracted, organic forms. Among curvilinear linework, I see a flower bud slumping toward the ground; a sun setting behind a mountain ridge; and a root system taking form. By illustrating elements of natural environments, the artist alludes to the ways in which each of Toomer's characters reflects the topography of their surroundings—in their physical features, their behaviors, and their disposition. At the same time, Puryear articulates the multifaceted dimensions with which Toomer infused each of these women: at once strong, sexualized, intelligent, oppressed, mythic, beautiful, and sublime.

It is against and within this cross-generational and visionary backdrop that the Studio Museum in Harlem presented *Martin Puryear: The Cane Project* in 2000 (fig. 21). I was the museum's deputy director at the time, and Puryear figured centrally in the art histories that created me, so when I was given the opportunity to insert his work into our exhibition programming, it felt like an overly ambitious goal. Puryear's response to our exhibition proposal was characteristic of what I have experienced in our decades-long relationship: he was deeply generous, incredibly soulful, and fully committed to the many possibilities that art presents its audiences.[1]

Though this exhibition was small in size—literally, as it took up only one room—it looms large in the history of this institution. It gave us the chance to reintroduce an iconic and formative novel of the Harlem Renaissance to those within the very same space that inspired much of Toomer's writing, in turn enabling Harlem's past to reappear in its present, and those in its present to reimagine a critical period in Harlem's history. *The Cane Project* also exemplified so much of what lies at the core of the Studio Museum and cites itself within a lineage of exhibitions that continually honor Harlem as not just a geographical space but a space of intellectual construction and imagination; a space that remains redolent of Black feeling, thought, and ideas. Showcasing Puryear's work at the Studio Museum therefore felt like a homecoming. In these ways, *The Cane Project* was momentous, and, like the works of Puryear and Toomer, it vividly "told other folks just what it is to live."[2]

1. *Martin Puryear: The Cane Project*, curated by Thelma Golden, was on view at the Studio Museum in Harlem from October 11, 2000, to January 8, 2001.

2. Jean Toomer, *Cane* (1923; New York: Liveright, 2011), 7.

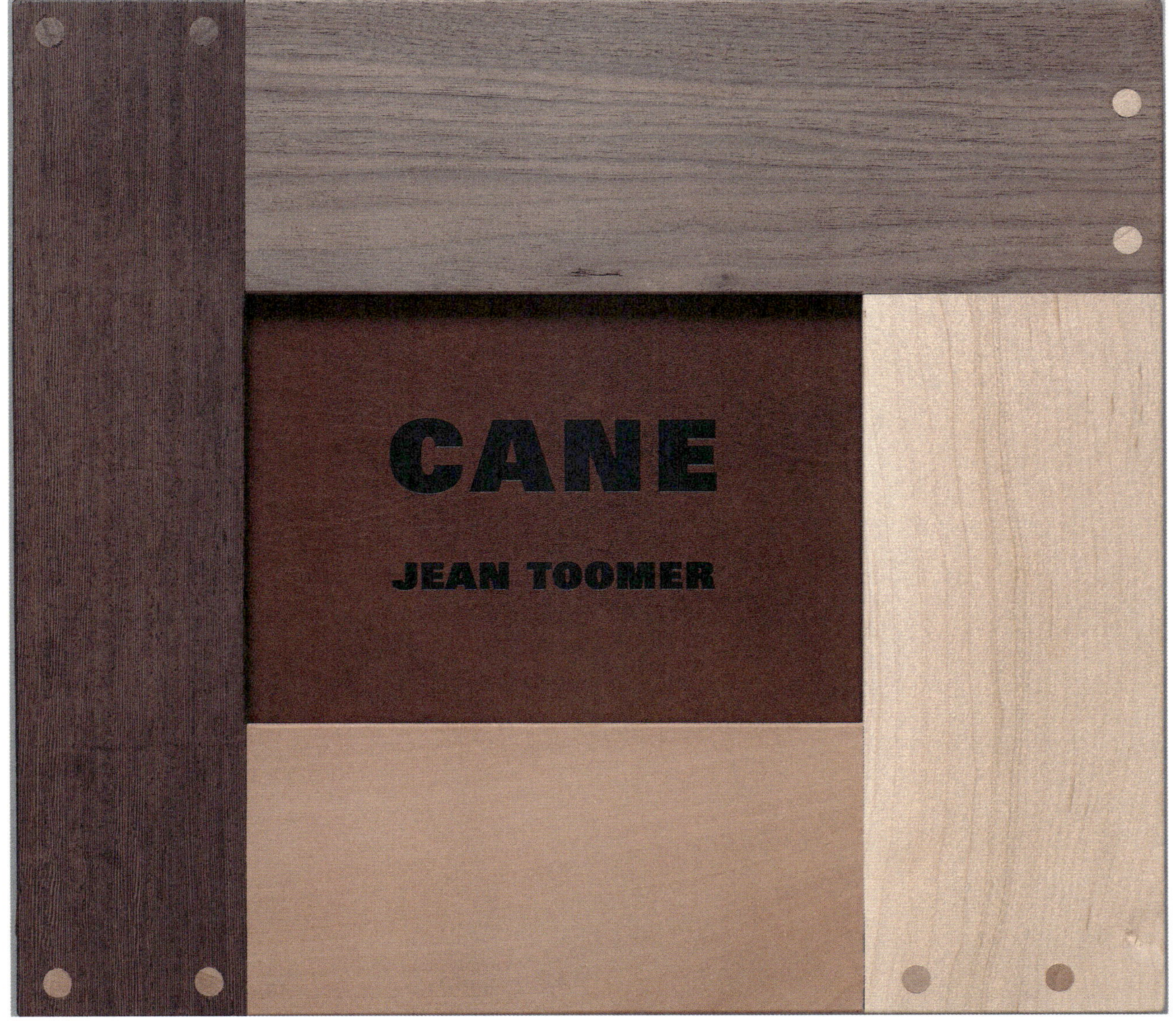

38

Cane, 2000

Deluxe edition illustrated book, by Jean Toomer and illustrated by Martin Puryear, printed and published by Arion Press, San Francisco

Bound in full brown goatskin with artist-designed wooden case, and separate portfolio of woodcuts; closed: 30.2 x 35.9 x 2.9 cm. Wooden slipcase: African wenge, Swiss pear, American black walnut, and sugar maple; overall: 34.9 x 38.4 x 4.8 cm.

Museum of Fine Arts, Boston, Lee M. Friedman Fund, 2002.904.1, 2002.904.10

Photo © 2025 Museum of Fine Arts, Boston

"Thats just it, Bona. We have our team."

"Well, team or no team, I want to play and thats all there is to it."

She snatches the ball from Helen's hands, and charges down the floor.

Helen shrugs. One of the weaker girls says that she'll drop out. Helen accepts this. The team is formed. The whistle blows. The game starts. Bona, in center, is jumping against Paul. He plays with her. Out-jumps her, makes a quick pass, gets a quick return, and shoots a goal from the middle of the floor. Bona burns crimson. She fights, and tries to guard him. One of her team-mates advises her not to play so hard. Paul shoots his second goal.

Bona begins to feel a little dizzy and all in. She drives on. Almost hugs Paul to guard him. Near the basket, he attempts to shoot, and Bona lunges into his body and tries to beat his arms. His elbow, going up, gives her a sharp crack on the jaw. She whirls. He catches her. Her body stiffens. Then becomes strangely vibrant, and bursts to a swift life within her anger. He is about to give way before her hatred when a new passion flares at him and makes his stomach fall. Bona squeezes him. He suddenly feels stifled, and wonders why in hell the ring of silly gaping faces that's caked about him doesnt make way and give him air. He has a swift illusion that it is himself who has been struck. He looks at Bona. Whir. Whir. They seem to be human distortions spinning tensely in a fog. Spinning . . dizzy . . spinning . . . Bona jerks herself free, flushes a startling crimson, breaks through the bewildered teams, and rushes from the hall.

2

Paul is in his room of two windows.

Outside, the South-Side L track cuts them in two.

Bona is one window. One window, Paul.

Hurtling Loop-jammed L trains throw them in swift shadow.

Paul goes to his. Gray slanting roofs of houses are tinted lavender in the setting sun. Paul follows the sun, over the stock-yards where a fresh stench is just arising, across wheat lands that are still waving above their stubble, into the sun. Paul follows the sun to a pine-matted hillock in Georgia. He sees the slanting roofs

80 ◆ CANE

Figure 22. "Bona," in Jean Toomer (American, 1894–1967), *Cane*, illustrated by Martin Puryear (San Francisco: Arion Press, 2000)

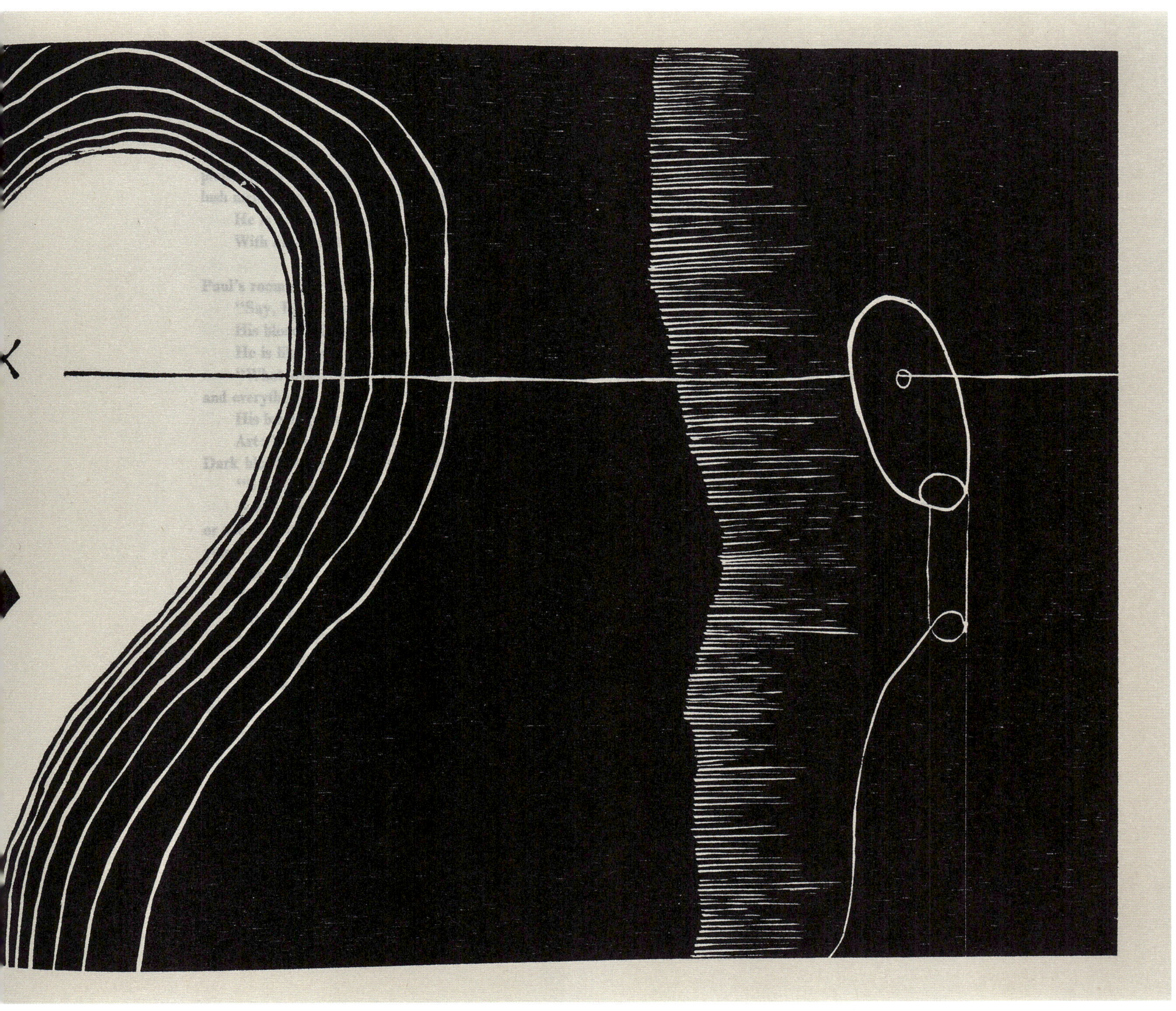

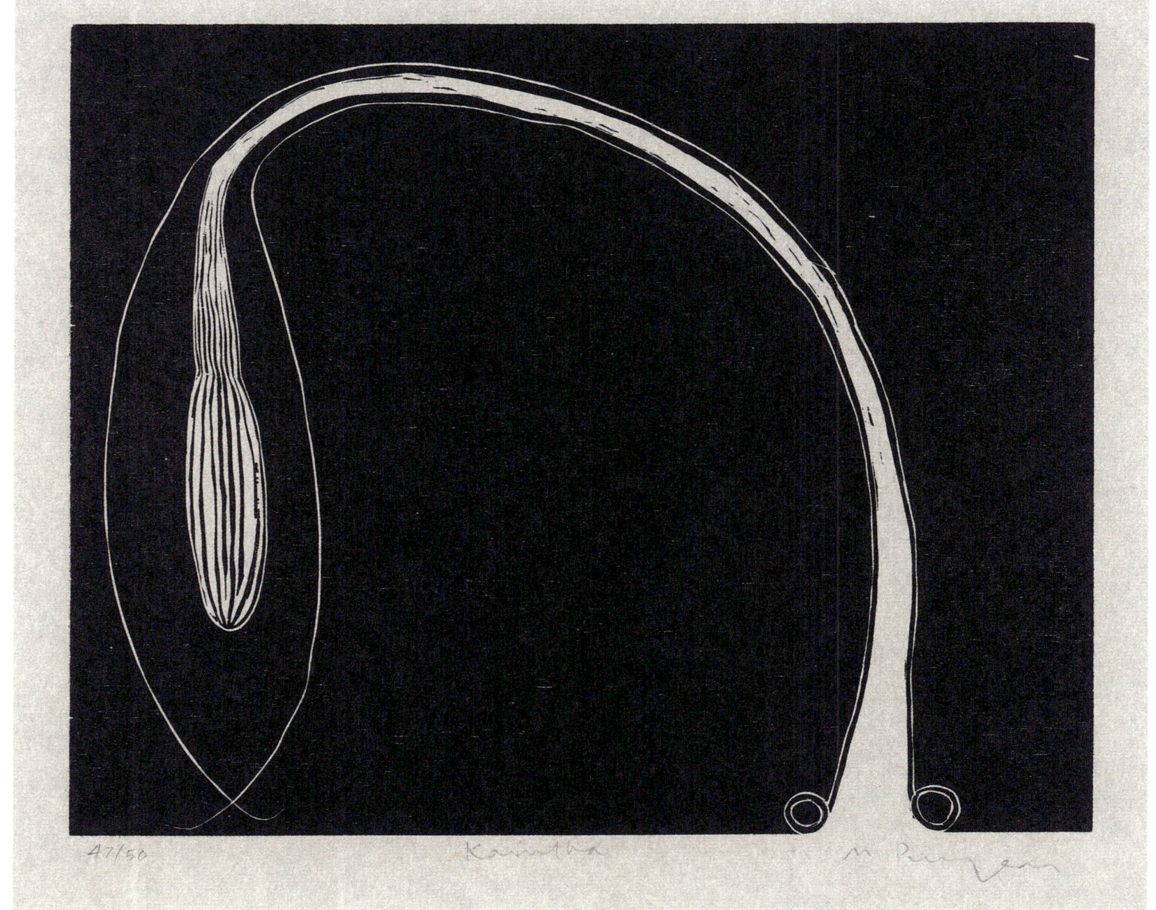

39

Karintha, from *Cane*, 2000

Woodcut on Japanese paper; image / plate: 26.7 x 33 cm; sheet: 43.2 x 52.1 cm

Museum of Fine Arts, Boston, Lee M. Friedman Fund, 2002.904.2

Photo © 2025 Museum of Fine Arts, Boston

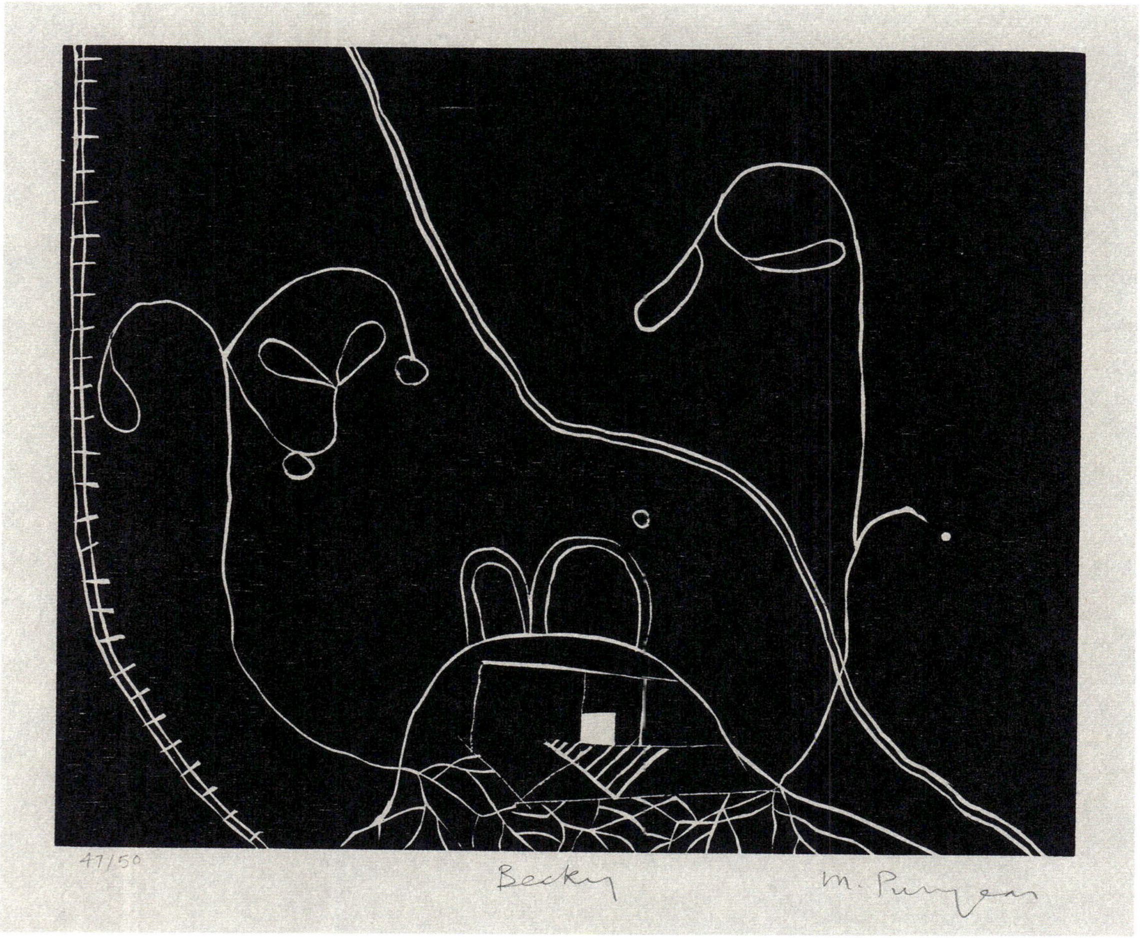

40

Becky, from *Cane*, 2000

Woodcut on Japanese paper; image / plate: 26.7 x 33 cm; sheet: 43.2 x 52.1 cm

Museum of Fine Arts, Boston, Lee M. Friedman Fund, 2002.904.3

Photo © 2025 Museum of Fine Arts, Boston

41

Carma, from *Cane*, 2000

Woodcut on Japanese paper; image / plate: 26.7 x 33 cm; sheet: 43.2 x 52.1 cm

Museum of Fine Arts, Boston, Lee M. Friedman Fund, 2002.904.4

Photo © 2025 Museum of Fine Arts, Boston

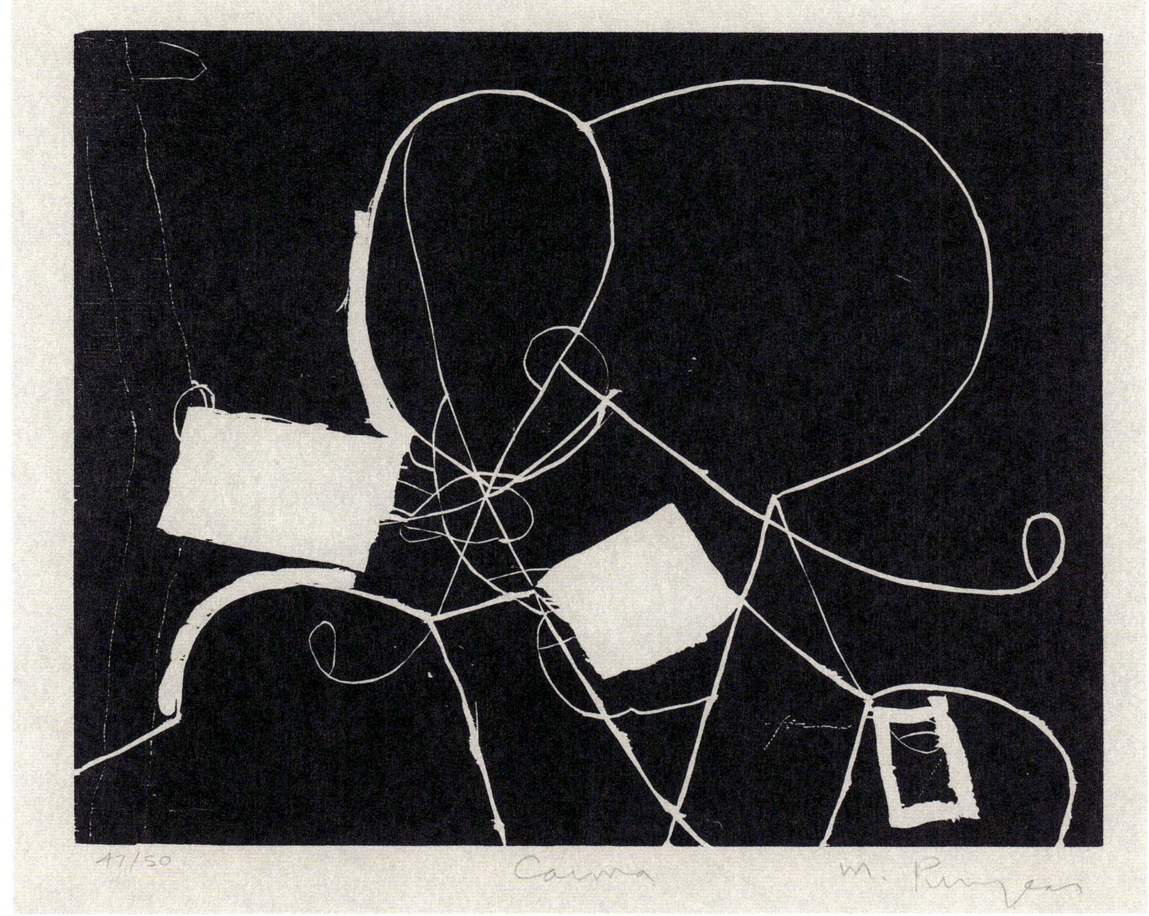

42

Fern, from *Cane*, 2000

Woodcut on Japanese paper; image / plate: 26.7 x 33 cm; sheet: 43.2 x 52.1 cm

Museum of Fine Arts, Boston, Lee M. Friedman Fund, 2002.904.5

Photo © 2025 Museum of Fine Arts, Boston

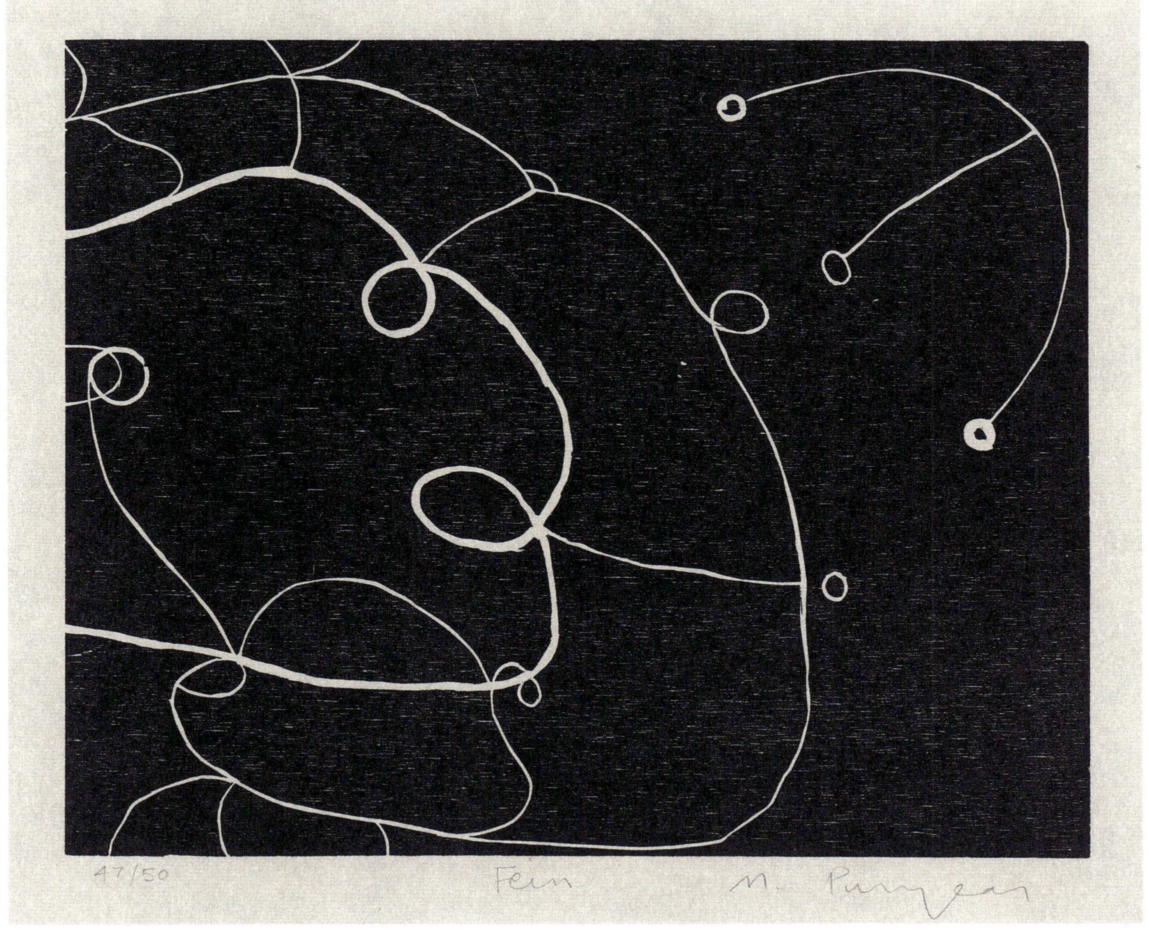

43

Esther, from *Cane*, 2000

Woodcut on Japanese paper; image / plate: 26.7 x 33 cm; sheet: 43.2 x 52.1 cm

Museum of Fine Arts, Boston, Lee M. Friedman Fund, 2002.904.6

Photo © 2025 Museum of Fine Arts, Boston

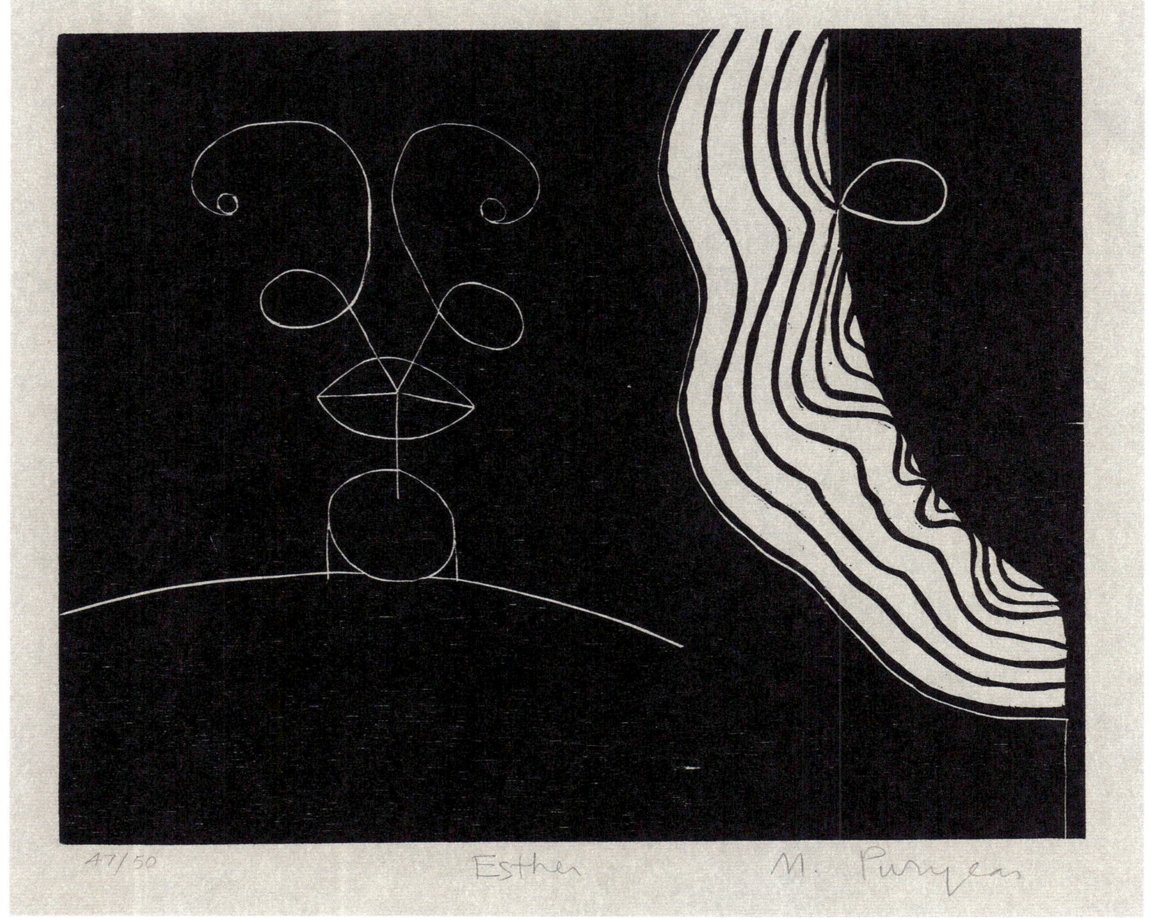

44

Avey, from *Cane*, 2000

Woodcut on Japanese paper; image / plate: 26.7 x 33 cm; sheet: 43.2 x 52.1 cm

Museum of Fine Arts, Boston, Lee M. Friedman Fund, 2002.904.7

Photo © 2025 Museum of Fine Arts, Boston

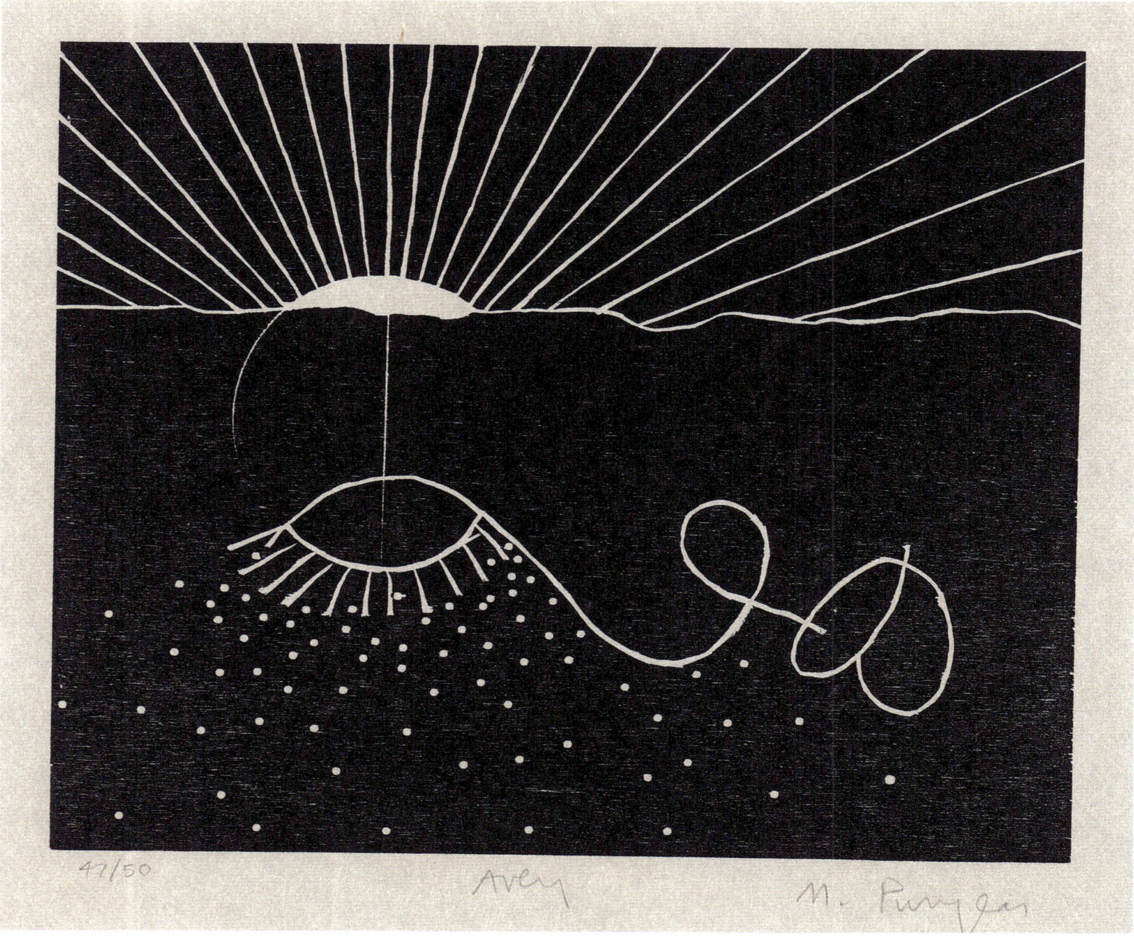

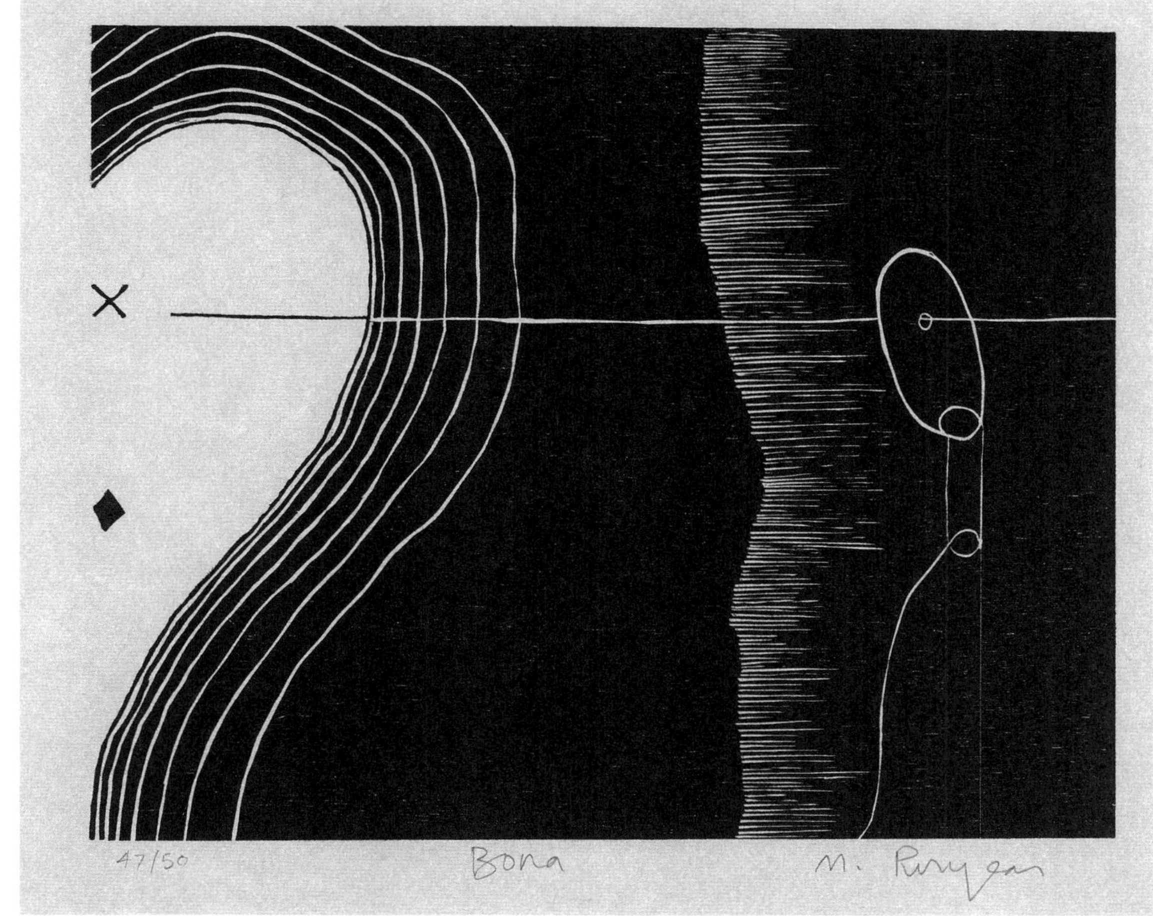

45

Bona, from *Cane*, 2000

Woodcut on Japanese paper; image / plate: 26.7 x 33 cm; sheet: 43.2 x 52.1 cm

Museum of Fine Arts, Boston, Lee M. Friedman Fund, 2002.904.8

Photo © 2025 Museum of Fine Arts, Boston

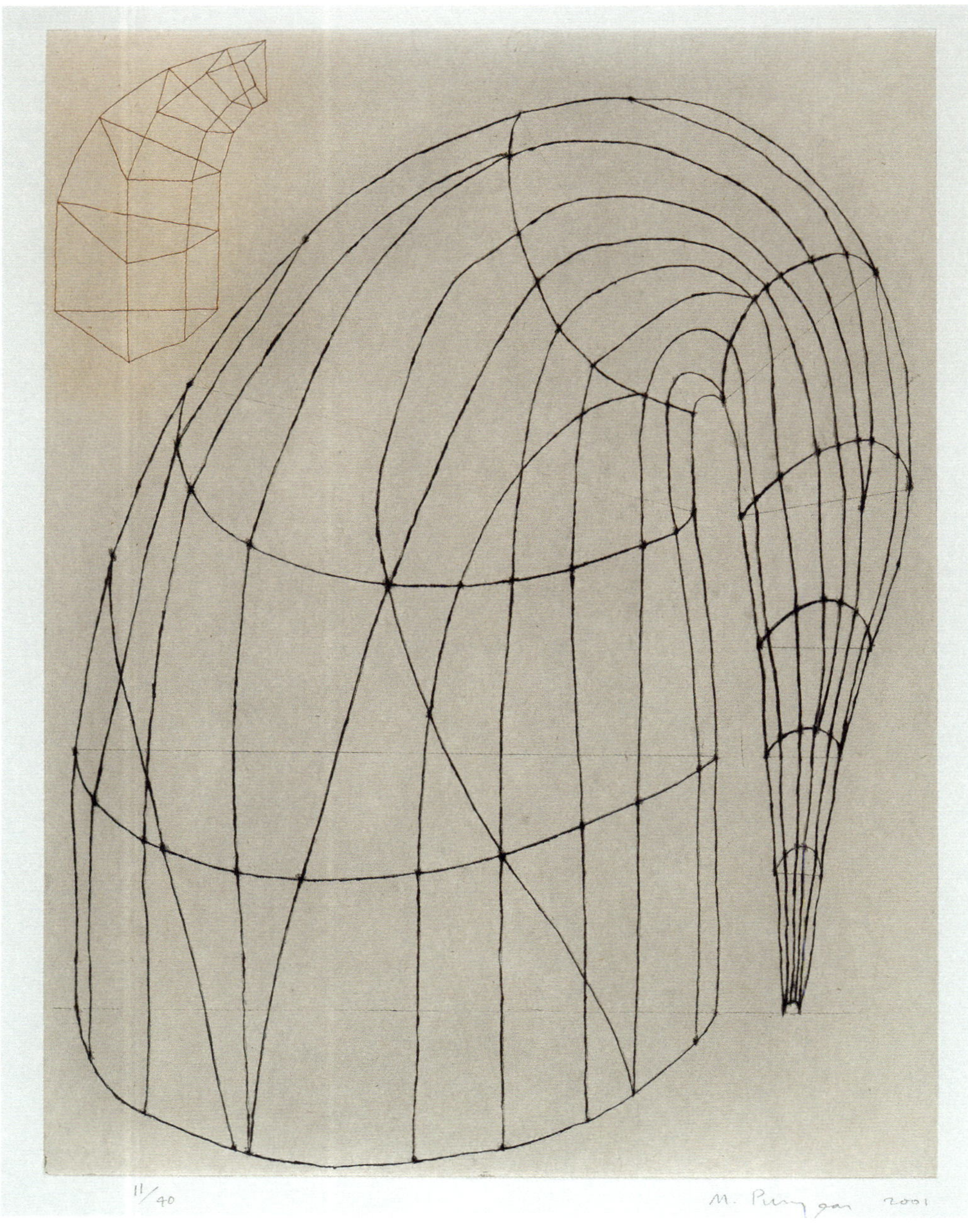

46

Untitled, 2001

Printer and publisher: Paulson Bott Press, Berkeley, CA

Color hard and soft ground etching, with drypoint (and chine collé); image / plate: 60.5 x 45.5 cm; sheet: 88.5 x 70.8 cm

The Art Institute of Chicago, Mr. and Mrs. Robert O. Delaney Fund, 2007.90

Photo: The Art Institute of Chicago / Art Resource, NY

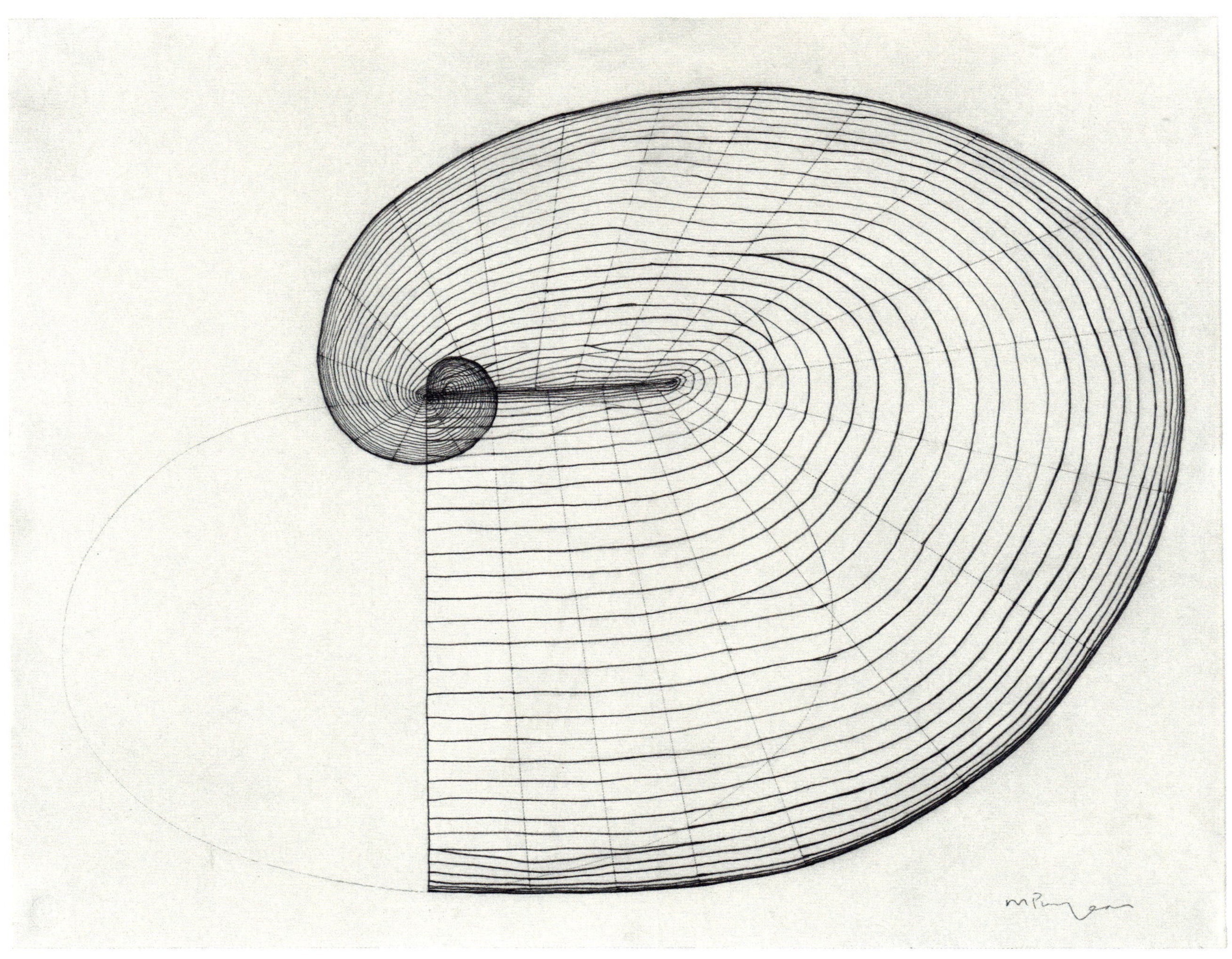

47

Untitled, c. 2003

Graphite on paper;
58.4 x 73.5 cm

Collection of the artist

Photo: The Art Institute of Chicago

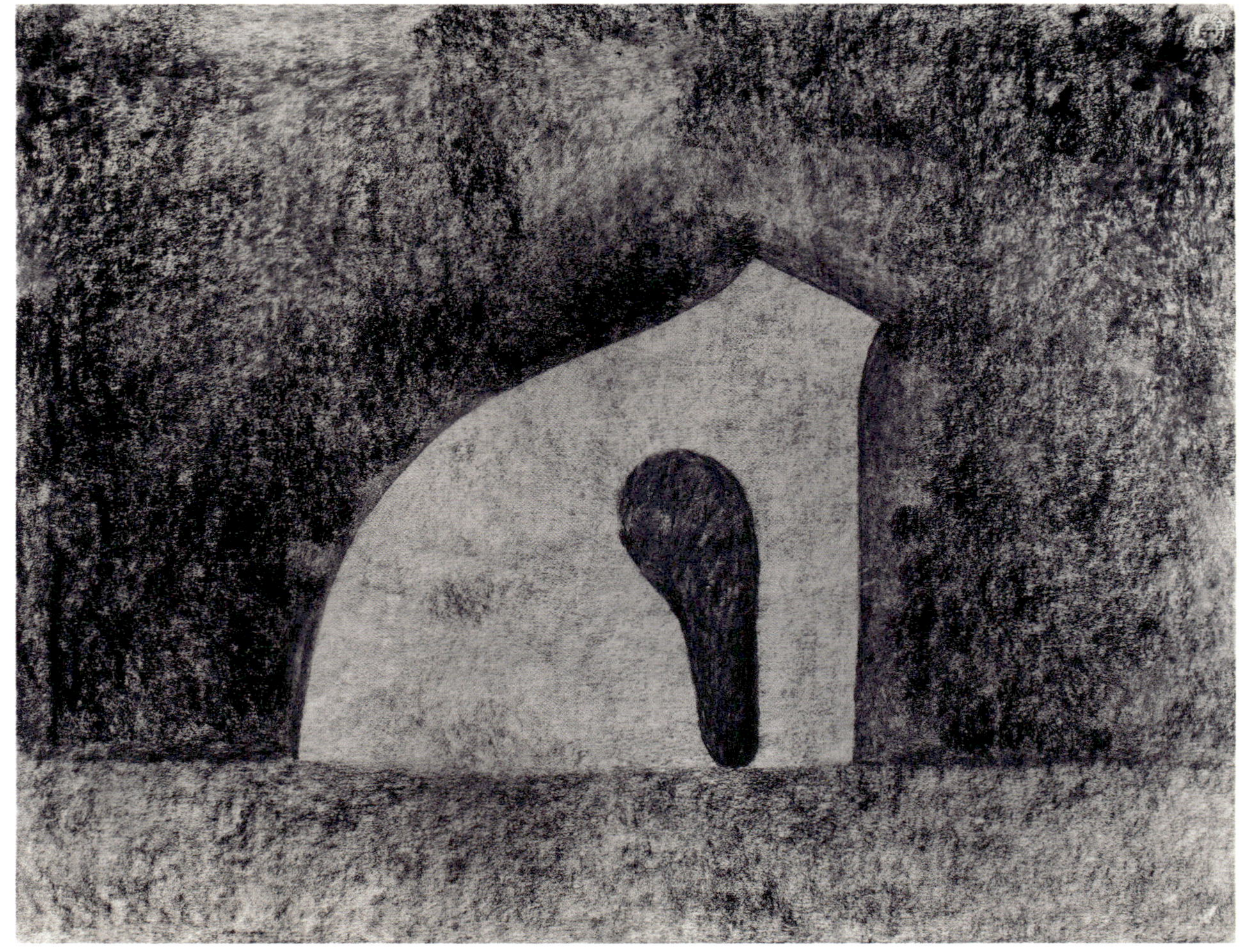

48

Drawing for *Untitled*, c. 2003

Charcoal and pastel on paper; 58.4 x 73.6 cm

Collection of the artist

Photo: The Art Institute of Chicago

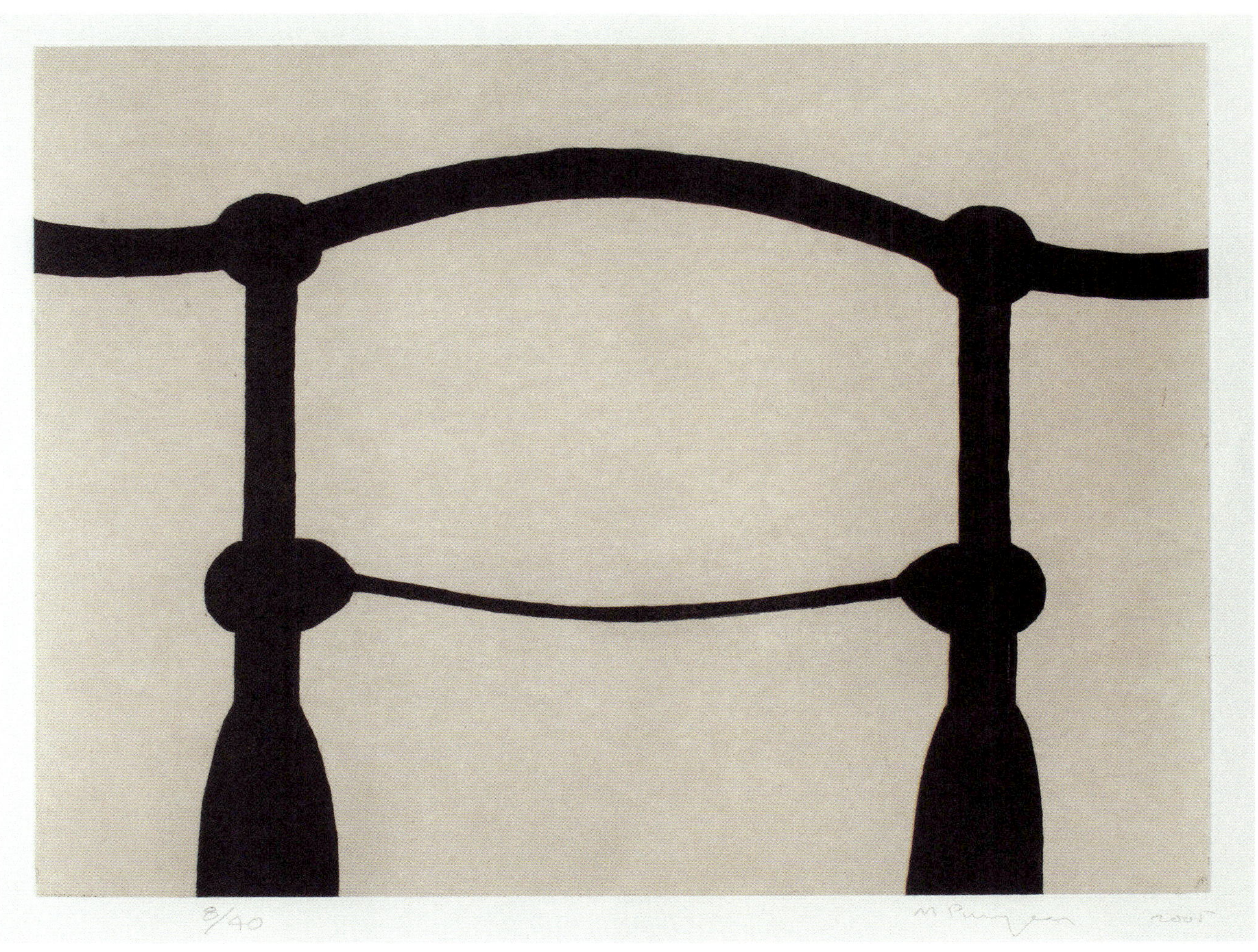

49

Shoulders (State 2), 2005

Printer and publisher: Paulson Bott Press, Berkeley, CA

Drypoint, with soft ground etching and chine collé; image / plate: 45.5 x 60.5 cm; sheet: 73.5 x 86 cm

The Art Institute of Chicago, Mr. and Mrs. Robert O. Delaney Fund, 2007.102

Photo: The Art Institute of Chicago / Art Resource, NY

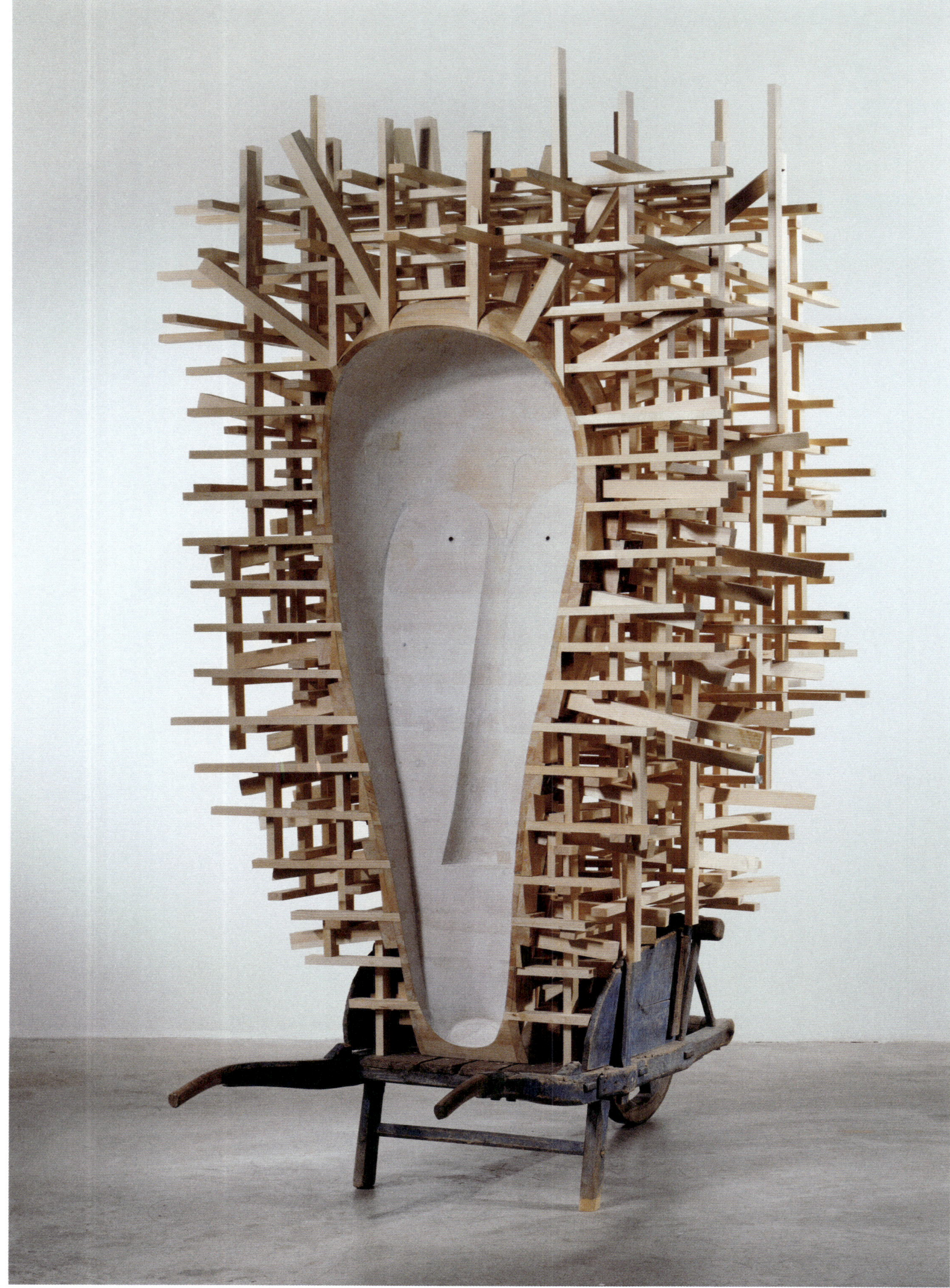

50

C.F.A.O., 2006–7

Painted and unpainted pine and found wheelbarrow; 255.9 x 196.9 x 154.9 cm

The Museum of Modern Art, New York, Gift of Sid Bass, Leon D. Black, Donald L. Bryant, Jr., Kathy and Richard S. Fuld, Jr., Agnes Gund, Mimi Haas, Marie-Josée and Henry R. Kravis, Jo Carole and Ronald S. Lauder, Donald B. Marron and Jerry Speyer on behalf of the Committee on Painting and Sculpture in honor of John Elderfield, 2008, 553.2008

Photos: Richard Goodbody

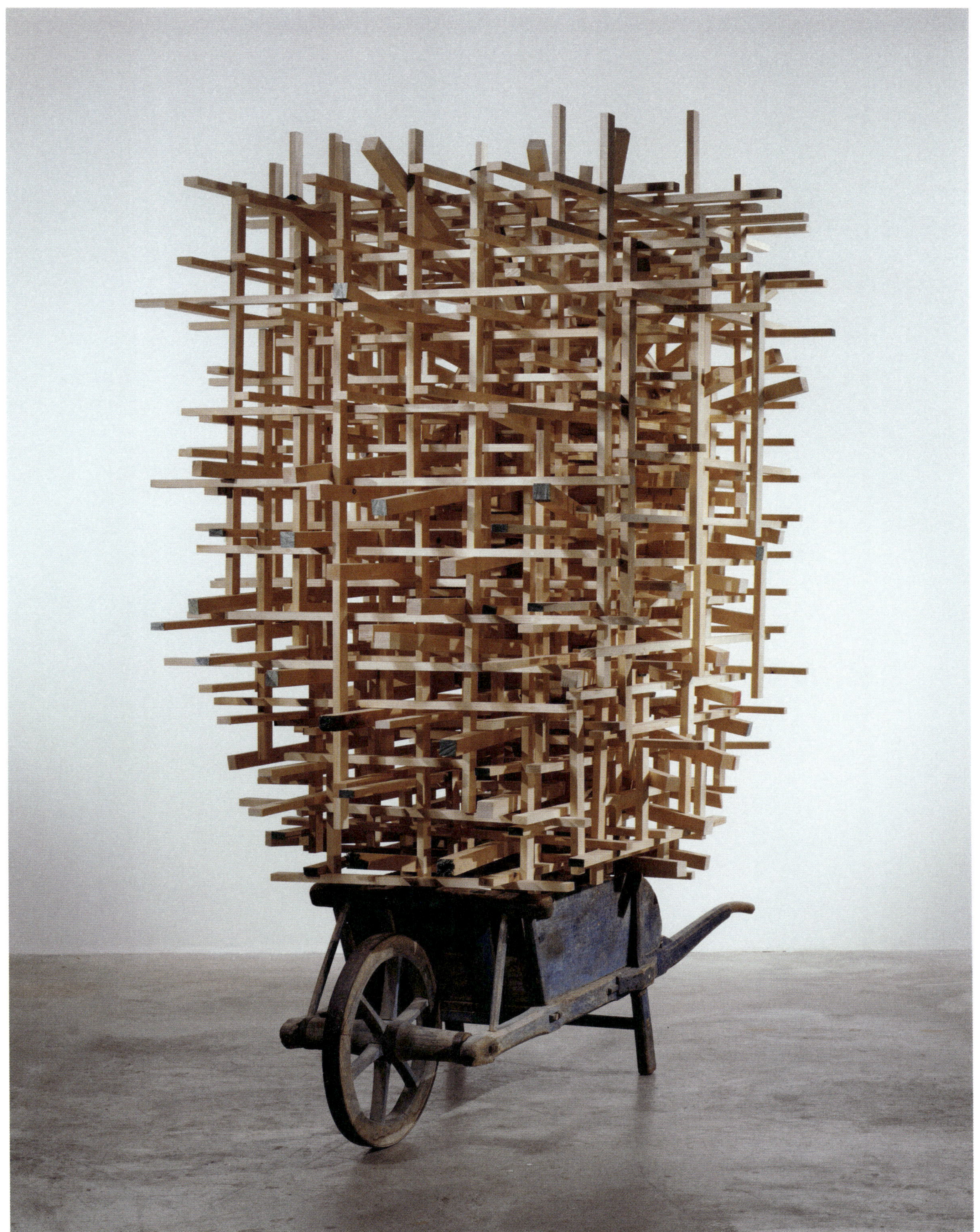

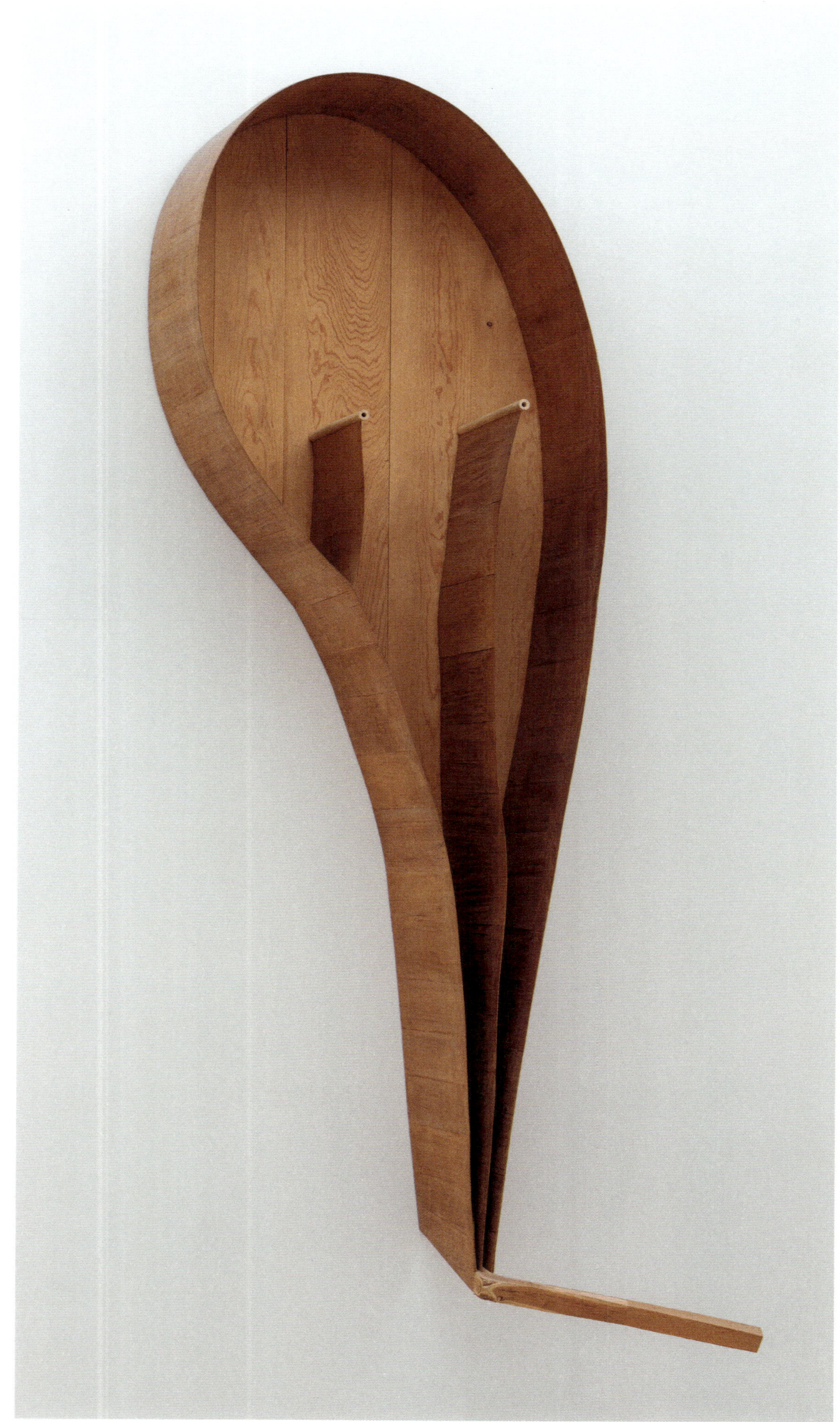

51

Malediction, 2006–7

Red cedar, pine, black locust, ash, and rattan; 318.77 x 151.1 x 65.1 cm
San Francisco Museum of Modern Art, The Doris and Donald Fisher Collection at the San Francisco Museum of Modern Art, FC.842

Photo: Katherine Du Tiel

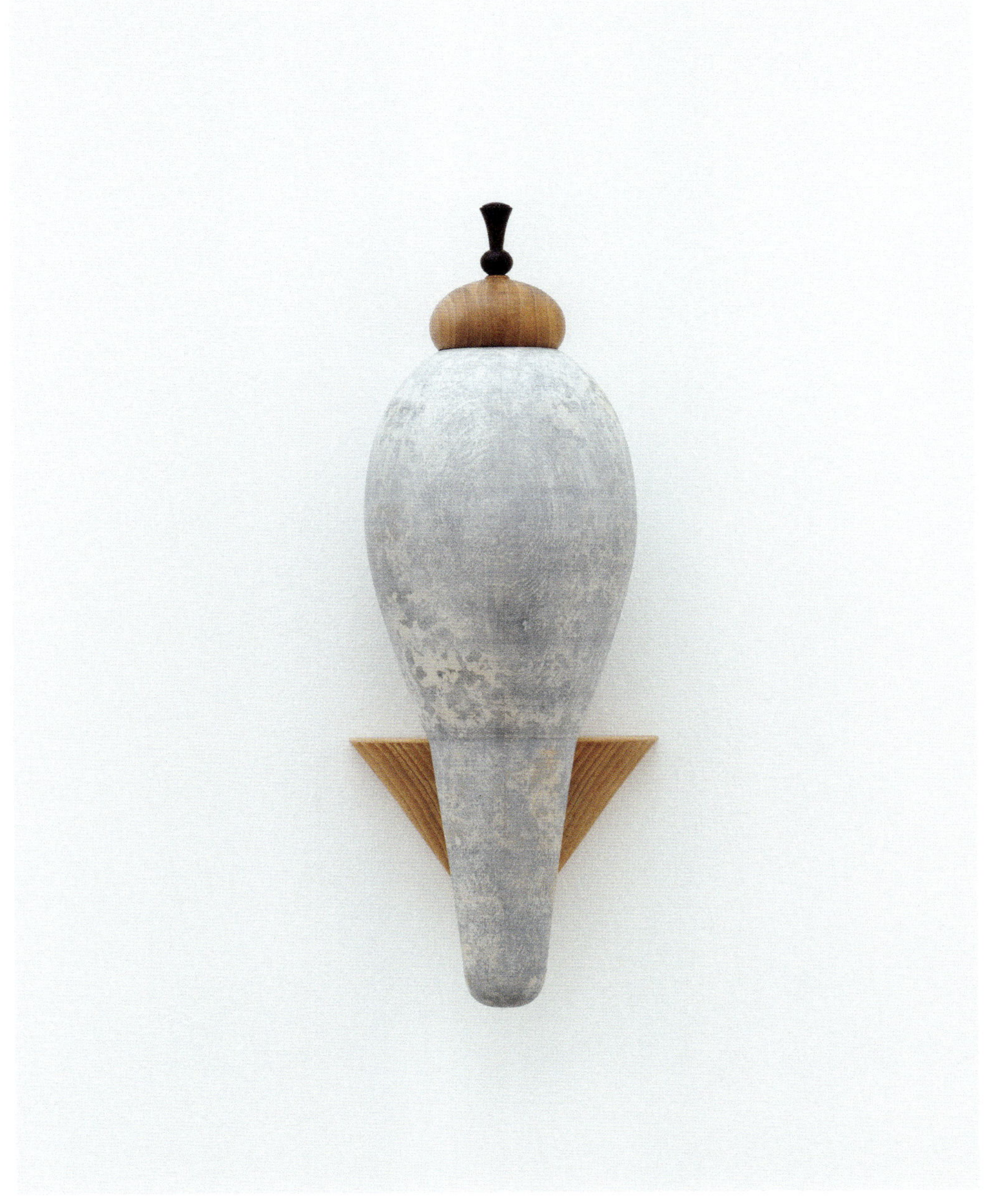

52

Untitled, 2009

Alaskan yellow cedar, milk paint, Swiss pear, and lignum vitae; 43.2 x 16.5 x 15.2 cm

Private collection

Photo: Antoine van Kaam

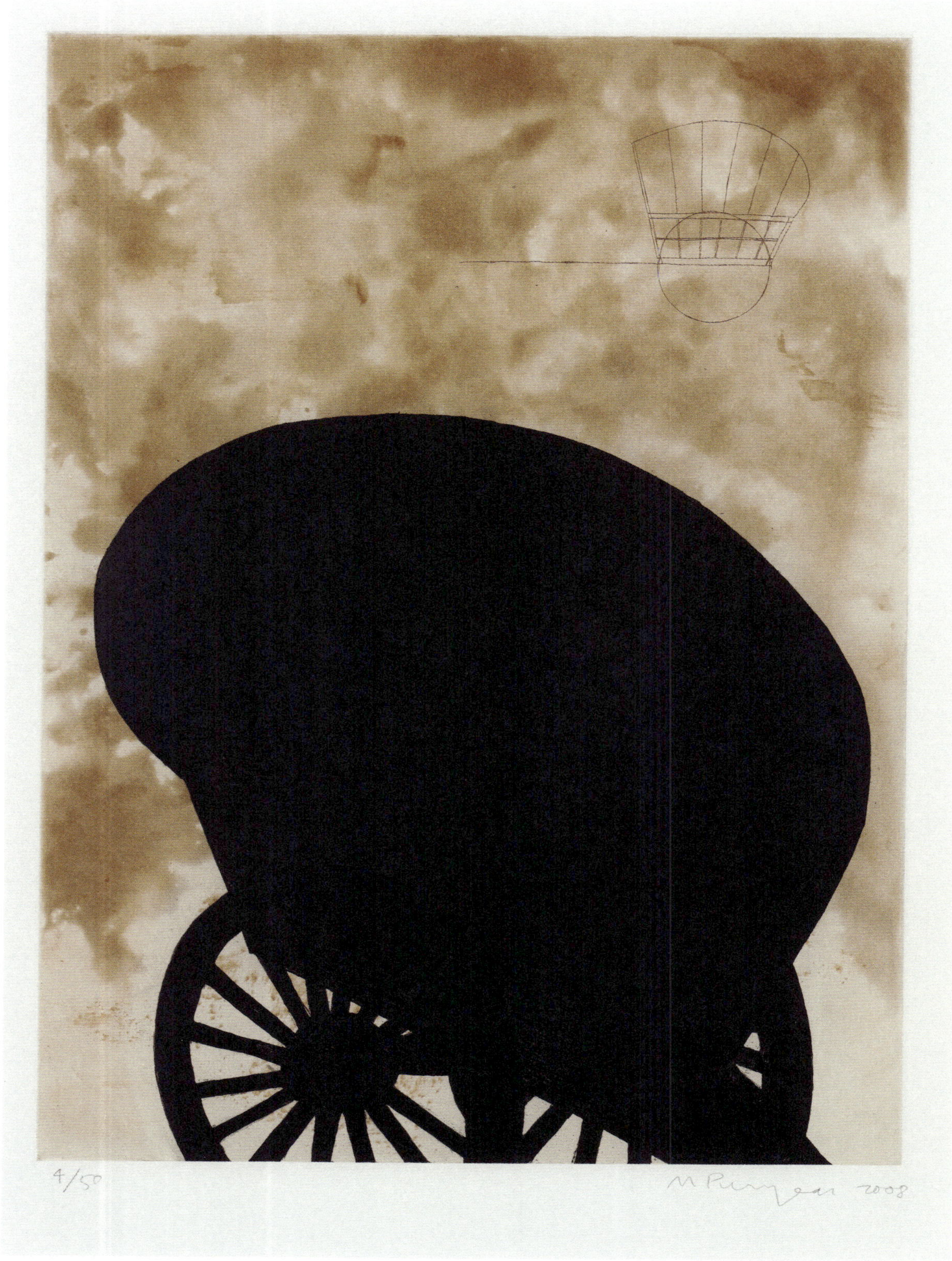

53

Black Cart, 2008

Printer and publisher: Paulson Bott Press, Berkeley, CA

Aquatint etching with chine collé; image / plate: 60.3 x 45 cm; sheet: 88.5 x 70.2 cm

The Art Institute of Chicago, Purchased with funds provided by Kaye and Howard Haas, 2009.665

Photo: The Art Institute of Chicago

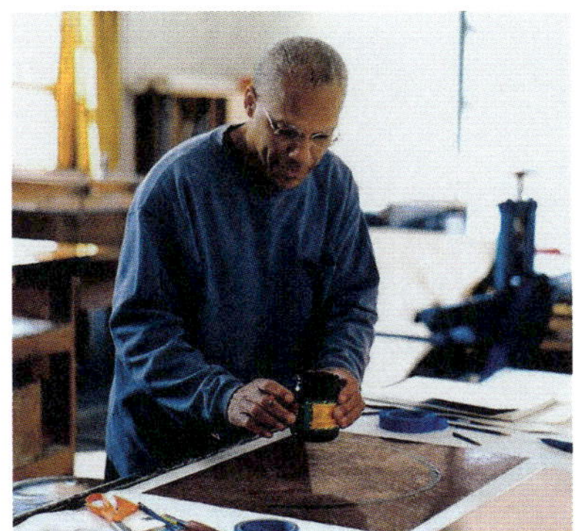

Martin Puryear at Paulson Fontaine Press

Pam Paulson

When Martin Puryear first visited Paulson Fontaine Press in 2001, he made a beeline to the print dryer. This is a very utilitarian and somewhat graceless contraption of horizontal boards clamped together with the modern equivalent of medieval thumbscrews. But Puryear seemed intrigued by it—drawn to understanding how the dryer functioned, and its efficacy at the press.

For me, Puryear's fascination with the print dryer beautifully embodies his endless fascination with techniques of making, no matter how mundane. He has a deep understanding of and care for materials—their distinctive properties and histories—evidenced in his craftsmanship. Through dedicated study, he has become fluent in traditional methods of making, including woodworking, weaving, and stone masonry. On a recent trip to Puryear's studio, I was reminded of the breadth of his inquiry into materials, objects, and their makers: his extensive library of reference books and collections of man-made objects underscore his reverence for artisanal craft traditions. His attention to the symbolic is grounded in creative processes.

Figure 23. Martin Puryear at Paulson Fontaine Press studio, 2007

At Paulson Fontaine Press, the properties of copper, acid, paper, and ink define the task.

Since Puryear began working with us in 2001, he has explored various intaglio printmaking techniques. He has enjoyed working in drypoint, responding to the malleability of copper and the way it yields beneath a steel needle. He incises directly onto the plate to enhance a line, stipple in texture, and encase an area in a deep layer of inky blackness. Drypoint allows for complete control, yet Puryear has also been inspired to let the spontaneity of acid interact with his compositions. In many prints, Puryear has utilized spit bite, the process of painting with acid directly onto an aquatint plate, to create increasingly complex atmospheric spaces.

Soft ground has also been a generative process in Puryear's repertoire. In soft ground, soft wax is applied to a copperplate. A piece of paper is then placed on top of the plate for the artist to draw on. When the paper is removed, it lifts away the wax ground wherever the pencil or other instrument has touched, exposing the copper beneath. The plate is then submerged in an acid bath and etched. Puryear's *Black Cart* (2008) is the result of four twenty-four- by eighteen-inch plates printed on top of one another. Several stages of soft ground drawings were used to describe the interior shape and structure of a cart. Each layer covered up the intricate details of the previous one until the black silhouette of the cart dominated the image. As the first plate was printed, a sheet of Japanese gampi paper, cut flush to the plate, was glued in place. This strong yet delicate paper adds a natural tone to the background and enhances the printing of the smokey subtleties of the spit bite plate. In the upper right corner of the image, Puryear includes a hard-ground line drawing of the plan view of the cart shape.

Puryear has featured the cart motif in several sculptures (see for example, [50]). The cart and covered wagon evoke the history of colonial trade and slavery. They also conjure the journey of pioneers—autonomous individuals changing their location, escaping to safety, and heading toward an uncharted future.

It has been an incredible experience to work with Martin for over two decades, to see his ideas gestate and become realized across mediums and disciplines including printmaking.

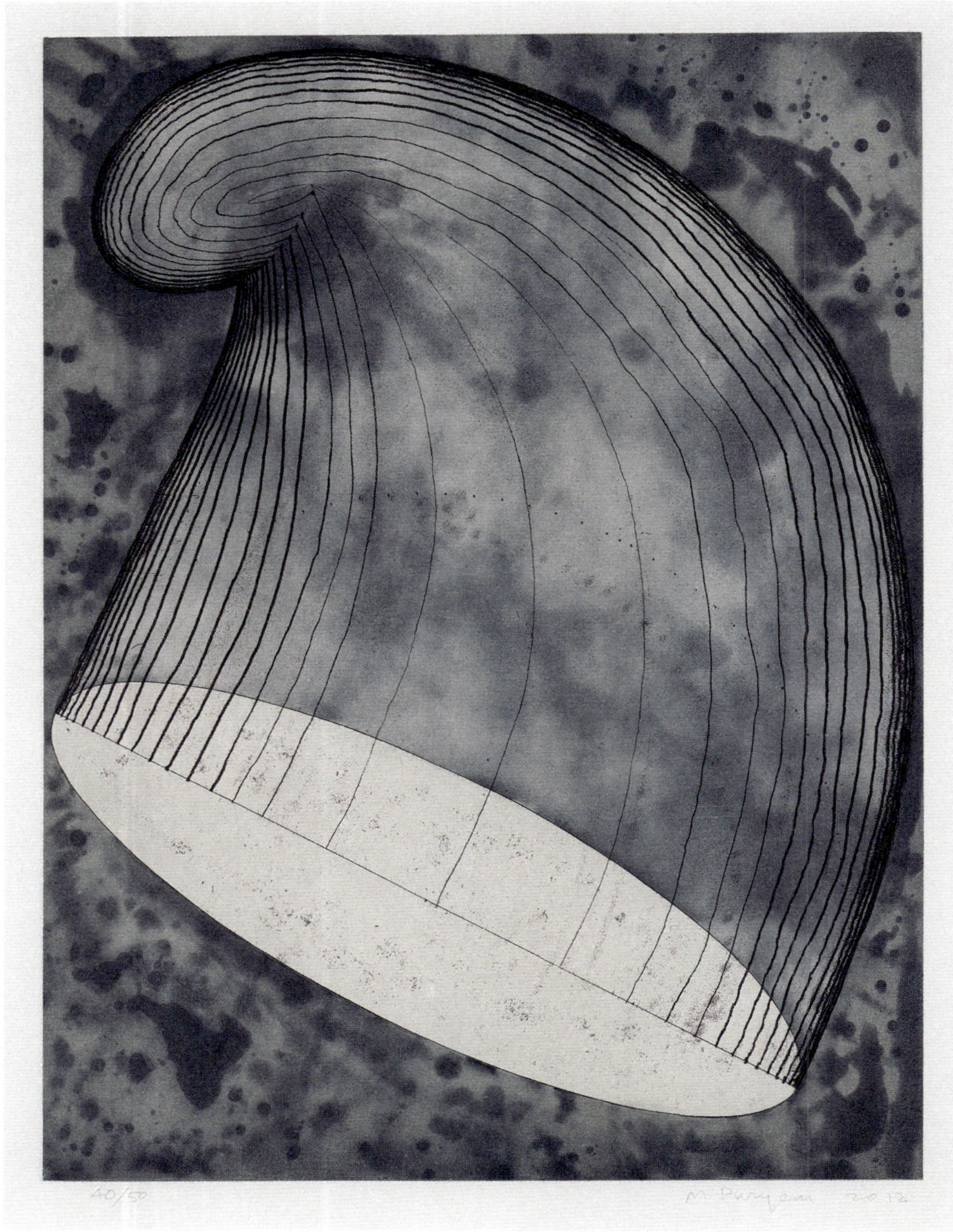

54

Phrygian (Cap in the Air), 2012

Printer and publisher: Paulson Bott Press, Berkeley, CA

Etching with aquatint and drypoint; platemark: 60.5 x 45.2 cm; sheet: 88.6 x 70.8 cm

Museum of Fine Arts, Boston, Lee M. Friedman Fund, 2016.13

Photo © 2025 Museum of Fine Arts, Boston

55

Big Phrygian, 2010–14

Painted red cedar; 147.3 x 101.6 x 193 cm

Glenstone Museum, Potomac, Maryland

Photo: Ron Amstutz

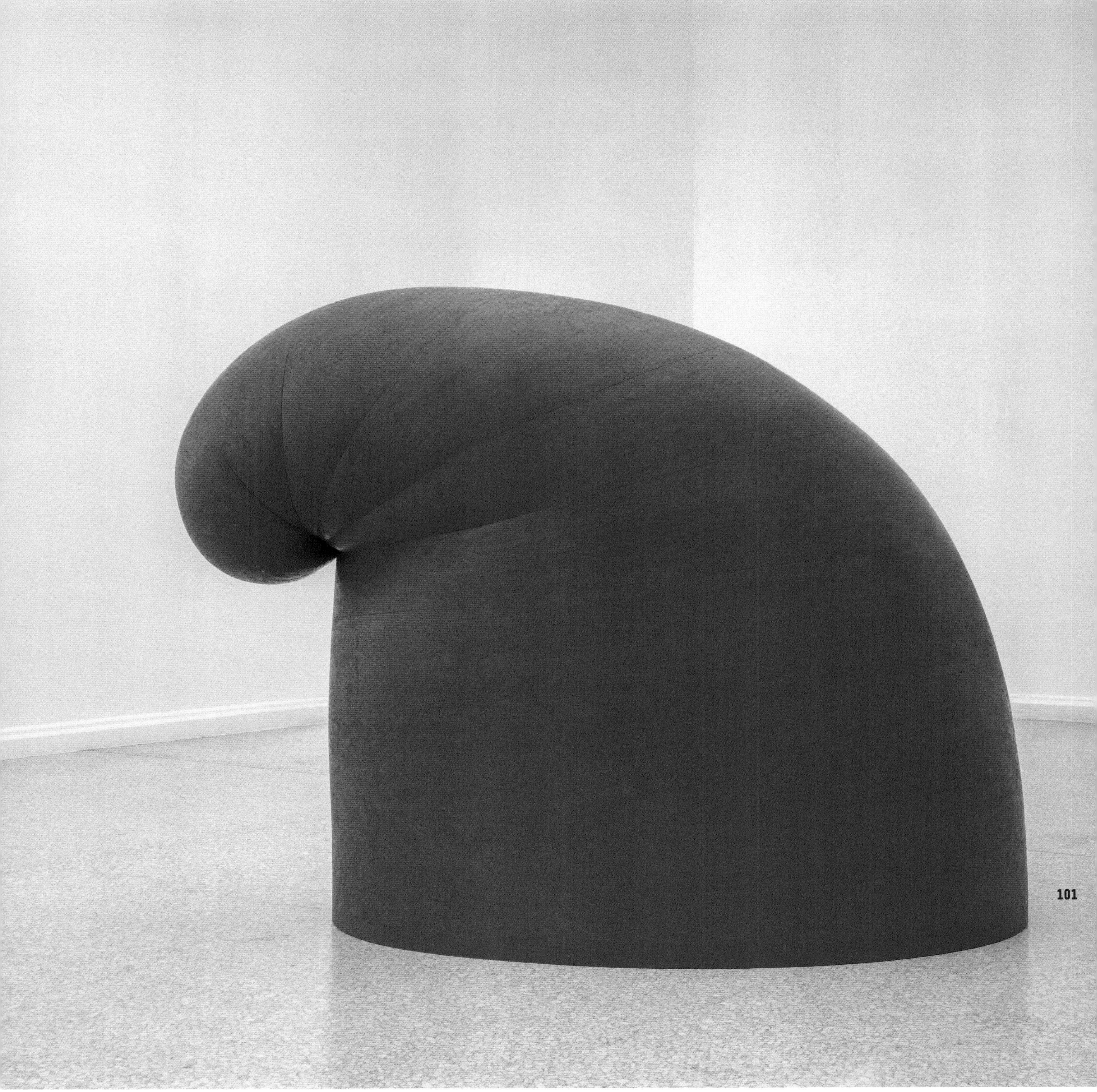

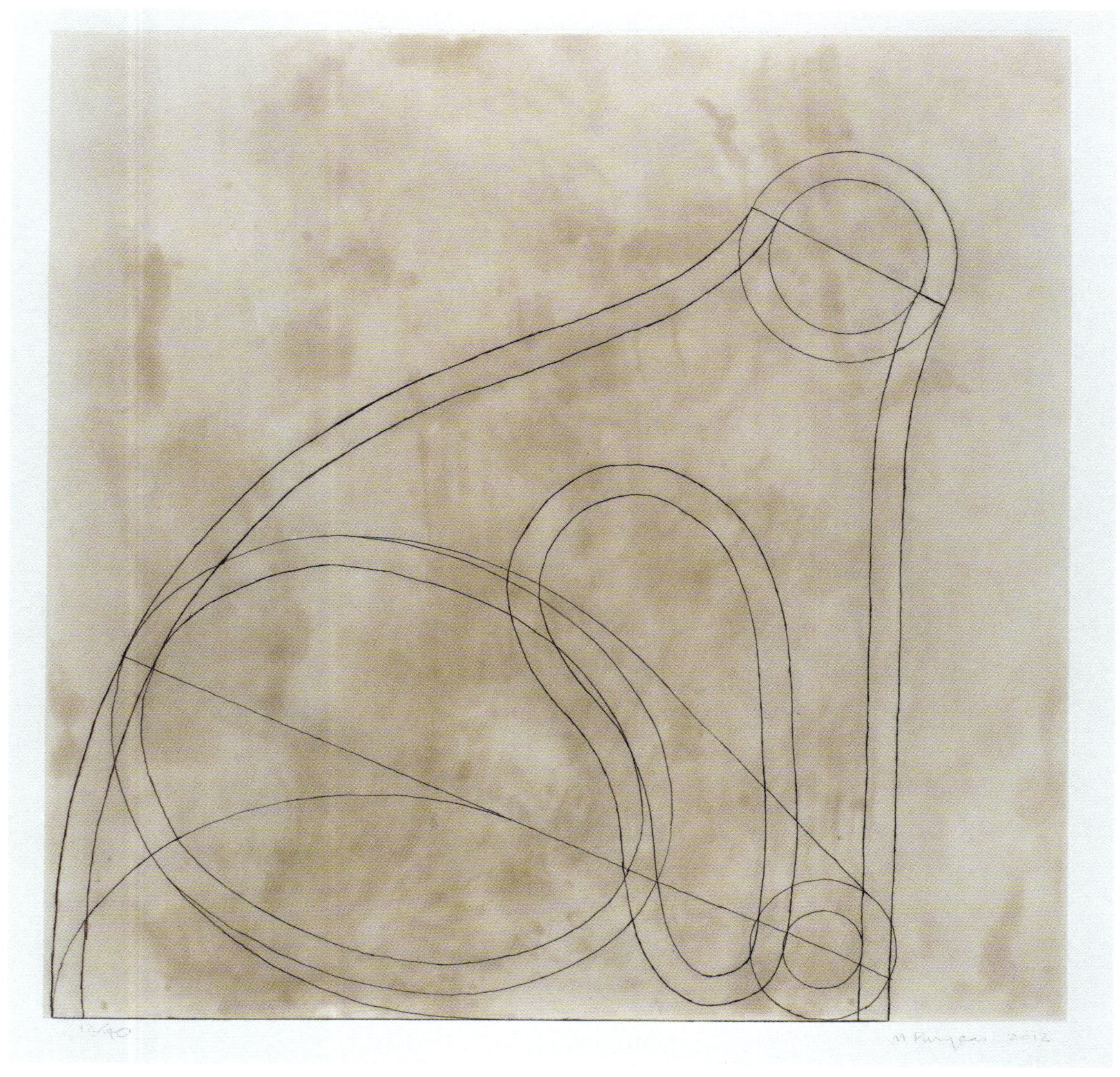

56

Untitled VI (State 1), 2012

Printer and publisher: Paulson Bott Press, Berkeley, CA

Soft ground etching, drypoint, and spit bite with chine colle; image / plate: 80.4 x 80.3; sheet: 109.1 x 103.8 cm

The Art Institute of Chicago, The John H. Wrenn Memorial, Helen Davis Baily, and Albert H. Wolf funds, 2013.180

Photo: The Art Institute of Chicago / Art Resource, NY

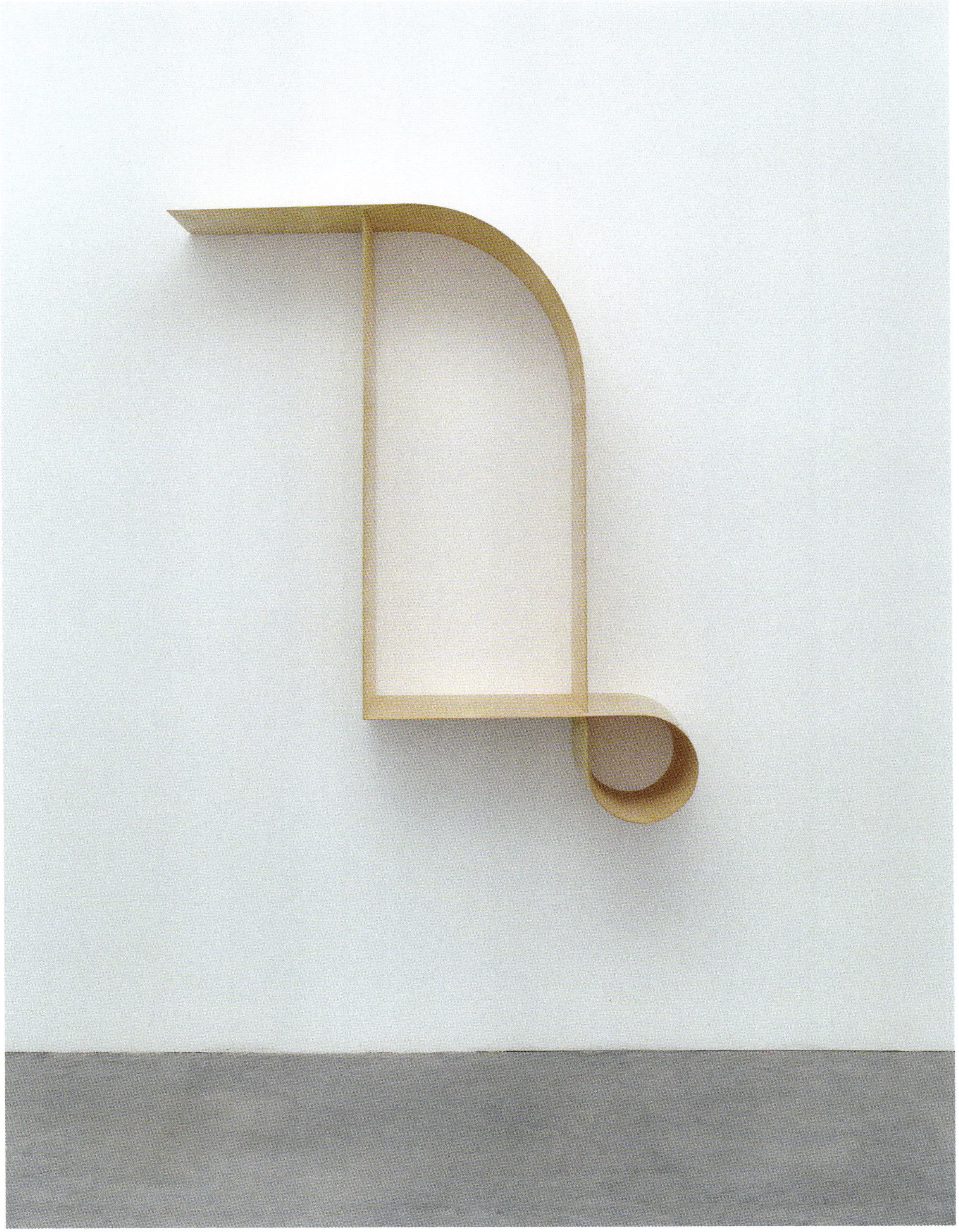

57

Cascade, 2013

Alaskan yellow cedar;
167.6 x 139.1 x 43.2 cm

Collection of the artist

Photo: Ron Amstutz

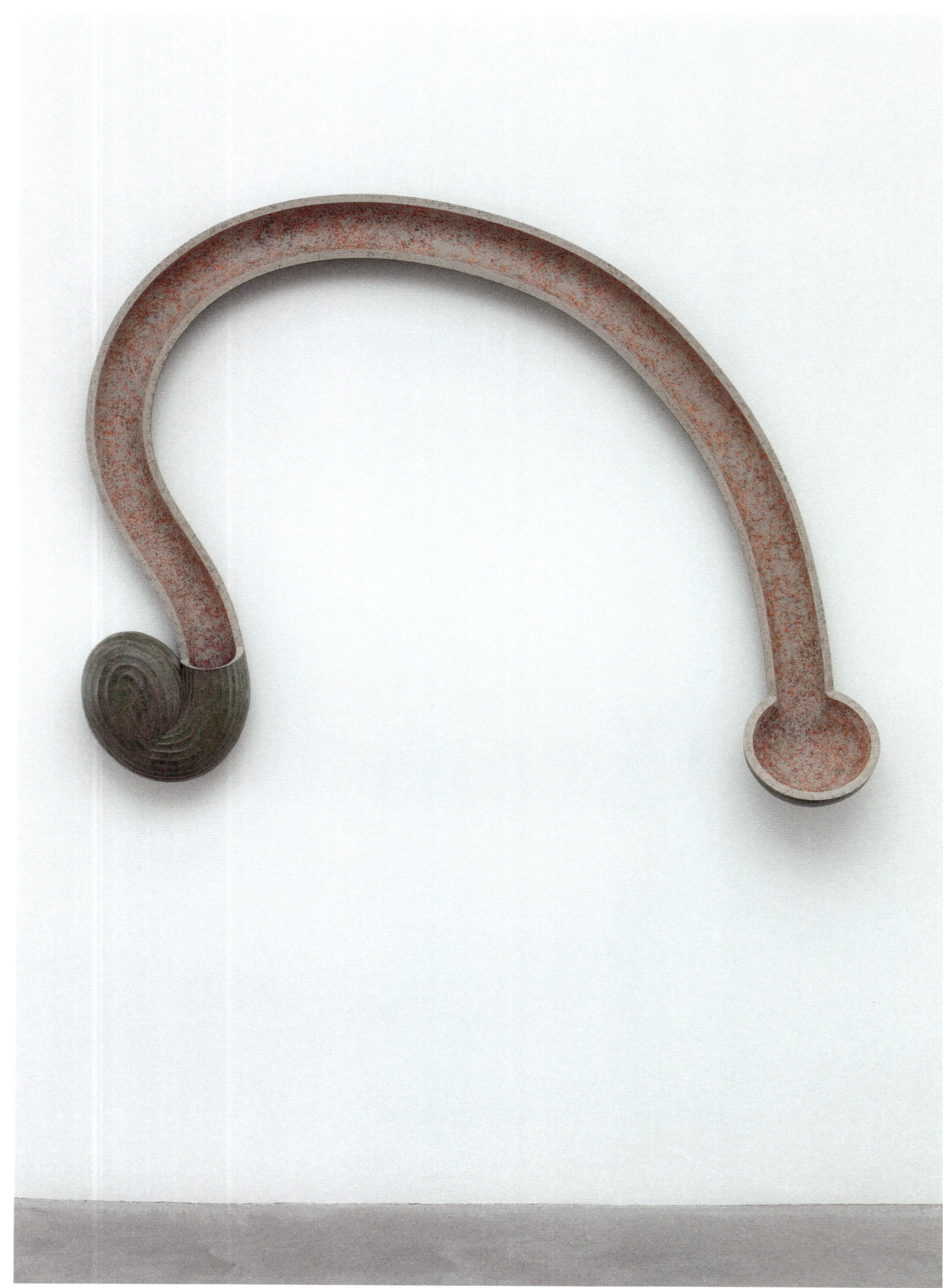

58

Shell Game, 2014

Tulip poplar and milk paint;
142.9 x 182.9 x 24.1 cm

Collection of Scott Mueller

Photo: Ron Amstutz

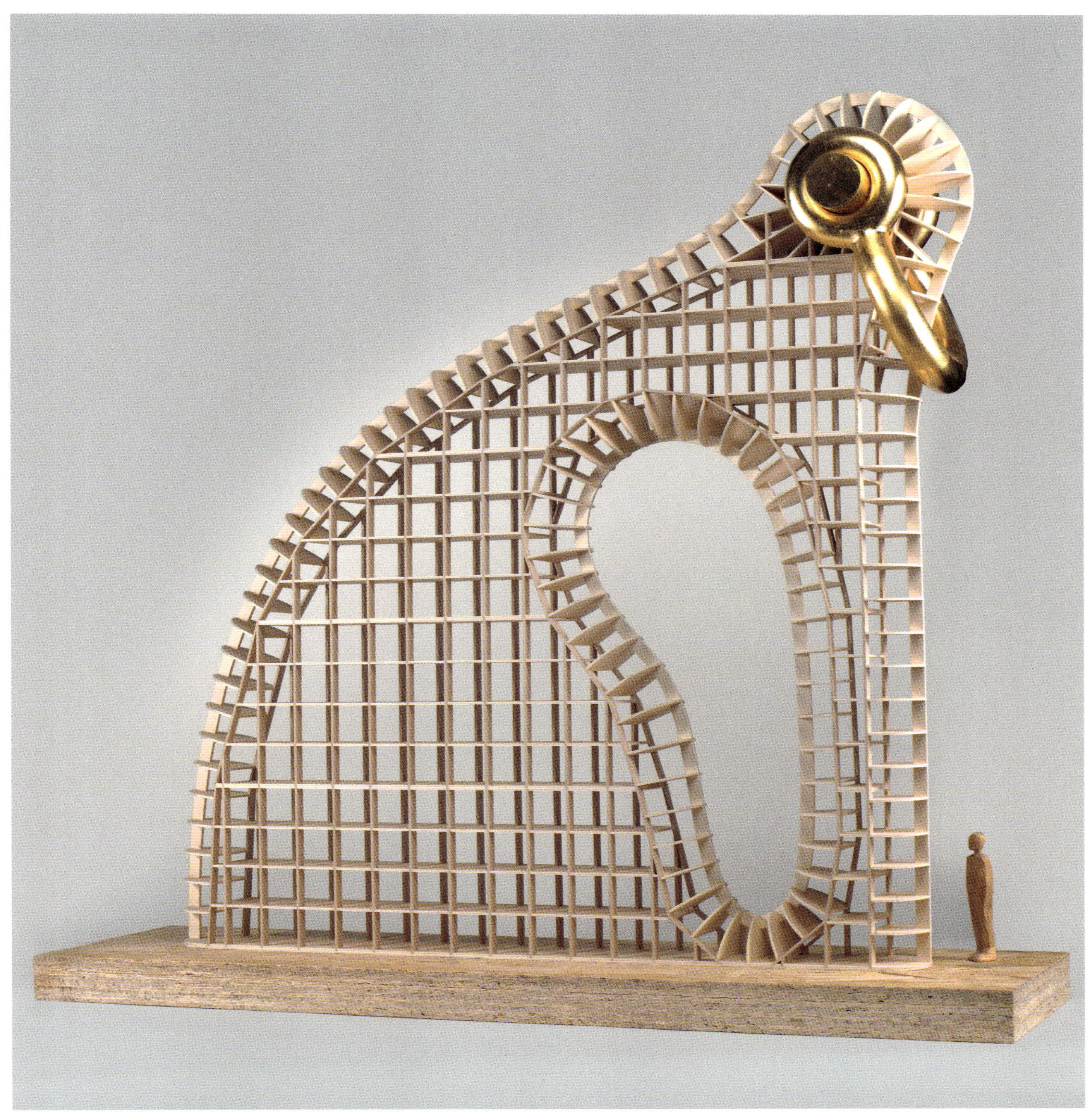

59

Maquette for Big Bling, 2014

Birch plywood, maple, and 22 karat gold leaf; 102.9 x 23.2 x 101.6 cm

Collection of the artist

Photo: Jamie Stukenberg

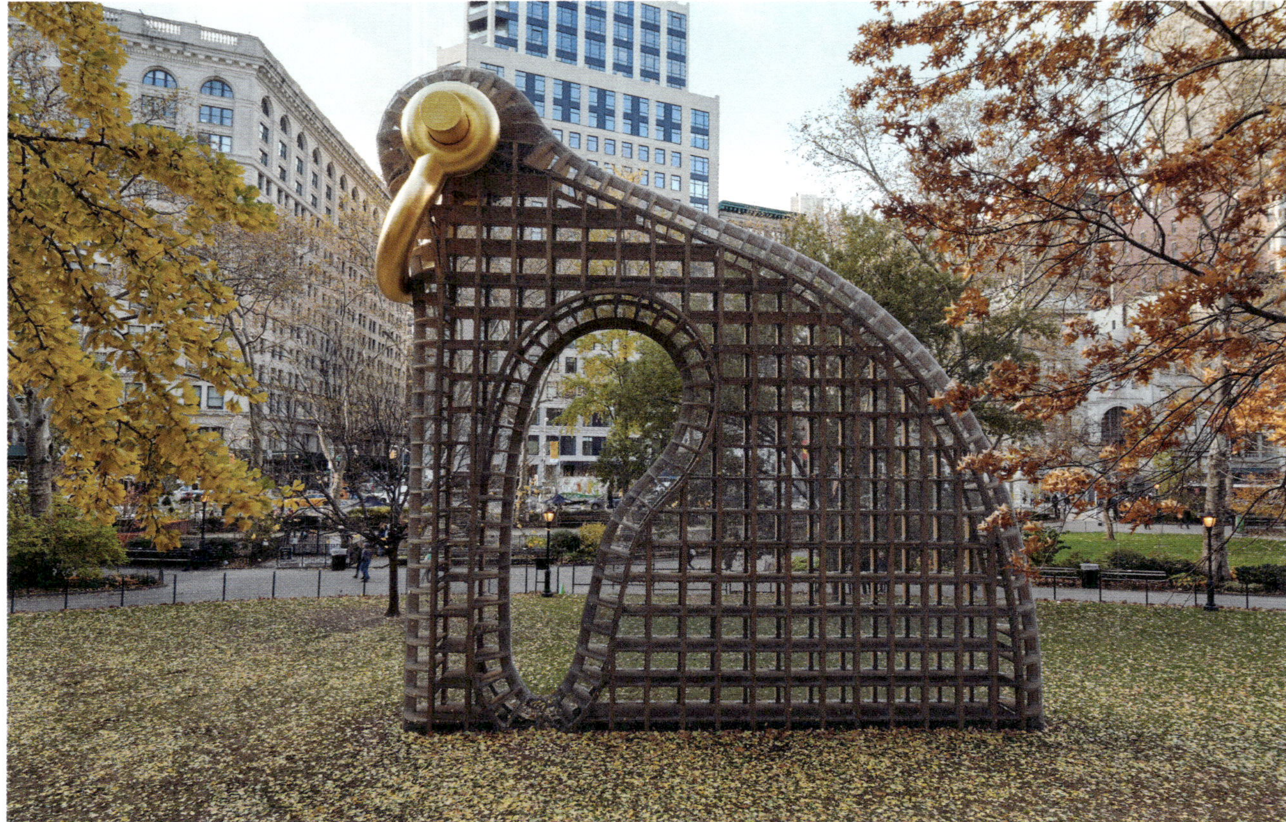

Figure 24. Installation view of *Big Bling* (2016) in Madison Square Park, New York. Martin Puryear. Pressure-treated laminated timbers, plywood, chain-link fencing, fiberglass, and gold leaf, 12.2 x 3 x 11.6 m. Photo: Jordan Tinker. Courtesy Madison Square Park Conservancy

Figure 25. Installation view of *Big Bling* (2016) on Kelly Drive, Philadelphia, presented by the Association for Public Art, 2017. Photo: James Ewing / JBSA © 2017 for aPA

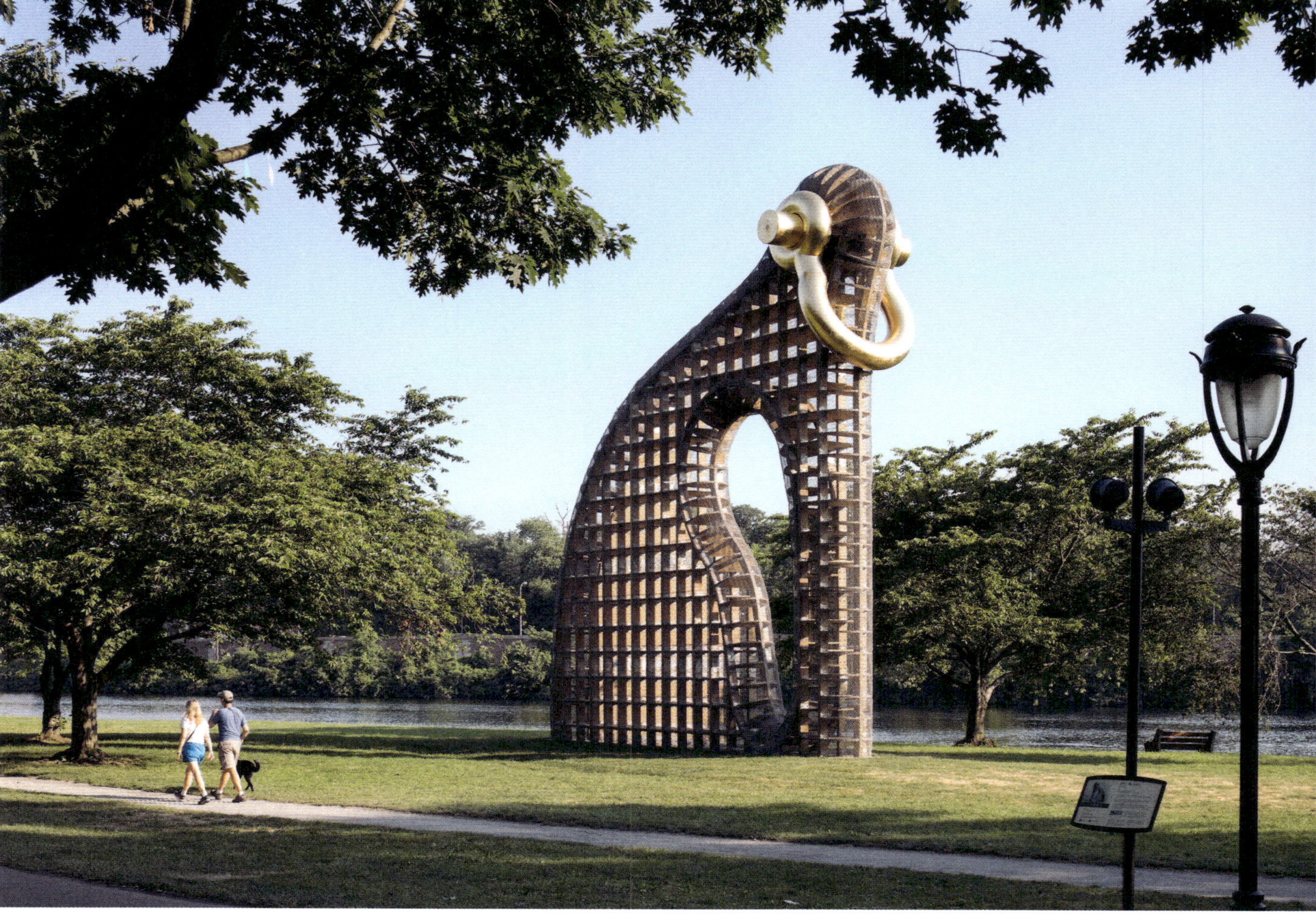

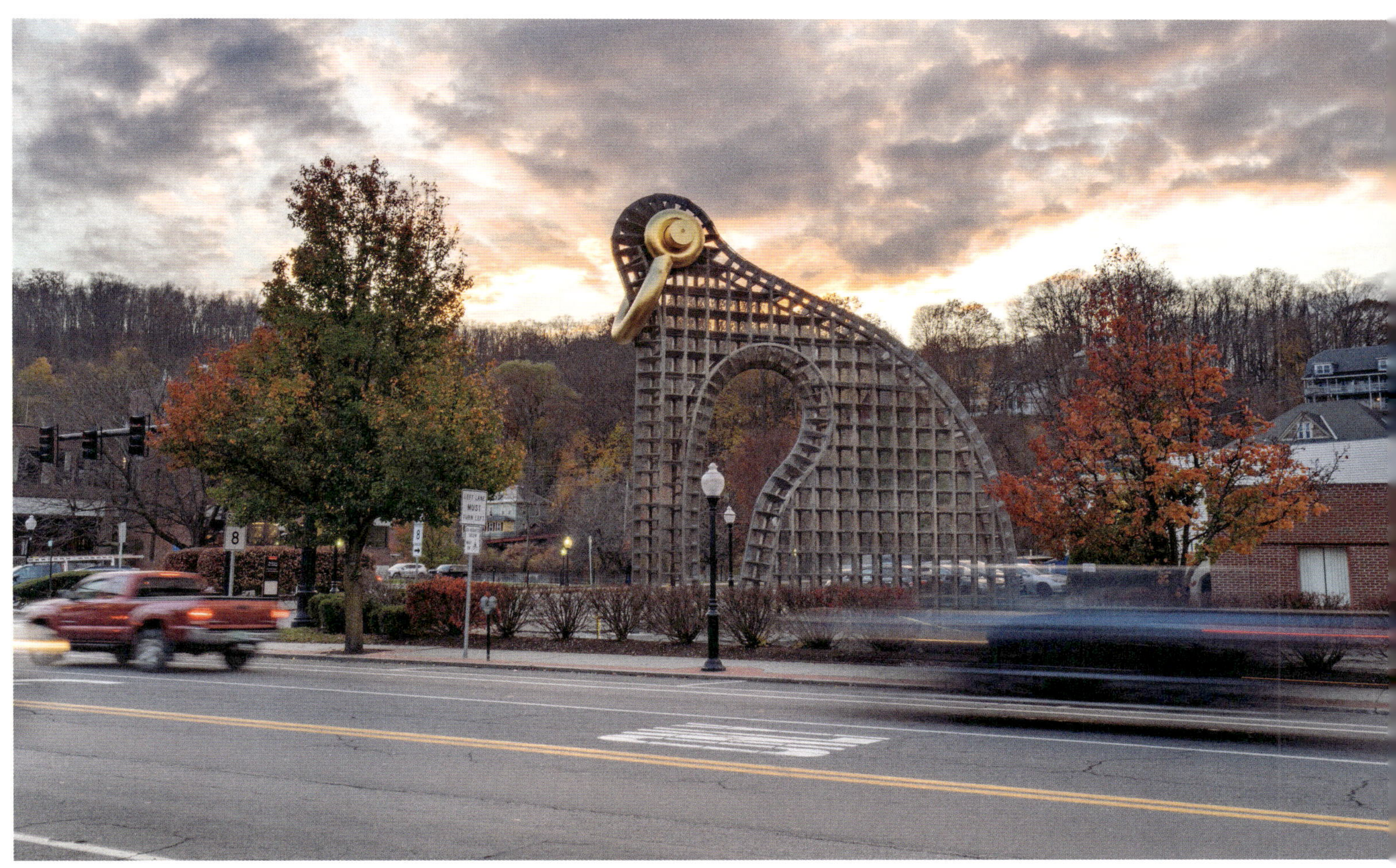

Figure 26. Installation view of *Big Bling* (2016) outside of MASS MoCA, North Adams, Massachusetts, 2019. Photo: Kaelan Burkett

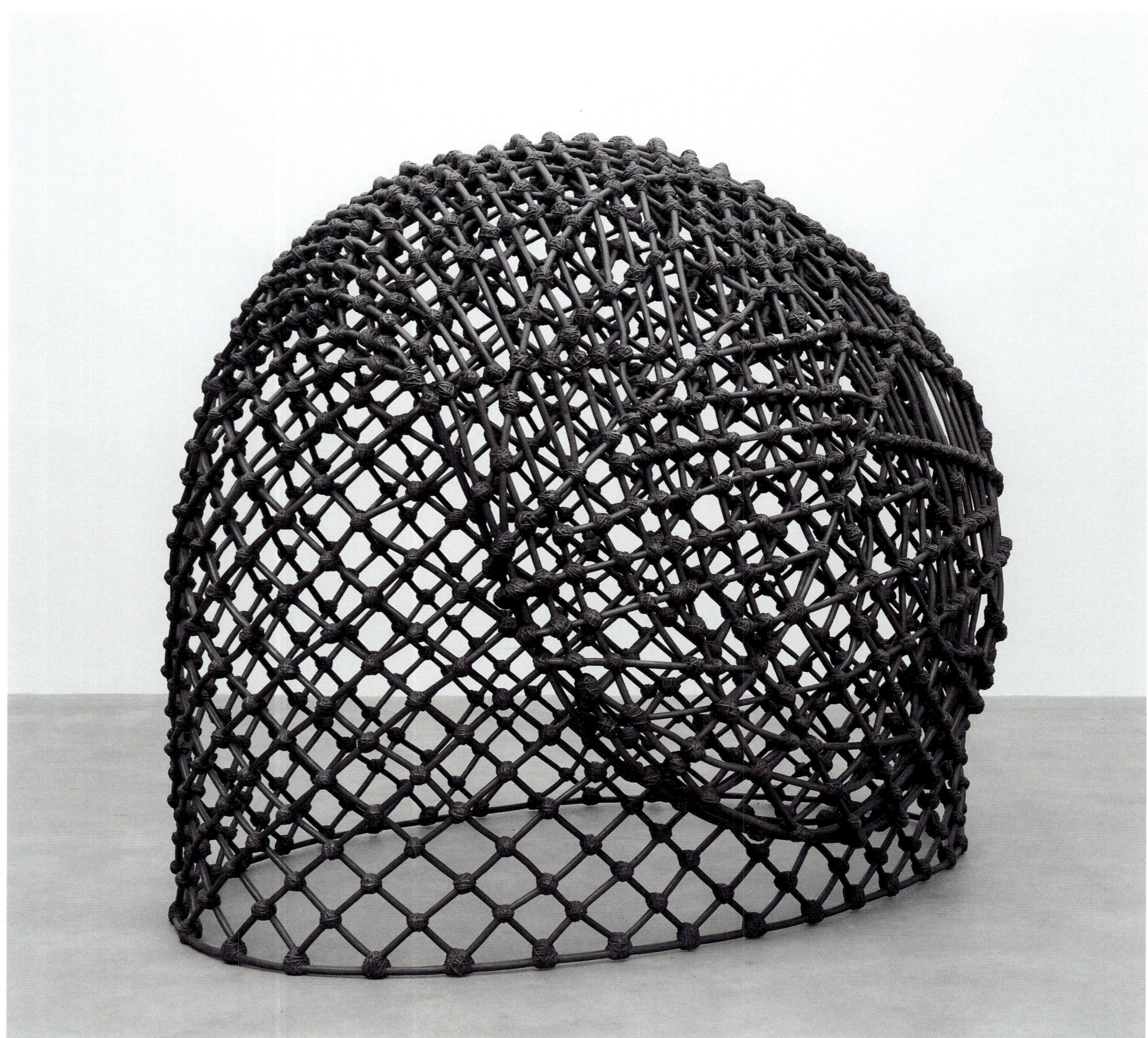

60

Aso Oke, 2019

Bronze; 213.4 x 261.6 x 189.2 cm

Jack Shear Collection

Photo: Matthew Marks Gallery

Aso Oke

Julia Phillips

Martin Puryear's *Aso Oke* (2019) was inspired by a *fila gobi* cap, a type of headwear worn by West Africa's Yoruba people at ceremonial occasions, a status symbol of sorts (see fig. 56). The title of the sculpture, which literally translates to "top/precious layer," hints at the work's interplay between structure and surface.

The draping form of *Aso Oke*, evocative of soft matter, suggests a malleable shell slumping over, drooping down its side–a cartoonish softness reminiscent of an aging body or a depleted volume folding in on itself. There is an erotic quality to this mount-like shape, the downward movement climaxing in a form that hovers about a foot above the floor. If one imagines this sculpture in human scale, its facial features would sit below ground level.

Encompassing complex negative space, the sculpture could be described as an airy volume defined by a net. The viewer is confronted with a grid that is tight enough to confine or keep out but large enough for one to reach through. The original positive was constructed out of rattan bars held together at each juncture by individually hand-tied twine knots. The bronze cast abstracts these intricate knots down to their surface layer, an accumulated volume of threads (fig. 27).

The material translation from rattan to bronze changes the makeup of the sculpture's weight; it introduces an element of surreality, a perceptible heaviness that seems to contradict the qualities of delicate rattan grain and plied twine texture. In the bronze cast the knots become significant additions to the sculpture's weight (fig. 27), almost like padlocks added to a bridge, seemingly subverting the original engineering.

Standing up close to *Aso Oke*, experiencing its haptic presence, the sound of rattling comes to mind. There is a narrow air gap within the "cap's" fold, prompting a series of questions regarding this form and its experiential aspect. Does this structure bounce? Does the fold ever touch the rest of the form? If moving like a fabric cap on a human head, how would the bronze sound rubbing up against itself?

As a graphic play, the bending and overlapping net oscillates between organic order and idiosyncratic pattern with unexpected horizontal and arched lines. The dramatic turning point, the moment gravity gets the best of the volume, is a recurring theme in the artist's work, as in pieces like *Big Phrygian* (2010–14; [55]) and *Untitled* (2014; no longer extant; see fig. 115), a hardwood sapling/cordage sculpture.

A drooping cap, a seemingly casual sculptural gesture, is carefully calibrated not only with regard to materials but also in its historical reference to sociopolitical questions. In ancient Rome, the Phrygian cap signified formerly enslaved people who were freed through manumission. During the French Revolution, the headwear was adopted as a symbol of liberty and democracy. In a different way, the fold of the *fila gobi* cap conveys social rank, and the tilt direction marks societal distinctions such as hierarchical orders, marriage status, and seniority. *Aso Oke*'s material negates the notion of softness and malleability while underscoring its role as a metaphor for unfixed status.

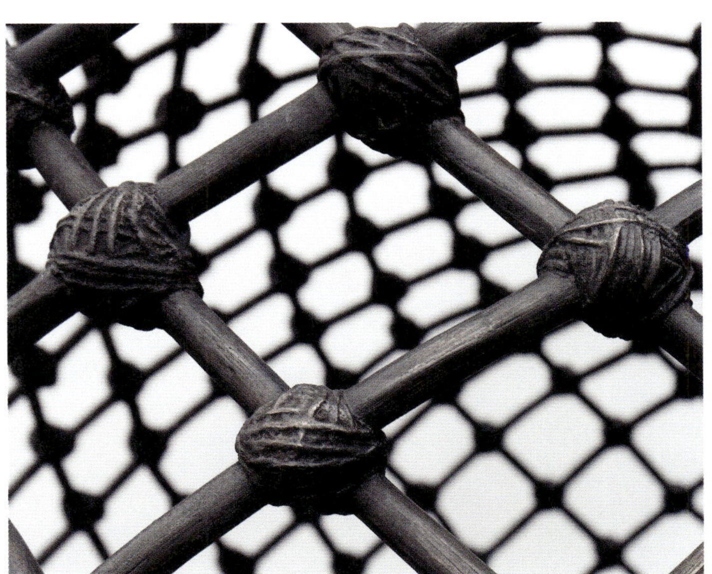

Figure 27. Detail of *Aso Oke* (2019). Photo: Matthew Marks Gallery

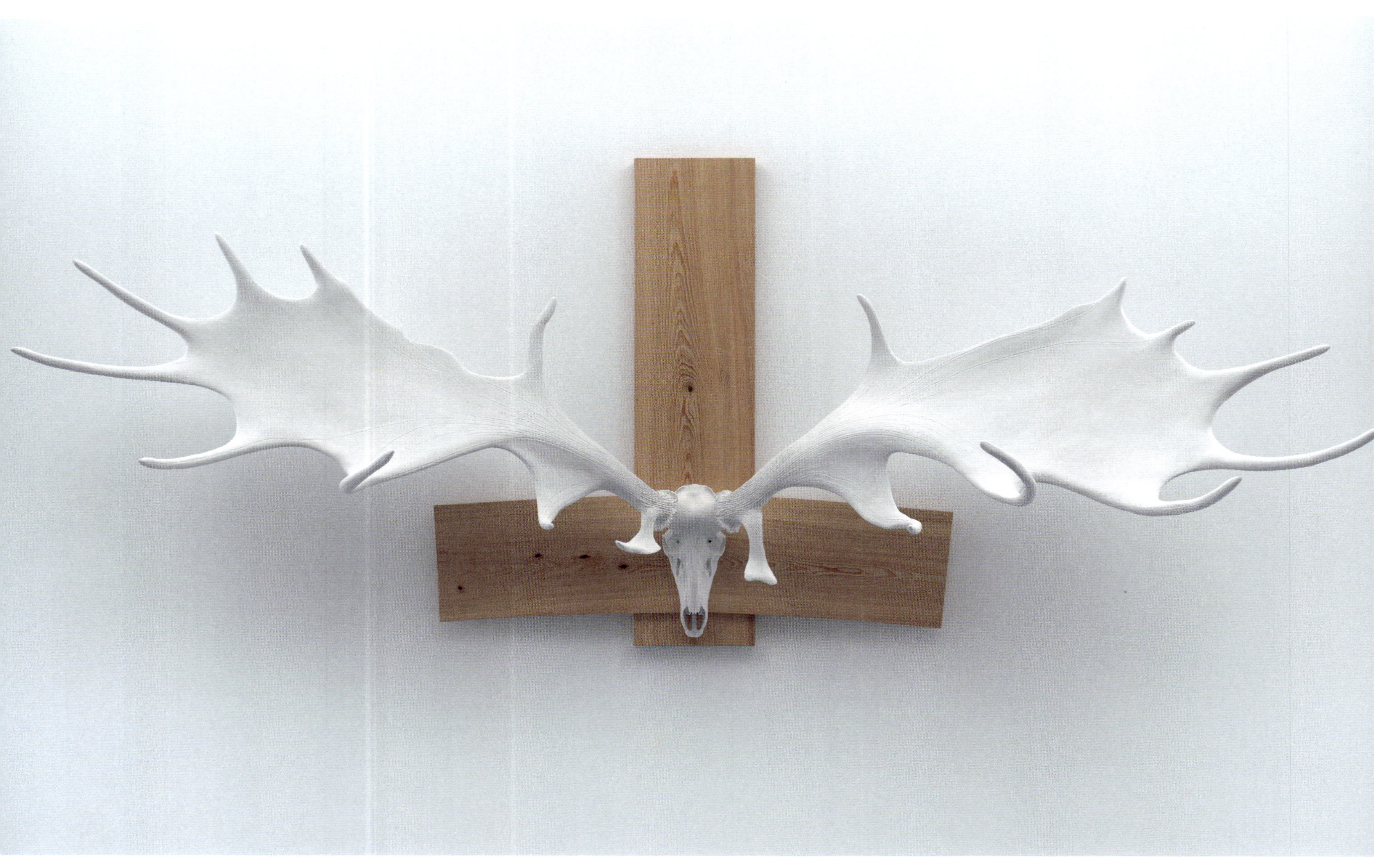

61

Hibernian Testosterone, 2018

Painted cast aluminum and American cypress; 144.8 x 358.1 x 113 cm

Courtesy the artist and Matthew Marks Gallery

Photo: Ron Amstutz

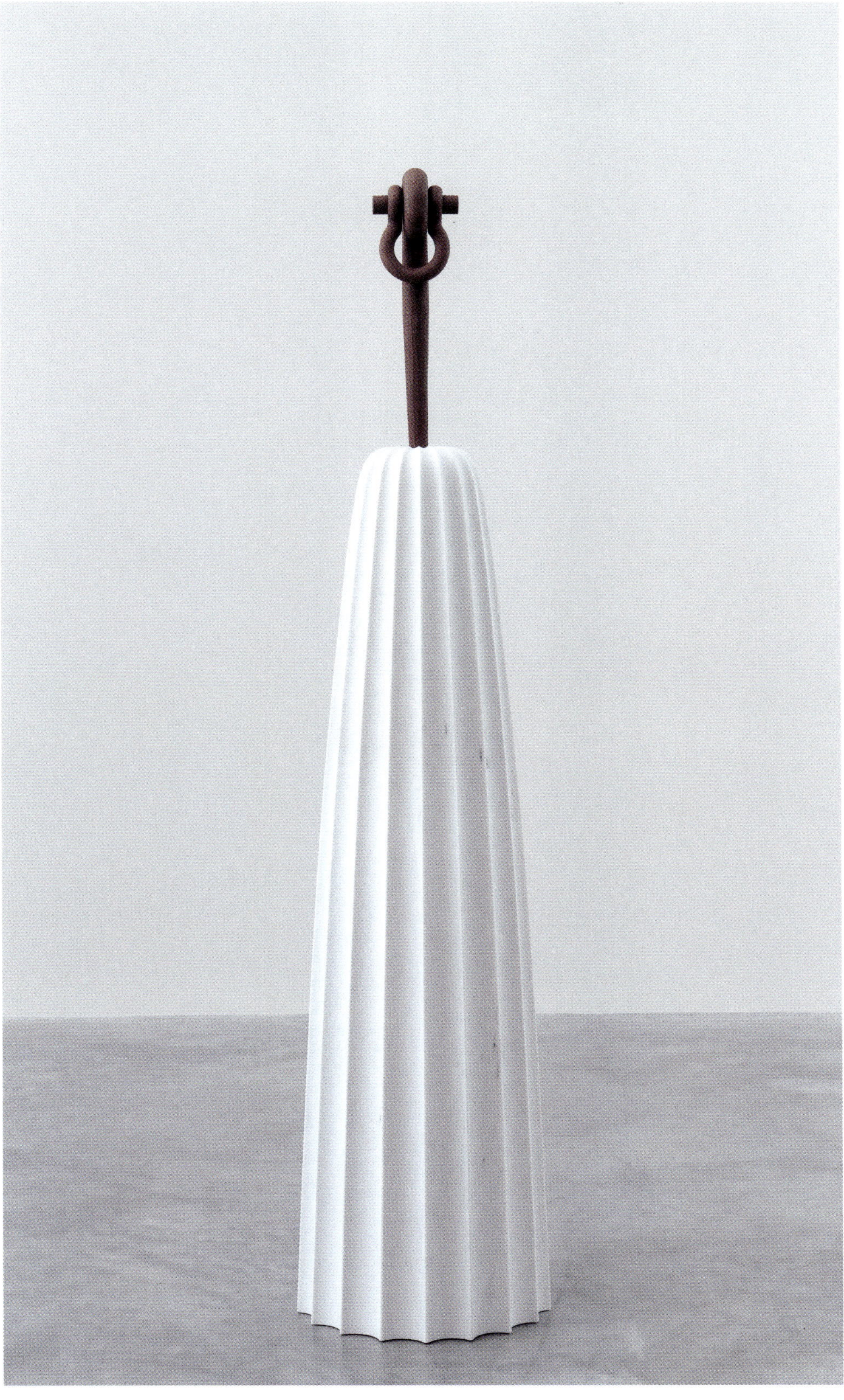

62

A Column for Sally Hemings, 2021

Marble and cast iron; 201.3 x 43.8 x 43.8 cm

Collection of the artist

Photo: Matthew Marks Gallery

63

Maquette for *Swallowed Sun (Monstrance and Volute)*, 2018. Oriented strand board, pine, maple, paint, and laser-cut acrylic; 59.7 x 99.7 x 139.7 cm

Collection of the artist

Photo: Jeanne Englert

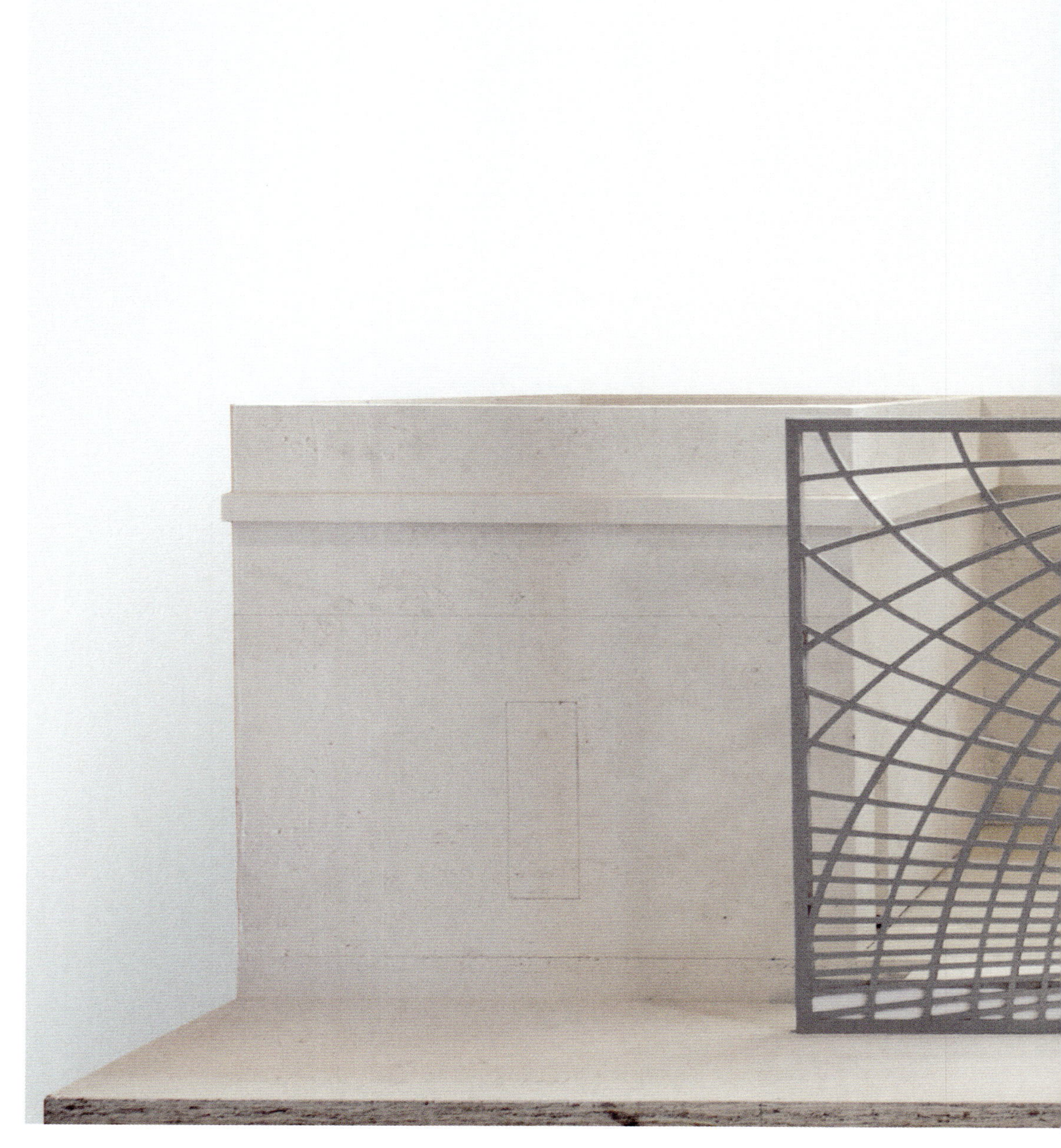

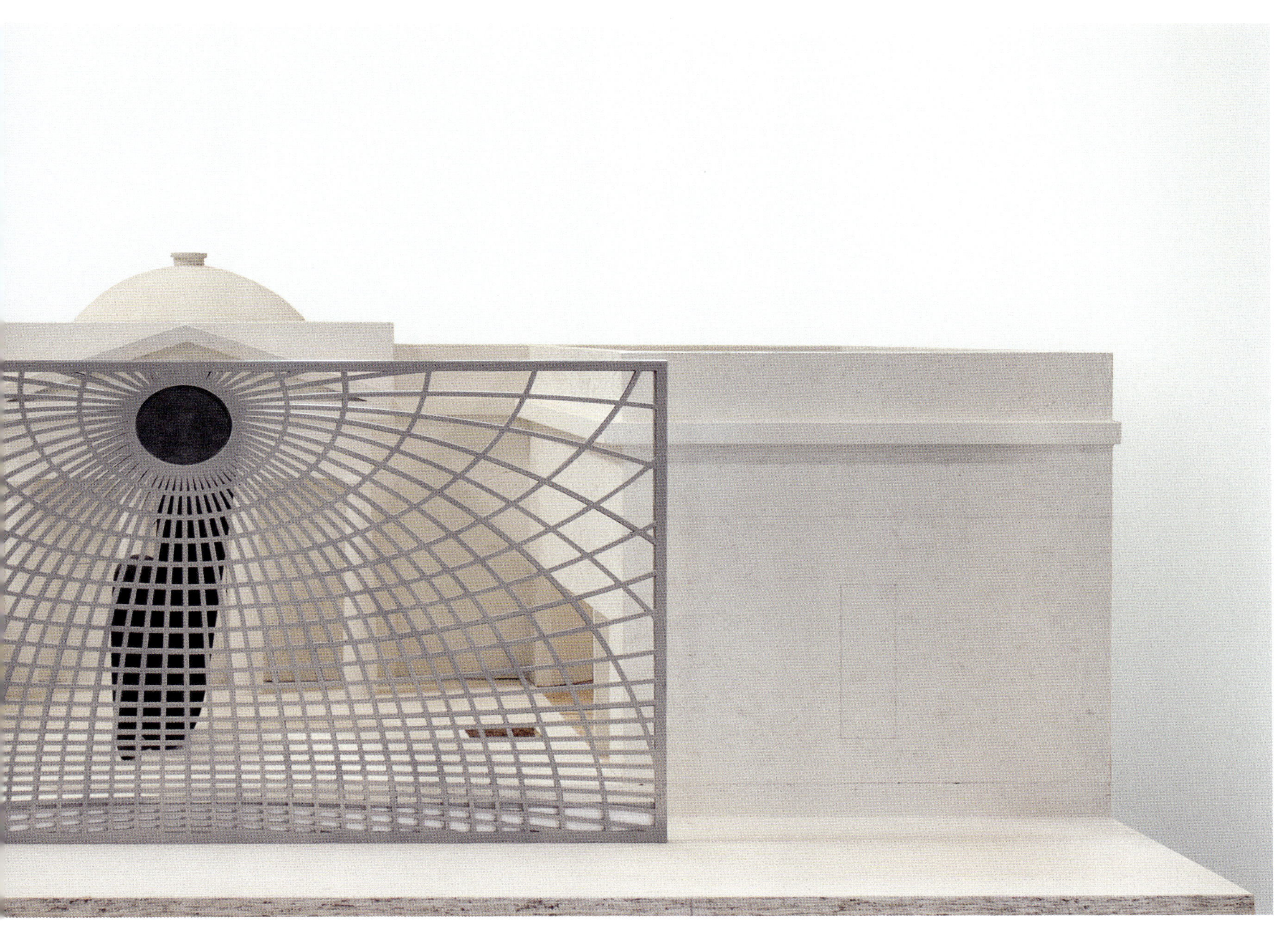

64

Untitled Drawing for "Swallowed Sun (Monstrance and Volute)," 2018

Graphite on tracing paper; 25.4 x 40 cm

Collection of the artist

Photo: Matthew Marks Gallery

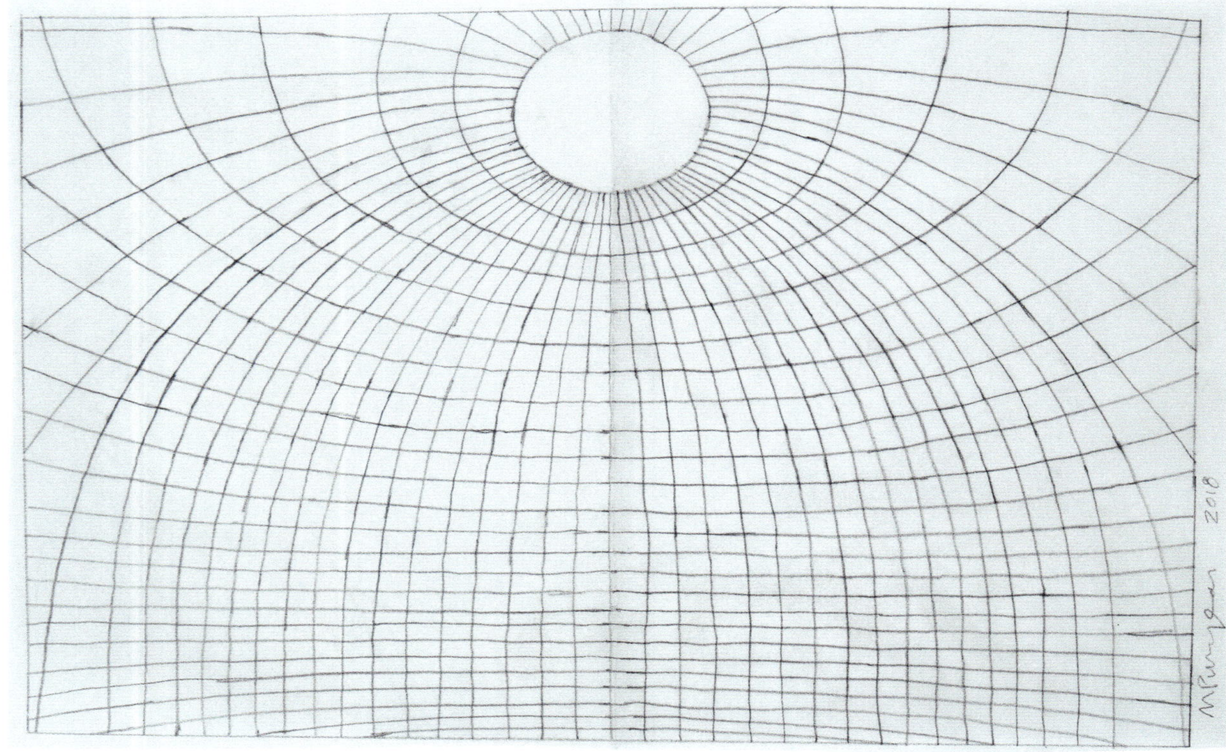

65

Untitled, Drawing for "Swallowed Sun (Monstrance and Volute)," 2018

Graphite on paper; 27.9 x 33 cm

Collection of the artist

Photo: Matthew Marks Gallery

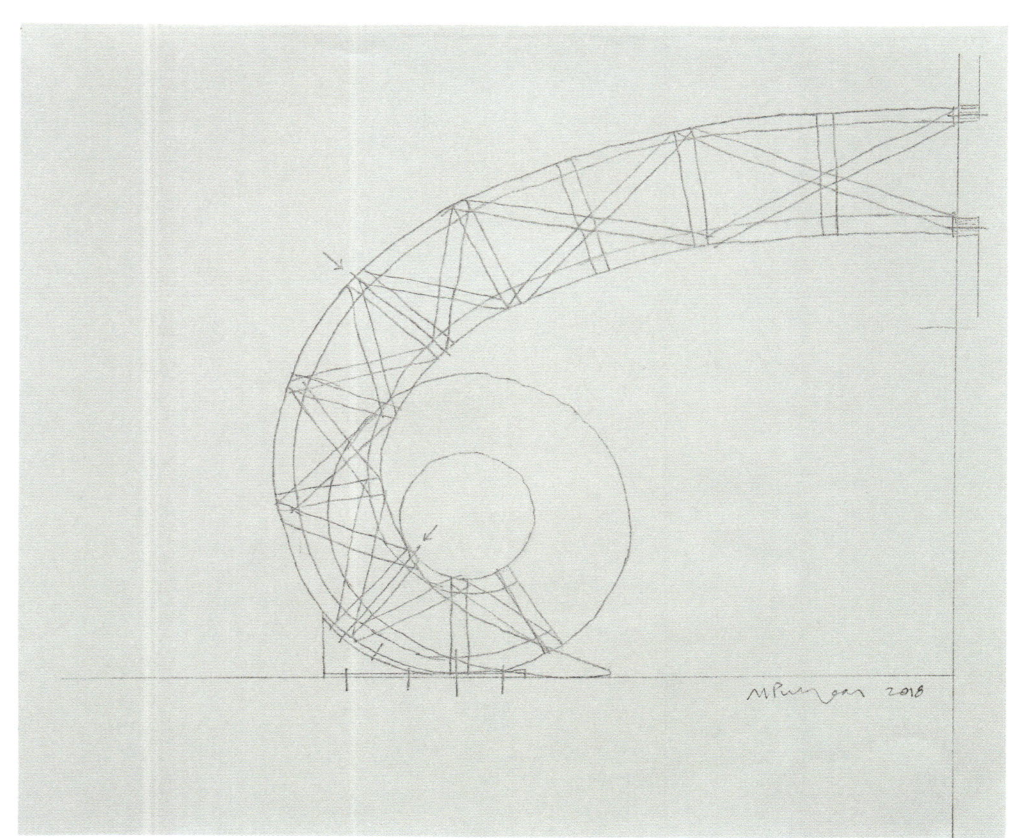

Figure 28. Installation view of *Swallowed Sun (Monstrance and Volute)* (2019) in the American Pavilion, Venice Biennale, 2019. Martin Puryear. Southern yellow pine, steel, polyester, and rope; two parts, overall 691.1 x 1341.1 x 739.1 cm. Photo: Joshua White

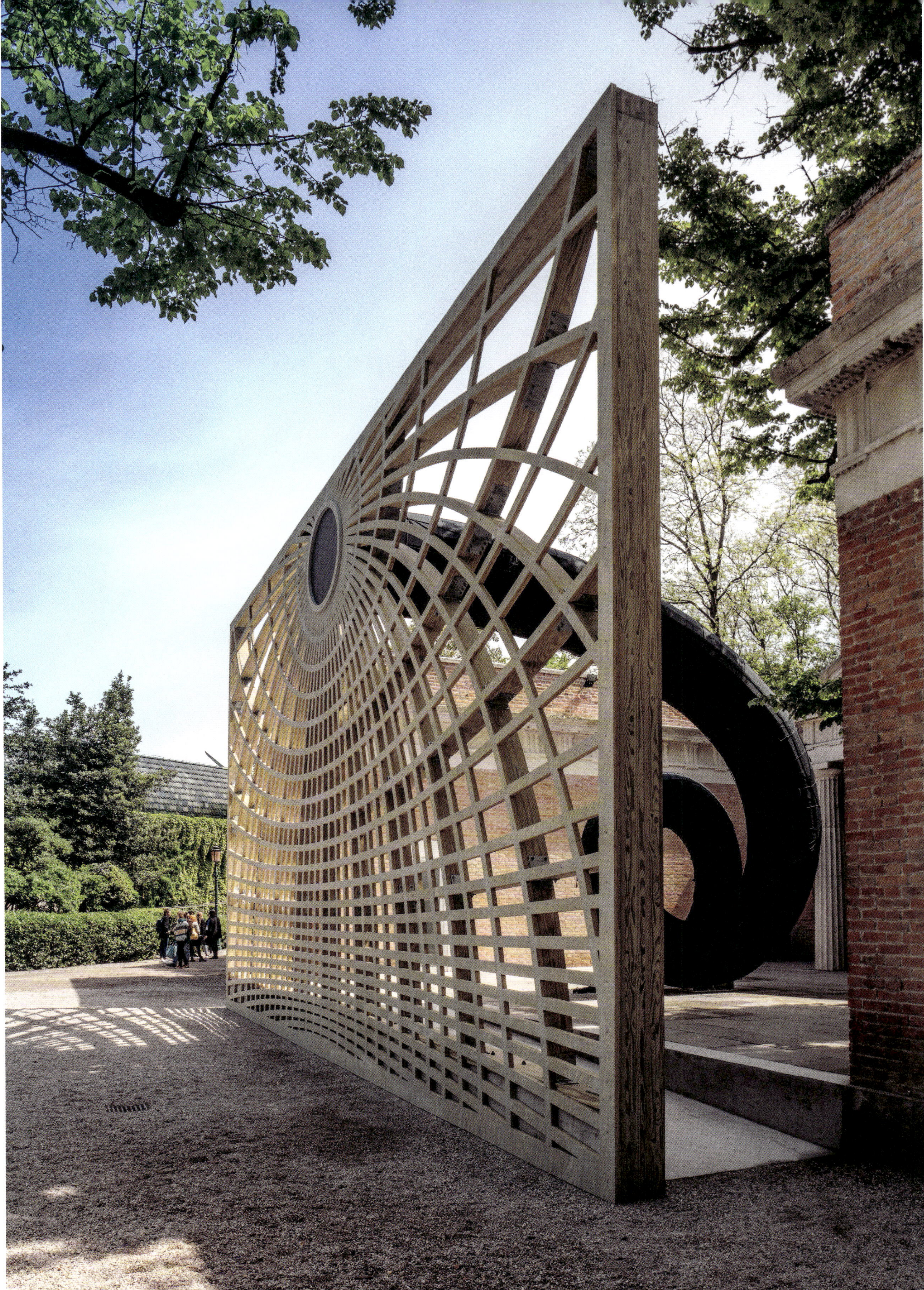

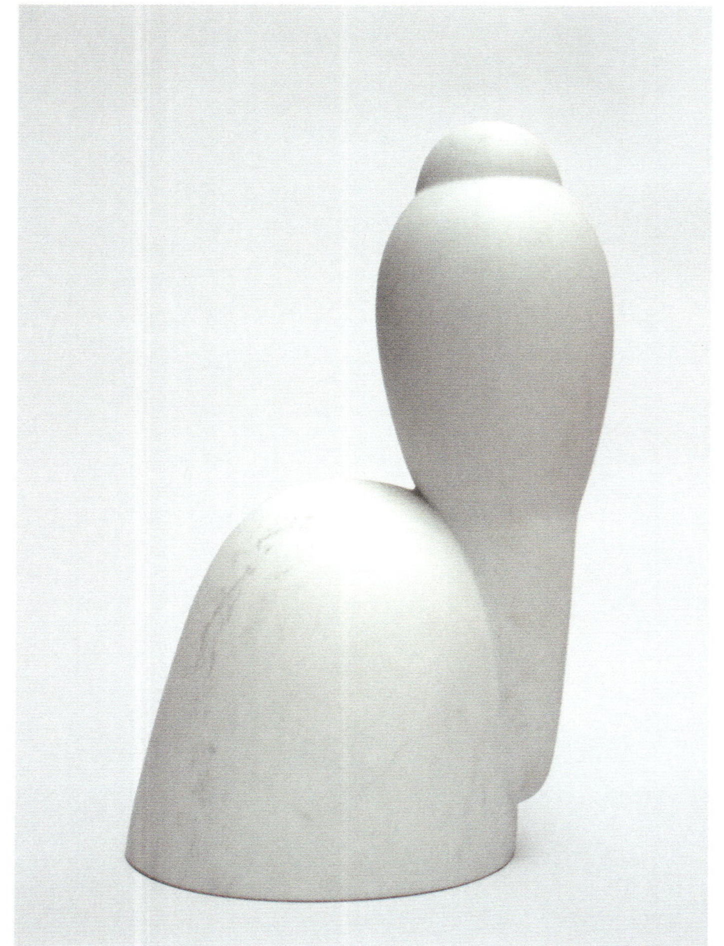

66

On the Tundra (Winter), 2022

Marble; 48.3 x 31.8 x 25.4 cm

Collection of the artist

Photo: Jeanne Englert

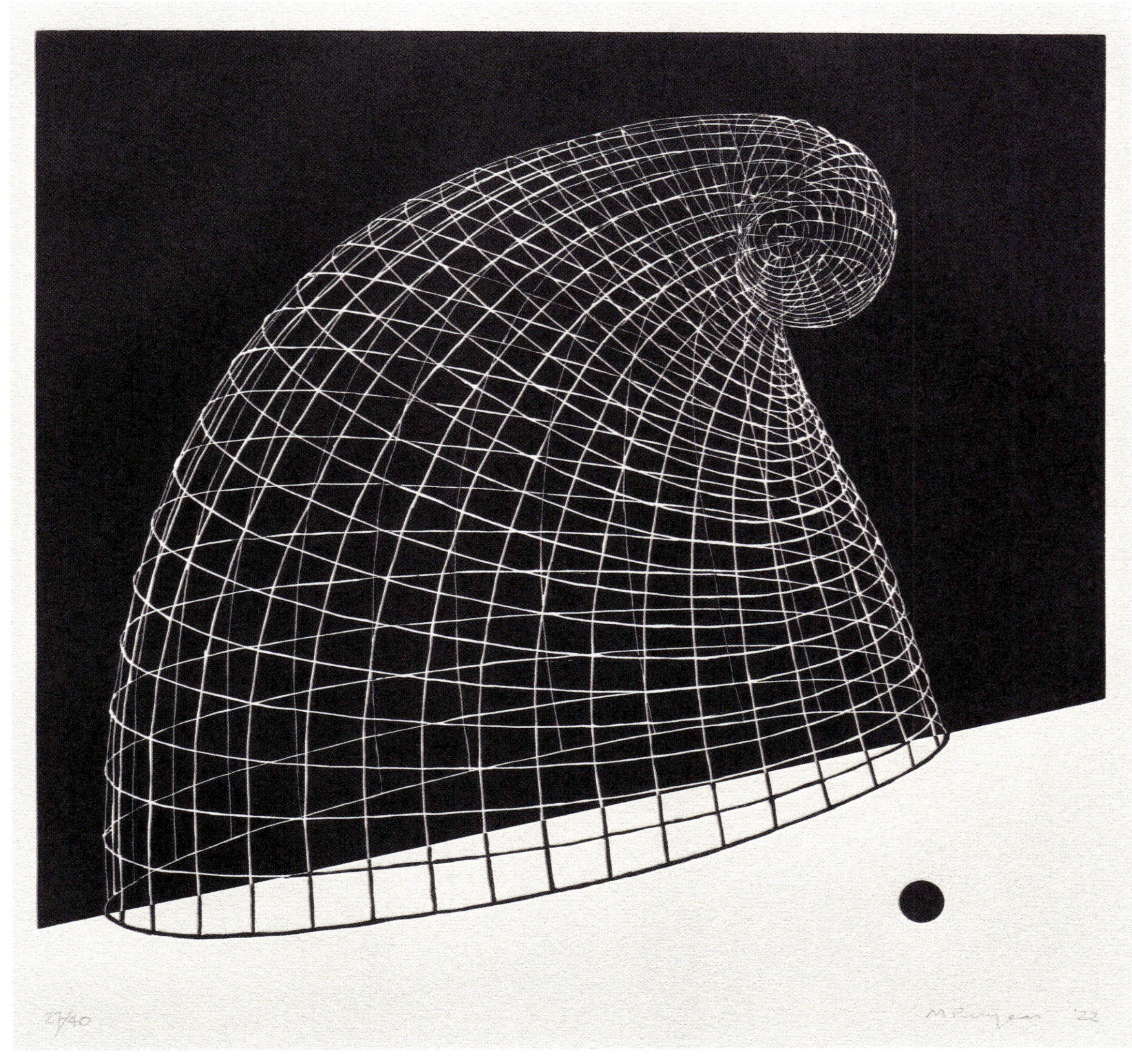

67

Untitled, 2022

Printer: Universal Limited Fine Arts; publisher: Studio in a School

Woodcut; 71.4 x 74 cm

The Cleveland Museum of Art, Anonymous Gift, in honor of Agnes Gund, Holly Peterson, and Studio in a School, 2023 2023.150

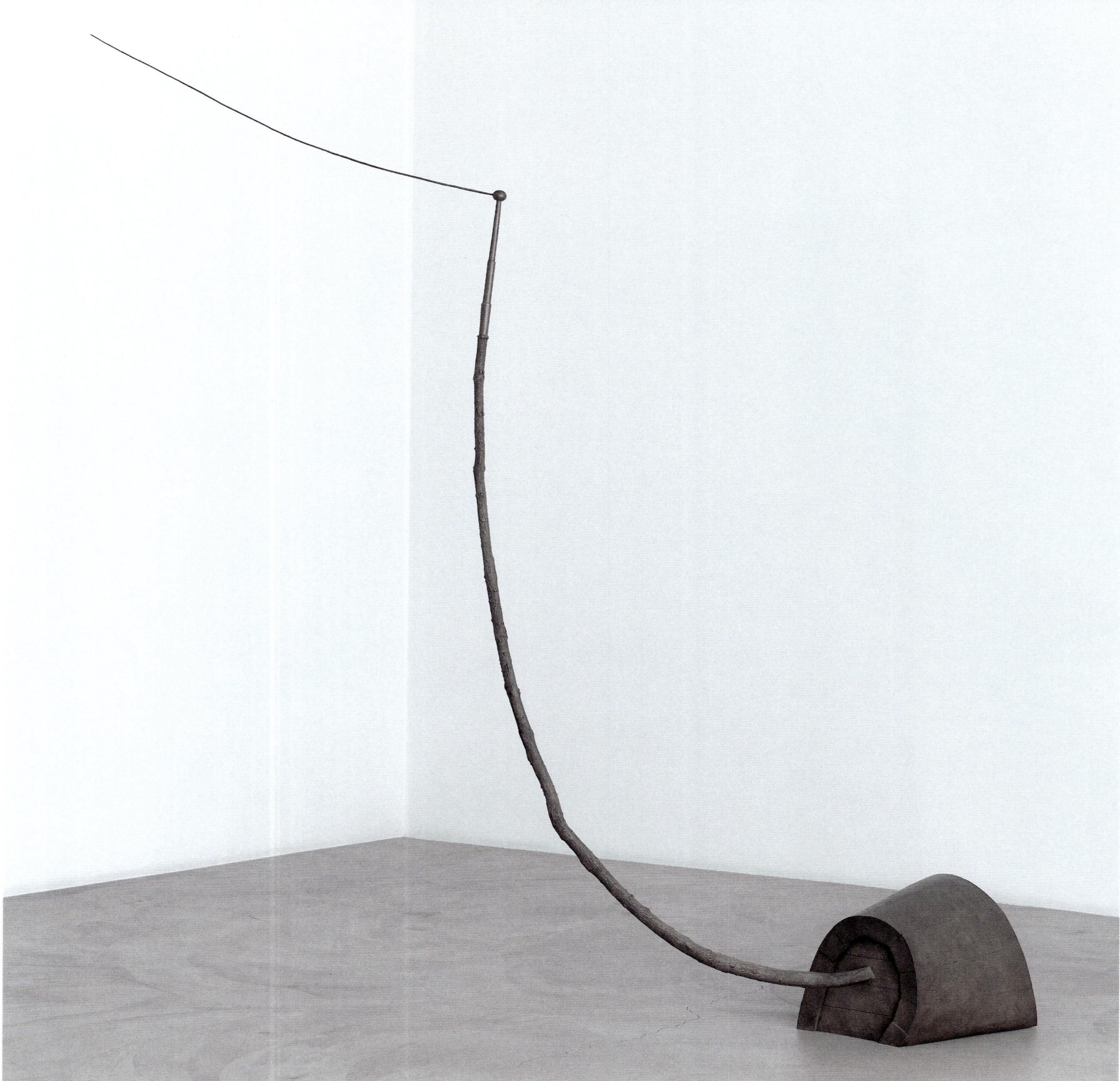

68

The Way, 2022

Bronze; 260 x 61 x 244 cm

Courtesy the artist and
Matthew Marks Gallery

Photo: Lee Thompson

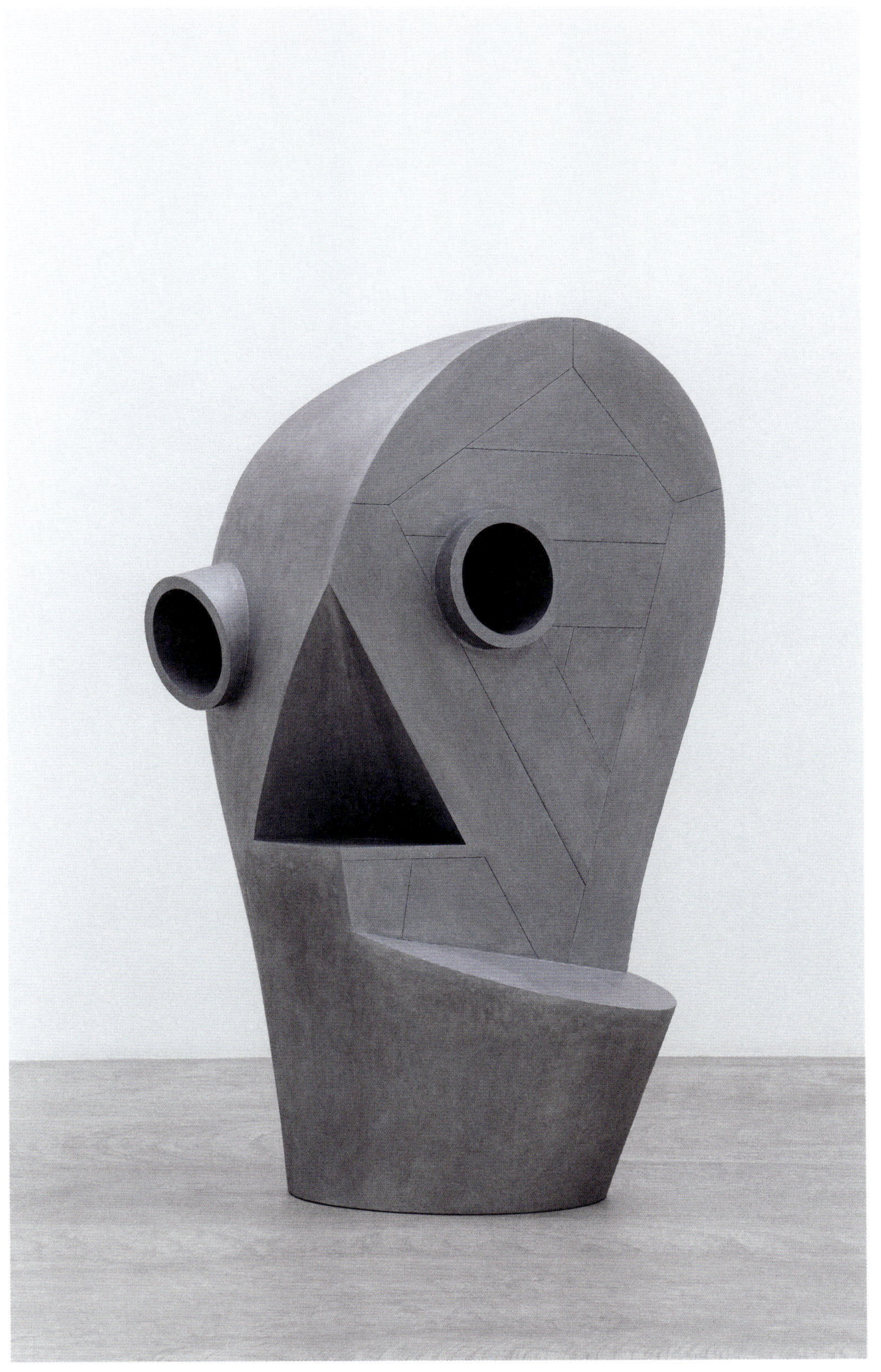

69

Looking Askance, 2023

Painted red cedar and pine; 180.3 x 109.2 x 104.1 cm

Courtesy the artist and Matthew Marks Gallery

Photo: Lee Thompson

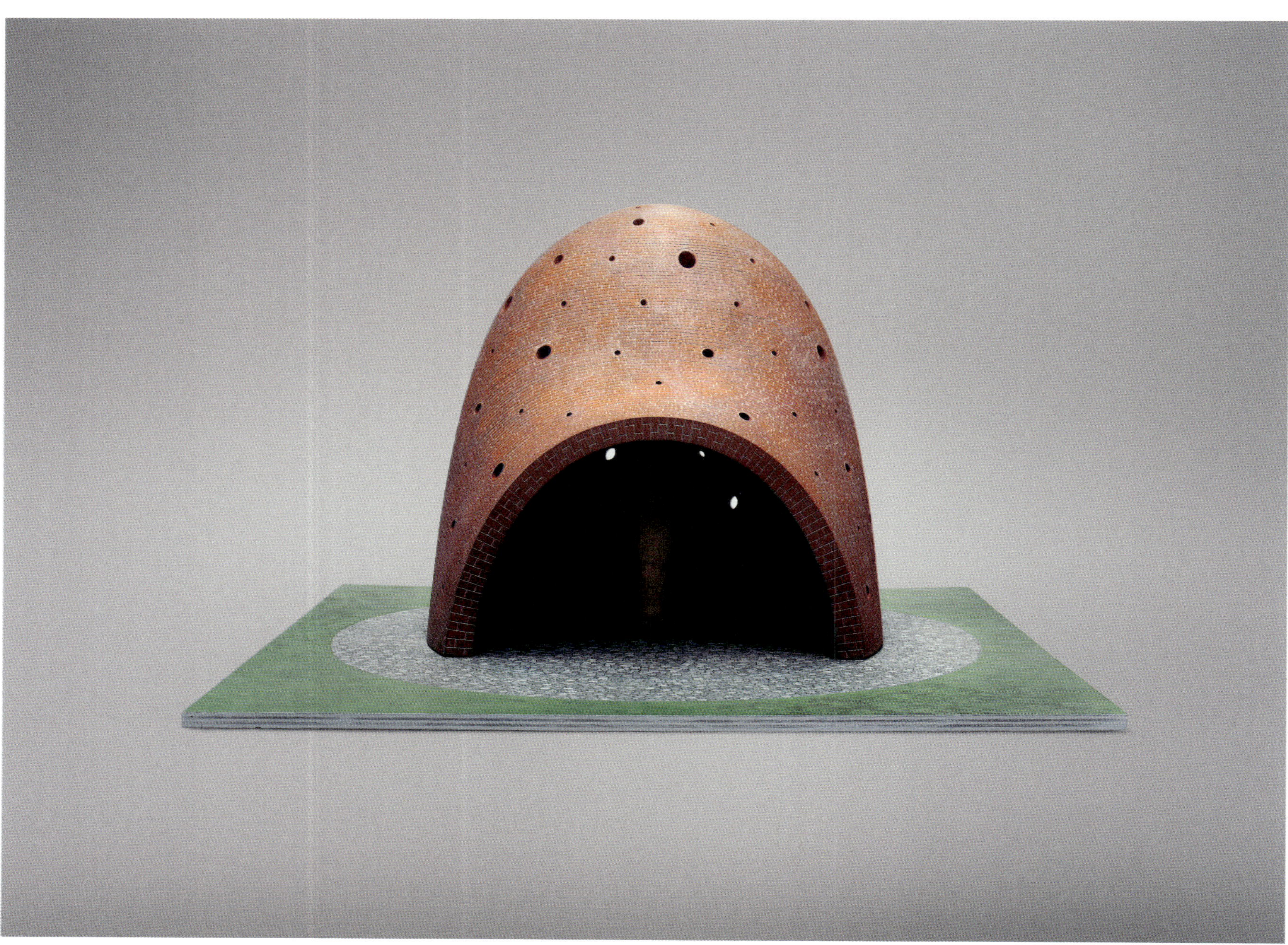

70

Maquette for Lookout,
2018

Painted high-density urethane foam and painted wood; 49.5 x 81.3 x 86.4 cm

Collection of the artist

Photo: Jeffrey Jenkins, courtesy of Storm King Archives

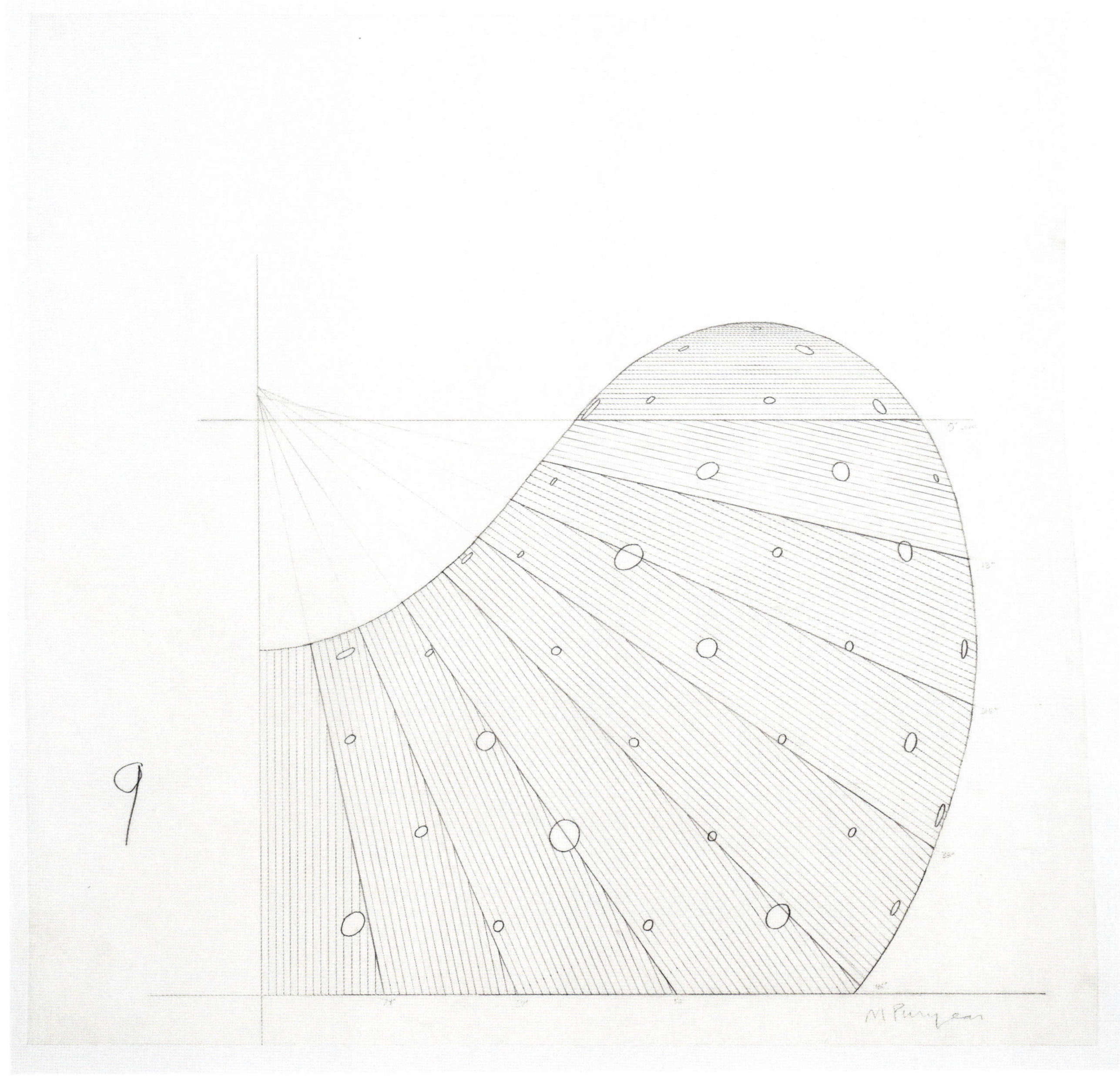

71

Brick Sculpture for Storm King Art Center (Nine Segments), 2021

Graphite on vellum; 58.4 x 73.7 cm

Collection of the artist

Photo: Jeffrey Jenkins, courtesy of Storm King Archives

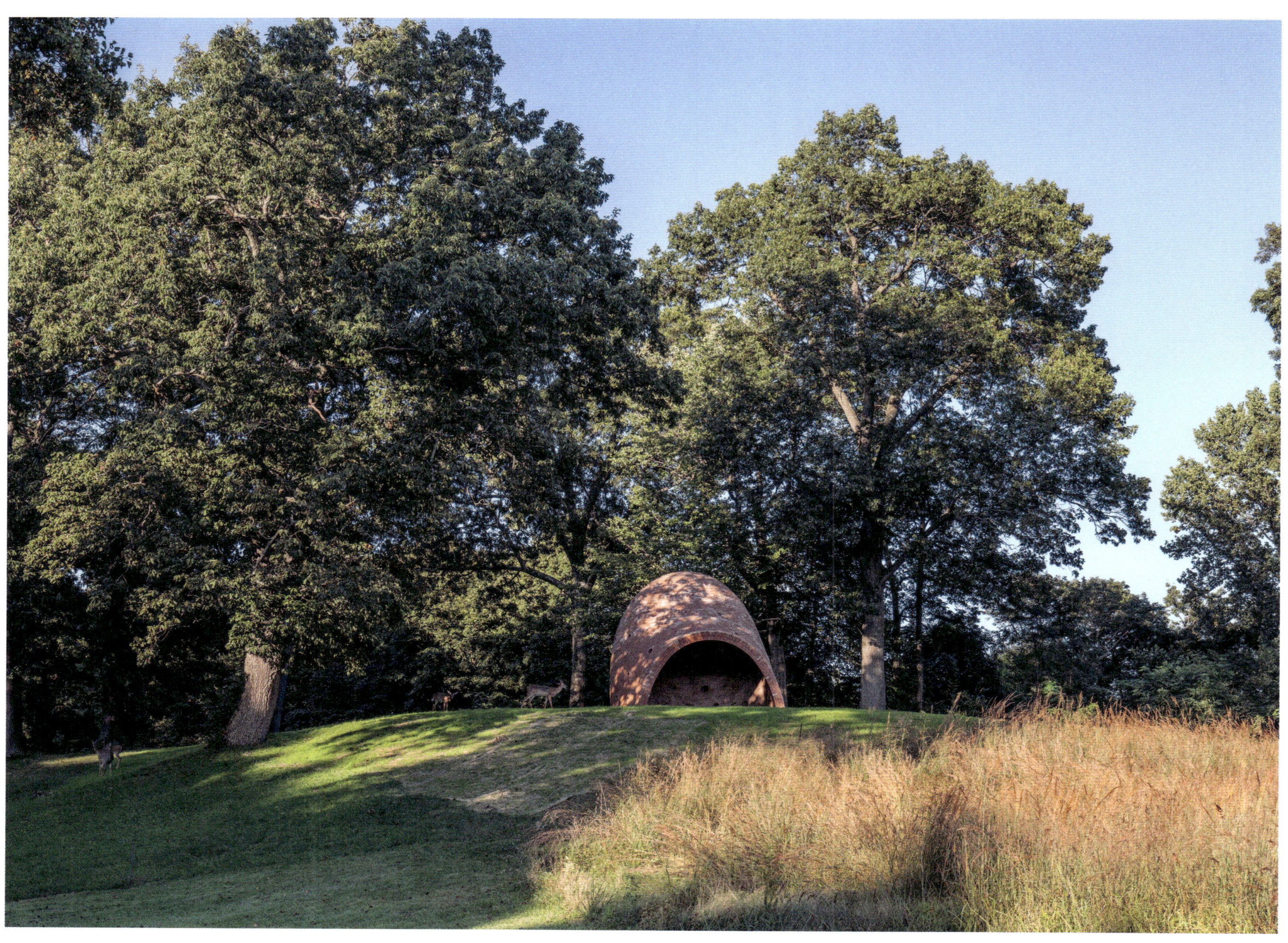

Figures 29a–c. Installation views of *Lookout* (2023) at Storm King Art Center, New Windsor, New York, 2023. Martin Puryear. Brick, concrete, and cobblestone; 609.6 cm (height). Photos: Jeffrey Jenkins, courtesy of Storm King Archives

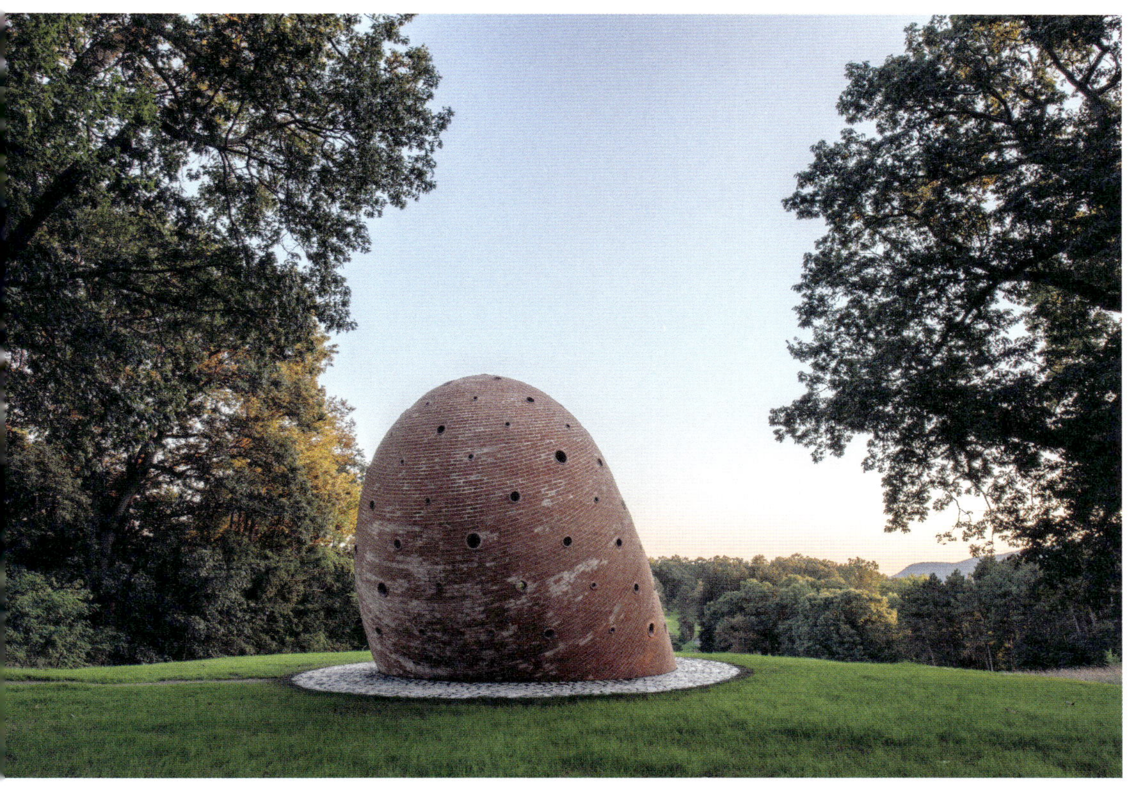

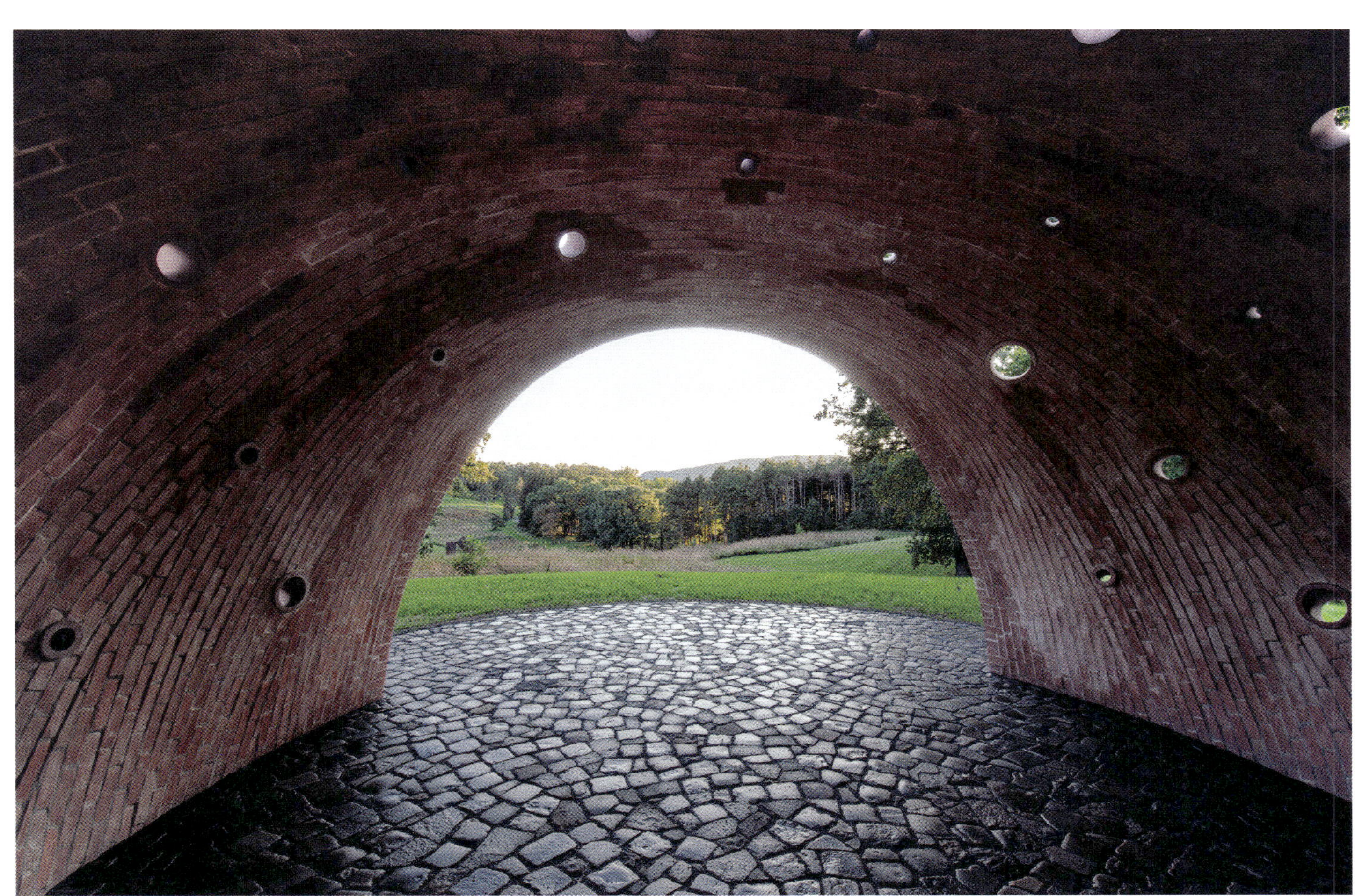

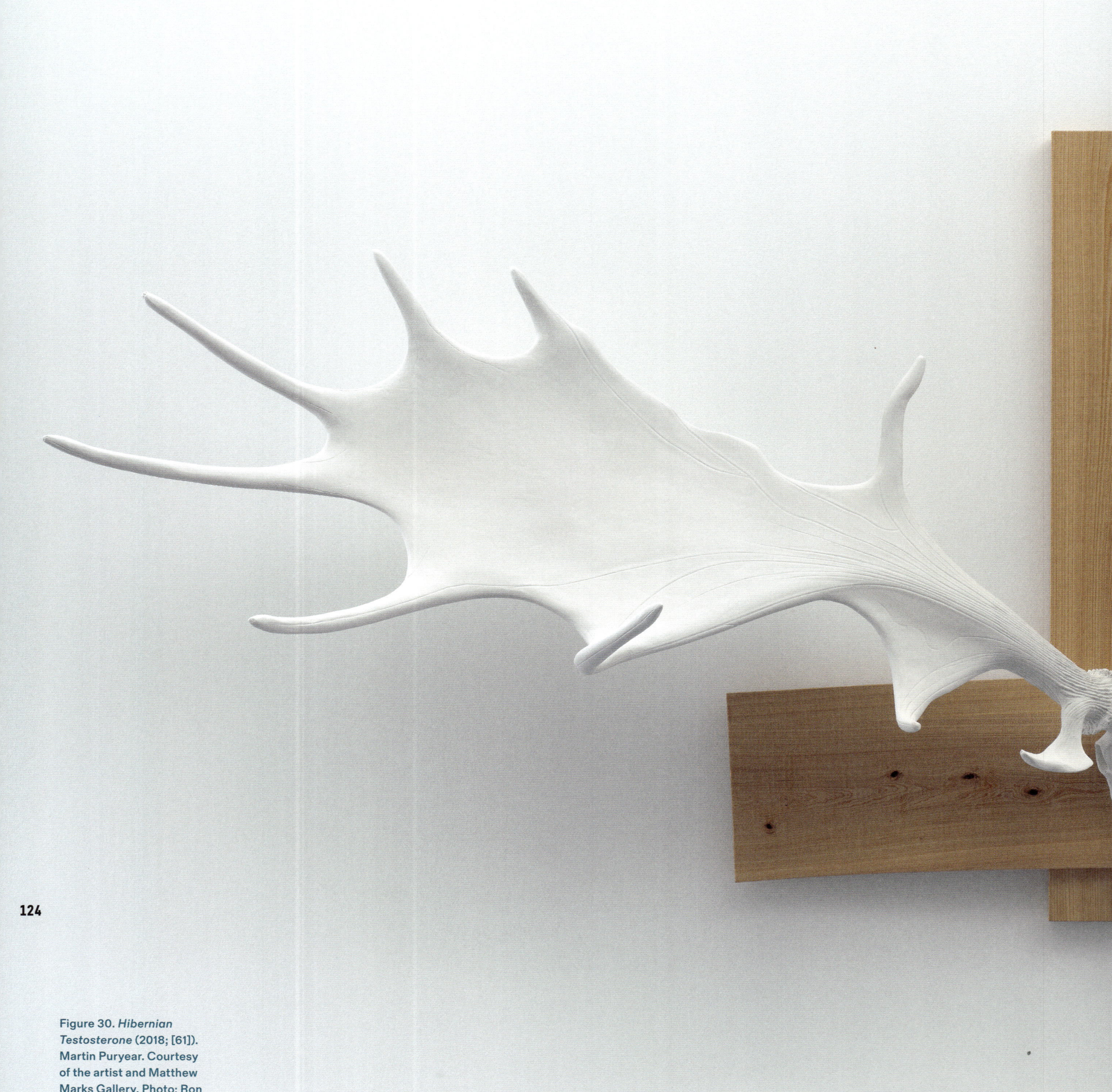

Figure 30. *Hibernian Testosterone* (2018; [61]). Martin Puryear. Courtesy of the artist and Matthew Marks Gallery. Photo: Ron Amstutz

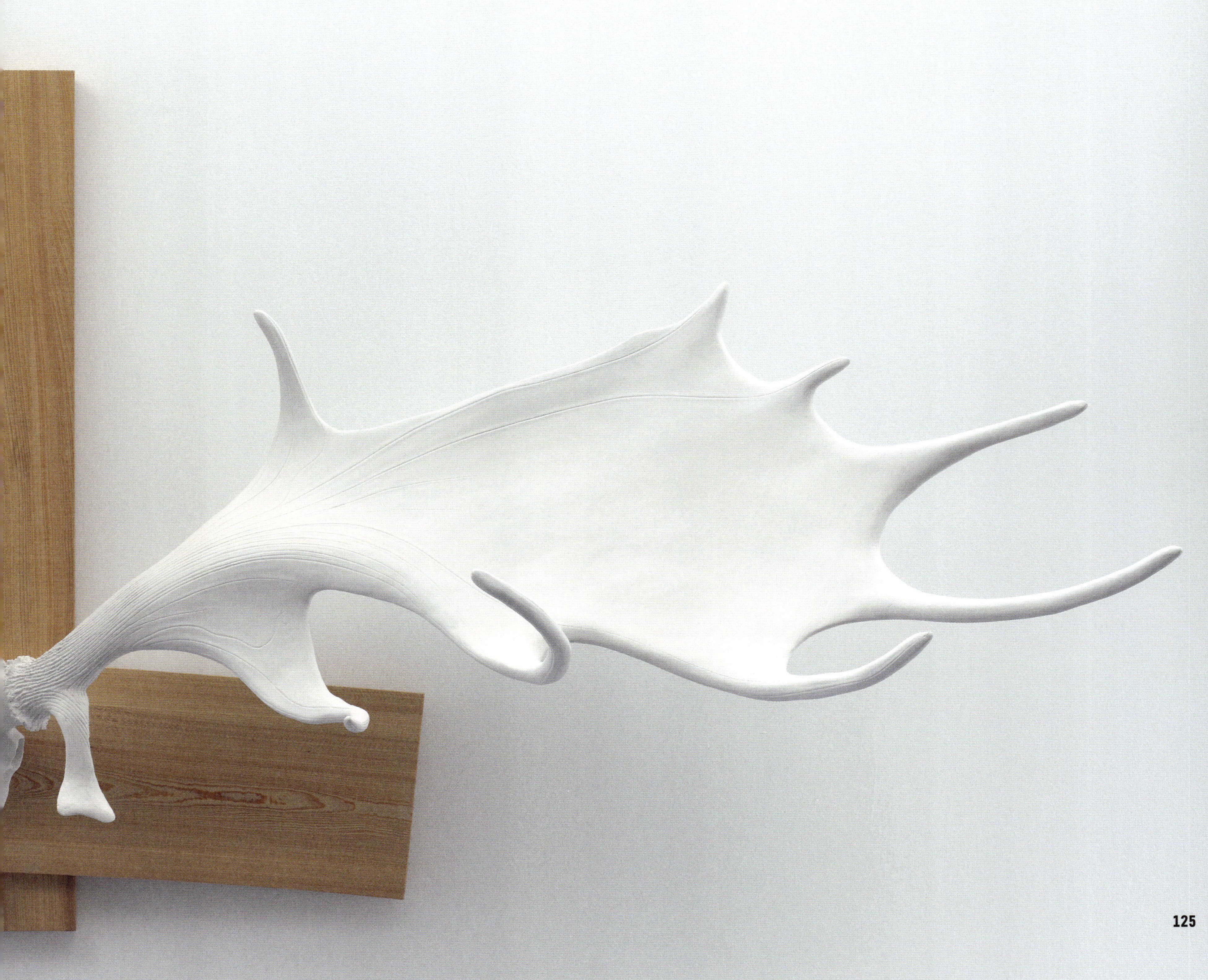

Martin Puryear's Joining of Natural and Social Worlds

Emily Liebert

"Far in the Northern Land / By the wild Baltic's strand, / I, with my childish hand, Tamed the gerfalcon [gyrfalcon]."[1] Martin Puryear recalls his seventh-grade teacher reading these lines aloud from "The Skeleton in Armor," a poem by Henry Wadsworth Longfellow (1807–1882) about a Viking crossing North America, his mind troubled by thoughts of lost love. When Puryear's teacher came to the end of the stanza she paused, unsure what a "gerfalcon" might be. Puryear raised his hand and enlightened the class about the key traits and habits of this largest species of falcon.[2] As he briefly inhabited the role of teacher, Puryear discovered what it felt like to possess with confidence a body of knowledge.

Seventy years later, the experience remains vivid for the artist. It mirrors back to him the feeling of enjoying a budding mastery over a subject, the result of voracious reading from a young age. This anecdote encompasses two intertwined endeavors that will guide my reading of Puryear's oeuvre: the artist's focused pursuit of knowledge and his profound engagement with the natural world. Before we turn to their expressions in Puryear's mature work, let us linger a bit longer in his childhood.

Born in Washington, DC, in 1941, Puryear recalls feeling that he was "growing up in the wrong place."[3] The urban environment lacked the power and authenticity he found in rural settings, in the midst of nature. He relished periods of respite when his parents would take him and his six younger siblings on camping trips. Between such excursions, books were a source of escape and inspiration. A regular visitor to the DC public libraries, the young Puryear read constantly about wilderness, wildlife, and the natural world.[4] He later put himself through college at the Catholic University of America in DC by working in circulation in the library system that he had gotten to know as a child.

In 1949, as a third grader in DC's William Syphax School, Puryear gained his first artistic recognition. A painting he made, titled *Jungle Dream*, earned him fourth place in a nationwide art contest run by the Young American Junior Readers, which published a classroom news weekly.[5] To this day, Puryear can describe *Jungle Dream*'s depiction of a quintessential explorer—pith helmet and all—sleeping under a tree as the elephants and snakes produced by his unconscious wander around him.[6] The prize, which he also remembers, was a fountain pen.

When he began to consider his future, Puryear had the idea that he might become a professional artist. In particular, he saw himself as a wildlife illustrator. This vocation, he thought, would enable him to earn a living by combining his interests in drawing, painting, and nature. Puryear's undergraduate program of study at Catholic University likewise reflects these different pulls: he started out as a biology major but changed his major to art in his junior year.

It was around the time of *Jungle Dream* that Puryear discovered the gyrfalcon through the folios of John James Audubon's (1785–1851) *Birds of America*, housed at the Smithsonian Museum of Natural History. Among the 435 life-size renderings of bird species, two pictures stood out to him: renderings of the same species of gyrfalcon, one white and one black (figs. 31 and 32). As he would learn, the stark contrast in plumage that caught his attention is determined by each bird population's particular habitat among the Arctic regions where the species thrives: the purest white gyrfalcons typically reside in Greenland, and the darkest in Labrador. Growing up Black in segregated Washington, DC, this evolutionary adaptation struck Puryear. "I made a connection about human racial difference by way of these species," the artist explains.[7]

Figure 31. Gyrfalcon, illustrated in *The Birds of America*, Havell plate 366, ca. 1835–36. John James Audubon (French-American, 1785–1851). Watercolor, gouache, and graphite on paper; sheet: 132.1 x 96.5 cm. The New York Historical, Purchased for the Society by public subscription from Mrs. John J. Audubon. Photo © The New York Historical

Figure 32. Labrador falcon, illustrated in *The Birds of America*, plate 196, 1827–30. Robert Havell Jr. (American, 1793–1878), after John James Audubon. Etching and hand-colored aquatint; sheet: 101.6 x 71.1 cm. The Museum of Fine Arts, Boston, Gift of William Hooper, 21.11772.196. Photo © 2025 MFA Boston

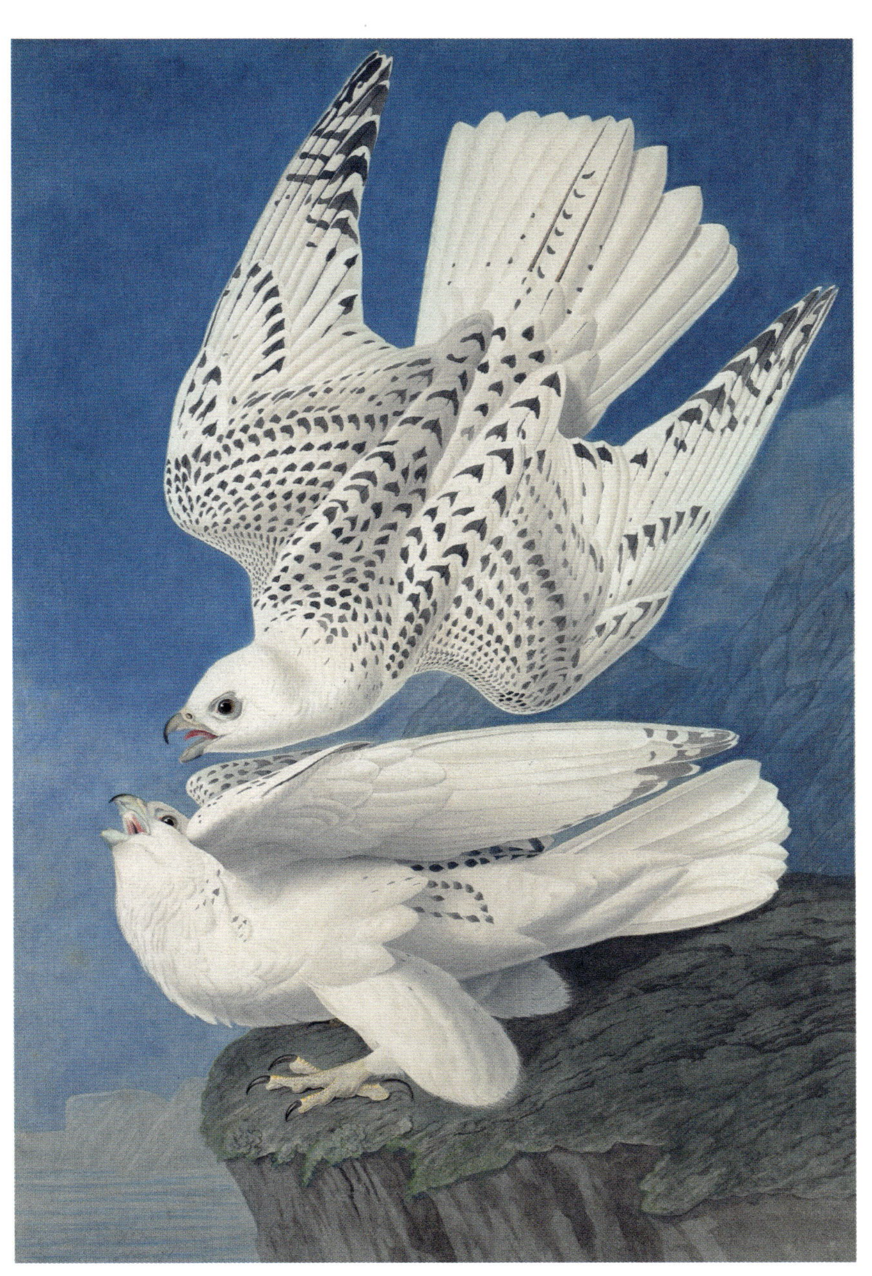

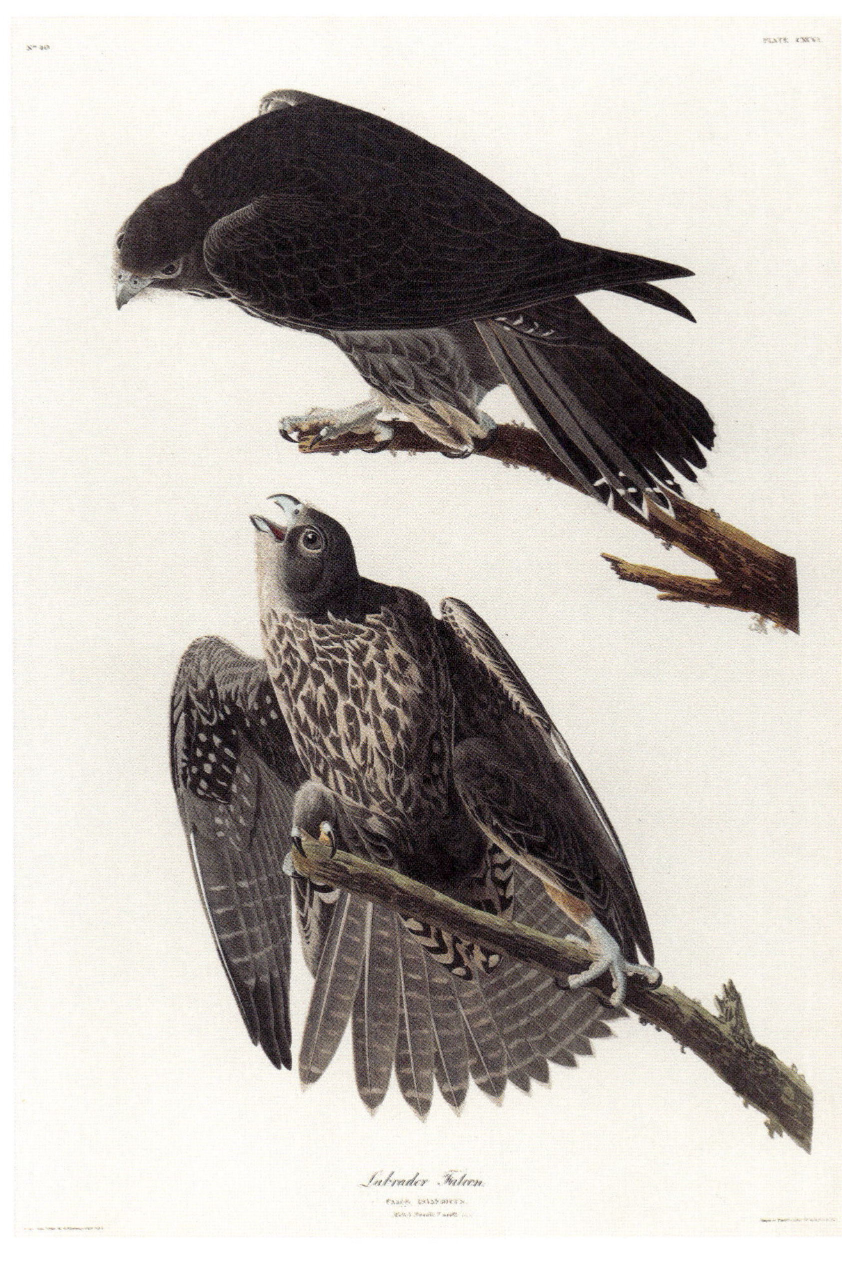

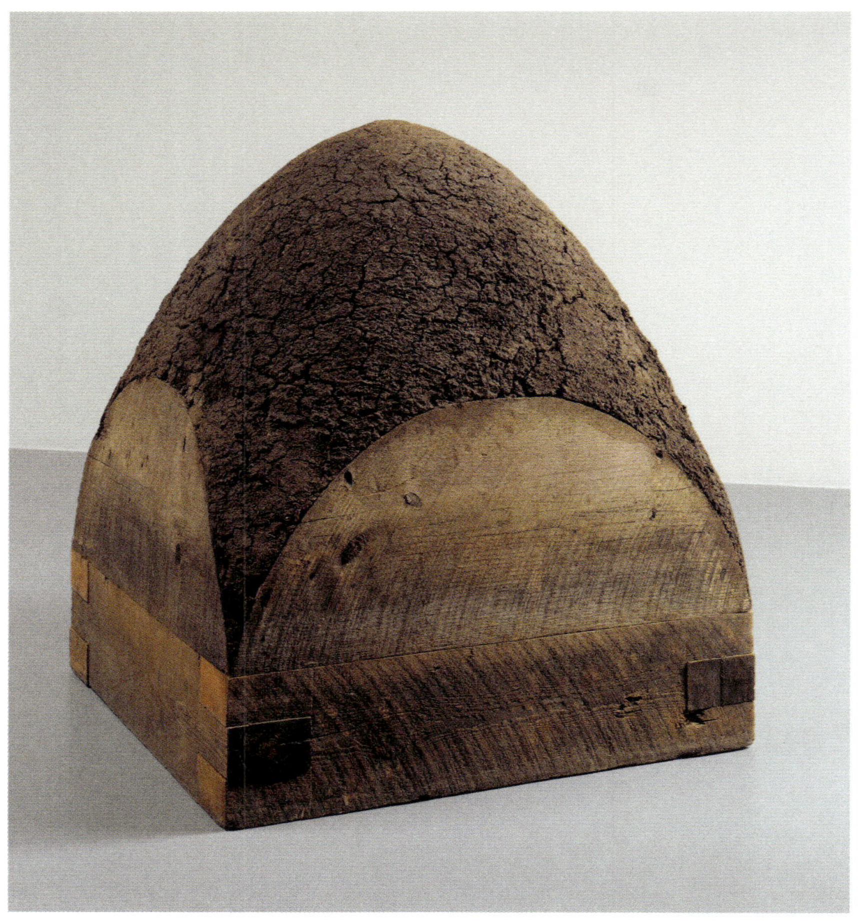

Figure 33. *For Beckwourth* (1980). Martin Puryear. Turf, oak, and pitch pine; 101.6 x 88.9 x 88.9 cm. Collection of the artist. Photo: Michael Tropea

Today, prints of Audubon's white and black gyrfalcons hang in Puryear's home and studio. Puryear also maintains a robust section in his own library devoted to Audubon. One of the titles is *Two Centuries of Black American Art: 1750–1950*, the catalogue for an exhibition curated by the late artist and art historian David C. Driskell (1931–2020), who had been a friend of Puryear's since college. Audubon's inclusion in this touring exhibition, which premiered at the Los Angeles County Museum of Art in 1976, was a surprise to many visitors unaware of Audubon's full biography and was challenged by Audubon's descendants.[8] Audubon was born Jean Rabin in Sainte-Domingue (now Haiti) in 1785, to a French sea captain and his mistress, a Creole chambermaid, who died before he was a year old. After growing up in France, Audubon immigrated to the United States at the age of eighteen under a false passport to avoid conscription into Napoleon's army. On American soil, Audubon fashioned the identity for which he is best known: pioneering chronicler of the natural world.[9] Given Puryear's initial encounter with Audubon's representations of the gyrfalcon, it is no surprise that the naturalist's autobiography would resonate as a meaningful frame through which to read Audubon's work—as underscored by Puryear's decision to classify Driskell's exhibition catalogue as Audubon literature.

Puryear's early discovery that the natural world could illuminate social experience led to what has become a recurrent theme—even a guiding tenet—in his art of the last half-century, which challenges the age-old dichotomy of nature versus culture. In material, form, and content, Puryear intertwines these supposed opposites, rendering them mutually dependent in his art. Some works, especially recent ones, propose that the natural world holds meaningful lessons to absorb in our constructed environments.

Herein lies a distinction that is as important as it is subtle: though Puryear's art invites us to reflect on social relations including racial difference through aspects of nature, it does not *naturalize* race. On the contrary, it treats race as a representation—a social construct whose histories shape the world we inhabit and therefore merit close consideration. This became vividly clear to Puryear when he served in the Peace Corps in Sierra Leone from 1964 to 1966:

> It was very interesting to me that as Black Americans in the Peace Corps we were often not considered Black by the local people. There was a word in the Mende language that meant white man or foreigner, European, and that word could be used as readily for a Black American as for a white American. That was further evidence of how the concept of race is a constructed reality.[10]

"Moving as You Work"

Puryear's interest in the natural world crucially informed his choice of materials. Since his earliest days as a sculptor, wood has been Puryear's primary medium.[11] Wood is unrefined and therefore close to its source in a living organism, in contrast to other materials, such as bronze and other metals, that are common to sculpture. Indeed, Puryear is aware of "working with something that has recently been alive."[12] Possessing a vast knowledge of wood, he is attuned to the life cycles of the trees from which he sources his woods, which he can also distinguish by their moisture levels and scents.[13] Puryear has made sculptures from many wood species, most often cedar and pine, although ash, maple, and poplar make frequent appearances as well. He typically determines which wood he will use based on whether its physical properties lend themselves to the form he has envisioned for a given work. Listening to Puryear describe such decisions, one has the sense that he, as the maker, regards his relationship with material as a collaboration with an animate partner. The artist has explained that wood is "moving . . . as you work. It's shrinking and swelling all the time."[14]

Puryear's interest in the transition from living material to sculptural matter prompted him to make his own rawhide while he was living in Nashville, Tennessee, teaching at Fisk University, during the early 1970s: "I was really interested in working with animal skins to actually see what it felt like to take the skin right off the animal."[15] He would purchase animal carcasses from a local butcher, then clean and dry the skin, creating a material whose malleability and transparency were utilized to great effect in sculptures such as *Some Lines for Jim Beckwourth* (1978; [15]).[16] Composed of seven long, thin pieces of twisted rawhide stretched taut on a wall and stacked one above the other, *Some Lines for Jim Beckwourth* evokes an oversize block of text or a blank musical score. Its pared-down formal quality relates to Minimalist and Post-Minimalist work of that era. At the same time, the congruence between animal skin and notation connects the piece to what Puryear has described as "a primal impulse" across cultures to create functional objects from natural materials—bricks made of mud, as well as clothes, vessels, and weapons crafted from the skin of animals.[17]

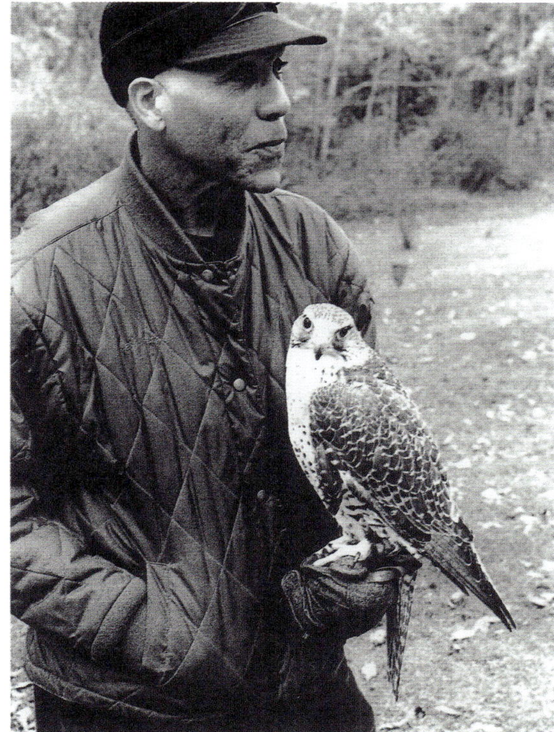

Figure 34. Martin Puryear with falcon, Upstate New York, 2010. Photo: Sascha Puryear

Some Lines for Jim Beckwourth and *For Beckwourth* (1980; fig. 33), a low, compact floor sculpture made of oak, pine, and cracked sod, are named after a nineteenth-century biracial frontiersman whose mother was enslaved and father a slaveowner.[18] Jim Beckwourth (1798–1866) was born into slavery, emancipated by his father, and went on to play a notable role in the exploration of the American West as well as became closely acquainted with the Crow Nation.[19] As Holland Cotter observes, Beckwourth was an individual who "managed to transcend the constraints built into a unitary racial identity."[20] As with Audubon, Beckwourth's social ascent and his ability to inhabit multiple cultures were functions of his adeptness at straddling the realms of wilderness and built civilization, markers of which unite in Puryear's work.

Mobility, Migration

Alongside his ongoing material experimentation, Puryear continued his study of the natural world. His early commitment to learning about the gyrfalcon did not diminish in adulthood. In 1981, he and his brother Michael traveled to Alaska to see gyrfalcons up close. Later, he became a trained falconer (fig. 34).[21] His library features an entire section dedicated to the gyrfalcon, including books of various genres and vintages on the subject.[22]

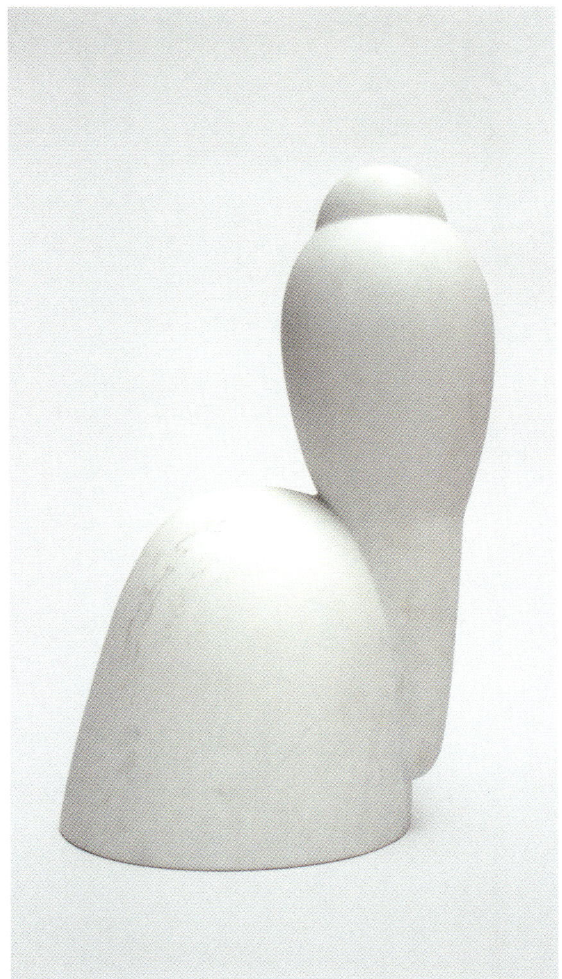

Figure 35. *On the Tundra (Winter)* (2022; [66]). Martin Puryear. Marble; 48.3 x 31.8 x 25.4 cm. Collection of the artist. Photo: Jeanne Englert

Puryear's interest in the gyrfalcon's plumage motivated his creation of *On the Tundra* (1986; [26]), an abstracted form suggesting a falcon perched on a rock. Departing from his usual material of wood, Puryear made the sculpture in cast iron, which gave it added weight and solidity. This material also allowed him to create editions of the work—there are five in total—with subtly varied patinas. From the outset, Puryear had intended to reflect the full spectrum of that plumage through the form of *On the Tundra*. As often happens with the artist, the idea percolated for many years until he made an iteration of the piece in white marble in 2022 (fig. 35; [66]).[23]

Along with the two versions of *On the Tundra*, Puryear has created dozens of other bird effigies, varying in scale, material, and the degree of abstraction [see 29, 31, 52]. These have flocked to several exhibitions, including *Connections: Martin Puryear* at the Museum of Fine Arts, Boston, in 1990.[24] *Connections* was the first in a series of exhibitions developed by Kathy Halbreich, the museum's then-curator of contemporary art, that put the work of living artists in dialogue with historical work from the MFA Boston's encyclopedic collections.

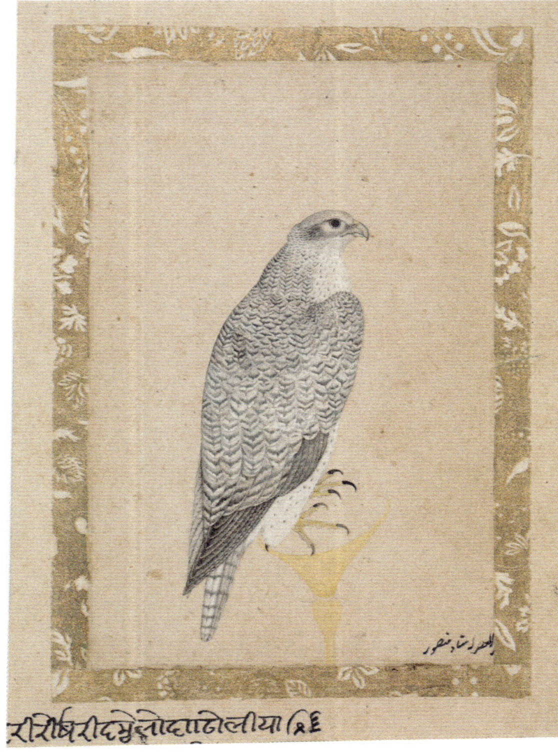

Figure 36. *Portrait of a gyrfalcon*, 1619. Mansur (Indian, active c. 1590–1630). Ink, color, and gold on paper; 29 x 20.3 cm. Museum of Fine Arts, Boston, Museum purchase with funds from the Francis Bartlett Donation of 1912 and by contribution, 14.683. Photo © 2025 MFA Boston

Upon receiving the invitation to participate in the series, Puryear did not have to think long about which work he would select. A decade prior, he had encountered the Mughal court painter Mansur's (active c. 1590–1630) depiction of the gyrfalcon in the MFA's collection (1619; fig. 36). This image had captured Puryear's attention because he knew that the gyrfalcon is not native to India. Having studied the biological and cultural histories of the gyrfalcon, Puryear determined that the painting likely depicts a bird that arrived in India via diplomatic-trade channels from Europe, a common occurrence since medieval times. Mansur's painting—a reproduction of which hangs in Puryear's studio—was immediately compelling for Puryear, not only within the history of ornithological portraiture but also as a representation of geopolitical trade routes. Trade histories are of enduring interest for Puryear because they map the regions of the world by their Indigenous resources, techniques of production, and values.[25] This interest is part of a body of research that Puryear has nurtured through his own avid pursuit of travel since his early adult years.

Connections presented Puryear's bird sculptures in conversation with the Mansur painting and three Audubon prints—of the black gyrfalcon, the white gyrfalcon, and the great-footed hawk, or peregrine falcon. The installation was anchored by Puryear's sculptural equivalent of a yurt, a form of portable housing invented by ancient nomadic peoples of Central Asia (fig. 37). Puryear created the yurt in 1981, several years after a fire in his Brooklyn studio that

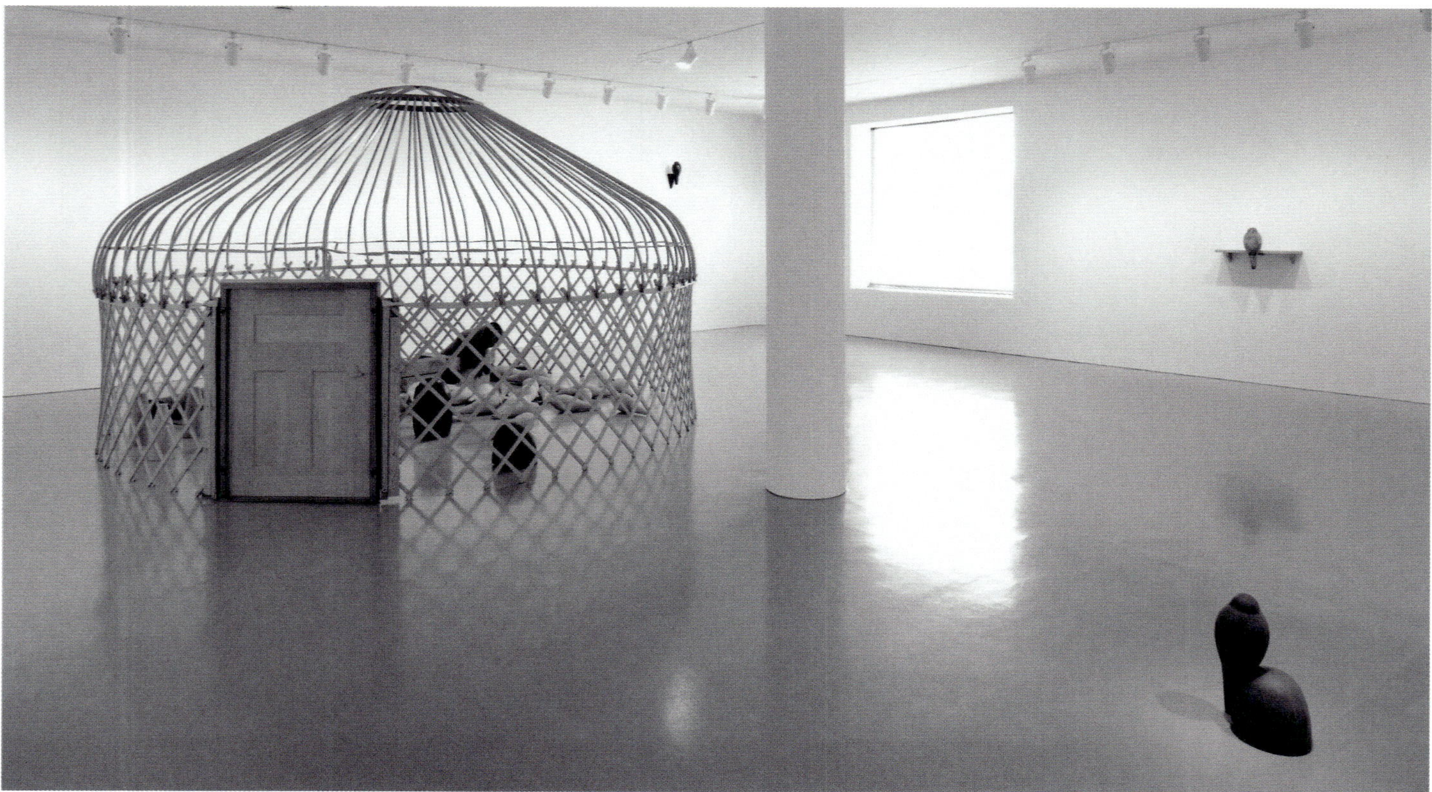

Figure 37. Installation view of *Connections: Martin Puryear*, Museum of Fine Arts, Boston, 1990. Pictured: *Where the Heart Is (Sleeping Mews)* (1990), *Untitled* (1987), *Untitled* (1986), *On the Tundra* (1986; [26]). Photo © 2025 Museum of Fine Arts, Boston

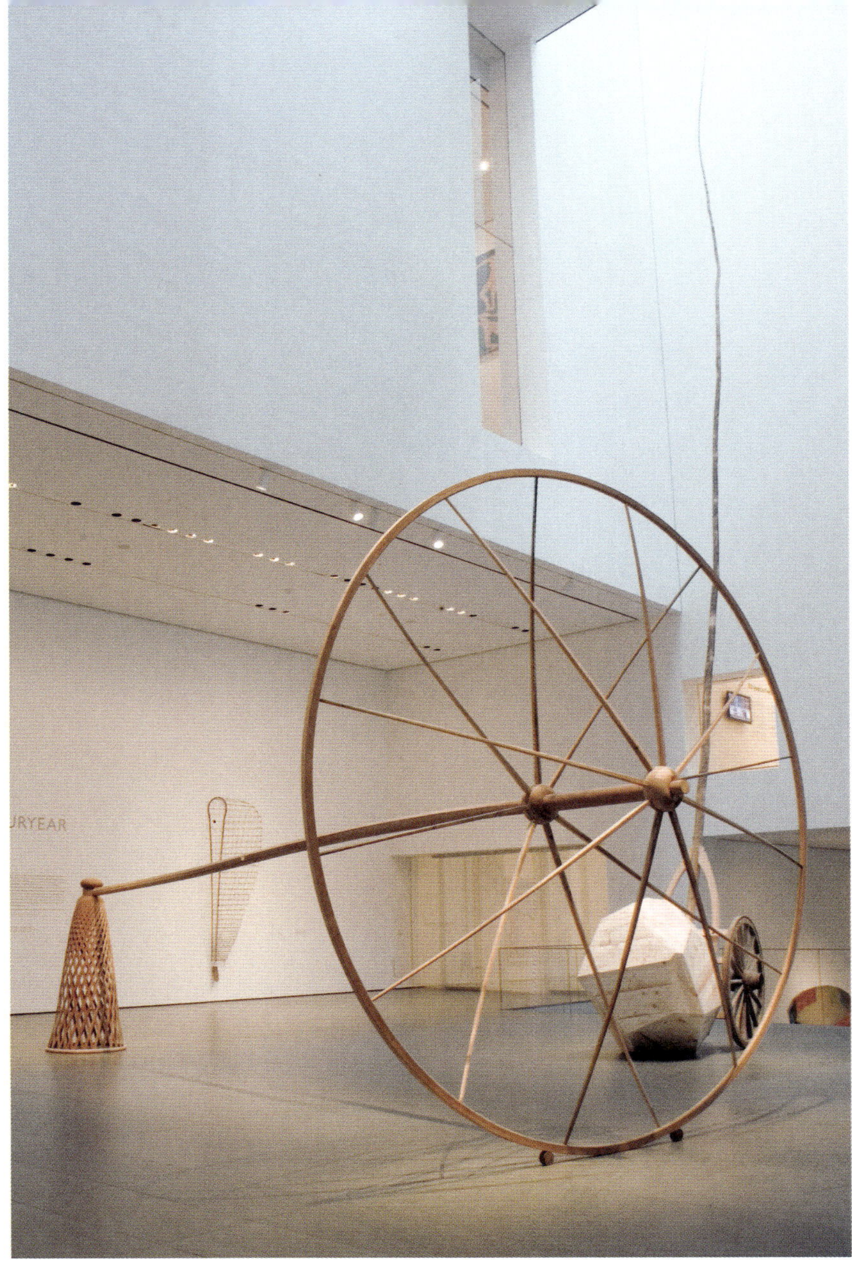

Figure 38. Installation view of *Martin Puryear*, The Museum of Modern Art, New York, 2008. Pictured: *Desire* (1981), *Greed's Trophy* (1984), and *Ad Astra* (2006–2007). Digital Image © The Museum of Modern Art / Licensed by SCALA / John Wronn / Art Resource, NY

Figure 39. *The Load* (2012). Martin Puryear. Wood, steel, and glass; 231.1 x 469.9 x 188 cm. Glenstone Museum, Potomac, Maryland. Photo: Christian David Erroi

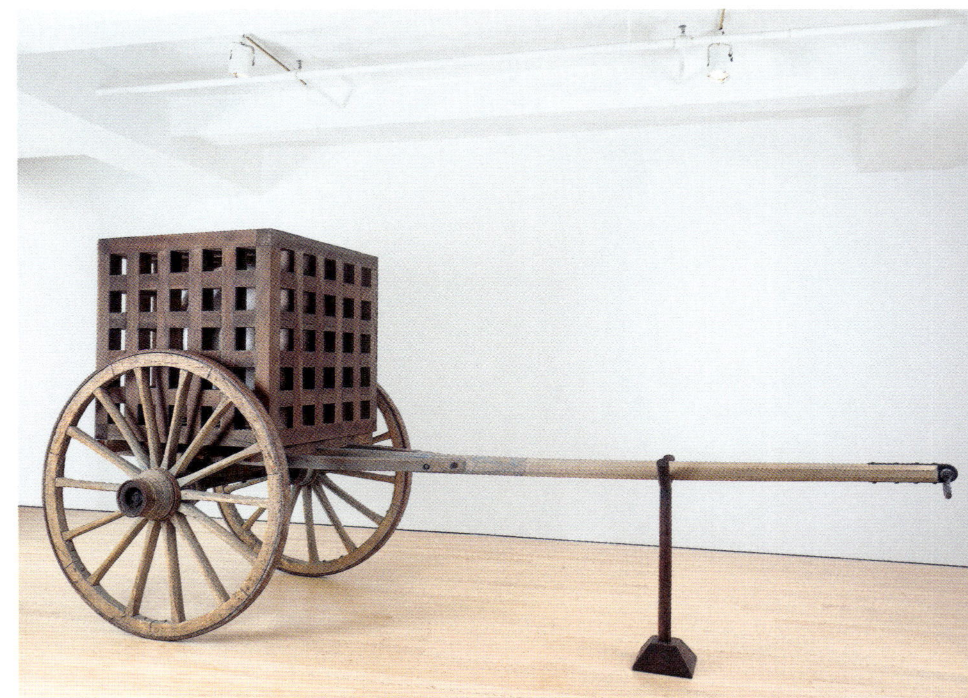

destroyed most of his work and belongings. The artist recently described the making of that yurt as a "survival imperative" in the aftermath of the fire—a way to reassure himself that he could always have in his possession a dwelling suitable for immediate relocation.[26] Puryear has created yurt installations on multiple occasions, in every instance alongside a selection of his bird sculptures.[27] The association between this architectural innovation and natural symbols of flight foreground a freedom located in mobility that has long enthralled Puryear, both inside and outside the studio.

Soon after making his yurt, Puryear introduced into his artistic vocabulary the most basic structure of mobility—the wheel. *Desire* (1981; fig. 38) comprises a massive wheel, sixteen feet in diameter, held in place by a thirty-two-foot-long beam anchored by an inverted basket. Ever since, wheels have repeatedly surfaced in Puryear's art, introducing the potential for movement into static forms. Over the last two decades, Puryear has connected the physical act of moving to histories of migration in a succession of works in which wheels support cart-and-wagon structures. *Ad Astra* (2007; fig. 38), *The Rest* (2009–10; Whitney Museum of American Art), *Vehicle for Reflection* (2012; private collection), *The Load* (2012; fig. 39), and *New Voortrekker* (2018; fig. 40) give form to the hopes and obstacles embedded in the complex migratory journeys Puryear has studied since childhood.[28]

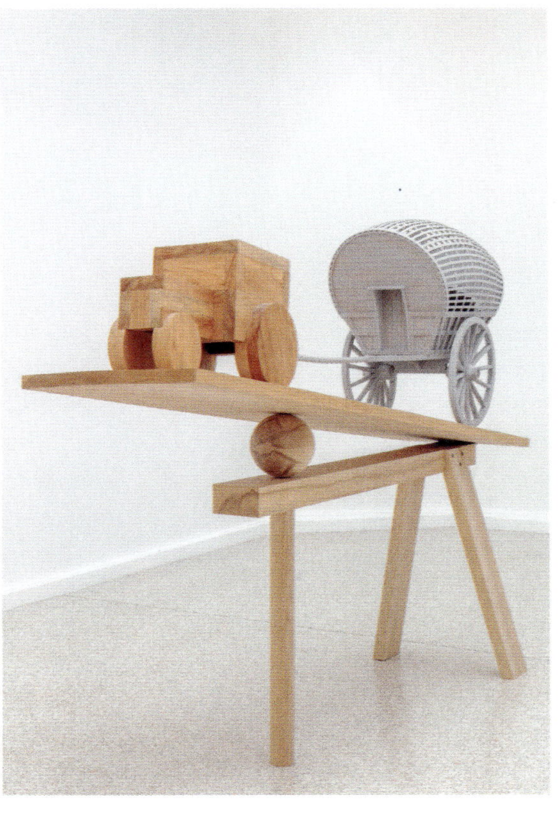

Figure 40. *New Voortrekker* (2018). Martin Puryear. Ash, American cypress, maple, pine, and mirror; 182 x 236.2 x 56 cm. Courtesy the artist and Matthew Marks Gallery. Photo: Joshua White

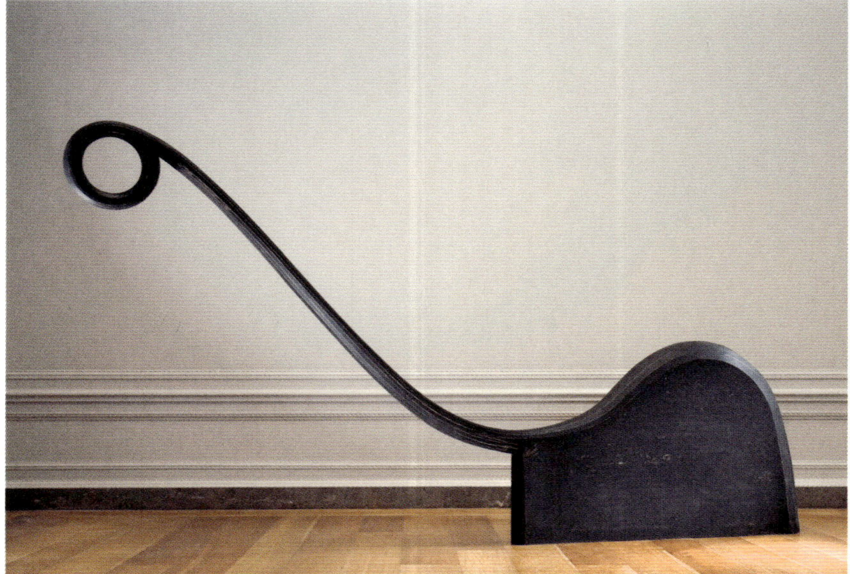

Figure 41. *Lever No. 3* (1989). Martin Puryear. Carved and painted wood; 214.6 x 411.5 x 33 cm. National Gallery of Art, Washington, Gift of the Collectors Committee, 1989.71.1

Creatures

"A zoo can be as stimulating as an art museum," Puryear once said.[29] It is no surprise, then, that birds are not the only animals to have found their way into his oeuvre. Indeed, when hints of representation arise in Puryear's abstract art, it is often to evoke animals. *Old Mole* (1985; see fig. 2) and *Cask Cascade* (1985; private collection), for example, depict, in different ways, a cylindrical core that resolves in a point resembling a mole's head. Soon after making these works, Puryear created *Lever No. 3* (1989; fig. 41), initiating an ongoing series that conjures, among other associations, a creature arching its long neck forward. In the following decades this form would return in *Untitled* (1997–2001; fig. 42) and *Untitled* (2000; private collection) and again a few years later in *Le Prix* (2005; Yale University Art Gallery).

Among Puryear's most striking animal evocations, which he has explored in sculpture, prints, and drawings since the early 2000s, is what can be seen as a crouching creature (figs. 43 and 44). This form is best known from the monumental public outdoor sculpture *Big Bling* (2016; see fig. 46). Commissioned by the Madison Square Park Conservancy in New York City, the soaring forty-foot work traveled to Philadelphia and then to North Adams, Massachusetts, where it now resides in the care of the Massachusetts Museum of Contemporary Art (MASS MoCA). Among *Big Bling*'s most prominent features is a gleaming gold-leafed shackle that hangs from the topmost point of the sculpture's core structure—where an animal's head would be if this were a representational work. This composition follows from a diminutive sculpture, measuring a little more than two feet tall, titled *Shackled* (2014; fig. 45). In both pieces, the integration of organic form and shackle conjure the violent history of restraining living things—a history that, as we shall see, the artist continues to excavate.

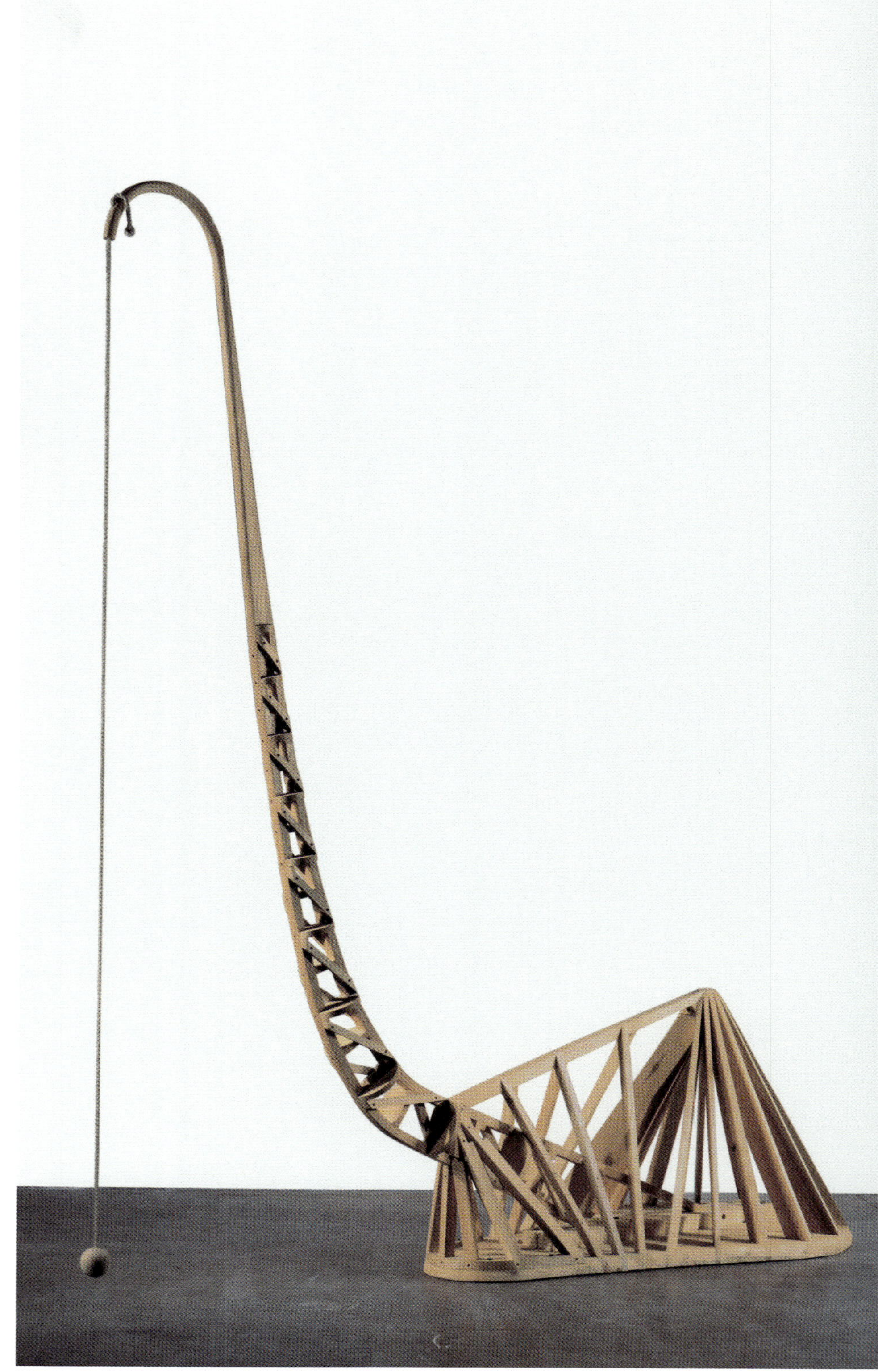

Figure 42. *Untitled* (1997–2001). Martin Puryear. Ash, pine, cypress, and rope; 364.5 x 111.8 x 335.3 cm. The Newark Museum of Art, Purchase 2006 Helen McMahon Brady Cutting Fund, 2006.52. Photo: Collection of the Newark Museum of Art / Art Resource, NY

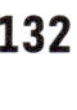

Figure 43. *Untitled* (2003). Martin Puryear. Charcoal and Conté crayon on tan wove paper; 127 x 116.8 cm. The Museum of Modern Art, New York, The Judith Rothschild Foundation Contemporary Drawings Collection Gift 2005, 2835.2005. Digital Image © The Museum of Modern Art / Licensed by SCALA / Art Resource, NY

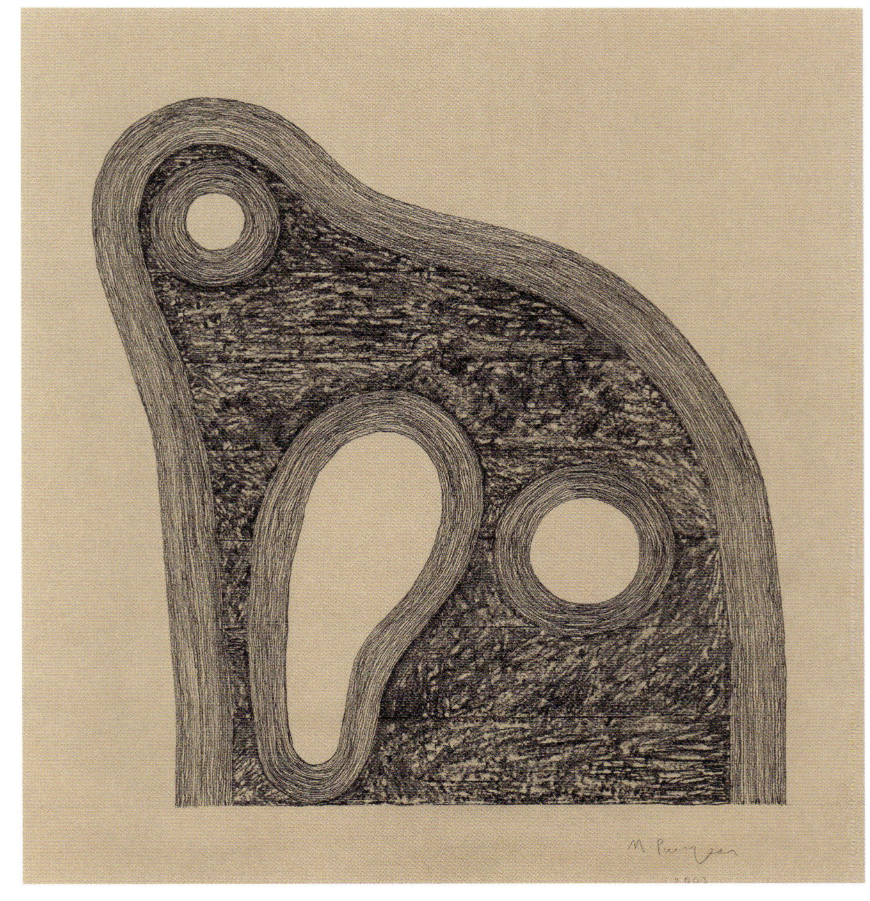

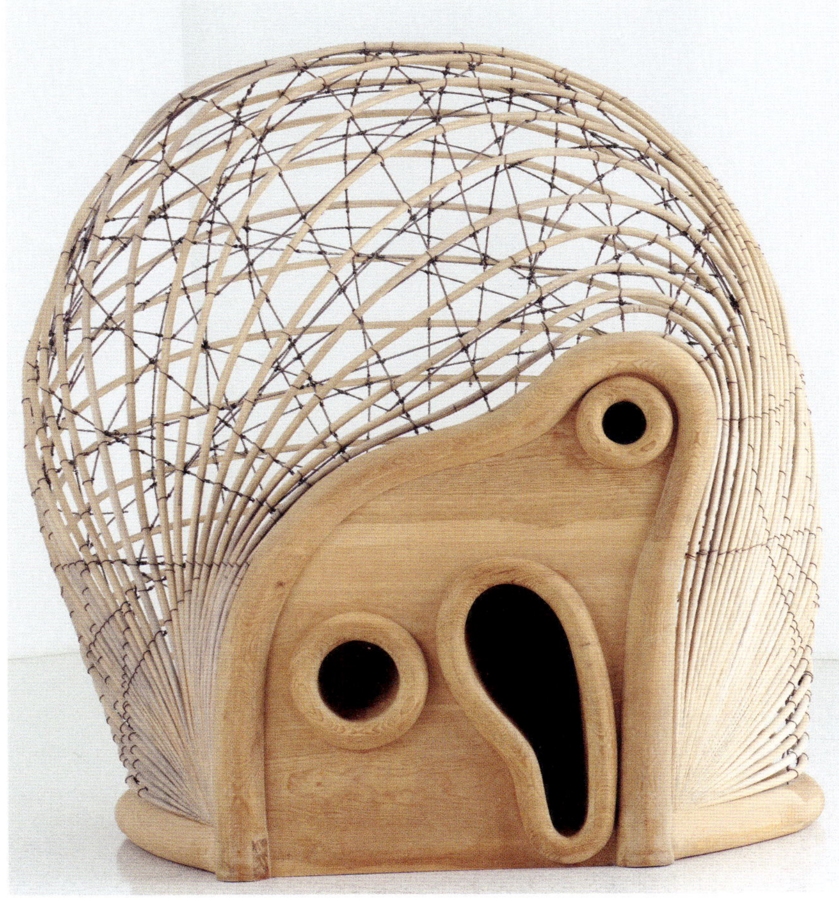

Figure 44. *Untitled* (2005). Martin Puryear. White pine, wire, and rattan; 160 x 152.4 x 137.2 cm. Walker Art Center, Gift of the Gabbert Family, John, Martha, Laura, and Anne, 2019, 2019.105. Courtesy Walker Art Center, Minneapolis

Figure 45. *Shackled* (2014). Martin Puryear. Iron; 70 x 78 x 21 cm. Private collection. Image courtesy of the artist and Matthew Marks Gallery. Photo: Ron Amstutz

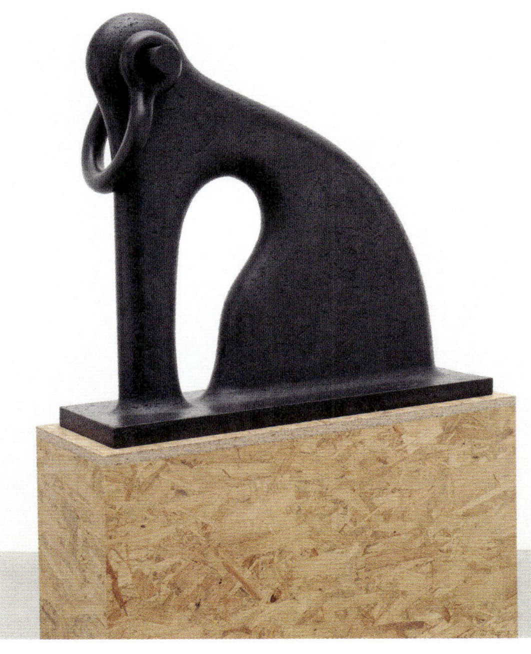

Figure 46. Installation view of *Big Bling* (2016), at Madison Square Park, New York. Martin Puryear. Pressure-treated laminated timbers, plywood, chain-link fencing, fiberglass, and gold leaf; 112.2 x 3 x 11.6 m. Photo: Yasunori Matsui. Courtesy Madison Square Park Conservancy

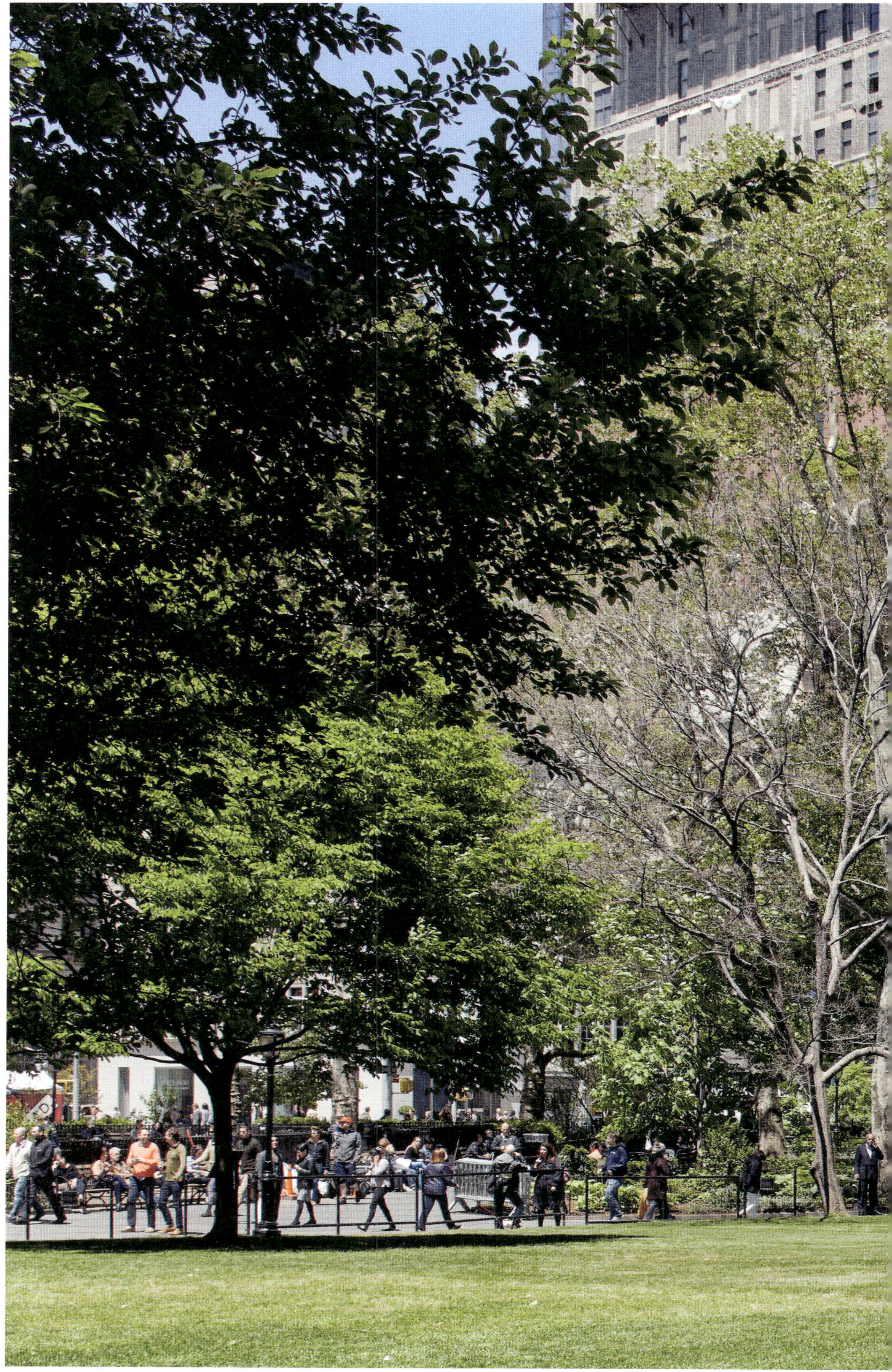

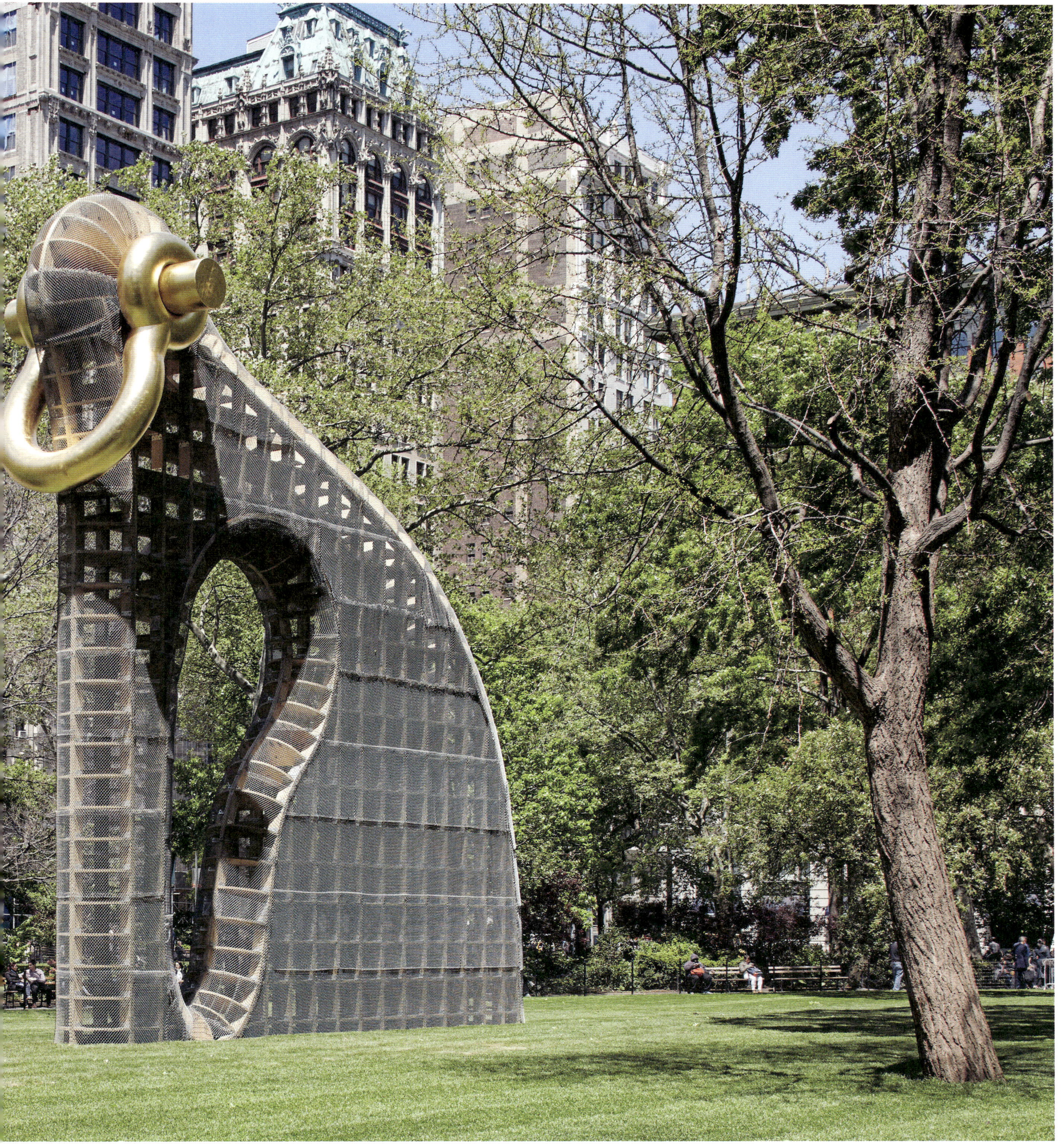

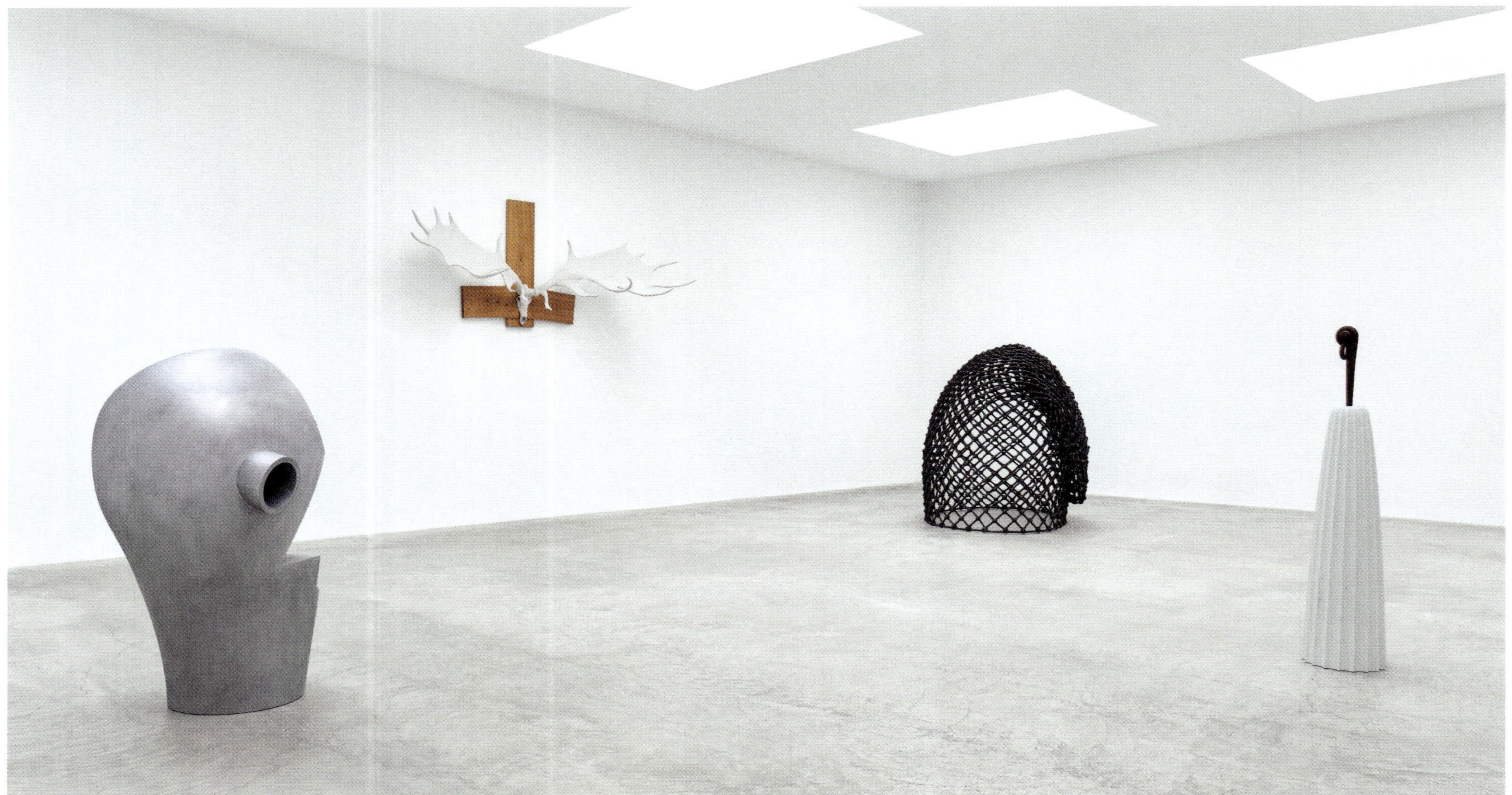

Figure 47. Installation view of *Martin Puryear*, Matthew Marks Gallery, Los Angeles, 2023. Pictured: *Looking Askance* (2023; [69]), *Hibernian Testosterone* (2018; [61]), *Aso Oke* (2019; [60]), *A Column for Sally Hemings* (2021; [62]). Photo: Lee Thompson

For its fidelity to its source of inspiration, *Hibernian Testosterone* (2018; [61]) stands out among Puryear's works that derive from the animal world. This colossal, wall-mounted sculpture reproduces in full scale the twelve-foot antlers of the Irish elk, an extinct species of deer common during the Ice Age. Scientists believe that the size of the Irish elk's antlers, which evolved to help the species survive combat and demonstrate sexual prowess, contributed to its extinction.[30] Eventually, the antlers, whose growth was propelled by testosterone, became too heavy for the animal to hold its head up and at times it also became tangled in trees. Puryear distills this parable-like history from the animal kingdom into a straightforward visual statement, for, just as the work's form and scale reflect a fact of nature, its surface, white-painted aluminum, is wholly unembellished. The antlers are suspended from an inverted cross, a form with a vast range of symbolic associations, from humility as in the biblical story of St. Peter, to rebellion or the occult in the popular imagination.

Hibernian Testosterone debuted at the 58th Venice Biennale, where Puryear represented the United States in 2019. Puryear has discussed his ambivalence in accepting this honor while Donald Trump was America's president.[31] Puryear's art is never overtly political, but in that setting the work's stark and monumental evocation of excessive aggression and perilous machismo invited reflection on our own moment in history—as did, more broadly, what we might interpret as a cautionary tale of a species that evolved to its own extinction.

A presentation of *Hibernian Testosterone* at the Matthew Marks Gallery in Los Angeles four years later amplified the work's social resonance (fig. 47). There, in a spare installation, it hung directly across from *A Column for Sally Hemings* (2021; fig. 48 and [62]). Hemings (1773–1835) was an African American woman enslaved at Thomas Jefferson's Virginia estate, Monticello. Famously, she and Jefferson had an ongoing relationship, and she was the mother of at least six of the former president's children.[32] One of Puryear's few indoor site-specific sculptures, the first edition of *A Column for Sally Hemings* was created for the American Pavilion at the 2019 Venice Biennale where it debuted with *Hibernian Testosterone*. Responding to the pavilion's architecture, which was modeled on Monticello, the work's fluted base echoes the Doric columns between which visitors passed to enter the exhibition space (fig. 49). The base of the sculpture's column tapers at the top, suggesting a body wearing a crisply

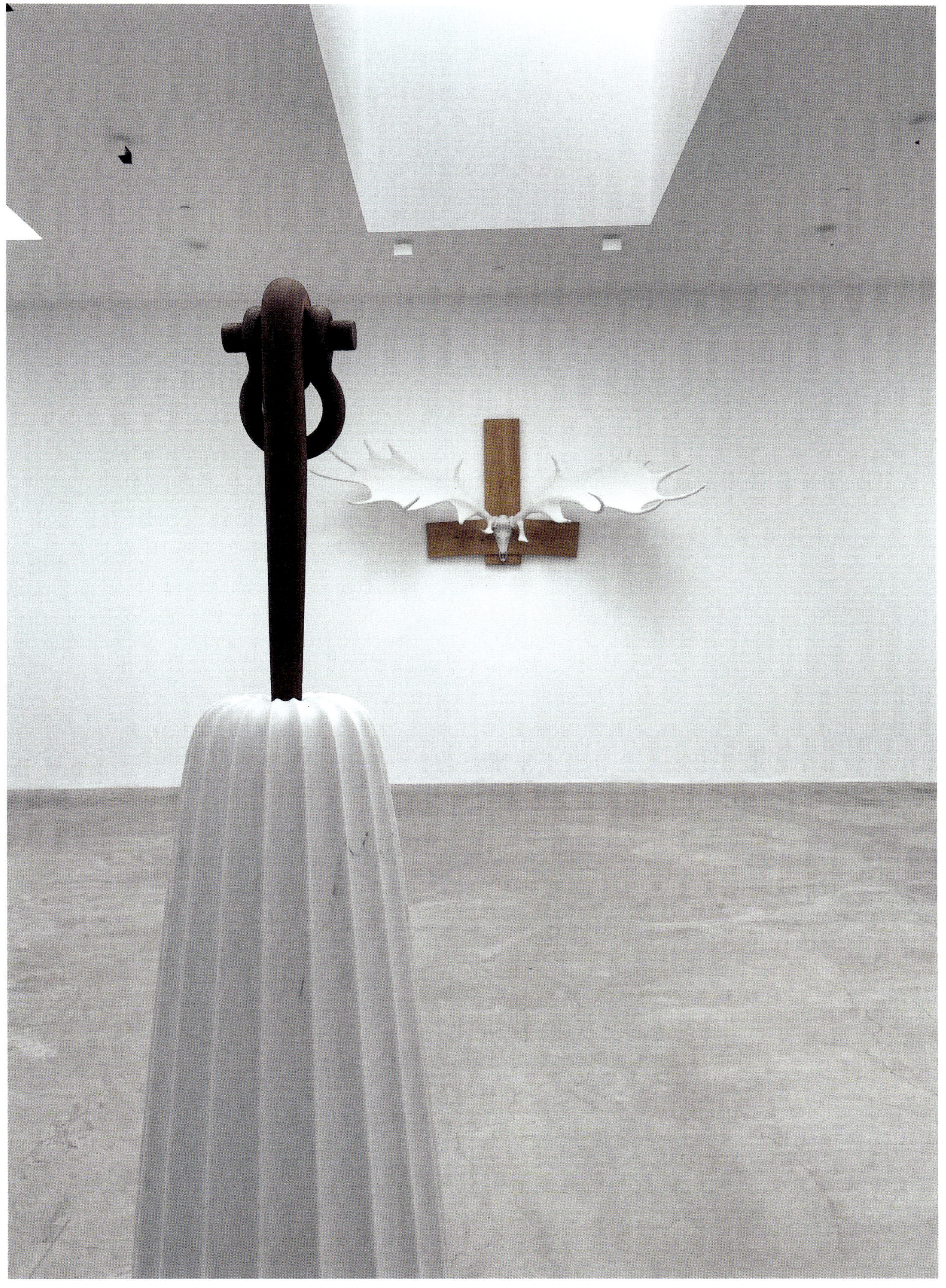

Figure 48. Installation view of *Martin Puryear*, Matthew Marks Gallery, Los Angeles, 2023. Pictured: *A Column for Sally Hemings* (2021; [62]) and *Hibernian Testosterone* (2018; [61]). Photo: Emily Liebert

Figure 49. Facade of American Pavilion at the Venice Biennale in Giardini, Venice. Photo: Eden Breitz / Alamy

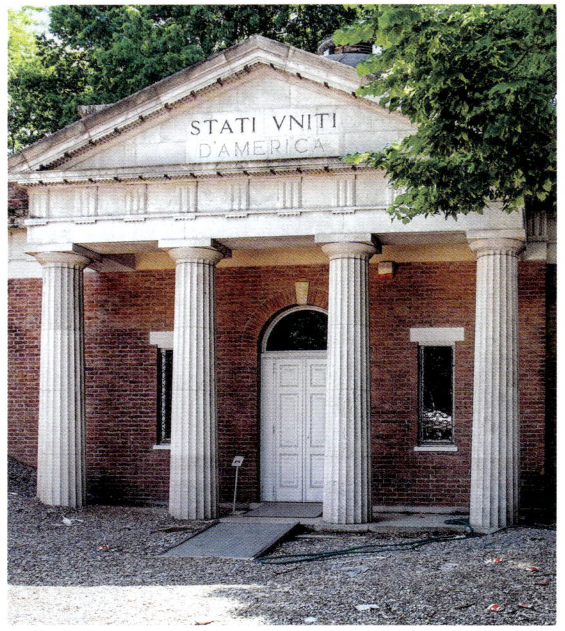

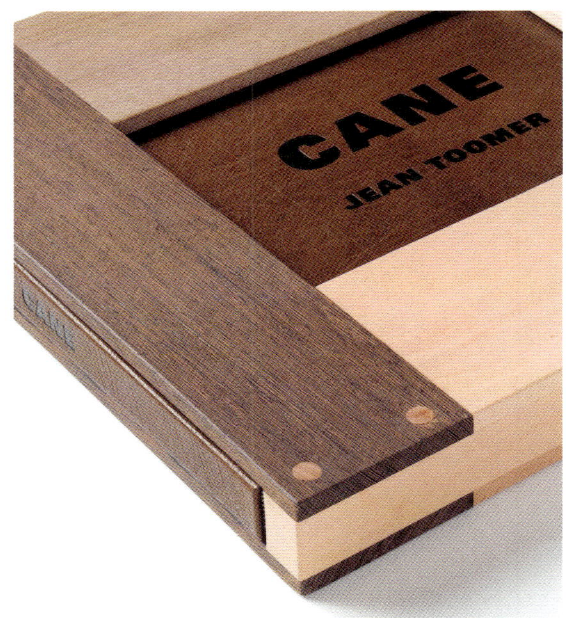

Figure 50. Detail of *Cane* (2000; [38]). Martin Puryear. Photo: Courtesy of Reynolda House Museum of American Art, Affiliated with Wake Forest University, Winston-Salem, North Carolina

pleated skirt. Thrust into this sleek form—initially made in white-painted poplar and later in white marble—is a cast-iron stake and, again, a shackle. Brooke Kamin Rapaport, the curator of *Big Bling* and Puryear's Biennale presentation, describes the impact of this point of contact between sculptural elements, observing that the shackled stake "destabilize[d] the pristine purity of the column's classic form."[33]

The juxtaposition—or face-off—between *Hibernian Testosterone* and *A Column for Sally Hemings* sets into relief the gendered and racial histories of physical aggression and vulnerability that the works summon. Insofar as the Irish elk's evolutionary narrative can serve as a metaphor for the iniquities of the human world, *Hibernian Testosterone* brings us full circle from Puryear's primal encounter with the gyrfalcon.

"No Less Real"

Like many artists, Puryear owns objects by other artists and artisans whom he admires. During a recent conversation, when I asked Puryear about his collections, his response surprised me: "My richest collection is between the bindings of books in my library." He elaborated, "The objects you see are a drop in the bucket. In books I have the things I can never own. It's conceptual more than material, but it's no less real."[34]

Of course, libraries do have a physical life, and with Puryear this is impossible to overlook given the vast quantity of books in his possession. Puryear has organized his copious volumes with a precision that harks back to his days as an employee of the Washington, DC, public libraries. It is important to the artist that he knows the location of every volume because he frequently pulls books from their shelves to look something up or to illustrate a point in conversation.

For Puryear, books are not only conceptual but also tactile objects to be held and handled, respected and savored. Like the birds, yurts, wheels, and wagons and carts that populate his art, books can transport readers out of their surroundings, enabling them to gain a wider perspective on the world. Puryear's most direct artistic engagement with a book took form in 2000, when Arion Press invited him to create illustrations for a new edition of the Harlem Renaissance writer Jean Toomer's (1894–1967) experimental novel *Cane*, from 1923 [38].[35] This highly influential work of literature is composed of a series of vignettes, each comprising what was at the time a radical blend of poetry and prose to narrate African American experience in the southern and northern United States during the Great Migration.[36] Puryear created seven woodcut portraits of some of Toomer's Black women characters [39–45]. The prints, which are abstract but feature hints of figuration, were bound into a deluxe limited edition.

As part of the *Cane* project, Arion Press published a second portfolio of prints, housed in a box that Puryear made by joining four kinds of wood: African wenge, American black walnut, sugar maple, and Swiss pear (fig. 50; [38]). Creating a color spectrum that ranges from beige to dark brown, the artist selected the different woods to represent different skin tones. Just as Puryear had located a metaphor for racial difference in a bird species all those years earlier, in his *Cane* case, wood species evoke a central aspect not only of the book's narrative but also of Toomer's own biography. A light-skinned African American man of mixed racial descent, Toomer was identified throughout his life as both Black and white, a fact that became central to his public persona and critical reception.[37]

Speaking of form and material, Puryear has noted his enduring fascination with the interplay between "transparency and solidity."[38] This interest is also manifested in his engagement with subject matter when specific histories are present yet subtle—expressed in harmony with the visual, physical, technical, and metaphorical languages of each work. Through that balance, Puryear upends conventional depictions of social experience, including racial difference, demonstrating the capacity of abstraction to help us see our world anew.

I am grateful to Rosalyn Deutsche, Key Jo Lee, and Bibiana Obler for their incisive comments on earlier versions of this essay.

1. Henry Wadsworth Longfellow, "The Skeleton in Armor," in *The Skeleton in Armor* (Boston: James R. Osgood & Co., 1877), 4.

2. Martin Puryear, conversation with the author, July 18, 2024.

3. Martin Puryear, conversation with the author, October 6, 2023.

4. As an adult, Puryear has collected many of the books that were most important to him as a child, and to this day he appreciates their stories and illustrations. Of particular interest to Puryear, then and now, are books by Francis Lee Jaques (1887–1969).

5. See Philip H. Love, "Just Between Ourselves . . . ," *Sunday Star* (Washington, DC), February 27, 1949.

6. Puryear, conversation with the author, July 18, 2024.

7. Puryear, conversation with the author, July 18, 2024. For an earlier reflection by Puryear on this connection, see Hugh M. Davies and Helaine Posner, "Conversations with Martin Puryear," in *Martin Puryear*, exh. cat. (Amherst: University Gallery, Fine Arts Center, University of Massachusetts, Amherst, 1984), 29–30.

8. See letter from Audubon's great-great-great-grandson Walter Audubon to *Sunday News Magazine*, July 26, 1977. David C. Driskell Papers, MS01.05.00, box 2, folder 4, The Driskell Center at the University of Maryland, College Park. I first learned of the Audubon family's response to this exhibition through Puryear's own recollections, and I thank Gabriella Shypula for locating a letter documenting that response.

9. Audubon's biography remains the subject of controversy, as seen in a recent movement to rename the National Audubon Society (NAS) because Audubon enslaved people and publicly espoused racist views of Black and Indigenous peoples. In March 2023, NAS announced their decision to retain their current name. Local chapters of the organization, however, have opted to change theirs. See "National Audubon Society Announces Decision to Retain Current Name," National Audubon Society, March 16, 2023, https://www.audubon.org/press-room/national-audubon-society-announces-decision-retain-current-name, and Jesus Jiménez, "Audubon Society Keeps Name Despite Slavery Ties, Dividing Birders," *New York Times*, March 15, 2023.

10. Puryear, conversation with the author, October 6, 2023.

11. Other materials that have played a significant role in Puryear's sculpture include aluminum, brick, bronze, iron, marble, rattan, rawhide, tar, and wire mesh.

12. Michael Brenson, "Maverick Sculptor Makes Good," *New York Times*, November 1, 1987. See also Paul Richard's account of *Cedar Lodge* (1977) in "A Shrine of Cedar and Hide," *Washington Post*, July 30, 1977. Richard is particularly attuned to the sensory aspects of Puryear's organic materials, noting, for example, that because of the fresh cedar from which the work was made, it "smells like sharpened pencils."

13. This aspect of Puryear's work prompts consideration of the artist's place in a modernist sculptural lineage. The art historian Anne Wagner notes that Puryear's "animate abstraction" connects his work with that of Jean (Hans) Arp (1886–1966) and Constantin Brâncuși (1876–1957), both influential on Puryear, as well as a history of vitalism that regards sculpture as alive. See Anne Wagner, "The Self in Sculpture," in Brooke Kamin Rapaport et al., *Martin Puryear: Liberty / Libertà*, exh. cat. (New York: Madison Square Park Conservancy and Gregory R. Miller; Berlin: Hatje Cantz, 2019), 88. Puryear himself has noted the resonance of his work with that of Barbara Hepworth (1903–1975) and Henry Moore (1898–1986), both of whom characterized their own art in vitalist terms. See Richard J. Powell, "A Conversation with Martin Puryear," in *Martin Puryear*, ed. John Elderfield, exh. cat. (New York: Museum of Modern Art, 2007), 108.

14. Brenson, "Maverick Sculptor Makes Good." Puryear's dynamic conception of materials also foregrounds the temporal aspect of his practice, placing him in a modernist sculptural tradition famously articulated by Rosalind Krauss. "Sculpture," wrote Krauss in 1977, just as Puryear's work was maturing, "is a medium peculiarly located at the juncture between stillness and motion, time arrested and time passing." Rosalind Krauss, *Passages in Modern Sculpture* (New York: Viking, 1977), 5. The trajectory that Krauss outlines begins with Arp, Brâncuși, and David Smith (1906–1965) and ends with Puryear's Post-Minimalist peers, including Richard Serra (1938–2024) and Robert Smithson (1938–1973). Puryear, however, is absent from her highly influential account.

Puryear's indebtedness to the global traditions of handmade artisanal crafts and functional objects—alongside the sculptures of Arp, Brâncuși, and Smith—sets his work apart from that of leading Post-Minimalist artists. The entrance of craft histories into mainstream art history has played an important role in introducing previously marginalized figures into the dominant accounts of modernist sculpture. See Lynne Cooke, *Woven Histories: Textiles and Modern Abstraction* (Chicago: University of Chicago Press, 2023).

15. Puryear, conversation with the author, February 20, 2024. In 1980, soon after making sculptures out of rawhide, Puryear spoke in depth of his fascination with the material in a lecture at the Skowhegan School of Painting and Sculpture, Maine. See Martin Puryear, 1980, Skowhegan School of Painting and Sculpture Lecture Archive, The Museum of Modern Art Archives, New York. Puryear also reflects on his use of the material in Powell, "A Conversation with Puryear," 104–5.

16. Rawhide was also a primary material in *Cedar Lodge* (1977 see figs. 99a, b) and *Rawhide Cone* (1980; [18]).

17. Puryear, conversation with the author, July 18, 2024.

18. These works, together with *Rawhide Cone* [18], comprised the installation *Equation for Jim Beckwourth*, which debuted at the Museum of Contemporary Art Chicago in 1980.

19. See James Beckwourth and T. D. Bonner, *The Life and Adventures of James P. Beckwourth: Mountaineer, Scout and Pioneer, and Chief of the Crow Nation of Indians* (London: T. Fisher Unwin, 1902). It is widely held that this account is a mix of fact and fiction. See, for example, Judith Madera, *Black Atlas: Geography and Flow in Nineteenth-Century African American Literature* (Durham, NC: Duke University Press, 2015), 75–76. I thank Gabriella Shypula for pointing me toward these references.

20. Holland Cotter, "Martin Puryear, Citizen-Sculptor," *New York Times*, May 3, 2019.

21. Puryear reached the class of General falconer and then decided not to continue this pursuit to the next and highest level of Master falconer. Puryear, conversation with the author, February 19, 2025.

22. On a 2024 visit, Puryear asked if I had time to look at a book on the gyrfalcon. When I said I did he disappeared into his library, returning not with one book but a stack of ten. A foundational text for Puryear on the gyrfalcon, and in particular its cultural history, is Gyorgy P. Dementiev's *The Gyrfalcon*, published in Russian in 1951 and later translated into German and English. Puryear owns copies of this text in both the original Russian and its English translation. Another key text for Puryear is Ronald Stevens, *The Taming of Ghengis* (London: Faber & Faber, 1956).

23. Puryear, conversation with the author, July 18, 2024. Puryear's interest in natural manifestations of black and white at the time he made *On the Tundra* is evident in another work made just two years earlier, *Night and Day* (1984; [25]). This wall sculpture's semicircular arch is divided into two halves, one black and one white. Alongside *On the Tundra*, *Night and Day*'s sweeping form might even be interpreted as a bird's line of flight.

24. The other exhibitions that brought together Puryear's bird effigies are: *Martin Puryear* (and/or gallery, Seattle, May 21–June 13, 1981); *Public and Personal* (Chicago Public Library Cultural Center, February 7–April 4, 1987); Documenta IX (Palais Bellevue, Kassel, Germany, June 13–September 20, 1992); and *Martin Puryear* (Museum Voorlinden, Wassenaar, The Netherlands, January 20–May 27, 2018).

25. Puryear's interest in trade is at the heart of his iconic work *C.F.A.O.* (2006–7; [50]). The initials in the sculpture's title refer to the Compagnie Française de L'Afrique Occidentale, a nineteenth-century trading company that sailed between Marseille and West Africa with ports in Sierra Leone that Puryear knew from his time in the Peace Corps. These points of cultural contact and exchange are reflected in the work's materials and imagery. A wheelbarrow Puryear found in 1993, when he was an artist in residence at Alexander Calder's (1898–1976) studio in Saché, France, supports an oversize construction of a mask in the style of the Fang people of Gabon, West Africa.

26. Puryear, conversation with the author, November 27, 2024.

27. This is the same exhibition history listed in endnote 24.

28. For an incisive account of the imagery in these works, see Brooke Kamin Rapaport, "Martin Puryear: Liberty / Libertà," in Rapaport et al., *Martin Puryear: Liberty / Libertà*, 44–47.

29. Puryear quoted in Nancy Princenthal, "Intuition's Disciplinarian," *Art in America* 78, no. 1 (January 1990): 134.

30. See Silvia Gonzalez, Andrew C. Kitchener, and Adrian M. Lister, "Survival of the Irish Elk into the Holocene," *Nature* 405 (2000): 753–54; Carl Zimmer, "The Allure of Big Antlers," The Loom (blog), *National Geographic*, September 2, 2008, https://www.nationalgeographic.com/science/article/the-allure-of-big-antlers; and Richard Grant, "Not a Huge Advantage," *Smithsonian Magazine* 52, no. 3 (June 2021): 20–22.

31. Puryear, conversation with the author, June 14, 2024.

32. Puryear first learned about Sally Hemings through the artist Barbara Chase-Riboud's (b. 1939) novel *Sally Hemings* (Chicago: Chicago Review, 1979). For a biographical account of Hemings, see Annette Gordon-Reed, *The Hemingses of Monticello: An American Family* (New York: W. W. Norton, 2009).

33. Rapaport, "Martin Puryear: Liberty / Libertà," 42.

34. Puryear, conversation with the author, May 20, 2024.

35. See also Thelma Golden in this volume, 82.

36. For a thorough account of *Cane*, including its reception history and legacy, as well as biographical background on Jean Toomer, see Jean Toomer, *Cane*, ed. Rudolph P. Byrd and Henry Louis Gates Jr. (1923; New York: W. W. Norton, 2011).

37. See Rudolph P. Byrd and Henry Louis Gates Jr. "'Song of the Son': The Emergence and Passing of Jean Toomer," and "Jean Toomer's Racial Self-Identification: A Note on the Supporting Materials," in Toomer, *Cane*, xix–lxvi; lxvi–lxx. See also Richard Eldridge and Cynthia Earl Karman, *Jean Toomer: A Hunger for Wholeness* (Baton Rouge: Louisiana State University Press, 1987).

38. Puryear, conversation with the author, July 18, 2024.

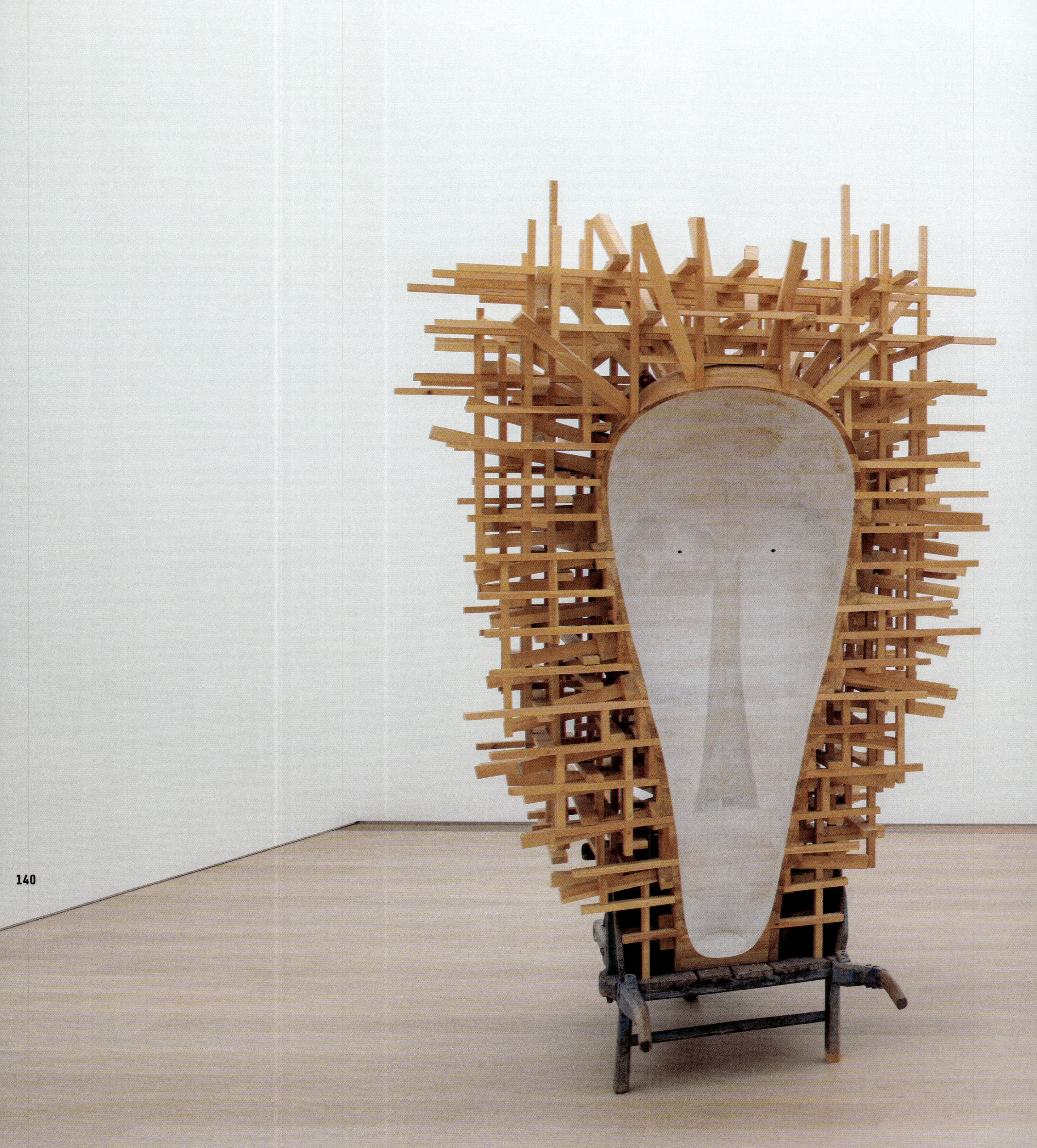

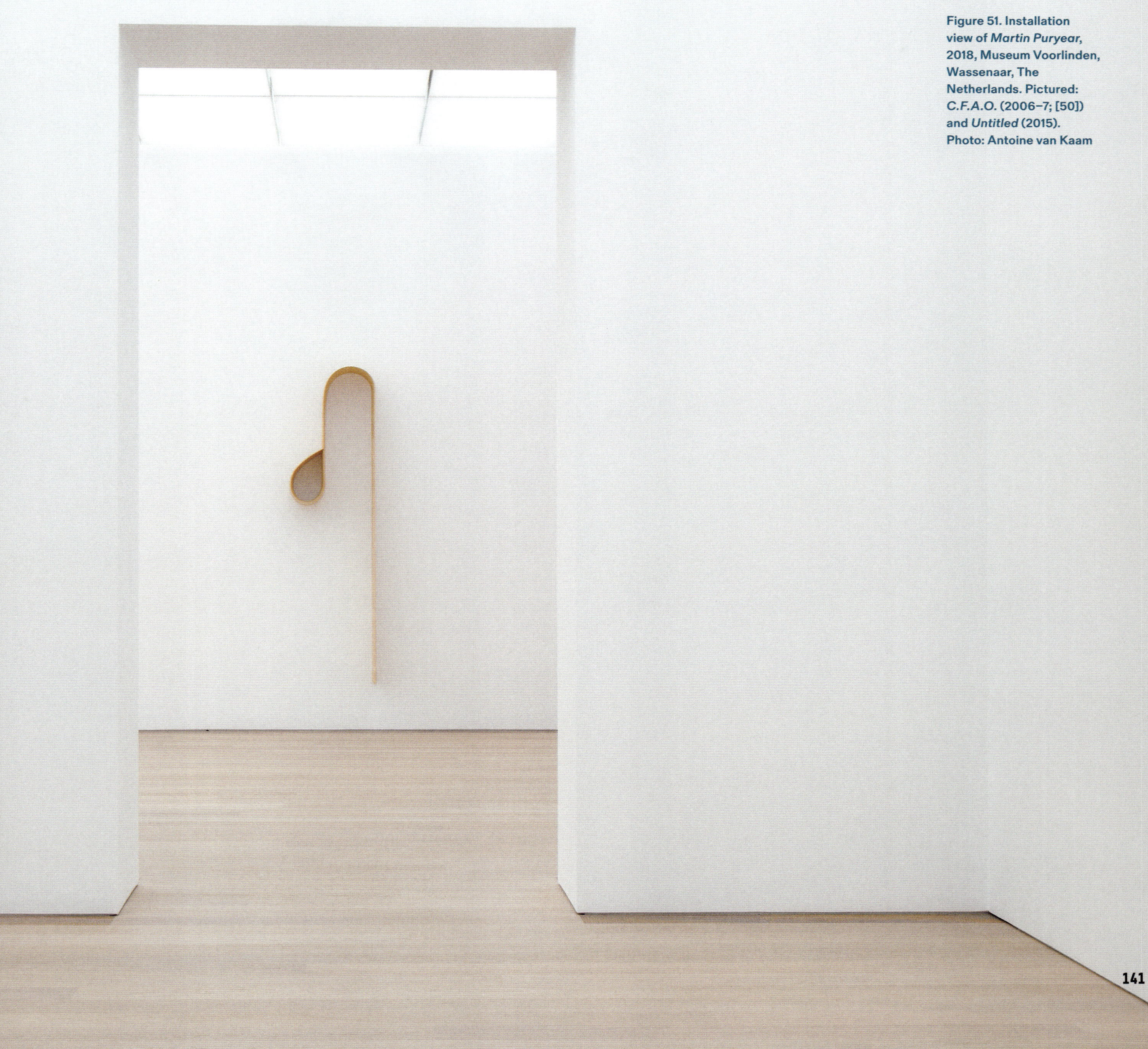

Figure 51. Installation view of *Martin Puryear*, 2018, Museum Voorlinden, Wassenaar, The Netherlands. Pictured: *C.F.A.O.* (2006–7; [50]) and *Untitled* (2015). Photo: Antoine van Kaam

Martin Puryear and Africa

Ugochukwu-Smooth Nzewi

> I came from a generation where the work was itself the information, and so there remains this belief that the work itself can have an identity that can hopefully speak.[1]
>
> —Martin Puryear

For many artists, art is a solitary endeavor. This holds true for Martin Puryear, whose creative process is slow and deliberate. His practice remakes ideas into form and, in many ways, reflects his psychological attributes. He dances in and out of categories, understanding the rules of the canon yet thwarting any preconceived notions. The art historian Elizabeth Reede reminds us that by weaving in and out of oppositions and dualities, perhaps in an effort to challenge his viewers to be open-minded and seek out the logic of the work from within the work itself, Puryear stymies any attempt to approach his art by means of familiar formalist tools of analysis.[2] Though fully cognizant of the twentieth-century history of modern sculpture, Puryear creates work that articulates its own terms of engagement. This stems from his global travels, curiosity, intellectual pursuits, and avid reading, all of which have yielded various cultural references outside the Western canon. Africa is a crucial context for him, as I explore in this text.[3]

Puryear set off for West Africa as a Peace Corps volunteer in 1964—a time of great optimism and sweeping political and social change on the continent, characterized by anticolonial struggles and the emergence of newly independent states. Drawn to the nascent reality of freedom in Africa and its exciting potential, many African American artists, such as Jacob Lawrence (1917–2000), John Biggers (1924–2001), Melvin Edwards (b. 1937), and Barbara Chase-Riboud (b. 1939), also visited West Africa around this time.

Living in Sierra Leone from 1964 to 1966 and traveling through West Africa during this heady period, Puryear experienced the world opening up to him in ways not previously possible or imagined in America.[4] As he later realized, connecting with Africa was very important in enabling him to address the unhealed wound and stigma of being a Black American whose African heritage has been severed and cannot be traced to a particular root or source in Africa due to the Middle Passage. For Puryear, going to West Africa was part of a difficult but necessary homecoming.[5]

The experience also instilled in Puryear a sense of possibility that abstraction could provide freedom by other means. Abstraction arguably enables creative latitude that representational art does not typically offer because of certain assumptions of visual legibility, which may suggest directed meaning or a singular lens of interpretation. In addition, abstraction affords multiple entry points in confronting and interpreting reality, something very familiar to African artists, who in the past and present, have always drawn inspiration from their natural environment, using it as a repository of ideas and materials that they distill to vital notations or essences. A hallmark of the African aesthetic system is the notion that materials hold memory and information, whereby we find meaning between the tangible and the abstract. This knowledge grounds Puryear's artistic pursuits, especially his desire to create abstract art underpinned by narratives sourced from reality, in which formal questions hold deeper humanistic meaning. Speaking about his African sojourn, the artist explained, "It was during my time in Africa that my work actually began to open up. It never became abstract purely, but it began to show some openness to breaking up form and seeing form for their own sake."[6]

The Grammar of Form

The seed of Puryear's use of reductive forms and elemental approach to object-making, with its marrying of art and craft, was planted during his time in

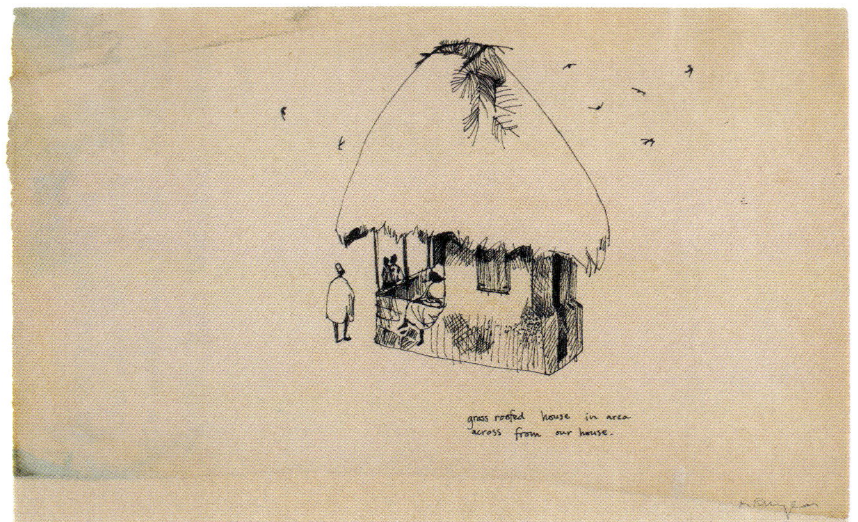

Figure 52. *Untitled* (1964/1966). Martin Puryear. Pen and black ink on tan wove paper; 21.3 x 34 cm. Collection of the artist. Photo: The Art Institute of Chicago

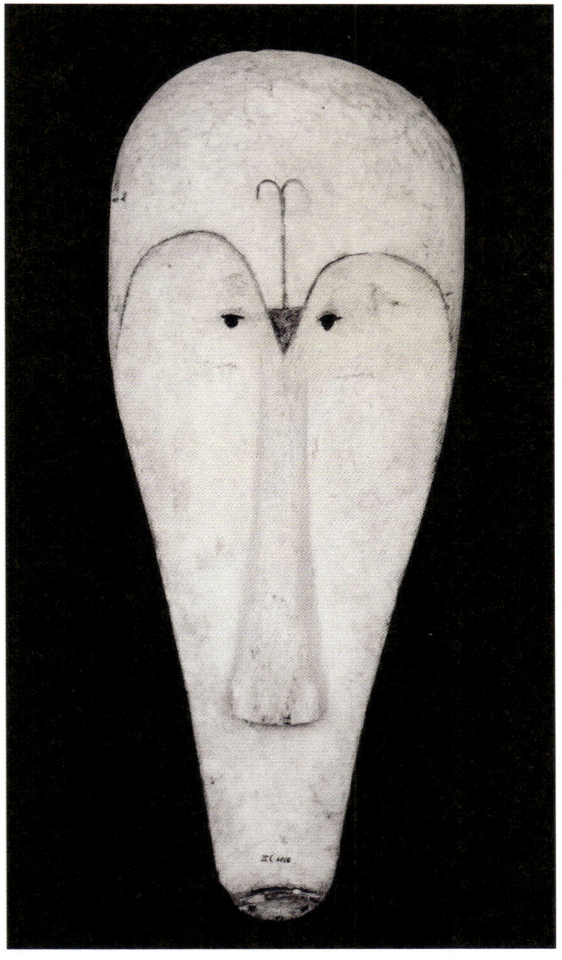

Figure 53. Mask, 19th century. Fang peoples (Gabon or Cameroon). Wood and lime (or chalk); 78 cm (height). Ethnologisches Museum, Staatliche Museen du zu Berlin. Photograph by Walker Evans, 1935. Victoria and Albert Museum, London. © Walker Evans Archive, The Metropolitan Museum of Art

the Segbwema village, in the eastern province of Sierra Leone, where he taught biology, French, and English; ran an art club; and managed a library in the local secondary school—and, in turn, learned from local wood-carvers, carpenters, potters, and weavers (fig. 52). His sculpture *C.F.A.O.* (2006–7 [50]; fig. 51) harkens back to this seminal period. It comprises a dense scaffolding constructed from an interlocking thicket of milled wood cut to different sizes and arranged on an old wheelbarrow. Approached from the side, the thicket looks like a carefully arranged jigsaw atop the wheelbarrow. The scaffold nestles the reverse side of a sculptural representation of a large Fang *ngil* mask, a ritual object representing an ancestral spirit. The white mask is distinguished by its intense geometric form, featuring a large, rounded forehead, a tapering face, slit eyes, and a line-nose (fig. 53). Gracefully embedded, the *ngil* mask gives the appearance of an architectural recess. Its elegance pushes softly against the density of the scaffold, and its whiteness provides a jarring contrast to the soft brown of the scaffolding.

Made around the same time as *C.F.A.O.*, *Malediction* (2006–7; [51]) also borrows its reductive form from the Fang *ngil* mask. But in contrast to *C.F.A.O.*, Puryear focuses solely on the objectness of the mask form, turning it inside out and using the mask's interior. He created it by bending flat cedarwood strips to suggest essential aspects of the original mask form. Wood is a material of choice for Puryear because of its simplicity and malleability; the artist bends it at will. Although elongated like the original *ngil*, *Malediction*'s form tapers at the bottom to combine with a piece of jutting wood. This intervention transforms the original mask, demonstrating the artist's visual elocution and attention to detail.

Puryear is drawn to African sculpture for its form as well as its intrinsic visual integrity.[7] His exploration of canonical African art, as with the recognizable Fang mask in *C.F.A.O.* and *Malediction*, stems from what he describes as African art's innate integrity—a genuineness that may not be physically accessible on the surface.[8] He also considers this integrity to be what binds African sculpture to its source culture. Puryear is thus interested in how form and purpose intersect in African art.[9] Artworks are visual texts through which these societies inscribe themselves into history, manifest their humanity, and communicate that humanity to their neighbors and the world. African art embodies its communities' worldviews, philosophy, ethics, norms, idiosyncrasies, and sense of being. It also serves as a conduit for the reenactment of aspects of communal life, from performing rituals in which communal bonds are renewed to affirming relationships with ancestors, along with playing a vital role in secular events, social pacts, and in the general well-being of their source communities.[10] The *ngil* mask, for example, worn by the Ngil secret male society, was used to administer justice and to police and protect the community before the secret society was outlawed by French colonial authorities in the 1920s. Referring to the act of placing a curse, the title *Malediction*—an interesting choice for Puryear—could be understood as an attempt by the artist to root the work in the function of its African referent. Here, meaning grounds form, and its form is anchored in a referent—a coda that he embraces.

What also stayed with Puryear from his time in Africa was how rich life was with little or no means or technological resources, and how vital the making of utilitarian objects was to the ecosystem. People were highly skilled at making things from natural and humble materials. For example, it was in Sierra Leone

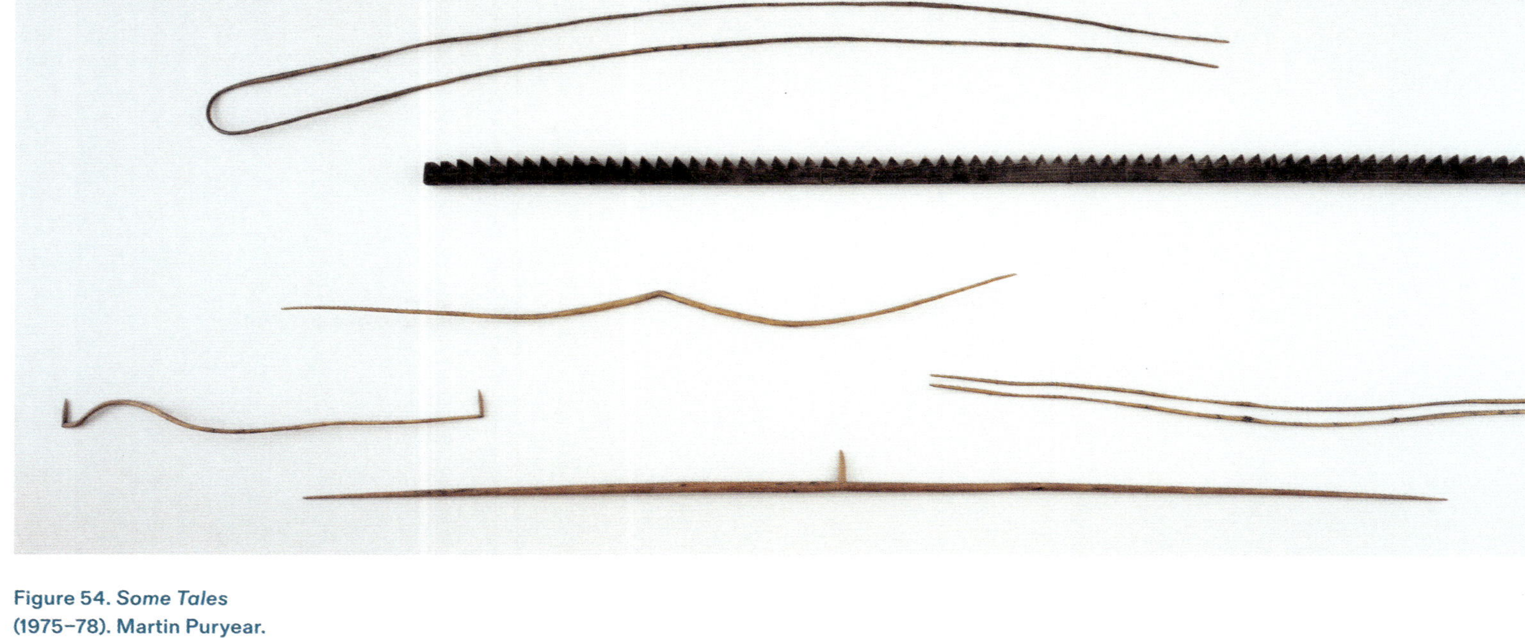

Figure 54. ***Some Tales*** **(1975–78). Martin Puryear. Yellow pine, ash, and hickory (6 parts); dimensions variable, approx. 400.5 x 1,000 x 13 cm. Panza Collection. Photo: Giorgio Colombo, Milan**

that Puryear learned the basic techniques of joinery that would become integral to his work. He got to know the local carpenter, James Garner, who made the shelves, chairs, and tables for the classrooms in which Puryear taught. As a show of appreciation for all he learned through observation in Garner's shop, Puryear helped Garner make a guitar with locally available materials and parts that he ordered from England.[11]

For a long time, Puryear's work consisted of, in his words, wood "wedged together, balanced, or stacked and held by gravity and friction without recourse to glue or sophisticated joinery."[12] Take, for example, *Some Tales* (1975–78; fig. 54), composed of six wooden pieces of varying shapes, lengths, and sizes, ranging from one that looks like hacksaw teeth to others that evoke simple marks or gestures, all hanging horizontally on the wall. Or *Alien Huddle* (1993–95; [30]), a volumetric construction consisting of three interlocking spheres. Or *Brunhilde* (1998–2000; see fig. 3), featuring open latticework that evokes a woven basket, created from thin strips of laminated cedarwood joined together with glue and staples.

During his time in West Africa, Puryear was especially struck by handwoven textiles, which have remained one of his long-standing interests and in which he found an Indigenous functional art form that served multiple purposes in the sacral and secular lives of the people (fig. 55).[13] He absorbed the meticulous, protracted, and incremental nature of textile weaving. *Aso Oke* (2019; [60])—a monumental bronze sculpture first exhibited in *Martin Puryear: Liberty / Libertà*, the artist's solo presentation in the United States Pavilion at the Venice Biennale in 2019—is an exercise in form and perception that takes its title from a prestigious handwoven fabric of the Yoruba people of Nigeria. The fabric is created using two main weaving techniques: carryover (*njawu*) and openwork (*eleya*), which together manipulate the warp and weft threads. Puryear repurposes the openwork technique in *Aso Oke*.

The sculpture borrows its form from the *fila gobi*, the ceremonial cap worn by Yoruba men that reflects sartorial comportment and display. When tilted to the left, as it does here, the cap's flap represents how a married man wears it (fig. 56). In this formal borrowing, *Aso Oke* also assumes a philosophical undertone. Yoruba art emphasizes the head (*orí*). For the Yoruba, the head is a bifurcated ensemble that best represents the intertwining of spirit and matter, mind and body. The inner head (*orí inú*) is the site of consciousness and as such gives force to the human being. The outer or corporeal head (*orí òde*) is the physical manifestation of consciousness and, therefore, a vehicle of perception, identity, and interaction with reality. It is this essence—the intersection of the inner and outer heads mirrored in the interweaving of *njawu* and *eleya* techniques—that Puryear channels in *Aso Oke*'s open latticework, achieving an eloquence of form and a balance of material and space. *Aso Oke*—and, by extension, *C.F.A.O.* and *Malediction*—suggest African referents while invoking deeper social history as well as metaphysical concepts.

C.F.A.O. constitutes an attempt by the artist to convey a sense of his time in Sierra Leone while alluding more broadly to the colonial experience in Africa. The title refers to the Compagnie Française de L'Afrique Occidentale (often abbreviated to C.F.A.O.), a conglomerate founded by the French industrialist and mogul Charles-Auguste Verminck in 1845, which started out as a trading

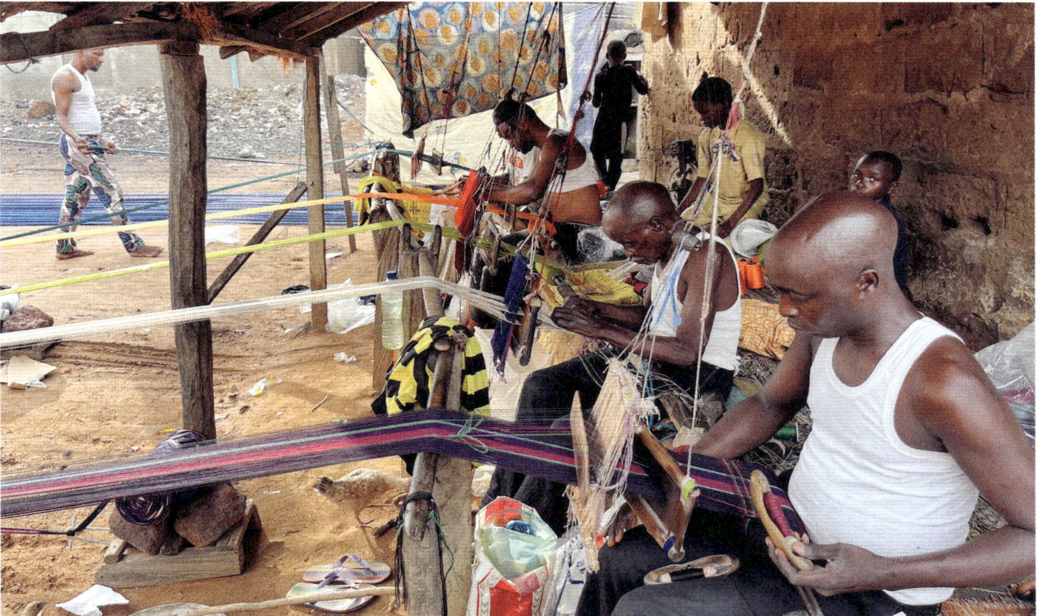

Figure 55. Weaving workshop, Ilorin, Kwara State, Nigeria, October 2022. Photo: Courtesy of Tony Agbapuonwu

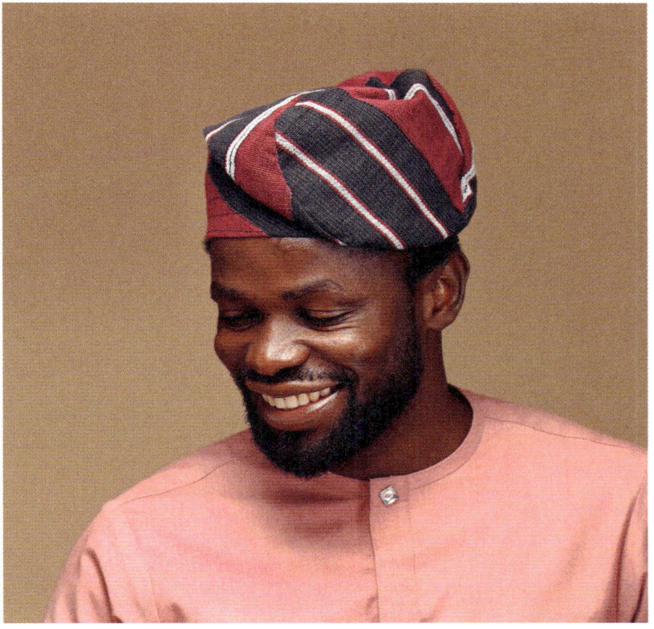

Figure 56. Nigerian artist Andrew Esiebo wearing a *Fila gobi* ceremonial cap. Photo: The Yudel Media/ iStock

post in Senegal and later expanded across West Africa amid the European colonial scramble for Africa. C.F.A.O. had a warehouse in the village of Segbwema. For Puryear, the rusting warehouse—which locals called "French company"—helped him understand the dynamics of colonialism, which is not only about extracting cheap raw materials but also about creating markets for finished goods.[14] The worn-down, ready-made wheelbarrow in *C.F.A.O.*—which Puryear found in Saché, France, in 1993 while doing an artist residency at the Atelier Calder (see fig. 68)—acts as a trope of colonial labor and extraction. This, combined with the Fang mask, signifies colonial expropriation and the dispersal of African art, which became a global commodity at the turn of the twentieth century.

C.F.A.O.'s examination of Africa's colonial history aligns with Puryear's ongoing address of bleak chapters of global history as they have impacted the Black experience. So, too, *Shackled* (2014; fig. 57), a blackened iron measuring roughly two feet high, set on a wood plinth. At the top is a metal hoop, suggestive of the cuffs once used to restrain enslaved persons onboard slave vessels. The hoop drops down the vertical side of the sculpture. The other side slides into a smooth curve. In profile, the sculpture forms a stooped figure, reminiscent of prints of kneeling slaves in chains or breaking loose of the chains. Seemingly cold and removed, *Shackled* is a searing commentary on the history of slavery, a recurring motif in Puryear's work.

A Column for Sally Hemings (2021; [62]) continues along similar lines. It is a mixed-media sculpture consisting of a rusty-looking hoop, like the one in *Shackled*, and is also fashioned from cast iron. It sits atop a fluted plinth (first constructed in white-painted wood, and later in marble; fig. 58). As the title

Figure 57. Detail of *Shackled* (2014). Martin Puryear. Iron; 70 x 78 x 21 cm. Private collection. Photo: Ron Amstutz

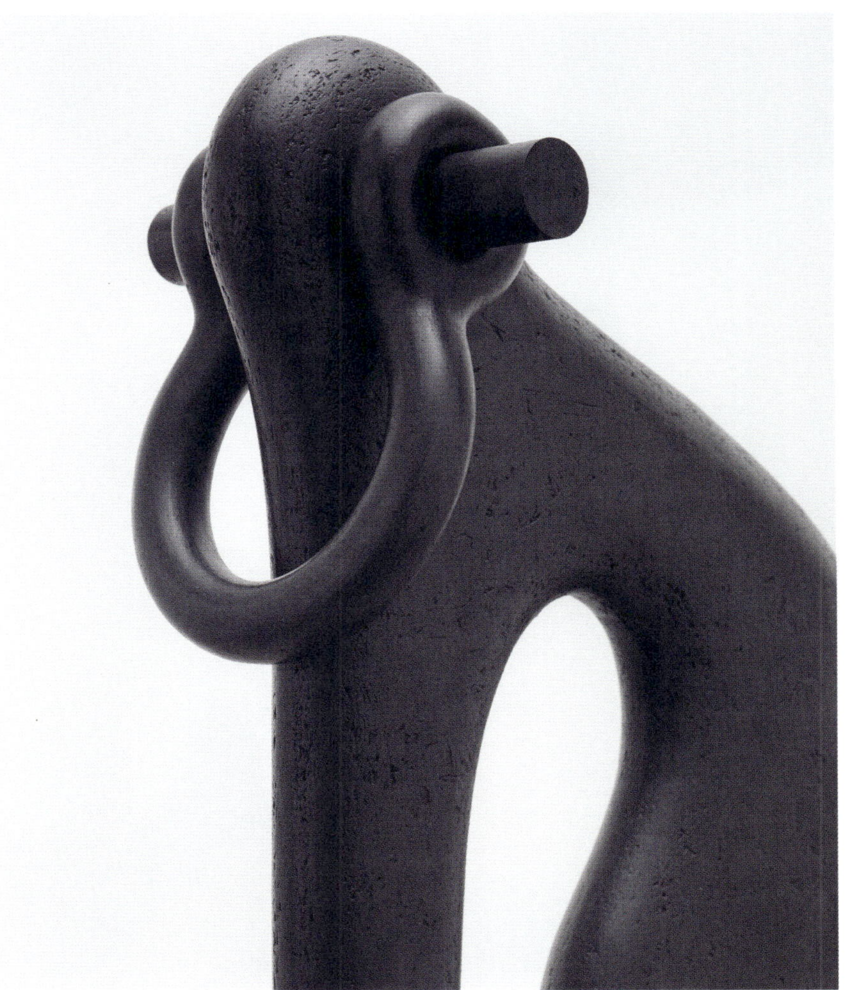

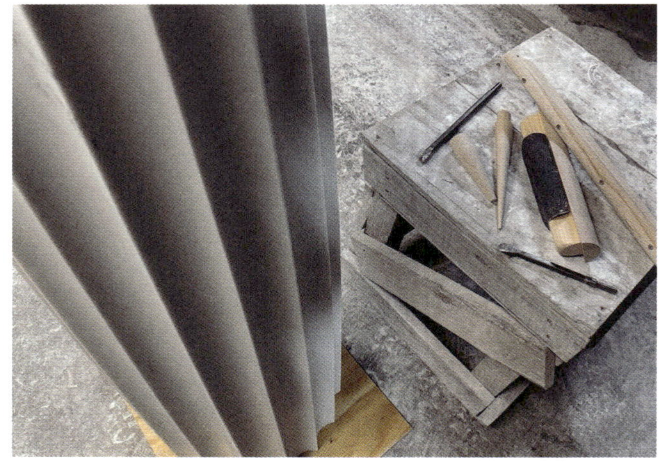

Figure 58. *A Column for Sally Hemings* (2021) in process at Quarra Stone Company workshop, Madison, Wisconsin. Photo: Quarra Stone

Figure 59. Monticello, Thomas Jefferson's home, Charlottesville, Virginia, c. 1980–2006. Photo: Carol M. Highsmith Archive, Library of Congress Prints and Photographs Division, Washington, DC

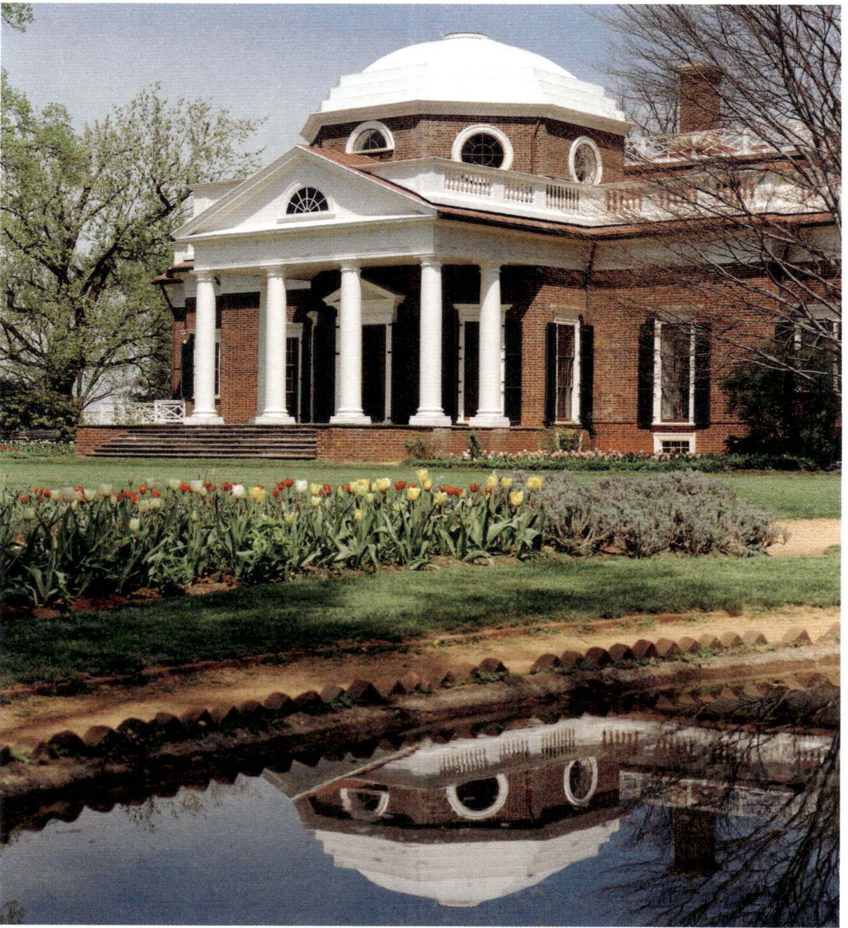

suggests, the work refers to Sally Hemings (1773–1835), the Black woman enslaved to President Thomas Jefferson with whom she bore at least six children.[15] The sleek marble base of the sculpture nods to the Doric columns of Monticello, President Jefferson's residence (fig. 59).[16] Stoic in its aura, presence, and repose, the sculpture evokes an altar as if offering supplication to a higher power. Puryear treats the work's subject with care and reverence while taking the viewer on an excursion through a dark era of American history.

On Beauty and Moral Authority

In many ways, Puryear's sculptures summon African aesthetic principles that combine formal quality with a moral underpinning. Writing on this topic, the art historian Susan Vogel argues that African art is expected to express moral values and that its beauty lies in expressing them through appropriate forms.[17] That is, a work of African art embodies moral traits by demonstrating characteristics such as excellent finish, skilled workmanship, innovation, and invention.[18] Vogel further suggests that the overlap of form (external appearance) and content (signification of something good) unleashes a work of art's full aesthetic values.[19] Extending this argument, the art historian Chika Okeke-Agulu proposes the notion of "aesthetic-ethics," which he describes as a "fundamental and synergistic fusion of aesthetics and ethics that reflects the widespread African insistence on the pursuit of the beautiful (aesthetics) and the good (ethics) as unitary endeavors."[20] Puryear's work likewise demonstrates the fusion of the sensorial ("formal appearance and optical affirmation") with the "condition of 'being' good."[21] He tests the limits of physical beauty (incredible craftsmanship), purity of form (form for form's sake), and the ways in which a work of art participates in a broader discursive space (moral basis).

A work of absolute craftsmanship and impeccable fabrication, *A Column for Sally Hemings* is an excellent example of this. The shackled cast-iron hoop seems to pierce the classical fluted marble base like a stake. Hovering, as the curator Brooke Kamin Rapaport puts it, "between beauty and brutality," the work's striking visual beauty is in tension with the morbid history it narrates.[22] However, it is this tension that evokes the moral implications of the work. As a memorial, *A Column for Sally Hemings* reminds viewers of America's original sin of enslavement. As a visual text, it reinscribes this event of the past that previously circulated as rumors and was not well known until Annette Gordon-Reed's groundbreaking book, *Thomas Jefferson and Sally Hemings* (1997). Puryear thereby reintroduced this particular individual from history to contemporary consciousness in a profound way. It is telling that the work first came to public attention when it was featured on an auspicious occasion and at an august venue—in Puryear's *Liberty / Libertà* at the Venice Biennale in 2019 (fig. 60).

Although *A Column for Sally Hemings* does not address an African theme in its form and content, it invites comparison with the manner in which votive figures in African art, such as the *mbulu ngulu* reliquary ensemble of the Fang people of Central Africa or the *waka snan* male figure of the Baule people of West Africa, honor the memory of ancestors (figs. 61 and 62). *Ladder for Booker T. Washington* (1996; see fig. 18) offers a similar proposition. With its curving sides made from golden-ash saplings, this soaring thirty-six-foot sculpture delineates a ladder reaching toward the ceiling and suspended from the ground with wires. The ladder creates an illusion of perspective as it ambles toward the top, becoming ever narrower. The title of the work, named for influential

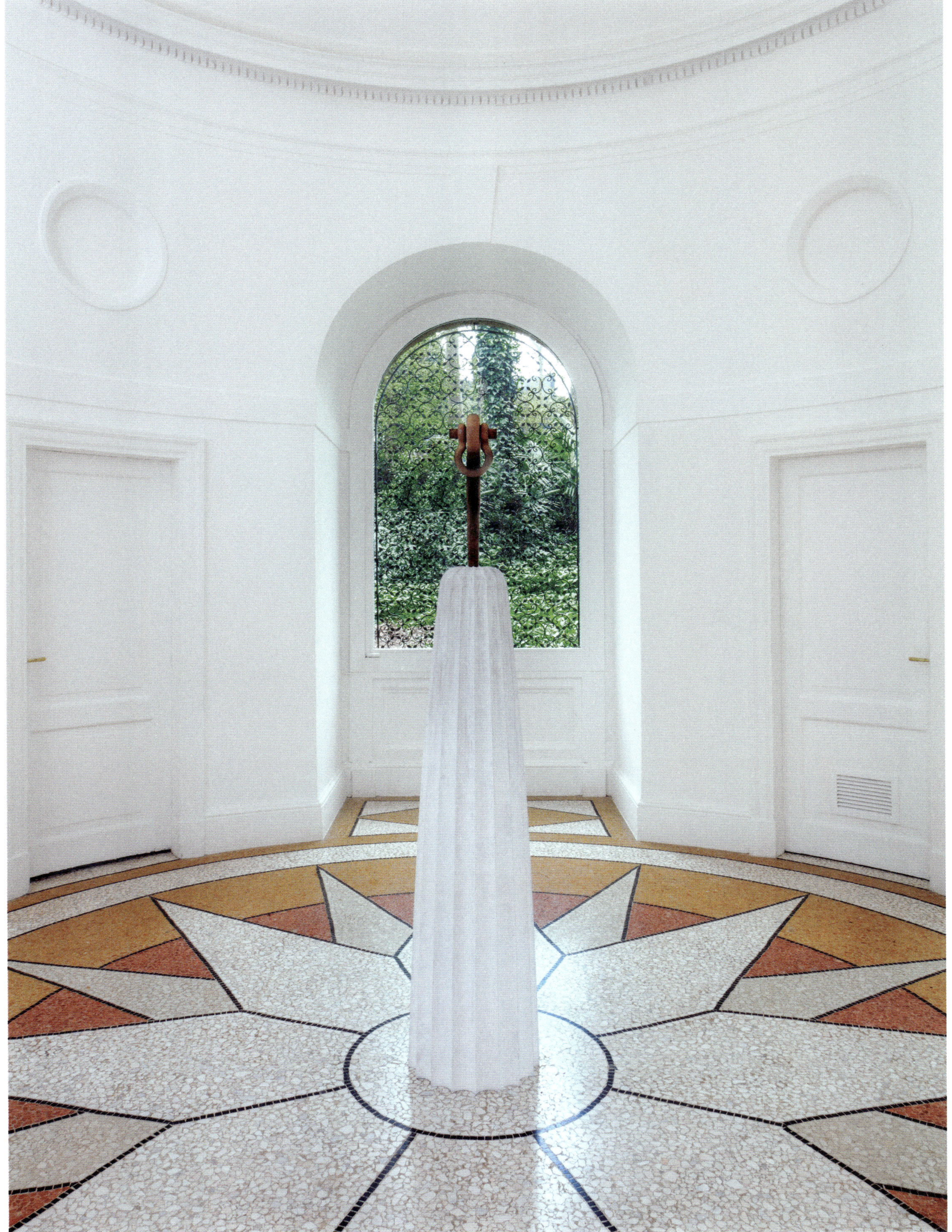

Figure 60. Installation view of *A Column for Sally Hemings* (2019), at the American Pavilion, Venice Biennale, 2019. Martin Puryear. Cast iron, painted tulip poplar; 201.3 x 43.8 x 43.8 cm. Photo: Joshua White

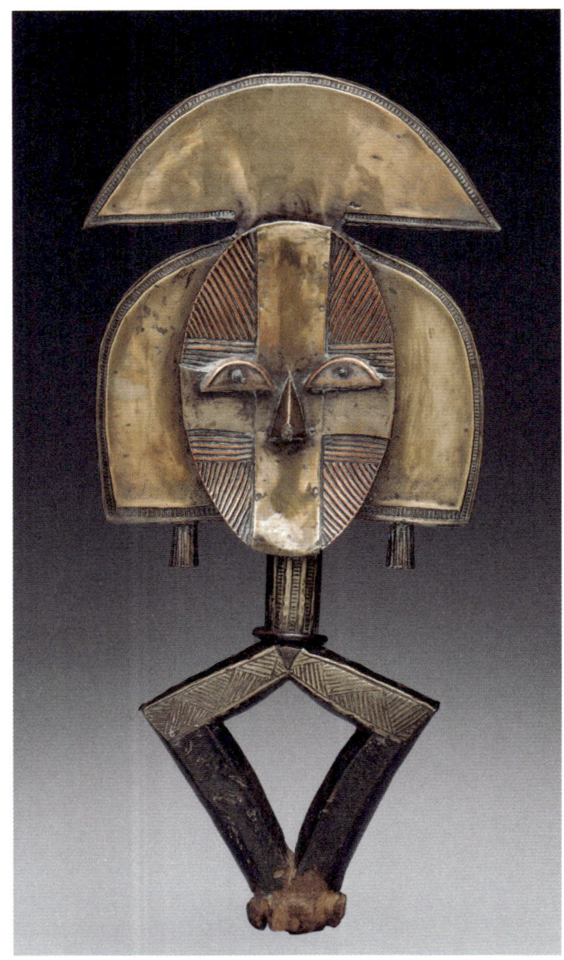

Figure 61. Sculptural element from a reliquary ensemble (*mbulu ngulu*), probably 1800s. Gabon, Kota style. Wood, copper alloy, and iron; 61 x 27.5 x 3 cm. The Cleveland Museum of Art, Purchase from the J. H. Wade Fund 2005.2

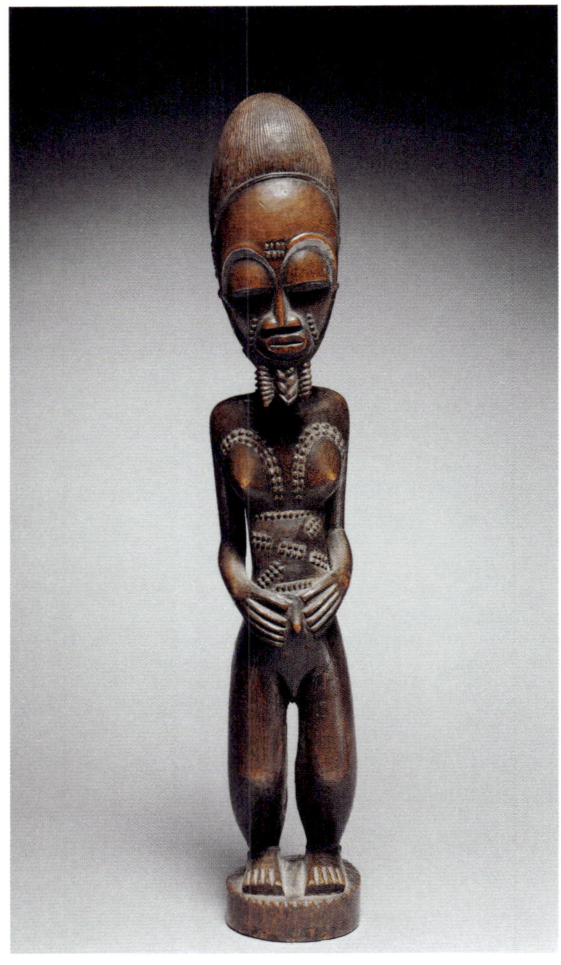

Figure 62. Male figure, by 1931. Totokro Master. Wood; 44.8 x 9.3 x 7.7 cm. The Cleveland Museum of Art, Gift of the African Art Sponsors of Karamu House 1931.204

African American educator Booker T. Washington (1856–1915), was given after the sculpture was realized, and it gestures to Washington's ideas regarding racial progress. Washington believed that progress should be gradual and emphasized economic advancement and vocational skills. Puryear conceived of this work as a dialogue between Washington's vision and its antithesis, the more proactive, radical stance on the struggle for racial equality championed by W. E. B. Du Bois (1868–1963). The two thinkers' divergent positions shaped the Black discursive space at the turn of the twentieth century. With *Ladder for Booker T. Washington*, Puryear invokes these historical subjects whose lives offer useful lessons for the present moment.

I suspect that the moral authority of art to operate in a public space also underpins *Lookout* (2023; fig. 63), Puryear's site-specific sculpture commission at Storm King Art Center. Using bricks for the first time, Puryear created a structure with an archway that curves and rises nearly twenty feet high to form a dome. Each course of bricks props the next course with no internal framework except for a concrete-reinforced rebar wedged within the double-walled structure. The monumental sculpture has ninety perforations through the walls that let light and air into the interior. To achieve this complex result, the artist adopted the Nubian vaulting technique of laying bricks at an angle instead of flat, a building method developed in the upper Nile Delta of Egypt several millennia ago. He also looked to the history of brick structures in locales ranging from the Hudson Valley and New York City's Upper East Side to Stoke-on-Trent, England. A 2009 visit to Mali, however, where a local roofing technique greatly impressed him, was what directly sparked Puryear's approach to *Lookout* (fig. 64). "I saw a roof being made in a village, and it had no internal framework—that was a significant moment to unlock the structural principles of this piece," he explained.[23] Puryear was excited that Africa was the source of this technique.[24] Set on a hilltop and sloping backward, the eye-catching sculpture rises from the ground to command the surrounding picturesque environment. The artist expects *Lookout* to be an enduring fixture at Storm King that visitors will encounter for years to come.

Human Connections and Cultural Syntaxes

Underscoring art's role in society, the artist Melvin Edwards asserts, "Art doesn't make art; people make art."[25] He continues, "Names of places show up in my work in reference to history but also to my personal experience rooted in places that I have visited."[26] Edwards is African American and an abstract sculptor like Puryear, with a similar trajectory of engagement with Africa since the 1960s. Both have seemingly sought recourse to broader conceptual ideas and aesthetic principles in African art.

Puryear pursues the formal possibilities of abstraction in sculpted form, but his investment in abstraction should be understood as a profound quest for clarity regarding the world. There is a reason why the African worldview recognizes the depth of the universe as an inscrutable vastness with a moving spirit.

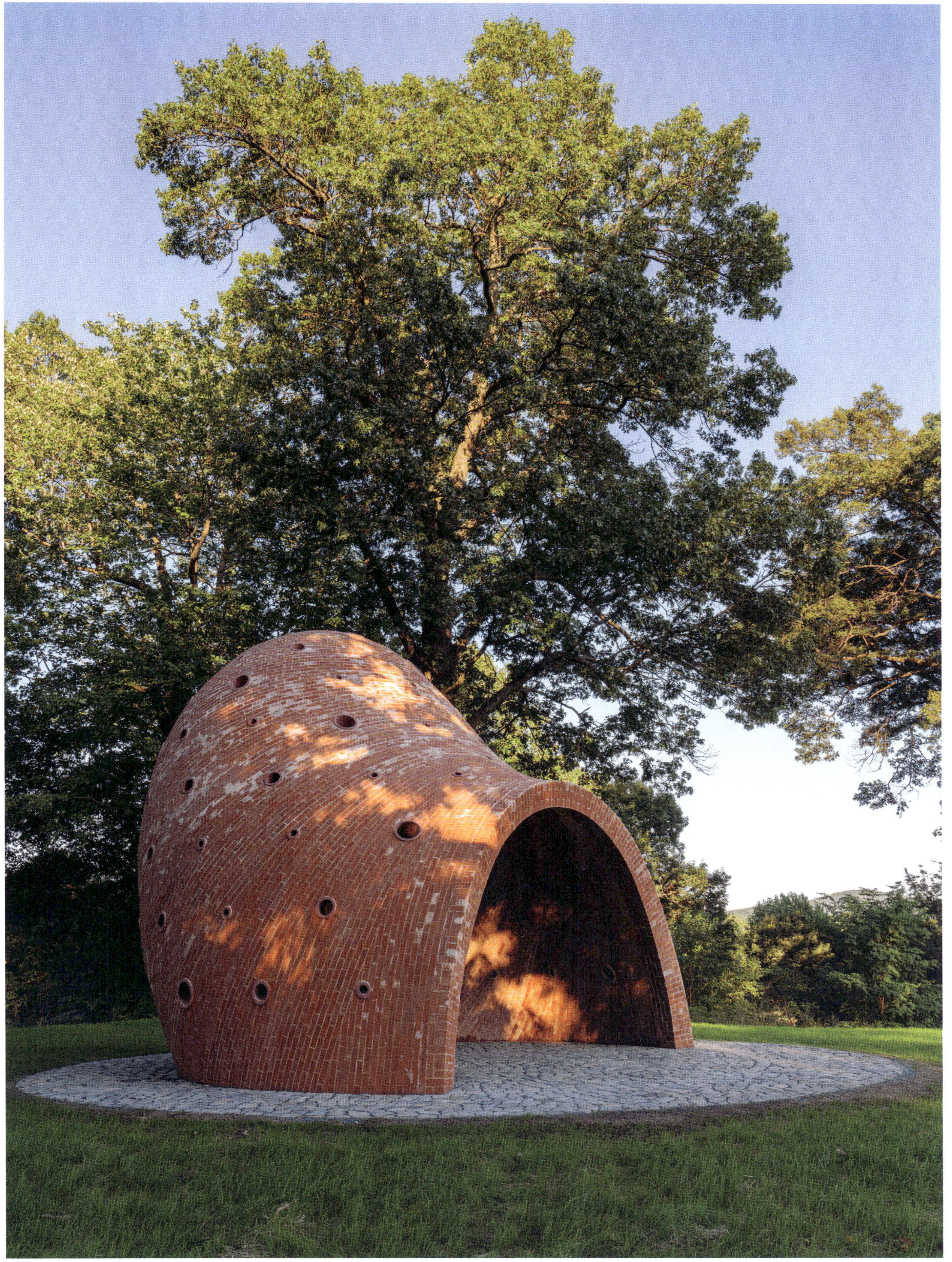

Figure 63. Installation view of *Lookout* (2023), at Storm King Art Center, New Windsor, New York, 2023. Martin Puryear. Brick, concrete, and cobblestone; 609.6 cm (height). Photo: Jeffrey Jenkins, courtesy of Storm King Archives

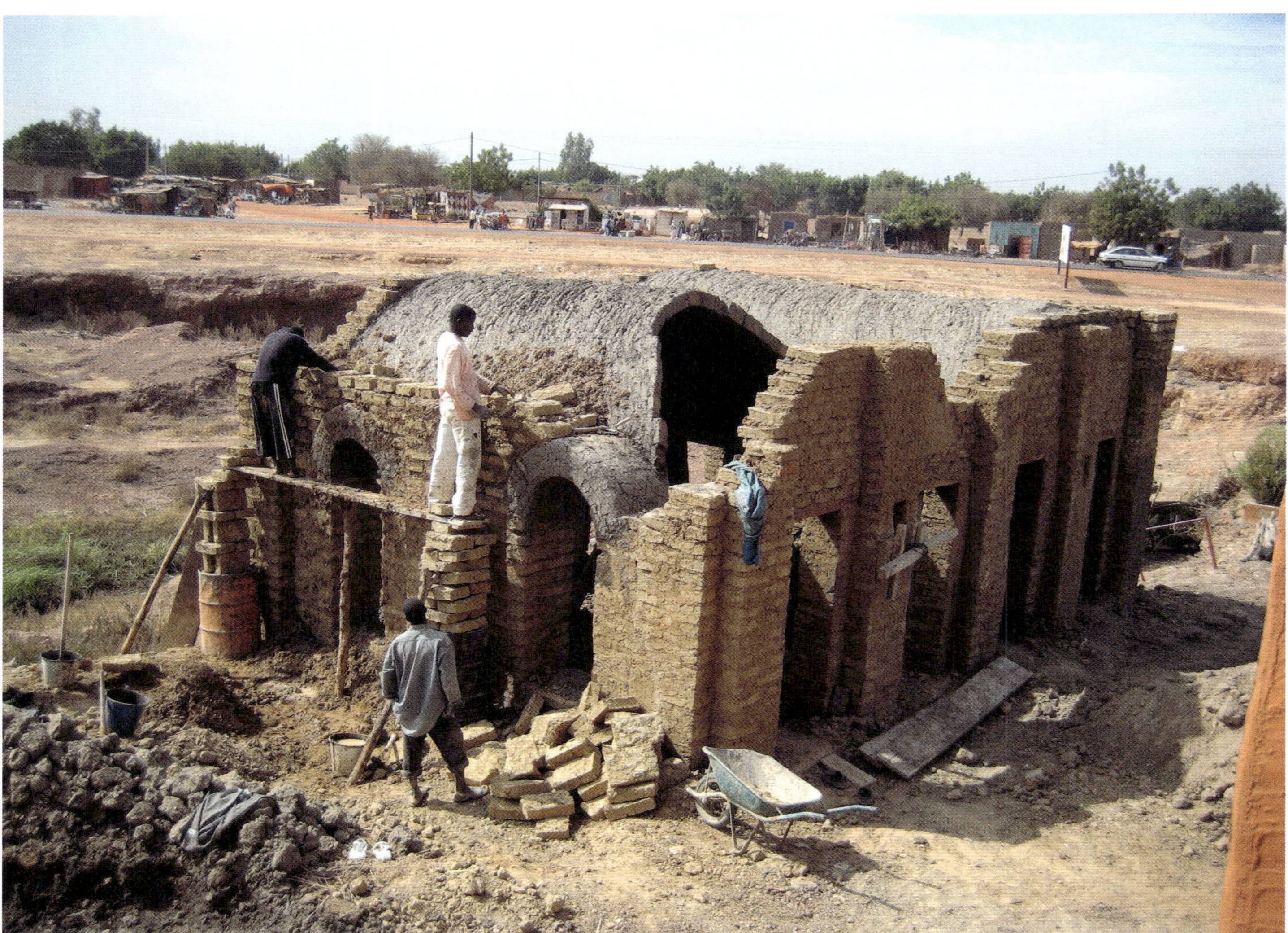

Figure 64. Construction of a mud brick house, photographed by Martin Puryear during a trip to Mali, 2009. Collection of the artist

The Igbo of Nigeria have a term for this level of depth: *omimi*, meaning that the world is deep. The Igbos also believe that when one thing stands, another stands by it. Perhaps this idea of the double as a frame for producing meaning is the key lesson Puryear internalized from his time in Africa. His oeuvre oscillates between defiance of labels and resistance to associations—a play with paradox and contradictions, call-and-response, double meaning, structuralist duality or binary opposition are all immanent in his work.

In many respects, Puryear's art invokes Krio, the English-based creole spoken in Sierra Leone, which he learned there; Krio has variants known as pidgin in the English-speaking West African countries of Nigeria and Ghana. Creole emerged as a language of commerce on the West African coast during the early contact period between West African societies and European colonial powers. There is a uniqueness and shared ownership because it is a mélange of Indigenous languages bound by the dominant colonial language, be it English or French. It has since become the lingua franca spoken by many in West Africa.

Puryear has always been fascinated by the complex matrices engendered by first contact, both in human terms when cultures and people interact and in terms of creative strategies in which ideas, materials, and techniques intertwine. His comprehension of several European languages, stemming from his formative knowledge of Latin and his retention of Krio sixty years after learning it, speaks to how he has integrated diverse modes of thinking into his creative process.[27] Puryear stands on a cultural *métissage* comprising the colossal memory of the Middle Passage that has shaped the Black experience in America; the history of modern sculpture; his experience of Africa, where he opened himself up to abstraction as a way to make art; his artistic training in Sweden and the United States; and his abiding interests in myriad forms of knowledge.

1. Martin Puryear, "Interview: Abstraction and 'Ladder for Booker T. Washington,'" *Art21*, November 2011, https://art21.org/read/martin-puryear-abstraction-and-ladder-for-booker-t-washington/.

2. Elizabeth Reede, "Jog and Switchbacks," in *Martin Puryear*, ed. John Elderfield, exh. cat. (New York: Museum of Modern Art, 2007), 74–75.

3. A lot has been written about Puryear and African art. In many interviews, he has described his formative experience in Africa in the 1960s and the importance of his subsequent visits. For an especially compelling exchange on this topic, see Richard J. Powell, "A Conversation with Martin Puryear," in Elderfield, *Martin Puryear*, 100–102.

4. Martin Puryear, conversation with the author, July 17, 2024.

5. Powell, "A Conversation with Martin Puryear," 100.

6. Puryear, conversation with the author, July 17, 2024.

7. Puryear has expressed discomfort with the market commodification of objects that were once meant for ritual purposes. Martin Puryear, conversation with the author, August 26, 2024.

8. Puryear, conversation with the author, July 17, 2024.

9. Puryear, conversation with the author, August 26, 2024.

10. Ancestors are patron saints who ensure that the community maintains its spiritual moorings and replenishes its relationship with its corporeal and metaphysical source as a cultural group.

11. Puryear, conversation with the author, July 17, 2024.

12. Powell, "A Conversation with Martin Puryear," 104.

13. Puryear, conversation with the author, July 17, 2024.

14. Martin Puryear, "In Conversation," interviewed by David Levi Strauss, *Brooklyn Rail*, November 2007, https://brooklynrail.org/2007/11/art/martin-puryear-with-david-levi-strauss/.

15. Puryear first learned about Sally Hemings's history through Barbara Chase-Riboud's 1979 novel on the subject. See Emily Liebert's essay in this volume, p. 139n32.

16. Monticello's architecture inspired the American Pavilion, where the work was first displayed and to which it responds.

17. Susan Vogel, "African Aesthetics," in *African Aesthetics* (New York: Center for African Art, 1986), xii-xiii.

18. Vogel, "African Aesthetics," xvi-xvii.

19. Vogel, "African Aesthetics," xvi.

20. Chika Okeke-Agulu, "Foreword—Sue Willamson, Art and the Ethical Imperative," in *Sue Williamson: Life and Work*, ed. Mark Gevisser (Milan: Skira Editore, 2015), 8.

21. Okeke-Agulu, "Foreword," 8.

22. Brooke Kamin Rapaport, "Martin Puryear: Liberty / Libertà," in Brooke Kamin Rapaport et al., *Martin Puryear: Liberty / Libertà*, exh. cat. (New York: Madison Square Park Conservancy and Gregory R. Miller; Berlin: Hatje Cantz, 2019), 42.

23. Ted Loos, "Brick by Brick, a Sculpture at Storm King, by Way of Africa," *New York Times*, September 14, 2023.

24. Loos, "Brick by Brick."

25. *Some Bright Morning: The Art of Melvin Edwards*, directed by Lydia Diakhaté (USA/France, 2016), film.

26. *Some Bright Morning*.

27. "Also one of the things I think that learning language got me, is to realize that it gives you a currency that you can move in the world," Puryear said. He speaks French and Swedish and understands written and spoken Italian and Spanish. Puryear, conversation with the author, July 17, 2024.

Martin Puryear, James Krenov, and Postwar Craft

Michelle Millar Fisher

I. Meeting James Krenov

In the abundant literature on Martin Puryear's decades-long career, the mention of the artist's time as a student in Sweden in the mid-1960s is frequent but perfunctory. Yet, within this formative moment spent in northern climes lies a critical connection between the artist and the field of contemporary craft. Well-known are the two years Puryear spent as a printmaking student at the Royal Academy of Fine Arts in Stockholm between 1966 and 1968. Rarely acknowledged, however, is that during this time he had a series of brief but impactful encounters with the acclaimed woodworker, educator, and writer James Krenov (1920–2009).

These occasional mentions of Krenov usually fail to recognize his significance in the world of contemporary craft, and they often elide the difference between the geographic, cultural, and design context of Scandinavia and Krenov's own identity.[1] While Krenov lived in Stockholm for several decades at midcentury and studied at the renowned Verkstadsskola, founded by Swedish designer Carl Malmsten (1888–1972), he was Siberian by birth and grew up in Alaska and Seattle (fig. 65). Krenov was also well traveled and widely influenced, as Puryear himself would become. When Puryear sought him out, the

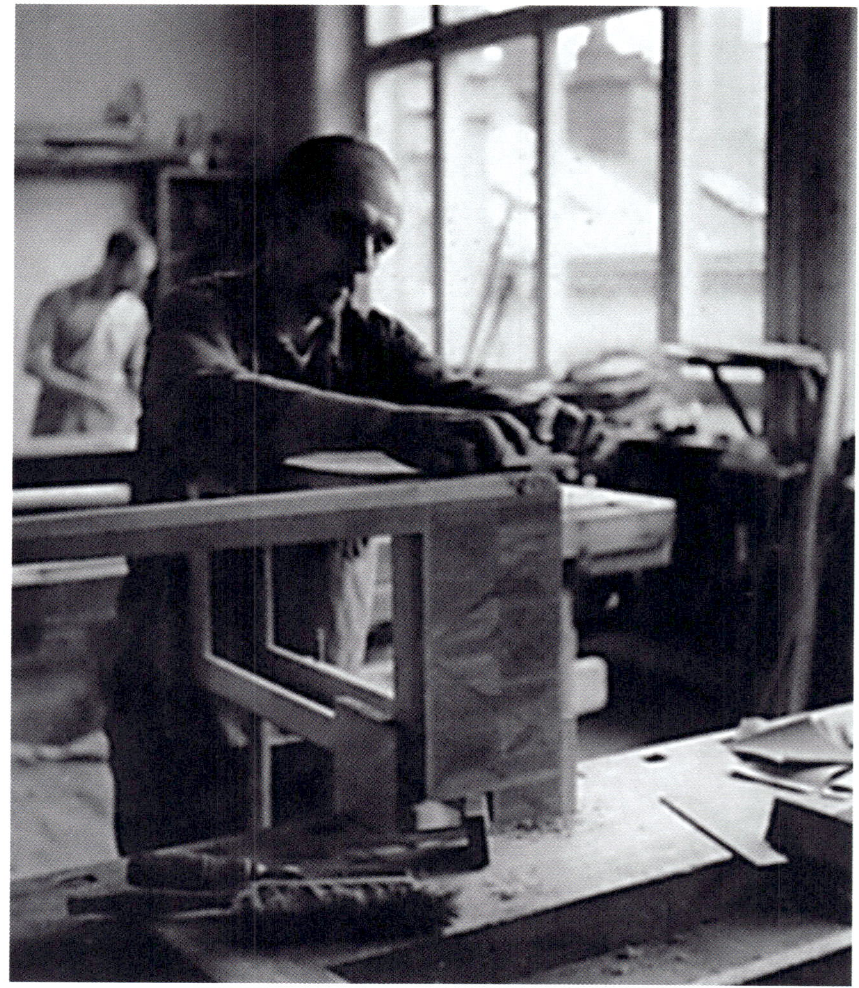

Figure 65. James Krenov at work on one of Carl Malmsten's desk designs from the 1940s, the "Nefertiti" desk. The desk's elaborate marquetry required technical skill and a time-intensive finishing process. Photo: Courtesy of the Krenov family

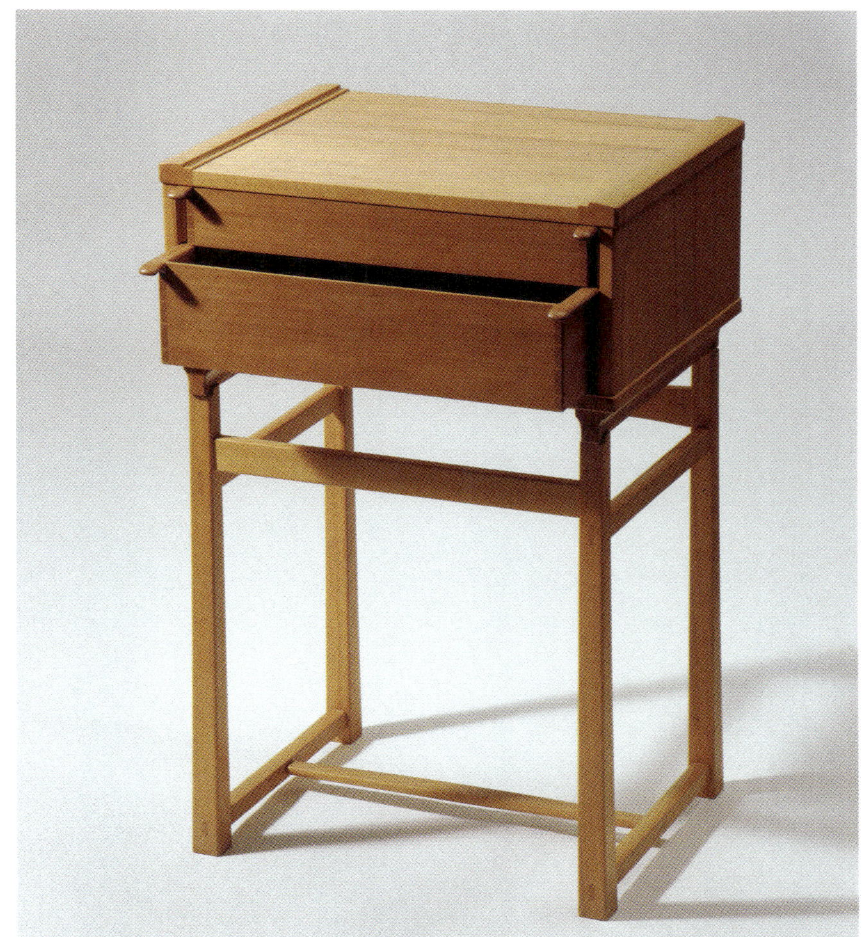

Figure 66. Casket, 1965. James Krenov (American, born Russia, 1920–2009). Chestnut and pearwood; 77 x 47.5 x 38 cm. Collection of the Nationalmuseum Stockholm, Sweden, Gift of The Craft Association of Stockholm City, 1967, NMK 181/1967. Photo: Hans Thorwid / Nationalmuseum

Russian-born woodworker and craft philosopher twenty years his senior was well on his way to becoming a giant in contemporary craft in Europe and the United States.[2]

A relationship of mutual respect and reciprocity between these two men continued to develop through episodic encounters in the decades after both relocated to North America. Krenov's furniture output certainly impacted Puryear. Yet, it is the woodworker's poetic treatises on craftsmanship and his attitude in the studio that are the more significant points of connection.[3] Krenov famously encouraged his students to "leave fingerprints" and foregrounded hand skills over power tools. We find this approach in Puryear's own rejection of the machined, outsourced aesthetics of Minimalism, which he "spat out" in favor of honesty and respect for—but never a fetishization of—his materials.[4] Krenov also wrote about the sensual and emotional capacity of wood, which made way for Puryear's own sensitive engagement with the material in ways that transcend technique alone.

This essay remedies the fact that no writing on the work of Martin Puryear has yet explored the impact of this meeting of minds early in the artist's career. Considering the touchpoint between Krenov and Puryear highlights influences that both artists felt deeply. Meeting Krenov augmented Puryear's existing curiosity regarding craft and helped him think through the approaches to hands-on making he wanted to embrace—and those he would reject—in his own work.[5] It also connected the artist to American Studio Craft, a post–World War II moniker for artists using wood, clay, glass, metal, and fiber. These artists laid claim to an equal status with their fine-art peers who worked conceptually, independently, and with institutional opportunities, such as the market and the museum, that were usually foreclosed to those in the realm of craft.[6] The movement blossomed concurrently with Puryear's own multifaceted practice yet is rarely present (let alone foregrounded) in writing on his work.[7]

Where craft appears in Puryear's historiography, it is often as a specter accompanied by semantic anxiety or as an essentialized conception of the term and its histories.[8] Instead, the story that follows here reflects upon a compelling human connection linking the artist to the field of contemporary craft. This tale is grounded in an affinity between two makers rather than comparison of material or technique. Considering their shared ethos moves us beyond artificial and unproductive debates of "art versus craft." Rather, it accounts for Puryear's omnivorous regard for creative practices and philosophies—a regard that suffuses his every work.

II. First Encounters

As Puryear tells it, an epiphany in his creative practice occurred in the galleries of the Nationalmuseum in Stockholm in 1967.[9] He was a year into his printmaking studies at the Royal Academy and a regular visitor to the museum's encyclopedic collections. On one particular visit he chose to wander through its extensive decorative-arts holdings. There, he was stopped in his tracks by a pearwood-and-chestnut casket designed to hold silver flatware made by James Krenov two years earlier (fig. 66).

Though the young artist had never seen or heard of Krenov's work, it made an immediate impression on him. The casket's clean, simple lines and chest-on-stand form would become that maker's trademarks.[10] The cabinet was "so sensitive . . . not imposing in scale," recalled Puryear over a half century later.[11]

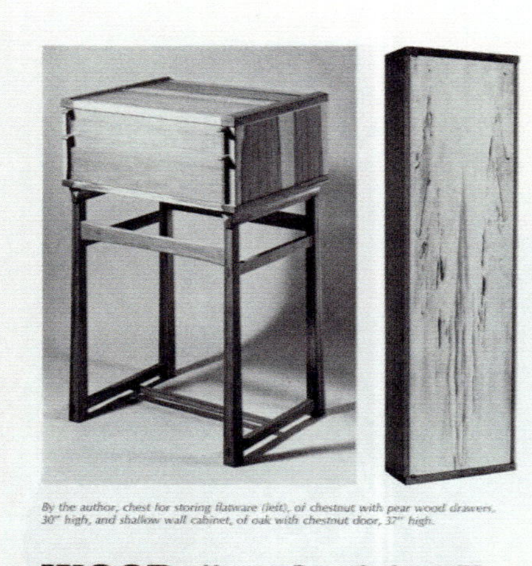

Jim Krenov, who lives and works just outside of Stockholm, is a cabinetmaker with an additional talent for writing. His essays, which express the involvement, the rewards, and the trials that many of us have in common as craftsmen, have appeared in European publications. As a former student of Krenov's, it gives me pleasure to introduce him to the readers of CRAFT HORIZONS.

Krenov selects wood with unusually beautiful grain and color. His work is characterized by a particular surface quality, which he achieves with hand planes he makes himself, and exacting joinery.

Born in an igloo in Siberia, he moved with his family to Alaska and later to Seattle, where he learned the love of handwork by building and repairing fishing boats. When Krenov emigrated to Sweden after World War II, he studied furniture making at the Malmsten School. This summer his work will be shown in the U.S. for the first time at The Three Crowns, Pittsford, New York.
—CRAIG McART

By the author, chest for storing flatware (left), of chestnut with pear wood drawers, 30" high, and shallow wall cabinet, of oak with chestnut door, 37" high.

WOOD: ". . . the friendly mystery . . ."

by James Krenov

The plank lying on my workbench is heavy—and hard. I strike it with my knuckles, hear the sound of solid, unyielding wood. Two inches thick, three meters long, this plank cut somewhere in a far corner of the world. There is a patch of clear brownish-yellow showing against the otherwise grimy and weather-darkened surfaces—that is where I first planed through the roughness and discovered the treasure underneath. A treasure buried as it was in dust amid a pile of odds-and-ends cast aside in a far corner of the lumberyard. Large importers of hardwoods receive so many shipments, such a multitude of fine wood! Yet somehow, mysteriously, no two pieces are quite alike. And in each shipment there are apt to be one or two planks different from the rest of their kind, misfits, so to speak, that nobody seems to want. Rational production of furniture requires wood that is uniform, obedient. Thus our misfit pieces are cast aside, to gather dust until some odd patterner comes along with his rule and his plane, turning over planks, tapping, scraping surfaces—generally disturbing the order of things. Lately, though, I have noticed a glint in the foreman's eye, as if he secretly approves my pleasure over having found something special, a piece of wood whose origin might be vague, but whose promise he and I can wordlessly share.

The other day a man contacted me about a cabinet. It should contain his collection of silver; otherwise, he had only a vague notion of what it was to be like. I sketched several suggestions, one of them seemed to point in the right direction. Still I could promise nothing—and said so. A sketch is a sketch, you see; the same applies to a working drawing. Out of definite lines and proportions we may make a cabinet. Yes, already on paper we see how it will look; a few sections, details, assure us of its usability. As to material, I bring some samples of wood, and we decide on one whose tone and texture pleases us. But if we let it go at that, entrust the rest to mere workmanship, the result can very well be a rather ordinary cabinet. Regardless of the price.

I suggested that he come to my workshop. Together we considered many sorts of fine wood, trying to imagine how each would look in the light of our idea and that old silver. . . . Finally we decided upon the plank here before me, brownish, with odd shadows flickering diagonally over its mild surface, enlivening the refined tone and stubborn hardness. We dabbed a little oil on it, rubbed—and saw the color deepen as the wood slowly became translucent, amber-like, glowing.

If I want it milder, I can use polish. All depends on what it will call for. What it will be. . . .

Our sketch, this wood—and then a rough, full-scale drawing which we hung on the wall. Here was a start! I felt a first

28

Figure 67. James Krenov (introduced by Craig McArt), "The Friendly Mystery of Wood," *Craft Horizons* 27, no. 2 (March/April 1967): 28

"I was struck by the way that he used the grain of the wood as a pattern to work with like a painter or a mosaicist would. . . . His joinery was just flawless, absolutely flawless. I was blown away."[12]

Shortly after this encounter, Puryear visited the library in the US Embassy in Stockholm and flipped through issues of *Craft Horizons*, the genre-defining shelter magazine for American Studio Craft founded in New York in 1941.[13] There, in the March/April issue from 1967, his eyes alighted upon an image of the very same cabinet he had seen in the museum gallery. It illustrated a pithy, two-page encomium by Krenov himself on "the friendly mystery" of wood (fig. 67).[14]

In his essay, among lyrical, detailed, and heady descriptions of the thickness, grain, and coloration of various woods, Krenov cautioned the reader against entrusting any engagement with such a special material to "mere workmanship." As if speaking to Puryear directly from the page about his recent experience in the gallery, Krenov acknowledged that "in museums we ordinarily see the notice: 'Do not touch'. . . . [yet when] we touch . . . the sculptor, [he] feels our appreciation . . . When we have every technical aid, all the know-how—what now? The answer, perhaps, is in a touch of the hand."[15] This was all the encouragement the young artist needed to translate this meeting with object and text into a more human connection.

Energized by his two encounters with Krenov's work, Puryear looked up the woodworker in the phone book and found that he lived in Bromma, a suburb of Stockholm only two subway stops from his own student apartment. Puryear turned up unannounced at the elder's door with a portfolio of his current work. Surprisingly, given Krenov's legendary spikiness, he invited Puryear in for the first of several visits. The two recognized in one another the potential not only for shared conversations about a material of mutual interest and kindred childhood experiences (both had built wooden boats early in their lives, appreciated vernacular forms, and sought out experiences in nature), but also for the kind of expatriate talk they missed in Stockholm.[16]

Thus began a lifelong connection that would ebb and flow over the years but that remained relevant and alive to both men. Before Puryear graduated and returned to the United States in 1968, Krenov attended exhibitions of Puryear's work in Stockholm, and Puryear joined the Krenov family for dinners. When they both moved back to the US, they remained in touch, with Krenov visiting Puryear in Chicago (they spent an afternoon wandering through the Art Institute's collection of Chinese furniture) and Puryear making a return visit to Krenov's school of woodworking that he founded in Fort Bragg, California, in 1981.

III. An Inheritance

What did Puryear glean from his encounters with Krenov? A solitary craftsman working by hand in his woodshop, Krenov epitomized the ideal of the postwar Studio Craft movement, in which makers created one-of-a-kind, conceptually driven works. Far more important, though, was the fact that he modeled a deliberate and daily practice that kept him in immediate, embodied dialogue with making. This impressed his young visitor. Indeed, Puryear has used "maker," a term historically associated with craft, to describe himself, and his working environment has more in common with Krenov's than with that of other artists of his stature whose studios teem with assistants. Not so for Puryear, who notes, "I have two people working for me, I work with my hands, I work slowly."[17]

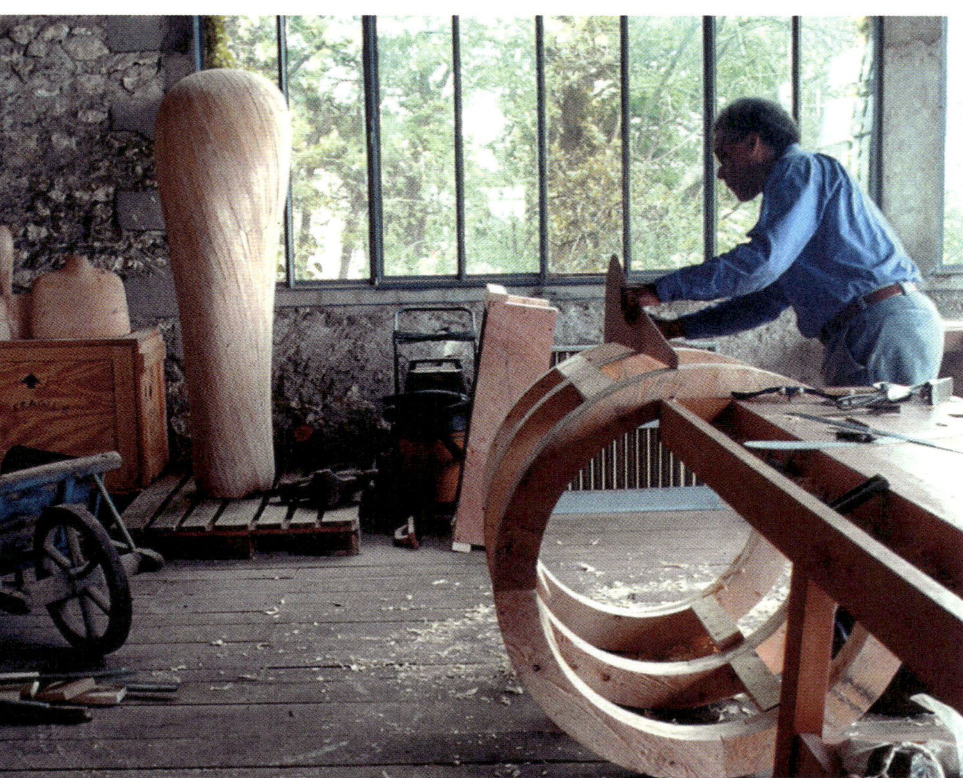

Figure 68. Martin Puryear at Atelier Calder, Saché, France, 1992-93. Photo: Atelier Calder

Figure 69. An early photo of Krenov's workshop, showing his bench space in the basement and piles of wood being shuffled around for consideration in an upcoming piece and to check on their dryness. Photo: Courtesy of the Krenov family

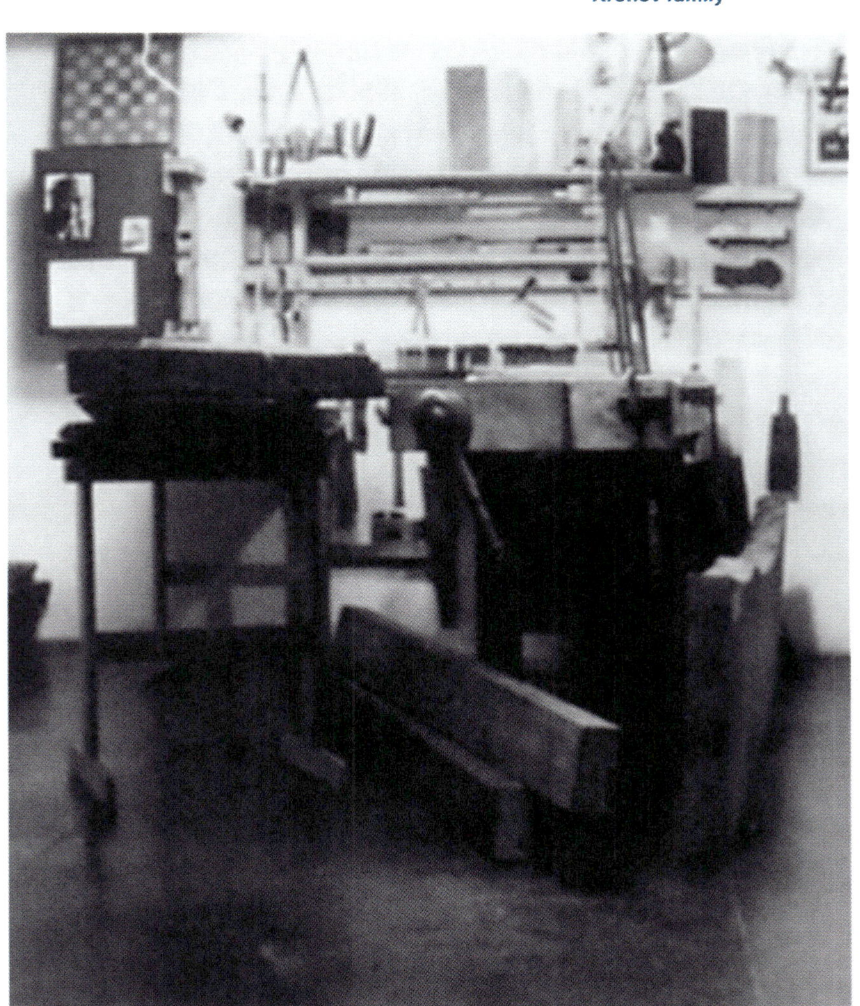

Robert Storr also uses this craft descriptor—Puryear "is a maker not a manufacturer of sculptures"—to highlight an important distinction regarding the presence of the artist's hand in the context of the Minimalist legacy that Puryear's oeuvre dances beside and around.[18]

Skill, technique, and tools are crucial to this kind of studio practice (fig. 68). While Puryear learned in many places in his formative years, Krenov was an essential source. "I was deeply interested in what he did and how he did it. . . . We had wonderful lunches together," remembered Puryear of his visits to Krenov's Stockholm workshop (fig. 69). "I watched him work. I can't say that I studied with him because he never really taught, but I saw how he worked [and he gave] me a chore. . . of sharpening some of his carving tools."[19] The maintenance of the master's tools, akin to the work of an apprentice, situates this exchange within a craft idiom. So too this method of learning by osmosis, in quietude and close observation rather than in group critique. The former was a pedagogical approach that remained central to postwar craft programs even while it fell out of fashion in MFA classrooms of the same period—including the one that Puryear encountered during his graduate studies at Yale University.[20]

While tools and technique often equal tradition, in this story they signify the inheritance of an attitude or a way of living with and within one's craft. Puryear's encounter with Krenov in Stockholm intensified the young artist's awareness of how he wanted to pursue his practice, materially, and spiritually. He recalled a wooden hand plane Krenov helped him make during this time and, through it, a creeping awareness that he had begun "to value wood surfaces finished with sharp edge tools rather than rasps and sandpaper, both for furniture, but more significantly for my sculpture in wood."[21] This echoes Krenov's own words in

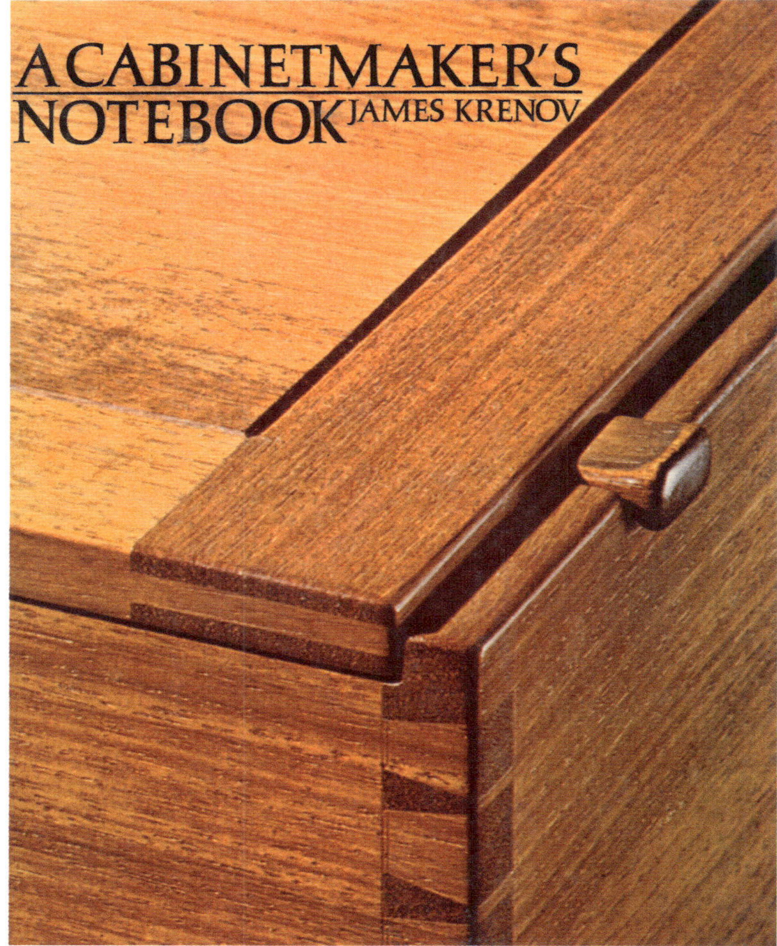

Figure 70. Cover of James Krenov, *A Cabinetmaker's Notebook* (New York: Van Nostrand Reinhold, 1976). Cover design: Bengt Carlen

his 1967 essay in *Craft Horizons*, in which he extols "an edge cut rounded, but not sandpapered—a sensitive finger will understand its living imperfections and be pleased at the traces left by sharp steel on hardwood."[22]

It is important, however, to avoid transposition of these affinities into too-literal points of inheritance that can be "read into" Puryear's work. Such an approach is an art historian's gambit that privileges form and reads craft as concerned *only* with the transmission of technique.[23] In contrast, Puryear was interested in what might be termed an ethos of craft. It is an embodied and intellectual engagement not only with material but also with the time and manner of working it and the ideas that shape it. Recognizing this as Puryear's primary craft inheritance does not discount technique but it does refuse essentialized identification of elements from one maker's work surfacing in another's. Instead, it centers the way in which hands, heart, and head synthesize to produce form and meaning.

Puryear's hands-on approach to material was already latent in his upbringing and early training by the time he lived in Stockholm. His father was shut out of a career as an electrical contractor because of racism in all-white unions and instead went to work for the US Postal Service in Washington, DC. He had seven children and so, the artist recalled, "he was a handy father . . . when he needed something done around the house he'd go to the library and get a book . . . buy some tools—and I grew up watching a man teaching himself to build things and do things and that was invaluable to me."[24] This experience of making do with what was at hand was reaffirmed during his two years with the Peace Corps in Sierra Leone, where Puryear observed woodworkers without access to electricity using old imported British and American hand tools to create forms that combined vernacular, utilitarian, and aesthetic elements. In these ways, working with one's hands and with traditional tools engaged aesthetic and historical approaches that might be called "craft." More importantly, though, they were acts of working-class self-determination and practical necessity that had both personal and political resonance.

Accessibility and autonomy were foundational beliefs for Krenov, too, in ways that Puryear came to admire. Beyond his own studio, Krenov realized his commitment to accessible education most powerfully in his deliberate choice to found his eponymous school in 1981 within the context of a community college in California. There, he reasoned, he could build a culture of making that was the exact opposite of the then-flourishing "privately endowed [craft] schools where it cost a student ten to twenty thousand dollars just to walk through the door."[25]

This independent spirit was crystallized in a series of well-received books on woodworking and teaching that Krenov published starting in the 1970s (fig. 70).[26] Puryear read them eagerly as they came out, and fifty years later, he has every book Krenov ever wrote.[27] The artist calls Krenov's writing "spiritual," referring to Krenov's belief in the emotional and humanistic potential of using one's hands.[28] Puryear shares that belief, as evidenced by his recollection of his own father's need to be "handy" or his description of the poetic synthesis of form and meaning when making a sculpture.

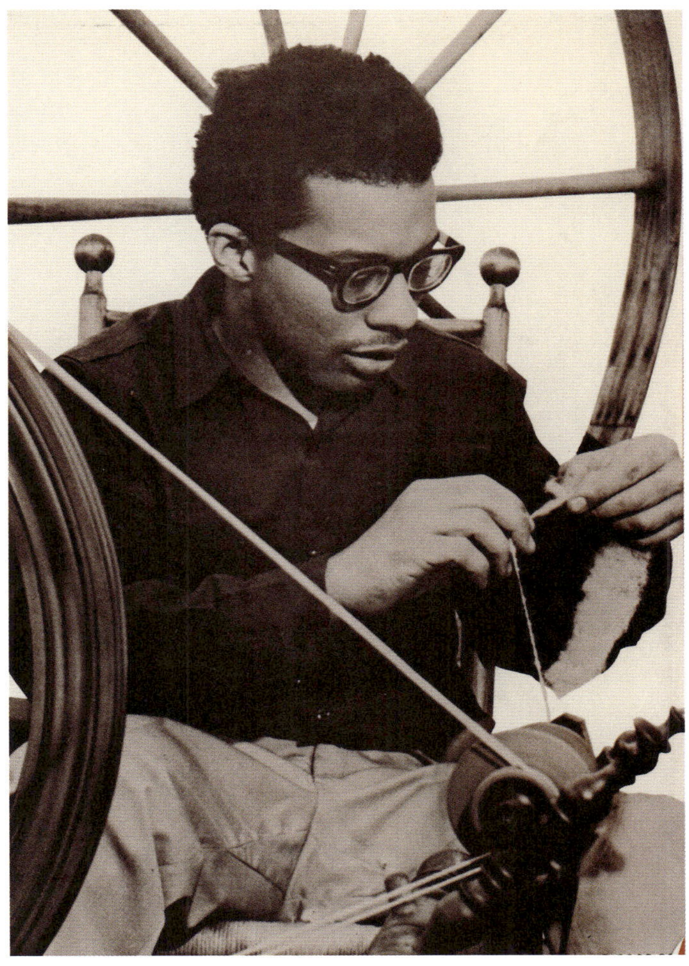

Figure 71. Allen Fannin, 1970. As illustrated on the back cover of Allen Fannin, *Handspinning: Art & Technique* (New York: Van Nostrand Reinhold, 1970)

IV. Craft Disclaimers

While craft offers a lens through which to view Puryear's oeuvre, it is also a vantage point that is not without significant tension. Even as they found confluence, Puryear recognized in Krenov a level of obsession with material execution that he did not wish to emulate. He characterizes Krenov as a "rare exception" who "trained in what would be called a trade . . . [and] elevated it [to] the level of fine art."[29] In contrast, Puryear was from the start avowedly an artist—a painter-turned-sculptor and self-taught woodworker. Accordingly, he pursued an education at the Royal Academy, not Stockholm's highly regarded design school Konstfackskolan or a trade school such as Verkstadsskola, the one Krenov attended under Carl Malmsten. The latter marked its graduates as designer-draftsmen who outsourced making or, worse, craftsmen who might be ignorantly dismissed by art-world gatekeepers.[30]

Puryear's self-definition recasts the serious debates and significant amount of spilled ink that constructed artificial boundary lines between art and craft in the postwar period. In Puryear's telling, "I was hungry for a broader engagement with different kinds of things in the world," an indication that he did not wish to be pigeonholed, as someone like Krenov was, within the field of craft alone.[31] It is one thing to self-identify as a maker and wholly another to be labeled as one without your permission.

Puryear engages with the history of trade education and, by extension, the interpolation of craft and social status in his celebrated ash-wood sculpture, *Ladder for Booker T. Washington* (1996; see fig. 18). The sinewed thirty-six-foot-long form is deliberately unclimbable, attenuating from a two-foot width at its base to one inch at its crown. The work's title references the eponymous educator and author who championed industrial training for Black Americans as a form of racial and social uplift, self-sufficiency, and assimilation at the turn of the twentieth century. In the words of the scholar Marie Lo, Booker T. Washington "merged labor and art into a mutually ennobling and democratizing vision," much like the proponents of the British Arts and Crafts Movement a generation earlier, including John Ruskin (1819–1900) and William Morris (1834–1896).[32]

Lo has written of Washington's complicated and conflicted relationship with craft. While he rejected "the soullessness of mechanized labor" in the period of Reconstruction following the American Civil War, he also "redefined the binary of 'free' and 'unfree' labor in terms of an affective relation to work, now conceived as 'willing' and 'unwilling' labor" that did not always benefit his fellow Black and newly freed Americans.[33]

Washington gave rise to the ideal of the Black craftsman as someone who embraced "pleasure and dignity in 'intelligent labor.'"[34] In doing so, he opened himself up to criticism for using trade education to cultivate a willing workforce easily assimilated into white capitalism rather than creating a more radical paradigm of freedom for Black Americans.

Almost a century later, Brooklyn-based weaver Allen Fannin (1940–2004; fig. 71) sized up the sociopolitical stakes of craft much more forcefully than Washington ever did. Fannin was asked to recommend participants to a

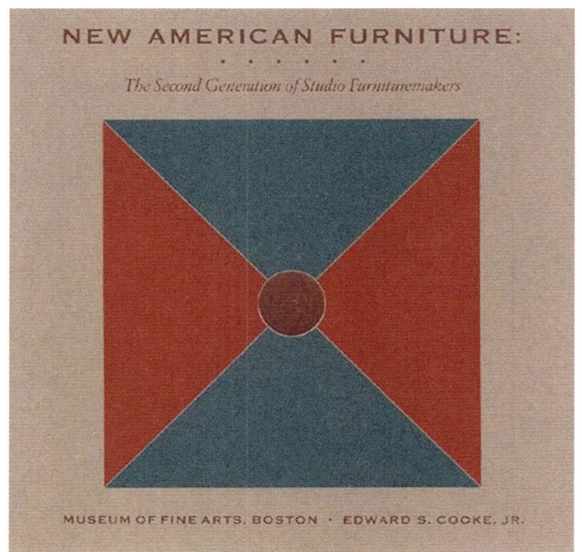

Figure 72. Cover of Edward Cooke, *New American Furniture: The Second Generation of Studio Furnituremakers*, exh. cat. (Boston: Museum of Fine Arts, Boston, 1989)

symposium on African makers at Maine's venerated Haystack Mountain School of Crafts in 1972. Writing to Haystack's director, Fran Merritt, who had reached out to Fannin for help in recruiting teachers and students, Fannin was unsparing in his critique of the contemporary craft world. Fannin framed craft, and the Studio Craft movement in particular, as full of hobbyists who had no need to make a living through crafts and populated by predominantly white makers who were inured to the "very basic human needs" of his fellow Black Americans.[35] "The first factor that is the hardest to take," he wrote, "is the almost total and complete dominance of the craft world by middle and upper crust whites who are, despite seeming indications to the contrary, quite conservative in their lifestyles."[36]

While Puryear's ladder remains an enigmatic critique of incremental social change as it pertains to wider civil rights, his assessment of the craft world is, like Fannin's, much more direct. Puryear is less concerned by the homogeneity produced by the field's historical whiteness. Instead, where his discomfort with craft exists, is rooted in the way in which material intelligence becomes synonymous with repetition and refinement, or so broadly generous in its reach that it encompasses dabblers and dilettantes of all ages and stages. As he puts it, "the word 'craft' has too many meanings. It's a minefield . . . some of the ways craft is understood are quite trivial."[37]

V. Attitude Before Form

Many of Puryear's art-historical interlocutors—and the artist himself—have thus sought to maintain a division between sculpture and furniture in his oeuvre. The historical reticence of writers to substantively engage craft history in relation to Puryear's work is especially understandable when framed by the artist's own caution in this regard.

Such anxiety brings to mind the critic Arthur C. Danto's response to a seminal exhibition of contemporary craft held at the Museum of Fine Arts, Boston, in 1989. The exhibition, *New American Furniture,* invited artists trained in wood to choose works from the museum's permanent collection (whose decorative-arts holdings Puryear knows well) and reinterpret them in the present. The results were put on display in pairs (fig. 72).

After his visit, Danto praised the exhibition as "alive to the referential powers of furniture as a bearer of meaning" and used the opportunity to interrogate art museums' disdain for work perceived as craft. He pointed out that Sandro Botticelli's (1444/45–1510) celebrated late-fifteenth-century panel painting *Primavera* was originally part of an elaborate settle (in Italian, *lettucio*) in the bedchamber alcove of a Florentine patron. He marveled that the furniture element has been consigned to obscurity within art history, "as if the boundary between the bottom edge of *Primavera* and the upper edge of the lettucio's cornice was a metaphysical boundary that divides spirit from crass body—as if, indeed, lettucio and painting together compose a kind of monster, like the centaur, half beast and half human."[38] Reconnecting the dots between Puryear and Krenov not only substantively recuperates craft within a historiography dominated by art history but, like Danto's smart critique of an art-historical blind spot, challenges the very notion that the two could ever have been separated in the first place.

When the polymath Richard Sennett wrote persuasively that craft is not just a set of techniques or relationships with material, but a spirit of care and intention that cuts a far wider swathe, he pinpointed what Krenov offered Puryear.[39] The young artist did not turn up at his elder's studio in Stockholm all those years ago to debate the distance between sculpture and furniture making or the difference between art and craft. He was there to understand what compelled the woodworker to make—and, in turn, to explore what motivated his own making as well. Ultimately, the tools he inherited were those that shaped attitude before they came to mold form.

1. For example, the brief mention that Puryear "even met cabinet maker James Krenov" during his time as a student at the Royal Academy of Fine Arts, Stockholm. See Chase Quinn, "What Is and What Could Be: The Enduring Legacy of Martin Puryear," *Callaloo* 40, no. 5 (2017): 77.

2. James Krenov's achievements as an artist, writer, and educator in the field of craft are many. For an excellent overview of his life and career, see Brendan Gaffney's biography on the maker, *James Krenov: Leave Fingerprints* (Covington, KY: Lost Art Press, 2020). Gaffney trained at Krenov's school of woodworking in Fort Bragg, California, and is a very talented woodworker in his own right.

3. For those unfamiliar with the postwar American Studio Craft movement, a good starting point is Janet Koplos, Bruce Metcalf, and Center for Craft Creativity & Design, *Makers: A History of American Studio Craft* (Chapel Hill: University of North Carolina Press, 2010).

4. Martin Puryear quoted in Michael Brenson, "Maverick Sculptor Makes Good," *New York Times*, November 1, 1987.

5. While Puryear would create his own network within contemporary craft circles, meeting Krenov was a significant entry point into a world of American craft that remained with and sustained the younger artist's interest throughout his subsequent practice. Puryear went on to become aware of important galleries for studio furniture like Peter Joseph Gallery in New York; became friends and collaborators with significant second-generation figures in the Studio Furniture movement such as Michael Hurwitz (b. 1955, a peer of Puryear's brother Michael Puryear, who was also a furniture maker); and had on his bookshelf seminal catalogues such as the Museum of Fine Arts, Boston's 1989 exhibition *New American Furniture*, curated by Edward Cooke, which introduced a new generation of United States-based woodworkers.

6. Puryear's relationship to craft is complicated by his own astute acknowledgment of such hierarchies. Krenov was himself likely leery of artificial taxonomies and externally imposed value systems, including those of the Studio Craft movement itself.

7. Gaffney's excellent and comprehensive biography of James Krenov is the only place where any substantive mention of the meeting between Krenov and Puryear appears; see Gaffney, *Leave Fingerprints*, 103–5. As such, this encounter remains hidden to most art historians writing on Puryear. Puryear knows Gaffney well. They both live in Upstate New York, and the artist is the proud owner of a number of Gaffney's greenwood chairs.

8. I am grateful for the opportunity to speak with Martin Puryear as part of the research for this essay. He is an artist who has proven far better able to engage in interdisciplinary conversations about his work than many of his critical and curatorial interlocutors.

9. Martin Puryear, interview with the author, August 15, 2024.

10. Krenov's cabinet was gifted to the museum by the Craft Association of Stockholm City in 1967. As Gaffney notes, this "silver chest" designed to store flatware was shown as part of the Hanverkslotteriets exhibition, which was an annual showcase for Swedish craft. It is a specific form within Krenov's oeuvre that "provided large uninterrupted show surfaces to showcase fine woods. . . more technically challenging than its relatively simple form implies—the carved pulls are integrally dovetailed into the drawers and function as the drawer runners, a complicated dual purpose that highlights Krenov's technical abilities." Gaffney, *Leave Fingerprints*, 77.

11. Puryear, interview with the author, August 15, 2024.

12. Puryear, interview with the author, August 15, 2024.

13. *Craft Horizons* was founded in 1941 by philanthropist and potter Aileen Osborn Webb (1892–1979), who also created a raft of other booster associations for postwar craft including America House, a retail and exhibition space opposite the Museum of Modern Art (MoMA) in Midtown Manhattan, in operation from 1940 to 1971.

14. This was an early crossover moment for his writing, which had already appeared in Europe but was newer to American audiences. See James Krenov (introduced by Craig McArt), "The Friendly Mystery of Wood," *Craft Horizons* 27, no. 2 (March/April 1967): 28–29, 54.

15. Krenov, "The Friendly Mystery of Wood," 54.

16. Both had an interest in and a reverence for the wilderness, Krenov from his childhood in Siberia and Alaska and Puryear through his travels in young adulthood. As Puryear noted, "His craftsmanship in the very beginning was connected with an Indigenous vernacular engagement with materials. . . . and it's something that had fascinated me as well." Puryear, interview with the author, August 15, 2024.

17. Lenore Metrick-Chen, "Artworks, Artworking, and Race: A Conversation Between Martin Puryear and Theaster Gates," *International Review of African American Art* 26, no. 3 (Summer 2016): 48. See also a 1997 conversation between the artist and MoMA curator Roxana Marcoci: "Brancusi was a person working with his own hands. I saw all his tools in the studio. This was crucial to me. I felt I was doing the same with my work. Today too many artists have become executives." Roxana Marcoci, "The Anti-Historicist Approach: Brancusi, 'Our Contemporary,'" *Art Journal* 59, no. 2 (Summer 2000): 33. On a recent studio visit with Boston-based artist Venetia Dale, Marcoci noted that Dale's craft-oriented graduate program at SUNY New Paltz was a source for Puryear's studio assistants.

18. Robert Storr quoted in Karen Wilkin, "Martin Puryear at MoMA," *New Criterion* 26, no. 5 (January 2008): 43. See also Judith Russi Kirshner, "Martin Puryear in the American Grain," *Artforum* 30, no. 4 (December 1991): 58–63. Kirshner notes that while Puryear's "logical artistic inheritance is Minimalism . . . his work is more individualistic than that of the Minimalists proper, more expressive, if in an austere and subtle way. Though his touch is usually camouflaged by his surface treatment, his art is also more involved with hand work than is Minimalism—his procedures are often drawn from carpentry and boatbuilding. Finally, he appears to have an aversion to the kind of mass or serial production associated with Minimalist artists" (58).

19. Puryear, interview with the author, August 15, 2024.

20. A seminal text by Howard Singerman, a historian of art pedagogy, is helpful here. In the 1960s and 1970s, when, per Singerman, MFA students were deskilling in the studio and centering theory and language rather than physical artworks in their critiques, Puryear did the opposite. See Howard Singerman, *Art Subjects: Making Artists in the American University* (Berkeley: University of California Press, 1999).

21. Gaffney, *Leave Fingerprints*, 104.

22. Krenov continued, "Through the years this edge will be polished, change tone, gleam in mellowness. It will always be the mark of my favorite tool." Krenov, "The Friendly Mystery of Wood," 29.

23. To wit, in a review of Puryear's 2007 MoMA retrospective, Nancy Princenthal invokes craft when she contrasts her view of the "exceptionally elegant construction" of *Bower* (1980; [19]) with what she terms "rough-hewn beams doweled together willy-nilly" in *Thicket* (1990; Seattle Art Museum). Her choice of adjectives to make these distinctions—"raw" versus "cooked," "painstaking craft" versus "untutored workmanship"—elides a stickier but more substantive interpretation of what Puryear took from craft and Krenov, which is the desire to honor and interrogate *process*. This is different than simply aping the mastery Puryear recognized when he made his pilgrimage to Krenov's workbench. Nancy Princenthal, "Puryear's Tall Tales," *Art in America* 96, no. 2 (February 2008): 120.

24. "Artworks, Artworking, and Race," 48.

25. His vision continues to thrive—annual in-state tuition costs less than $1,000.

26. See James Krenov, *A Cabinetmaker's Notebook* (New York: Van Nostrand Reinhold, 1976); *The Fine Art of Cabinetmaking* (New York: Van Nostrand Reinhold, 1977); and *The Impractical Cabinetmaker* (New York: Van Nostrand Reinhold, 1979).

27. As Puryear told me, "I have his last one, which I found interesting because it has work that does not all bear his stamp. It's his students' work . . . [which was] wonderful to see because that was a real testament to a certain kind of openness that I wouldn't have necessarily expected from a person with that rigid set of standards." Puryear, interview with the author, August 15, 2024.

28. The spiritual nature of Krenov's writing is vivid in the following passage: "Rational production of furniture requires wood that is uniform, obedient . . . [but] wood is a subtle material. It wants to express itself, to be made into subtle things . . . if we are to retain, in what we make, all the beauty and life of wood, then the inner, living message of the word must be important to us as craftsmen. And we can't guess at that—we have to listen." Krenov, "The Friendly Mystery of Wood," 29.

29. Puryear, interview with the author, August 15, 2024.

30. While midcentury Scandinavian furniture design was (and is) renowned, it remained a trade rather than an art. Designers created sketches and prototypes but usually sent off their products to be carefully mass-produced.

31. Puryear, interview with the author, August 15, 2024.

32. Marie Lo, "Handcrafting Whiteness: Booker T. Washington and the Subject of Contemporary Craft," *ASAP/Journal* 5, no. 2 (2020): 429. I am grateful to Juliarose Triebes for making me aware of this essay.

33. Lo, "Handcrafting Whiteness," 430.

34. Lo, "Handcrafting Whiteness," 433.

35. Lo, "Handcrafting Whiteness," 433.

36. Sonya Clark, Wesley Clark, Bibiana Obler, Mary Savig, Joyce J. Scott, and Namita Gupta Wiggers, "'The Black Craftsman Situation': A Critical Conversation About Race and Craft," in *The New Politics of the Handmade: Craft Art and Design*, eds. Anthea Black and Nicole Burisch (London: Bloomsbury Visual Arts, 2021), 250.

37. Puryear, interview with the author, August 15, 2024.

38. Arthur C. Danto, "Furniture as Art," *Nation* 250, no. 16 (April 23, 1990): 571–75. For Danto's reflections on Puryear's work in relation to craft, see his "Martin Puryear," *Nation* 256, no. 1 (January 4 & 11, 1993): 30–32.

39. See Richard Sennett, *The Craftsman* (New Haven, CT: Yale University Press, 2008).

You Are Here: The Greater Asias of Martin Puryear

Joan Kee

Martin Puryear's worldliness is its own continuous odyssey. Not for nothing does *Guardian Stone* (2001–3; fig. 73), his first large-scale carved stone sculpture, anticipate the shape of the locational Google Maps pin designed by Jens Eilstrup Rasmussen. Situated on a crescent-shaped plot of land once home to the Mori family residence in central Tokyo's Roppongi Hills, *Guardian Stone* stands just outside the TV Asahi building (2003), headquarters of a major television network designed by the architect Fumihiko Maki (1928–2024). A proponent of what he called "collective form," in which the city figures as a dynamic of interrelated forces rather than as a single, stationary location, Maki invited Puryear to create a sculpture as part of the art program launched by the developer of Roppongi Hills, where TV Asahi would be located. Puryear designed *Guardian Stone* in response, and presented a large wooden model of the work to Maki and his associates.[1] Assisted by Masami Shiraishi (b. 1948), president of the gallery SCAI the Bathhouse, whom Puryear had met in New York City in 2000, the artist traveled to Japan and China, choosing, shaping, and assembling eighteen stone blocks into the final work on the north side of the TV Asahi building, opposite its entrance.[2]

Drawing from years of extensive looking, thinking, reading, and traveling, including time spent in Alaska, Finland, France, Japan, Morocco, Poland, Russia, Sierra Leone, and Sweden, Puryear ranks among the most cosmopolitan of American artists. By this I mean that his works occupy a position equidistant to a range of approaches to making from different places and times. I borrow the word "equidistance" from the architect Arata Isozaki (1931–2022), whose storied 1979 exhibition, *MA: Space / Time in Japan*, at the Cooper Hewitt Museum, New York, overlapped with Puryear's participation at the Whitney Biennial that same year.[3] Realizing that "two types of architecture from different places (spatiality) and times (temporality) can be equidistant from my position," Isozaki saw architecture as a cartographic problem.[4] But it is Puryear's long-standing engagement with Asian techniques of working with spaces and shapes that suggests how allusion and influence manifest kinship beyond inherited ties.

Assisted by a Guggenheim Foundation grant, Puryear embarked on a month of self-directed travel in Japan in the fall of 1983. Gardens figured prominently in his travels, and the impact of his close looking may be the invisible hand behind *Guardian Stone*. Although Puryear titled the work after completing the sculpture, *Guardian Stone* had always been destined to preside over the Japanese garden facing the huge, curving glass atrium of TV Asahi.[5] Responsible for cohering a garden's ecology of forms, a guardian stone in Japanese landscape architecture traditionally serves as an anchoring presence, as in the manner outlined by the British architect Josiah Conder (1852–1920) in his copiously illustrated treatise of 1893.[6] A case in point is *Stone no. 41* in the Meiji-era Kiyosumi Garden, which was among the sites Puryear visited (fig. 74). There, the guardian stone energizes the space without dominating it, an apt metaphor for how influence operates throughout Puryear's oeuvre.

Figure 73. Installation view of *Guardian Stone* (2001–3) outside of the TV Asahi headquarters, Tokyo. Martin Puryear. Black granite; 550 x 370 x 300 cm. Photo: Shigeo Anzai

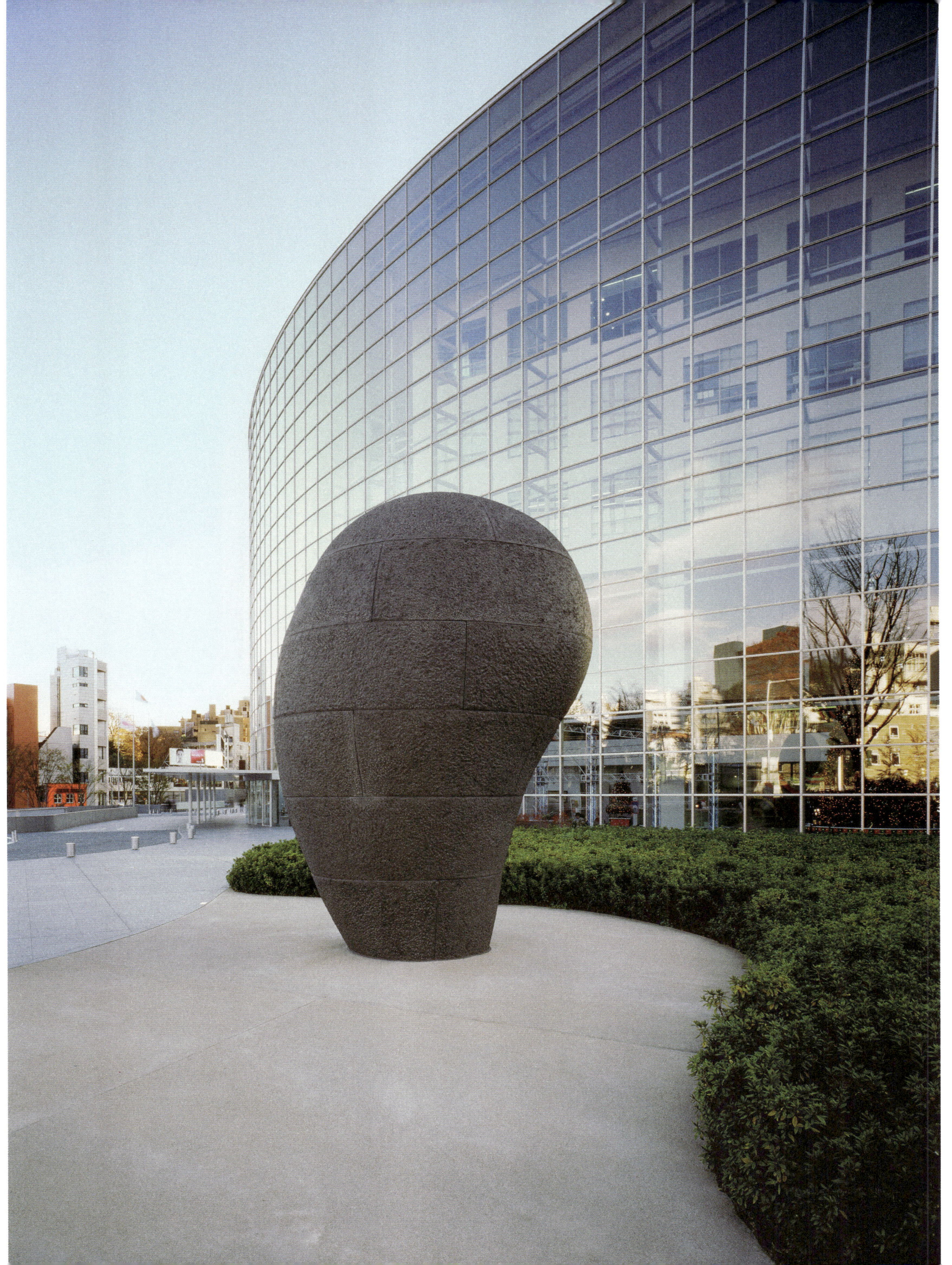

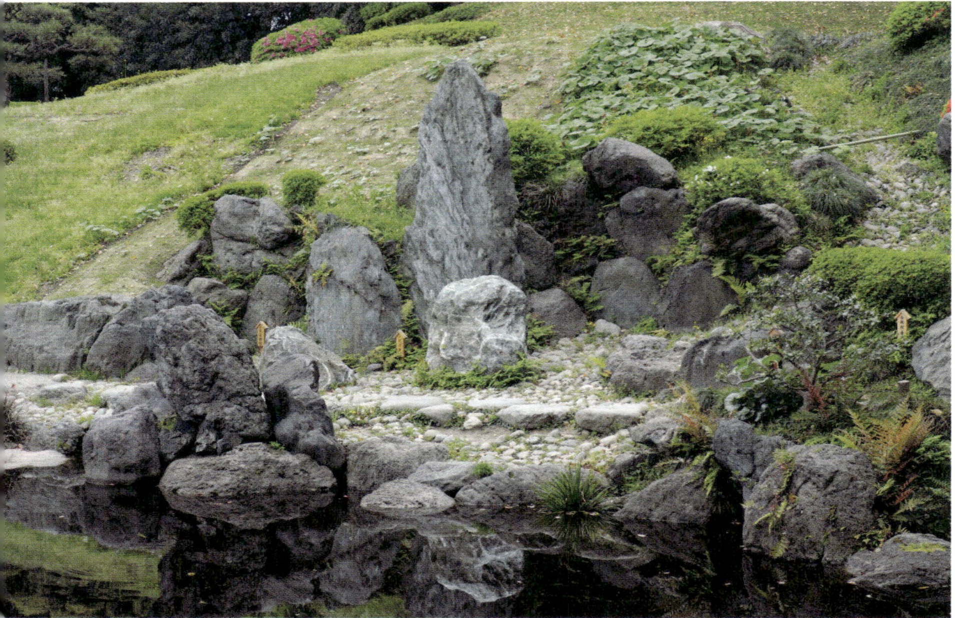

Figure 74. *Stone no. 41*, Kiyosumi Garden, Tokyo, Meiji era, 1868–1912. Photo: Thomas S. Elias

By alluding so strongly to Japanese gardens, *Guardian Stone* declares itself cultural kin to a long history of placemaking. In the process, it defies myopic readings of artistic possibility that entertain the question of influence only when it appears to confirm preconceptions arising from cursory attention to an artist's cultural, national, and racial heritages. Indeed, *Guardian Stone* demonstrates the relevance of Black intellectual vitality for audiences invested in what the art historian Toshio Watanabe implies is a critical question embodied by the Japanese garden: how to balance a sense of uniqueness primarily ascribed to Japanese culture with a belief in the "universality of Japanese civilization."[7] Irreducible to representation affirmed through physical resemblance, influence in Puryear's hands is a tool of social possibility. The forms to which he commits connect him, in turn, with audiences not expecting someone like him to produce work so deeply empathetic to their most cherished histories.

The poet John Yau (b. 1950) writes that "it is not an 'I' using the form to speak, but a diverse and complex 'we' speaking through the form" of Puryear's works.[8] But where Yau suggests that "we" encompasses "anonymous workers and history" who made possible certain ways of seeing and making, Puryear carefully notes how the refinement of technique—what he terms "reverence"—must often yield to an entire regime of specialization.[9] Long acquainted with Japanese landscapes and woodworking approaches furthered by his visits to Bay Area woodworkers specializing in temple carving and other related techniques, the artist admires the difficulty of lengthening wood he characterizes as "not wanting to be interrupted."[10] In a 2018 conversation, he spoke feelingly about the patience needed to develop what he called a "system" of strengthening an "inherently weak connection" between two pieces of fibrous wood.[11]

Yet, Puryear has long resisted converting his interest into a single-minded pursuit of expertise. Although he learned woodworking in Sierra Leone and Sweden, early on the artist recognized the risks of perfection partly through the extent to which technique in Japan approached a "devotional practice" of sorts.[12] Of his experiences creating *Guardian Stone*, he remarks how "the level of craft that's practiced there [in Japan] is so extraordinary that, if you have the right kind of mind, you really just get pulled along into that."[13] In many respects the pursuit of knowledge entails a loss of self or, as Puryear puts it, the "submission of one's ego."[14] At worst it devolves into "tunnel vision."[15] The dark side of expertise is its subordination to what Puryear characterizes as an "idealized view of the world" in which the rationale for action and even existence depends on their "perfectibility."[16] Powerful enough to warp artistic engagement so that the resulting work can only look residual in comparison to a more ideal referent, the enterprise of perfectible craft struck Puryear as a closed game, whereby craft was not an open-ended play but an established set of means to achieve a defined end. His encounters with Japanese carpentry and wood carving foreground the paradoxical nature of competence: as one becomes more comfortable navigating increasing levels and forms of difficulty, one must also develop vigilance against letting expertise petrify too quickly into an unyielding professionalism.

Puryear distinguishes between the unforgiving hierarchy on which many forms of expertise depend and the authority that accrues when visibly demonstrating skill. Neither amateurish nor obsessive, his works physically record intellectual and technical competence. Highly indicative of his approach to knowledge is his engagement with the yurt, the tentlike form of mobile dwelling used by nomadic communities throughout Central Asia. Assembled within days or even

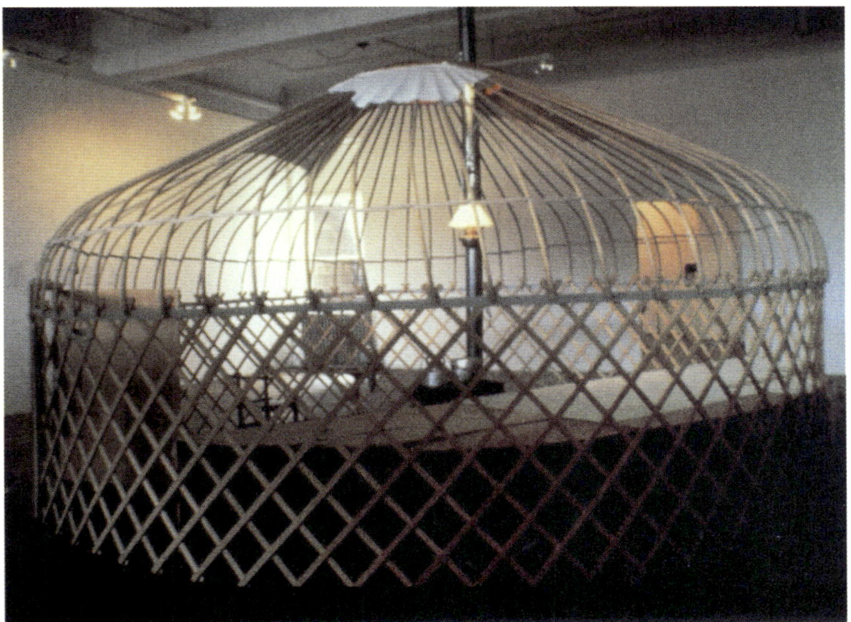

Figure 75. Installation view of *Martin Puryear*, and/or gallery, Seattle, 1981. Pictured: *Where the Heart Is* (1981). Yurt, mixed media; 548.6 cm (diameter), no longer extant

hours, a yurt consists of a portable wooden-and-bamboo frame in a lattice pattern to ensure even weight distribution; animal skins or cloth traditionally insulated the wooden frame. The yurt captured the artist's attention from a very young age, and Puryear revisited the form after a devastating fire in his Brooklyn studio in 1977. Puryear made a yurt-like sculpture in 1981, displaying it for the first time that year in Seattle (fig. 75), and later in 1990 for the Museum of Fine Arts, Boston (see fig. 37), in 1992 for that year's edition of Documenta, and in 2018 for an exhibition at the Museum Voorlinden in the Netherlands.[17] Compelling visual resemblance between the functioning yurt and Puryear's 1981 take, *Where the Heart Is*, compresses the geographical—and to a lesser degree—chronological distance separating the two. Whereas the lattice of a functional yurt is intended as a scaffold awaiting final cover, the artist typically leaves his uncovered. We see its fragility and its collapsibility.

There is also buoyancy in Puryear's yurt sculpture. At first glance, the wooden lattice in *Where the Heart Is* tapers to sharp points that only kiss the gallery floor. Stay a while longer, however, and the entire assembly appears on the verge of levitation, its attachment to the ground noncommittal at best. Puryear suggests as much in his 1990 presentation of the yurt at the Museum of Fine Arts, Boston.[18] There, guided by a rendering of a falcon by the legendary Mughal painter and naturalist Mansur (active c. 1590–1630; see fig. 36), the yurt escapes the load-bearing implications of the word "influence." Puryear's commitment to the yurt bridges multiple parallel histories of making ordinarily separated from one another because of geography and time period. What initially reads as unilateral influence is but a symptom of the work's transversal force cutting across both a relatively brief history of modern sculpture configured through US and European Minimalisms and a history of housing architecture in Central Asia spanning thousands of years. More a dynamic companion than a placid source, the yurt surfaces as an instance of how traditions read more strongly as endurances.

Something of this endurance resounds even more forcefully when considering *Guardian Stone* alongside the obelisk designed by Isamu Noguchi (1904–1988), an artist whose protean movement across sculpture, public art, furniture, and craft has long appealed to Puryear (fig. 76).[19] Channeling the flow of pedestrian traffic through the Japanese American Cultural and Community Center Plaza

Figure 76. Installation view of *To The Issei*, 1980–83, Japanese American Cultural and Community Center Plaza, Los Angeles. Isamu Noguchi (American, 1904–1988; sculptor). Exterior design with basalt sculptural elements and water; horizontal sculpture: 121.9 x 355.6 x 137.2 cm; vertical sculpture: 365.8 x 152.4 x 96.5 cm. © 2025 The Isamu Noguchi Foundation and Garden Museum, New York / Artists Rights Society (ARS), New York. Photo: Courtesy of Esoteric Survey

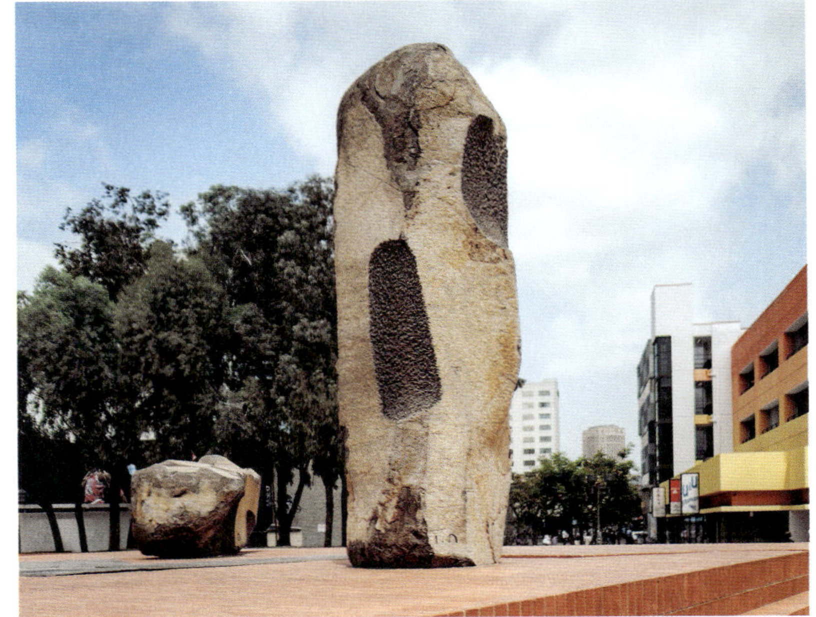

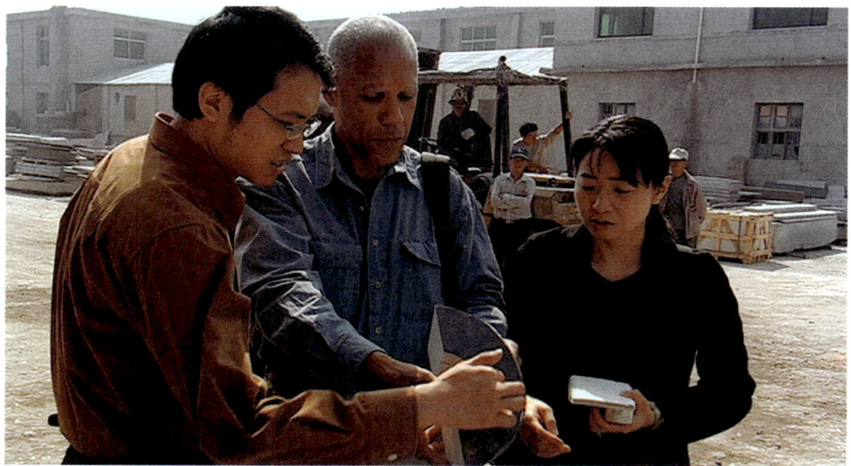

Figure 77. Martin Puryear working in a stone yard in Xiamen, China, 2002. Production still from the Art21 television series *Art in the Twenty-First Century*, season 2, "Time." © Art21, Inc. 2003.

in Los Angeles's Japantown, Noguchi's obelisk acts as a pivot point much like *Guardian Stone* does for the Roppongi Hills complex. Realized between 1980 and 1983, the obelisk and its loyal companion draw on Noguchi's interest in veneration structures in ways that both anticipate and follow Puryear's extended visual engagement with the temples of Nara and the seventeenth-century Katsura Imperial Villa. Standing upright like a sentry, it casts shadow onto the orange-brick plaza like a gnomon does onto a sundial. The Shanxi black granite used for *Guardian Stone* absorbs sunlight while also reflecting light particles so that the work appears to shimmer like a beacon from a distance. The subdued gleam of the highly durable granite from north China, known for its deep-black hue with minimal veining, counters the transparency of Maki's enormous glass atrium as well as the shiny reflective surfaces of the neighboring fifty-four-story Mori Tower.

Whereas Noguchi's basalt elements emerge from monolithic, independent stone forms, *Guardian Stone* is a composite produced from numerous blocks manually aggregated into a single shape. The work posed significant challenges for Puryear. Despite Puryear having provided a maquette to Chinese fabricators in Xiamen (fig. 77), manual labor could not precisely translate the artist's vision at the scale desired. *Guardian Stone* arose from a succession of balancing acts such that to behold the work is also to participate in the process of its continuous realization. By way of comparison, consider *Untitled* from 1997 [34]. Shown indoors, *Untitled* discloses the inadequacy of the museum gallery as its proper dwelling even as its apparent mass enhances the perception of institutional gravity. Puryear revels in the conflicting impressions his sense of scale produces; one could even claim that these impressions are exactly what enables his works to model forbearance and generosity toward viewers eager to "read into" what it is they see.

A favorite curatorial game is to collect the references Puryear's work seems to so easily accrue. Treating his sculptures as if they were lost ships in need of interpretive rescue, some authors mistake allusion in his work for an act of citation or as a residual visual echo. Think, for instance, of how *Pavilion in the Trees* (1993; fig. 78), Puryear's model for an outdoor project proposed in 1981, was, in one writer's description, conflated with a Sámi storehouse and a *honden*, the most sacred structure in a Shinto temple.[20] But contrary to both the storehouse and the *honden*, whose very existence as a sanctuary for divine spirits depends on barring public access, Puryear's work maximizes the everyday pleasures of egress. Intended to dissolve into the wooded surroundings, the visible structure is only one part of a multisensorial passage. While a surveyor understands the land using geodetic calculations and meridian designations, Puryear trails the logic of the Japanese garden in which space is not a pictorial depiction but an irreproducible passage through time.

Puryear constantly revisits allusion and influence, two of the most common strategies for understanding the presence of art in the world. When *Guardian Stone* was first installed, Puryear was relatively unknown in Japan despite having participated in the group exhibition *Weaving the World: Contemporary Art of Linear Construction* at the Yokohama Museum of Art in 1999. But as Shiraishi observed, *Guardian Stone* quickly became its own center of gravity.[21] Part of its pull owes much to what it so forcefully says and does not say about influence. Just as allusion becomes more fathomable as a sign of kinship, influence cannot be explained only through identifiable resemblances. Rather, it concerns the interdependence of admission and denial. We hear

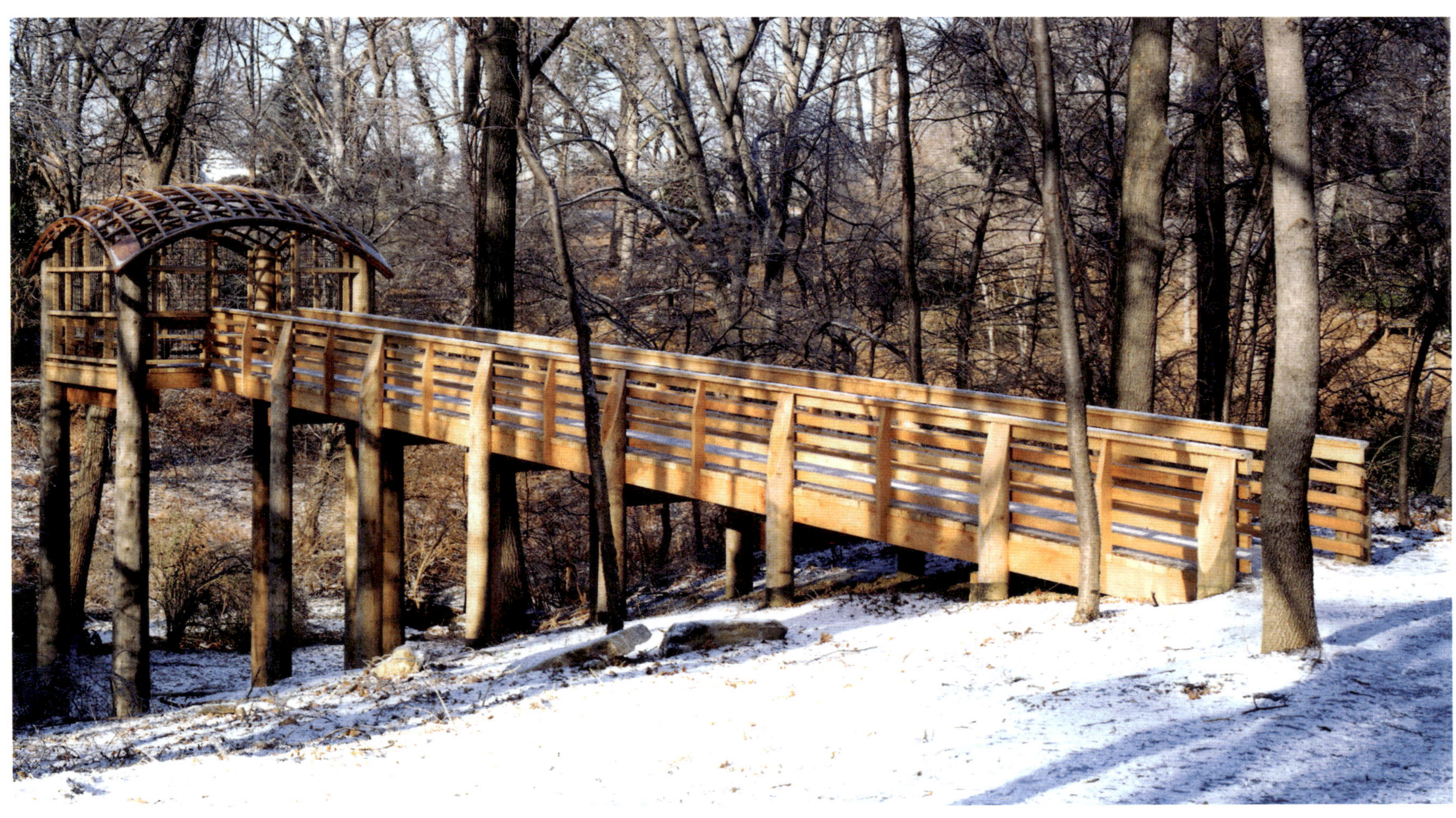

Figure 78. Installation view of *Pavilion in the Trees* (1983) at Fairmount Park, Philadelphia, 1994. Martin Puryear. Debarked western red cedar, white oak, heart redwood, and chain-link fencing; walkway: 152.4 cm (width), 1828.8 cm (length); deck: 34.3 x 34.3 cm; 731.5 cm (aboveground); latticed canopy: 335.3 x 487.7 x 487.7 cm; overall: approximately 1066.8 cm (height). Photo © Wayne Cozzolino, 1994, courtesy of the Association for Public Art

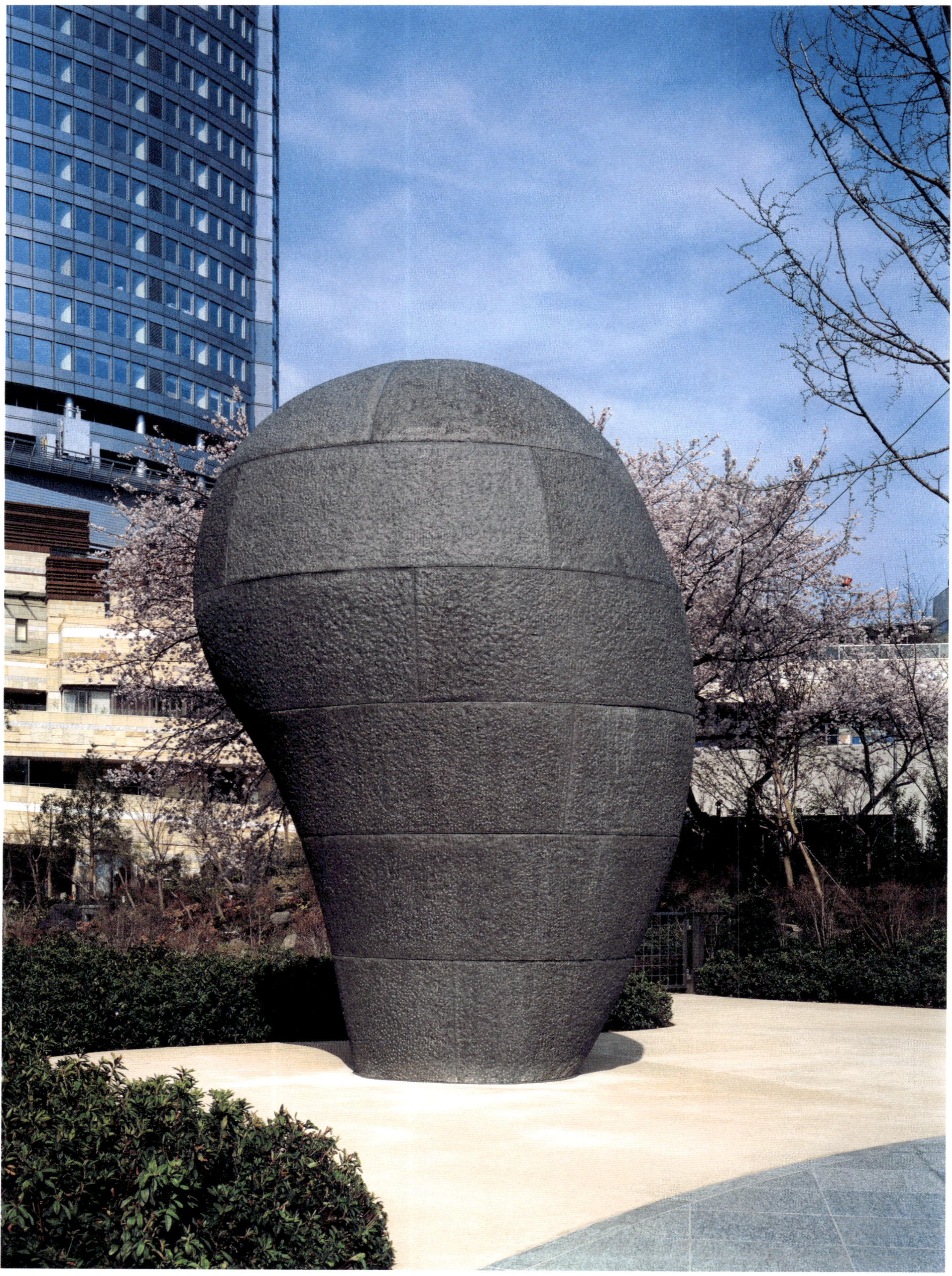

Figure 79. Installation view of *Guardian Stone* (2001–3) outside of the TV Asahi headquarters, Tokyo. Photo: Shigeo Anzai

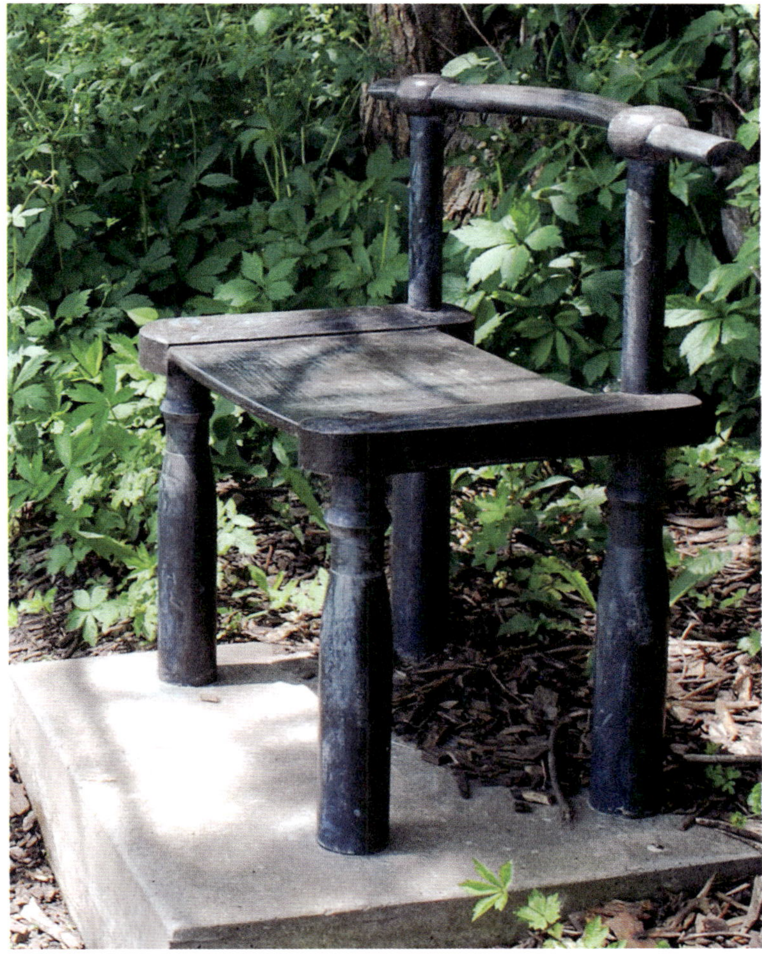

Figure 80. Detail view of the chair in *Bodark Arc* (1982) at the Nathan Manilow Sculpture Park, Governors State University, University Park, Illinois. Martin Puryear. Cast bronze; 64.8 x 64.8 x 38.1 cm. Photo: Courtesy of Nathan Manilow Sculpture Park

this in Puryear's incisive observations on the outsize impact of Minimalism on histories of modern and contemporary art that are given precedence in museum collections and university syllabi. When Puryear first saw the work of Donald Judd (1928–1994), "it cleared the air" for him to pursue "purity and simplicity" in his work.[22] Yet purity qua Minimalism read increasingly as a system of disqualifications, banishments, and exclusions. Puryear states, "you can only rarify something so much before you have nothing left. And I'm really committed to *objects*, not to dogma."[23]

He accordingly works with a much broader time frame than can be comfortably inferred from Minimalism or the art histories it serves. *Guardian Stone* looks as if it is locked in ceaseless internal debate with itself and its own shadow as to what form it should finally take. Is it a tilted sphere elongating into a column, or is it an upright columnar shape bulging at one end? Puryear recounts long discussions during the work's assembly in China over how the contours did not sufficiently bulge in certain places while being too straight in others.[24] All of Puryear's works are treasuries of allusion. But the artist sternly guards against the possibility of their becoming diffuse; hence, the deliberation over whether a voluminous shape should be more globular or whether an edge is too straight.

Guardian Stone proposes we consider influence as a model of mutual intelligibility. Recalling some theories of intertextuality, such a model deemphasizes a work's relation to prior texts in favor of attending to how the work actively participates in spaces defined by other cultural priorities.[25] At stake is not how Japanese aesthetics may have shaped Puryear's thinking but, on the contrary, how his work has amplified or reframed such aesthetics so that even the most knowledgeable theorists could be reenchanted by what they might ordinarily regard as examples of routine or habit. It was hardly a coincidence that Maki was so taken by Puryear's work. For Puryear understands how placemaking exceeds the physical construction of human-made things to honor unoccupied space for its past and future potentials. Another way to think about influence, then, depends less on centering what one receives, absorbs, or takes away and more on how the resulting work replenishes the sources from which it draws.

While firmly stating that his work is not Japanese but "American," Puryear nevertheless wills into being sculptures unintentionally more faithful than many of its Japanese analogues to the Zen Buddhist concept of *yūgen*, or "mysterious profundity."[26] Curiously apropos of Puryear's work is Allen Weiss's observation of how the quality of mystery in Japanese gardens feeds on "the tension between iconography and abstraction" (fig. 79).[27] Much of *Guardian Stone*'s potency turns on how it verges on human form without demanding that human proportions determine our measure of the world. Despite towering over the average adult viewer, *Guardian Stone* remains deeply connected to human scale. Small wonder, then, that Maki should see the work as having a "human face."[28]

Puryear's sculptures toggle between referentiality as a form of disclosure and concealment that denies such referentiality full expression. When ambling through *Bodark Arc* (1982) in the Nathan Manilow Sculpture Park in University Park, Illinois, we might stumble across a low bronze chair (fig. 80). Though styled after a West African throne, the work withholds any explanation as to how or why it came to be. The chair tugs on our imagination, bringing us closer to the histories of chairs associated with the Dan people of West Africa and of *ukibori*, a Japanese relief-carving technique used to embellish wood. Here, allusion is

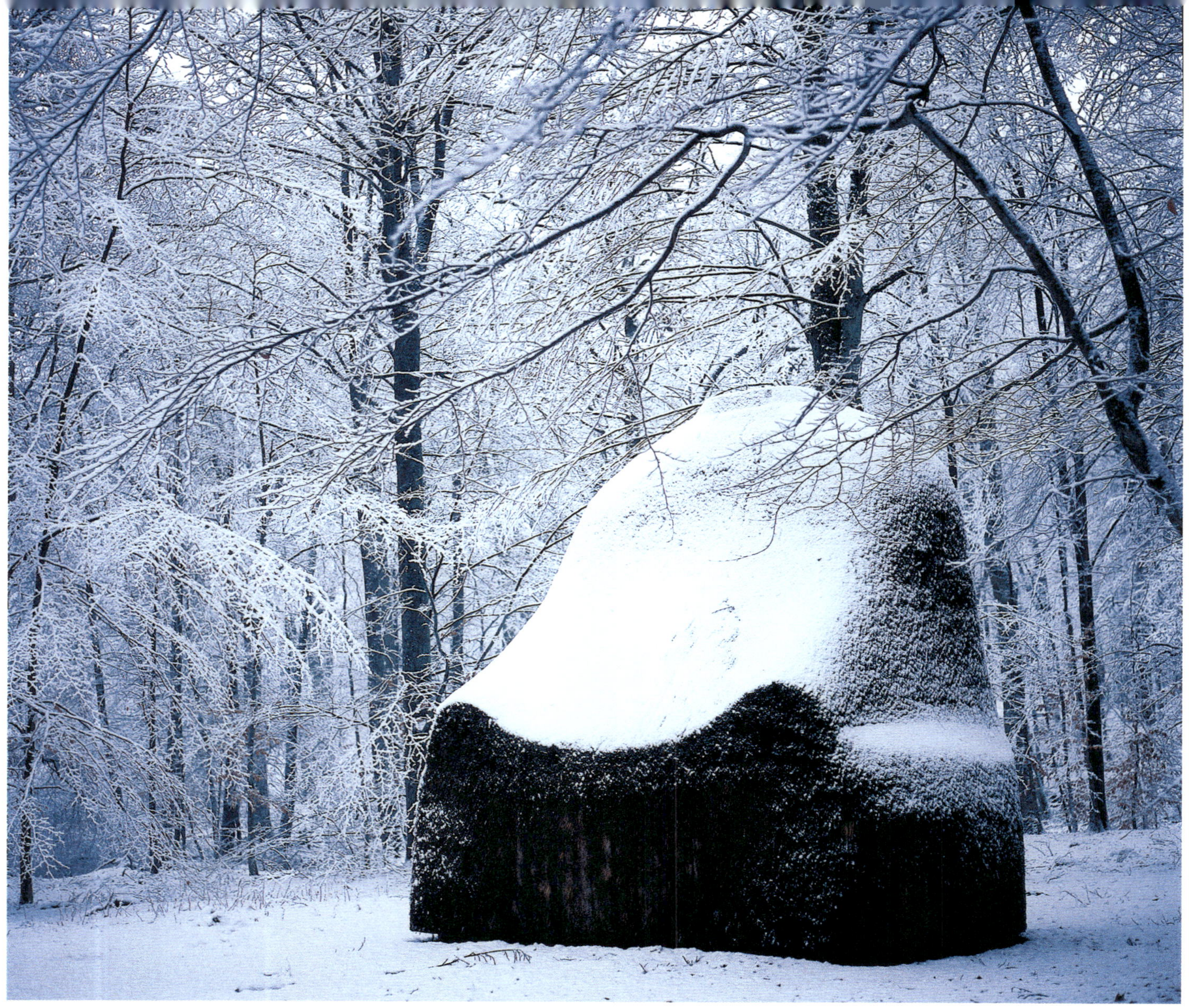

Figure 81. Installation view of *Meditation in a Beech Wood* (1996) at the Wanås Foundation, Knislinge, Sweden. Martin Puryear. Water reed thatched over timber frame (wood, concrete, and steel); 444.8 x 500.4 x 340.4 cm. Photo: Anders Norrsell

a two-step process. Viewers first become attuned to other histories with which the work coexists, then find themselves overwhelmed by the vast scope of these histories and what they imply. Our tongues are stilled in a manner perhaps akin to Isozaki's conception of "complete silence" as "extravagance."[29]

Arguably the most silent of Puryear's works is the enormous thatched-reed structure known as *Meditation in a Beech Wood* (1996; fig. 81).[30] Nestled in a beech forest in Knislinge, Sweden, its bell shape invokes a seated Buddha sans head or legs. Puryear never formally studied or practiced Buddhism. Yet the viewing experience *Meditation in a Beech Wood* affords is perhaps best apprehended in light of Theravada meditation techniques, based on calming the mind and seeking to know the true nature of things. Together with its distinctive form, the largeness of the work demands undistracted attention from the viewer, who develops their powers of attention by withdrawing their focus from other thoughts or objects so that the mind has a chance to slow down. To see the work, one must refrain from speaking. The Buddha-like figure fills and enlivens space otherwise mistaken for a lapse, or as simply nonexistent, by inducing viewers to dwell on its susceptibility to the vagaries of weather, time, and animal life. Prolonged viewing highlights the impermanence of the work that mechanical or digital technologies cannot properly record. Viewing thus begins to resemble the kind of training undertaken through Vipassana practice that encourages the acceptance of change, including mortality. In this way, *Meditation in a Beech Wood* turns on how scale bridges mysticism, or a state of consciousness ascribed to personal spiritual transformation, and empiricism rooted in verifiable observation and measurement.

Silence connotes evasion. Even under the brightest daylight, *Guardian Stone* possesses an opacity in the vein described by the critic Greg Tate. Writing of the unprecedented visibility of Black artists in the United States including Terry Adkins (1953–2014), who studied with Puryear at Fisk University in the early 1970s, Sanford Biggers (b. 1970), Kerry James Marshall (b. 1955), and Kara Walker (b. 1969), Tate hoped for what he called a "utopic leap forward" in which Black artistic mystery "may be so abstracted and encoded as to be invisible to the nakedly ethnographic eye."[31] The referential instability of *Guardian Stone* deflects the rapacious demands such an eye makes of anything it hopes to pillage for digestible meaning. Rejecting systems of classification and preservation that coerce assemblies of form and spirit to perform as specimens under glass, a defiance borne of reticence energizes Puryear's works. The receptivity of Puryear's oeuvre to Asian and African forms especially fly outside the purview of ethnographic insistences on fixed location. Managing multiple relationships to different scales, as well as rates, of operation, *Guardian Stone* sets its own pace. We gladly follow its lead, trusting it will bring us far beyond where we started.

1. Gary Kamemoto, principal of Maki and Associates, email to the author, April 4, 2024.

2. Masami Shiraishi recalls meeting Puryear in 2000 in New York. Email to the author, December 15, 2023.

3. Puryear was aware of Isozaki but neither knew of nor attended the 1979 exhibition in New York. Martin Puryear, conversation with the author, February 21, 2024.

4. Arata Isozaki, *The Island Nation Aesthetic* (London: Wiley, 1996), 7.

5. Puryear, conversation with the author, February 21, 2024. Puryear has also stated that artwork titles are usually "afterthoughts." Richard J. Powell, "A Conversation with Martin Puryear," in *Martin Puryear*, ed. John Elderfield, exh. cat. (New York: Museum of Modern Art, 2007), 107.

6. Josiah Conder, *Landscape Gardening in Japan* (Tokyo: Kelly and Walsh, 1893).

7. Toshio Watanabe, "The Modern Japanese Garden," in *Since Meiji: Perspectives on the Japanese Visual Arts, 1868–2000*, ed. J. Thomas Rimer (Honolulu: University of Hawai'i Press, 2012), 349.

8. John Yau, "Some Thoughts About Richard Serra and Martin Puryear (Part 2: Puryear)," *Hyperallergic* (November 16, 2014), https:// hyperallergic.com/162494/some-thoughts-about-richard-serra-and-martin-puryear-part-2-puryear/.

9. Puryear, conversation with the author, February 21, 2024.

10. Puryear, "A Conversation with Martin Puryear," interviewed by Billie Tsien, June 27, 2018, published on July 16, 2018, Architectural League of New York, https://vimeo.com/280212494?share=copy.

11. Puryear, "A Conversation with Martin Puryear."

12. Puryear, conversation with the author, February 21, 2024.

13. Martin Puryear, "Interview: Stone Carving," *Art 21*, September 2003, https://art21.org/read/martin-puryear-stone-carving/.

14. Puryear, conversation with the author, February 21, 2024.

15. Puryear, "Interview: Stone Carving."

16. Puryear, "Interview: Stone Carving."

17. For a chronology of Puryear's yurt installations, see Emily Liebert's essay in this volume, pp. 130–21, p. 139n24, n27. Founded in 1955, Documenta is one of the world's premier recurring showcases for contemporary art, taking place every five years in Kassel, Germany.

18. The work inaugurated *Connections*, a series hosted by the museum that invited artists to design an installation based on a historical object or image important to their work.

19. Puryear intended to visit Noguchi's studio in Shikoku, but unfortunately did not have enough time during his Japan travels. Puryear, conversation with the author, February 21, 2024.

20. Neal Benezra, "'The Thing Shines, Not the Maker': The Sculpture of Martin Puryear," in Neal Benezra and Robert Storr, *Martin Puryear*, exh. cat. (New York: Thames & Hudson; Chicago: Art Institute of Chicago, 1991), 34.

21. Shiraishi, email to the author, December 15, 2023.

22. Martin Puryear, quoted in Steven Henry Madoff, "Sculpture Unbound," *ARTnews* 85, no. 9 (November 1986): 104–5.

23. Martin Puryear, quoted in Madoff, "Sculpture Unbound," 105.

24. Puryear, conversation with the author, February 21, 2024.

25. Jonathan Culler, "Presupposition and Intertextuality," in *The Pursuit of Signs: Semiotics, Literature, Deconstruction* (Ithaca, NY: Cornell University Press, 1981), 103.

26. Puryear, conversation with the author, February 21, 2024.

27. Allen Weiss, *Zen Landscapes: Perspectives on Japanese Gardens and Ceramics* (London: Reaktion Books, 2013), 76.

28. Iris Brooks, "'Artelligent' Living," *Washington* 18, no. 9 (September 2003): 70, 72, 77.

29. Arata Isozaki, "Arata Isozaki—TIME SPACE EXISTENCE," 2017, published on September 23, 2024, Thisispaper, https://www.youtube.com/watch?v=alr02PQrd1k.

30. For further discussion of *Meditation in a Beech Wood*, see Maya Lin in this volume, p. 74.

31. Greg Tate, "To Bid a Poet Black and Abstract," in *Flyboy 2: The Greg Tate Reader* (Durham and London: Duke University Press, 2016), 212.

Martin Puryear: Refractions of the Historical Present

Rizvana Bradley

The most interesting art for me retains a flickering quality, where opposed ideas can be held in tense coexistence.[1]

—Martin Puryear

To write about Martin Puryear and the impact of his sculptural practice requires a reconsideration of the social and political import of Black cultural and artistic forms in the making *and* unmaking of American life. Puryear's art, which builds upon an extended tradition of Black cultural and artistic interrogations of the given orders of meaning, history, and lived experience, references the conflicting, incongruous, and unresolvable histories of Black striving and struggle. On the one hand, his sculptures bear the unique imprints of the past in the present. On the other, they retain, materially, the inscriptive power and poetic resonance of absented lives and lost registers of experience. This essay argues for a nuanced approach to Puryear's work that differentially emphasizes history, ecology, and craft as form.

Exploring the evolution of his work across nearly five decades, this essay highlights Puryear's legacy as an artist, designer, architect, and philosopher of and for the historical present. Puryear's work does not merely reflect the progression of history nor does it seek to redeem the past or yearn for a future yet to arrive. Rather, his practice holds open the present as a means of restoring to consciousness what has been and continues to be elided, absented, or voided from historical memory.

The following meditation on Puryear's practice begins by turning toward traditions of Black radicalism in a global, transnational frame that elude historical documentation but that have become inescapably crucial to the realization of various expressions of Black artistry. It then shifts to take up those neglected ecologies that are gathered within and threaded through Black quotidian life-worlds by placing Puryear's practice in conversation with discourses that have taken shape within environmental philosophy, ecopoetry, and critical theories of ecology. Finally, the text concludes by reconsidering Puryear's work with respect to the aesthetic valuations of and distinctions between art and craft. Far from suggesting the harmonious complementarity of "art" and "craft," my reading emphasizes Puryear's refusal/reversal of the dualistic distinction between, and hierarchical ordering of, art and craft as axiomatic aesthetic tropes.[2]

I.

Ladder for Booker T. Washington (1996; figs. 82 and 83) stands out as one of Martin Puryear's most significant works. Twisting insistently into space, the sculptural composition evokes a sense of the metaphysical, of infinity, at the same time that it registers to the eye as a delimited structure. Puryear engineers a trick of the eye, or trompe l'oeil, rather than anchor the viewer in space. The ladder induces a strange kind of vertigo. Its unusual curvature creates a general feeling of disorientation, and its extreme verticality foregrounds a formal precarity with respect to both scale and perspective. While the title of the sculpture might lead one to read the work as a metaphor for collective Black striving toward the attainment of political, economic, and social equality within the context of American democracy at the turn of the twentieth century, Puryear would likely welcome a more nuanced interpretation.

The artist has insisted that *Ladder*'s title not be taken as indexical to the material and conceptual thrust of the sculpture itself, explaining that he wanted to "[make] a work that had a kind of artificial perspective, a forced perspective—an exaggerated perspective that made it appear to recede into space faster than, in fact, it does."[3] He continues:

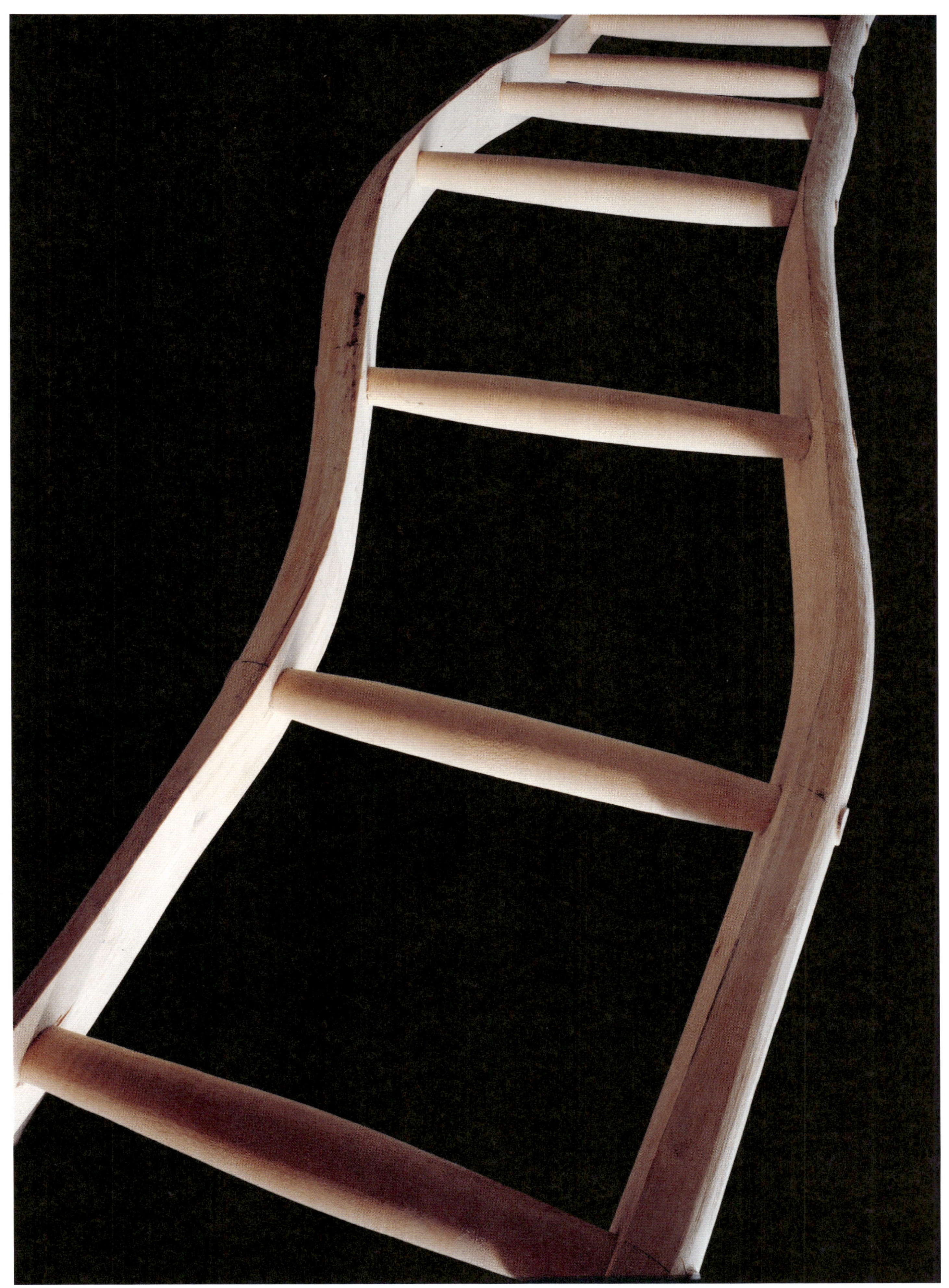

Figure 82. Detail of *Ladder for Booker T. Washington* (1996). Martin Puryear. Ash and maple; 1097.3 x 60.3 x 7.6 cm. Photo: Katherine Wetzel, © Virginia Museum of Fine Arts

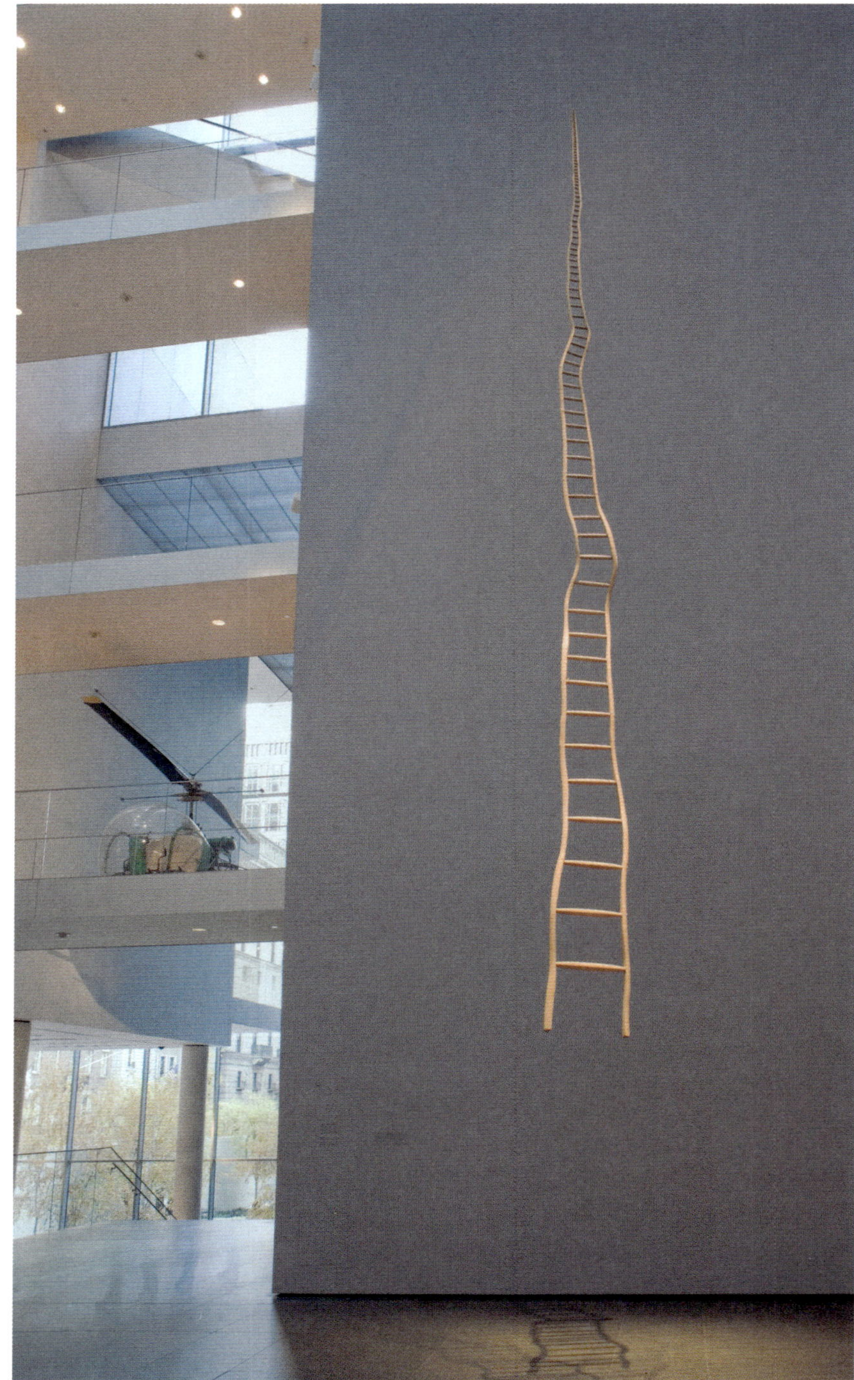

Figure 83. Installation view of *Ladder for Booker T. Washington* (1996) in *Martin Puryear*, The Museum of Modern Art, New York, 2008. Digital Image © The Museum of Modern Art / Licensed by SCALA / Art Resource, NY

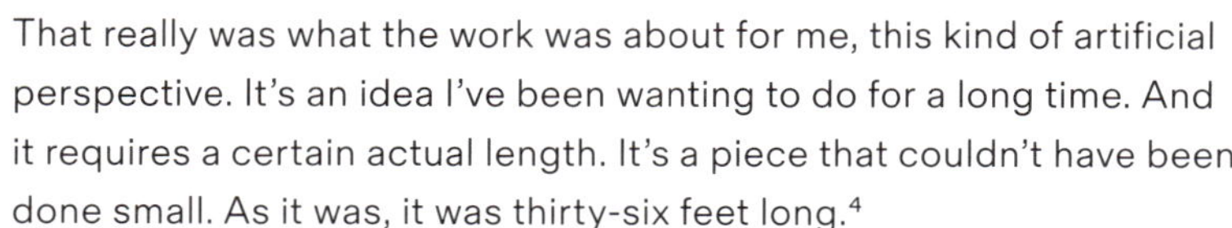

> That really was what the work was about for me, this kind of artificial perspective. It's an idea I've been wanting to do for a long time. And it requires a certain actual length. It's a piece that couldn't have been done small. As it was, it was thirty-six feet long.[4]

What becomes evident is an artistic choice to refuse to subsume *Ladder* and its formal attributes under the rubric of a narrow historicity or archivalism—in other words, *Ladder*, as a sculpture, should not be read as a transparent historical document or biographical index.

I begin with an extended consideration of *Ladder*'s prominence within Puryear's oeuvre because of the way in which the work unveils a conceptual register that exceeds the metaphorical and the allegorical. Puryear elaborates:

> People who see it want to know what it's about. It's a curiosity when they see a title as specific as that. It's been written about a couple of times. In fact, there's a wall label in the [Museum of Modern of Art] . . . that talks about Booker T. Washington more than it talks about the work, which I find interesting. . . . But I think the urgency of the historical information about Booker T. Washington is . . . what the museum thinks the public would want to know, or should know about it and, I think, in this case eclipses what's going on within the object. I found that kind of interesting.[5]

What strikes me with regard to Puryear's assertions about the sculpture is a certain slippage between the public perception of the work and the overdetermination of Blackness within the available frameworks of contemporary art discourses.

The predicament that plagues the reception of work such as Puryear's within these discourses is the selective privileging of historical events that prefigure dominant patterns of interpretation. This seems to persist across critical assessments of Black art at the same time that the more minor registers of Black lived experience remain unavailable to art-historical inquiry. As the art historian Darby English has diagnosed the problem: "We do not yet have a way of tending openly and honestly to historical events and developments on the near side of racism—that is, exhortations to and about black artists and their work in the name of safeguarding this supposed distinctness—within the framework of dominant patterns of thinking 'black art,' 'racial representation,' and other like categories."[6]

Crucially, Puryear's practice gestures to the slippage between the work and its interpretation in a way that betrays an even larger problem pertaining to the discursive unavailability of Blackness within the onto-epistemology—the available knowledges and empirical frameworks that ground what is taken for reality—of various art-historical conceptualisms. The formal innovations that underpin *Ladder for Booker T. Washington*, particularly the trick of the eye that the work engineers, cannot be considered apart from its reflexive interrogation of the field of overdetermined meaning within which it is always already poised to circulate. Indeed, the key to apprehending *Ladder* is understanding how Puryear anticipates these very problematics and allows them to be the subject of the sculpture.

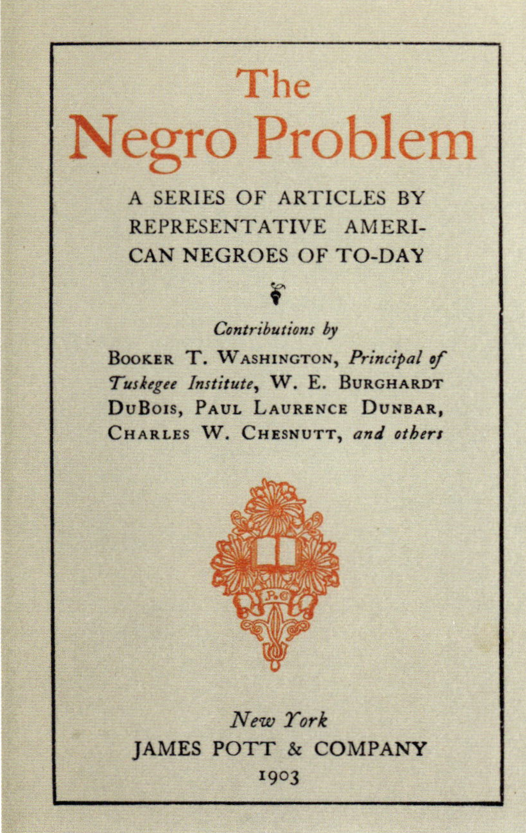
The
Negro Problem
A SERIES OF ARTICLES BY REPRESENTATIVE AMERICAN NEGROES OF TO-DAY
Contributions by
BOOKER T. WASHINGTON, *Principal of Tuskegee Institute*, W. E. BURGHARDT DUBOIS, PAUL LAURENCE DUNBAR, CHARLES W. CHESNUTT, *and others*
New York
JAMES POTT & COMPANY
1903

Figure 84. Booker T. Washington, ed., *The Negro Problem* (New York: James Pott, 1903), featuring W. E. B. Du Bois's essay "The Talented Tenth." Photo: Courtesy of Wellesley College Archives

As noted above, the title of the work stands out—as perhaps it should. "Ladder for Booker T. Washington" is part homage, part critique, part tongue-in-cheek rehearsal of the opposing ideologies of racial uplift and Black struggle emblematized most clearly in the contrasting expressions of Black leadership offered by Booker T. Washington (1856–1915) and W. E. B. Du Bois (1868–1963). The disparate views of Washington and Du Bois have been taken up by numerous scholars and continue to figure prominently in the countless social histories of Black intellectuals. Washington was famously a proponent of, in the words of the political scientist Martin Kilson, an "accommodationist black leadership methodology."[7] Contra Du Bois's philosophical convictions, this ideology advocated *against* "advancing the development of the country's poor black proletarians through the application of democratic citizenship and political rights."[8]

Ladder's contrapuntal, ascending and descending momentum could be said to reflect these dissenting positions around Black leadership within its form. Indeed, at first blush, Puryear's sculptural engagement with that history would seem to house the contradictions of an elite Black class whose attendant qualifications for a "Talented Tenth" would lead the Black masses to freedom (fig. 84).[9] That is, *Ladder for Booker T. Washington* would immediately appear to allegorize what the scholar and theorist Joy James has described as a "historical mandate" that required "the black intellectual to be a race leader."[10] Yet my wager is that Puryear's sculpture does more than simply personify and metaphorically signal a history of "black elites progressing up the mythic American ladder, and 'lifting as they climbed.'"[11] His artistic gesture masterfully encompasses a dual critique. The work speaks to the specificity of the history within which it is embedded—the imposed requirements and demands upon Black leadership at the turn of the twentieth century. Even so, it underscores, as the professor of Black studies and political science Cedric Robinson put it, that "Black radicalism . . . cannot be understood within the particular context of its genesis."[12] *Ladder for Booker T. Washington* thereby brings together a conceptual understanding as well as critique of linear historicism. This problem, or what the German philosopher and Frankfurt School intellectual Walter Benjamin (1892–1940) memorably characterized as a crisis of historicism, ranges across contemporary art discourses.[13] In other words, the problem with this kind of linear historicism is its failure to attend to the irregular, unconventional, and contradictory expressions that undergird more minor figurations of Black life, art, and culture.

Here we are compelled to return to Puryear's formulation concerning "interesting art," which reemerges as crucial in this regard. For Puryear, such art "retains a flickering quality, where opposed ideas can be held in tense coexistence." One cannot help but hear an echo of Benjamin's celebrated account of images of the past as fleeting illuminations that can only be truly grasped in the midst of their disappearance: "The true picture of the past flits by. The past can be seized only as an image which flashes up at the instant when it

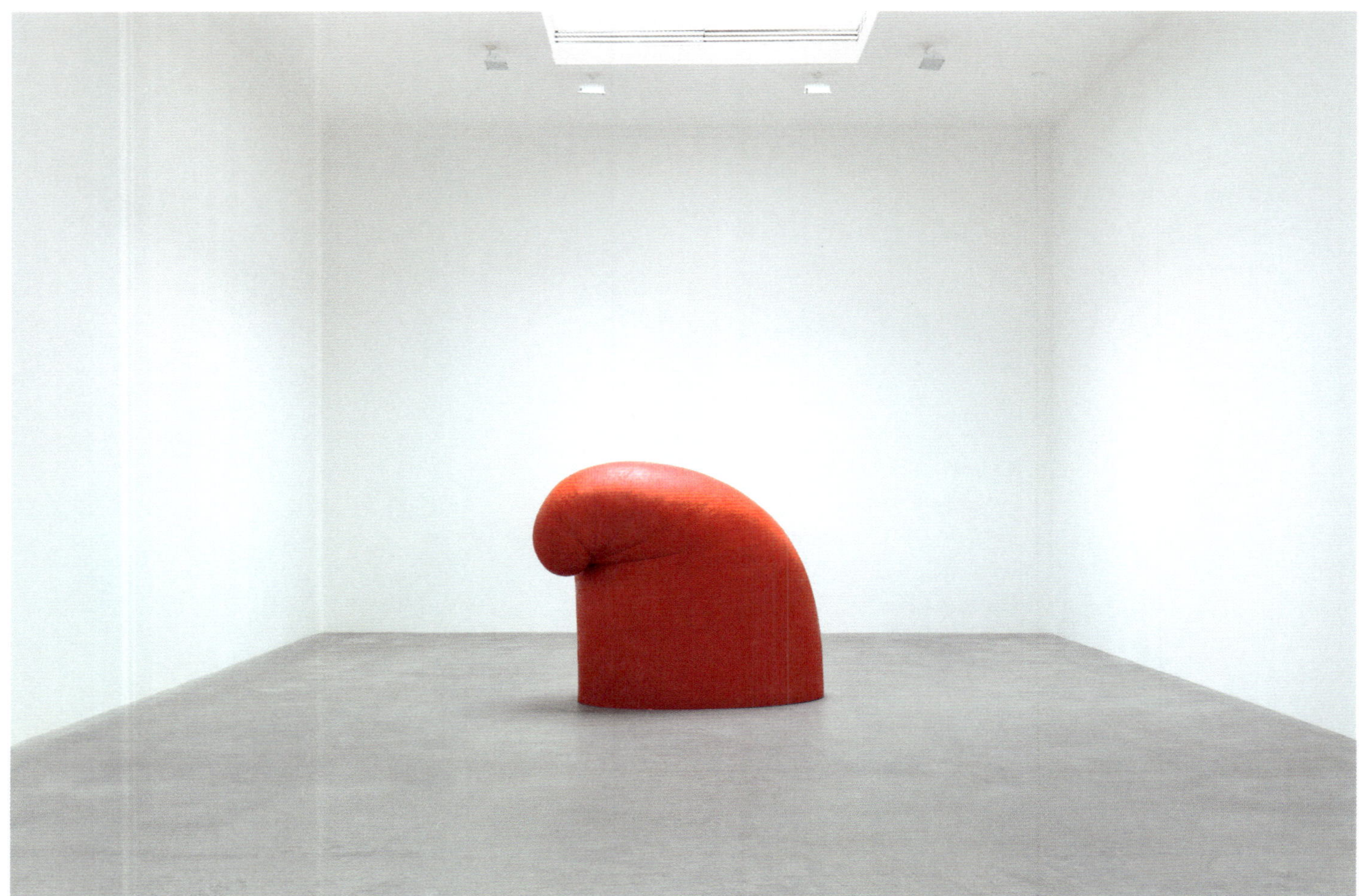

Figure 85. Installation view of *Big Phrygian* (2010–14; [55]) in *Martin Puryear*, Matthew Marks Gallery, New York, 2015. Photo: Ron Amstutz

can be recognized and is never seen again."[14] As with Benjamin, at stake in Puryear's work is nothing less than the flickering, even fleeting illumination of what is not readily apparent or decipherable to us—the past as unfixed from the prerequisites of legibility.

II.

The Phrygian cap has a lineage as both object and idea within the repertoire of global political insurgencies that shaped eighteenth- and nineteenth-century Black liberation struggles. Puryear has engaged with this lineage in sustained fashion throughout his career, most dramatically in *Big Phrygian* (2010–14; [55]). On first glance, the sculpture's colossal red protrusion seems overbearing in relation to the gallery's ascetic, slate-gray concrete floors and white walls—excessively robust in contrast to the stark spatial symmetricality of the gallery-as-white cube (fig. 85). Throughout Puryear's oeuvre, the political and cultural meanings that have accrued to the irreverently misshapen conical cap are implicitly tracked—from its Greek, Roman, and Persian references in antiquity (fig. 86) to its more radical circulation in the context of modernity, where, during the French and American Revolutionary periods (fig. 87), the cap, as a sartorial signifier, gradually assumed its bona fide status as an international symbol of resistance to persecution. Ultimately, the Phrygian cap would come to emblematize the ambitions and potential of distinctly *non-European* revolutionary multitudes against the imperial, state-sanctioned consolidation of tyranny and oppression.

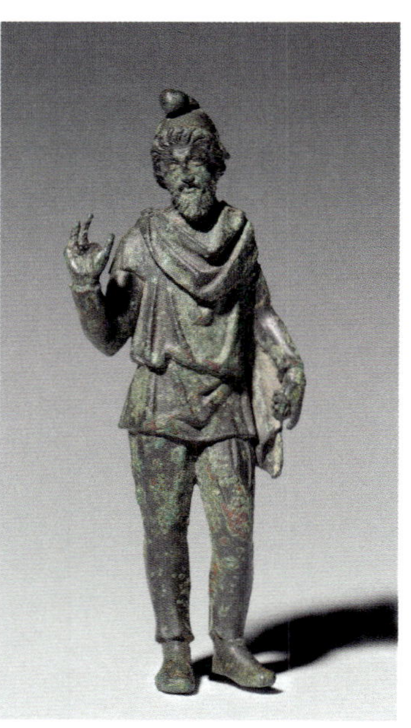

Figure 86. *Barbarian*, 1–100 CE. Rome. Bronze; 8.5 x 3.3 x 1.8 cm. The Cleveland Museum of Art, Purchase from the J. H. Wade Fund, 1987.64

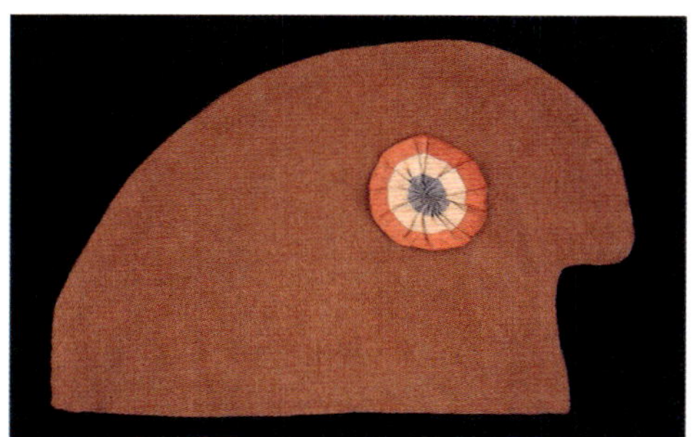

Figure 87. Revolutionary cap, late 1880s. France. Wool plain weave, cotton plain weave, and silk plain weave; 56 cm; legacy dimension: 20.3 x 27. cm. The Museum of Fine Arts, Boston, The Elizabeth Day McCormick Collection, 45.298. Photo © 2025 Museum of Fine Arts, Boston

Belonging to an artistic repertoire that spans some forty-plus years, the permutations of the Phrygian cap in *Self* (1978; [14]) and *Untitled* (1997; [34]), variously rendered through stained and painted red cedar, pine, and mahogany, are magnified and polished in order to accentuate the historical resonance of the form's profile and outline.

Puryear's iterative citations of the Phrygian cap (fig. 88) retain historical iconography while reimagining the cultural and political dialogues within and across the layered global expressions of Blackness in the makings of diaspora, engaging the history of the cap's circulation without overdetermining its symbolism. This is no mean feat given the obscure material and historical transits that have forged the transatlantic legacy and specificity of its objecthood as well as the figurations of Blackness that obtain within its fold. The cultural and political relays between Black America and Haiti in the constellation of historical memory with respect to the Haitian Revolution may serve as a reference point. Julius S. Scott's writing on the Haitian Revolution proves indispensable here, and his field-changing book, *The Common Wind* (2018), which details the ineffable transfer and passage of ideas and news of the Haitian Revolution to the New World, is worth noting. For just as Puryear's *Ladder* generates an alternative image of the past flashing before us, *Big Phrygian* similarly retains this "flickering quality," enabling us to glimpse the shadowy outlines of history's most ephemeral figurations.

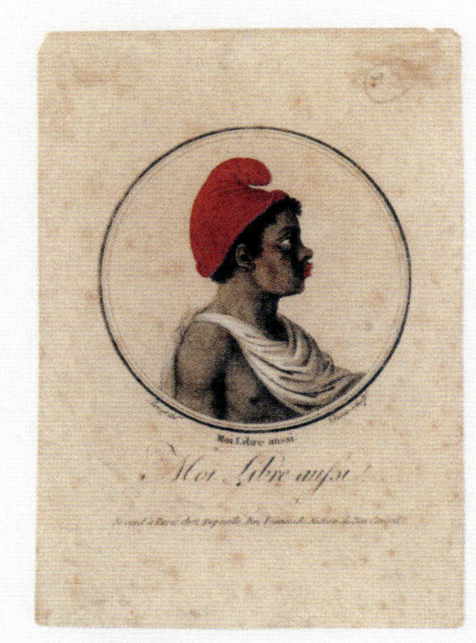

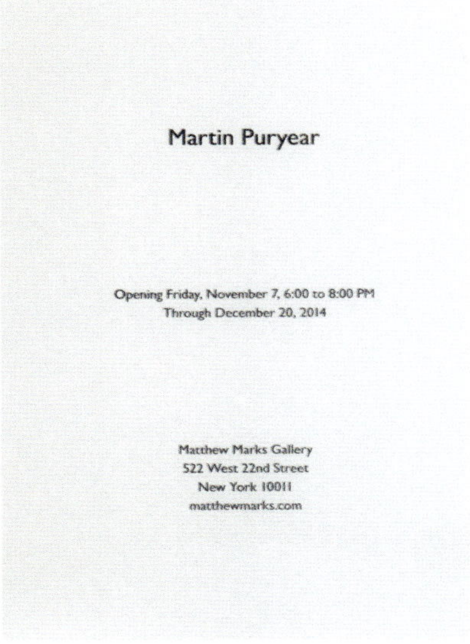

Figure 88. Invitation to opening reception for *Martin Puryear*, Matthew Marks Gallery, New York, November 7, 2014. Pictured: *Print of a Free Man*, 1794. Louis Simon Boizot (French, 1743–1809). Engraving; 9 cm (diameter). Bibliothèque Nationale de France, Paris, Département des Estampes et de la Photographie

For the historian Marcus Rediker, Scott's unprecedented study of the forms of ephemeral knowledge that "circulated on 'the common wind'" enabled Blacks in the New World to "[link] news of English abolitionism, Spanish reformism, and French revolutionism to local struggles across the Caribbean" such that "subversive networks" of communication were expanded into an "imaginative transnational geography of struggle."[15] Scott's and Rediker's scholarly observations allow us to discern the contours of a new epistemology—one that suggests not only a deep interconnectedness between those enslaved in the Americas and those struggling for freedom in the Caribbean, but also a paradigmatic shift in the epistemologies that undergird cartographies of Black struggle.[16] That global Black liberation struggles were shaped by precarious cultural and aesthetic practices, routinely repressed and effaced, returns us to Puryear's *Big Phrygian*, in particular the work's ability to constellate and synthesize these oblique histories anew.

Big Phrygian exaggerates the dimensions and mass of the cap's peak in an almost comical way. Jutting out from the massive flush of red, the bulge that extends the cap appears disproportionate to the rest of its form. The resonance between *Big Phrygian* and the latticed geometry that furnishes the facade of another of Puryear's sculptures, *Aso Oke* (2019; [60]), permeates the gallery space with a poetic openness; a trace of the Phrygian cap can be discerned in the latter, in the delicate contouring of rattan and twine, later cast in bronze. While the form of the cap here is seemingly more provisional, the bronze *Aso Oke* assumes an air of regality that one might associate with the metallic crowns or outsize headdresses of the African Yoruba, whose textile cultures *Aso Oke* explicitly references in its title. Here, the relays between Africa, the Caribbean, and African America are palpable, held in the texture and opened by the intricacies of latticework. Puryear thereby weaves the history of the cap through the present, preserving and conserving its heterogeneous legacy.

If Puryear's sculptures feel infinite and familiar, it is because they bear the traces of forms of life and practices remaindered. Wresting the beauty of blackened forms from the ensnarement of an anti-Black world is the weight with which his various works are freighted.

III.

Puryear's work potentiates fresh inquiries into the relationships between culture and nonhuman environments. The works loosely belonging to the Phrygian series, as well as those that could be regarded as variations on the cap, provide ample opportunities for a consideration of political ecologies of conversation that embrace "cultural" formations typically positioned against the "natural." In fact, a great many of Puryear's sculptures bear ecological histories wherein history and culture, language and meaning are inseparable from nonhuman ecologies. In this respect, Puryear's artistic repertoire finds common ground with Black ecological poetry and poetics. Consider, for a moment, the contrapuntal momentum that animates Camille T. Dungy's (b. 1972) poem "this beginning may have always meant this end":

> coming from a place where we meandered mornings and met quail, scrub jay, mockingbird, i knew coyote, like everyone else, i knew cactus, knew tumbleweed, lichen on the rocks and pill bugs beneath, rattlers sometimes, the soft smell of sage and the ferment of cactus pear. coming from this place, from a place where grass might grow greener on the hillside in winter than in any yard, where, the whole rest of the year, everything i loved, chaparral pea, bottle brush tree, jacaranda, mariposa, pinyon and desert oak, the kumquat in the back garden and wisteria vining the porch, the dry grass whispering long after the last rains, raccoons in and out of the hills, trash hurled by the hottest wind, the dry grass tall now and golden, lawn chairs, eucalyptus, everything, in a place we knew, every thing, we knew, little and large and mine and ours, except horror, all of it, everything could flame up that quickly, could flare and be gone.[17]

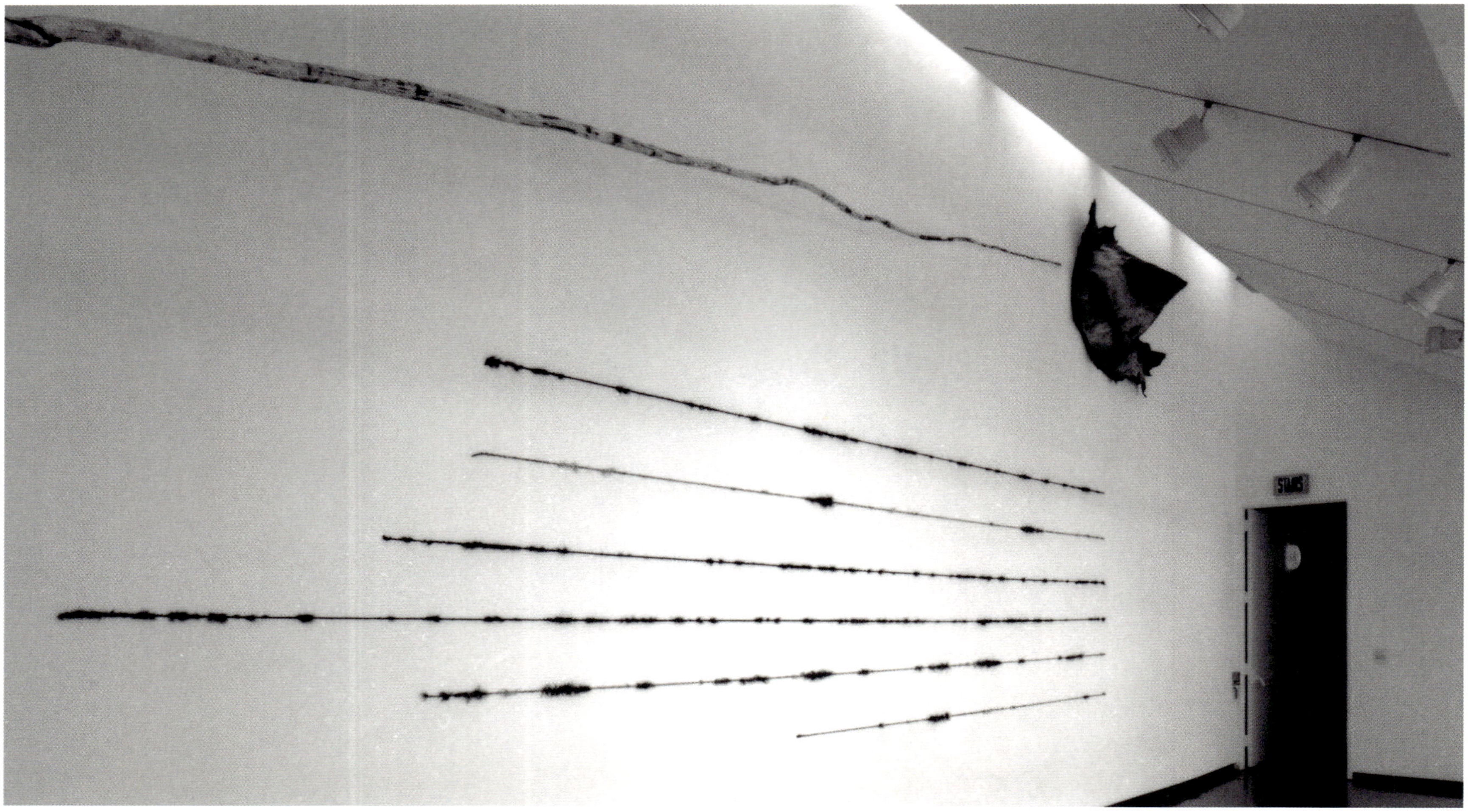

Figure 89. Installation view of *Options 2: Martin Puryear* at MCA Chicago, 1980. Pictured: Some *Lines for Jim Beckwourth* (1978; [15]) and *Rawhide Cone* (1980; [18]). Photo: Museum of Contemporary Art Chicago / Art Resource, NY

Whereas Dungy's poetics hold space for what is most fragile and provisional, Puryear's works manage to stir the inexpressible and resonate with the unsayable.

Reading between poet and artist, between the lines of a call-and-response that inheres in a tradition they differentially share, it is possible to discern the makings of a Black ecology that understands "the designation Black" as that which the scholars J. T. Roane and Justin Hosbey describe, "marks the outside within the ecologies of living—the spaces that sustain and reproduce normative forms of biological and social existence."[18] In their attempt to define Black ecologies, Roane and Hosbey note that Black ecological formations and knowledges must be both prescriptive and instructive: "As a naming of the outside and the bottom, Black ecologies are foremost sites . . . [that] form the critical ecologies of the damned, sites wherein ordinary Black people articulate alternative maps—dissonant and heterodox ecological grammars as well as vision for a different order."[19] If the reigning ecological order is predicated upon the dispossession and extraction of histories of Black organization and struggle, the shaping of Black ecologies demands the derangement of that normative ecology and its order of forms.

Puryear's artistry holds out the possibility for such derangement. His sculptures seem to organically grow and extend into and recede from space, their undulating movement simultaneously foregrounding scale and immeasurability. His work gestures toward the earth and earthly materiality. Consider, for example, *Rawhide Cone* (1980; [18]): the transfiguration of molded rawhide seems to abstractly convey both the passage of matter as well as the felt traces of the human within nature. The hide's raw texture alludes to uncommon and quotidian variations of natural forms that extend our inevitable entanglement with earthly phenomena. As general knowledge would have it, the violence of slavery is linked to the materiality of rawhide in ways that make clear that *Rawhide Cone* can be read as a testament to the brutalities of enslavement—the violence of the whip and the lash to which so many souls were forcibly subjected. Yet, this is a work that takes shape from that history but is not reducible to the brutality of its inscriptions. As with Puryear's *Some Lines for Jim Beckwourth* (1978; fig. 89 and [15]), though the violent sundering of human from animal, of civilization from nature has been materialized on Black backs as *if* this sadistic penmanship were the sign of property, there is no act of terror that can master the language of these hieroglyphic scarrings, which insist on speaking in tongues.[20]

Puryear's oeuvre suggests a relationship to the serial progression of Black ecological forms severed from the world—ecological forms forcibly made to bend with and toward worldly violence. His sculptures, which manage to convey both a calculated weightiness and weightlessness, seem almost paradoxical. Characterized by their ineffable transparency as much as their proverbial solidity, they revel in the contradictions and ambiguities of form. Works such as *Bower* (1980; [19]) or *Sanctuary* (1982; [22]) draw our gaze toward nature's unpredictability. Indeed, the beauty of Puryear's craft attends to nature's irreducibility. At the same time, this irreducibility is restrained precisely in order to showcase the rootedness of various forms. These sculptural works are expressly non-narrative and reflect those difficulties of form that bespeak the loss of narratable histories. They are sculptural forms that at once manage to make room for archival absences while prefiguring the vastness and uncertainty of the future.

Many of Puryear's works are iterative; they involve repetition and variation, and seem to flit at the edges of history. The apparent circularity of works such as *Nexus* (1979; [16]), *Cerulean* (1982; fig. 90), *Sanctuary* (1982; [22]), and *Untitled* (1982; [21]) lay bare these contradictions within sculpture while tending to the movement of resolution and synthesis. Puryear renders formal contradictions with a simplicity and abstract asceticism (not to be confused with Minimalism) that have come to singularly define his formal craft. He features maple sapling, pear wood, yellow cedar, polychromed pine, and stained, ebonized, gessoed yellow cedar—all while tarrying with the interplay of color and blackness (the presumed absence of color), extemporaneously applied to natural surfaces. Ebonizing (fig. 91) involves staining a material black in imitation of ebony, whereas polychroming (fig. 92) entails the application of color. Their playful interanimation spans a sculptural repertoire in which indeterminate forms seem to swerve, dance, and strain against the confines of representation. As Puryear has attested: "I value the referential qualities of art, the fact that a work can allude to things or states of being without in any way representing them."[21]

IV.

If works such as *Nexus*, *Cerulean*, *Sanctuary*, and *Untitled* express a precision and exactitude, it is due to Puryear's indomitable skill as a craftsman. Craft has long endured a devalued status among the rankings of the fine arts, often forced to straddle the distinctions between high and low culture and relegated to the domestic because of its proximity to unskilled artistic labor. Writing on craftsmanship at the intersection of artistic formalism, Alex Potts states: "For Puryear, a commitment to workmanship is not just a matter of aesthetics but also has significant ethical implications."[22] As Potts notes, Puryear studied African craftsmanship and techniques while working in the Peace Corps in Sierra Leone in the 1960s, which the artist described thus:

> In West Africa, I encountered skilled joiners and carpenters making everything of wood that the community needed, without fanfare or preciousness or self-consciousness but with a lot of skill. It was both inspiring and instructive. Part of the inspiration for me was that I saw people working without the benefit of sophisticated tools producing work of a fairly high order.[23]

In Potts's assessment, craft or workmanship might be regarded as "the antithesis of artistic virtuosity or portentousness."[24] However, as the late art historian Robert Farris Thompson has written in his extensive studies of West African

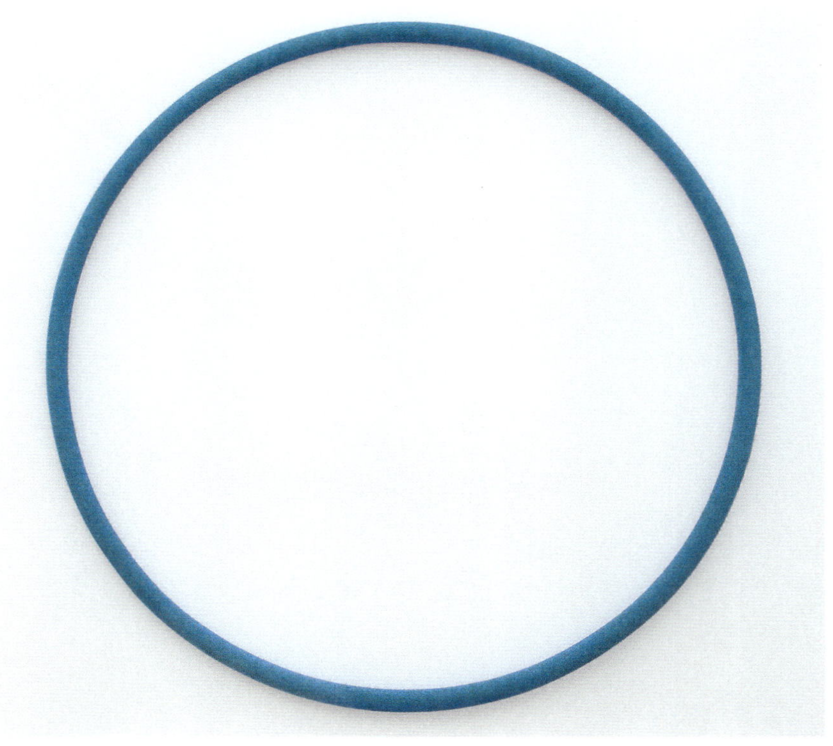

Figure 90. *Cerulean* (1982). Martin Puryear. Polychromed pine; 161.9 x 160.7 x 4.4 cm. Panza Collection. Photo: Antoine van Kaam

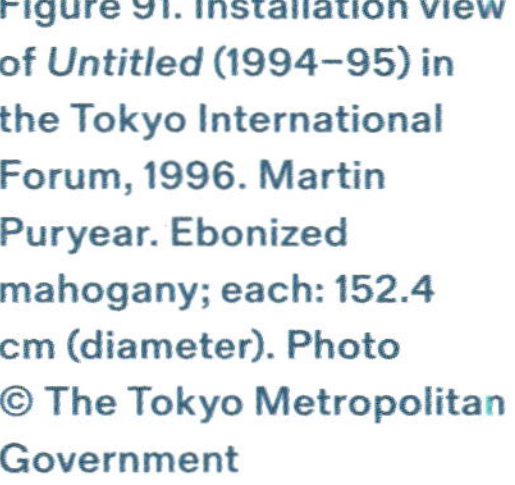

Figure 91. Installation view of *Untitled* (1994–95) in the Tokyo International Forum, 1996. Martin Puryear. Ebonized mahogany; each: 152.4 cm (diameter). Photo © The Tokyo Metropolitan Government

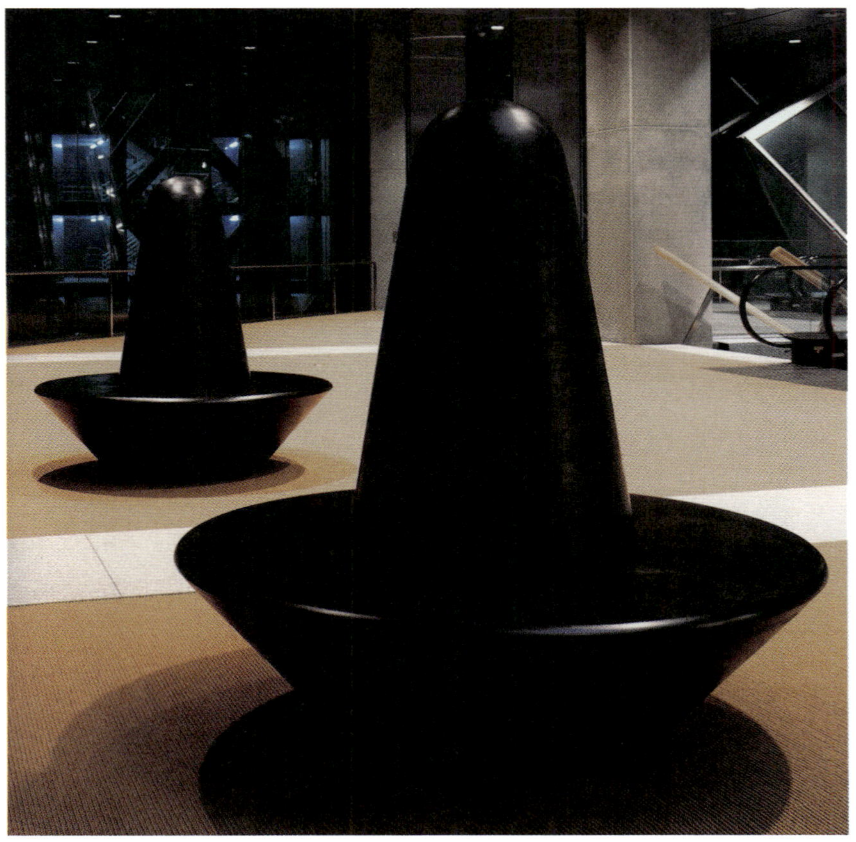

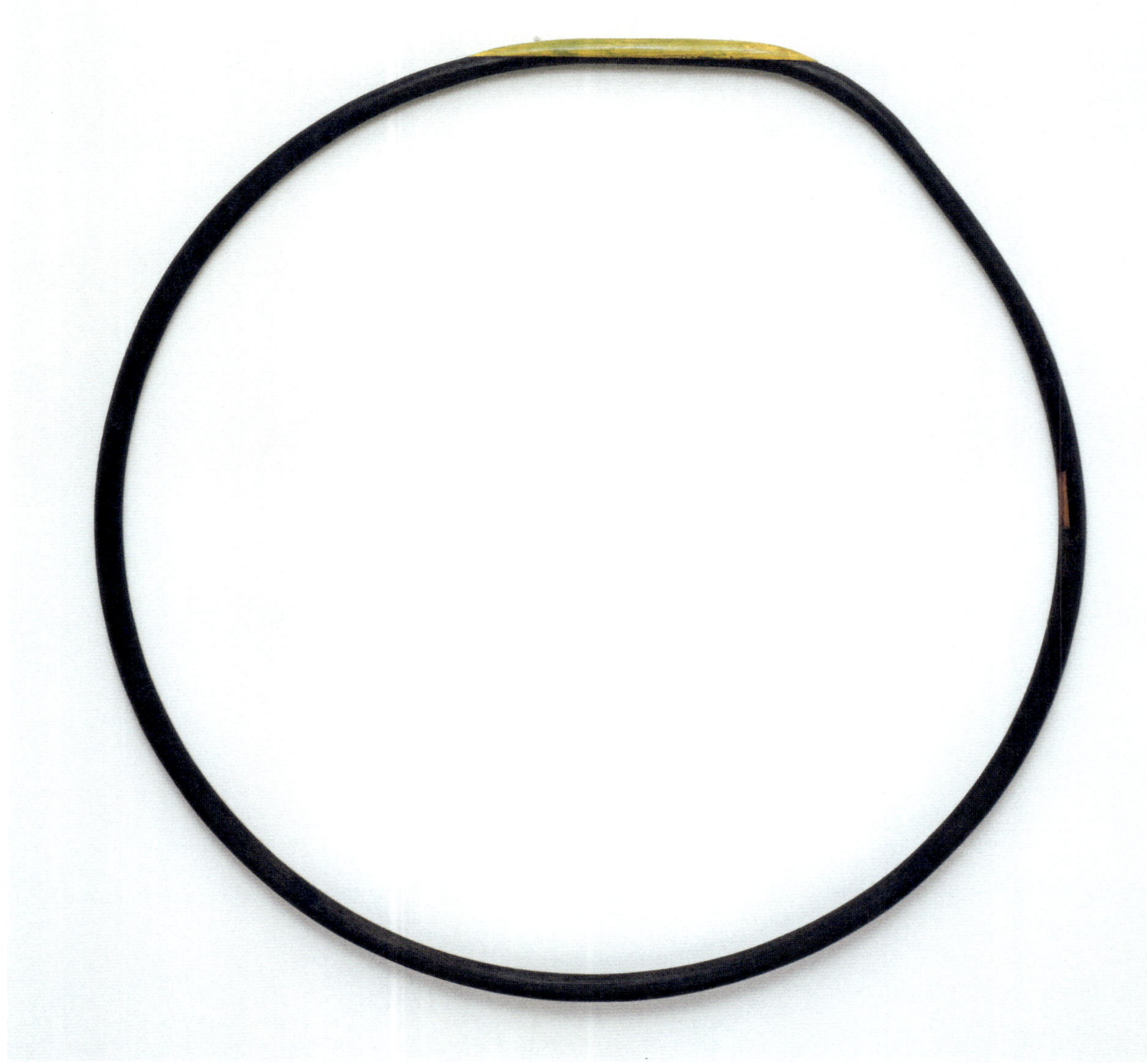

Figure 92. ***Blue Blood*** **(1979). Martin Puryear. Polychromed pine and red cedar; overall: 168.6 x 5.1 cm (diameter x depth). National Gallery of Art, Washington, DC, Corcoran Collection (Gift of the Truland Foundation), 2014.136.288**

art traditions, such workmanship—specifically the conception, development, execution, and transformation of African *crafted* forms, from masks to figures to panels—involved nothing less than an expert "handling" of "embellishment and openwork with the economy and sophistication of a highly developed craft tradition."[25] Thompson's meticulous studies of African art are attuned to the regional specificity of the variegated histories of African artistic expression, while his observations sustain a deep commitment to considering the implications of the devaluation of *craft* in a Western art-historical context.

At stake in the contrast between Potts's and Thompson's analyses is a misreading of Puryear's work that maintains a problematic dualism premised upon a hierarchical distinction between art and craft—a misreading that merely inverts that hierarchy instead of problematizing the aesthetic and philosophical foundations that undergird the dualism as such. Following Thompson, rather than interpret the transposition of African craft to the field of African American sculpture as "the antithesis . . . of artistic virtuosity," we are compelled to think differently about the cultural and epistemic transits between Africa and a diaspora whose artistic practices demand more careful consideration of the interleaving of North American, continental African, and more globally expansive Black vernacular traditions that remain largely understudied.

If, guided by Puryear's oeuvre, we allow ourselves to tarry with the philosophical interventions already advanced by these vernacular traditions, we might begin to notice how the opposition of art and craft surreptitiously contains enmities that are, in many ways, at the root of the global ecological crisis—the violent aesthetic differentiation of the truly historical from the prehistorical or ahistorical, of the social from the natural, of the civilized from the savage, of formal refinement from base materiality. Puryear's practice disabuses its viewers of such dualistic tropes and marks the fissures in the racial and colonial order onto which they have been mapped. In that offering, there is a murmur or murmuration of earthly movement not yet stilled by the worldly.

1. Martin Puryear, quoted in Elizabeth Reede, "Jogs and Switchbacks," in *Martin Puryear*, ed. John Elderfield, exh. cat. (New York: Museum of Modern Art, 2007), 77, 96n13.

2. For a recent meditation on the stakes of such an intervention in the context of feminist material cultures across the Americas in the 1970s, 1980s, and 1990s, see Julia Bryan-Wilson, *Fray: Art + Textile Politics* (Chicago: University of Chicago Press, 2017).

3. Martin Puryear, "Interview: Abstraction and 'Ladder for Booker T. Washington,'" *Art21*, November 2011, https://art21.org/read/martin-puryear-abstraction-and-ladder-for-booker-t-washington/.

4. Puryear, "Interview: Abstraction and 'Ladder for Booker T. Washington.'"

5. Puryear, "Interview: Abstraction and 'Ladder for Booker T. Washington.'"

6. Darby English, *How to See a Work of Art in Total Darkness* (Cambridge, MA: MIT Press, 2007), 5.

7. Martin Kilson, *Transformation of the African American Intelligentsia, 1880–2012* (Cambridge, MA: Harvard University Press, 2014), 4.

8. Kilson, *Transformation of the African American Intelligentsia*, 53.

9. W. E. B. Du Bois, "The Talented Tenth," from Booker T. Washington (ed.), *The Negro Problem: A Series of Articles by Representative Negroes of To-day* (New York, 1903). See also W. E. B. Du Bois, *The Souls of Black Folk* (Chicago: A. C. McClurgh, 1903), 105.

10. Joy James, *Transcending the Talented Tenth: Black Leaders and American Intellectuals* (New York and London: Routledge, 1997), 6.

11. James, *Transcending the Talented Tenth*, 6.

12. Cedric J. Robinson, *Black Marxism: The Making of the Black Radical Tradition* (1983; Chapel Hill: University of North Carolina Press, 2000), 106.

13. Walter Benjamin, "Theses on the Philosophy of History," in *Illuminations*, ed. Hannah Arendt, trans. Harry Zohn (New York: Schocken Books, 1955), 255.

14. Benjamin, "Theses on the Philosophy of History," 255.

15. Marcus Rediker, "Foreword," in Julius S. Scott, *The Common Wind: Afro-American Currents in the Age of the Haitian Revolution* (New York: Verso Books, 2018), xi.

16. Such scholarship dispels the myth that those enslaved on plantations in the colonies were unaware of the monumental events unfolding beyond America's shores. As Scott writes: "the beckoning call of the Haitian revolutionaries, this appealing image of Saint-Domingue as a center of antislavery and black self-determination in the hemisphere, reached a wider audience than simply the French Negroes in the Spanish section of Hispaniola. News of the decisive events of 1793 soon made the revolution in Saint-Domingue an object of identification for Afro-Americans throughout the New World." Julius S. Scott, "'Know Your True Interests': Saint Domingue and the Americas, 1793–1800," in *The Common Wind : Afro-American Currents in the Age of the Haitian Revolution* (New York: Verso Books, 2018), 169.

17. Camille T. Dungy, "this beginning may have always meant this end," from *America, a Love Story* © Camille T. Dungy, (Middletown, CT: Wesleyan University Press, forthcoming in 2026) and used by permission.

18. J. T. Roane and Justin Hosbey, "Mapping Black Ecologies," *Current Research in Digital History* 2 (2019), https://crdh.rrchnm.org/essays/v02-05-mapping-black-ecologies/.

19. Roane and Hosbey, "Mapping Black Ecologies."

20. For more on this latter interpretation of Hortense Spillers's celebrated rumination on the "hieroglyphics of the flesh," see Rizvana Bradley, *Anteaesthetics: Black Aesthesis and the Critique of Form* (Stanford, CA: Stanford University Press, 2023); and Hortense J. Spillers, "Mama's Baby, Papa's Maybe: An American Grammar Book," in *Black, White, and in Color: Essays on American Literature and Culture* (Chicago: University of Chicago, 2003), 203–29.

21. Martin Puryear, quoted in "Our Picks of the Must-See Shows to See in New York in November," *Art Newspaper* (November 1, 2020), https://www. theartnewspaper.com/2020/11/01/our-picks-of-the-must-see-shows-to-see-in-new-york-in-november.

22. Alex Potts, "The Persistence of Sculpture," in *Martin Puryear*, ed. Craig Garrett (New York: Matthew Marks Gallery, 2016), 27.

23. Puryear, quoted in Reede, "Jogs and Switchbacks," 77, 96n13.

24. Martin Puryear, "Shaping the Future of Craft: Keynote Address," in *Shaping the Future of Craft: 2006 National Leadership Conference*, eds. Monica Hampton and Lily Kane (New York: American Craft Council, 2006), 26.

25. Robert Farris Thompson, *African Art in Motion: Icon and Art* (Los Angeles, Berkeley, and London: University of California Press, 1974), 106.

Chronology

Gabriella Shypula

Exhibitions, Commissions, and Special Projects

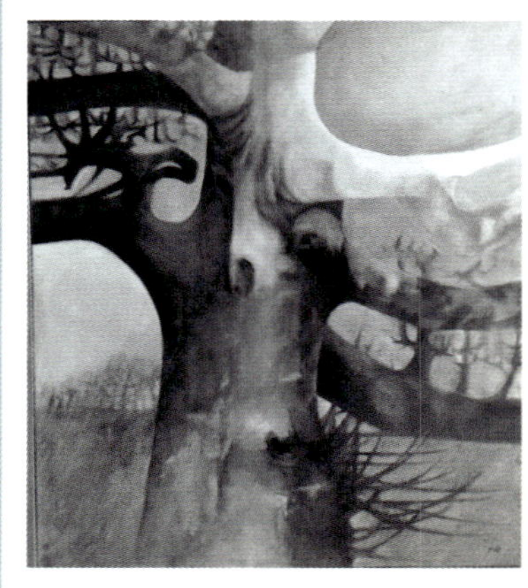

Figure 93. *Tree* (1963). Martin Puryear. Oil on canvas; dimensions unknown, which won the Maryland Chapter, American Institute of Interior Decorators Award at the Maryland Regional, 31st Annual, 1963. Exhibitions Photographs Collection, Archives and Manuscripts Collections, Baltimore Museum of Art, Box N5, PC_EX_N5_118.

1962

Anthony Camisa, Martin Puryear, David Raymond, M. C. Termini
Adams-Morgan Gallery, Washington, DC
June 25–July 20

1963

Maryland Regional, 31st Annual
Baltimore Museum of Art
March 10–April 7
• Fig. 93

1965

Group Exhibition
United States Information Service (U.S.I.S.) Gallery, Freetown, Sierra Leone

1967

Spring Exhibition
Royal Academy of Fine Arts, Stockholm
June 1–9

1968

Stockholm Salon Exhibition
Liljevalchs Konsthall, Stockholm
February 16–March 17

Martin Puryear
Gröna Paletten Galleri, Stockholm
May 18–31

Spring Exhibition
Royal Academy of Fine Arts, Stockholm
June 1–9
• Fig. 94

1969

Group Exhibition
Lunn Gallery, Washington, DC

1972

Martin Puryear: Wood work
Henri 2 Gallery, Washington, DC
January 8–February 4
• Figs. 95–97

Prints and Paintings
[Group Exhibition]
UW Union South Gallery, Second Annual Black Arts Festival, University of Wisconsin, Madison
February 7–25

Fisk University Faculty Art Work
Guerry Hall Gallery of Fine Arts, University of the South, Sewanee, TN
April 2–26

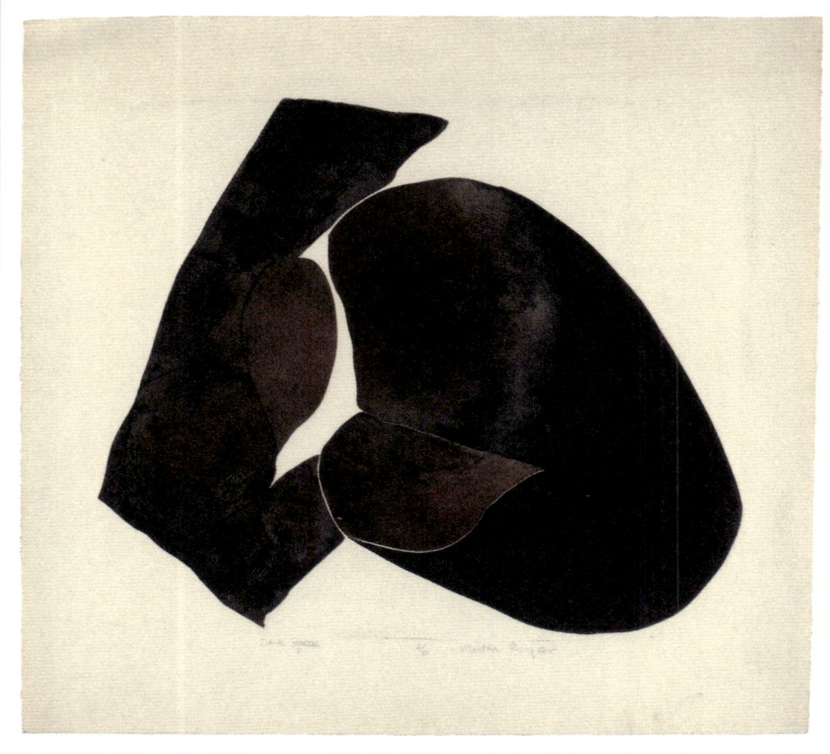

Figure 94. *Dark Squeeze* (1966–67). Martin Puryear. Color intaglio on paper; 41.7 x 49.4 cm, presented at the Spring Exhibition, Royal Academy of Fine Arts, Stockholm, 1968. Photo: Jamie Stukenberg

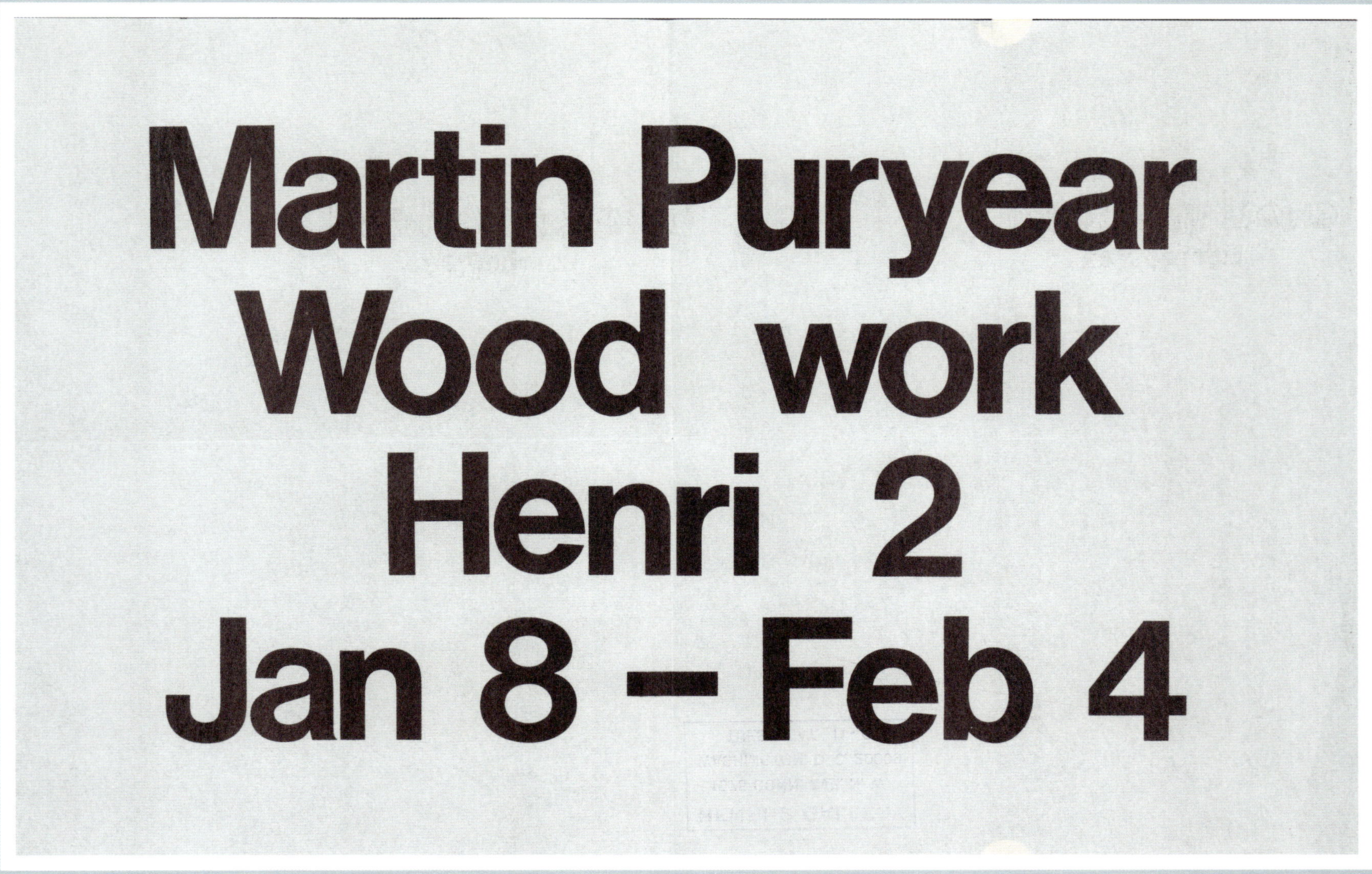

Martin Puryear
Wood work
Henri 2
Jan 8 – Feb 4

Figure 95. Exhibition flyer for *Martin Puryear: Wood work*, Henri 2 Gallery, 1972. Archives of American Art, Smithsonian Institution, Henri Gallery records, circa early 1900s, 1940–1966, bulk 1957–1995

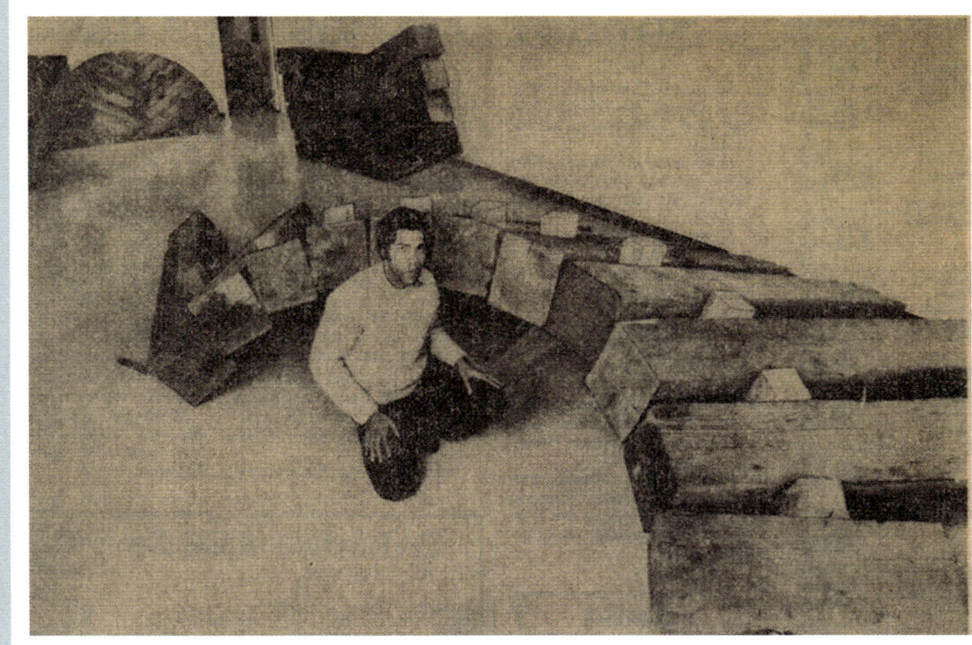

Figure 96. Martin Puryear in *Martin Puryear: Wood work*, Henri 2 Gallery, 1972. Pictured: *Untitled* (1971) [back left]; *Fir Beams* (1972) [back right]; *Untitled* (1971–72) [front right, next to Puryear]. Photo: Larry Morris, The Washington Post. Courtesy of the David C. Driskell Center for the Visual Arts and Culture of African Americans and the African Diaspora

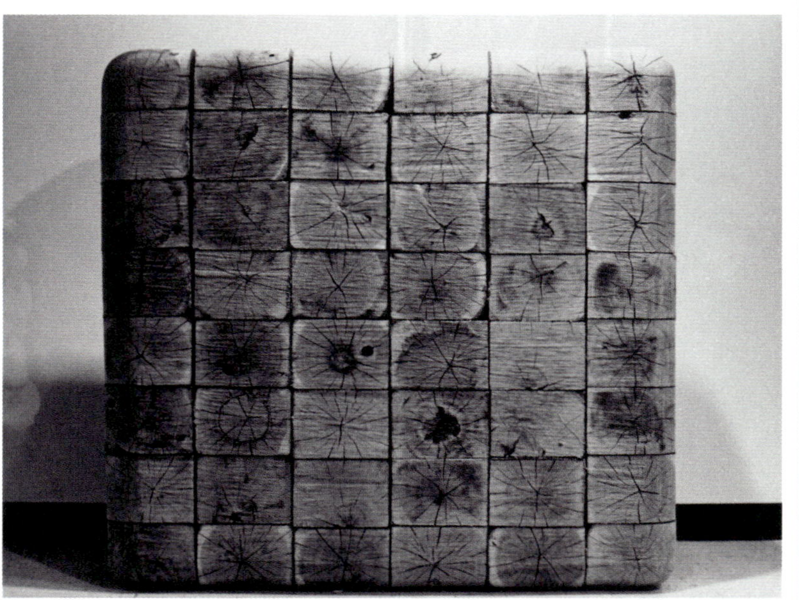

Figure 97. Installation view of *Carved Woodpile* (1971–72) in *Martin Puryear: Wood work*, Henri 2 Gallery, 1972, which was also presented in *Stephanie Pogue and Martin Puryear*, Carl Van Vechten Gallery, Fisk University, 1972. Oak; 121.9 x 68.6 x 35.6 cm. Archives of American Art, Smithsonian Institution, Henri Gallery records, circa early 1900s, 1940–1966, bulk 1957–1995

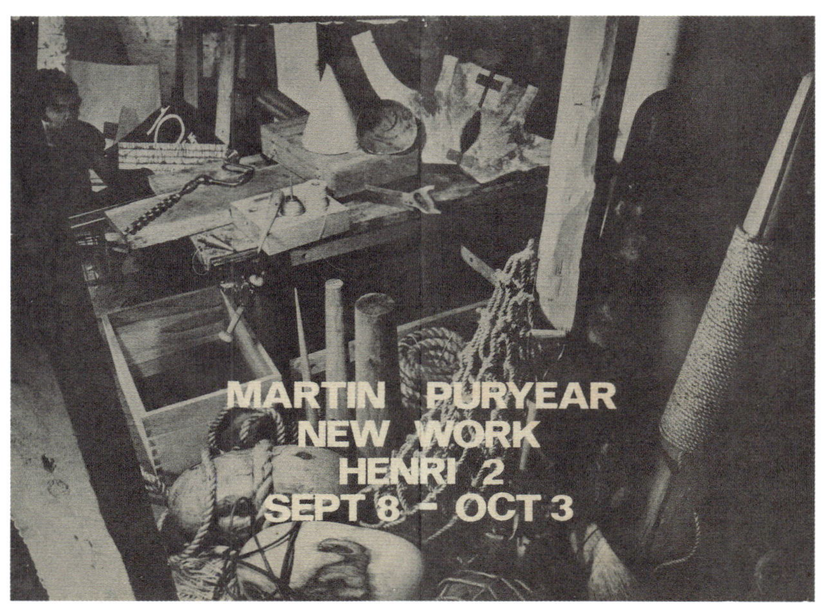

Figure 98. Exhibition flyer for *Martin Puryear: New Work*, Henri 2 Gallery, 1973. Courtesy of the David C. Driskell Center for the Visual Arts and Culture of African Americans and the African Diaspora

Stephanie Pogue and Martin Puryear
Carl Van Vechten Gallery, Fisk University, Nashville
November 5–26

• Fig. 97

1973

Martin Puryear: New Work
Henri 2 Gallery, Washington, DC
September 8–October 3

• Fig. 98

1974

Group Exhibition
Lincoln Gallery, National Collection of Fine Arts (NCFA), Smithsonian Institution, Washington, DC
August–July 1977

New Talent at Maryland
[Group Exhibition]
Art Gallery, University of Maryland, College Park
September 30–October 26

1977

The Material Dominant: Some Current Artists and Their Media
Museum of Art, The Pennsylvania State University, University Park
January 29–March 27

Martin Puryear
Corcoran Gallery of Art, Washington, DC
July 30–September 18

• Figs. 99a, b

Box and Pole
Temporary outdoor installation as part of monthlong residency at Artpark, Lewiston, NY
August 4–September 11

• For further installation details, see [12]; figs. 10–12

1978

Young American Artists: 1978 Exxon National Exhibition
Solomon R. Guggenheim Museum, New York
May 5–June 16

• See fig. 125

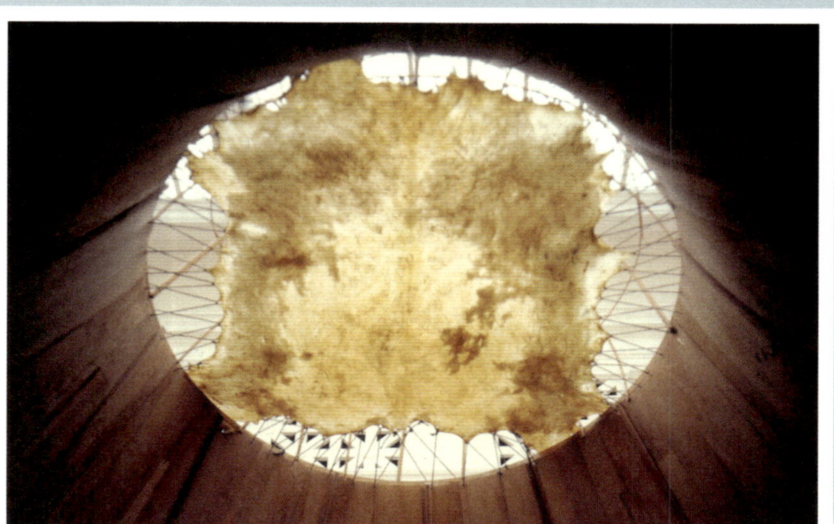

Figures 99a, b. Installation views of the interior and exterior of *Cedar Lodge* (1977) in *Martin Puryear*, Corcoran Gallery of Art, Washington, DC, 1977. Douglas fir and rawhide; 554 x 503 cm, no longer extant. Photo: Special Collections Research Center, Gelman Library, The George Washington University

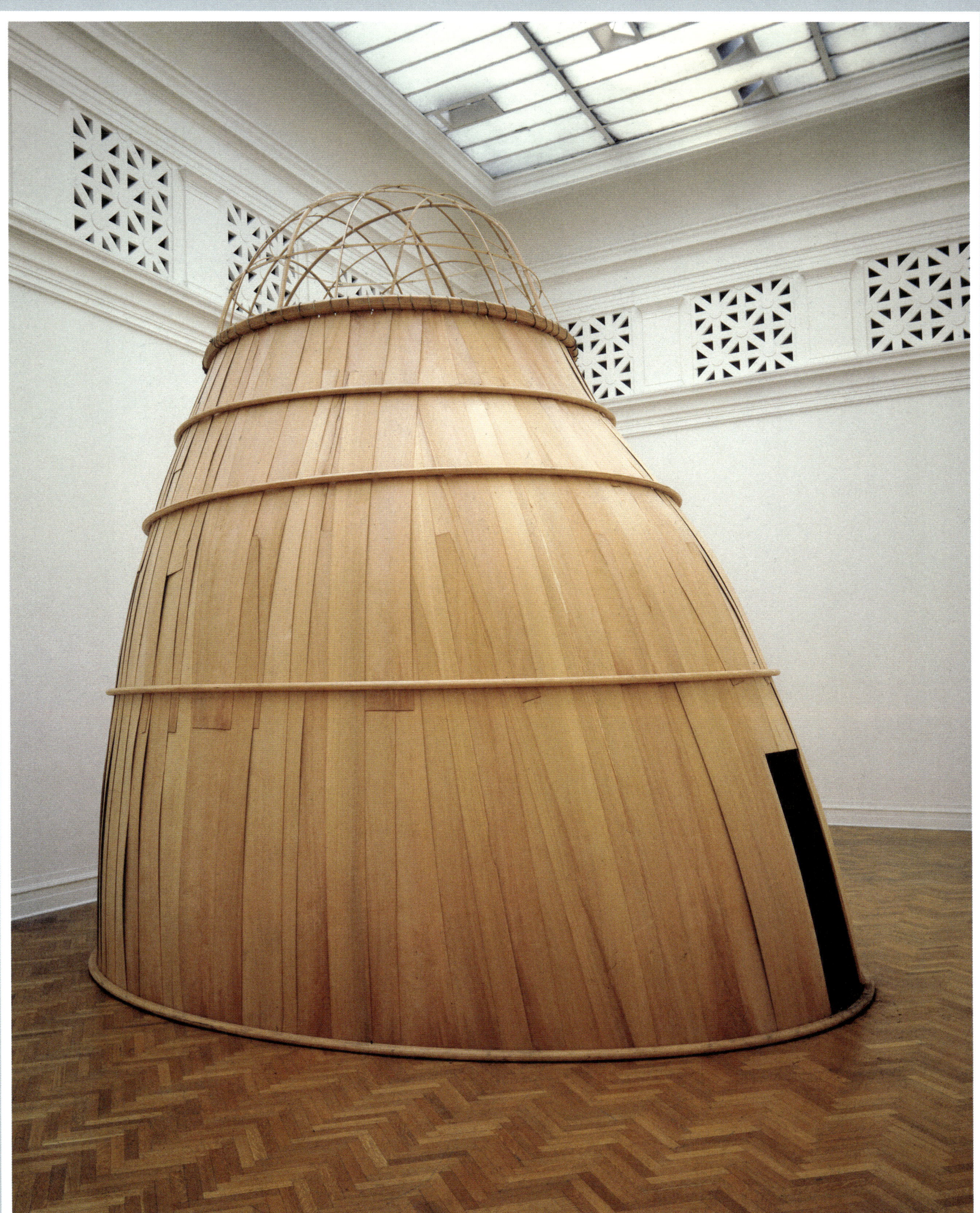

1979 BI
ENNIAL
EXHIBI
TION

Figure 100. Exhibition catalogue cover for the Whitney Biennial 1979, Whitney Museum of American Art, 1979. Digital image © Whitney Museum of American Art / Licensed by Scala / Art Resource, NY

Martin Puryear: Sculpture; Elizabeth Voelker: No Series—Collage
Protetch-McIntosh Gallery,
Washington, DC
May 9–June 3

The Presence of Nature
[Group Exhibition]
Whitney Museum of American Art,
Downtown Branch, New York
December 14–January 17, 1979

Untitled
Temporary outdoor installation at the Center Campus courtyard, Macomb Community College, Warren, MI
1978–c. 1980s

Collaboration with Macomb Community College students during artist visit

Hemlock; 3.1 x 3.1 x 3.1 m

Relocated to: University Center, Center Campus, Macomb Community College, 1993–2000; Michigan Legacy Art Park, Thompsonville, MI, donated by Macomb Community College, 2000–2015 (destroyed)

1979

Art and Architecture: Space and Structure
Protetch-McIntosh Gallery,
Washington, DC
January 16–February 3

Whitney Biennial 1979
Whitney Museum of American Art,
New York
February 6–April 1

● Fig. 100

Custom and Culture 2
[Group Exhibition]
Temporary indoor installation at U.S. Custom House, New York
May 3–June 17

Organized by Creative Time

She, 1979. Red cedar and Douglas fir; height 265.4 cm

Her, 1979. Red cedar and Douglas fir; height 182.9 cm

Wave Hill: The Artist's View
[Group Exhibition]
Temporary outdoor installation at Wave Hill, Bronx, NY
May 15–October 28

Equivalents, 1979. Canadian hemlock; box: 137.2 x 137.2 x 137.2 cm; cone: 222.3 x 190.5 x 190.5 cm

New Work by Martin Puryear
Protetch-McIntosh Gallery,
Washington, DC
November 20–December 15

1980

Drawings: 13 Washington Sculptors
Diane Brown Gallery,
Washington, DC
January 8–February 2

Options 2: Martin Puryear
Museum of Contemporary Art
Chicago
February 1–March 11

● See fig. 89

The Black Circle
[Group Exhibition]
A. Montgomery Ward Gallery,
University of Illinois at Chicago
February 4–February 29

Afro-American Abstraction
Institute for Art and Urban Resources, P.S. 1 Contemporary Art Center, Long Island City, New York
February 17–April 6

Traveled to: Everson Museum of Art, Syracuse, NY, February 6–March 29, 1981; Los Angeles Municipal Art Gallery, July 1–August 30, 1982; Oakland Museum of California, November 13, 1982–January 2, 1983; Brooks Memorial Art Gallery, Memphis, February 10–March 24, 1983; The Art Center, South Bend, IN, September 4–October 16, 1983; Toledo Museum of Art, OH, January 22–February 26, 1984; Bellevue Art Museum, WA, March 25–May 6, 1984; Laguna Gloria Museum, Austin, TX, June 1–July 15, 1984; Mississippi Museum of Art, Jackson, September 14–November 4, 1984

● Fig. 101

Martin Puryear
Young Hoffman Gallery, Chicago
May 2–31

I-80 Series: Martin Puryear
Joslyn Art Museum, Omaha
August 2–September 14

Chicago / Chicago
[Group Exhibition]
Contemporary Arts Center,
Cincinnati
October 3–November 9

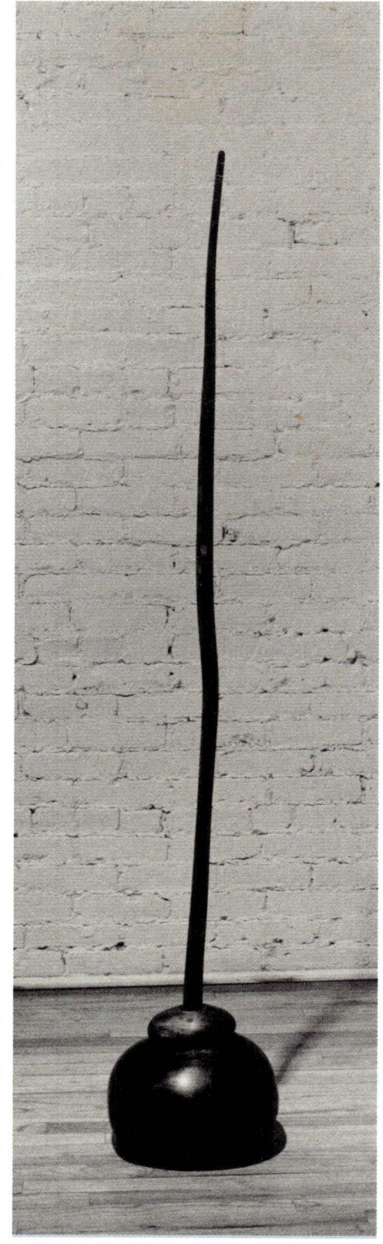

Figure 101. Installation view of *Untitled* (1978) in *Afro-American Abstraction*, P.S.1, 1980. Martin Puryear. Osage orange, yellow pine, maple, ash; overall: 170.2 x 35.6 cm (height x diameter). Digital Image © The Museum of Modern Art/Licensed by SCALA / Art Resource, NY

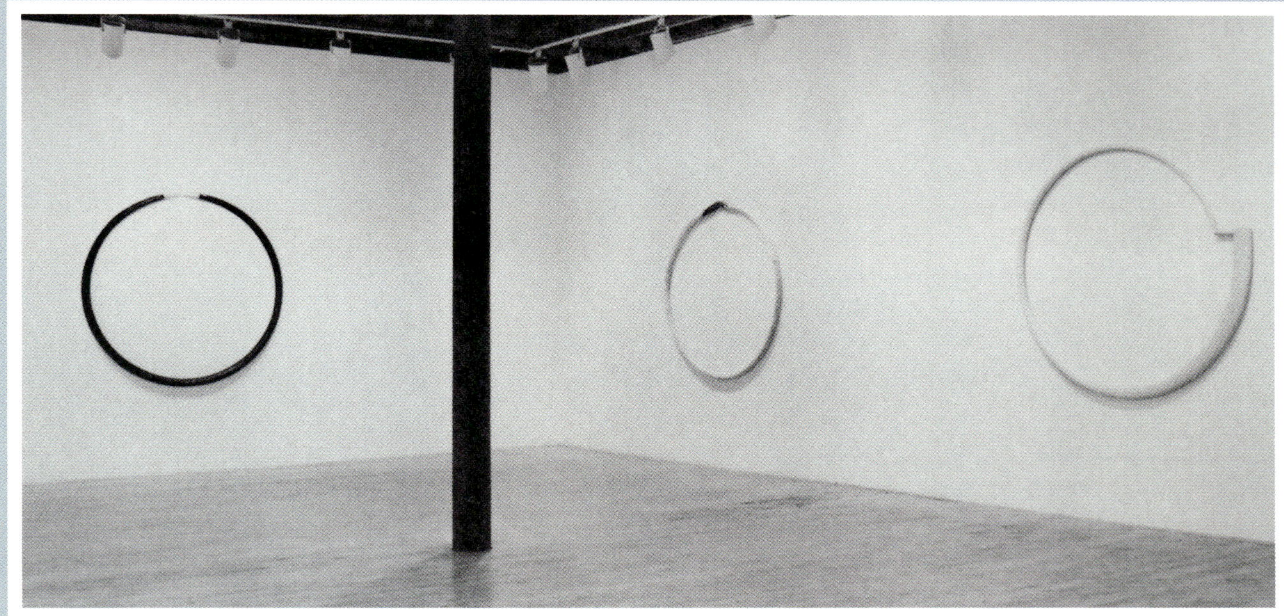

Figure 102. Installation view of *Martin Puryear*, Young Hoffman Gallery, 1982. Pictured: *Tango* (1982); *Kiruna* (1982); *Simple Gift* (1982)

1981

Whitney Biennial 1981
Whitney Museum of American Art, New York
January 20–April 12

Sculptural Density
[Group Exhibition]
Visual Arts Museum, School of Visual Arts (SVA), New York
March 30–April 24

Artists' Gardens and Parks
Museum of Contemporary Art Chicago
April 18–June 14

Martin Puryear
and/or gallery, Seattle
May 21–June 13

• See fig. 75

City Sculpture
[Group Exhibition]
Chicago Public Library Cultural Center
July 18–September 5

The New Spiritualism: Transcendent Images in Painting and Sculpture
Oscarsson Hood Gallery, New York
September 9–26

Traveled to: Jorgensen Gallery, University of Connecticut, Storrs, November 16–December 31; Robert Hull Fleming Museum, University of Vermont, Burlington, February 4–March 28, 1982

Instruction Drawings: The Gilbert and Lila Silverman Collection
Cranbrook Academy of Art Museum, Bloomfield Hills, MI
September 20–November 1

Martin Puryear: Recent Sculpture
Delahunty Gallery, Dallas
October 10–November 11

***Duncan Plaza Project*, 1980–81**
Invited proposal for Duncan Plaza, New Orleans

Collaboration with landscape architect Charles Caplinger

Concrete and plantings
Unrealized

1982

Invitational
[Group Exhibition]
Bell Gallery, List Art Center, Brown University, Providence, RI
January 15–February 14

Martin Puryear: Sculpture
McIntosh-Drysdale Gallery, Washington, DC
February 6–March 3

Form and Function: Proposals for Public Art for Philadelphia
Pennsylvania Academy of the Fine Arts, Philadelphia
February 19–April 18

Mayor Byrne's Mile of Sculpture
Navy Pier, Chicago
May 13–29

Organized by the Chicago Sculpture Society, concurrent with Art 1982 Chicago, Chicago International Art Exposition

Martin Puryear: Sculpture
Young Hoffman Gallery, Chicago
May 21–July 6

• Fig. 102

N.A.M.E. Gallery in Pittsburgh
Hewlett Gallery, College of Fine Arts, Carnegie Mellon University, Pittsburgh
June 1–July 22

74th American Exhibition
Art Institute of Chicago
June 12–August 1

Works in Wood
[Group Exhibition]
Margo Leavin Gallery, Los Angeles
July 10–September 11

American Abstraction Now
Institute of Contemporary Art of the Virginia Museum, Richmond
September 1–October 3

Directions in Afro-American Abstract Art
Carl Van Vechten Gallery, Fisk University, Nashville, TN
October 17–November 17

Bodark Arc
Outdoor installation at Nathan Manilow Sculpture Park, University Park, IL

Commissioned by Governors State University

• For further installation details, see [24]; figs. 13–15, 80

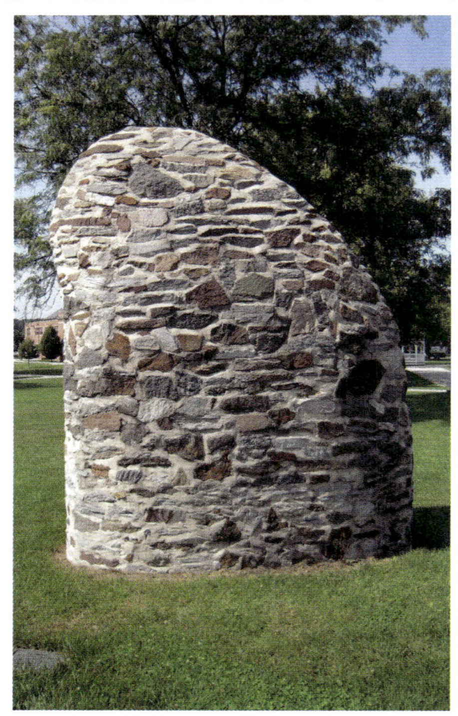

Figure 103. Installation view of *Sentinel* (1982). Martin Puryear. Mortared fieldstone; 3.2 x 2.6 x 106.7 m. Photo: Courtesy of Special Collections and College Archives, Musselman Library, Gettysburg College, PA

Sentinel
Outdoor installation at Gettysburg College, PA

Commissioned by Gettysburg College

● Fig. 103

1983

Five Sculptors / N.O.A.A. Collaboration
Seattle Center Pavilion, Seattle Art Museum, Seattle
January 27–February 27

Knoll for NOAA
Outdoor installation at Western Regional Center, NOAA, Seattle

Commissioned by Seattle Arts Commission and National Oceanic and Atmospheric Administration (NOAA), U.S. Department of Commerce

Concrete, inlaid glass, and plantings; knoll, diameter 13.7 m, height 137.2 cm

● Fig. 104

Invitational Exhibition
[Group Exhibition]
Grace Borgenicht Gallery, New York
June 1–30

Bruce Nauman / Martin Puryear
Donald Young Gallery, Chicago
September 24–October 18

Beyond the Monument
Hayden Gallery, Massachusetts Institute of Technology, Cambridge
October 8–November 13

Traveled to: Stamford Museum and Nature Center, CT, March 24–May 12, 1985

Sensuous Art
Fayerweather Gallery, University of Virginia, Charlottesville
November 4–23

1984

Martin Puryear
University Gallery, Fine Arts Center, University of Massachusetts, Amherst
February 4–March 16

Traveled to: Berkshire Museum, Pittsfield, MA, April 7–May 27; Museum of the National Center of Afro-American Artists, Boston, June 10–July 15; New Museum of Contemporary Art, New York, July 28–September 9; as *Martin Puryear: Selected Sculpture of the Last Decade*, La Jolla Museum of Contemporary Art, CA, October 13–December 9

● Figs. 105–6

Transformation of the Minimal Style: Materials & Meaning
[Group Exhibition]
SculptureCenter in collaboration with Art Across the Park, New York
February 7–28

American Sculpture
[Group Exhibition]
Donald Young Gallery, Chicago
April 28–June 30

An International Survey of Recent Painting and Sculpture
Museum of Modern Art, New York
May 17–August 19

Projects: World's Fairs, Waterfronts, Parks, and Plazas
Rhona Hoffman Gallery, Chicago
June 20–July 31

American Sculpture
[Group Exhibition]
Margo Leavin Gallery, Los Angeles
July 17–September 15

East-West Contemporary American Art
California Museum of Afro-American History, Los Angeles
July 22–January 15, 1985

"Primitivism" in 20th Century Art: Affinity of the Tribal and the Modern
Museum of Modern Art, New York
September 27–January 15, 1985

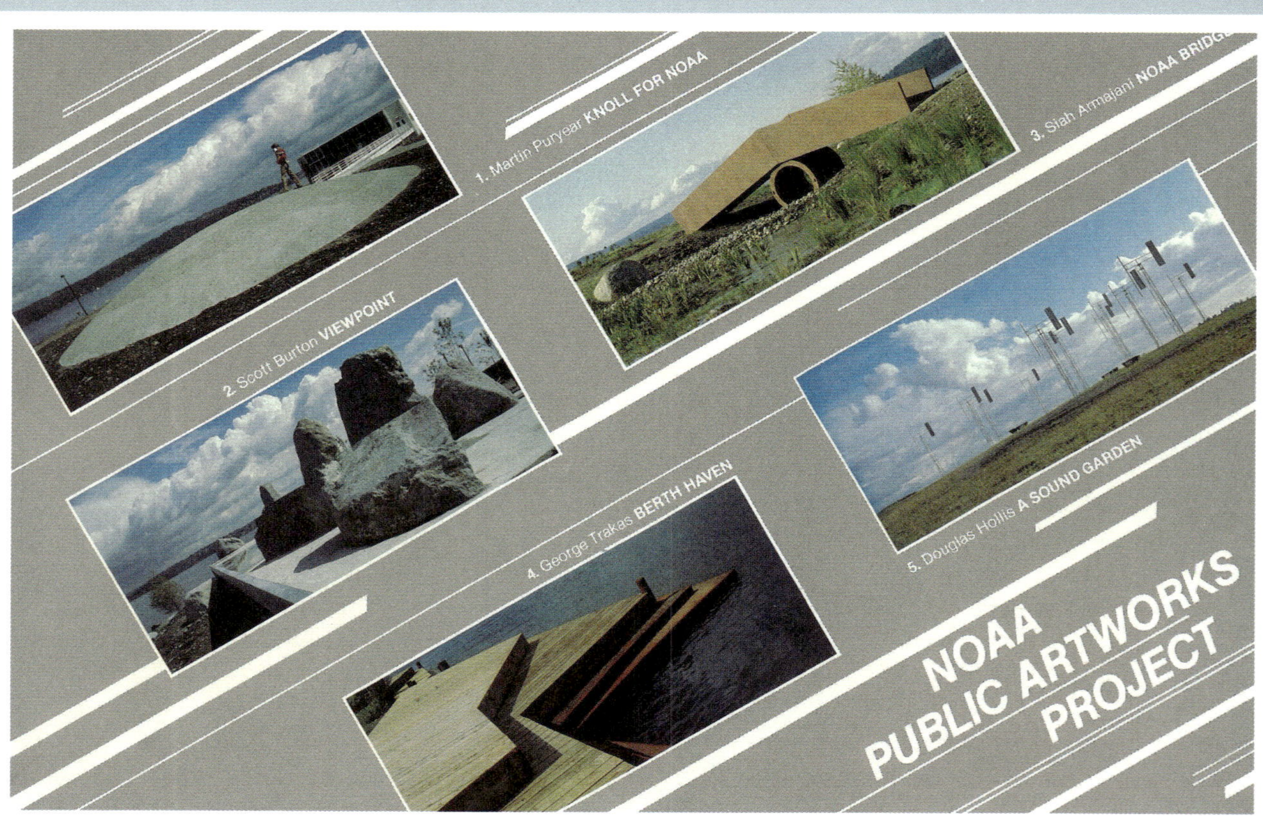

Figure 104. Postcard for "NOAA Public Artworks Project," National Oceanic and Atmospheric Administration, 1983

Eccentric Images
[Group Exhibition]
Margo Leavin Gallery, Los Angeles
October 20–November 24

***No Small Plans*, 1982–84**
Invited proposal for the Committee on Arts for the Light Rail Transit System, Port Authority of Allegheny County, Penn Park Station, Pittsburgh

Welded steel
Unrealized

1984 Summer Olympic Games Poster
Commissioned by the Los Angeles Olympic Organizing Committee (LAOOC) for the Games of the XXIII Olympiad

Paper; 61 cm x 91.4 cm; part of a fifteen-poster set

1985

Martin Puryear: Nature and Artifice
Margo Leavin Gallery, Los Angeles
January 12–February 16

The Artist as Social Designer: Aspects of Public Urban Art Today
Los Angeles County Museum of Art
February 7–March 17

Basically Wood
[Group Exhibition]
Thomas Segal Gallery, Boston
March 2–April 10

Overview 1985: A Survey of Sculpture
Evanston Art Center, IL
April 14–May 19

Selections from the William J. Hokin Collection
Museum of Contemporary Art Chicago
April 20–June 16

Chicago Sculpture International, Mile 4
State Street Mall, Chicago
May 9–June 9

Anniottanta
[Group Exhibition]
Gallerie Salamon Agustoni Algranti, Bologna, Italy
July 4–September 30

Martin Puryear / MATRIX 86
University Art Museum, University of California, Berkeley
August 1–September 22

Inaugural Exhibition
[Group Exhibition]
Tyler Gallery, Temple University, Philadelphia
October 1–November 8

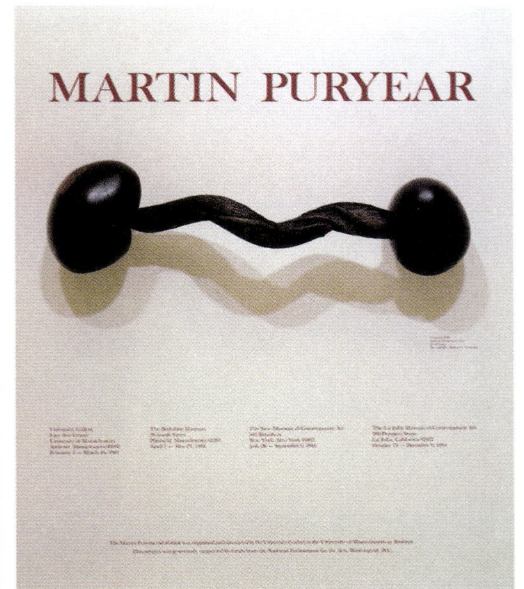

Figure 105. Exhibition poster for *Martin Puryear*, University Gallery, Fine Arts Center, University of Massachusetts, Amherst, 1984. Pictured: *Untitled* (1978). Photo: Stephen Petegorsky, courtesy of the University Museum of Contemporary Art, University of Massachusetts, Amherst

Artists + Architects: Challenges in Collaboration
Cleveland Center for Contemporary Art
October 4–November 16

Martin Puryear: New Sculpture
Donald Young Gallery, Chicago
October 11–November 9

Transformations in Sculpture: Four Decades in American and European Art
Solomon R. Guggenheim Museum, New York
November 22–February 16, 1986

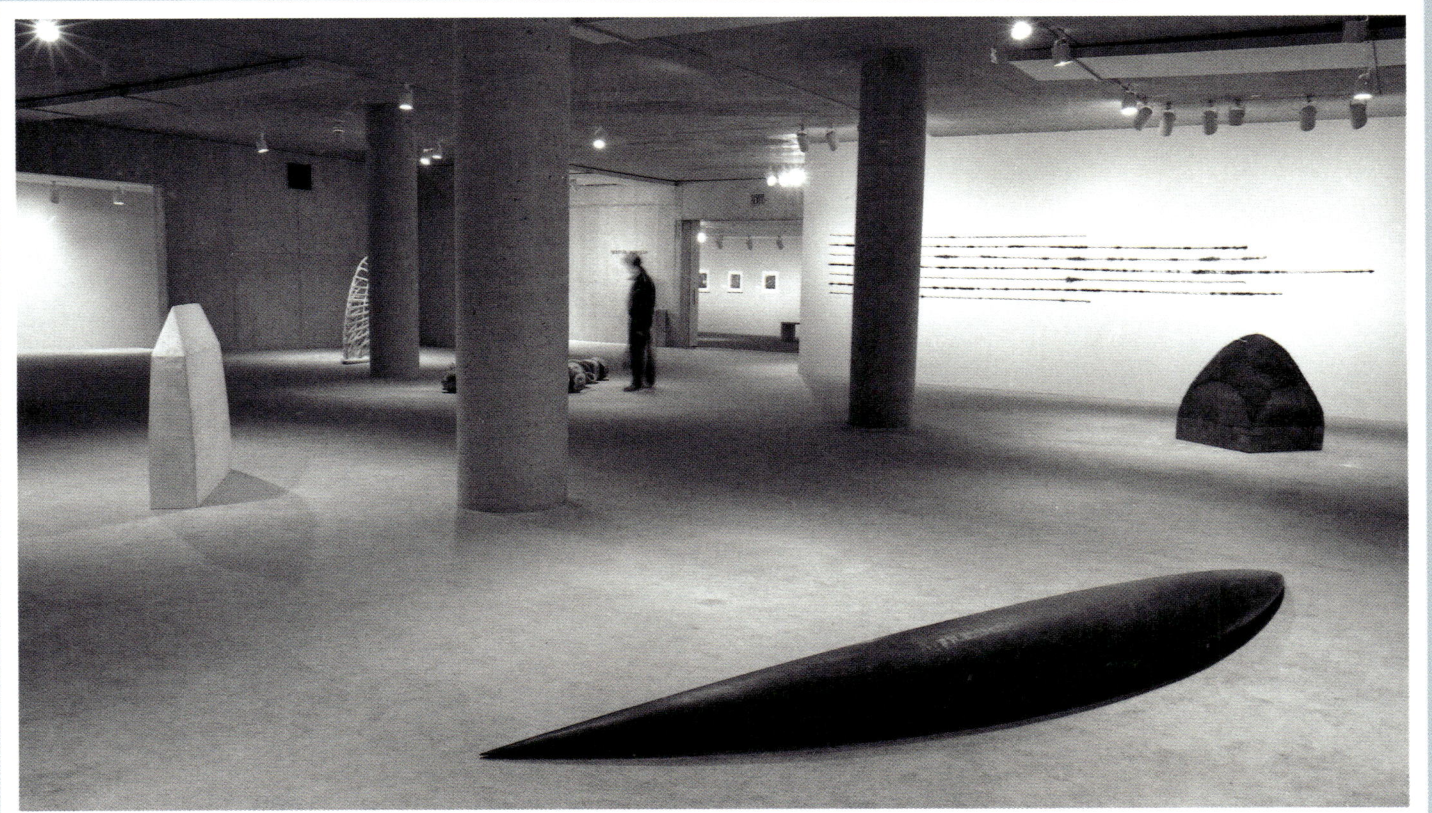

Figure 106. Installation view of *Martin Puryear*, University Gallery, Fine Arts Center, University of Massachusetts, Amherst, 1984. Pictured: *Reliquary* (1980; [17]); *Bower* (1980; [19]); *Osage Beadwork* (1973); *Some Lines for Jim Beckwourth* (1978; [15]); *For Beckwourth* (1980); *Bask* (1976; [11]). University Photo Negatives Collection, Robert S. Cox Special Collections and University Archives Research Center, UMass Amherst Libraries

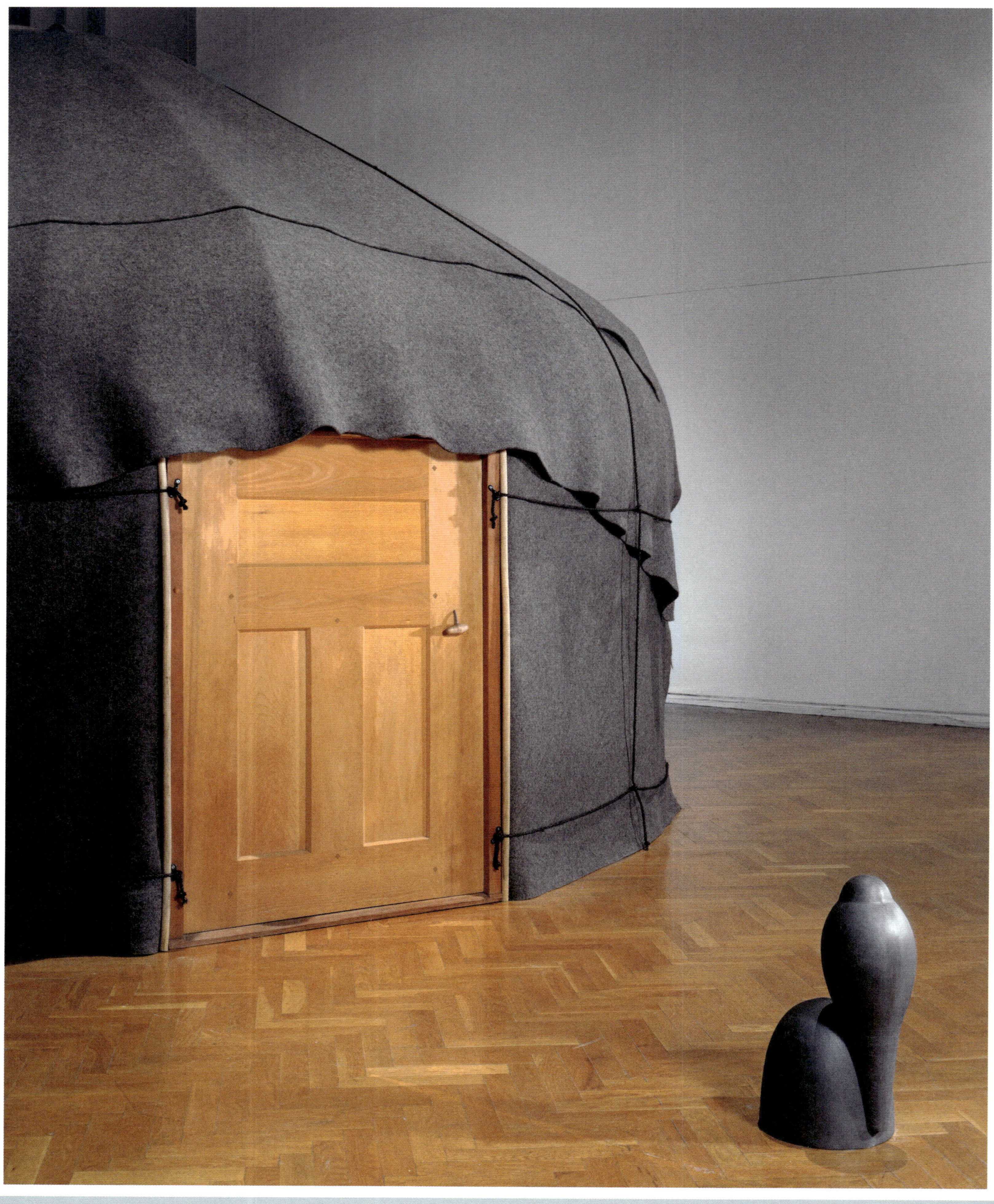

River Road Ring
Indoor installation at the River Road Station, Chicago O'Hare Transit Line, Chicago

Commissioned by the City of Chicago

Honduras mahogany; 8.4 m x 8.4 m x 15.2 m
Dismantled in 2010 (no longer extant)

Stone Bow
Invited proposal for Tufts University, Medford, MA

Stainless steel cable and granite
Unrealized

1986

Choosing: An Exhibit of Changing Perspectives in Modern Art and Art Criticism by Black Americans, 1925–1985
Hampton University Art Gallery, VA
January 29–February 28

Traveled to: Portsmouth Community Arts Center, Portsmouth Museums, VA, February 1–March 31; President's Gallery, Chicago State University, May 1–31; Gallery of Art, Howard University, Washington, DC, September 16–November 23

Recent Acquisitions
[Group Exhibition]
Donald Young Gallery, Chicago
January 31–March 1

Sculpture on Stetson
[Group Exhibition]
Two Illinois Center, Chicago
January–January 1987

After Nature
[Group Exhibition]
Germans van Eck Gallery, New York
February 1–28

Black Creativity, Generations in Transition: 80 Years of Black American Expression
Museum of Science and Industry, Chicago
February 1–March 2

Installations and Sculpture
[Group Exhibition]
Donald Young Gallery, Chicago
May 2–31

Natural Forms and Forces: Abstract Images in American Sculpture
Hayden Gallery, List Visual Arts Center, Massachusetts Institute of Technology, Cambridge
May 9–June 19

Personal References: Raymond Saunders, Phyllis Bramson, Martin Puryear
Charlotte Crosby Kemper Gallery, Kansas City Art Institute, MO
September 6–October 5

Individuals: A Selected History of Contemporary Art, 1945–1986
Museum of Contemporary Art, Los Angeles
December 10–January 10, 1988

1987

Public and Personal
[Solo Exhibition]
Chicago Public Library Cultural Center
February 7–April 4

• Figs. 107a, b

Martin Puryear: Sculpture / Drawings
Carnegie Mellon University Art Gallery, Pittsburgh
April 12–May 30

Structure to Resemblance: Work by Eight American Sculptors
Albright-Knox Art Gallery, Buffalo
June 13–August 23

Emerging Artists 1978–1986: Selections from the Exxon Series
Solomon R. Guggenheim Museum, New York
September 3–November 1

Martin Puryear
Donald Young Gallery, Chicago
September 11–October 17

Martin Puryear: Stereotypes and Decoys
David McKee Gallery, New York
November 6–December 12

Fifty Years of Collecting: An Anniversary Selection; Sculpture of the Modern Era
Solomon R. Guggenheim Museum, New York
November 13–March 13, 1988

1988

Private Works for Public Spaces: Drawings, Maquettes and Documentation for Unrealized Public Artworks
R. C. Erpf Gallery, New York
February 19–March 19

Martin Puryear: New Wall Sculpture
McIntosh-Drysdale Gallery, Washington, DC
March 12–April 2

Vital Signs: Organic Abstraction from the Permanent Collection
Whitney Museum of American Art, New York
April 28–July 10

1988: The World of Art Today
Milwaukee Art Museum
May 6–August 28

Australian Biennale 1988, *From the Southern Cross; A View of World Art c. 1940–1988*
Art Gallery of New South Wales, Sydney and Pier 2/3, Walsh Bay, Sydney, Australia
May 18–July 3

Traveled to: National Gallery of Victoria, Melbourne, Australia, August 4–September 18

Sculpture Inside Outside
[Group Exhibition]
Walker Art Center, Minneapolis
May 22–September 18

Traveled to: Museum of Fine Arts, Houston, December 10–March 5, 1989

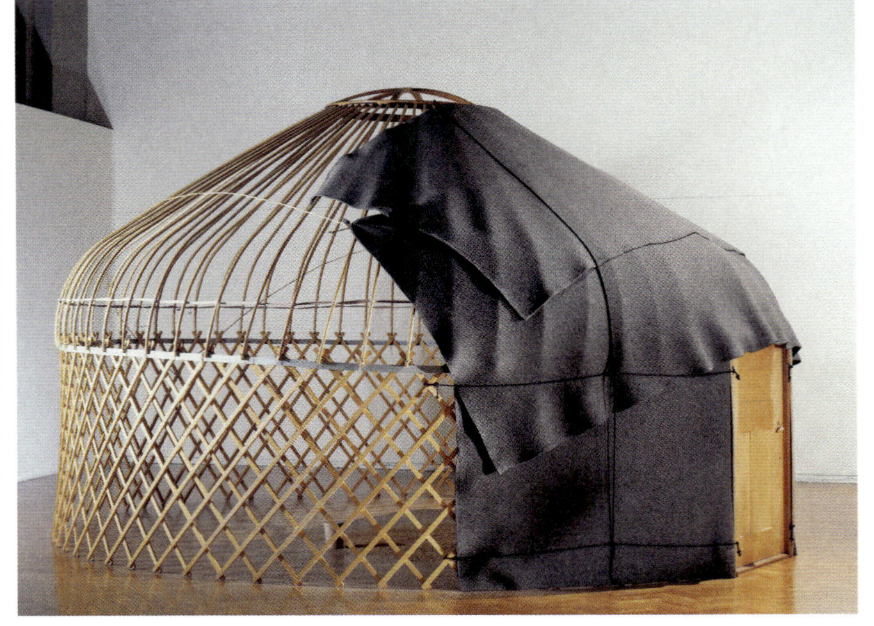

Figures 107a, b. Installation views of *Where the Heart Is (Sleeping Mews)* (1987) with *On the Tundra* (1986; [26]) in *Public and Personal*, Chicago Public Library Cultural Center, 1987. Mixed materials; yurt: diameter 5.5 m; other dimensions variable. Photos: © Russell Phillips Photography

Figure 108. Installation view of *Martin Puryear*, Hirshhorn Museum and Sculpture Garden, Smithsonian Institution, Washington, DC, 1992. Pictured: *Lever #2* (1989); *Empire's Lunch* (1987); *Sharp and Flat* (1987); *Rawhide Cone* (1980; [14]); *Some Lines for Jim Beckwourth* (1978; [15]); *For Beckwourth* (1980). Photo: Hirshhorn Museum and Sculpture Garden

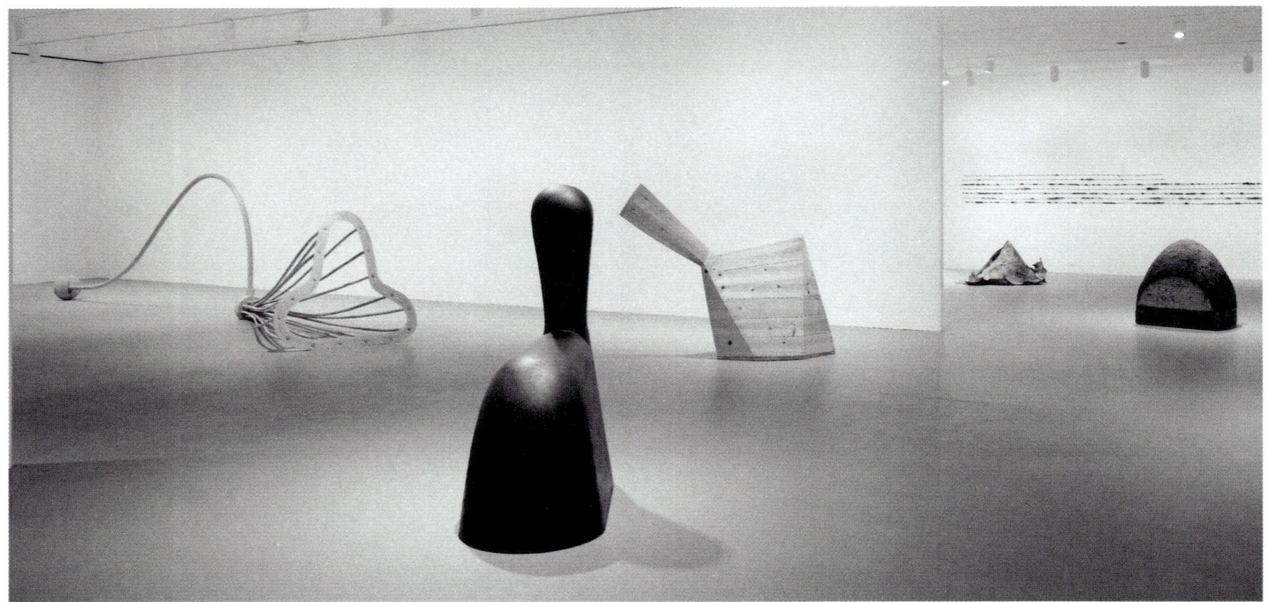

Skulptur: Material und Abstraktion; 2 x 5 Positionen
Aargauer Kunsthaus Aarau, Switzerland
June 18–July 31

Traveled to: Musée cantonal des beaux-arts, Lausanne, Switzerland, October 27–December 11; Swiss Institute and City Gallery, Department of Cultural Affairs, New York, January 5–February 10, 1989

New Sculpture / Six Artists
Saint Louis Art Museum
September 23–October 30

Innovations in Sculpture, 1985–1988
Aldrich Museum of Contemporary Art, Ridgefield, CT
September 24–December 31

Mary Beth Edelson, Martin Puryear, Italo Scanga, Robert Stackhouse
Corcoran Gallery of Art, Washington, DC
October 13–December 31

Enclosing the Void: Eight Contemporary Sculptors
Whitney Museum of American Art at Equitable Center, New York
November 11–January 25, 1989

Martin Puryear
Grand Lobby installation, Brooklyn Museum, New York
November 18–February 13, 1989

Gog & Magog (Ampersand), 1987–88
Outdoor installation at the Minneapolis Sculpture Garden, Walker Art Center, Minneapolis

Commissioned by the Walker Art Center, Minneapolis. Gift of Margaret and Angus Wurtele, 1988

Granite; east column: 414 x 91.4 x 91.4 cm; west column: 424.2 x 91.4 x 96.5 cm

Ark
Ceiling-mounted indoor installation at the North Mall Atrium, Academic Core Building, York College, City University of New York (CUNY), Jamaica, Queens

Commissioned by Dormitory Authority of the State of New York / (CUNY) Construction Fund for York College, CUNY with support from National Endowment for the Arts, Visual Arts Program, Art in Public Places

Copper pipe and suspension cables; 21.9 x 9.1 x .9 m

1989

Introspectives: Contemporary Art by Americans and Brazilians of African Descent
California Afro-American Museum, Los Angeles
February 11–September 30

Traditions and Transformations: Contemporary Afro-American Sculpture
Bronx Museum of the Arts, New York
February 21–May 27

Martin Puryear: New Works
Margo Leavin Gallery, Los Angeles
April 15–May 20

Whitney Biennial 1989
Whitney Museum of American Art, New York
April 18–July 16

Tony Cragg, Richard Deacon, Martin Puryear, Susana Solano
Donald Young Gallery, Chicago
May 3–May 27

Art in Place: 15 Years of Acquisitions
Whitney Museum of American Art, New York
July 27–October 22

20th Bienal Internacional de São Paulo
Ciccillo Matarazzo Pavilion, Parque do Ibirapuera, São Paulo
October 14–December 10

United States Exhibition, organized by the Jamaica Arts Center, Queens, New York

• See pp. 4–5

Max Protetch Gallery: 20 Years
Max Protetch Gallery, New York
December 9–January 13, 1990

1990

Objects of Potential: Five American Sculptors from the Anderson Collection
Wiegand Gallery, College of Notre Dame, Belmont, CA
February 6–March 30

Connections: Martin Puryear
Museum of Fine Arts, Boston
March 17–July 8

• See fig. 37

Black USA
Museum Overholland, Amsterdam
April 7–July 29

The Decade Show: Frameworks of Identity in the 1980s
Studio Museum in Harlem, New York
May 18–August 19

Organized by the New Museum, the Museum of Contemporary Hispanic Art, and the Studio Museum in Harlem (Puryear featured at the Studio Museum)

On the Road: Selections from the Permanent Collection of the San Diego Museum of Contemporary Art
Duke University Museum of Art, Durham, NC
September 7–November 4

Traveled to: J.B. Speed Art Museum, Louisville, KY, December 4–January 27, 1991; Springfield Museum of Fine Arts, MA, March 3–May 19, 1991; traveled as *On the Road: Selections from the Permanent Collection*, San Diego Museum of Contemporary Art, La Jolla, CA, June 8–August 4, 1991; Memorial Art Gallery, University of Rochester, NY, September 28–November 17, 1991; Utah Museum of Fine Arts, University of Utah, Salt Lake City, May 18–June 28, 1992; Philbrook Museum of Art, Tulsa, OK, July 17–September 1, 1992

***Chevy Chase Garden Plaza*, 1985–86, completed 1990**
Outdoor installation at the Chevy Chase Garden Plaza, Bethesda, MD

Commissioned by Chevy Chase Federal Savings & Loan, Maryland

Fountain, stainless steel and rippled granite; sculpture: approx. 3 x 3 x 3 m; base: approx. height .9 m; diameter 1.5 m

Four curved benches, granite; each approx. 35.6 cm x 213.4 cm x 483 cm

Trellis, steel and concrete sculpture: approx. 3.7 x 5.5 x 14.6 m; bases, each approx. 1.5 x .2 m

Knot installed on the roof of a pavilion, copper and bronze; 1.2 x .9 x .3 m

1991

Martin Puryear
Art Institute of Chicago
November 2–January 5, 1992

Traveled to: Hirshhorn Museum and Sculpture Garden, Smithsonian Institution, Washington, DC, February 4–May 10, 1992; Museum of Contemporary Art, Los Angeles, August 2–October 11, 1992; Philadelphia Museum of Art, November 8, 1992–January 3, 1993

● Fig. 108

Devil on the Stairs: Looking Back at the Eighties
Institute of Contemporary Art, Philadelphia
October 4–January 5, 1992

Traveled to: Newport Harbor Art Museum, CA, April 16–June 21, 1992

Reprise: The Vera G. List Collection
David Winton Bell Gallery, List Art Center, Brown University, Providence, RI
October 12–November 24

Small Scale Sculpture
[Group Exhibition]
Sewell Art Gallery, Rice University, Houston
October 24–December 14

Griot New York
World premiere: Brooklyn Academy of Music (BAM), BAM Next Wave Festival, New York, December 4–7

Co-commissioned by the Brooklyn Academy of Music (BAM), the Vienna Festival–Tanz '92, the Houston International Festival, the University of the Arts (Philadelphia / Festival Mythos), and the University of Kansas Concert Series

Concept and choreography by Garth Fagan; music composed, arranged and performed by Wynton Marsalis; sets and costumes by Martin Puryear; lighting design by C. T. Oakes; with Garth Fagan Dance and the Wynton Marsalis Septet; scenic design associate: Michael Puryear; custom design associate: Charles Schoonmaker

● Figs. 109a, b

Proposal for Holocaust Memorial Museum
Invited proposal by the United States Holocaust Memorial Museum, Washington, DC

Charred wood to have been cast in bronze and patinated black
Unrealized

1992

Group Show
Donald Young Gallery, Seattle
January 17–April 8

Allegories of Modernism: Contemporary Drawing
Museum of Modern Art, New York
February 16–May 5

Exhibition of Works by Newly Elected Members and Recipients of Honors and Awards
American Academy and Institute of Arts and Letters, New York
May 20–June 14

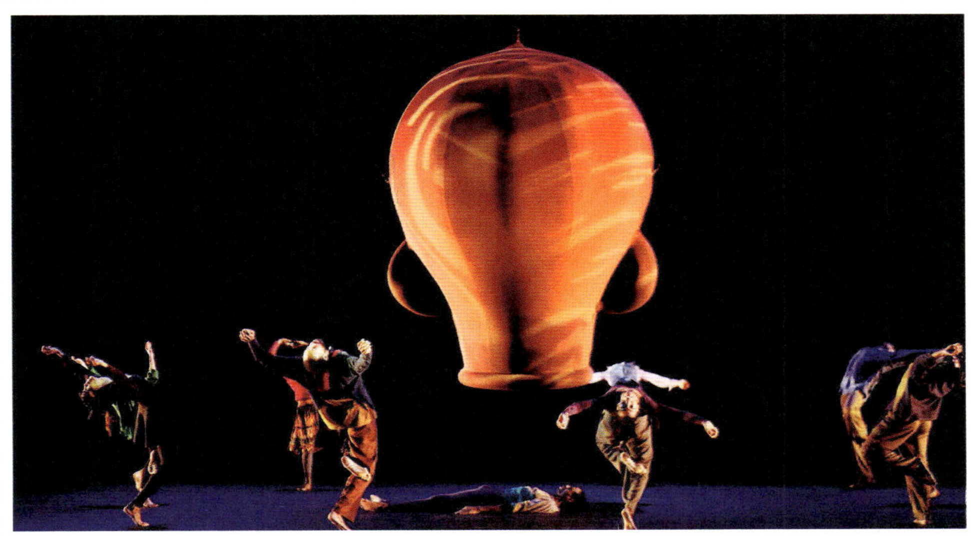

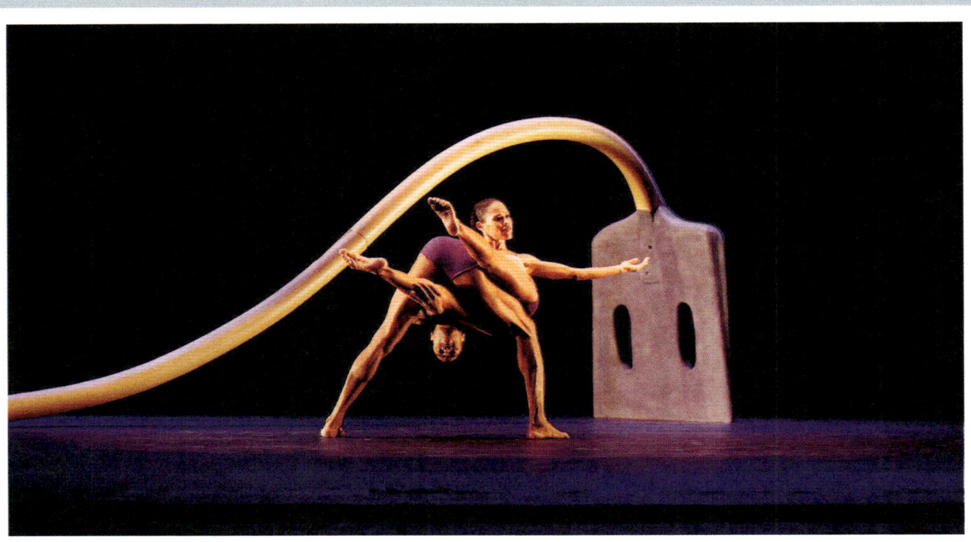

Figure 109a, b. Scenes from *Griot New York* (1991) performed in BAM Next Wave Festival, 2012. Garth Fagan (choreography) with Wynton Marsalis (music) and Martin Puryear (set and costume design). Photos: Basil Childers

Process to Presence: Issues in Sculpture, 1960 to 1990
Locks Gallery, Philadelphia

In conjunction with the 14th International Sculpture Conference
June 3–July 17

Documenta IX
Palais Bellevue, Kassel, Germany
June 13–September 20

1993

Collective Pursuits: Mount Holyoke Investigates Modernism
Mount Holyoke College Art Museum, South Hadley, MA
April 3–May 30

Yale Collects Yale
Yale University Art Gallery, New Haven, CT
April 30–July 31

American Art in the 20th Century: Painting and Sculpture 1913–1993
Martin-Gropius-Bau, Berlin, Germany
May 8–July 25

Traveled to: Royal Academy of Arts, London, and Saatchi Gallery, London, September 16–December 12

Group Show
Donald Young Gallery, Seattle
May

Drawing the Line Against AIDS
Peggy Guggenheim Collection, Venice, Italy
June 8–13

In conjunction with the 45th Venice Biennale

Traveled to: Guggenheim Museum SoHo, New York, October 6–19

Living with Art: The Collection of Ellyn & Saul Dennison
Morris Museum, Morristown, NJ
October 16–November 21

Martin Puryear
Cleveland Center for Contemporary Art
November 19–January 23, 1994

Pavilion in the Trees
Outdoor installation at Fairmount Park, Philadelphia; first proposed for Cliveden Park, Philadelphia, in 1981

Commissioned by the Fairmount Park Association, Philadelphia

• For further installation details, see fig. 78

1994

Putting Things Together: Recent Sculpture from the Anderson Collection
Art Museum of Santa Cruz County, CA
April 23–June 26

Visions of America: Landscape as Metaphor in the Late Twentieth Century
Organized by the Columbus Museum of Art and the Denver Art Museum

Traveled to: Denver Art Museum, May 14–September 11; Columbus Museum of Art, OH, October 16–January 5, 1995

Group Exhibition
Donald Young Gallery, Seattle
June 1–November 12

Drawings in Black and White: A Selection of Contemporary Works from the Collection
Museum of Modern Art, New York
September 22–February 7, 1995

1995

Martin Puryear: New Sculpture
McKee Gallery, New York
March 3–April 15

American Color: A Late 20th Century Perspective
Louis Stern Fine Arts, Los Angeles
April 22–June 7

Adding It Up: Print Acquisitions 1970–1995
Museum of Modern Art, New York
May 27–September 5

25th Anniversary Show: An Exhibition of Selected Works
Margo Leavin Gallery, Los Angeles
September 23–October 28

New Works on Paper
[Group Exhibition]
Donald Young Gallery, Seattle
September 23–November 22

Twentieth Century American Sculpture at The White House, Exhibit III Southwest and West Regions
Jacqueline Kennedy Garden, The White House, Washington, DC
October–March 1996

The Material Imagination
Guggenheim Museum SoHo, New York
November 18–January 28, 1996

***Untitled*, 1994–95**
Outdoor installation at Oliver Ranch, Geyserville, CA

Commissioned by the Oliver Ranch Foundation

Mortared fieldstone and red cedar, 5.5 x 5.2 x 7.3 m

North Cove Pylons
Outdoor installation at Battery Park City, New York

Commissioned by Battery Park City Authority, New York

Granite and stainless steel; north pylon: 22 x 1.7 m; south pylon: 17.3 x 2.1 x 2.1 m

Tokyo International Forum Proposal
Invited proposal for the atrium of the Tokyo International Forum

Unrealized

• For further proposal details, see [33]

Figure 110. Two students seated on Martin Puryear's stainless steel bench in the Vera List Courtyard, New School for Social Research, New York, c. 1997. Photo: Shannon Von Ronne. Courtesy of The New School photograph collection, The New School Archives and Special Collections, The New School, New York, NY

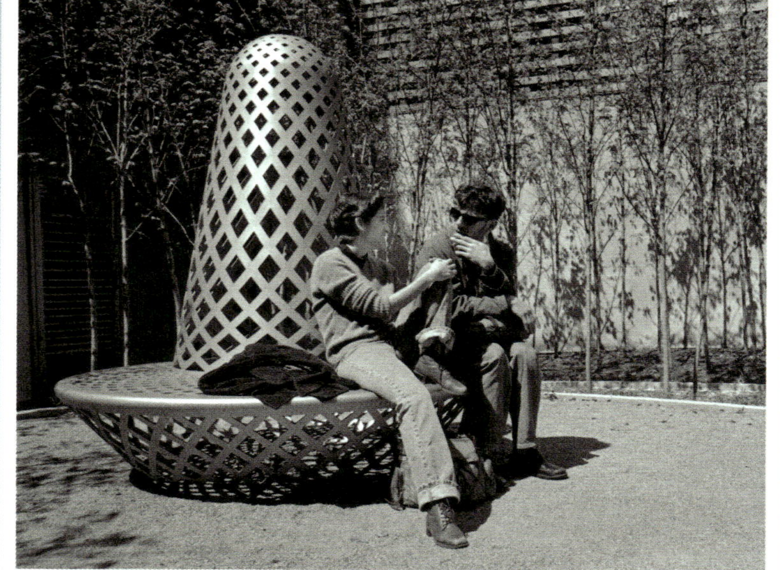

1996

Abstraction in the Twentieth Century: Total Risk, Freedom, Discipline
Solomon R. Guggenheim Museum, New York
February 8–May 12

Group Exhibition
McKee Gallery, New York
April 5–26

Wanås 1996
Wanås Foundation, Knislinge, Sweden
May 26–October 20

Thinking Print: Books to Billboards, 1980–1995
Museum of Modern Art, New York
June 20–September 10

Outdoor Sculpture
[Group Exhibition]
Elena Zang Gallery, Woodstock, NY
July 6–October 15

Masterworks of Modern Sculpture: The Nasher Collection
California Palace of the Legion of Honor, Fine Arts Museums of San Francisco
October 26–January 12, 1997

Traveled as *A Century of Sculpture: The Nasher Collection* to: Solomon R. Guggenheim Museum, New York, February 7–June 1, 1997

Art in Chicago, 1945–1995
Museum of Contemporary Art Chicago
November 16–March 23, 1997

Group Exhibition
McKee Gallery, New York
April 5–26

Group Exhibition
Fendrick Gallery, Washington, DC

Meditation in a Beech Wood
Outdoor installation at the Wanås Foundation, Knislinge, Sweden

Commissioned by the Wanås Foundation, Knislinge

Restored in June 2024

• For further installation details, see figs. 19, 81, 121

1997

Martin Puryear
Donald Young Gallery, Seattle
February 28–May 3

Selections from the Permanent Collection: Identity / Identidad
Museum of Contemporary Art San Diego, La Jolla, CA
April 6–July 9

Sol LeWitt / Iglesias / Puryear
Donald Young Gallery, Seattle
May

Envisioning the Contemporary: Selections from the Permanent Collection
Museum of Contemporary Art Chicago
June 21–April 5, 1998

American Stories: Amidst Displacement and Transformation / Amerikan sutōrī: idō to hen yō no naka de
Setagaya Bijutsukan, Tokyo
August 30–October 19

Traveled to: Chiba City Museum of Art, Chiba, Japan, November 1–December 23; Fukui Fine Arts Museum, Fukui, Japan, April 29–May 24, 1998; Kurashiki City Art Museum, Okayama, Japan, June 13–July 26, 1998; Akita Prefectural Integrated Life Cultural Hall, Akita, Japan, August 7–September 6, 1998

A Decade of Collecting: Recent Acquisitions in Contemporary Drawing
Museum of Modern Art, New York
September 8–January 20, 1998

Martin Puryear
Fundación "la Caixa," Madrid
November 14–January 11, 1998

Nunzio, Martin Puryear: Forma Lignea
American Academy in Rome
December 19–February 22, 1998

Vera List Courtyard
Three benches installed in courtyard located between Alvin Johnson / J. M. Kaplan Hall and Eugene Lang College of Liberal Arts, The New School, New York

Commissioned by The New School Art Collection; collaboration with landscape architect Michael Van Valkenburgh

Bench, granite, 157.5 x 157.5 x 157.5 cm

Bench, stainless steel, 157.5 x 157.5 x 157.5 cm

Bench, maple, 157.5 x 157.5 x 157.5 cm

• Fig. 110

Everything That Rises
Outdoor installation at the Physics and Astronomy Building, University of Washington, Seattle

Commissioned by the University of Washington, Seattle

Formed plate bronze; height 5.7 m

1998

Group Exhibition
McKee Gallery, New York
January

The African American Odyssey: A Quest for Full Citizenship
Library of Congress, Washington, DC
February 5–May 5

The Edward R. Broida Collection: A Selection of Works
Orlando Museum of Art
March 12–June 21

Face to Face: Art in Public
Marlborough Chelsea, New York
May 9–June 27

Essence of the Orb
[Group Exhibition]
Michael Rosenfeld Gallery, New York
June 4–August 20

Giacometti to Judd: Prints by Sculptors
Museum of Modern Art, New York
June 9–October 13

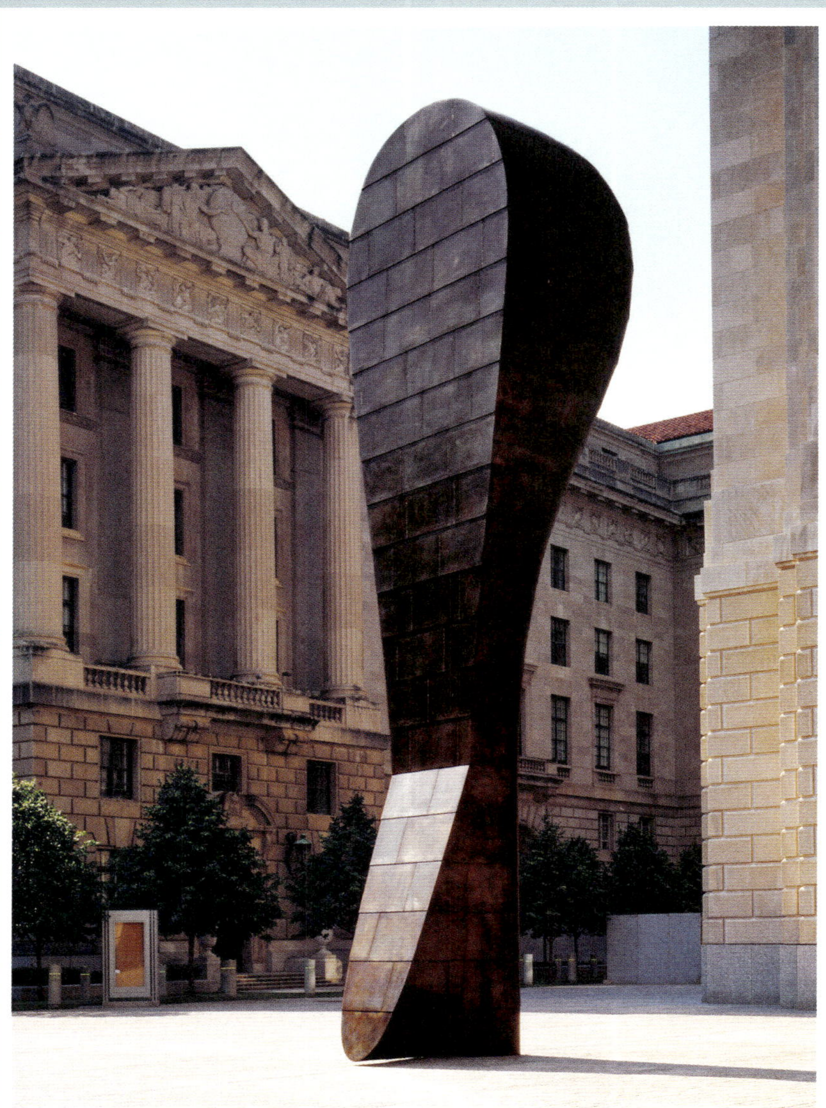

Figure 111. Installation view of *Bearing Witness* (1994–98) at the Reagan Building and International Trade Center, Washington, DC. Martin Puryear. Hammer-formed, welded bronze plate; 12.2 x 3 x 4.3 m. Photo: Robert Laufman

Narratives of African American Art and Identity: The David C. Driskell Collection
Art Gallery, University of Maryland, College Park, MD
October 22–December 19

Traveled to: African American Museum, Dallas, March 13–June 19, 1999; Colby College Museum of Art, Waterville, ME, July 21–October 17, 1999; M.H. de Young Memorial Museum, Fine Arts Museums of San Francisco, November 13, 1999–February 13, 2000; Cincinnati Art Museum, March 17–May 14, 2000; High Museum of Art, Atlanta, June 13–September 24, 2000; Newark Museum, NJ, October 25, 2000–February 25, 2001; Virginia Museum of Fine Arts, Richmond, July 8–September 30, 2001; Naples Museum of Art, FL, October 15, 2001–January 13, 2002; Mint Museum of Art, Charlotte, NC, August 23–October 25, 2002

***Bearing Witness*, 1994–98**
Outdoor installation at Reagan Building and International Trade Center, Washington, DC

Commissioned by the General Services Administration, Washington, DC

• Fig. 111

1999

Drawings into Sculpture: Martin Puryear
Contemporary Arts Center, Cincinnati
June 19–August 29

Weaving the World, Contemporary Art of Linear Construction
Yokohama Museum of Art, Japan
June 26–August 22

ARTIST BOXES: Intimate Spaces
Lynn Tendler Bignell Gallery, Brookfield Craft Center, CT
September 11–October 24

The American Century: Art & Culture, 1950–2000
Whitney Museum of American Art, New York
September 26–February 13, 2000

This Mortal Coil
Temporary indoor installation at Chapelle Saint-Louis de la Salpêtrière, Paris
September 24–November 1

Commissioned for the Festival d'Automne à Paris

• For further installation details, see [35]; fig. 20

Martin Puryear: Commission for the Getty Center
J. Paul Getty Museum at the Getty Center, Los Angeles
November 23–January 9, 2000

That Profile
Outdoor installation at J. Paul Getty Museum, Los Angeles

Commissioned by The J. Paul Getty Trust, Los Angeles

• Fig. 112

2000

Making Choices
Museum of Modern Art, New York
March 16–September 26

Strength and Diversity: A Celebration of African American Artists
Carpenter Center for the Visual Arts, Harvard University, Cambridge, MA
April 6–May 5

New Works by Vija Celmins, Annette Lemieux, Loren Madsen, Martin Puryear, William Tucker, Daisy Youngblood
McKee Gallery, New York
November 9–December 21

Celebrating Modern Art: The Anderson Collection
San Francisco Museum of Modern Art
October 7–January 15, 2001

The Cane Project
Studio Museum in Harlem, New York
October 11–January 8, 2001

• See fig. 22

NEW
[Group Exhibition]
McKee Gallery, New York
November 9–December 21

2001

New•Land•Marks: Public Art, Community, and the Meaning of Place
Pennsylvania Academy of the Fine Arts, Philadelphia
February 10–April 15

The Draftsman's Colors: Fourteen New Acquisitions from Johns to Chong
Whitney Museum of American Art, New York
March 2–July 7

Martin Puryear
Virginia Museum of Fine Arts, Richmond
March 6–May 27

Traveled to: Miami Art Museum, June 21–August 19, 2001; traveled as *Martin Puryear: Sculpture of the 1990s*, University of California, Berkeley Art Museum and Pacific Film Archive, September 12–January 13, 2002; Des Moines Art Center, February 1–April 14, 2002

Figure 112. Installation view of *That Profile* (1999) at J. Paul Getty Museum, Los Angeles. Martin Puryear. Stainless steel and bronze; 13.7 x 9.1 x 3.5 m. The J. Paul Getty Trust, Los Angeles, 99.SI.51. Photo: Lynn Davis

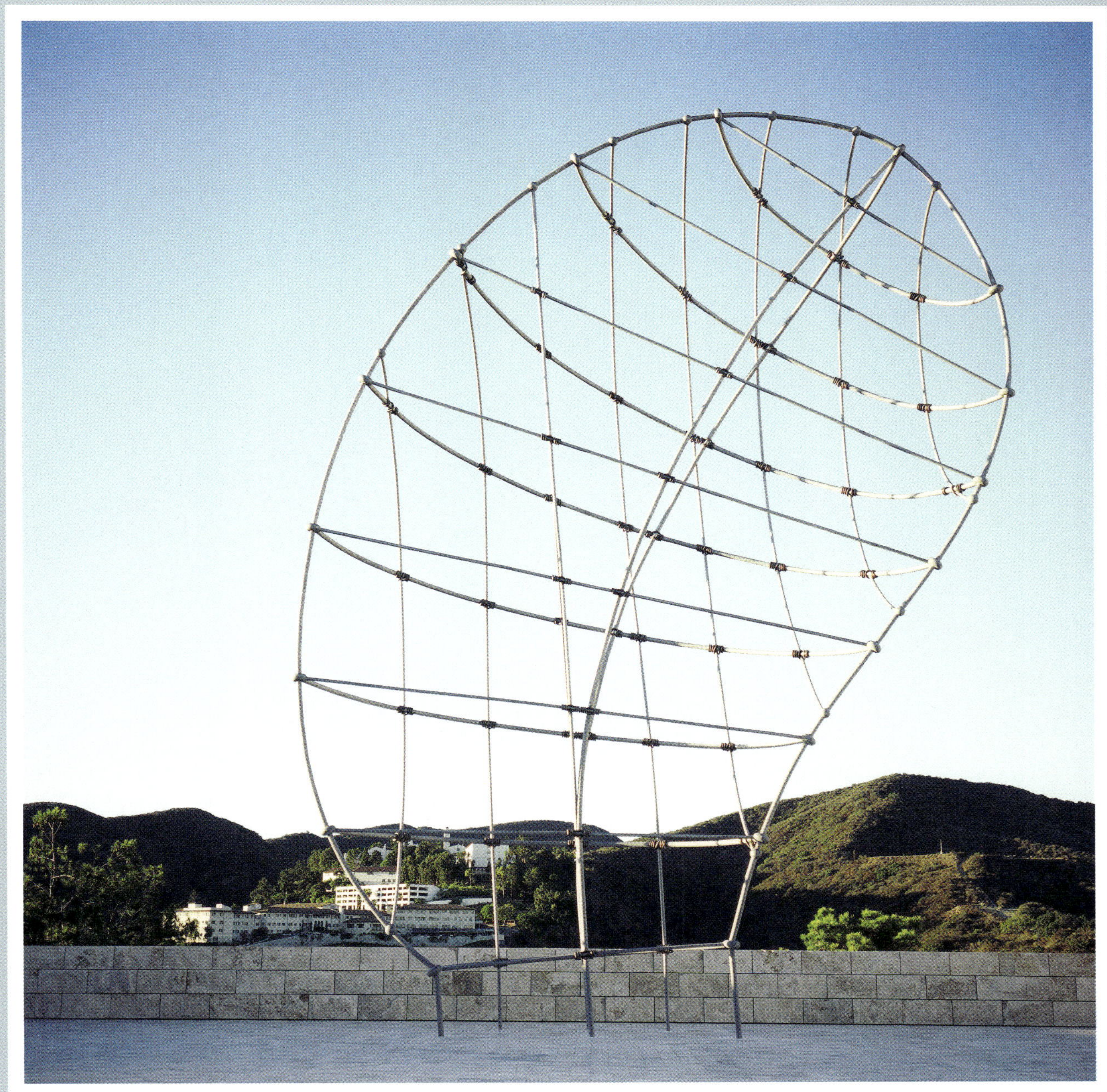

Yale University School of Art Alumni Choice Exhibition
Yale University Art Gallery, New Haven, CT
October 1–28

New to the Modern: Recent Acquisitions from the Department of Drawings
Museum of Modern Art, New York
October 25–January 8, 2002

The Cane Project
Temple Gallery, Tyler School of Art, Temple University, Philadelphia
November 2–December 15

2002

In the Spirit of Martin: The Living Legacy of Dr. Martin Luther King, Jr.
Charles H. Wright Museum of African American History, Detroit
January 12–August 4

Traveled to: Bass Museum, Miami Beach, September 7–December 1; Frederick R. Weisman Art Museum, University of Minnesota, Minneapolis, January 19–April 6, 2003; International Gallery, Smithsonian Institution, Washington, DC, May 14–July 27, 2003; Memphis Brooks Museum of Art, TN, August 30–November 30, 2003; Montgomery Museum of Fine Arts, AL, January 30–March 30, 2004

Martin Puryear: New Sculpture
McKee Gallery, New York
April 25–June 21

New Work by Gallery Artists
Donald Young Gallery, Chicago
May 4–September 21

To Be Looked At: Painting and Sculpture from the Collection
Museum of Modern Art, New York
July 3–September 6, 2004

Gifts in Honor of the 125th Anniversary of the Philadelphia Museum of Art
Philadelphia Museum of Art
September 29–December 8

110 Years: The Permanent Collection of the Modern Art Museum of Fort Worth
Modern Art Museum of Fort Worth, Fort Worth, TX
December 14–March 9, 2003

2003

African American Art in the Collection of the Art Institute of Chicago
Art Institute of Chicago
February 15–May 27

New Prints
[Group Exhibition]
McKee Gallery, New York
March 1–29

Material Differences: Art and Identity in Africa
Museum for African Art, New York
April 10–October 6

Drawings
[Group Exhibition]
Donald Young Gallery, Chicago
April 26–May 31

Gyroscope
[Solo Exhibition]
Hirshhorn Museum and Sculpture Garden, Smithsonian Institution, Washington, DC
May 19–January 4, 2004

Martin Puryear: Prints
Hemphill Gallery, Washington, DC
May 28–June 26

According with Nadelman: Contemporary Affinities
June Kelly Gallery, New York
July 1–August 1

Breathless
[Group Exhibition]
Neuberger Museum of Art, Purchase College, State University of New York
August 17–February 15, 2004

Martin Puryear: New Works
Baltic Centre for Contemporary Art, Gateshead, England
September 27–November 30

Traveled to: Irish Museum of Modern Art, Dublin, January 21–May 9, 2004

Guardian Stone, 2001–3
Outdoor installation at TV Asahi headquarters, Tokyo

Commissioned by TV Asahi, Tokyo

• For further installation details, see figs. 73, 77, 79

2004

Contemporary Art and Furniture Design in Dialogue
Senior & Shopmaker Gallery, New York
January 22–March 27

Prints
Elena Zang Gallery, Woodstock, NY
May–July

Art by MacArthur Fellows
Carl Solway Gallery, Cincinnati
May 7–July 31

Love / Hate: From Magritte to Cattelan: Masterpieces from the Collection of the Museum of Contemporary Art, Chicago
Villa Manin–Centro d'Arte Contemporanea, Passariano, Udine, Italy
May 30–November 7

Group Exhibition
McKee Gallery, New York
June 4–July 30

Artists & Prints: Masterworks from The Museum of Modern Art, Part 1
Museum of Modern Art, New York
November 20–March 14, 2005

Africa in America
Seattle Art Museum
December 18–December 11, 2005

2005

Sculpture: An Intuitive View
McKee Gallery, New York
September 17–October 27

Prints
Elena Zang Gallery, Woodstock, NY
September–November

Between Representation and Abstraction
Museum of Modern Art, New York
October 19–January 9, 2006

In conjunction with *Focus: Elizabeth Murray*

Martin Puryear
Donald Young Gallery, Chicago
December 10–February 11, 2006

• Fig. 113

Martin Puryear
San Jose Museum of Art, CA
February 9–May 1

2006

Against the Grain: Contemporary Art from the Edward R. Broida Collection
Museum of Modern Art, New York
May 3–July 10

The Persistence of Geometry: Form, Content and Culture in the Collection of the Cleveland Museum of Art
Museum of Contemporary Art, Cleveland
June 9–August 20

Prints
Elena Zang Gallery, Woodstock, NY
June–September

Selections from the Collection of Edward R. Broida
National Gallery of Art, Washington, DC
August 24–November 12

2007

Works on Paper by African American Artists
Snite Museum of Art, University of Notre Dame, South Bend, IN
January 14–February 25

Commemorating 30 Years: Part One: 1976–1980
Rhona Hoffman Gallery, Chicago
March 9–April 7

Summer Group Show
McKee Gallery, New York
June 27–August 3

Martin Puryear
Museum of Modern Art, New York
November 4–January 14, 2008

Traveled to: Modern Art Museum of Fort Worth, February 24–May 18, 2008; National Gallery of Art, Washington, DC, June 22–September 28, 2008; San Francisco Museum of Modern Art, November 8, 2008–January 25, 2009

• See figs. 7, 38, 83, 124

Early Signs: Celmins, Puryear, Youngblood
McKee Gallery, New York
November 10–December 21

Figure 113. Installation view of *Martin Puryear.* Donald Young Gallery, Chicago, 2006. Pictured: *Untitled* (2005); *A Distant Place* (2005). Photo: Donald Young Gallery

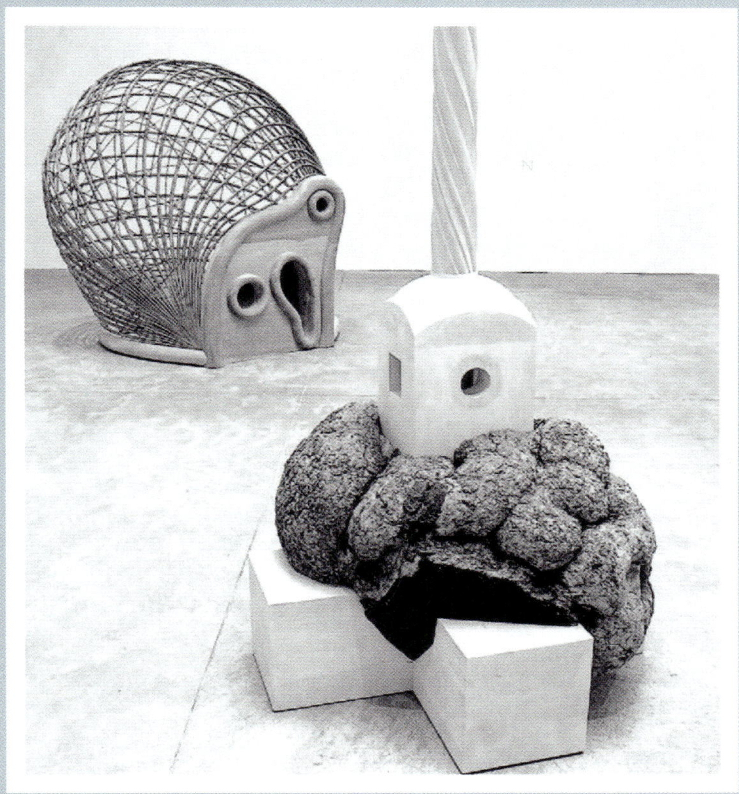

2008

Paintings, Drawings and Sculpture
[Group Exhibition]
John Berggruen Gallery, San Francisco
March 1–28

Martin Puryear Prints
de Young Museum, Fine Arts Museums of San Francisco
September 13–January 11, 2009

Origins
[Group Exhibition]
Hudson Valley Center for Contemporary Art, Peekskill, NY
September 13–July 26, 2009

Art for Yale: Collecting for a New Century
Yale University Art Gallery, New Haven, CT
September 18–January 13, 2009

2009

The Sculptor's Hand
[Group Exhibition]
Tasende Gallery, La Jolla, CA
January 9–February 28

I Have a Dream
Gabarron Foundation, Carriage House Center for the Arts, New York
January 12–March 8

Traveled to: Power House Memphis, March 21–May 3; Martin Luther King, Jr. National Historic Site, Atlanta, May 16–July 19; Rosa Parks Museum, Montgomery, AL, August 1–September 13; Chicago Matt Lamb Museum of Art, September 24–November 8

A Force for Change: African American Art and the Julius Rosenwald Fund
Spertus Museum, Chicago
February 6–August 16

Traveled to: Allentown Art Museum, PA, September 13–January 10, 2010; Montclair Art Museum, NJ, February 6–July 25, 2010

Die Gegenwart der Linie: Eine Auswahl neuerer Erwerbungen des 20. und 21. Jahrhunderts
Staatliche Graphische Sammlung, Pinakothek der Moderne, Munich
March 19–June 21

Artists and the Natural World
McKee Gallery, New York
April 2–May 2

The Endless Renaissance
[Group Exhibition]
Bass Museum of Art, Miami Beach
April 17–October 4

Group Show
Donald Young Gallery, Chicago
April

Art at Colby: Celebrating the 50th Anniversary of the Colby College Museum of Art
Colby College Museum of Art, Waterville, ME
July 11–February 21, 2010

Martin Puryear: A Survey of Prints
Woodstock Byrdcliffe Guild, Kleinert / James Art Center, Woodstock, NY
September 12–October 18

Sculpture
[Group Exhibition]
Barbara Mathes Gallery, New York
September 24–October 24

New Prints 2009 / Autumn
[Group Exhibition]
International Print Center New York (IPCNY), New York
October 30–December 12

Figure 114. Installation view of *Vessel* (1997–2002) in *Vessel*, 'T' Space, Rhinebeck, NY, 2012. Martin Puryear. Eastern white pine, mesh, tar; 2.1 x 4.6 x 1.7 m. Photo: Susan Wides and 'T' Space Rhinebeck

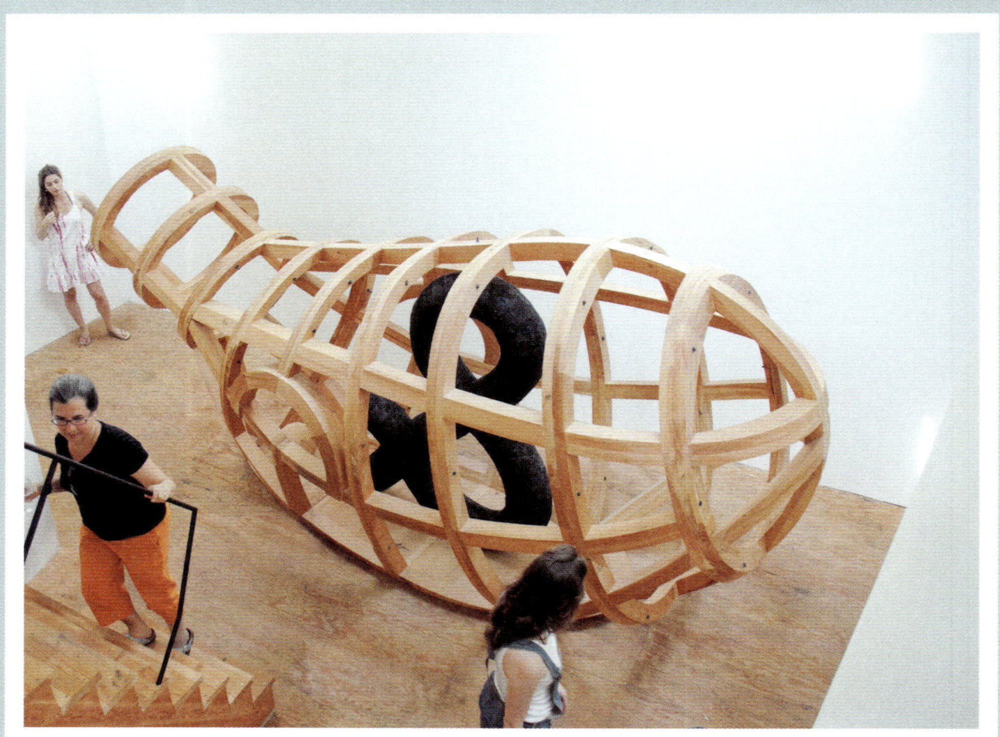

2010

The Contemporary Figure
[Group Exhibition]
Donald Young Gallery, Chicago
January 23–February 20

Martin Puryear Prints
Cincinnati Art Museum
January 30–June 13

Summer Group Show
McKee Gallery, New York
July 1–September 16

Sculpture
[Group Exhibition]
McKee Gallery, New York
November 6–December 18

Martin Puryear Prints: Selections from the JPMorgan Chase Collection
Montclair Art Museum, NJ
February 7–July 25

Paintings, Drawings and Sculpture
[Group Exhibition]
John Berggruen Gallery, San Francisco
August 6–28

2011

Winter Group Show
McKee Gallery, New York
January 14–February 19

Legacy: The Emily Fisher Landau Collection
Whitney Museum of American Art, New York
February 10–May 1

Traveled to: Norton Museum of Art, West Palm Beach, FL, February 21–June 2, 2013; Asheville Art Museum, NC, June 15–September 8, 2013; Joslyn Art Museum, Omaha, NE, September 28, 2013–January 5, 2014

Multiplicity
[Group Exhibition]
Smithsonian American Art Museum, Smithsonian Institution, Washington, DC
November 11–March 11, 2012

Traveled as *Multiplicity: Contemporary Prints from the Smithsonian Art Museum*: Arkansas Arts Center, Little Rock, November 20, 2012–January 6, 2013; Patty & Jay Baker Naples Museum of Art, FL, April 6–July 7, 2013; Akron Art Museum, OH, November 23, 2013–March 16, 2014; Virginia Museum of Contemporary Art, Virginia Beach, May 29–August 18, 2014

2012

Winter Group Show
McKee Gallery, New York
January

Printin'
[Group Exhibition]
Museum of Modern Art, New York
February 15–May 14

In conjunction with the exhibition *Print / Out*

Wish You Were Here: The Buffalo Avant-garde in the 1970s
Albright-Knox Art Gallery, Buffalo, NY
March 29–July 8

Martin Puryear: New Sculpture
McKee Gallery, New York
May 3–June 29

Group Show
McKee Gallery, New York
July

Vessel
[Solo Exhibition]
'T' Space, Rhinebeck, NY
August 4–September 30

• Fig. 114

Against the Grain: Wood in Contemporary Art, Craft and Design
Organized by the Museum of Arts and Design, New York

Traveled to: Mint Museum, Charlotte, NC, September 1–January 6, 2013; Museum of Arts and Design, New York, March 19–July 7, 2013; Museum of Art Fort Lauderdale, FL, October 12, 2013–January 20, 2014

African American Art Since 1950: Perspectives from The David C. Driskell Center
David C. Driskell Center for the Visual Arts and Culture of African Americans and the African Diaspora, University of Maryland, College Park
September 20–December 14

Traveled to: Taft Museum of Art, Cincinnati, February 15–April 28, 2013; Harvey B. Gantt Center for African-American Arts, Charlotte, NC, January 16–June 15, 2014; Figge Art Museum, Davenport, IA, September 15, 2014–January 4, 2015; Polk Museum of Art, Lakeland, FL, March 21–June 29, 2015; Susquehanna Museum of Art, Harrisburg, PA, October 7, 2016–January 22, 2017

Lighthouse / Lightning Rod and Griot New York (excerpts)
Brooklyn Academy of Music (BAM), BAM Next Wave Festival, New York
September 27–30

• Figs. 109a, b

Winter Group Show
McKee Gallery, New York
January

2014

Our Stories: African American Prints and Drawings
Cleveland Museum of Art
January 26–May 18

Sculpture: Katharina Fritsch, Robert Gober, Jasper Johns, Ellsworth Kelly, Martin Puryear, Charles Ray
Matthew Marks Gallery, New York
February 8–April 19

Dick Polich: Transforming Metal into Art
Samuel Dorsky Museum of Art, State University of New York, New Paltz
August 27–December 14

A Drawing Show
Matthew Marks Gallery, New York
October 4–November 29

Martin Puryear
Matthew Marks Gallery, New York
November 8–January 10, 2015

• Fig. 115; see figs. 85, 88

Conversations: African and African American Artworks in Dialogue
Smithsonian National Museum of African Art, Washington, DC
November 9–January 24, 2016

Inaugural Exhibition
[Group Exhibition]
Anderson Collection at Stanford University, Palo Alto, CA
September 14–July 13, 2015

Slavery Memorial, Brown University
Outdoor installation at Brown University, Providence, RI

Commissioned by Brown University, Providence, RI

Ductile cast iron, stainless steel, and granite, sculptural element; 1.4 x 2. x 2.4 m

2015

Represent: 200 Years of African American Art
Philadelphia Museum of Art
January 10–April 5

River Crossings: Contemporary Art Comes Home
Thomas Cole National Historic Site and Olana State Historic Site, Catskill and Hudson, NY
May 3–November 1

10 Sculptures
Matthew Marks Gallery, Los Angeles
July 11–August 29

Prints and Drawings Spanning 500 Years
Portland Art Museum, OR
August 8–December 13

The Ceramic Presence in Modern Art: Selections from the Linda Leonard Schlenger Collection and the Yale University Art Gallery
Yale University Art Gallery, New Haven, CT
September 4–January 3, 2016

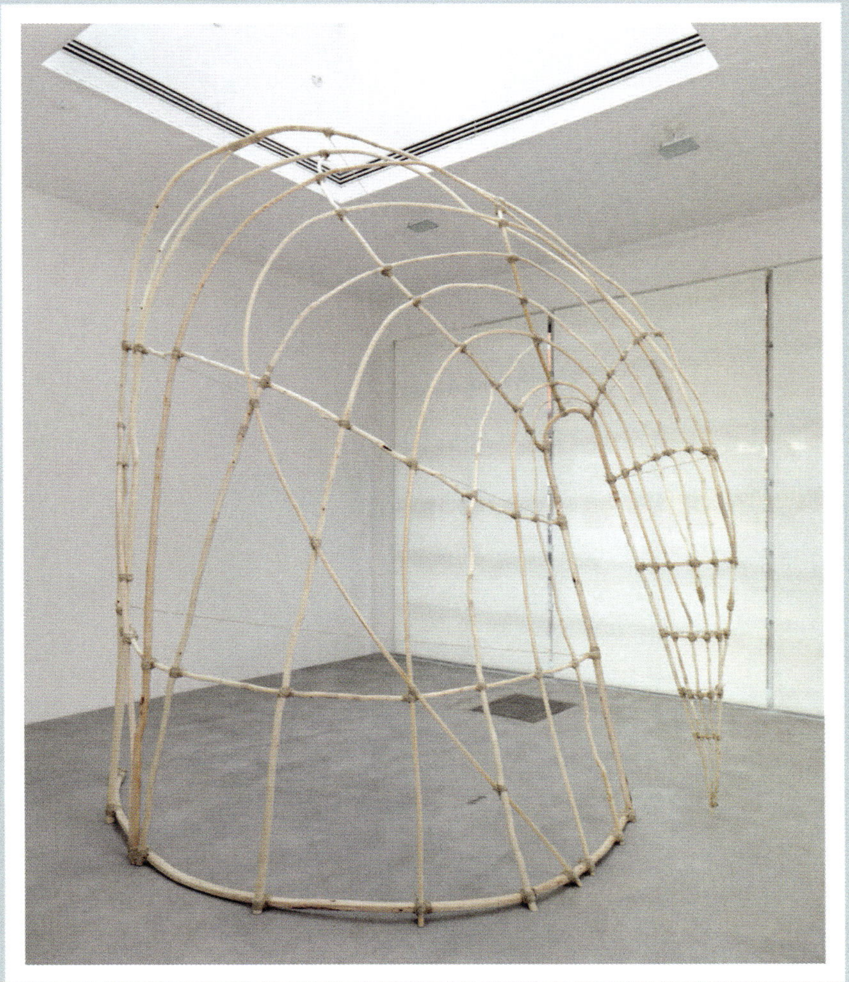

Figure 115. Installation view of *Untitled* (2014), at *Martin Puryear*, Matthew Marks Gallery, New York, 2015. Hardwood saplings, cordage; 443 x 376 x 132 cm, no longer extant. Photo: Matthew Marks Gallery

Black Fire: A Constant State of Revolution
Sheldon Museum of Art, University of Nebraska, Lincoln
September 11–January 3, 2016

Martin Puryear: Multiple Dimensions
Organized by the Art Institute of Chicago

Traveled to: Morgan Library & Museum, New York, October 9–January 10, 2016; Art Institute of Chicago, February 5–May 1, 2016; Smithsonian American Art Museum, Smithsonian Institution, Washington, DC, May 26–September 4, 2016

• Fig. 116

Group Exhibition: Robert Adams, Vincent Fecteau, Robert Gober, Martin Puryear, Charles Ray, Anne Truitt, and Terry Winters
Matthew Marks Gallery, New York
October 31–December 24

One Handed Stool
Produced by Lisa Ivorian Jones in limited edition of 25; proceeds benefit the New Museum, New York

Pine and maple with steel rod spine, lathe turned by hand, finished with hand-painted milk paint and Japan Color in several color layers/patterns, and hand rubbed; height 37.8 cm, diameter 12.1 cm

2016

Abstracting Nature
[Group Exhibition]
Newark Museum, NJ
January 12–January 18, 2017

Master Works
LongHouse Reserve, East Hampton, NY
April 30–July 18

Approaching American Abstraction: The Fisher Collection
San Francisco Museum of Modern Art
May 14–May 14, 2020

Dimensions of Black: A Collaboration with the San Diego African American Museum of Fine Art
Museum of Contemporary Art, San Diego
December 16–April 30, 2017

Big Bling
Outdoor installation at the Madison Square Park, New York
May 16–April 2, 2017

Commissioned by the Madison Square Park Conservancy, New York

Traveled to: Kelly Drive, presented by the Association for Public Art, Philadelphia, June 8, 2017–November 13, 2017; MASS MoCA, North Adams, MA, May 2020–ongoing

• For further installation details, see [59]; figs. 24, 25, 26, 46

2017

Recent Acquisitions: Martin Puryear, Prints
Bates College Museum of Art, Lewiston, ME
January 13–March 18

A BIT OF MATTER: The MoMA PS1 Archives, 1976–2000
MoMA PS1, New York
April 9–September 10

Soul of a Nation: Art in the Age of Black Power
Tate Modern, London
July 12–October 22

Traveled to: Crystal Bridges Museum of American Art, Bentonville, AR, February 3–April 23, 2018; Brooklyn Museum, New York, September 14, 2018–February 3, 2019; The Broad, Los Angeles, March 23–September 1, 2019; de Young Museum, Fine Arts Museums of San Francisco, November 9, 2019–March 15, 2020; Museum of Fine Arts, Houston, June 27–August 30, 2020

One of Many: Recent Acquisitions of Prints and Portfolios
Ackland Art Museum, University of North Carolina at Chapel Hill
July 7–September 10, 2017

Martin Puryear: Prints, 1962–2016
Print Center, Philadelphia
September 8–November 18

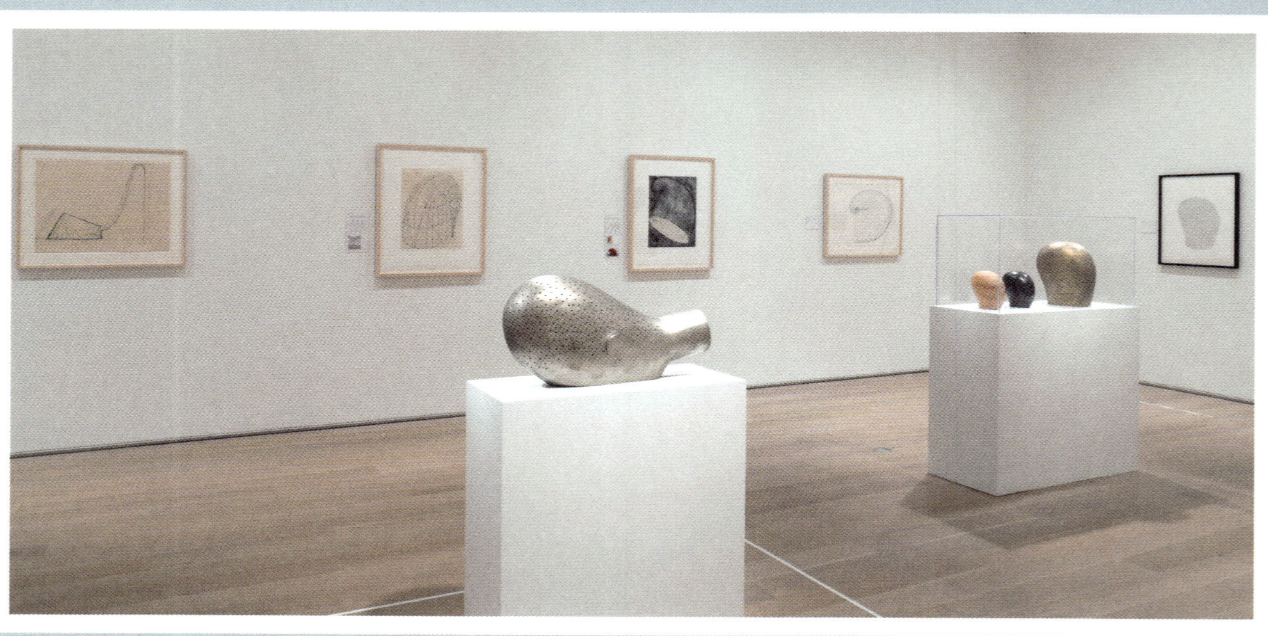

Figure 116. Installation view of *Martin Puryear: Multiple Dimensions*, The Art Institute of Chicago, 2016. Pictured (left to right): *Drawing for Untitled 1997–2001* (1992); *Untitled* (2001; [46]); *Face Down* (2008); *Phrygian (Cap in the Air)* (2012; [54]); *Untitled* (c. 2003; [47]); *Untitled* (2009); *Untitled* (2009); *Untitled* (2009); *Untitled* (1996). Photo: The Art Institute of Chicago / Art Resource, NY

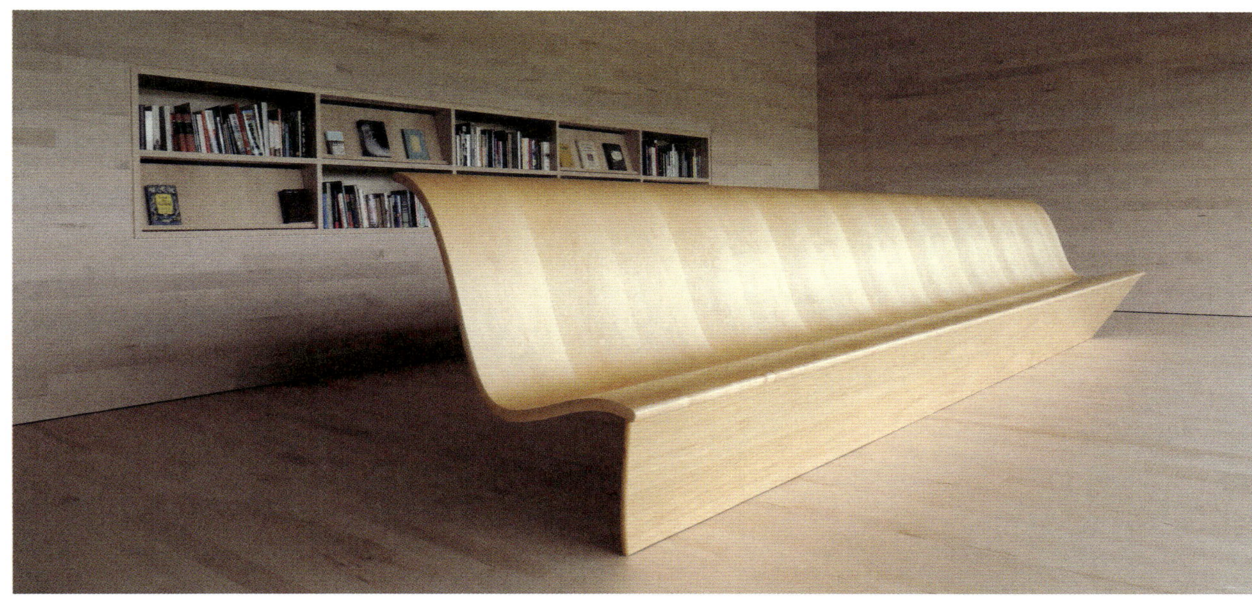

Figure 117. Installation view of Room 7 Bench (2014), Glenstone Museum, Potomac, MD. Martin Puryear in collaboration with Michael Hurwitz (fabricator). Hickory [base] and maple [seat]; 1.1 x .8 x 5.5 m. Photo: Paul Clemence

Thomas Demand, Katharina Fritsch, Robert Gober, Brice Marden, Ken Price, Martin Puryear, Charles Ray, Paul Sietsema, Anne Truitt, Terry Winters
Matthew Marks Gallery,
Los Angeles
September 14–October 21

Martin Puryear
Parasol Unit Foundation for Contemporary Art, London
September 19–December 6

Seeking Stillness
[Group Exhibition]
Museum of Fine Arts, Boston
September 24–September 3, 2018

The Long Run
[Group Exhibition]
Museum of Modern Art, New York
November 11–May 5, 2019

Untitled
Invited proposal for outdoor installation in San Francisco

Stock parts of large diameter galvanized steel pipe welded together

Unrealized

2018

Martin Puryear
Museum Voorlinden, Wassenaar, The Netherlands
January 20–May 27

• See figs. 8, 51, 122

Modern and Contemporary Art: Selected Works from the Permanent Art Collection
University Archives and Special Collections Gallery, University of the South, Sewanee, TN
February 5–July 31

Contemporary Highlights
Colby College Museum of Art, Waterville, ME
April 10–August 26

Personal to Political: Celebrating the African American Artists of Paulson Fontaine Press
Bedford Gallery at the Lesher Center for the Arts, Walnut Creek, CA
April 15–June 24

Traveled to: Krasl Art Center, St. Joseph, MI, September 1–November 25; Gallery 360, Northeastern University, Boston, January 17–March 11, 2019; Las Cruces Museum of Art, NM, May 10–July 20, 2019; Museum of Arts and Sciences, Daytona Beach, FL, August 31–October 27, 2019; Charles H. Wright Museum of African American History, Detroit, December 19, 2019–April 5, 2020; Montgomery Museum of Fine Arts, AL, May 2–August 2, 2020; Art Museum of West Virginia University, Morgantown, August 29–December 13, 2020; Robert and Frances Fullerton Museum of Art, California State University, San Bernardino, January 16–April 11, 2021; Fort Wayne Museum of Art, IN, May 8–July 18, 2021; DeVos Art Museum, Northern Michigan University, Marquette, August 16–October 31, 2021; Mills College Art Museum, Oakland, CA, January 18–March 12, 2022; Bakersfield Museum of Art, CA, April 28–August 20, 2022; Monterey Museum of Art, CA, September 17–November 27, 2022; California Museum, Sacramento, December 15, 2023–March 24, 2024; Hearst Center for the Arts, Rapid City, IA, June 7–September 1, 2024; Lyman Allyn Art Museum, New London, CT, October 13, 2024–January 5, 2025; Pauly Friedman Art Gallery, Misericordia University, Dallas, PA, February 1–March 29, 2025; Sarasota Art Museum, FL, May 4–August 10, 2025

Studio Visit: Selected Gifts from Agnes Gund
Museum of Modern Art, New York
April 29–July 22

Almanach 18
Le Consortium, Dijon, France
June 22–October 14

Crossroads: Carnegie Museum of Art's Collection, 1945 to Now
Carnegie Museum of Art, Pittsburgh
June 22–ongoing

Art in Dialogue: Robert Indiana and Martin Puryear
Patricia & Phillip Frost Art Museum at Florida International University, Miami
June 30–August 19

Beyond Borders: Global Africa
University of Michigan Museum of Art, Ann Arbor
August 11–November 25

Recent Acquisitions: Paintings, Ceramics, and Works on Paper
Museum of Fine Arts, St. Petersburg, FL
September 8–December 30

Second Look, Twice: Selections from the Collections of Jordan D. Schnitzer and His Family Foundation
Museum of the African Diaspora, San Francisco
September 19–December 16

Martin Puryear
Glenstone Museum, Potomac, MD
October 4–March 17, 2019

Bench designs for Glenstone, 2013–18
Designed for the Pavilions, Glenstone Museum, Potomac, MD, opened in 2018

In collaboration with fabricator Michael Hurwitz, Philadelphia

Commissioned by Glenstone Museum

Passage Benches (2015), Port Orford cedar [seat] and maple [legs]; .5 x .6 x 3.7 m

Benches for the Entry Pavilion (2015), Port Orford cedar [seat] and maple [legs]; .5 x .6 x 2.5 m

Room 7 Bench (2014), hickory [base] and maple [seat]; 1.1 x .8 x 5.5 m

Pond Platform Bench (2018), teak; length 5.5 m

• Fig. 117

Connecting
Outdoor installation at the U.S. Embassy, Beijing

Commissioned by FAPE (Federation for Art and Preservation in Embassies)

Stainless steel with granite bases; height 9.4 m

2019

Five Ways In: Themes from the Collection
Walker Art Center, Minneapolis
February 14–May 5, 2024

Front Room: The Mary and Paul Roberts Collection
Baltimore Museum of Art
April 3–June 30

Martin Puryear: Liberty / Libertà
American Pavilion, 58th Venice Biennale
May 11–November 24

• See [63–65]; figs. 5–6, 28, 60

Artistic License: Six Takes on the Guggenheim Collection
[Group Exhibition]
Solomon R. Guggenheim Museum, New York
May 24–January 12, 2020

Puryear featured in section curated by Carrie Mae Weems

Rosebud
[Group Exhibition]
Matthew Marks Gallery, Los Angeles
July 13–August 24

Generations: A History of Black Abstract Art
Baltimore Museum of Art
September 29–January 19, 2020

Afrocosmologies: American Reflections
Wadsworth Atheneum Museum of Art, Hartford, CT
October 19–January 20, 2020

Contemporary Art: Five Propositions
Museum of Fine Arts, Boston
October 26–March 12, 2020

One hundred drawings
[Group Exhibition]
Matthew Marks Gallery, New York
November 8–January 18, 2020

Detroit Collects: Selections of African American Art from Private Collections
Detroit Institute of Arts
November 12–March 15, 2020

Bound to the Earth: Art, Materiality, and the Natural World
Museum of Contemporary Art San Diego
November 21–March 19, 2020

Making Knowing: Craft in Art, 1950–2019
Whitney Museum of American Art, New York
November 22–February 20, 2022

2020

Making Community: Prints from Brandywine Workshop and Archives, Brodsky Center at PAFA, and Paulson Fontaine Press
Pennsylvania Academy of the Fine Arts, Philadelphia
February 1–April 12

James Prosek: Art, Artifact, Artifice
Yale University Art Gallery, New Haven, CT
February 14–February 28, 2021

Duro Olowu: Seeing Chicago
[Group Exhibition]
Museum of Contemporary Art Chicago
February 29–May 10

Riffs and Relations: African American Artists and the European Modernist Tradition
Phillips Collection, Washington, DC
February 29–January 3, 2021

Presence: African American Artists from the Museum's Collection
Honolulu Museum of Art
March 7–July 5

PICTURE ID: Contemporary African American Works on Paper
Toledo Museum of Art, OH
August 4–January 17, 2021

Martin Puryear
Matthew Marks Gallery, New York
November 12–January 30, 2021

• See fig. 120

Creature from Iddefjord
Outdoor installation at Deichman Library, Oslo, Norway

Commissioned by Sparebankstiftelsen

• Fig. 118

2021

Nasher Mixtape
Nasher Sculpture Center, Dallas
February 6–September 26

Recent Acquisitions: Modern and Contemporary Drawings and Prints
Morgan Library & Museum, New York
June 25–October 3

ART + NATURE + HOME
Foreland, Catskills, NY
May 29–June 13

Subliminal Horizons
Alexander Gray Associates, Germantown, NY
July 3–August 15

Martin Puryear: 40 Years Since Sentinel
Schmucker Art Gallery, Gettysburg College, PA
September 10–November 6

2022

Toni Morrison's Black Book
David Zwirner, New York
January 20–February 26

Uncombed Unforeseen Unconstrained
Conservatorio di Musica Benedetto Marcello di Venezia, Italy
April 19–November 27

A Decade of Acquisitions of Works on Paper—Part II
Hammer Museum, Los Angeles
May 22–August 21

Past Is Present: Black Artists Respond to the Complicated Histories of Slavery
Herron School of Art + Design, Indianapolis
September 28–January 14, 2023

Joan Didion: What She Means
Hammer Museum, Los Angeles
October 11–February 19, 2023

Traveled to: Pérez Art Museum, Miami, July 13, 2023–January 7, 2024

Figure 118. Installation view of *Creature from Iddefjord* (2020) at Deichman Library, Oslo , Norway. Martin Puryear. Granite; 7.6 x 6.7 x 3.7 m. Photo: Kenneth Myhre Pram via Shutterstock

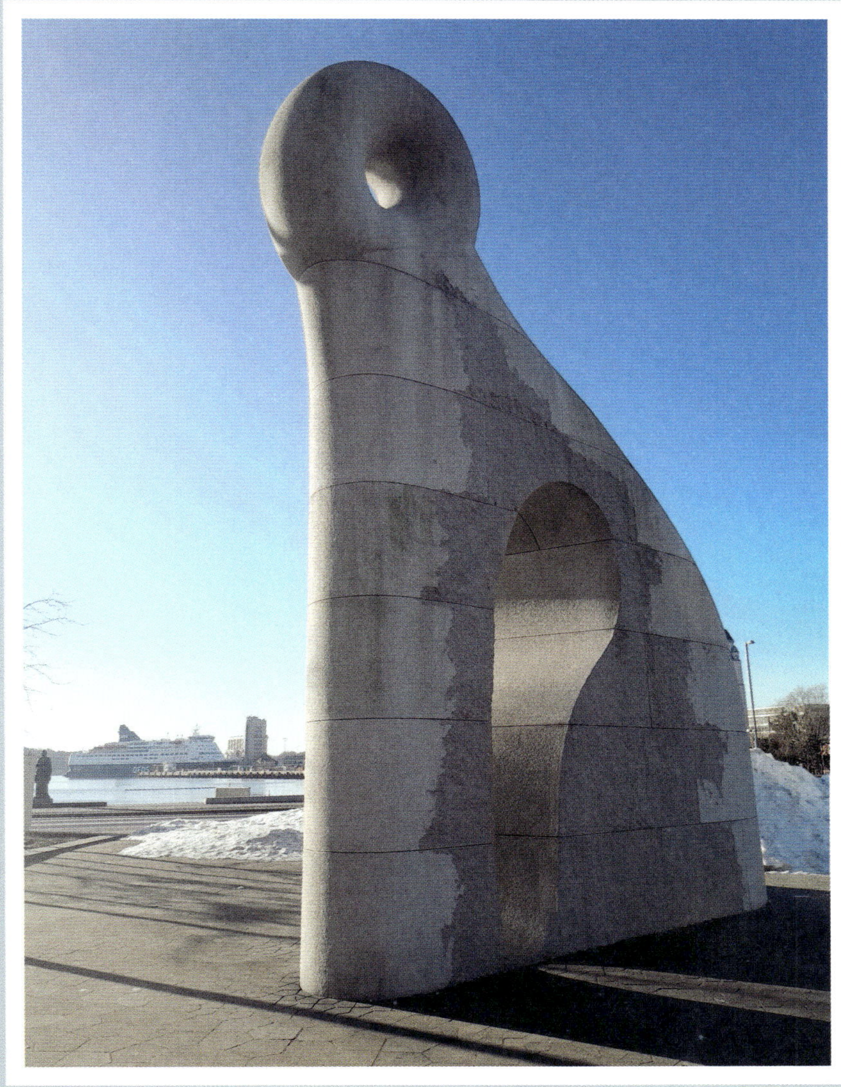

2023

The Searchers
Philadelphia Art Alliance at University of the Arts
January 27–March 16

Martin Puryear
Matthew Marks Gallery, Los Angeles
February 16–April 8

• See figs. 47, 48

Woven Histories: Textiles and Modern Abstraction
Organized by the National Gallery of Art, Washington, DC

Traveled to: Los Angeles County Museum of Art, September 17–January 21, 2024; National Gallery of Art, Washington, DC, March 17–July 28, 2024; National Gallery of Canada, Ottawa, October 24–March 2, 2025; Museum of Modern Art, New York, April 20–September 13, 2025

Martin Puryear: Process and Scale
[Solo Exhibition]
Storm King Art Center, New Windsor, NY
September 23–December 17

Lookout
Outdoor installation at Storm King Art Center, New Windsor, NY

Commissioned by Storm King Art Center

• For further installation details, see [70, 71]; figs. 29a–c, 63

Iconoclasts: Selections from Glenstone's Collection
Glenstone Museum, Potomac, MD
November 16–ongoing

2024

Unprecedented: Art in Times of Crisis
Sheldon Museum of Art, University of Nebraska–Lincoln
January 24–July 6

Sum of the Parts: Serial Imagery in Printmaking, 1500 to Now
Hammer Museum, Los Angeles
July 13–November 24

Edges of Ailey
Whitney Museum of American Art, New York
September 25–February 9, 2025

Project A Black Planet: The Art and Culture of Panafrica
Art Institute of Chicago
December 22–March 30, 2025

2025

Thinking Eye, Seeing Mind: The Medford and Loraine Johnston Collection
High Museum of Art, Atlanta
January 17–May 25

Other Octaves: Curated by Jennie C. Jones
[Group Exhibition]
Pulitzer Arts Foundation, Saint Louis
September 5–February 1, 2026

Martin Puryear: Nexus
Organized by the Cleveland Museum of Art and the Museum of Fine Arts, Boston

Traveled to: Museum of Fine Arts, Boston, September 27–February 1, 2026; Cleveland Museum of Art, April 12–August 9, 2026; High Museum of Art, Atlanta, GA, September 25, 2026–January 17, 2027

Exhibition Checklist

All works by Martin Puryear
(American, b. 1941)

As of June 13, 2025
Not all works are exhibited at all venues.

1
Bull, 1962
Woodcut on Japanese paper;
block: 27.5 x 49 cm; sheet: 35 x 54.4 cm
Collection of the artist

3
Untitled, 1964/1966
Pen and black ink; 21.9 x 34 cm
Collection of the artist

5
Untitled, 1964/1966
Charcoal on paper; 35.1 x 21.9 cm
Collection of the artist

4
Untitled, 1965
Pen and black ink; 34.3 x 21.6 cm
Collection of the artist

2
Head, 1965
Woodcut (*ARTnews* wrapper);
block: 27 x 22 cm; sheet: 29.9 x 24 cm
Collection of the artist

6
Untitled (Joseph Momoh), 1965
Pen and ink; 41.9 x 29.6 cm
Collection of the artist

9
Gate, 1966
Soft ground etching, with burnishing;
image/plate: 10.5 x 12.6 cm; sheet: 23.5 x 38.4 cm
Collection of the artist

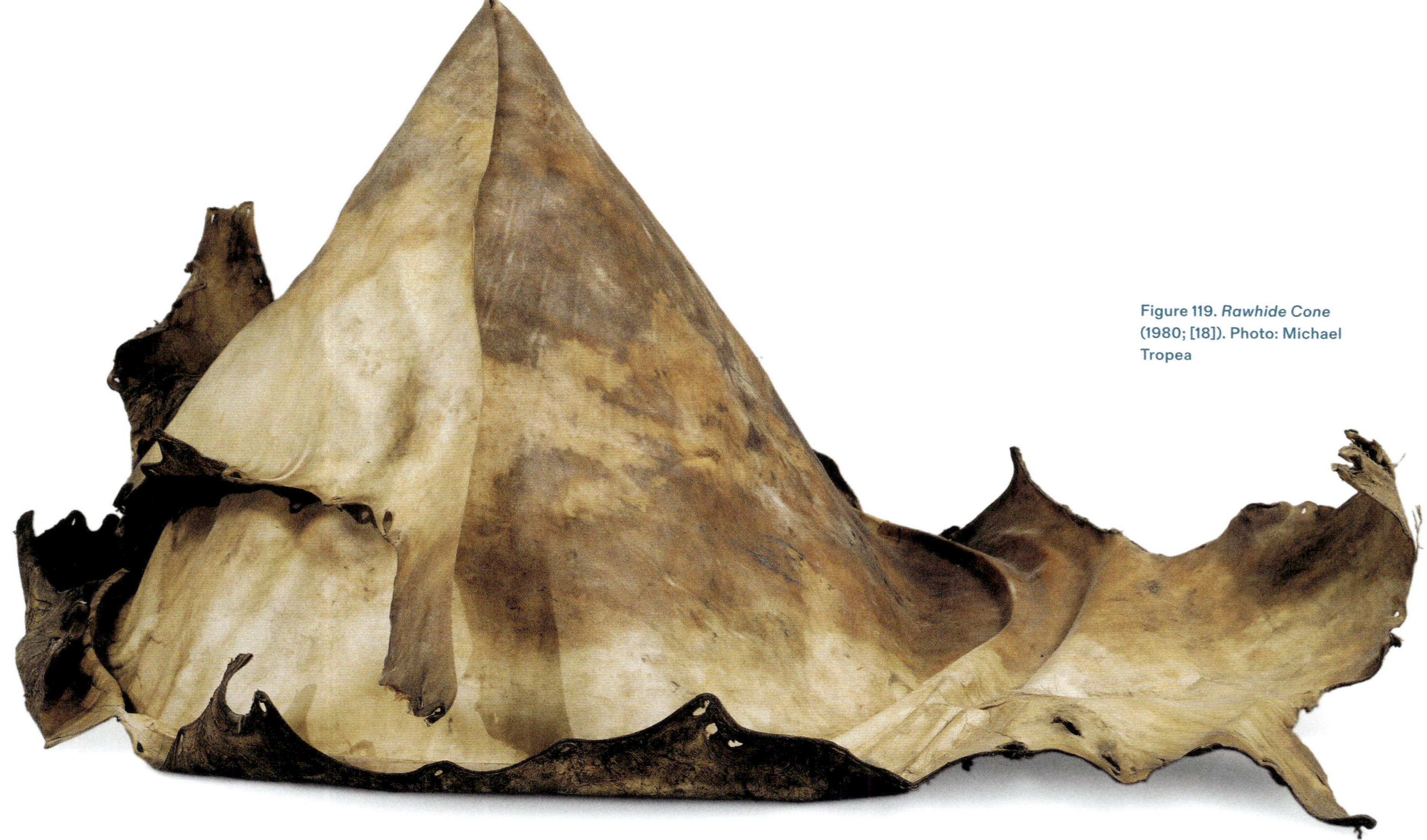

Figure 119. *Rawhide Cone* (1980; [18]). Photo: Michael Tropea

8
Rune Stone, 1966
Soft ground etching, aquatint, and open bite; image/plate: 49.3 x 37 cm; sheet: 59.2 x 46 cm
Collection of the artist

7
Quadroon, 1966–67
Soft ground etching and aquatint; image/plate: 39 x 40.1 cm; sheet: 55.4 x 56.2 cm
Collection of the artist

10
Bound Cone, 1972–73
Red oak and hemp rope; 176.53 x 27.94 x 27.94 cm
Toledo Museum of Art, Ohio, Gift of David K. and Georgia E. Welles, 2025.14

11
Bask, 1976
Stained pine; 30.5 x 372.7 x 55.9 cm
Solomon R. Guggenheim Museum, New York, Exxon Corporation Purchase Award 1978, 78.2430

12
Drawing for *Box and Pole*, 1977
Graphite on paper; 73.7 x 53.3 cm
Collection of the artist

13
Believer, 1977–82
Tulip poplar and pine; 59.1 x 59.4 x 44.1 cm
Collection of the artist

14
Self, 1978
Stained and painted red cedar and mahogany; 175.3 x 121.9 x 63.5 cm
Joslyn Art Museum, Omaha, Nebraska, Museum purchase in memory of Elinor Ashton, 1980.63

15
Some Lines for Jim Beckwourth, 1978
Twisted rawhide; 690.9 cm (length); height variable
Collection of the artist

16
Nexus, 1979
Alaskan yellow cedar, pigment, and gesso; 114.3 x 114.3 x 3.8 cm
Collection of halley k harrisburg and Michael Rosenfeld, New York

17
Reliquary, 1980
Gessoed pine; 106.7 x 120.7 x 22.9 cm
Andrew L. and Gayle Shaw Camden Collection

19
Bower, 1980
Sitka spruce, pine, and copper tacks; 163.3 x 240.2 x 66 cm
Smithsonian American Art Museum, Washington, DC, Museum purchase made possible through the Luisita L. and Franz H. Denghausen Endowment, Alexander Calder, Frank Wilbert Stokes, and the Ford Motor Company, 2002.18

18
Rawhide Cone, 1980
Molded rawhide; 74.9 x 152.4 x 116.8 cm
Collection of the artist

24
Drawing for *Bodark Arc*, 1982
Graphite on paper; 15.2 x 22.9 cm
Collection of the artist

22
Sanctuary, 1982
Pine, maple, and cherry; 320 x 61 x 45.7 cm
The Art Institute of Chicago, Mr. and Mrs. Frank G. Logan Purchase Prize Fund, 1982.1473

23
Untitled, drawing for *Sanctuary*, c. 1982
Graphite on paper; 58.7 × 73.8 cm
The Art Institute of Chicago, Gift of Martin Puryear, 1996.641

20
Azul-Azul, 1981
Painted basswood; 162.5 x 162.5 x 4.4 cm
Collection of Pamela and Arthur Sanders

21
Untitled, 1982
Maple sapling, pear wood, and yellow cedar; 149.9 x 167.6 x 12.7 cm
Yale University Art Gallery, Gift of the Neisser Family, Judith Neisser, David Neisser, Kate Neisser, and Stephen Burns, in memory of Edward Neisser, B.A. 1952, 2019.123.2

26
On The Tundra, 1986
Cast iron; 49.5 x 24.1 x 29.2 cm
Museum of Fine Arts, Boston, Curator's Grant Program of the Peter Norton Family Foundation, 1991.620

25
Night and Day, 1984
Painted pine and wire; 212.1 x 301 x 12.7 cm
Nasher Sculpture Center, Dallas, Raymond and Patsy Nasher Collection, NC.1985.A.04

27
Noblesse O., 1987
Red cedar and aluminum paint; 249.9 x 147.3 x 116.8 cm
Dallas Museum of Art, General Acquisitions Fund and a gift of The 500, Inc., 1987.350

28
Lever #1, 1988–89
Red cedar, cypress, poplar, and ash; 429.3 x 340.4 x 45.1 cm
The Art Institute of Chicago, A. James Speyer Memorial, UNR Industries in honor of James W. Alsdorf, and Barbara Neff Smith and Solomon Byron Smith funds, 1989.385a–b

29
Untitled, 1992
Glass and wood; 81.3 x 27.9 x 35.6 cm
Collection of Margaret V. B. Wurtele

31
Untitled, 1993
Bronze; 196.8 x 14 x 34.9 cm
Collection of the artist

30
Alien Huddle, 1993–95
Red cedar and pine, 134.6 x 162.6 x 134.6 cm
The Cleveland Museum of Art, Gift of Agnes Gund and Daniel Shapiro, 2002.65

33
Drawing for *Tokyo International Forum*, 1995
Graphite on tracing paper; 38.4 x 237.5 cm
Collection of the artist

32
Confessional, 1996–2000
Wire mesh, staples, nails, steel rods, tar, and various woods; 196.2 x 247 x 114.3 cm
Museum of Fine Arts, Boston, Museum purchase with funds donated by the Ives Family Fund, Towles Contemporary Art Fund, Catherine and Paul Buttenwieser Fund, The Heritage Fund for a Diverse Collection, Joyce Linde, Carol Wall, and partial gift of Mickey Cartin, 2012.1019
Boston only

34
Untitled, 1997
Painted red cedar and pine;
172.7 x 144.8 x 129.5 cm
The Museum of Modern Art, New York, Gift of Agnes Gund in honor of Tom Cahill, 1997, 651.1997

35
Drawing for *This Mortal Coil*, 1998
Graphite on paper; 35.6 x 27.9 cm
Collection of the artist

36
Untitled (LA MoCA Portfolio), 1999
Printer: Jacob Samuel, Lapis Press, Venice, California. Publisher: Museum of Contemporary Art, Los Angeles.
Hard and soft ground etching and aquatint with chine collé; platemark: 61 x 45.4 cm; sheet: 76.3 x 55.3 cm
Museum of Fine Arts, Boston, Museum purchase with funds donated by the Board of Trustees in honor of Stokley Towles, Chair of the Board of Trustees, 2007–2010, and Sylvia Quarles Simmons, Chair of the Board of Overseers, 2008–2010, 2010.625

38
Cane, 2000
Deluxe edition illustrated book, by Jean Toomer (American, 1894–1967) and illustrated by Martin Puryear. Printer and publisher: Arion Press, San Francisco
Bound in full brown goatskin with artist-designed wooden case, and separate portfolio of woodcuts; closed: 30.2 x 35.9 x 2.9 cm
Museum of Fine Arts, Boston, Lee M. Friedman Fund, 2002.904.1

Wooden slipcase for the leather-bound edition of *Cane*, by Jean Toomer and illustrated by Martin Puryear, 2000
African wenge, Swiss pear, Italian walnut, and maple; 34.9 x 38.4 x 4.8 cm
Museum of Fine Arts, Boston, Lee M. Friedman Fund, 2002.904.10

39
Karintha, from *Cane*, 2000
Woodcut on Japanese paper;
image/plate: 26.7 x 33 cm; sheet: 43.2 x 52.1 cm
Museum of Fine Arts, Boston, Lee M. Friedman Fund, 2002.904.2

40
Becky, from *Cane*, 2000
Woodcut on Japanese paper;
image/plate: 26.7 x 33 cm; sheet: 43.2 x 52.1 cm
Museum of Fine Arts, Boston, Lee M. Friedman Fund, 2002.904.3

41
Carma, from *Cane*, 2000
Woodcut on Japanese paper;
image/plate: 26.7 x 33 cm; sheet: 43.2 x 52.1 cm
Museum of Fine Arts, Boston, Lee M. Friedman Fund, 2002.904.4

42
Fern, from *Cane*, 2000
Woodcut on Japanese paper;
image/plate: 26.7 x 33 cm; sheet: 43.2 x 52.1 cm
Museum of Fine Arts, Boston, Lee M. Friedman Fund, 2002.904.5

43
Esther, from *Cane*, 2000
Woodcut on Japanese paper;
image/plate: 26.7 x 33 cm; sheet: 43.2 x 52.1 cm
Museum of Fine Arts, Boston, Lee M. Friedman Fund, 2002.904.6

44
Avey, from *Cane*, 2000
Woodcut on Japanese paper;
image/plate: 26.7 x 33 cm; sheet: 43.2 x 52.1 cm
Museum of Fine Arts, Boston, Lee M. Friedman Fund, 2002.904.7

45
Bona, from *Cane*, 2000
Woodcut on Japanese paper;
image/plate: 26.7 x 33 cm; sheet: 43.2 x 52.1 cm
Museum of Fine Arts, Boston, Lee M. Friedman Fund, 2002.904.8

37
Jug, 2001
Printer and publisher: Paulson Bott Press, Berkeley, CA
Hard and soft ground etching, with drypoint and chine collé; image/plate: 60.3 x 45 cm; sheet: 87.8 x 70.1 cm
The Art Institute of Chicago, Mr. and Mrs. Robert O. Delaney Fund, 2007.91

46
Untitled, 2001
Color hard and soft ground etching, with drypoint and chine collé; image/plate: 60.5 x 45.5 cm; sheet: 88.5 x 70.8 cm
The Art Institute of Chicago, Mr. and Mrs. Robert O. Delaney Fund, 2007.90

48
Drawing for *Untitled*, c. 2003
Charcoal and pastel on paper; 58.4 x 73.6 cm
Collection of the artist

47
Untitled, c. 2003
Printer and publisher: Paulson Bott Press, Berkeley, CA
Graphite on paper; 58.4 x 73.5 cm
Collection of the artist

49
Shoulders (State 2), 2005
Printer and publisher: Paulson Bott Press, Berkeley, CA
Drypoint, with soft ground etching and chine collé; image/plate: 45.5 x 60.5 cm; sheet: 73.5 x 86 cm
The Art Institute of Chicago, Mr. and Mrs. Robert O. Delaney Fund, 2007.102

50
C.F.A.O., 2006–7
Painted and unpainted pine and found wheelbarrow; 255.9 x 196.9 x 154.9 cm
The Museum of Modern Art, New York, Gift of Sid Bass, Leon D. Black, Donald L. Bryant, Jr., Kathy and Richard S. Fuld, Jr., Agnes Gund, Mimi Haas, Marie-Josée and Henry R. Kravis, Jo Carole and Ronald S. Lauder, Donald B. Marron and Jerry Speyer on behalf of the Committee on Painting and Sculpture in honor of John Elderfield, 2008, 553.2008

51
Malediction, 2006–7
Red cedar, pine, black locust, ash, and rattan; 318.77 x 151.1 x 65.1 cm
San Francisco Museum of Art, The Doris and Donald Fisher Collection at the San Francisco Museum of Modern Art, FC.842

53
Black Cart, 2008
Printer and publisher: Paulson Bott Press, Berkeley, CA
Aquatint etching with chine collé;
image/plate: 60.3 x 45 cm; sheet: 88.5 x 70.2 cm
The Art Institute of Chicago, Purchased with funds provided by Kaye and Howard Haas, 2009.665

52
Untitled, 2009
Alaskan yellow cedar, milk paint, Swiss pear, and lignum vitae; 43.2 x 16.5 x 15.2 cm
Private collection

55
Big Phrygian, 2010–14
Painted red cedar; 147.3 x 101.6 x 193 cm
Glenstone Museum, Potomac, Maryland

54
Phrygian (Cap in the Air), 2012
Printer and publisher: Paulson Bott Press, Berkeley, CA
Etching with aquatint and drypoint;
platemark: 60.5 x 45.2 cm; sheet: 88.6 x 70.8
Museum of Fine Arts, Boston, Lee M. Friedman Fund, 2016.13
The edition presented at the Cleveland Museum of Art was lent from the collection of the artist.

56
Untitled VI (State 1), 2012
Printer and publisher: Paulson Bott Press, Berkeley, CA
Soft ground etching, drypoint, and spit bite with chine collé; image/plate: 80.4 x 80.3; sheet: 109.1 x 103.8 cm
The Art Institute of Chicago, The John H. Wrenn Memorial, Helen Davis Baily, and Albert H. Wolf funds, 2013.180

57
Cascade, 2013
Alaskan yellow cedar; 167.6 x 139.1 x 43.2 cm
Collection of the artist

58
Shell Game, 2014
Tulip poplar and milk paint; 142.9 x 182.9 x 24.1 cm
Collection of Scott Mueller

59
Maquette for Big Bling, 2014
Birch plywood, maple, and 22 karat gold leaf; 102.9 x 23.2 x 101.6 cm
Collection of the artist

61
Hibernian Testosterone, 2018
Painted cast aluminum and American cypress; 144.8 x 358.1 x 113 cm
Courtesy the artist and Matthew Marks Gallery

70
Maquette for Lookout, 2018
Painted high-density urethane foam and painted wood; 49.5 x 81.3 x 86.4 cm
Collection of the artist

63
Maquette for Swallowed Sun (Monstrance and Volute), 2018
Oriented strand board, pine, maple, paint, and laser-cut acrylic; 59.7 x 99.7 x 139.7 cm
Collection of the artist

64
Untitled, Drawing for "Swallowed Sun (Monstrance and Volute)," 2018
Graphite on tracing paper; 25.4 x 40 cm
Collection of the artist

65
Untitled, Drawing for "Swallowed Sun (Monstrance and Volute)," 2018
Graphite on paper; 27.9 x 33 cm
Collection of the artist

60
Aso Oke, 2019
Bronze; 213.4 x 261.6 x 189.2 cm
Jack Shear Collection

62
A Column for Sally Hemings, 2021
Marble and cast iron; 201.3 x 43.8 x 43.8 cm
Collection of the artist

71
Brick Sculpture for Storm King Art Center (Nine Segments), 2021
Graphite on vellum; 58.4 x 73.7 cm
Collection of the artist

66
On the Tundra (Winter), 2022
Marble; 48.3 x 31.8 x 25.4 cm
Collection of the artist

67
Untitled, 2022
Printer: Universal Limited Fine Arts; publisher: Studio in a School
Woodcut; 71.4 x 74 cm
The Cleveland Museum of Art, Anonymous Gift, in honor of Agnes Gund, Holly Peterson, and Studio in a School, 2023 2023.150

68
The Way, 2022
Bronze; 260 x 61 x 244 cm
Courtesy the artist and Matthew Marks Gallery

69
Looking Askance, 2023
Painted red cedar and pine; 180.3 x 109.2 x 104.1 cm
Courtesy the artist and Matthew Marks Gallery

Figure 120. Installation view of *Martin Puryear*, Matthew Marks Gallery, New York, 2021. Pictured: *Aso Oke* (2019; [60]) and *Happy Jack* (2020). Photo: Matthew Marks Gallery

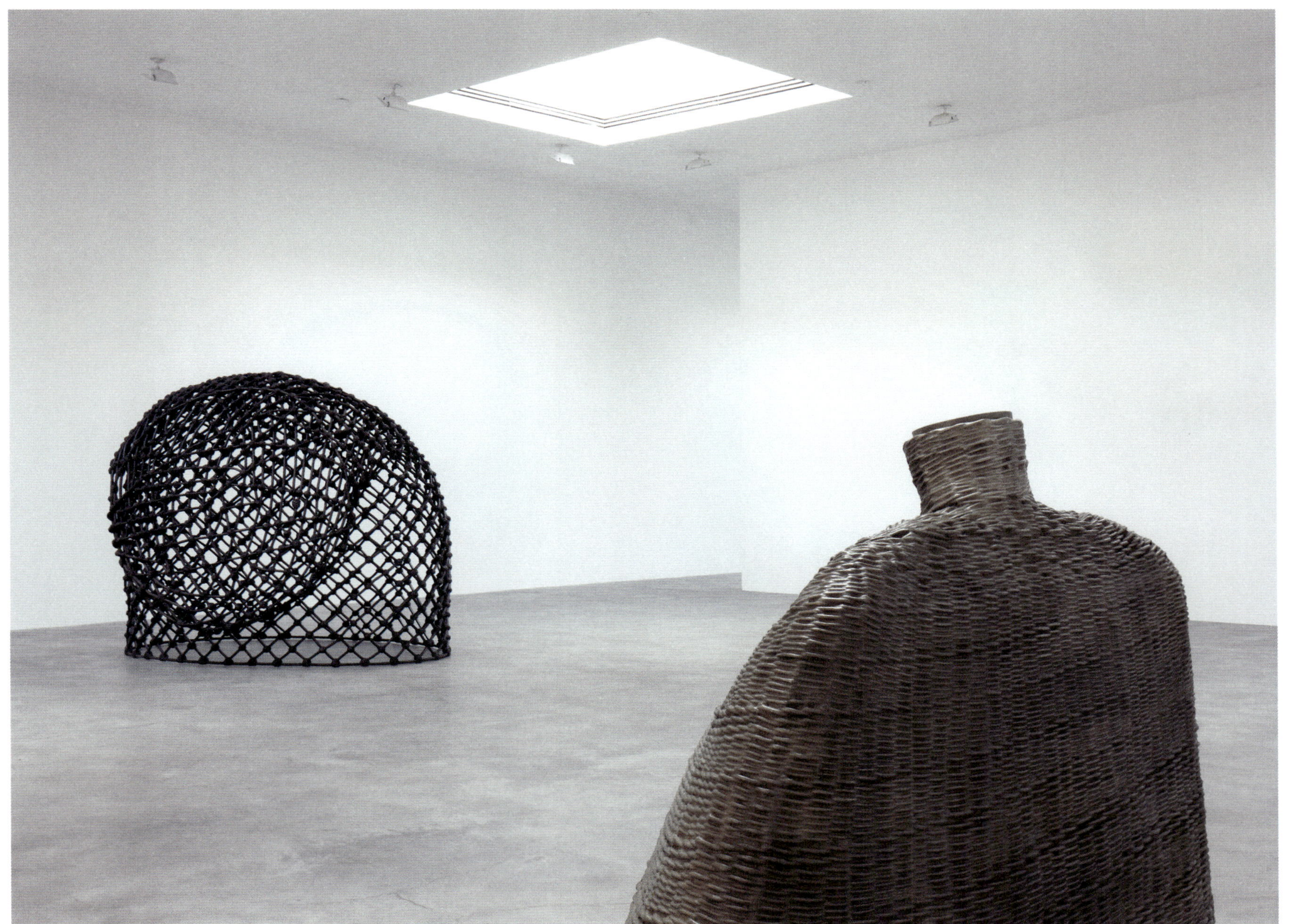

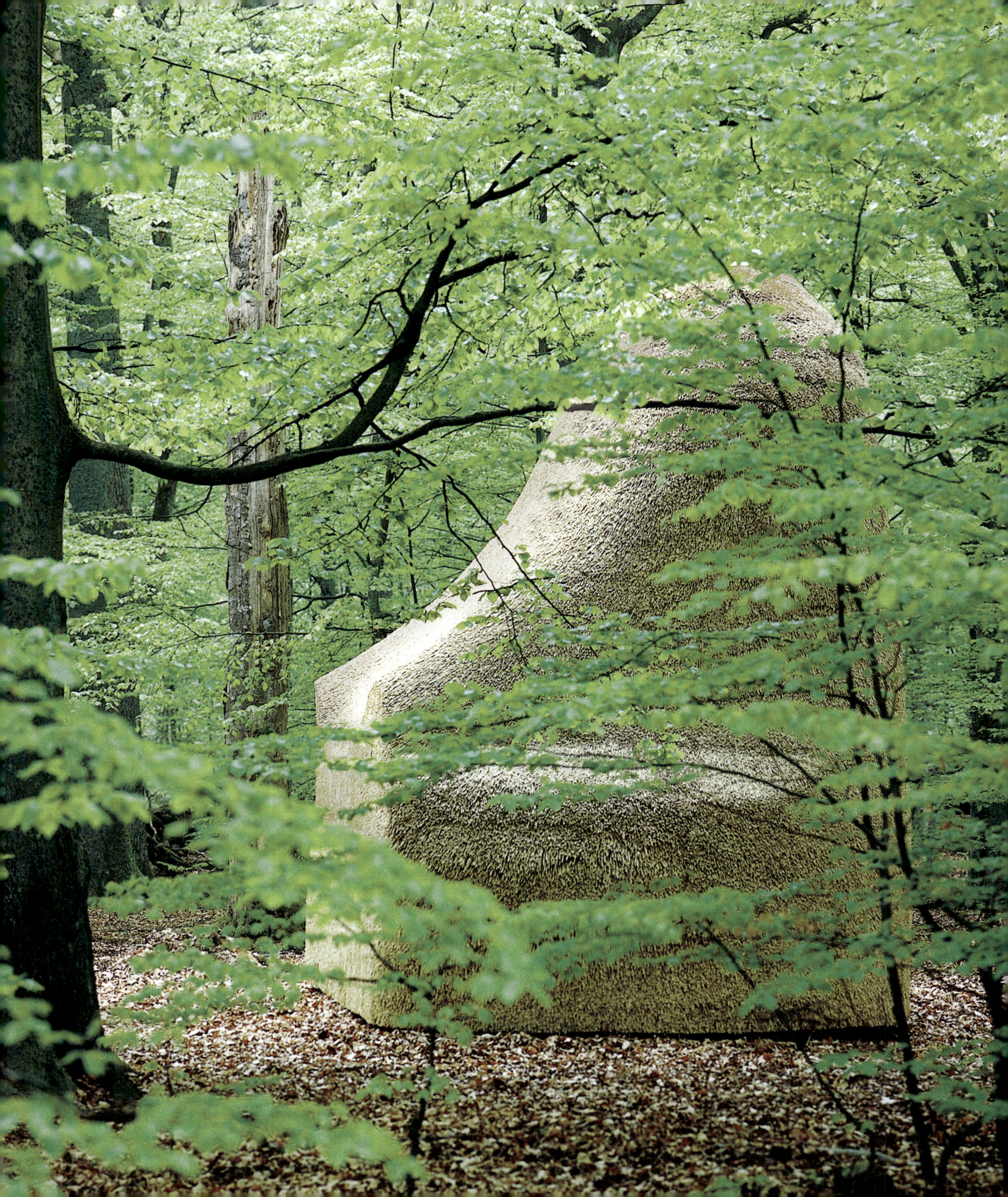

Selected **Bibliography**

Figure 121. Installation view of *Meditation in a Beech Wood* (1996) at the Wanås Foundation, Knislinge, Sweden. Martin Puryear. Water reed thatched over timber frame (wood, concrete, and steel); 444.8 x 500.4 x 340.4 cm. Photo: Anders Norrsell

Interviews, Lectures, and Artist Writings

Adamson, Glenn. "Martin Puryear in Conversation." In *Lookout*, by Nora Lawrence, Amy S. Weisser, Glenn Adamson, et al., 37–40. Exhibition catalogue. New Windsor, NY: Storm King Art Center; New York: Gregory R. Miller & Co., 2024.

"Artist Conversation: Martin Puryear and Theaster Gates." Video recording. Published on February 16, 2016. Art Institute of Chicago. https://www.youtube.com/watch?v=_LVmdOrC91c.

Auping, Michael. "A Form of Carving." In *30 Years: Interviews and Outtakes*, 248–57. Fort Worth: Modern Art Museum of Fort Worth, 2007.

Baker, Kenneth. "Puryear Opens Up." *San Francisco Chronicle,* November 2, 2008.

Berger, Laurel. "In Their Sights." *ARTnews* 96, no. 3 (March 1997): 94–100.

Breerette, Geneviève. "Dans l'espace intérieur de Martin Puryear." *Le Monde*, September 18, 1999.

Colker, Ed. "Present Concerns in Studio Teaching: Artist's Statements." *Art Journal* 42, no. 1 (March 1982): 36–37.

"A Conversation with Martin Puryear." Interviewed by Billie Tsien, June 27, 2018. Video recording. Published on July 16, 2018. Architectural League of New York. https://vimeo.com/280212494?share=copy.

Davies, Hugh M., and Helaine Posner. "Conversations with Martin Puryear." In *Martin Puryear*, 23–40. Exhibition catalogue. Amherst: University Gallery, Fine Arts Center, University of Massachusetts at Amherst, 1984.

Fine, Ruth. "Artist Panel: The African American Art World in Twentieth-Century Washington, DC, March 17, 2017." *Studies in the History of Art* 83 (2023): 16–47.

Gast, Dwight V. "Martin Puryear: Sculpture as an Act of Faith." *Journal of Art* 2, no. 1 (September–October 1989): 6–7.

Horsfield, Kate, and Lyn Blumenthal. *Martin Purear* [*sic*]. From the series *On Art / Artists*. Video recording. 1978. Video Data Bank, The School of the Art Institute of Chicago.

Marcoci, Roxana. "The Anti-Historicist Approach: Brancusi, 'Our Contemporary.'" *Art Journal* 59, no. 2 (Summer 2000): 33.

Metrick-Chen, Lenore. "Artworks, Artworking, and Race." *International Review of African American Art* 26, no. 3 (Summer 2016): 46–49.

"Martin Puryear." In *Art21: Art in the Twenty-First Century*, edited by Marybeth Sollins, 2:198–209. New York: Harry N. Abrams, 2003.

"Martin Puryear, Clarissa Wittenberg, and Mary Swift." July 13, 1978. Audio recording. Mary Swift papers, 1973–2004. Archives of American Art, Smithsonian Institution.

"NSE #88 | Martin Puryear with Jason Rosenfeld." *Brooklyn Rail*. Video recording. Published on July 17, 2020. https://www.youtube.com/watch?v=eo6QIra-qaQ.

Powell, Richard J. "A Conversation with Martin Puryear." In *Martin Puryear*, edited by John Elderfield, 99–110. Exhibition catalogue. New York: Museum of Modern Art, 2007.

Puryear, Martin. "Artist's Statement." In *Martin Puryear: Big Bling*, by Brooke Kamin Rapaport, Martin Puryear, and Harry Cooper, 10–11. Exhibition catalogue. New York: Madison Square Park Conservancy, 2016.

Puryear, Martin. "Foreword." In *Ruth Duckworth: Modernist Sculptor*, by Jo Lauria and Tony Birks, 6. Exhibition catalogue. Aldershot, UK: Lund Humphries; Los Angeles Art Options Foundation, 2004.

Puryear, Martin. "Interview: Abstraction and 'Ladder for Booker T. Washington.'" *Art21*, November 2011. https://art21.org/read/martin-puryear-abstraction-and-ladder-for-booker-t-washington/.

Puryear, Martin. "Interview: Stone Carving." *Art21*, September 2003. https://art21.org/read/martin-puryear-stone-carving/.

Puryear, Martin. Interviewed by John Elderfield, October 2007. Video recording. Museum of Modern Art Archives, New York.

Puryear, Martin. Interviewed by Tom Ferguson, July 1, 1975, Michigan State University. Audio recording. From the series *Artists and Critics*. Michigan State University Libraries.

Puryear, Martin. Interviewed by Miles Thurlow, September 26, 2003. Video recording. Baltic Archive, Baltic Centre for Contemporary Art.

Puryear, Martin. Interviewed on completion of *Sentinel*, Sesquicentennial Sculpture, Gettysburg College, October 1982. *MS-288 Creation and Preservation of Martin Puryear's Sentinel.* Special Collections and College Archives, Musselman Library, Gettysburg College.

Puryear, Martin. "Introduction." In Richard J. Powell, *Homecoming: The Art and Life of William H. Johnson*, by Richard J. Powell, xix–xxi. Exhibition catalogue. Washington, DC: National Museum of American Art, Smithsonian Institution; New York: Rizzoli, 1991.

Puryear, Martin. Lecture, 1980. Audio recording. Skowhegan School of Painting and Sculpture Lecture Archive. The Museum of Modern Art Archives, New York.

Puryear, Martin. "Louise Bourgeois: A Living Legacy." *Sculpture* (July–August 1994): 35.

Puryear, Martin. "Shaping the Future of Craft: Keynote Address." In *Shaping the Future of Craft: 2006 National Leadership Conference*, edited by Monica Hampton and Lily Kane, 25–39. New York: American Craft Council, 2006.

Shearer, Linda. "Martin Puryear." In *Young American Artists: 1978 Exxon National Exhibition*, 54–57. Exhibition catalogue. New York: Solomon R. Guggenheim Museum, 1978.

Strauss, David Levi, "In Conversation." Martin Puryear interviewed by David Levi Strauss. *Brooklyn Rail*, November 2007. https://brooklynrail.org/2007/11/art/martin-puryear-with-david-levi-strauss/.

Swift, Mary, and Clarissa Wittenberg, "An Interview with Martin Puryear." *Washington Review of the Arts* 4, no. 2 (August–September 1978): 33–34.

"Talking with the Artists II: Martin Puryear, Sol Le Witt [*sic*], Charles Simonds." In *The Sculptor's Eye: Looking at Contemporary American Art*, by Jan Greenberg and Sandra Jordan, 67–69. New York: Delacorte, 1993.

Articles, Reviews, and Other Publications

Ables, Kelsey. "Public Art Hides in Plain Sight." *Washington Post*, August 7, 2020.

Adam, Alfred Mac. "Martin Puryear." *ARTnews* 114, no. 2 (February 2015): 78.

Aguilar, Nelson. "Puryear e Klein Atraem Visitante da 20a Bienal." *Folha de S. Paulo*, October 18, 1989.

"Alice Walton, Martin Puryear, and Kwame Anthony Appiah Receive Getty Medals." *Artforum* (February 27, 2020). https://www.artforum.com/news/alice-walton-martin-puryear-and-kwame-anthony-appiah-receive-getty-medals-246702/.

Allen, Terry Y. "The Unconventional Eye." *Amherst Magazine* 42, no. 4 (Summer 1990): 14–17.

Allende, Margaret. "Sculpting Success." *Connoisseur* 221, no. 957 (October 1991): 141.

Als, Hilton. "At the Galleries." *New Yorker* 96, no. 43 (January 4 & 11, 2021): 8.

Anderáos, Ricardo. "Puryear se diz 'constructor'." *Folha de S. Paulo*, October 12, 1989.

Anders, Gigi. "Adoration of the Artist." *Washington Post*, February 5, 1992.

Arner, Mark. "Curiosity About Making Things Spurs Artist." *Blade-Tribune* (Oceanside, CA), October 18, 1984.

Artner, Alan G. "Art Galleries: Martin Puryear." *Chicago Tribune*, June 25, 1982.

Artner, Alan G. "Jury to Select 'Mile 4' Winner." *Chicago Tribune*, May 23, 1985.

Artner, Alan G. "Massive Work a Visual Odyssey." *Chicago Tribune*, September 17, 1987.

Artner, Alan G. "N.Y.'s 'Primitive' Show a Modern Masterpiece." *Chicago Tribune*, November 4, 1984.

Artner, Alan G. "On Form and Function: The Finely Sculpted Thoughts of Martin Puryear." *Chicago Tribune*, November 3, 1991.

Artner, Alan G. "Perfection Is Hallmark of Puryear's Sculpture." *Chicago Tribune*, October 25, 1985.

Artner, Alan G. "Photographer's Composite Images Are Crafted Cliches." *Chicago Tribune*, February 22, 1980.

Artner, Alan G. "Public Sculpture's Changing Face: It's Time to Rethink the Art We Put in Public Places." *Chicago Tribune*, August 26, 1990.

Artner, Alan G. "A Sculptor's 2 Sides: Martin Puryear on His Public and Private Art." *Chicago Tribune*, February 1, 1987.

Artner, Alan G. "Shaping Up." *Chicago Tribune*, October 1, 1989.

Ash, John. "Martin Puryear." *Artforum* 34, no. 2 (October 1995): 98.

Ashbery, John. "The Sculptures of Summer." *New York Magazine* 12, no. 29 (July 23, 1979): 57–58.

Ashbery, John. "Visions of the Olympics." *Newsweek* 101, no. 4 (January 24, 1983): 74.

Ashton, Dore. "Pandemonium of the MoMA." *Arts Magazine* 59, no. 1 (September 1984): 108–11.

"Awards." *Art in America* 77, no. 6 (June 1989): 206.

Baker, Kenneth. "Journal of the Puryear." *Boston Phoenix*, July 10, 1984.

Baker, Kenneth. "The Language of the Eye." *Boston Phoenix*, April 2, 1985.

Baker, Kenneth. "Martin Puryear: Sympathy and Common Ground." *Artspace* 16, no. 4 (July–August 1992): 32–35.

Baker, Kenneth. "Prime Displays of Anti-Minimalist Art on the Peninsula." *San Francisco Chronicle*, March 21, 1990.

Baker, Kenneth. "Sculpture in Right Direction." *San Francisco Chronicle*, November 8, 2008.

Belik, Hélio. "Representante dos EUA na Bienal chega sábado para estudar espaço." *Folha de S. Paulo*, February 19, 1989.

Berkowitz, Marc. "São Paulo Biennale: No Hidden Corners." *ARTnews* 89, no. 2 (February 1990): 167.

Berkson, Bill. "Seattle Sites." *Art in America* 74, no. 7 (July 1986): 68–83, 133–35.

Bertolucci, Lucia. "Martin Puryear . . . Washington's Own National Inspiration." *Uptown Citizen*, March 5, 1992.

Beuttenmuller, Alberto. "A Bienal, Como Retrospectiva dos Ultimos 20 Anos." *O Estado de S. Paulo*, October 24, 1989.

Beuttenmuller, Alberto. "Richard Hamilton e eventos Salvam a Bienal." *O Estado de S. Paulo*, October 15, 1989.

Bodick, Noelle. "Shows That Matter: Martin Puryear at the Morgan Library." *Artinfo*, October 19, 2015.

Bois, Yve-Alain. "La Pensée Sauvage." *Art in America* 73, no. 4 (April 1985): 178–98.

Bonesteel, Michael. "Summer Solstice for Chicago Art." *New Art Examiner* 9, no. 1 (October 1981): 1, 6–7.

Bonetti, David. "Back to Natural: Sculpture Takes on the World." *Boston Phoenix*, June 3, 1986.

Bourdon, David. "Martin Puryear at Henri 2." *Art in America* 62, no. 1 (January–February 1974): 110.

Bourdon, David. "Washington Revisited." *Art in America* 66, no. 4 (July–August 1978): 95–99.

Brenson, Michael. "Art: The Human Form in the Work of 12 Sculptors." *New York Times*, February 1, 1985.

Brenson, Michael. "Art View: How Sculpture Freed Itself from the Past." *New York Times*, December 15, 1985.

Brenson, Michael. "Critic's Notebook: Doors of Art Opening (Ignore the Squeaks)." *New York Times*, October 16, 1989.

Brenson, Michael. "Gallery View: Sculptors Find New Ways to Work with Wood." *New York Times*, December 2, 1984.

Brenson, Michael. "Gallery View: Shaping the Dialogue of Mind and Matter." *New York Times*, November 22, 1987.

Brenson, Michael. "Maverick Sculptor Makes Good." *New York Times Magazine*, November 1, 1987.

Brenson, Michael. "Memory of the Hand." *Sculpture* 14 (May–June 1995): 28-35.

Brenson, Michael. "Revue / Art: Sculptural Interiors." *New York Times*, November 18, 1988.

Brenson, Michael. "A Sculptor to Represent the U.S. at São Paulo Biennale." *New York Times*, November 22, 1988.

Brenson, Michael. "A Sculptor's Struggle to Fuse Culture and Art." *New York Times*, October 28, 1989.

Brenson, Michael. "Sculpture Breaks the Mold of Minimalism." *New York Times*, November 23, 1986.

Brenson, Michael. "Sculpture: Puryear Postminimalism." *New York Times*, August 10, 1984.

Brenson, Michael. "Season Preview: Art, Familiar and Unknown." *New York Times*, August 30, 1987.

Brenson, Michael. "The Unpredictable on View in São Paulo." *New York Times*, October 23, 1989.

Brenson, Michael. "Works for Urban College Raise Hard Questions." *New York Times*, April 8, 1988.

Bright, Deborah. "Bruce Nauman, Martin Puryear." *New Art Examiner* 11, no. 3 (December 1983): 17.

Brown, Mark. "Grants Give 'Geniuses' Freedom." *Chicago Sun-Times*, July 18, 1989.

Budick, Ariella. "In Search of the Instagrammable Moment: How Open-Air Art Came of Age." *Financial Times*, January 4, 2019. https://www.ft.com/content/26886370-0eac-11e9-b2f2-f4c566a4fc5f.

Bui, Phong. "ArtSeen: Martin Puryear, New Sculpture." *Brooklyn Rail*, June 2012. https://brooklynrail.org/2012/06/artseen/martin-puryear-new-sculpture/.

Burchard, Hank. "On the Wings of a Sculptor." *Washington Post*, February 7, 1992.

Calo, Carole Gold. "Martin Puryear: David McKee Gallery." *New Art Examiner* 15, no. 6 (February 1988): 65.

Calo, Carole Gold. "Martin Puryear: Private Objects, Evocative Visions." *Arts Magazine* 62, no. 6 (February 1988): 90-93.

Campbell, Adrianna. "Martin Puryear." *Artforum* (January 2015). https://www.artforum.com/events/matthew-marks-gallery-502-w-22nd-street-208585/.

Camper, Fred. "Ideograms in a New Language." *Chicago Reader*, December 5, 1991.

Carboni, Massimo. "Nunzio / Martin Puryear." *Artforum* 36, no. 8 (April 1998): 124.

Carrier, David. "Martin Puryear: New York and Fort Worth." *Burlington Magazine* 150, no. 1259 (February 2008): 138–39.

Castro, Jan Garden. "Martin Puryear: Spirit, Personhood, and History." *Sculpture* 27, no. 1 (January–February 2008): 52–57.

Castro, Jan Garden. "Martin Puryear: The Call of History." *Sculpture* 17, no. 10 (December 1988): 16–21.

Catlin, Roger. "Joslyn Opens Small Show." *Sunday World Herald Magazine*, August 24, 1980.

"Chicago Sculptor Puryear Wins Top Prize in Sao Paulo." *Chicago Sun-Times*, October 15, 1989.

Clark, Vicky A. "Primal Forms." *Dialogue* 10, no. 5 (September–October 1987): 52.

Comodo, Roberto. "A Festa da Nova Forma." *Jornal do Brasil*, October 14, 1989.

Conn, Sandra. "Move to State Street Boosts Mile of Sculpture's Image." *Crain's Chicago Business* 8, no. 11 (March 18, 1985): 16.

Considine, Austin. "Martin Puryear." *Art in America* 103, no. 3 (March 2015): 156–57.

Cotter, Holland. "Black Artists: Three Shows." *Art in America* 78, no. 3 (March 1990): 164–71, 217.

Cotter, Holland. "Martin Puryear." *New York Times*, December 12, 2014.

Cotter, Holland. "Martin Puryear, Citizen-Sculptor." *New York Times*, May 5, 2019.

Cotter, Holland. "Report from New York: A Bland Biennial." *Art in America* 77, no. 9 (September 1989): 80–87.

Crary, Jonathan. "Martin Puryear's Sculpture." *Artforum* 18, no. 2 (October 1979): cover, 28–31.

Cullinan, Helen. "Getting to Know an Award-Winning Sculptor, Martin Puryear." *Plain Dealer* (Cleveland), December 26, 1993.

Dale, Steve. "A New Look to State Street: Sculpture Invitational Debuts." *Chicago Tribune*, May 10, 1985.

Danoff, I. Michael. "How the Sculptures Were Selected for State St. Exhibit." *Sunday Sun-Times* (Chicago), May 5, 1985.

Danto, Arthur C. "Martin Puryear." *Nation* 256, no. 1 (January 4 & 11, 1993): 30–32.

Danto, Arthur C. "Tilted Ash." *Nation* 285, no. 2 (December 31, 2007): 27–30.

Danto, Ginger. "What Becomes an Artist Most." *ARTnews* 86, no. 9 (November 1987): 149–53.

Davis, Robert. "$355,000 Grant Lets Teacher Know She's Really Worth It." *Chicago Tribune*, July 18, 1989.

Dean, Andrea Oppenheimer. “Turning Point.” *Landscape Architecture* 88, no. 10 (October 1998): 48–55.

Dickinson, Carol. “The Landscape as Metaphor.” *ARTnews* 93, no. 8 (October 1994): 194–96.

Donohue, Marlena. “The Galleries.” *Los Angeles Times*, April 21, 1989.

Drohojowska-Philip, Hunter. “Building a Vision from the Ground Up.” *Los Angeles Times*, December 5, 1999.

Dudar, Helen. “‘Griot New York’ Sets the City’s Rhythm to Dance.” *Smithsonian* 23, no. 6 (September 1992): 102–9.

Duncan, Michael. “New Puryear for the Getty.” *Art in America* 88, no. 1 (January 2000): 23.

Ebony, David. “David Ebony’s Top 10 New York Gallery Shows for November.” *Artnet News* (November 21, 2014). https://news.artnet.com/art-world/david-ebonys-top-10-new-york-gallery-shows-for-november-176536.

Enslow Bell, Daphne. “Five Artworks for NOAA.” *Seattle Arts* 7, no 3 (November 1983): 1, 3.

Estorick, Alex. “Martin Puryear.” *Frieze*, no. 192 (January–February 2018): 156–57.

Failing, Patricia. “Black Artists Today: A Case of Exclusion.” *ARTnews* 88, no. 3 (March 1989): 124–31.

Farago, Jason. “Committed to Sculpture, Even in Two Dimensions.” *New York Times*, December 25, 2015.

FDV [Lanny Frances DeVuono]. “The Decade Show.” *ARTnews* 89, no. 9 (November 1990): 165–66.

Feldman, Hannah. “This Will Have Been: Art, Love & Politics in the 1980s.” *Artforum* 50, no. 10 (Summer 2012): 308–9.

Felsenthal, Julia. “Head to Head with Martin Puryear at the Morgan Library.” *Vogue*, October 15, 2015. https://www.vogue.com/article/martin-puryear-morgan-library-multiple-dimensions.

Flam, Jack. “The View from the Cutting Edge.” *Wall Street Journal*, May 10, 1989.

Fleming, Lee. “Martin Puryear, McIntosh/Drysdale Gallery, 406 7th Street, NW, February 1982.” *Washington Review* 7, no. 6 (April–May 1982): 28.

Forgey, Benjamin. “Craft Comes Full Circle to Art.” *Washington Post*, February 24, 1982.

Forgey, Benjamin. “Draftsmanship and Woodsmanship.” *ARTnews* 77, no. 1 (January 1978): 118–22.

Forgey, Benjamin. “Gallery Roundup: A Young Artist Arrives.” *Washington Star-News*, September 19, 1973.

Forgey, Benjamin. “Martin Puryear’s Show: An Artist Comes Home.” *Evening Star* (Washington, DC), January 12, 1972.

Forgey, Benjamin. “Puryear’s Circles: Subtle, Brooding Presence.” *Washington Star*, December 7, 1979.

Francblin, Catherine. “Martin Puryear: Globe-Sculpteur.” *Beaux Arts Magazine*, no. 185 (October 1999): 36.

Frank, Peter. “To Be Young, Gifted.” *Village Voice* (New York), June 12, 1978.

Freire, Norma. “Roupa Suja se Lava Numa Bienal de Arte.” *O Estado de S. Paulo*, October 17, 1989.

Frick, Thomas. “Martin Puryear.” *MOCA Contemporary* 1, no. 5 (June–July 1992): 4–5.

Friedman, Martin L. “Growing the Garden.” *Design Quarterly* 141 (1988): cover, 4–15, 20–42.

Glueck, Grace. “Artists of the Custom House.” *New York Times*, May 4, 1979.

Glueck, Grace. “Serving the Environment.” *New York Times*, June 27, 1982.

Goodman, Jonathan. “Martin Puryear: David McKee.” *ARTnews* 94, no. 7 (September 1995): 142–43.

Gopnik, Blake. “Martin Puryear’s ‘Big Bling’: Manhattan’s Spirit Animal?” *Artnet News* (October 19, 2016). https://news.artnet.com/art-world-archives/martin-puryear-big-bling-madison-square-park-709211.

Gross, Jennifer. “Introduction: The Field of Sculpture.” *2009, State of the Art: Contemporary Sculpture Yale University Art Gallery Bulletin* (2009): 26–33.

Gross, Jennifer. “Martin Puryear: Museum of Modern Art.” *Modern Painters* 20, no. 1 (February 2008): 90–91.

Hawkins, Margaret. “In-spired Sculpture: Puryear Tops Rare Show with Piece That Has Viewers Looking Up.” *Chicago Sun-Times*, December 30, 2005.

Harnish, Anne. “Commissions.” *Sculpture* 13, no. 4 (July–August 1994): 40–41.

Hellman, Marla. “LMJCA & Puryear: What a Combination.” *UCSD Guardian* 53, no. 16 (November 8, 1984): 3.

Herbert, Martin. “Previewed.” *ArtReview* 69, no. 6 (September 2017): 41–46.

Holland, Laura. “Berkshire Museum / Pittsfield. Martin Puryear: Sculpture.” *Art New England* 5, no. 6 (May 1984): 12.

Holg, Garrett. “Art in Chicago, 1945–1955.” *ARTnews* 96, no. 4 (April 1997): 137.

Holg, Garrett. “Chicago: Martin Puryear, Art Institute.” *ARTnews* 91, no. 2 (February 1992): 139.

Homes, A. M. “Hirshhorn Museum, Washington, D.C.: Exhibit.” *Artforum* 31, no. 1 (September 1992): 102.

Holst-Ekström, Måns. “Knislinge, Sweden: Eight American Artists in Sweden.” *Sculpture* 15, no. 8 (October 1996): 70–71.

Honan, William H. "The New School Challenges a Restriction on Arts Grants." *New York Times*, May 24, 1990.

Horn, Miriam. "New Cultural Worlds." *U.S. News and World Report* 105, no. 25 (December 26, 1988): 101–2.

Hudson, Suzanne. "Martin Puryear: Museum of Modern Art, New York, and Modem Art Museum of Fort Worth." *Artforum* 46, no. 9 (May 2008): 374.

Huebner, Jeff. "Abstract Thinking." *Chicago Reader*, February 4, 2000.

Hughes, Robert. "America's Best Artist: Martin Puryear." *Time* 158, no. 1 (July 9, 2001): 78–80.

Hughes, Robert. "Art: Delight in a Shaping Hand." *Time* 139, no. 9 (March 2, 1992): 61–63.

Hughes, Robert. "Going Back to Africa—as Visitors." *Time* 115, no. 13 (March 31, 1980): 72.

Hunsecker, J. J. "Naked City." *Spy Magazine* (April 1990): 48.

Huntington, Richard. "Albright-Knox Turns Good Idea into Fine Show." *Buffalo News*, August 2, 1987.

James, Curtia. "Hirshorn Museum and Sculpture Garden, Washington, D.C.; Traveling Exhibit." *New Art Examiner* 20, no. 2 (October 1992): 26–27.

Jamie, Rasaad. "Making It in the American Grain." *Times Literary Supplement*, September 25, 1992.

JP [James Panero]. "The Critic's Notebook." *New Criterion,* December 8, 2020. https://newcriterion.com/dispatch/the-critics-notebook-11997/.

Johnson, Jory. "Formal Objects, Public Visions." *Landscape Architecture* 82, no. 2 (February 1992): 50–53.

Johnson, Ken. "Martin Puryear." *New York Times*, June 8, 2012.

Joselit, David. "Lessons in Public Sculpture." *Art in America* 77, no. 12 (December 1989): 130–35.

Kangas, Matthew. "Martin Puryear." *Vanguard* 10, no. 7 (September 1981): 42.

Kangas, Matthew. "Martin Puryear." *Sculpture* 16, no. 6 (July–August 1997): 61–62.

Karmel, Pepe. "The Stuff of Dreams and the Natural World." *New York Times*, January 5, 1996.

Kaufman, Jason Edward. "XXth São Paulo Bienal." *Art Papers* 14, no. 1 (January–February 1990): 69–70.

Kelley, Jeff. "Puryear's Sculpture Casts a Spell." *Los Angeles Times*, October 29, 1984.

Kennicott, Philip. "America Picked Artist Martin Puryear's Work for the Venice Biennale—and He's Everything America Is Not." *Washington Post*, May 16, 2019.

Kennicott, Philip. "The America You Have to Go to Venice to See." *Washington Post*, May 22, 2019.

Kennicott, Philip. "A Sculptor in Rare Form, Even in 2-D." *Washington Post*, May 31, 2016.

Kennicott, Philip. "A Sculptor's Work, Seen in Two and Three Dimensions." *Washington Post*, May 27, 2016.

Kimmelman, Michael. "Abstraction, Without the Mess." *New York Times*, February 9, 1996.

Kimmelman, Michael. "The Force of Conviction Stirred by the 80's." *New York Times*, May 27, 1990.

Kimmelman, Michael. "Martin Puryear." *New York Times*, December 2, 1988.

Kimmelman, Michael. "Martin Puryear." *New York Times*, March 10, 1995.

Kimmelman, Michael. "The Softly Spoken Message of Martin Puryear." *New York Times*, March 1, 1992.

Kingsley, April. "Public Acres of Art: Artpark and the Leisure Landscape." *Artxpress* 2, no. 3 (May–June 1982): 26–29.

Kingsley, April. "'The Shape Arise!'" *Village Voice* (New York), July 30, 1979.

Kirshman, Cindy. "Earthworks Art Sways with Its Dimension." *Chicago Tribune*, April 3, 1987.

Kirshner, Judith Russi. "Martin Puryear in the American Grain." *Artforum* 30, no. 4 (December 1991): 58–63.

Kirshner, Judith Russi. "Martin Puryear, Margo Leavin Gallery." *Artforum* 23, no. 10 (Summer 1985): 115.

Klawans, Stuart. "Museums." *New York Daily News*, March 25, 1995.

Knight, Christopher. "'Afro-American Abstraction': More Abstract than African." *Los Angeles Herald Examiner*, July 14, 1982.

Knight, Christopher. "Martin Puryear: A Paean to Craftsmen." *Los Angeles Times*, July 30, 1992.

Knight, Christopher. "Monumental Greeting." *Los Angeles Times*, November 26, 1999.

Knight, Christopher. "Sculptures with a Touch of Nature." *Los Angeles Herald Examiner*, May 12, 1989.

Koplos, Janet. "Martin Puryear's 'Ars Poetica.'" *Art in America* 89, no. 12 (December 2001): 74–79.

Krainak, Paul. "Contraprimitivism and Martin Puryear." *Art Papers* 13, no. 2 (March–April 1989): 39–40.

Kuijken, Ilse. "Documenta IX." *Kunst & Museum Journaal* 3, no. 6 (1992): 1–11.

Landecker, Heidei. "Waterfront Connection." *Architecture* 84, no. 8 (August 1995): 56–61.

Lautman, Victoria. "Martin Puryear: Chicago Public Library Cultural Center." *Sculpture* 6, no. 4 (July–August 1987): 28–29.

Leffingwell, Edward. "Report from Brazil: Tropical Bazaar." *Art in America* 78, no. 6 (June 1990): 87–95.

Levin, Kim. "Martin Puryear: Museum of Modern Art." *ARTnews* 107, no. 1 (January 2008): 119.

Lewinson, David. "Two Artists Vividly Combine—Painter, Sculptor Show Well Together." *San Diego Union*, November 4, 1984.

Lewis, Jo Ann. "Galleries: Natural Talent." *Washington Post*, March 9, 1985.

Lewis, Jo Ann. "Shards and Epistles." *Washington Post*, November 24, 1979.

Lewis, Jo Ann. "Washington, D.C." *ARTnews* 79, no. 3 (March 1980): 147–50.

Litt, Steven. "Museum Adds Major Sculpture, Painting." *Plain Dealer* (Cleveland), June 5, 2002.

Loos, Ted. "Brick by Brick, a Sculpture at Storm King, by Way of Africa." *New York Times*, September 15, 2023.

Loos, Ted. "Making Bricks Do What They Don't Want to Do." *New York Times*, September 15, 2023.

Love, Philip H. "Just Between Ourselves . . ." *Sunday Star* (Washington, DC), February 27, 1949.

Luecking, Stephen. "Monumental Sculpture: Speaking the Language of Wood." *Fine Woodworking*, no. 50 (January–February 1985): 66–69.

Madoff, Steven Henry. "Sculpture Unbound." *ARTnews* 85, no. 9 (November 1986): 103–9.

Mais, Leia. "20a Bienal é aberta sem estar pronta; somem duas obras de Dale Chihuly." *Folha de S. Paulo*, October 15, 1989.

Margarido, Orlando C. "Bienal Toda a Arte do Mundo em São Paulo." *Manchete*, no. 1959 (November 4, 1989): 70–76.

Martin, Mary Abbe. "Splendor in the Grass." *ARTnews* 87, no. 8 (October 1988): 126–30.

"Martin Puryear." *New Yorker* 88, no. 16 (June 4 & 11, 2012): 24.

"Martin Puryear." *New Yorker* 90, no. 40 (December 15, 2014): 8.

Maxwell, Jessica Ann. "Heterogeneous Objects: The Sculptures of Martin Puryear." PhD dissertation. Art and Archaeology Department, Princeton University, 2013.

McGill, Douglas C. "Art People." *New York Times*, January 29, 1988.

Melrod, George. “Martin Puryear.” *World Art*, no. 3 (1995): 99.

Melrod, George. “Martin Puryear: The Art of the Decoy.” *Sculpture* 10, no. 5 (September–October 1991): 32–39.

Melrod, George. “Searching for a Center.” *ARTnews* 92, no. 8 (October 1993): 117–18.

Melrod, George. “Skill, Vision, and Craft: Martin Puryear Lets His Sculpture Speak for Itself.” *Art & Antiques* 18, no. 6 (June 1995): 39-43.

Menzies, Neal. “Unembellished Strength of Form.” *Artweek* 16, no. 5 (February 2, 1985): 4.

Merritt, Robert. “Fall Art Season Under Way.” *Richmond Times-Dispatch*, August 29, 1982.

Miller, Donald. “Related Shows Center on Subway Art.” *Pittsburgh Post-Gazette*, April 18, 1987.

Mizota, Sharon. “Martin Puryear Prints at the Fine Arts Museum of San Francisco.” *Art on Paper* 13, no. 3 (January–February 2009): 82–83.

Morgan, Ann Lee. “Sculpture as Elemental Expression.” *New Art Examiner* 14, no. 9 (May 1987): 27–29.

Morgan, Robert C. “American Sculpture and the Search for a Referent.” *Arts Magazine* 62, no. 3 (November 1987): 20–23.

Morrison, Keith. “The Emerging Importance of Black Art in America.” *New Art Examiner* 7, no. 9 (June 1980): 1, 4–5.

Morrison, Keith. “Question the Quality Canon.” *New Art Examiner* 18, no. 2 (October 1990): 24–27.

Moser, Charlotte. “Martin Puryear: Donald Young.” *ARTnews* 85, no. 1 (January 1986): 116.

Muchnic, Suzanne. “The Abstract Shapes of Familiar Mysteries.” *Los Angeles Times*, January 15, 1985.

Muchnic, Suzanne. “The Handyman.” *Los Angeles Times*, August 2, 1992.

Muchnic, Suzanne. “Olympic Posters: A Celebration of Creativity.” *Los Angeles Times*, July 24, 1983.

Nadelman, Cynthia. “Broken Premises: ‘Primitivism’ at MoMA.” *ARTnews* 84, no. 2 (February 1985): 88–95.

Naves, Mario. “Exhibition Notes.” *New Criterion* 13, no. 9 (May 1995): 47–48.

Nayeri, Farah. “Martin Puryear’s Works Mine African-American History.” *New York Times*, October 15, 2017.

Nemser, Mary Rebecca. “Flying High: Martin Puryear Makes the Right ‘Connections.’” *Boston Phoenix*, March 23, 1990.

“New Sculpture Nears Completion.” *GSU Landscapes* 1, no. 1 (October 2, 1981): 1.

Nuridsany, Michel. “Martin Puryear: La Séduction de la spiritualité.” *Le Figaro*, September 28, 1999.

Opincar, Randy. “The Puryear Exhibition.” *San Diego Reader* 13, no. 40 (October 11, 1984): 1, 12.

Ottinger, Didier. “The Chimeras of Martin Puryear.” Translated by C. Penwarden. *Art Press*, no. 345 (May 2008): 58–62.

Padon, Thomas. “Martin Puryear.” *Sculpture* 14, no. 3 (May–June 1995): 42.

Phillips, Patricia C. “Martin Puryear.” *Artforum* 29, no. 1 (October 1990): 172–73.

Plagens, Peter. “Grappling with America’s Past in Venice.” *Wall Street Journal*, May 29, 2019.

Plagens, Peter. “I Just Dropped in to See What Condition My Condition Was In. . .” *Artscribe International* 56 (February–March 1986): 23–29.

Plagens, Peter. “Sculpture Like It Oughta Be.” *Newsweek* 118, no. 20 (November 11, 1991): 73.

Pimenta, Angela, and Norma Freire. “A Dimensão Lírica No Cotidiano de Puryear.” *O Estado de S. Paulo*, October 12, 1989.

Pincus, Robert. “A Transformer of Minimalism.” *Los Angeles Times*, November 5, 1984.

Pogrebin, Robin. “Sculptor to Represent U.S. in Venice.” *New York Times*, August 16, 2018.

Princenthal, Nancy. “Intuition’s Disciplinarian.” *Art in America* 78, no. 1 (January 1990): 130–37, 181.

Princenthal, Nancy. “Martin Puryear.” *American Craft* 52, no. 1 (February–March 1992): 34–37.

Princenthal, Nancy. “Puryear’s Tall Tales.” *Art in America* 96, no. 2 (February 2008): 116–21, 165.

“Puryear Courtyard for New School.” *Art in America* 86, no. 2 (February 1998): 29.

“Puryear Retrospective.” *Flash Art* 24, no. 161 (November–December 1991): 146.

Quinn, Chase. “What Is and What Could Be: The Enduring Legacy of Martin Puryear.” *Callaloo* 40, no. 5 (2017): 76–80.

Raczka, Robert. “Martin Puryear.” *LA Weekly*, May 5–May 11, 1989.

Raymond, David. “Museum of Fine Arts, Boston, Connections: Martin Puryear.” *Art New England* 11, no. 6 (June 11, 1990): 30.

Raynor, Vivien. “Photos and Sculpture at the Aldrich.” *New York Times*, November 27, 1988.

Raynor, Vivien. “Print Exhibition at Brooklyn Museum.” *New York Times*, February 21, 1986.

Richard, Paul. “He Sawed & Conquered: Sculptor Martin Puryear’s Homecoming at the Hirshhorn.” *Washington Post*, February 5, 1992.

Richard, Paul. “Martin Puryear: A Master in Wood.” *International Herald Tribune*, February 15–16, 1992.

Richard, Paul. “The Sculptor’s Swell Curves.” *Washington Post*, March 11, 2001.

Richard, Paul. “The Sculpture of Longing: Martin Puryear, a Master of Woodwork, Making a Triumphal Return Home.” *Washington Post*, March 25, 1988.

Richard, Paul. “A Shrine of Cedar and Hide.” *Washington Post*, July 30, 1977.

Richard, Paul. “A Test in Connoisseurship.” *Washington Post*, January 29, 1972.

Rickey, Carrie. “Singular Work, Double Bind, Triple Thread.” *Village Voice* (New York), March 3, 1980.

Robbins, Eugenia S. “Who’s Who, Who’s Where, and What’s What.” *Artxpress* 2, no. 3 (May–June 1982): 12–15.

Robinson, Walter, and Cathy Lebowitz. “Puryear Chosen for São Paulo.” *Art in America* 77, no. 1 (January 1989): 180.

Rodney, Seph. “Finding the Heart of a Nation in Generations of Black Art.” *Hyperallergic*, December 14, 2018. https://hyperallergic.com/475761/.

Rosenfeld, Jason. “Martin Puryear: Big Bling.” *Brooklyn Rail*, July 11, 2016. https://brooklynrail.org/2016/07/artseen/martin-puryear-big-bling/.

Rossignol, Pascal. “Martin Puryear: Chapelle de la Salpêtrière, Paris.” *Art Press*, no. 252 (December 1999): 84–85.

Rubenfeld, Richard. “Martin Puryear.” *New Art Examiner* 9, no. 6 (April 1982): 15.

Rubenstein, Raphael. “Panza’s Gift to Italy.” *Art in America* 84, no. 9 (September 1996): 29.

Rugoff, Ralph. “See Me, Feel Me: Living in a Tactile World.” *LA Weekly*, August 21–27, 1992.

Russell, John. “Abstractions from Afro-America.” *New York Times*, March 14, 1980.

Russell, John. “American Art Through European Eyes.” *New York Times*, May 30, 1993.

“São Paulo Preview.” *Art in America* 77, no. 7 (July 1989): 168.

Saunders, Wade. “Art Inc.: The Whitney’s 1979 Biennial.” *Art in America* 67, no. 3 (May–June 1979): 96–99.

Sayej, Nadja. “Martin Puryear: The Cross-Cultural Artist Picked to Represent America.” *Guardian*, August 20, 2018.

Schjeldahl, Peter. “Seeing Things.” *New Yorker* 83, no. 35 (November 12, 2007): 94–95.

Schulze, Franz. “Puryear Works: Elegant Simplicity.” *Chicago Sun-Times*, May 18, 1980.

Schwabsky, Barry. “The Obscure Objects of Martin Puryear.” *Arts Magazine* 62, no. 3 (November 1987): 58–59.

Scott, Andrea K. “Greater New York” *New Yorker* 91, no. 34 (November 2, 2015): 16.

“Sculptor Puryear Celebrated at Biennial.” *Journal of Art* 2, no. 3 (December 1989): 4.

Sheets, Hilarie M. “Making Public Art a Contender.” *New York Times*, March 15, 2019.

Sheets, Hilarie M., and Randy Kennedy. “Mapplethorpe Print at Center of Culture Wars Returns to Public Eye.” *New York Times*, October 2, 2015.

Shere, Charles. “Absorbing Schools of Thought Exhibited in Berkeley.” *Oakland Tribune*, August 12, 1985.

Shipp, E. R. “Art for Those on the Go in Chicago.” *New York Times*, June 16, 1984.

“Sierra Leone.” “30th Anniversary Keepsake Edition,” *Peace Corps Times* (March 1, 1991): 52.

Silva, Jaime, and Elke Lopes Muniz. “Bienal: A Maneira Mais Fácil de Ver.” *O Estado de S. Paulo*, October 31, 1989.

Silverthorne, Jeanne. “Martin Puryear.” *Artforum* 23, no. 4 (December 1984): 82–83.

Simmons, Chuck. “Restriking Atavistic Chords.” *Artweek* 13, no. 42 (December 11, 1982): 4.

Smee, Sebastian. “A Portal That Leads to Introspection, Questions.” *Boston Globe*, December 24, 2013.

Smee, Sebastian. “Red, Right to the Liberated Heart.” *Washington Post*, December 22, 2021.

Smee, Sebastian, and Philip Kennicott. “Taking Risks Can Be Rewarding.” *Washington Post*, December 15, 2019.

Smith, Roberta. “Around Town.” *Village Voice* (New York), September 4, 1984.

Smith, Roberta. “Galleries: Martin Puryear.” *New York Times*, January 8, 2021.

Smith, Roberta. “Humanity’s Ascent, in Three Dimensions.” *New York Times*, November 2, 2007.

Smith, Roberta. “A Primitive Look at the Moderns.” *Village Voice* (New York), October 2, 1984.

Spector, Buzz. “Martin Puryear.” *New Art Examiner* 7, no. 7 (April 1980): 22.

Stapen, Nancy. “Making ‘Connections’ with Works of the Past.” *Boston Sunday Herald*, April 1, 1990.

Steinhauer, Jillian. “Martin Puryear to Represent US at Venice Biennale.” *Art Newspaper*, August 15, 2018. https://www.theartnewspaper.com/2018/08/15/martin-puryear-to-represent-us-at-venice-biennale.

Stern, William F. “Sculpture Inside Outside.” *Cite* 22 (Spring–Summer 1989): 20–21.

Sternefeld, Gayle. “1981 Biennial Exhibition.” *Art Papers* 5, no. 3 (May–June 1981): 13.

Strecker, Márion. “Bienal Abre Hoje Sob Tensão.” *Folha de S. Paulo*, October 14, 1989.

Strecker, Márion. “Mostra é a Única Janela Para o Mundo.” *Folha de S. Paulo*, February 19, 1989.

Swift, Barbara, and Rob Wilkinson. “The NOAA Program: Public Art on a Shoreline Site.” *Landscape Architecture* 78, no. 6 (September–October 1988): 98–100, 102–3.

Swift, Mary. “Martin Puryear, Protetch-McIntosh Gallery, Nov. 20–Dec. 15, 1979.” *Washington Review* 5, no. 5 (February–March 1980): 21.

Tanner, Marcia. “Vistas into Shared Terrain.” *Artweek* 21, no. 9 (March 8, 1990): 1, 28.

Tannous, David. “Martin Puryear at the Corcoran.” *Art in America* 66, no. 3 (May–June 1978): 119–21.

Tannous, David. “Sculpture Shows in Washington.” *AURA* (Winter 1980): 10–11.

Tannous, David. “Those Who Stay.” *Art in America* 66, no. 4 (July–August 1978): 78–85.

Tavares, Carlos. “A Madeira Viva de Martin Puryear na Bienal de SP.” *Correio Braziliense*, no. 9667, October 11, 1989.

Taylor, Robert. “Sculpture Show a Pioneering Effort.” *Boston Globe*, May 18, 1986.

Taylor, Sue. “Poetic Resonance Marks Puryear’s New Sculpture.” *Chicago Sun-Times*, October 23, 1985.

Taylor, Sue. “Report from Minneapolis: Garden City.” *Art in America* 76, no. 12 (December 1988): 28–36.

Teltsch, Kathleen. “MacArthur Foundation Honors Achievement.” *New York Times*, July 18, 1989.

Temin, Christine. “Puryear’s Primitive Sophistication.” *Boston Globe*, July 7, 1984.

Temin, Christine. “The Time of Martin Puryear.” *Boston Globe*, March 25, 1990.

Thalenberg, Eileen. “Site Work: Some Sculpture at Artpark.” *Artscanada* nos. 216–217 (October–November 1977): 16–20.

Thompson, David M. “Martin Puryear.” *Arts Magazine* 66, no. 6 (February 1992): 70.

Tomkins, Calvin, “The Art World: Perception at All Levels.” *New Yorker* 60, no. 42 (December 3, 1984): 176–81.

Tully, Judd. “The Chicago Art Scene.” *Flash Art*, no. 103 (Summer 1981): 23–26.

Tully, Judd. “On Custom and Culture.” *Skyline*, June 22, 1979.

Van Benthuysen, Daniel. “‘River Crossings,’ a Contemporary Art Exhibition at 2 Historic Sites of the Hudson River School.” *New York Times*, May 28, 2015.

Van Gelder, Lawrence. “This Week.” *New York Times*, November 22, 1999.

Vasconcelos, Cássio. “20: Bienal de São Paulo.” *Galeria* no. 13 (1989): 98–105.

Warren, Lynne, and Jeffrey Edelstein. “Artworld Chicago 1981.” *images & issues* 2, no. 3 (Winter 1981–82): 44–47.

Wasserman, Isabelle. "Puryear Sculpture Exhibit Will Open." *San Diego Union*, October 7, 1984.

Waxman, Sharon. "Getty, on the Grow: At 2, the Ambitious Art Center Shows Promising Signs of Filling Out." *Washington Post*, December 12, 1999.

Wei, Lilly. "Brunhilde Stripped Bare." *ARTnews* 100, no. 11 (December 2001): 98–100.

Weiss, Hedy. "City Sculpture." *New Art Examiner* 9, no. 1 (October 1981): 18.

Westerbeck, Colin. "Martin Puryear." *Artforum* 25, no. 9 (May 1987): 154.

Wilkin, Karen. "Martin Puryear at MoMA." *New Criterion* 26, no. 5 (January 2008): 43-46.

Wilkinson, Richard. "America's Best Artist." *CUA Magazine* 14, no. 1 (Spring 2002): 10–15.

Willig, Nancy Tobin. "Bordering on the Surreal." *ARTnews* 76, no. 9 (November 1977): 195–200.

Wingert, Pat. "Arty Stops in Store for Trains to O'Hare." *Sunday Sun-Times* (Chicago), July 17, 1983.

Wittenburg, Clarissa K. "Martin Puryear." *Art Voices / South* 1 (January–February 1979): 19.

Wood, Carol. "Martin Puryear." *New Art Examiner* 22, no. 9 (May 1995): 51–52.

Woodard, Josef. "Unusual Views." *Los Angeles Times*, December 24, 1999.

Wright, Martha McWilliams. "Washington Letter." *Art International* 22, no. 5 (October 1978): 57–65.

Wylie, Charles. "Contemporary American and European Art After 1980." *Saint Louis Museum of Art Bulletin* 21, no. 3 (Winter 1995): 1–60.

Yau, John. "John Keats and Martin Puryear, and the Latter's Renewal of Negative Capability." *Hyperallergic*, January 18, 2015. https://hyperallergic.com/175490.

Yau, John. "Martin Puryear Bears Witness" *Hyperallergic*, December 6, 2015. https://hyperallergic.com/258534.

Yau, John. "Some Thoughts About Richard Serra and Martin Puryear (Part 2: Puryear)." *Hyperallergic*, November 16, 2014. https:// hyperallergic.com/162494.

Yerebakan, O. C. "Martin Puryear Is on View at Matthew Marks Gallery Through January 10th, 2015." *Art Observed*, January 4, 2015. https://artobserved.com/2015/01/new-york-martin-puryear-is-on-view-at-matthew-marks-gallery-through-january-10th-2015/.

Yood, James. "Picturing America." *Art on Paper* 13, no. 1 (September–October 2008): 14, 16.

Zimmer, William. "Art for the Me Decade." *Soho Weekly News*, March 1, 1979.

Zimmer, William. "Art: Unity and Diversity in Sculpture." *New York Times*, December 20, 1992.

Zimmer, William. "Seventies Eclectics." *Soho Weekly News*, May 25, 1978.

Books and Exhibition Catalogues

Als, Hilton, Rob Perrée, and Suzanne Swarts. *Martin Puryear*. Exhibition catalogue. Wassenaar, The Netherlands: Museum Voorlinden, 2018.

Ardalan, Ziba, ed. *Martin Puryear*. Exhibition catalogue. London: Parasol Unit Foundation for Contemporary Art, 2017.

Armstrong, Richard, John G. Hanhardt, Richard Marshall, and Lisa Phillips. *1989 Biennial Exhibition*. Exhibition catalogue. New York: W. W. Norton and Whitney Museum of American Art, 1989.

Armstrong, Tom, and Susan C. Larsen. *Art in Place: Fifteen Years of Acquisitions*. New York: Whitney Museum of American Art, 1989.

Arnason, H. H. *History of Modern Art*. 3rd edition. New York: Harry N. Abrams, 1986.

Ater, Renée. "Tactility, Memory Work, and Martin Puryear's *Slavery Memorial*." In Brown University's *Slavery and Justice Report with Commentary on Context and Impact*, edited by Anthony Bogues, Cass Cliatt, and Allison Levy, 23–32. 2nd ed. Providence, RI: Brown University, 2021.

Auping, Michael. *Structure to Resemblance: Work by Eight American Sculptors*. Exhibition catalogue. Buffalo: Buffalo Fine Arts Academy and Albright-Knox Art Gallery, 1987.

Bach, Penny Belkin. *Form and Function: Proposals for Public Art for Philadelphia*. Philadelphia: Fairmount Park Art Association and Pennsylvania Academy of the Fine Arts, 1982.

Bach, Penny Belkin. *New•Land•Mark: Public Art, Community, and the Meaning of Place*. Exhibition catalogue. Philadelphia: Fairmount Park Art Association; Washington, DC: Editions Ariel, 2001.

Benezra, Neal, and Robert Storr. *Martin Puryear*. Exhibition catalogue. New York: Thames & Hudson; Chicago: Art Institute of Chicago, 1991.

Boyd, Julia. *American Abstraction Now*. Exhibition catalogue. Richmond: Institute of Contemporary Art of the Virginia Museum, 1982.

Boyden, Martha, ed. *Nunzio, Martin Puryear: Forma Lignea*. Exhibition catalogue. Milan: Electa; Rome: American Academy in Rome, 1997.

Brenson, Michael, and Enrique Juncosa. *Martin Puryear*. Exhibition catalogue. Madrid: Fundación "la Caixa," 1997.

Cateforis, David. *Objects of Potential: Five American Sculptors from the Anderson Collection*. Exhibition catalogue. Belmont, CA: Wiegand Gallery, College of Notre Dame, 1990.

Cooke, Lynne, ed. *Woven Histories: Textiles and Modern Abstraction*. Exhibition catalogue. Washington, DC: National Gallery of Art; Chicago and London: University of Chicago Press, 2023.

Crutchfield, Margo A. *Martin Puryear*. Exhibition catalogue. Richmond: Virginia Museum of Fine Arts, 2001.

Davies, Hugh M., and Helaine Posner. *Martin Puryear*. Exhibition catalogue. Amherst: University Gallery, Fine Arts Center, University of Massachusetts at Amherst, 1984.

Day, Holliday T. *I-80 Series: Martin Puryear*. Exhibition catalogue. Omaha: Joslyn Art Museum, 1980.

Desai, Vishakha N., and Kathy Halbreich. *Connections: Martin Puryear*. Exhibition catalogue. Boston: Museum of Fine Arts, Boston, 1990.

Diserens, Corinne. *Sculpture: Material and Abstraction; 2 x 5 Points of View*. Exhibition catalogue. Geneva: Black Cat Productions; Aarau, Switzerland: Aargauer Kunsthaus, 1985.

Driskell, David C., and Henry J. Drewel. *Introspectives: Contemporary Art by Americans and Brazilians of African Descent*. Exhibition catalogue. Los Angeles: California Afro-American Museum, 1989.

Edelman, Sharon. *Artpark 1977: The Program in the Visual Arts*. Exhibition catalogue. Lewiston, NY: Artpark, 1977.

Elderfield, John, ed. *Martin Puryear*. Exhibition catalogue. New York: Museum of Modern Art, 2007.

Fineberg, Jonathan. *Art Since 1940: Strategies of Being*. New York: Harry N. Abrams, 1995.

Fonvielle-Bontemps, Jacqueline , ed. *Choosing: An Exhibit of Changing Modern Art and Art Criticism by Black Americans, 1925–1985*. Exhibition catalogue. Hampton, VA: Hampton University, 1985.

French, Christopher. *Mary Beth Edelson, Martin Puryear, Italo Scanga, Robert Stackhouse*. Exhibition catalogue. Washington, DC: Corcoran Gallery of Art, 1988.

Friedman, Martin, Joan Simon, Carter Ratcliff, et al. *Sculpture Inside Outside*. Exhibition catalogue. Minneapolis: Walker Art Center; New York: Rizzoli, 1988.

Fuller, Patricia. *Five Artists at NOAA: A Casebook on Art in Public Places*. Seattle: Real Comet, 1985.

Garrels, Gary. *Beyond the Monument*. Exhibition catalogue. Cambridge, MA: Hayden Gallery, Massachusetts Institute of Technology, 1983.

Gentili, Carlo, ed. *Anniottanta*. Exhibition catalogue. Milan: Mazzotta; Bologna: Galleria Comunale d'Arte Moderna, Bologna, 1985.

Golden, Deven K., Judith Russi Kirshner, and Patricia Fuller. *Public and Personal*. Exhibition catalogue. Chicago: Chicago Office of Fine Arts, 1987.

Hall, Michael, and Roy Slade. *Instruction Drawings: The Gilbert and Lila Silverman Collection*. Bloomfield Hills, MI: Cranbrook Academy of Art, 1981.

Hanhardt, John G., Barbara Haskell, Richard Marshall, et al. *1979 Biennial Exhibition*. New York: Whitney Museum of American Art, 1979.

Hanhardt, John G., Barbara Haskell, Richard Marshall, et al. *1981 Biennial Exhibition*. New York: Whitney Museum of American Art, 1981.

Hannock, Stephen, Ken Burns, Jason Rosenfeld, et al. *River Crossings: Contemporary Art Comes Home*. Exhibition catalogue. New York: Artist Book Foundation, 2015.

Harris, Stacy Paleologos. *Insights / On Sights: Perspectives on Art in Public Places*. Washington, DC: Partners for Livable Places, 1984.

Herrera, María de, and Maurice Tuchman. *The Artist as Social Designer: Aspects of Public Urban Art Today*. Exhibition catalogue. Los Angeles: Los Angeles County Museum of Art, 1985.

Jones, Kellie. *EyeMinded: Living and Writing Contemporary Art*. Durham, NC: Duke University Press, 2011.

Jones, Kellie. *Martin Puryear*. Exhibition catalogue. Queens, New York: Jamaica Arts Center, 1989.

King, Elaine. *Martin Puryear: Sculpture and Works on Paper*. Exhibition catalogue. Pittsburgh: Carnegie Mellon University, 1987.

Kingsley, April. *Afro-American Abstraction*. Exhibition catalogue. San Francisco: Art Museum Association, 1982.

Kingsley, April. *The New Spiritualism: Transcendent Images in Painting and Sculpture*. Exhibition catalogue. Storrs: University of Connecticut; New York: Oscarsson Hood Gallery, 1981.

Kirshner, Judith Russi. *Options 2: Martin Puryear*. Exhibition catalogue. Chicago: Museum of Contemporary Art, Chicago, 1980.

Kline, Katy, and Douglas Dreishpoon. *Natural Forms and Forces: Abstract Images in American Sculpture*. Exhibition catalogue. Cambridge, MA: Massachusetts Institute of Technology, List Visual Arts Center, 1986.

Lawrence, Nora, Amy S. Weisser, Glenn Adamson, et al. *Martin Puryear: Lookout*. Exhibition catalogue. New Windsor, NY: Storm King Art Center; New York: Gregory R. Miller & Co., 2024.

Lewallen, Constance. *Martin Puryear: MATRIX / BERKELEY 86*. Exhibition catalogue. Berkeley, CA: University Art Museum, 1985.

Lopez, Merlyn Maldonado, and Shannon Egan. *Martin Puryear, 40 Years Since Sentinel*. Exhibition catalogue. Gettysburg, PA: Schmucker Art Gallery, Gettysburg College, 2021.

Lubowsky, Susan. *Enclosing the Void: Eight Contemporary Sculptors*. Exhibition catalogue. New York: Whitney Museum of American Art at Equitable Center, 1988.

Lucie-Smith, Edward. *Movements in Art Since 1945: Issues and Concepts*. 3rd edition. New York: Thames & Hudson, 1995.

Luecking, Stephen. *Sculpture Overview 1985*. Exhibition catalogue. Evanston, IL: Evanston Art Center, 1985.

Madoff, Steven Henry. *After Nature: Sculpture by Bård Breivik, Heide Fasnacht, Martin Puryear, Scott Richter, Mia Westerlund Roosen, Robert Therrien, Steve Wood*. Exhibition catalogue. New York: Germans Van Eck Gallery, 1986.

Mayer, Roger, and Ronald J. Onorato. *Laurie Anderson, Farrell Brickhouse, Scott Burton, Denise Green, Wolfgang Laib, Joshua Neustein, Lucio Pozzi, Martin Puryear, Haim Steinbach*. Exhibition catalogue. Providence, RI: Brown University, 1982.

McShine, Kynaston. *An International Survey of Recent Painting and Sculpture*. Exhibition catalogue. New York: Museum of Modern Art, 1984.

Martin, Sarah, ed. *Martin Puryear*. Gateshead, UK: Baltic Centre for Contemporary Art, 2003.

Neff, Terry Ann R., and Peter Schjeldahl. *The Nathan Manilow Sculpture Park*. University Park, IL: Governors State University, 1987.

New Sculpture: Six Artists: Richard Deacon, Rebecca Horn, Richard Long, Tom Otterness, Martin Puryear, James Turrell. Exhibition catalogue. Saint Louis: Saint Louis Art Museum, 1988.

Pascale, Mark, and Ruth Fine. *Martin Puryear: Multiple Dimensions*. Exhibition catalogue. Chicago: Art Institute of Chicago, 2015.

Patton, Sharon F. *African-American Art*. New York: Oxford University Press, 1998.

Peraza, Nilda, Marcia Tucker, Kinshasha Holman Conwill, et al. *The Decade Show: Frameworks of Identity in the 1980s*. Exhibition catalogue. New York: New Museum of Contemporary Art, 1990.

Phillips, Lisa. *Vital Signs: Organic Abstraction from the Permanent Collection*. Exhibition catalogue. New York: Whitney Museum of American Art, 1988.

Potts, Alex. *Martin Puryear*. Exhibition catalogue. New York: Matthew Marks Gallery, 2015.

Rapaport, Brooke Kamin, Darby English, Anne Middleton Wagner, et al. *Martin Puryear: Liberty / Libertà*. Exhibition catalogue. New York: Madison Square Park Conservancy and Gregory R. Miller; Berlin: Hatje Cantz, 2019.

Rapaport, Brooke Kamin, Martin Puryear, and Harry Cooper. *Martin Puryear: Big Bling*. Exhibition catalogue. New York: Madison Square Park Conservancy, 2016.

Richard, Frances, ed. *I Stand in My Place With My Own Day Here: Site-Specific Art at The New School*. Durham, NC: Duke University Press, 2019.

Rorimer, Anne, and A. James Speyer, eds. *74th American Exhibition*. Exhibition catalogue. Chicago: Art Institute of Chicago, 1982.

Rubin, William S., ed. *"Primitivism" in 20th Century Art: Affinity of the Tribal and the Modern*. Exhibition catalogue. New York: Museum of Modern Art, 1984.

Sandler, Irving. *Art of the Postmodern Era: From the Late 1960s to the Early 1990s*. New York: Harper Collins, 1996.

Shearer, Linda. *Young American Artists: 1978 Exxon National Exhibition*. Exhibition catalogue. New York: Solomon R. Guggenheim Museum, 1978.

Schwab, Cindy. *The Presence of Nature*. Exhibition catalogue. New York: Whitney Museum of American Art, 1978.

Shapiro, Michael Edward, Daniel A. Reich, and Maureen Megerian. *New Sculpture: Six Artists: Richard Deacon, Rebecca Horn, Richard Long, Tom Otterness, Martin Puryear, James Turrell*. Exhibition catalogue. Saint Louis: Saint Louis Art Museum, 1988.

Singerman, Howard, ed. *Individuals: A Selected History of Contemporary Art 1945–1986*. Exhibition catalogue. Los Angeles: Museum of Contemporary Art, 1986.

Strauss, David Levi. *Martin Puryear: New Sculpture*. Exhibition catalogue. New York: McKee Gallery, 2012.

Varnedoe, Krik. *Wave Hill: The Artist's View*. Exhibition catalogue. New York: Wave Hill, 1979.

Verre, Phillip, and George Nelson Preston. *Traditions and Transformations: Contemporary Afro-American Sculpture*. Exhibition catalogue. New York: Bronx Museum of the Arts, 1989.

Wachtmeister, Marika, Gregory Volk, Sune Nordgren, et al. *Konsten på Wanås*. Stockholm: Byggförlaget Kultur, 2001.

Waldman, Diane. *Emerging Artists 1978–1986: Selections from the Exxon Series*. New York: Solomon R. Guggenheim Museum, 1986.

Waldman, Diane. *Transformations in Sculpture: Four Decades in American and European Art*. New York: Solomon R. Guggenheim Museum, 1985.

Wheeler, Daniel. *Art Since Mid-Century: 1945–Present*. New York: Vendome Press, 1991.

Video and Audio Recordings

"'Big Bling': Martin Puryear." From the series *Extended Play*, from the PBS television series *Art21: Art in the Twenty-First Century*, June 10, 2016. https://art21.org/watch/extended-play/martin-puryear-big-bling-short/.

"Garth Fagan's Griot New York." From the series *Dance in America*. Sony Classical Film & Video, New York, 1995.

"The Leonard Lopate Show: Sculptor Martin Puryear at MoMA." November 29, 2007. Museum of Modern Art Archives, New York.

"Martin Puryear: A Panel," January 8, 2008. Museum of Modern Art Archives, New York.

"Martin Puryear Dinner @ MoMA," October 30, 2007. Museum of Modern Art Archives, New York.

Martin Puryear: Lookout. Directed by Susan Wald, Edgar Howard, and Thomas Piper. Checkerboard Films, 2023.

Martin Puryear: Meditation in a Beech Wood. Directed by Martin Lang. Wanås Foundation, 2024.

Martin Puryear: This Mortal Coil. Filmed and edited by Patrick Lecoq. Festival d'Automne à Paris, la Chapelle Saint-Louis de la Salpêtrière, 1999.

"Printmaking: Martin Puryear." From the series *Extended Play*, *Art21*, February 22, 2013.

"Rai News 24: Martin Puryear at MoMA," 2007. Museum of Modern Art Archives, New York.

"Time: Martin Puryear." Segment of season 2, *Stories, Loss, and Desire*, from the PBS television series *Art21: Art in the Twenty-First Century*, September 9, 2003. https://www.pbs.org/video/art21-time/.

Related Archival Repositories

Archive & Library, Royal Academy of Fine Arts, Stockholm

Archives and Manuscripts Collections, Baltimore Museum of Art

Archives of American Art, Smithsonian Institution, Washington, DC

Artpark Archival Collection, The Burchfield Penney Art Center Archives, SUNY Buffalo State University, Buffalo

Baltic Archive, Baltic Centre for Contemporary Art, Gateshead, United Kingdom

BAM Hamm Archives, Brooklyn Academy of Music, Brooklyn

Driskell Center at the University of Maryland, College Park

Getty Research Institute, Los Angeles

Governors State University Library, University Archives, University Park, IL

Kelvin Smith Library Special Collections, Case Western Reserve University, Cleveland

Museum of Modern Art Archives, New York

Musselman Library, Special Collections and College Archives, Gettysburg College, Gettysburg, PA

Ryerson and Burnham Art and Architecture Archives, The Art Institute of Chicago

Smithsonian Institution Archives (Smithsonian Libraries and Archives), Smithsonian Institution, Washington, DC

Special Collections Research Center, George Washington University, Washington, DC

University of Washington Libraries, Special Collections, Seattle

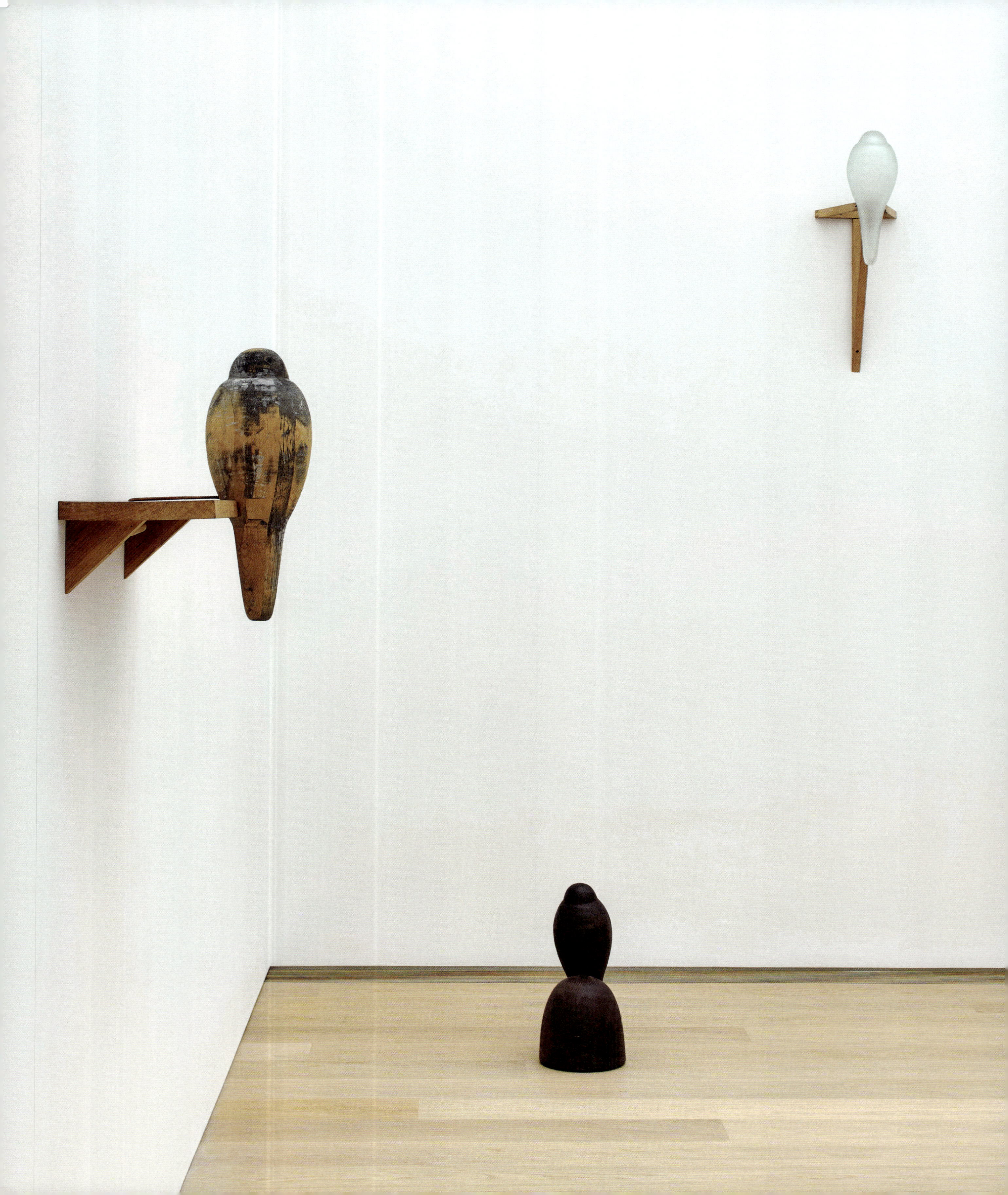

Index

Page numbers in *italics* refer to illustrations.

Figure 122. Installation view of *Martin Puryear*, Museum Voorlinden, Wassenaar, The Netherlands, 2018. Pictured: *Untitled* (1982); *Untitled* (1992; [29]); *On the Tundra* (1986; [26]). Photo: Antoine van Kaam

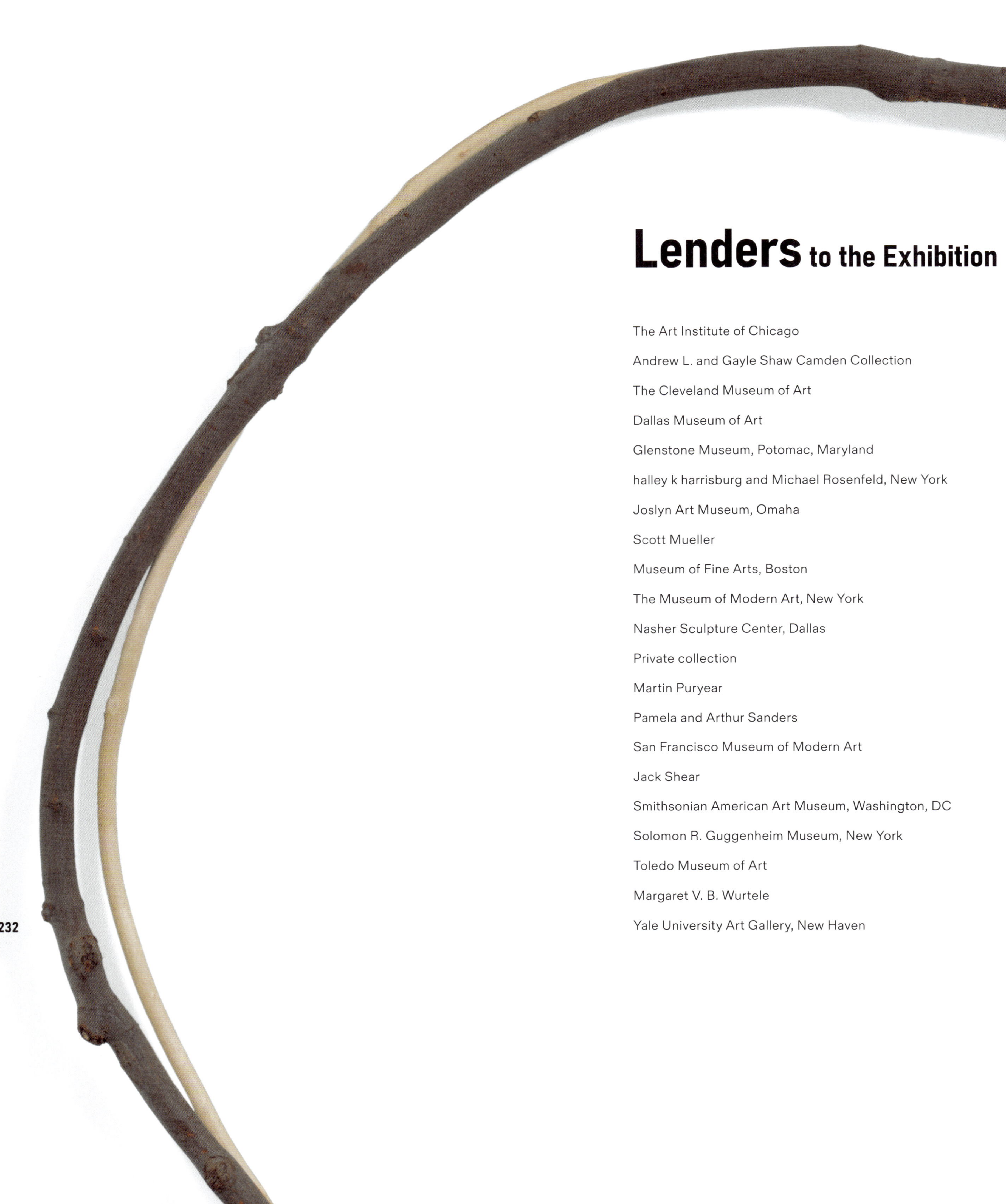

Lenders to the Exhibition

The Art Institute of Chicago

Andrew L. and Gayle Shaw Camden Collection

The Cleveland Museum of Art

Dallas Museum of Art

Glenstone Museum, Potomac, Maryland

halley k harrisburg and Michael Rosenfeld, New York

Joslyn Art Museum, Omaha

Scott Mueller

Museum of Fine Arts, Boston

The Museum of Modern Art, New York

Nasher Sculpture Center, Dallas

Private collection

Martin Puryear

Pamela and Arthur Sanders

San Francisco Museum of Modern Art

Jack Shear

Smithsonian American Art Museum, Washington, DC

Solomon R. Guggenheim Museum, New York

Toledo Museum of Art

Margaret V. B. Wurtele

Yale University Art Gallery, New Haven

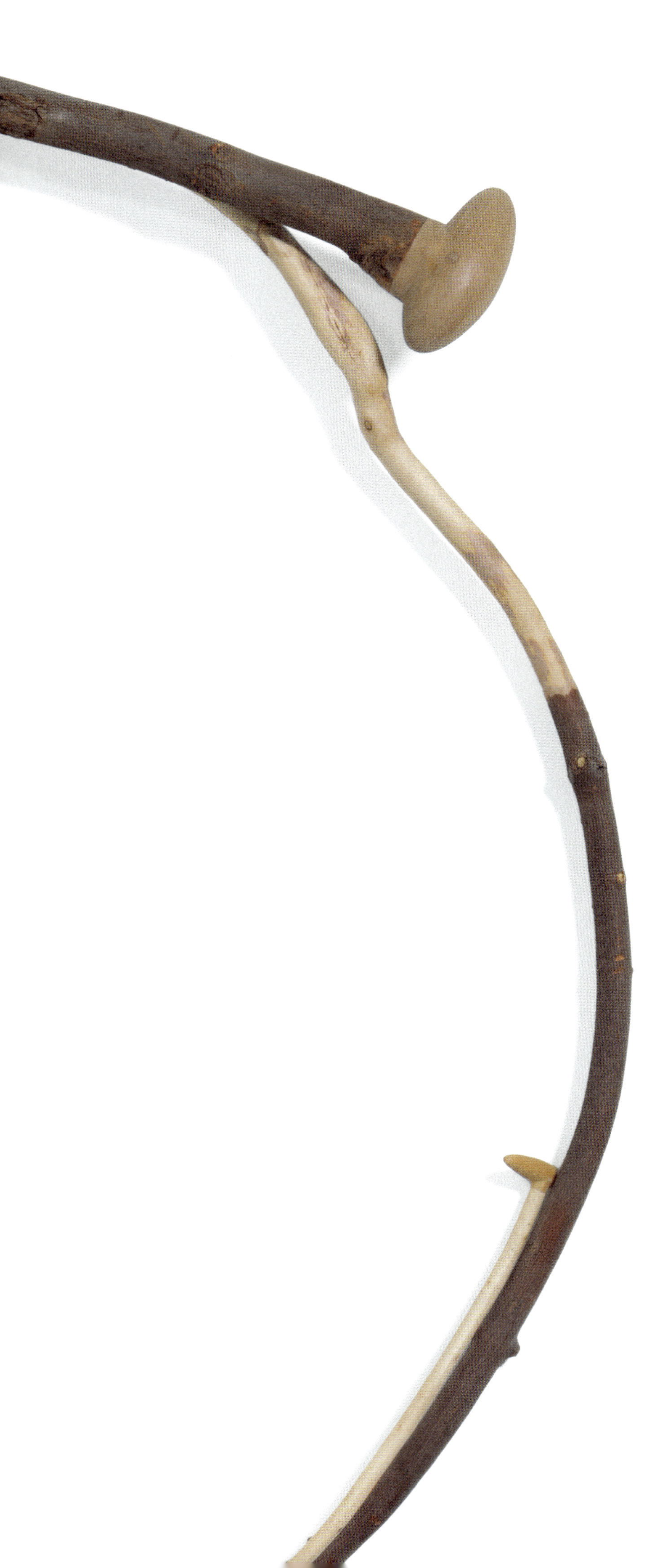

Figure 123. Detail of *Untitled*, (1982; [21]). Yale University Art Gallery, Gift of the Neisser Family, Judith Neisser, David Neisser, Kate Neisser, and Stephen Burns, in memory of Edward Neisser, B.A. 1952.

Boards of Trustees

The Cleveland Museum of Art

Museum of Fine Arts, Boston

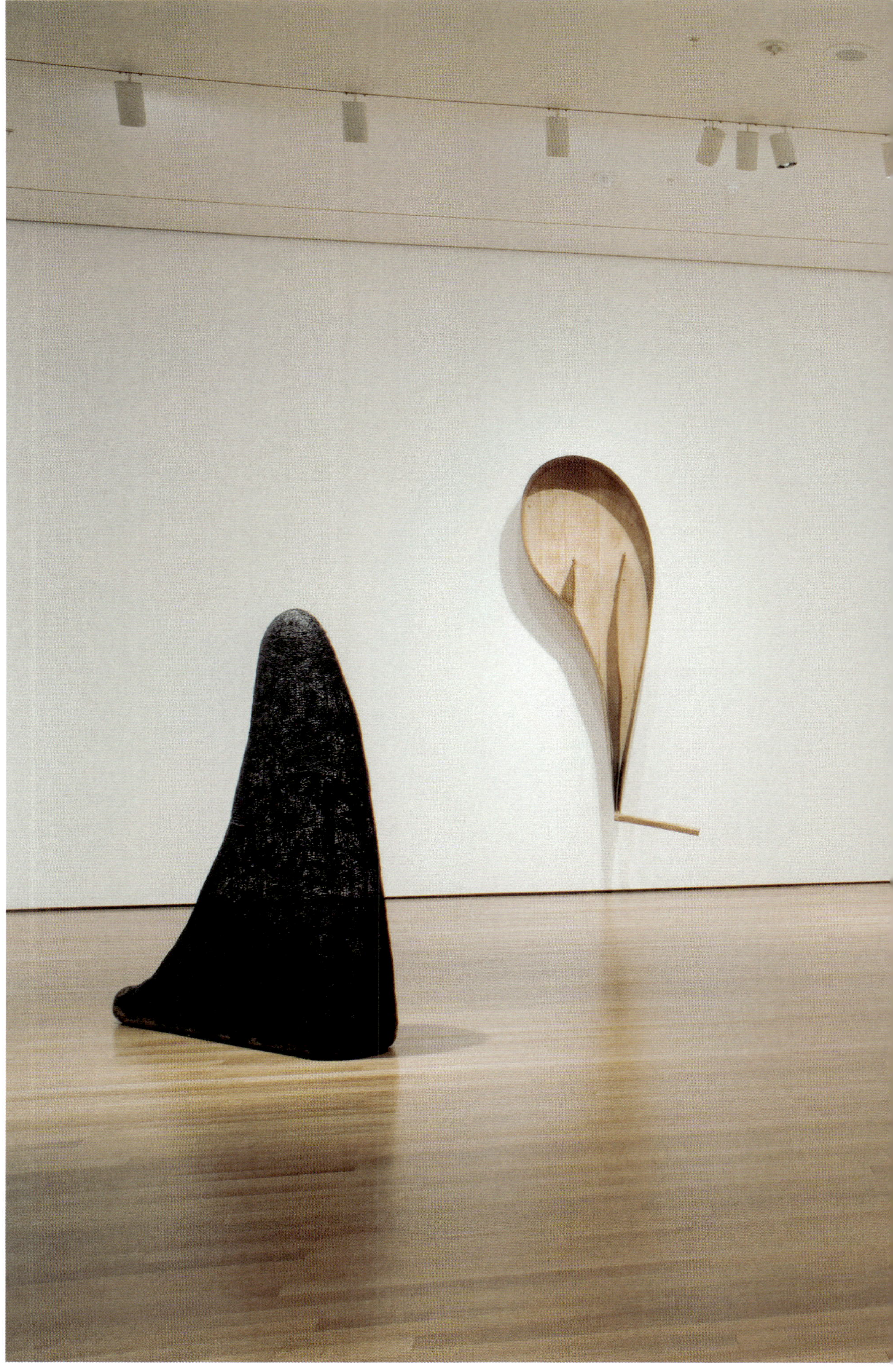

Figure 124. Installation view of *Martin Puryear*, The Museum of Modern Art, New York, 2008. Pictured: *Dowager* (1990); *Malediction* [51]; *In Sheep's Clothing* (1996); and *Alien Huddle* [30]. Digital Image © The Museum of Modern Art/ Licensed by SCALA / John Wronn / Art Resource, NY

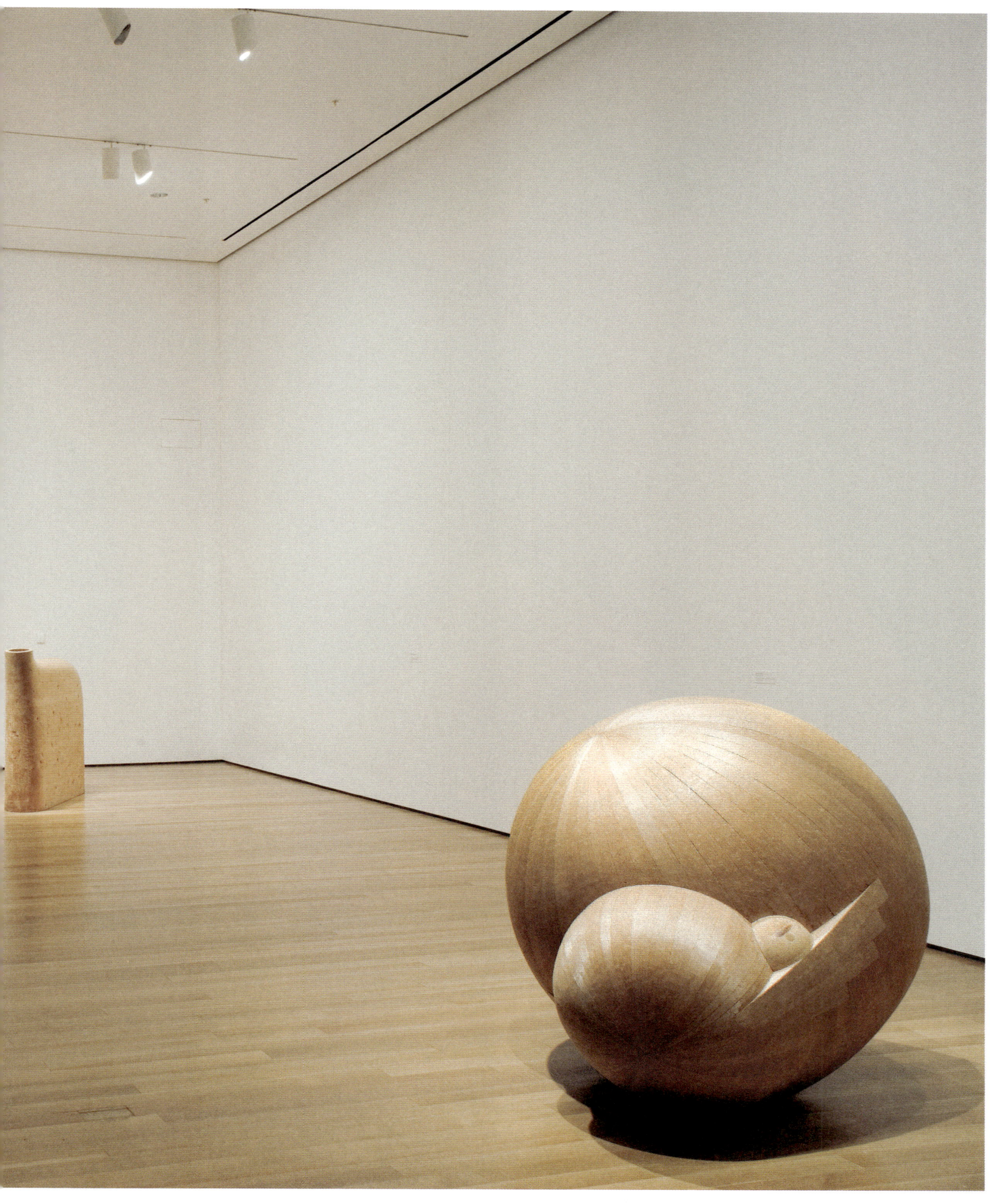

Contributor Biographies

Nairy Baghramian is an artist working across sculpture, installation, photography, and drawing. Her recent exhibitions include those at the Metropolitan Museum of Art, New York; the Aspen Art Museum; the Nasher Sculpture Center, Dallas; the Walker Art Center, Minneapolis; the Palacio de Cristal, Madrid; the Galleria d'Arte Moderna, Milan; and the Secession, Vienna, among others. She has also participated in major international exhibitions such as the Venice Biennale (2011, 2019), Documenta 14 (2017), and Skulptur Projekte Münster (2007, 2017).

Rizvana Bradley is Associate Professor of Film and Media Studies and Affiliated Faculty in the History of Art at the University of California, Berkeley. Bradley's *Anteaesthetics: Black Aesthesis and the Critique of Form* (2023) was named a Best Book of the Year by *Frieze* and shortlisted for the Modern Language Association Prize for a First Book. Her criticism appears in *Art in America*, *Artforum*, *e-flux*, *November*, *Parkett*, and *The Yale Review*.

Alex Da Corte is an artist who makes sculptures, paintings, installations, and films. Recent monographic exhibitions include surveys at the Louisiana Museum of Modern Art, Humlebæk, Denmark; the Modern Art Museum of Fort Worth, Texas; and the 21st Century Museum of Contemporary Art, Kanazawa, Japan. His long-form original writing has appeared in the catalogues for the touring exhibitions *Ellsworth Kelly at* 100 and *Marisol: A* Retrospective. He lives and works in Philadelphia.

Thelma Golden is the Ford Foundation Director and Chief Curator of the Studio Museum in Harlem, the world's leading institution devoted to visual arts by artists of African descent. Under her leadership, the Studio Museum has gained renown as a global leader in the exhibition of contemporary art and a cultural anchor in the Harlem community. Golden is a recognized authority on contemporary art by artists of African descent and an active lecturer and panelist. She also serves on the board of directors for the Barack Obama Foundation, the Crystal Bridges Museum of American Art, the Los Angeles County Museum of Art, and the Mellon Foundation.

Tom Joyce is an American sculptor working in a variety of media with a reverential preference for iron. In 2003 he was acknowledged through a MacArthur Foundation Fellowship as one of the foremost practitioners in the art and science of forging iron. Born in 1956, and initially trained as a blacksmith in his early teens, Joyce's innovations examine the corporeal, environmental, and historically charged implications of using iron as a fundamental medium.

Joan Kee is the Judy and Michael Steinhardt Director at the Institute of Fine Arts at New York University. A specialist in modern and contemporary art, her books include *Contemporary Korean Art: Tansaekhwa and the Urgency of Method* (2013); *Models of Integrity: Art and Law in Post-Sixties America* (2019); and *The Geometries of Afro Asia: Art Beyond Solidarity* (2023), which received the 2024 Robert Motherwell Book Award for an outstanding book in the history and criticism of modernism.

Emily Liebert is the Lauren Rich Fine Curator of Contemporary Art and Chair of Art of the Americas and Modern and Contemporary Art at the Cleveland Museum of Art (CMA). Her recent exhibitions include *Shahzia Sikander: Collective Behavior* (cocurated with Ainsley M. Cameron), a Collateral Event of the 2024 Venice Biennale; *Emeka Ogboh: Ámà; The Gathering Place* (cocurated with Ugochukwu-Smooth Nzewi), the CMA's inaugural commission in its Ames Family Atrium; and *Picturing Motherhood Now* (cocurated with Nadiah Rivera Fellah). Before joining the CMA, Liebert held positions at the Museum of Modern Art, New York, the Whitney Museum of American Art, New York, and the Chinati Foundation, Marfa, Texas. She holds a BA from Yale University and a PhD from Columbia University.

Maya Lin has been recognized for her distinct interdisciplinary aesthetic vision with groundbreaking works in art, architecture, and memorials. Nature is the context and source of inspiration for Lin's practice. A committed environmentalist, Lin is at work on her final memorial, focused on the environment, titled *What is Missing?*, a project that raises awareness of and poses solutions to biodiversity loss and climate change.

Kerry James Marshall was born in Birmingham, Alabama, and now lives in Chicago. Internationally renowned, Marshall's mastery as an artist has radically changed what he calls "the lack in the image bank" by foregrounding Black subjects in his paintings. His 2016 American retrospective traveled to the Metropolitan Museum of Art, New York; the Museum of Contemporary Art Chicago; and the Museum of Contemporary Art in Los Angeles. His 2025 European retrospective opens at the Royal Academy of Arts in London before traveling to the Kunsthaus Zurich and the Musée d'Art Moderne, Paris.

Michelle Millar Fisher is the Ronald C. and Anita L. Wornick Curator of Contemporary Decorative Arts at the Museum of Fine Arts, Boston. Previously, she worked at the Museum of Modern Art, the Philadelphia Museum of Art, and the Solomon R. Guggenheim Museum. Her work focuses on the intersections of people, power, and the material world. She holds a PhD from the Graduate Center at the City University of New York.

Ugochukwu-Smooth Nzewi is an artist, art historian, and the Steven and Lisa Tananbaum Curator in the Department of Painting and Sculpture at the Museum of Modern Art, New York (MoMA). He leads the Africa group in the museum's Contemporary and Modern Art Perspectives (C-MAP), MoMA's internal research and exchange initiative devoted to art in a global context. Before joining MoMA, Nzewi was the Curator of African Art at the Cleveland Museum of Art.

Pam Paulson is the founder of and Master Printer at Paulson Fontaine Press. Since 1996, the press has published more than six hundred editions with artists including Tauba Auerbach, Spencer Finch, Charles Gaines, the quilters of Gee's Bend, Kerry James Marshall, and Martin Puryear. Paulson was a Master Printer at Crown Point Press from 1987 to 1993. In 1982, she received her MFA in painting from the San Francisco Art Institute, where she worked as a teaching assistant for Robert Colescott. She received her BFA from the University of Texas at Arlington in 1979.

Julia Phillips is a Chicago-based artist, predominantly working with ceramics and metal. Inspired by functional objects, her sculptures are metaphors for social and psychological experiences. Her work is held in public collections, such as the Art Institute of Chicago, the Museum of Modern Art in New York, and the Moderna Museet in Stockholm. She published her first monograph, *Energy Exchange* (2023), with Mousse Publishing, Milan. She is on faculty at the University of Chicago.

Charles Ray grew up in Chicago and now lives in Los Angeles. His work has been shown at Documenta, Venice Biennales, and Whitney Biennials. His sculptures have been the subject of retrospectives, including at the Museum of Contemporary Art in Los Angeles (1998), Kunstmuseum Basel in Switzerland, and the Art Institute of Chicago (2014–15). In 2022, he had solo exhibitions at the Metropolitan Museum of Art, New York, the Glenstone Museum, Potomac, Maryland, the Centre Pompidou, Paris, and Bourse de Commerce, Paris.

Gabriella Shypula is the Leigh and Mary Carter Director's Research Fellow at the Cleveland Museum of Art and a PhD candidate at Stony Brook University. She has written on contemporary art and cocurated *Revisiting 5+1* at the Paul W. Zuccaire Gallery, presented in partnership with the Museum of Fine Arts, Boston. Previously, she has contributed to curatorial and research projects at the Smithsonian American Art Museum, Washington, DC, the San Francisco Museum of Modern Art, the Baltimore Museum of Art, and the Museum of Modern Art, New York.

Reto Thüring is the Head of Culture at the Foundation for Art, Culture, and History in Winterthur, Switzerland. He wrote his dissertation on sixteenth-century Venetian portraiture. From 2018 until 2023 he was the Beal Family Chair in the Department of Contemporary Art at the Museum of Fine Arts, Boston. Prior to that, he was Chair of Modern, Contemporary, Decorative Art and Performing Arts, Music, and Film at the Cleveland Museum of Art.

Billie Tsien, AIA, is an architect and founding partner of Tod Williams Billie Tsien Architects, Partners. Their studio is committed to reflecting the values of nonprofit, cultural, and academic institutions through an architecture that is serene and enduring. Some of their notable projects include the Barnes Foundation in Philadelphia, the US Embassy in Mexico City, and the Obama Presidential Center in Chicago. Tsien is devoted to cultivating a broader, more diverse cultural landscape through architecture.

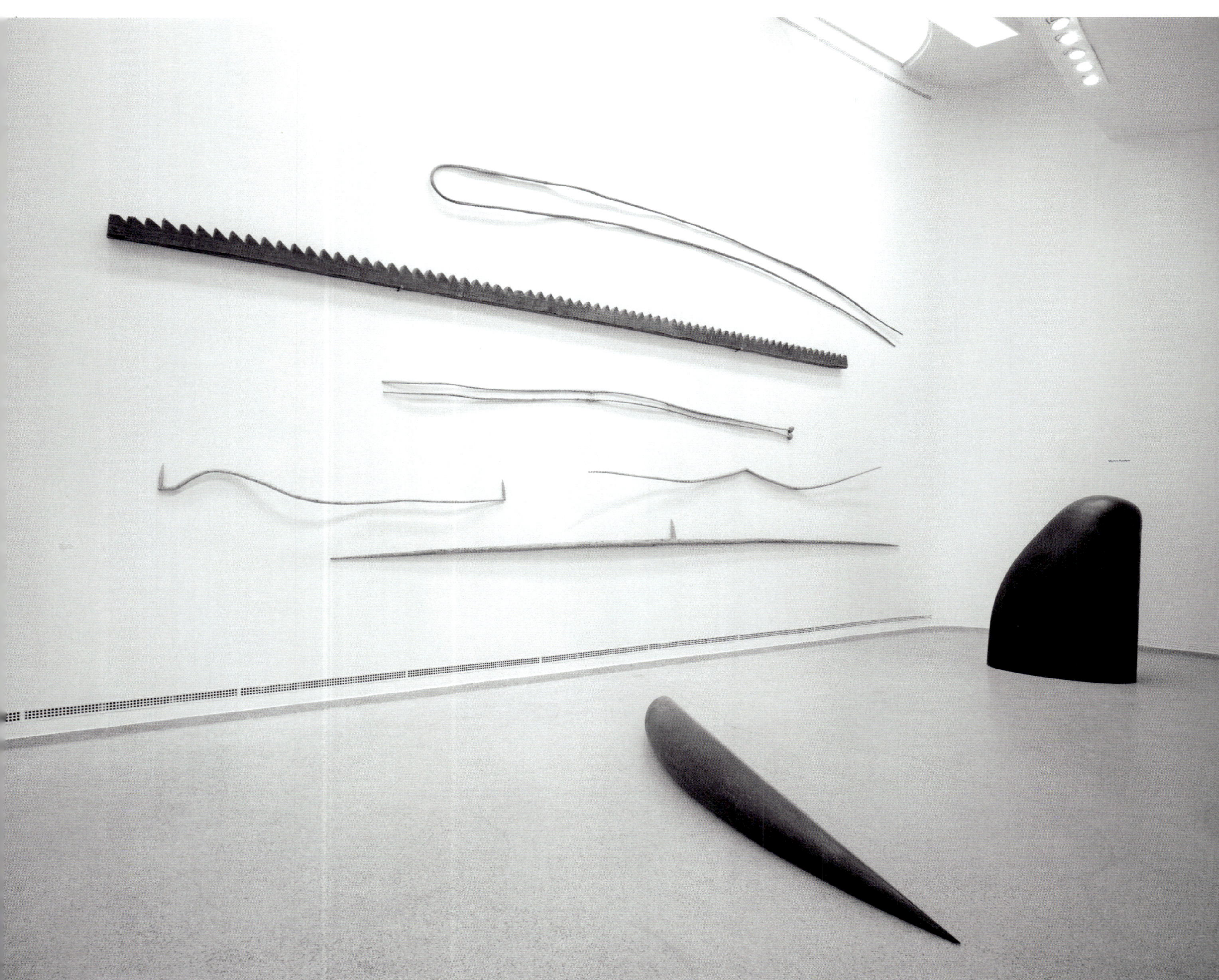

Figure 125. Installation view of *Young American Artists: 1978, Exxon National Exhibition*, Solomon R. Guggenheim Museum, New York, 1978. Pictured: *Some Tales* (1975–78); *Self* (1978; [14]); and *Bask* (1976; [11]). Photo: The Solomon R. Guggenheim Foundation / Art Resource, NY

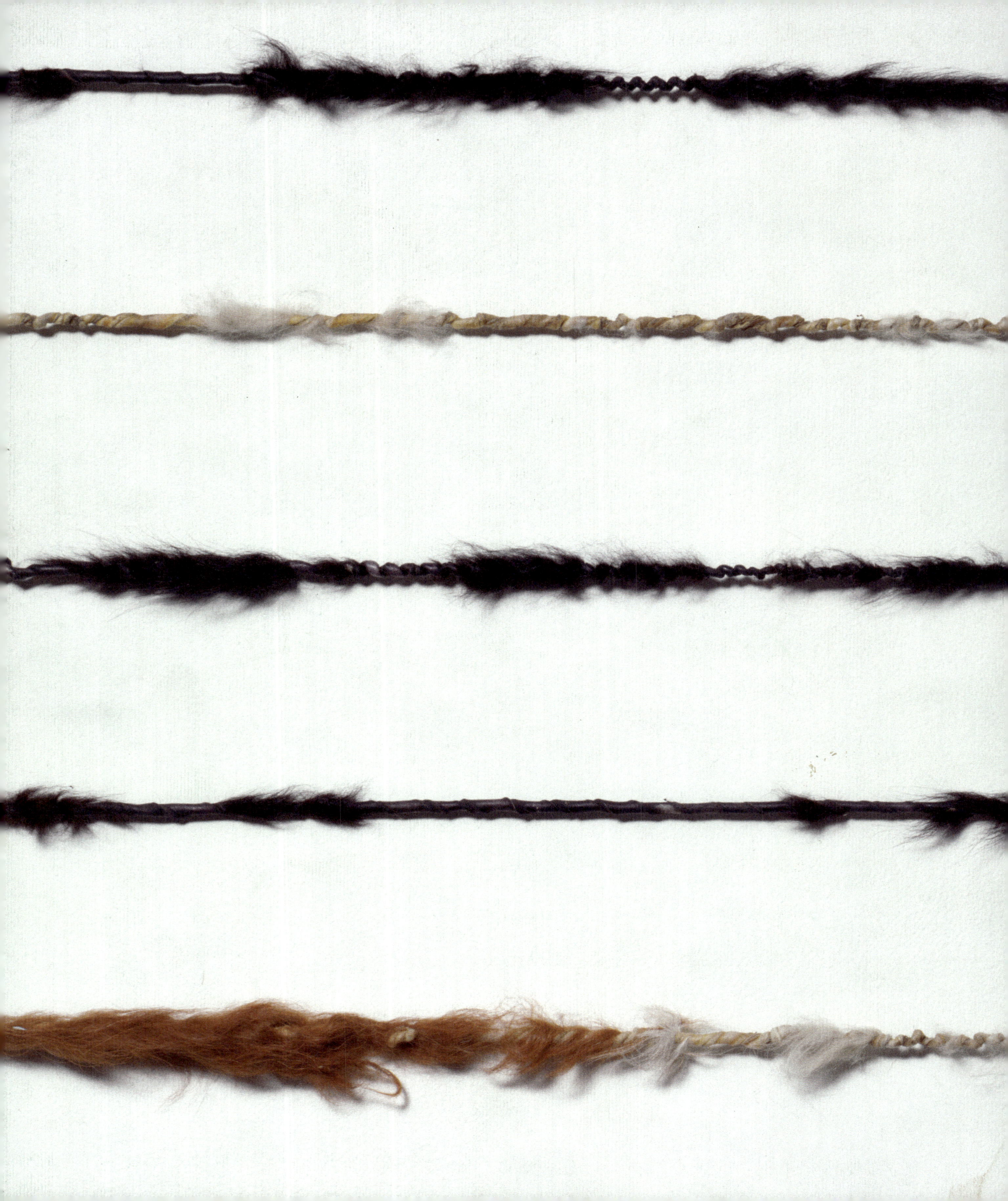